W9-BUY-443

ENGLISH RENAISSANCE PROSE FICTION, 1500-1660

an annotated bibliography of criticism

A
Reference
Publication
in
Literature

Marilyn Gaull
Editor

ENGLISH RENAISSANCE PROSE FICTION, 1500-1660

an annotated bibliography of criticism

JAMES L. HARNER

G.K.HALL&CO.

70 LINCOLN STREET, BOSTON, MASS.

Library of Congress Cataloging in Publication Data
Harner, James L
 English Renaissance prose fiction, 1500-1660.

 (A Reference publication in literature)
 Includes index.
 1. English fiction — Early modern, 1500-1700 —
History and criticism — Bibliography.   I. Title.
II. Series: Reference publications in literature.
Z2014.F4H37   [PR833]   016.823'2'09   78-2902
ISBN 0-8161-7996-4

This publication is printed on permanent/durable acid-free paper
MANUFACTURED IN THE UNITED STATES OF AMERICA

Contents

Contents

Contents

Contents

Contents

Introduction

The diversity of narrative types considered to be prose fiction
during the English Renaissance discourages attempts at precise definition: for along with the repentance tracts, novelle, travel accounts,
anatomies, utopias, romances, cony-catching pamphlets, jest books,
fables, histories, and criminal biographies are sub-types, hybrids,
and otherwise curious combinations of fictional elements.[1] Nevertheless, according to a consensus among scholars, the main body of
Renaissance prose fiction consists of imaginative narratives which
may be classified as novelle, romances, jest books, anatomies, histories, or some combination of these types.

Though works of prose fiction from 1500 to 1660 exhibit characteristics of the novel, they were never meant to be read as novels in any
modern sense of the term and were therefore generally neglected by
early literary historians, who held a limited generic view of fiction.
In their obligatory chapters on precursors of the form, historians of
the novel betrayed uneasiness with Arcadia, Euphues, The Unfortunate
Traveller, or Deloney's works, and rarely ventured beyond standard
clichés. Likewise, period historians virtually ignored prose fiction
except as sources for plays, illustrations of manners, specimens of
prose styles, or examples of Continental influence.

During the last twenty years, however, an increasing number of
scholars have realized that expectations based on the study of the
novel are inappropriate to this early fiction[2] and thus have discovered that many of these works are interesting in their own right
and worthy of detailed study. But the investigation of Renaissance
prose fiction is yet hampered by a lack of (1) broadly-based theoretical studies, (2) an adequate bibliography of primary works, (3) a detailed history of the subject, and (4) reliable scholarly editions.

Studies of the theoretical bases of Renaissance prose fiction
would provide the necessary groundwork for detailed analyses of individual works and authors. But little investigation of the early
theories of prose fiction has been done since Tieje's work (383–385
and 387) during the second decade of this century. Insufficient con-
sideration has been given to the Renaissance author's conception of
his craft, to his readers' expectations, or to the various influences

(social, moral, literary, and economic) on the production of prose
fiction. And too little is understood about the structures and conventions associated with the basic narrative types. Even romance,
the type most frequently encountered in the period and most examined
by scholars, has not been thoroughly analyzed. As F. D. Hoeniger
pointed out in 1976, "[a]ccounts of romances have been all too general, ignoring the vast differences in plot and characterisation and
tone between Alexandrian, pastoral and chivalric romance."[3]

An adequate bibliography is needed to bring obscure but important
works to light and to point up trends in the production and popularity
of types of fiction. Esdaile's A List of English Tales and Prose Romances Printed before 1740 (14), though an important pioneering work,
was incomplete even at publication. The prose fiction section in the
New Cambridge Bibliography of English Literature, I: 600-1660 (47)
excludes a number of works and includes others not in prose. Mish's
English Prose Fiction, 1600-1700 (26) and O'Dell's A Chronological
List of Prose Fiction...1475-1640 (28) together provide a convenient
overview of the period but are due for revision and updating now that
the new Short-Title Catalogues (19 and 50) are appearing. What is
needed is a revised, updated chronological list of editions--one that
would include full descriptive entries.

Basic accounts have been provided by Schlauch's Antecedents of
the English Novel (354) and the lengthy articles by her (356) and
Mish (298), but there is as yet no comprehensive, detailed history of
Renaissance prose fiction. What is required is a work offering an
historical overview of the development of fiction during the period,
an examination of relationships with later fiction (especially of the
eighteenth century), analyses of obscure as well as major works, discussions of pervasive themes, and a synthesis of the widely scattered
scholarship. Such a history would provide the background and stimulus
for detailed investigation of individual works and authors.

Finally, as the following reference guide shows, few of even the
major works are available in editions meeting the standards of modern
textual scholarship. There are reliable editions of Sidney's Old Arcadia, Deloney's works, and Nashe's The Unfortunate Traveller, but not
of most of the fiction of Lodge, Greene,[4] Dekker, or Lyly. Most works
are available only in their original editions, in inaccurate nine-
teenth-century reprints, or in unreliable facsimiles. At the very
least we should have a series of facsimile reprints with textual in-
troductions to serve until critical editions can be published.

Studies such as Davis's Idea and Act in Elizabethan Fiction (174),
Helgerson's The Elizabethan Prodigals (221), and Lawlis's Apology for
the Middle Class: The Dramatic Novels of Thomas Deloney (868) indi-
cate that the field will richly repay investigation. But much remains
to be done. Although considerable attention has been given to the
identification of works used as sources by dramatists and although the
discovery of new sources and analogues continues, the influence of the

drama upon characterization, themes, and structure in prose fiction remains to be analyzed. More general investigations of structural techniques, conventions of setting, themes,[5] and aspects of style are necessary. Finally, there are several authors and anonymous works (e.g., Robert Anton, William Baldwin, Cloria and Narcissus, John Hind, James Howell, The Life and Pranks of Long Meg of Westminster, and Robert Parry) still lacking significant study.

The following reference guide covers editions and studies (published between 1800 and 1976) of prose fiction in English--both original works and translations--written or printed in England from 1500 to 1660. Works and translations included are limited to those which may be classified as novelle, romances, histories, anatomies, or jest books (or some combination of these).[6] This limitation, though conservative, does include all individual works generally regarded as Renaissance prose fiction.

The entries are divided among four main sections: Bibliographies, Anthologies, General Studies, and Authors/Translators/Titles. In the first three sections, the entries are arranged alphabetically by author or editor. So that excessive cross-references may be avoided, works in these three divisions frequently appear also under one or more of the Author/Translator/Title listings; e.g., Davis's Idea and Act in Elizabethan Fiction is included among the general studies as well as in the listings for Sidney, Lodge, Greene, Gascoigne, Lyly, Rich, Nashe, Chettle, and Deloney, with an appropriate annotation for each.

The last section is arranged in one alphabetical sequence by author, or translator, or title (for an anonymous work or translation). The STC (19 and 31) and the Wing STC (49 and 50) have been used as authorities for the spelling of names of authors and translators, and of titles. Anonymous works are alphabetized according to the title of the earliest extant edition listed in the appropriate STC; in the notes titles are modernized.

Each Author/Translator/Title entry includes up to three subdivisions: Bibliographies (arranged alphabetically by author), Editions (arranged chronologically by date of publication), and Studies (arranged alphabetically by author). The Bibliographies section is confined to checklists of criticism and to descriptive bibliographies. Although the Editions section is generally limited to works which provide a complete text (abridgments, if they contain critical commentary, have been placed in the Studies section), some exceptions have been made for works of which few (or no) other editions are available.[7] Works which include a discussion (usually five pages or more in the case of a book or monograph) of an author/translator/title are listed in the Studies section.

Ph.D. dissertations (but not Master's theses[8]) are included; reprints or later editions of books are not noted unless they contain revisions or additions; information is provided on reprints of articles; reviews of studies or editions are included only if they contain important contributions to scholarship; those studies which discuss poems from prose fiction works only as poetry are excluded. Works not seen are marked by an asterisk, with sources of reference in the notes.[9]

A bibliographer is invariably faced with being unable to identify or locate all works pertinent to his subject. I would therefore welcome information on any study or edition which I have overlooked or been unable to locate.

NOTES

1. O'Dell's Introduction to A Chronological List of Prose Fiction... 1475-1640 (28) includes an interesting discussion of the problems of determining what is to be classified as prose fiction during the period.
2. The first chapter of Davis's Idea and Act in Elizabethan Fiction (174) is a particularly helpful introduction to the reading of Renaissance fiction.
3. "Shakespeare's Romances since 1958: A Retrospect," ShS, 29 (1976), 6.
4. The announced collection of Greene's works has not yet appeared; however, editions of most of his works are available as dissertations which were prepared for the collection.
5. Schlauch's "Themes of English Fiction, 1400-1600: Some Suggestions for Future Research" (357) includes a number of interesting topics for investigation.
6. Jest books have been included only when the jests are more than very short (four- or five-line) anecdotes. Authors/translators/ titles for which no editions or studies could be located are excluded.
7. Reprints of single tales from collections (such as Painter's Palace of Pleasure) are included in the Editions section. Anthologies intended for classroom use are excluded.
8. For a convenient list of Master's theses see: Patsy C. Howard, Theses in English Literature, 1894-1970 (Ann Arbor: Pierian Press, 1973).
9. Dissertations not seen may be located in one of the following: Hans Walter Gabler, English Renaissance Studies in German, 1945-1967: A Check-List of German, Austrian, and Swiss Academic Theses, Monographs, and Book Publications on English Language and Literature, c. 1500-1650, Schriftenreihe der Deutschen Shakespeare-Gesellschaft West, NS, 11 (Heidelberg: Quelle & Mayer, 1971); Lawrence F. McNamee, Dissertations in English and American Literature: Theses Accepted by American, British, and German Universities, 1865-1964 (New York: R. R. Bowker, 1968), Supplement

I, 1964–1968 (1969), Supplement II, 1969–1973 (1974); the various volumes of Comprehensive Dissertation Index (Ann Arbor: Xerox University Microfilms, 1973–); the various volumes of Index to Theses Accepted for Higher Degrees in the Universities of Great Britain and Ireland (London: Aslib, 1953–).

Acknowledgments

One of the pleasures of finishing a work such as this is the op-
portunity to recognize those individuals and institutions without
whose support it could not have been completed. I wish to acknowledge
the receipt of two research grants from the Faculty Research Committee, Bowling Green State University: one allowed me to hire a research assistant; the other provided for some released time during
the summer of 1977. I particularly wish to thank my colleagues in
the Department of English for releasing me from teaching duties during
the spring of 1977 and for granting me a research assistant during the
fall of 1977.

Diana Wyllie, who proved to be a most capable and good-humored
research assistant, patiently and efficiently searched a seemingly
endless number of bibliographies, catalogues, and lists, and typed
much of the preliminary card file. David Teisler, Crystal Walter,
Joann Sunderman, and Susan Gross assisted with various tasks. John
Moor, my present research assistant, has been helpful in the final
checking of some items and in proofreading. Mary Ann Grandjean translated articles in Hungarian, and Kathy Overhulse read works in Spanish. Brownell Salomon secured copies of some works from the British
Library. Donna Fricke, Douglas Fricke, Frank Baldanza, and Edgar
Daniels offered helpful comments on portions of the work, and Marilyn
Gaull saved me from some unfortunate lapses. Several individuals,
whom I must thank collectively, graciously answered queries, sent off-
prints, and offered words of encouragement.

Much of my reading was done in the libraries of Bowling Green
State University, Toledo University, Indiana University, Ohio State
University, the University of Illinois at Urbana-Champaign, and the
University of Michigan (where an appointment as a Visiting Scholar in
the Horace H. Rackham School of Graduate Studies allowed me faculty
privileges). Although most of the librarians who provided assistance
remain nameless, I owe a very special thanks to Dawn McCaghy, Inter-
Library Loan Librarian at Bowling Green, and her assistants, Mary
Mura and Kausalya Padmarajan, who when faced with a deluge of re-
quests--many with incomplete citations or for obscure works--patiently
and efficiently secured copies of all but a few works. Without their
dedicated assistance, many more items would be listed "not seen."

Acknowledgments

Finally, Rebecca Peters and Darinda Harner somehow managed to turn boxes of well-thumbed, much-edited index cards into a finished typescript. And I owe a special note to Darinda, my wife, who has given up too much of her leisure this past year and a half to type and file.

Abbreviations

ACF	Annali di Ca' Foscari
AF	Anglistische Forschungen
AL	American Literature
AN&Q	American Notes and Queries
Archiv	Archiv für das Studium der Neueren Sprachen und Literaturen
ARS	Augustan Reprint Society
AUMLA	Journal of the Australasian Universities Language and Literature Association
BB	Bulletin of Bibliography
BC	Book Collector
BCB	Boletín Cultural y Bibliográfico
BH	Bulletin Hispanique
BHR	Bibliothèque d'Humanisme et Renaissance
BHS	Bulletin of Hispanic Studies
BJRL	Bulletin of the John Rylands Library
BNYPL	Bulletin of the New York Public Library
BSDSL	Basler Studien zur Deutschen Sprache und Literatur
BSUF	Ball State University Forum
CA	Cuadernos Americanos
CahiersE	Cahiers Élisabéthains: Études sur la Pré-Renaissance et la Renaissance Anglaises
CalR	Calcutta Review
CJ	Classical Journal
CL	Comparative Literature
CLAJ	College Language Association Journal

CLC	Columbia Library Columns
CLS	Comparative Literature Studies
ČMF	Časopis pro Moderní Filologii
CoA	The Coat of Arms
CollG	Colloquia Germanica, Internationale Zeitschrift für Germanische Sprach- und Literaturwissenschaft
DM	The Dublin Magazine
DPL	De Proprietatibus Litterarum
DUJ	Durham University Journal
EA	Études Anglaises
E&S	Essays and Studies by Members of the English Association
EETS	Early English Text Society
EHR	English Historical Review
EigoS	Eigo Seinen [The Rising Generation] (Tokyo)
ELH	Journal of English Literary History
ElizS	Elizabethan & Renaissance Studies (University of Salzburg, Austria)
ELN	English Language Notes
ELR	English Literary Renaissance
EM	English Miscellany
ER	Études Rabelaisiennes
ES	English Studies
ESA	English Studies in Africa
ESELL	Essays and Studies in English Language and Literature (Tohoku Gakuin University, Sendai, Japan)
ESRS	Emporia State Research Studies
FAGAAS	Frankfurter Arbeiten aus dem Gebiete der Anglistik und der Amerika-Studien
FFC	Folklore Fellows Communications
FJS	Fu Jen Studies
FK	Filológiai Közlöny
ForumH	Forum (Houston)
GR	Germanic Review
HLB	Harvard Library Bulletin
HLQ	Huntington Library Quarterly

Abbreviations

HR	Hispanic Review
HSCL	Harvard Studies in Comparative Literature
ISLL	Illinois Studies in Language and Literature
IUHS	Indiana University Humanities Series
JEGP	Journal of English and Germanic Philology
JHI	Journal of the History of Ideas
JPC	Journal of Popular Culture
JWCI	Journal of the Warburg and Courtauld Institute
KN	Kwartalnik Neofilologiczny
Lang&S	Language and Style
LanM	Les Langues Modernes
LC	Library Chronicle (University of Pennsylvania)
LCrit	Literary Criterion
Library	The Library
LR	Les Lettres Romanes
LSE	Lund Studies in English
LSUSHS	Louisiana State University Studies, Humanities Series
M&H	Medievalia et Humanistica
M&L	Music and Letters
MLN	Modern Language Notes
MLQ	Modern Language Quarterly
MLR	Modern Language Review
MP	Modern Philology
MQR	Michigan Quarterly Review
MSpr	Moderna Språk
N&Q	Notes and Queries
Neophil	Neophilologus
NEQ	New England Quarterly
NM	Neuphilologische Mitteilungen
NS	Die Neueren Sprachen
PAPS	Proceedings of the American Philosophical Society
PBA	Proceedings of the British Academy
PBSA	Papers of the Bibliographical Society of America
PCP	Pacific Coast Philology

Abbreviations

PFLUS	Publications de la Faculté des Lettres de l'Université de Strasbourg
PLL	Papers on Language and Literature
PLPLS–LHS	Proceedings of the Leeds Philosophical and Literary Society, Literary & Historical Section
PMLA	PMLA: Publications of the Modern Language Association of America
PP	Philologica Pragensia
PQ	Philological Quarterly
PrS	Prairie Schooner
PURBA	Panjab University Research Bulletin (Arts)
RANAM	Recherches Anglaises et Américaines
RBPH	Revue Belge de Philologie et d'Histoire
RDM	Revue des Deux Mondes [Now Nouvelle Revue des Deux Mondes]
Ren&R	Renaissance and Reformation
RenB	The Renaissance Bulletin
RenP	Renaissance Papers
RenQ	Renaissance Quarterly
RES	Review of English Studies
RETS	Renaissance English Text Society
RFE	Revista de Filología Española
RHL	Revue d'Histoire Littéraire de la France
RLC	Revue de Littérature Comparée
RLMC	Rivista di Letterature Moderne e Comparate
RORD	Research Opportunities in Renaissance Drama
RR	Romanic Review
SAA	Schweizer Anglistische Arbeiten
SAB	South Atlantic Bulletin
SAQ	South Atlantic Quarterly
SB	Studies in Bibliography: Papers of the Bibliographical Society of the University of Virginia
SCB	South Central Bulletin
SCN	Seventeenth-Century News
SEL	Studies in English Literature, 1500–1900
SELit	Studies in English Literature (English Literary Society of Japan)

Abbreviations

SELL	Studies in English Literature and Language (Kyushu University, Fukuoka, Japan)
SEngL	Studies in English Literature (The Hague)
Serif	The Serif
SFQ	Southern Folklore Quarterly
ShN	Shakespeare Newsletter
SHR	Southern Humanities Review
ShS	Shakespeare Survey
SN	Studia Neophilologica
SNNTS	Studies in the Novel (North Texas State University)
SP	Studies in Philology
SQ	Shakespeare Quarterly
SR	Sewanee Review
SRO	Shakespearean Research Opportunities: The Report of the MLA Conference
SSe	Studi Secenteschi
SSF	Studies in Short Fiction
SSL	Studies in Scottish Literature
TCBS	Transactions of the Cambridge Bibliographical Society
TEAS	Twayne's English Author Series
TLS	[London] Times Literary Supplement
TN	Theatre Notebook
TPS	Transactions of the Philological Society
TSL	Tennessee Studies in Literature
TWA	Transactions of the Wisconsin Academy of Sciences, Arts, and Letters
UCTSE	University of Cape Town Studies in English
UMCMP	University of Michigan Contributions in Modern Philology
UMSE	University of Mississippi Studies in English
UNCSCL	University of North Carolina Studies in Comparative Literature
UNCSRLL	University of North Carolina Studies in Romance Languages and Literatures
UTQ	University of Toronto Quarterly
VP	Victorian Poetry

Abbreviations

VQR	Virginia Quarterly Review
WHR	Western Humanities Review
WP	Work in Progress
YES	Yearbook of English Studies
YSE	Yale Studies in English
ZAA	Zeitschrift für Anglistik und Amerikanistik

Bibliographies

1   ALLISON, A[NTONY] F[RANCIS]. English Translations from the
    Spanish and Portuguese to the Year 1700: An Annotated
    Catalogue of the Extant Printed Versions (Excluding Dramatic
    Adaptations). Folkestone: Dawsons of Pall Mall, 1974,
    224pp.
        Provides annotated listing (by author of original) of
    Renaissance translations.

2   BATESON, F[REDERICK] W[ILSE], ed. The Cambridge Bibliography
    of English Literature, I: 600-1660. New York: Macmillan;
    Cambridge: Cambridge University Press, 1941, 952pp.
        Includes section on prose fiction (pp. 726-36) with
    chronological listings of general studies, anthologies,
    original works (with entries on scholarship), and transla-
    tions; also includes listing of jest books (pp. 714-15).
    See 43. Revised as 47.

3   BEGLEY, WALTER. "Bibliography of Romance from the Renaissance
    to the End of the Seventeenth Century," in Nova Solyma, the
    Ideal City; Or Jerusalem Regained...Attributed to John
    Milton, Vol. II. Edited by Walter Begley. London: J.
    Murray, 1902, 355-400.
        Provides classified listing of romances, with biblio-
    graphical descriptions of some works.

4   BELL, INGLIS, and DONALD BAIRD. The English Novel, 1578-1956:
    A Check-List of Twentieth-Century Criticisms. Denver:
    Alan Swallow, 1958, 181pp.
        Includes highly selective listing of articles on Lyly
    and Sidney.

5   BENNETT, H[ENRY] S[TANLEY]. English Books & Readers, 1475-
    1557: Being a Study in the History of the Book Trade from
    Caxton to the Incorporation of the Stationers' Company.
    Cambridge: Cambridge University Press, 1952, 351pp.
        Includes appendix "Trial List of Translations into Eng-
    lish Printed between 1475-1560" (pp. 276-319), which in-
    cludes prose fiction.

6   BLUM, IRVING D. "English Utopias from 1551 to 1699: A Bibli-
     ography." <u>BB</u>, 21 (January 1955), 143–44.
         Provides annotated chronological checklist of twenty-six
     works (including some prose fiction).

7   BONHEIM, HELMUT. <u>The English Novel before Richardson: A
     Checklist of Texts and Criticism to 1970</u>. Metuchen, New
     Jersey: Scarecrow Press, 1971, 151pp.
         Provides selective listing of texts and criticism ar-
     ranged by author and subject headings.

8   CALVER, EDWARD THOMAS. "Translations into English, 1523–1600:
     A Catalogue Raisonné with a Bibliography of Secondary
     Sources." Ph.D. dissertation, University of Michigan, 1944,
     1146pp.
         Includes section on narrative prose and verse; lists
     translations chronologically by date of first publication.
     Provides notes on modern editions and scholarship (pp. 960–
     1013).

9   CHANDLER, FRANK WADLEIGH. <u>Romances of Roguery, an Episode in
     the History of the Novel: The Picaresque Novel in Spain</u>.
     Columbia University Studies in Literature. New York: Mac-
     millan Co., 1899, 493pp.
         In "A Bibliography of Spanish Romances of Roguery, 1554–
     1668, and Their Translations," pp. 399–469, provides de-
     scriptions of editions of English translations. (Appar-
     ently the second part, which was to treat the development
     of the type in English, was never published.)

10 CRANE, RONALD S[ALMON]. Review of <u>A List of English Tales and
     Prose Romances Printed before 1740</u>, by Arundell Esdaile.
     <u>MLN</u>, 29 (February 1914), 45–49.
         Provides additions and corrections to 14.

11 CRANE, RONALD S[ALMON]. <u>The Vogue of Medieval Chivalric Ro-
     mance During the English Renaissance</u>. Menasha, Wisconsin:
     Collegiate Press, 1919, 57pp.
         Includes a chronological, annotated list of "Editions of
     Romances Printed in England or for English Readers between
     1475 and 1640" (pp. 30–48).

12 EBISCH, WALTHER, and LEVIN L. SCHÜCKING. <u>A Shakespeare Bibli-
     ography</u>. Oxford: Clarendon Press, 1931, 312pp.
         Includes sections on sources (pp. 61–79), euphuism
     (p. 95) and "Literary Genesis" (for each play) which list
     several studies of Renaissance prose fiction. <u>See</u> 13.

13 EBISCH, WALTHER, and LEVIN L. SCHÜCKING. <u>Supplement for the
     Years 1930–1935 to A</u> Shakespeare Bibliography. Oxford:
     Clarendon Press, 1937, 108pp.
         Supplements 12.

2

14   ESDAILE, ARUNDELL [JAMES KENNEDY]. <u>A List of English Tales
     and Prose Romances Printed before 1740</u>. London: Blades,
     East, & Blades for the Bibliographical Society, 1912, 364pp.
        Provides alphabetical listing (by author) of editions;
     includes some locations. Divides listing into two parts:
     1475-1642 and 1643-1739. <u>See</u> 46, 35, and 10.

14a GARTENBERG, PATRICIA, and NENA [LOUISE] THAMES WHITTEMORE.
     "A Checklist of English Women in Print, 1475-1640." <u>BB</u>,
     34 (January-March 1977), 1-13.
        Includes listings for Tyler and Wroth.

15   GECKER, SIDNEY, EVA SCHMALBACH, and RUTH DUNCOMBE. <u>English
     Fiction to 1820 in the University of Pennsylvania Library:
     Based on the Collections of Godfrey F. Singer and John C.
     Mendenhall</u>. Philadelphia: University of Pennsylvania
     Library, 1954, 132pp.
        Provides short-title listing arranged alphabetically by
     author; includes several Renaissance works.

16   HALLIWELL[-PHILLIPS], JAMES ORCHARD. <u>Descriptive Notices of
     Popular English Histories</u>. Percy Society, 23. London:
     Richards for the Percy Society, 1848, 100pp.
        Provides annotated list of 118 popular histories--"nar-
     rative[s] especially intended for the instruction or the
     amusement of the unlearned." Several entries are descrip-
     tions of post-Restoration editions or chapbook adaptations
     of Renaissance prose fiction. Frequently discusses publi-
     cation history of work in notes.

17   HAZLITT, W[ILLIAM] CAREW. <u>Hand-Book to the Popular, Poetical,
     and Dramatic Literature of Great Britain, from the Invention
     of Printing to the Restoration</u>. London: J. R. Smith, 1867,
     713pp.
        Provides alphabetical listing by author or title: anno-
     tations frequently include information on editions, prove-
     nance, and location. Includes several works of Renaissance
     prose fiction.

18   HENINGER, S. K., JR. <u>English Prose, Prose Fiction, and Criti-
     cism to 1660: A Guide to Information Sources</u>. American
     Literature, English Literature, and World Literatures in
     English Information Guide Series, 2. Detroit: Gale Re-
     search Co., 1975, 265pp.
        In Part 8 ("Narrative Fiction," pp. 141-74) provides se-
     lective, sometimes annotated listing of editions and criti-
     cism; arranges author entries chronologically by date of
     publication of first prose fiction work. Includes some
     prose fiction listings in Part 11 ("Translations," pp. 197-
     216).

19 JACKSON, W[ILLIAM] A., F[REDERIC] S[UTHERLAND] FERGUSON, and
KATHARINE F. PANTZER. <u>A Short-Title Catalogue of Books
Printed in England, Scotland, & Ireland and of English Books
Printed Abroad, 1475-1640, II: I-Z</u>. 2d edition, revised
and enlarged. London: The Bibliographical Society, 1976,
506pp.
Considerably revised and enlarged edition of 31. Volume
I is scheduled for publication in the 1980s.

20 JONES, CLAUDE E. "Prose Fiction and Related Matters to 1832."
<u>BB</u>, 21 (May 1956), 234-36.
Provides chronological listing (by author and short-
title) "intended to organize the major types and writings
which feed into the novel proper." Covers period 1300 B.C.-
1832.

21 LATHROP, HENRY BURROWES. "Notes on Miss Palmer's List of Editions and Translations," in <u>Translations from the Classics
into English from Caxton to Chapman, 1477-1620</u>. University
of Wisconsin Studies in Language and Literature, 35. Madison: [University of Wisconsin], 1933, pp. 325-31.
Provides additions and corrections to 29.

22 LOWNDES, WILLIAM THOMAS. <u>The Bibliographer's Manual of English
Literature</u>. Revised by Henry G. Bohn. 6 vols. London:
H. G. Bohn, 1864, 3413pp.
Provides author/title/subject listings with many entries
pertinent to Renaissance prose fiction; includes section on
jest books (pp. 1200-1208). Annotations include collations,
notes on contents, and information on provenance of copies.

23 MANCINI, ALBERT N. "Il romanzo italiano nel seicento: Saggio
di bibliografia delle traduzioni in lingua straniera (Fran-
cia, Germania, Inghilterra e Spagna)." <u>SSe</u>, 16 (1975),
183-217.
Includes entries describing English translations of
Italian prose fiction, 1600-1699. Provides notes on contents and locations of copies.

24 MISH, CHARLES C[ARROLL]. <u>English Prose Fiction, 1600-1640</u>.
Charlottesville: Bibliographical Society of the University
of Virginia, 1952, 39pp.
Provides chronological list of editions. Revised in 26.

25 MISH, CHARLES C[ARROLL]. <u>English Prose Fiction, 1641-1660</u>.
Charlottesville: Bibliographical Society of the University
of Virginia, 1952, 24pp.
Provides chronological list of editions. Revised in 26.

26 MISH, CHARLES C[ARROLL]. <u>English Prose Fiction, 1600-1700: A
Chronological Checklist</u>. Charlottesville: Bibliographical
Society of the University of Virginia, 1967, 110pp.

Provides chronological short-title list of editions.
Revision and expansion of 24 and 25.

27   MORGAN, CHARLOTTE E. The Rise of the Novel of Manners: A
     Study of English Prose Fiction between 1600 and 1740. New
     York: Columbia University Press, 1911, 281pp.
          Includes "Chronological List of the Prose Fiction First
     Printed in England between 1600 and 1740" (pp. 154-246).
     Annotates some entries and provides location(s) or refer-
     ences to the Stationers' Register or Term Catalogues.

28   O'DELL, STERG. A Chronological List of Prose Fiction in Eng-
     lish Printed in England and Other Countries, 1475-1640.
     Cambridge: Technology Press of M.I.T., 1954, 153pp.
          Provides chronological list of editions with locations
     of copies. In "Introduction," pp. 1-22, discusses problems
     of classifying Renaissance prose fiction and of establishing
     principles of selection.

29   PALMER, HENRIETTA R[AYMER]. List of English Editions and
     Translations of Greek and Latin Classics Printed before
     1641. London: Blades, East, & Blades for the Bibliographi-
     cal Society, 1911, 151pp.
          Provides annotated list arranged alphabetically by ori-
     ginal author; includes listings of translations of prose
     fiction. See 21.

30   PEROTT, JOSEPH DE. "Notes on Professor M. A. Scott's Eliza-
     bethan Translations from the Italian." RR, 9 (July-Septem-
     ber 1918), 304-308.
          Provides additions and corrections to Scott's notes (37).

31   POLLARD, A[LFRED] W[ILLIAM], and G[ILBERT] R[ICHARD] REDGRAVE.
     A Short-Title Catalogue of Books Printed in England, Scot-
     land, & Ireland and of English Books Printed Abroad, 1475-
     1640. London: The Bibliographical Society, 1926, 625pp.
          Provides author listing; entry includes short-title, im-
     print information, and locations. Revised as 19.

32   Q., R. S. "Jest and Song Books." N&Q, 18 (20 October 1858),
     272-73.
          Provides list of jest books, including several from six-
     teenth and seventeenth century.

33   RAITH, JOSEF. Boccaccio in der englischen Literatur von
     Chaucer bis Painters Palace of Pleasure: Ein Beitrag zur
     Geschichte der italienischen Novelle in England. Aus
     Schrifttum und Sprache der Angelsachsen, 3. Leipzig:
     Robert Noske, 1936, 173pp.
          Includes list (by Italian author) of English translations
     and adaptations of Italian novelle to 1620 (pp. 114-35).

34   RANDALL, DALE B. J. The Golden Tapestry: A Critical Survey
      of Non-Chivalric Spanish Fiction in English Translation
      (1543-1657). Durham: Duke University Press, 1963, 272pp.
            In Appendix B provides "A List of Translations and
      Translators of Non-Chivalric Spanish Fiction with Dates of
      Editions through 1657" (pp. 234-39) and in Appendix C gives
      "A List of Chivalric Romances" translated from Spanish into
      English (pp. 240-42).

35   ROLFE, FRANKLIN P[RESCOTT]. "On the Bibliography of Seven-
      teenth-Century Prose Fiction." PMLA, 49 (December 1934),
      1071-86.
            Evaluates available bibliographies of seventeenth-cen-
      tury European prose fiction, noting lack of comprehensive,
      accurate works. Notes several French originals of transla-
      tions listed in Esdaile (14).

36   SAWYER, CHARLES J[AMES], and F[REDERICK] J[OSEPH] HARVEY
      DARTON. English Books, 1475-1900: A Signpost for Collec-
      tors. 2 vols. Westminster: Chas. J. Sawyer; New York:
      E. P. Dutton and Co., 1927, 384, 431pp.
            In Chapter IV ("The Renaissance," I, 63-110) includes
      several works of prose fiction in overview of high-spots
      for collectors; includes price(s) and sometimes indications
      of provenance.

37   SCOTT, MARY AUGUSTA. English Translations from the Italian.
      Vassar Semi-Centennial Series. Boston: Houghton Mifflin
      Co., 1916, 640pp.
            Revision of 38: adds nine entries (pp. 3-108). See 30.

38   SCOTT, MARY AUGUSTA. "Elizabethan Translations from the
      Italian: The Titles of Such Works now First Collected and
      Arranged, with Annotations [I. Romances]." PMLA, 10,
      no. 2 (1895), 249-93.
            Provides chronological checklist of seventy "Romances"
      with annotations on editions, Italian sources, and influ-
      ence on English drama. Revised in 37.

39   SMITH, GORDON ROSS. A Classified Shakespeare Bibliography,
      1936-1958. University Park: Pennsylvania State University
      Press, 1963, 844pp.
            Includes several studies of Renaissance prose fiction in
      section on Shakespeare's sources (pp. 151-217) and in
      "Literary Genesis and Analogues" section of listing for
      each play.

40   STUBBINGS, HILDA [RUBENA] U[REN]. Renaissance Spain in Its
      Literary Relations with England and France: A Critical
      Bibliography. Nashville: Vanderbilt University Press,
      1969, 154pp.

Provides annotated, selective, author-arranged list of
books and articles ("which can be found in at least the
larger American libraries") on Spanish-English literary relations. Includes several works which discuss English
translations of Spanish prose fiction. See 41.

41   STUBBINGS, HILDA RUBENA UREN. "A Selective and Annotated
     Bibliography of Articles, Monographs, and Books Dealing
     with the Influence of Peninsular Spanish Literature of the
     Golden Age (c. 1560 to c. 1681) on the Literatures of Eng-
     land and France During the Sixteenth, Seventeenth, and
     Eighteenth Centuries." Ph.D. dissertation, Vanderbilt Uni-
     versity, 1968, 176pp.
       See 40.

42   TIEJE, ARTHUR JERROLD. The Theory of Characterization in
     Prose Fiction Prior to 1740. University of Minnesota
     Studies in Language and Literature, 5. Minneapolis: Uni-
     versity of Minnesota, 1916, 131pp.
       In Appendix B (pp. 119-31) provides classified list of
     prose fiction to 1740: chivalric romance, pastoral ro-
     mance, allegorical romance, heroico-historical romance,
     satirical romance, educational-informational romance, reli-
     gious romance, picaresque tale, novel of manners, histori-
     cal-psychological novel, sentimental-psychological novel,
     letter fiction, chronique scandaleuse, voyage imaginaire,
     frame-work conte de fée, and collections of short tales.

43   TUCKER, JOSEPH E. "English Translations from the French, 1650-
     1700: Corrections and Additions to the C.B.E.L." PQ, 21
     (October 1942), 391-404.
       Provides several additions and corrections to 2.

44   TUCKER, JOSEPH E. "Wing's Short-Title Catalogue and Transla-
     tions from the French, 1641-1700." PBSA, 49 (First Quarter
     1955), 37-67.
       Includes several translations of prose fiction in list
     of additions and corrections to 49.

45   UNDERHILL, JOHN GARRETT. Spanish Literature in the England
     of the Tudors. Columbia University Studies in Literature.
     New York: Macmillan Co. for Columbia University Press,
     1899, 448pp.
       In "A Bibliography of the Spanish Works Published in the
     Original or in Translation in the England of the Tudors,"
     pp. 375-408, provides chronological listing which includes
     several prose fiction works. Includes notes on later edi-
     tions.

46   UPHAM, A[LFRED] H[ORATIO]. "Notes on Early English Prose Fic-
     tion." MLN, 30 (December 1915), 246-47.

Provides additions to Esdaile (14), some from an unpublished list by Augustus H. Shearer.

47   WATSON, GEORGE, ed. <u>The New Cambridge Bibliography of English Literature, I: 600–1660</u>. Cambridge: Cambridge University Press, 1974, 48pp., 2476 columns.
Revision of 2 (columns 2025–2030, 2049–2068).

48   WICKS, ULRICH. "A Picaresque Bibliography." <u>Genre</u>, 5 (June 1972), 193–216.
Provides bibliography of works on picaresque as form; includes several studies on English Renaissance prose fiction.

49   WING, DONALD. <u>Short-Title Catalogue of Books Printed in England, Scotland, Ireland, Wales, and British America and of English Books Printed in Other Countries, 1641–1700</u>. 3 vols. New York: Columbia University Press for The Index Society, 1945–1951, 580, 532, 533pp.
Provides author listing; entry includes short-title, imprint information, and locations. <u>See</u> 44. Revised as 50.

50   WING, DONALD. <u>Short-Title Catalogue of Books Printed in England, Scotland, Ireland, Wales, and British America and of English Books Printed in Other Countries, 1641–1700, I: A1–E2926</u>. Revised edition. New York: Index Committee of the Modern Language Association of America, 1972, 642pp.
Revised and enlarged edition of 49.

51   WORKMAN, SAMUEL K. "A List of Fifteenth Century English Prose Translations, with the Sources," in <u>Fifteenth Century Translation as an Influence on English Prose</u>. By Samuel K. Workman. Princeton Studies in English, 18. Princeton: Princeton University Press, 1940, pp. 166–206.
Includes several works of prose fiction published 1500–1530. Arranges entries alphabetically by original author; includes notes on source(s) and modern edition(s).

52   ZALL, P. M. "English Prose Jestbooks in the Huntington Library: A Chronological Checklist (1535?–1799)." <u>SRO</u>, No. 4 (1969), pp. 78–91.
Provides chronological, short-title list; indicates number of jests and nature.

Anthologies

53 ASHLEY, ROBERT, and EDWIN M. MOSELEY, eds. Elizabethan Fiction. San Francisco: Rinehart Press, 1953, 443pp.
    Provide partly modernized texts of: Gascoigne's The Pleasant Fable of Ferdinando Jeronimi, Lyly's Euphues: The Anatomy of Wit (omitting the concluding letters), Sidney's Arcadia (excerpts), Nashe's The Unfortunate Traveller, and Deloney's Jack of Newbury.

54 ASHTON, JOHN, ed. Humour, Wit, & Satire of the Seventeenth Century. London: Chatto and Windus, 1883, 462pp.
    Reprints several jests from Renaissance jest books. Arranges jests in no apparent order but does identify sources.

55 COLLIER, J[OHN] PAYNE, ed. Shakespeare's Library: A Collection of the Romances, Novels, Poems, and Histories Used by Shakespeare as the Foundation of His Dramas. 2 vols. London: T. Rodd, 1843 (several works separately paginated).
    Provides reprints of the following: Greene's Pandosto, Lodge's Rosalynde, The History of Hamlet, Prince of Denmark, Twine's The Pattern of Painful Adventures, Painter's "The Novel of Romeo and Julietta" and "The Story of Giletta of Narbona," Rich's "The History of Apolonius and Silla," and Whetstone's "The History of Promos and Cassandra." See 58.

*56 FERRARA, FERNANDO, ed. Burle e facezie del Cinquecento inglese. Poeti e Prosatori di Lingua Inglese, 1. Rome: Edizioni dell'Ateneo, 1973, 336pp.
    Not seen. Listed in National Union Catalog, 1973, vol. 4, 960.

57 HAZLITT, W[ILLIAM] CAREW, ed. Shakespeare Jest-Books. 3 vols. London: Willis & Sotheran, 1864, 302, 379, 475pp.
    Provides annotated reprints of: A Hundred Merry Tales, Merry Tales and Quick Answers, Merry Tales of Skelton, Scoggin's Jests, The Sackful of News, Tarlton's Jests, Peele's Merry Conceited Jests of George Peele, Jack of Dover, Borde's Merry Tales of the Mad Men of Gotham, Pasquil's Jests Mixed with Mother Bunch's Merriments, Johnson's The

9

Conceits of Old Hobson, and W. B.'s Certain Conceits and
Jests.

58   HAZLITT, W[ILLIAM] CAREW, ed. Shakespeare's Library: A Col-
     lection of the Plays, Romances, Novels, Poems, and Histories
     Employed by Shakespeare in the Composition of His Works.
     Edited by John Payne Collier. 2d edition revised. 6 vols.
     London: Reeves and Turner, 1875, 432, 353, 418, 448, 526,
     542pp.
          Reprints prose fiction in 55, with the exception that
     Rich's "Apolonius and Silla" is printed from the 1581 edi-
     tion of Farewell. See 2378.

59   LAWLIS, MERRITT [E.], ed. Elizabethan Prose Fiction. Indiana-
     polis: Odyssey Press, Bobbs-Merrill Co., 1967, 649pp.
          Reprints partly modernized texts of: The Sackful of
     News, Gascoigne's The Adventures of Master F. J., Lyly's
     Euphues: The Anatomy of Wit (omitting the concluding let-
     ters), Rich's "Of Apolonius and Silla," Greene's Pandosto,
     Lodge's Rosalynde, Nashe's The Unfortunate Traveller, and
     Deloney's Thomas of Reading. Includes textual notes on each
     work.

60   MISH, CHARLES C[ARROLL], ed. Short Fiction of the Seventeenth
     Century. Stuart Editions. New York: New York University
     Press, 1963, 458pp. [Reprinted: The Norton Library.
     New York: W. W. Norton & Co., 1968, 458pp.]
          Provides modernized texts of: The Famous and Renowned
     History of Morindos, Anton's Moriomachia, The Life and
     Pranks of Long Meg of Westminster, Reynolds's "Don Juan and
     Marsillia" from The Triumphs of God's Revenge against Mur-
     der, Godwin's The Man in the Moon, Allen's The History of
     Eurialus and Lucretia, The Pleasant History of Cawood the
     Rook, Hart's The Tragical-Comical History of Alexto and
     Angelica.

61   MORLEY, HENRY, ed. Early Prose Romances. Carisbrooke Library,
     4. London: G. Routledge, 1889, 446pp.
          Provides reprints of The History of Hamlet and The His-
     tory of Guy Earl of Warwick as well as selections from A
     Hundred Merry Tales. Reprints texts of Robert the Devil,
     Virgilius, The Famous History of Friar Bacon, and The His-
     tory of Friar Rush from 1858 edition of 66. In "Introduc-
     tion," pp. 11-30, traces development of each of the legends.
     Reprinted in 67.

62   O'BRIEN, EDWARD J[OSEPH], ed. Elizabethan Tales. London:
     G. Allen & Unwin, 1937, 317pp.
          Provides modernized texts of: Pettie's "Tereus and
     Progne," Rich's "Apolonius and Silla," Whetstone's "Promos
     and Cassandra," and excerpts from several longer works of

prose fiction to illustrate the art of the "short story" in Elizabethan England.

63 SPENCER, T[ERENCE] J. B., ed. <u>Elizabethan Love Stories</u>. Penguin Shakespeare Library. Harmondsworth: Penguin Books, 1968, 214pp.
    Includes modernized texts of: Painter's "Giletta of Narbona" and "Romeo and Julietta," Rich's "Apolonius and Silla," Whetstone's "Promos and Cassandra," Young's "The Story of Felix and Felismena" (from <u>Diana</u>), "The Story of Bernardo and Generva" (from 1620 <u>Decameron</u>).

64 <u>Shorter Novels: Elizabethan and Jacobean</u>. Introduction by George Saintsbury. Notes by Philip Henderson. Everyman's Library, 824. London: J. M. Dent & Sons; New York: E. P. Dutton & Co., 1929, 380pp.
    Provides partly modernized reprints of Deloney's <u>Jack of Newbury</u> and <u>Thomas of Reading</u>, Greene's <u>Card of Fancy</u>, and Nashe's <u>The Unfortunate Traveller</u>. Reprinted as 65.

65 <u>Shorter Novels: Elizabethan</u>. Introduction by George Saintsbury. Notes by Philip Henderson. Everyman's Library, 824. London: Dent; New York: Dutton, 1969, 380pp.
    Reprint of 64 with slight revisions in the "Introduction" and "Notes" by R[obert] G[uy] Howarth.

66 THOMS, WILLIAM J., ed. <u>A Collection of Early Prose Romances</u>. 3 vols. London: William Pickering, 1828, separately paginated. [Each work also published separately.]
    Provides reprints of: <u>The Life of Robert the Devil</u>, Deloney's <u>Thomas of Reading</u>, <u>The History of Friar Bacon</u>, <u>The Pleasant History of Friar Rush</u>, <u>Virgilius</u>, <u>The History of George a Green</u>, <u>Pindar of the Town of Wakefield</u>, Johnson's <u>The History of Tom a Lincoln</u>, Robert Copland's <u>The History of Helyas, Knight of the Swan</u>, P. F.'s <u>The History of the Life and Death of Doctor John Faustus</u>, <u>The Second Report of Doctor John Faustus</u>. Revised as 67; <u>see</u> 61.

67 THOMS, WILLIAM J., ed. <u>Early English Prose Romances</u>. Revised and enlarged edition. London: G. Routledge and Sons; New York: E. P. Dutton and Co., [1907], 958pp.
    Reprints contents of 61 plus works from 66 which Morley had omitted. Includes: <u>Robert the Devil</u>, <u>Virgilius</u>, <u>The History of Hamlet</u>, <u>The Famous History of Friar Bacon</u>, <u>The History of Guy Earl of Warwick</u>, <u>The History of Friar Rush</u>, Deloney's <u>Thomas of Reading</u>, <u>The History of George a Greene</u>, <u>Pindar of the Town of Wakefield</u>, Johnson's <u>The Pleasant History of Tom a Lincoln, the Red Rose Knight</u>, Robert Copland's <u>The Knight of the Swan</u>, P. F.'s <u>The History of the Damnable Life and Deserved Death of Doctor John Faustus</u>, <u>The Second Report of Doctor John Faustus</u>.

68   TREND, J[OHN] B[RANDE], ed. <u>Spanish Short Stories of the Six-</u>
     <u>teenth Century in Contemporary Translations</u>. World's Clas-
     sics, 326. Oxford: Oxford University Press, 1928, 373pp.
          Includes Rowland's translation of <u>Lazarillo de Tormes</u>
     and selections from the following translations: Young's
     <u>Diana</u>, Mabbe's <u>Exemplary Novels</u> and <u>The Rogue</u>, M. L.'s
     <u>Persiles and Sigismunda</u>, and Shelton's <u>Don Quixote</u>.

69   TURNER, ALBERT MORTON, and PERCIE HOPKINS TURNER, eds. <u>Malory</u>
     <u>to Mrs. Behn: Specimens of Early Prose Fiction</u>. Nelson's
     English Series. New York: T. Nelson and Sons, 1930, 418pp.
          Provides modernized texts of extracts from: Bourchier's
     <u>Huon of Bordeaux</u>, Lyly's <u>Euphues: The Anatomy of Wit</u>, Sid-
     ney's <u>Arcadia</u>, Nashe's <u>Unfortunate Traveller</u>, Deloney's
     <u>Jack of Newbury</u>, and Boyle's <u>Parthenissa</u>. Includes complete
     text of Lodge's <u>Rosalynde</u>.

70   WARDROPER, JOHN, ed. <u>Jest upon Jest: A Selection from the</u>
     <u>Jestbooks and Collections of Merry Tales Published from the</u>
     <u>Reign of Richard III to George III</u>. London: Routledge &
     Kegan Paul, 1970, 223pp.
          Provides annotated, modernized selections (arranged
     topically) from a variety of Renaissance jest books.

71   WINNY, JAMES, ed. <u>The Descent of Euphues: Three Elizabethan</u>
     <u>Romance Stories: Euphues, Pandosto, Piers Plainness</u>.
     Cambridge: Cambridge University Press, 1957, 205pp.
          Provides slightly modernized texts of Lyly's <u>Euphues:</u>
     <u>The Anatomy of Wit</u>, Greene's <u>Pandosto</u>, and Chettle's <u>Piers</u>
     <u>Plainness</u>.

72   ZALL, P. M., ed. A Hundred Merry Tales <u>and Other English</u>
     <u>Jestbooks of the Fifteenth and Sixteenth Centuries</u>. Lin-
     coln: University of Nebraska Press, 1963, 400pp.
          Provides modernized reprints of: <u>A Hundred Merry Tales</u>,
     William Copland's <u>Howleglas</u>, <u>Tales and Quick Answers</u>, <u>Merry</u>
     <u>Tales Made by Master Skelton</u>, and T. D.'s <u>Mirror of Mirth</u>
     (selections).

73   ZALL, P. M., ed. A Nest of Ninnies <u>and Other English Jestbooks</u>
     <u>of the Seventeenth Century</u>. Lincoln: University of
     Nebraska Press, 1970, 278pp.
          Provides modernized reprint of Armin's <u>A Nest of Ninnies</u>
     and selections from: Wilkins and Dekker's <u>Jests to Make</u>
     <u>You Merry</u>, Tarlton's <u>Tarlton's Jests</u>, Scoggin's <u>Scoggin's</u>
     <u>Jests</u>, and <u>A Banquet of Jests</u>.

General Studies

74   AARNE, ANTTI [AMATUS]. The Types of the Folk-Tale: A Classi-
      fication and Bibliography. Translated and Enlarged by
      Stith Thompson. FFC, 74. Helsinki: Suomalainen Tiedeaka-
      temia, Academia Scientiarum Fennica, 1928, 279pp.
         Translates and provides additions to 76.

75   AARNE, ANTTI [AMATUS]. The Types of the Folktale: A Classi-
      fication and Bibliography. Translated and Enlarged by Stith
      Thompson. Second revision. FFC, 184. Helsinki: Suoma-
      lainen Tiedeakatemia, Academia Scientiarum Fennica, 1961,
      588pp.
         Enlarged version of 74.

76   AARNE, ANTTI [AMATUS]. Verzeichnis der Marchentypen. FFC, 3.
      Helsinki: Suomalainen Tiedeakatemian Toimituksia, 1910,
      76pp.
         Provides list of narrative motifs, several of which are
      found in Renaissance prose fiction. Revised as 74 and 75.

77   ADAMS, ROBERT P. "Bold Bawdry and Open Manslaughter: The
      English New Humanist Attack on Medieval Romance." HLQ, 23
      (November 1959), 33-48.
         Examines methods and purpose of criticism by More, Eras-
      mus, and Vives of medieval romance.

78   ADOLPH, ROBERT. The Rise of Modern Prose Style. Cambridge:
      M. I. T. Press, 1968, 372pp.
         Studies development of modern prose style, arguing that
      "the ultimate influence on the new prose is neither 'science'
      nor 'Anti-Ciceronianism' but the new utilitarianism" of the
      seventeenth century. In discussion of differences between
      Elizabethan and modern fiction, focuses on changes in style
      and point of view. Characterizes sixteenth-century prose
      fiction as "a chain of static pictures, quite out of all
      time and space, connected by purely narrative links, with
      characterization generally a matter of frozen moral abso-
      lutes" (pp. 263-88).

79 ALLEN, H[ERBERT] WARNER. "The Picaresque Novel: An Essay in Comparative Literature," in Celestina or the Tragi-Comedy of Calisto and Melibea. Translated by James Mabbe. Edited by H[erbert] Warner Allen. London: George Routledge & Sons; New York: E. P. Dutton & Co. [1923], pp. xxi-lxxvi.
      Traces in general terms the "rise of realism in prose fiction" (rather than strictly picaresque narrative) in Spain, France, and England. Discusses lack of tendency toward picaresque in sixteenth-century fiction and surveys early seventeenth-century translations of Spanish picaresque novels. Precedes essay with table "A General Outline of the Rise of Realism in the Prose Fiction of Spain, England, and France as Illustrated by the Picaresque Novel and Kindred Works" (pp. vii-xix).

80 ALLEN, WALTER. The English Novel: A Short Critical History. New York: E. P. Dutton and Co., 1955, 478pp.
      In Chapter I ("The Beginnings") provides a brief overview of major authors of Renaissance prose fiction: focuses on prose style and discusses why each work cannot be called a novel. Argues that the dominance of the drama from 1580 to 1640, with its artistry in blank verse, hindered the development of prose fiction.

*81 AMOS, FLORA ROSS. "Early Theories of Translation." Ph.D. dissertation, Columbia University, 1920, 183pp.
      See 82.

82 AMOS, FLORA ROSS. Early Theories of Translation. Columbia University Studies in English and Comparative Literature. New York: Columbia University Press, 1920, 200pp.
      In Chapter III ("The Sixteenth Century," pp. 81-132) examines personal, cultural, and national factors which influenced translation and analyzes characteristics of the Elizabethan "theory" of translation.

83 ANDERS, H[EINRICH] R. D. Shakespeare's Books: A Dissertation on Shakespeare's Reading and the Immediate Sources of His Works. Berlin: Georg Reimer, 1904, 316pp.
      Intended work to be introduction to new edition of 58. Provides series of brief notes arranged by work on influences on Shakespeare's plays; includes several Renaissance prose fiction works.

84 ANON. "English Humor, 1500-1800." TLS, 21 May 1938, p. 360.
      Describes Renaissance jest books displayed at Bodleian exhibition illustrating English humor, 1500-1800.

85 ASHLEY, ROBERT, and EDWIN M. MOSELEY. "Introduction," in Elizabethan Fiction. Edited by Robert Ashley and Edwin M. Moseley. San Francisco: Rinehart Press, 1953, pp. vii-xx.

Provides overview of contributions of Gascoigne, Lyly,
Sidney, Nashe, and Deloney to the development of the novel.

86   ASHWORTH, ROBERT A. "The English Novel in the Time of Eliza-
      beth." SR, 3 (November 1894), 62-80.
           Provides an overview of characteristic works to illus-
      trate that in Elizabethan prose fiction one finds the "be-
      ginnings of the English novel of to-day." Discusses general
      characteristics (style, characterization, moralization) of
      the prose fiction of the period.

87   ATKINS, J[OHN] W[ILLIAM] H[EY]. "Elizabethan Prose Fiction,"
      in The Cambridge History of English Literature, III:
      Renascence and Reformation. Edited by A[dolphus] W[illiam]
      Ward and A[lfred] R[ayney] Waller. Cambridge: Cambridge
      University Press, 1909, 339-73.
           Provides overview of development of Elizabethan prose
      fiction from romance to realism. Examines influences on
      development, discusses major works, and stresses the ex-
      perimental nature of fiction of period.

88   AYRES, PHILIP J. "Degrees of Heresy: Justified Revenge and
      Elizabethan Narratives." SP, 69 (October 1972), 461-74.
           Examines treatment of revenge in several works of prose
      fiction to argue that "Elizabethans were reading of re-
      vengers whose actions were condoned by the authors and of
      whom the reader was often encouraged to approve."

89   BAHLSEN, LEO. "Spanische Quellen der dramatischen Litteratur,
      besonders Englands zu Shakespeares Zeit." Zeitschrift für
      Vergleichende Litteraturgeschichte, NS, 6 (1893), 151-59.
           Includes discussion of English translations of Spanish
      prose fiction in general overview of influence of Spanish
      literature on Renaissance drama.

90   BAKER, ERNEST A[LBERT]. The History of the English Novel,
      Vol. I. London: H. F. & G. Witherby, 1924, 336pp.
           Provides an overview of translations of French and
      Spanish romances, of early popular tales, and of jest books.
      Discusses relationship to the development of prose fiction,
      and argues for the continuity of English fiction from
      medieval romance to modern novel (passim).

91   BAKER, ERNEST A[LBERT]. The History of the English Novel,
      Vol. II. London: H. F. & G. Witherby, 1929, 303pp.
           Characterizes Elizabethan period as "one of haphazard or
      ill-directed experiment, of copious translation and adapta-
      tion." Provides an overview of various influences on and
      types of Elizabethan prose fiction; discusses translations,
      arcadian and euphuistic fiction, realistic fiction, charac-
      ter, and utopian fiction (passim).

92   BAKER, ERNEST A[LBERT]. The History of the English Novel,
         Vol. III. London: H. F. & G. Witherby, 1929, 278pp.
            Discusses the influence of the French heroic romance on
         English fiction and surveys the translations of anti-ro-
         mances and the types of rogue literature (pp. 11-49).

93   BAKER, SHERIDAN. "Fielding's Amelia and the Materials of
         Romance." PQ, 41 (April 1962), 437-49.
            Examines Fielding's use of conventions of earlier romance
         in Amelia.

94   BAKER, SHERIDAN. "The Idea of Romance in the Eighteenth-
         Century Novel." Papers of the Michigan Academy of Science,
         Arts, and Letters, 49 (1964), 507-22.
            Examines influence of earlier romances (especially seven-
         teenth-century French ones) on the eighteenth-century novel.

95   BAKER, SHERIDAN. "The Idea of Romance in the Eighteenth-
         Century Novel." SELit, 40 (1963), 49-61.
            Discusses the general influences of earlier romances on
         the eighteenth-century novel.

96   BALDWIN, CHARLES SEARS. Renaissance Literary Theory and Prac-
         tice: Classicism in the Rhetoric and Poetic of Italy,
         France, and England, 1400-1600. Edited by Donald Lemen
         Clark. New York: Columbia University Press, 1939, 265pp.
            Includes discussion of decorative style and lack of nar-
         rative power of Elizabethan prose fiction (passim).

97   BALDWIN, SPURGEON WHITFIELD, JR. "Brief Narrative Prose of
         the Fifteenth and Sixteenth Centuries." Ph.D. dissertation,
         University of North Carolina at Chapel Hill, 1962, 167pp.
            Attempts "to examine all forms of the brief narrative
         [in the period]...and to begin study which will eventually
         bridge the gap between the last of the collections of
         exempla and the short stories of the seventeenth century."
         Examines works "in connection with their expression of the
         social habits and customs" of the age.

*98   BATES, PAUL A. "Elizabethan Amorous Pastorals." Ph.D. disser-
         tation, University of Kansas, 1955.
            Abstract not available.

99   BEACH, DONALD MARCUS. "Studies in the Art of Elizabethan Prose
         Narrative." Ph.D. dissertation, Cornell University, 1959,
         237pp.
            "[A]ttempts to describe the art of prose narrative which
         developed in England between 1575 and 1600." Analyzes
         "plots of sentiment, separation,...[and] adventure."

100   BEACHCROFT, T[HOMAS] O[WEN]. The English Short Story. 2 vols.
      Writers and Their Work, 168–69. London: Longmans, Green
      for the British Council and the National Book League, 1964,
      85pp.
          Examines place of Elizabethan fiction in development of
      short story. Surveys briefly stylistic trends and types of
      fiction. Notes lack of emphasis on characterization and the
      "little attempt to build up scenes" (I, 22-28).

101   BEACHCROFT, T[HOMAS] O[WEN]. The Modest Art: A Survey of the
      Short Story in English. London: Oxford University Press,
      1968, 394pp.
          In Chapter 6 ("The Elizabethans: Through Pleasures and
      Palaces," pp. 58-75) provides survey of development of
      Elizabethan short prose fiction. Discusses types of short
      works, narrative techniques, and subject matter. Examines
      innovations in form and place in development of short story.

102   BEER, GILLIAN. The Romance. Critical Idiom, 10. London:
      Methuen, 1970, 96pp.
          Includes discussion of characteristics of and influences
      upon Elizabethan romance (pp. 31-38).

103   BENNETT, H[ENRY] S[TANLEY]. English Books & Readers, 1475-
      1557: Being a Study in the History of the Book Trade from
      Caxton to the Incorporation of the Stationers' Company.
      Cambridge: Cambridge University Press, 1952, 351pp.
          Considers several works of prose fiction in discussion
      of demand for and variety of books and translators and
      translations. Includes appendix "Trial List of Translations
      into English Printed between 1475-1560" (pp. 276-319), which
      lists prose fiction.

104   BENNETT, H[ENRY] S[TANLEY]. English Books & Readers, 1558-
      1603: Being a Study in the History of the Book Trade in
      the Reign of Elizabeth I. Cambridge: Cambridge University
      Press, 1965, 338pp.
          Includes discussion of prose fiction works in examination
      of factors affecting publishing of books (passim).

105   BENNETT, H[ENRY] S[TANLEY]. English Books & Readers, 1603-
      1640: Being a Study in the History of the Book Trade in
      the Reigns of James I and Charles I. Cambridge: Cambridge
      University Press, 1970, 267pp.
          Includes discussion of prose fiction in context of ex-
      amination of factors affecting publishing of books (passim).

106   BENNETT, H[ENRY] S[TANLEY]. "Introduction [to Romances and
      Tales]," in The Thought & Culture of the English Renais-
      sance: An Anthology of Tudor Prose, 1481-1555. Edited by
      Elizabeth M. Nugent. Cambridge: Cambridge University
      Press, 1956, pp. 563-70.

Discusses briefly the printing and publication of romances, their popularity, their didacticism, and their influence on national life.

107   BERNBAUM, ERNEST. "Recent Works on Prose Fiction before 1800."
      MLN, 42 (May 1927), 281-93.
      Review essay on works published 1925-1926.

108   BERNBAUM, ERNEST. "Recent Works on Prose Fiction before 1800."
      MLN, 43 (June 1928), 416-25.
      Review essay on works published 1927.

109   BERNBAUM, ERNEST. "Recent Works on Prose Fiction before 1800."
      MLN, 46 (February 1931), 95-107.
      Review essay on works published 1928-1930.

110   BERNBAUM, ERNEST. "Recent Works on Prose Fiction before 1800."
      MLN, 47 (February 1932), 104-13.
      Review essay on works published 1930-1931.

111   BERNBAUM, ERNEST. "Recent Works on Prose Fiction before 1800."
      MLN, 48 (June 1933), 370-78.
      Review essay on works published 1932-1933.

112   BERNBAUM, ERNEST. "Recent Works on Prose Fiction before 1800."
      MLN, 49 (December 1934), 523-34.
      Review essay on works published 1933-1934. Points out
      need for more work on history of early prose fiction.

113   BERNBAUM, ERNEST. "Recent Works on Prose Fiction before 1800."
      MLN, 51 (April 1936), 244-55.
      Review essay on works published 1935-1936.

114   BERNBAUM, ERNEST. "Recent Works on Prose Fiction before 1800."
      MLN, 52 (December 1937), 580-93.
      Review essay on works published 1936-1937.

115   BERNBAUM, ERNEST. "Recent Works on Prose Fiction before 1800."
      MLN, 55 (January 1940), 54-65.
      Review essay on works published 1938-1939.

116   BEVAN, ELINOR. "Revenge, Forgiveness, and the Gentleman."
      Review of English Literature, 8, no. 3 (1967), 55-69.
      Discusses "contemporary ideas about honourable revenge
      and forgiveness" as revealed through Italian novelle and
      sixteenth-century English prose fiction.

*117 BLACKBURN, A. L. "The Picaresque Novel: A Literary Idea,
      1554-1954." Ph.D. dissertation, Cambridge University-Fitz-
      william College, 1963.
      Abstract not available.

118   BLOOR, R[OBERT] H[ENRY] U[NDERWOOD]. The English Novel from
        Chaucer to Galsworthy. University Extension Library.
        London: I. Nicholson and Watson, 1935, 248pp.
             Includes overview of development of Elizabethan prose
        fiction from Painter through Deloney. Discusses tendency
        toward moralizing in works and argues that development of
        Elizabethan prose fiction reflects changes in society
        (pp. 58-111).

*119   BLUESTONE, MAX. "Adaptation of Prose Fiction in the Eliza-
        bethan Theatre." Ph.D. dissertation, Harvard University,
        1959.
             See 120.

120   BLUESTONE, MAX. From Story to Stage: The Dramatic Adaptation
        of Prose Fiction in the Period of Shakespeare and His Con-
        temporaries. SEngL, 70. The Hague: Mouton, 1974, 341pp.
             Attempts "to define and to demonstrate the qualitative
        nature of Elizabethan dramatic adaptation of prose fiction"
        and examines the problems involved in the "movement from
        one genre to another." Examines the emphasis on "sheer
        linear narrative," discusses the handling of time, and ana-
        lyzes the lack of attention to "material things" or "physi-
        cal action" and spatial details in Renaissance prose
        fiction. Not concerned with source study per se.

121   BOAS, FREDERICK S. "Aspects of Shakespeare's Reading," in
        Queen Elizabeth in Drama and Related Studies. By Frederick
        S. Boas. London: George Allen & Unwin, 1950, pp. 56-71.
             Devotes portion of essay to an overview of Shakespeare's
        reading of Renaissance prose fiction.

122   BONASCHI, ALBERTO C. Italian Currents and Curiosities in the
        English Literature from Chaucer to Shakespeare. New York:
        Italian Chamber of Commerce in New York, 1937, 25pp.
             Discusses in general terms Elizabethan translation of
        Italian prose fiction and its influence on the drama (par-
        ticularly Shakespeare).

123   BOOTHE, BERT E. "The Contribution of the Italian Novella to
        the Formation and Development of Elizabethan Prose Fiction,
        1566-1582." Ph.D. dissertation, University of Michigan,
        1936.
             Examines influences of Italian prose fiction on the de-
        velopment of Elizabethan prose fiction. Analyzes transla-
        tions and adaptations in relation to originals and examines
        the vogue of Italianate fiction in the 1580s.

124   BORINSKI, LUDWIG. "Diego de San Pedro und die euphuistische
        Erzählung." Anglia, 98, no. 2 (1971), 224-39.
             Examines influence of San Pedro's Arnalte y Lucenda and
        Cárcel de amor on the euphuistic novel.

125   BORINSKI, LUDWIG. "Mittelalter und Neuzeit in der Stilge-
       schichte des 16. Jahrhunderts." Shakespeare-Jahrbuch, 97
       (1961), 109-33.
            Includes discussion of increasing emphasis on realism as
       well as the psychological (and the effect on style) in
       Elizabethan prose fiction.

126   BORINSKI, LUDWIG. "The Origin of the Euphuistic Novel and Its
       Significance for Shakespeare," in Studies in Honor of T. W.
       Baldwin. Edited by Don Cameron Allen. Urbana: University
       of Illinois Press, 1958, pp. 38-52.
            Examines the place of Pettie, Lyly, and The Goodly His-
       tory of the Lady Lucrece in the development of the euphuis-
       tic novel. Analyzes the characteristics of the form and
       its influence on Shakespeare's works.

127   BORINSKI, LUDWIG. "Die Vorgeschichte des englischen Essay."
       Anglia, 83, no. 1 (1965), 48-77.
            Includes examination of contribution of Elizabethan prose
       fiction to development of essay; discusses use of moral dis-
       course and character portrait.

*128   BORINSKI, LUDWIG, and CLAUS UHLIG. Literatur der Renaissance.
       Studienreihe Englisch, 23. Düsseldorf: Bagel und Francke,
       1975, 187pp.
            Examines "increase in dramatic quality, psychology, and
       realism" in narrative prose, 1560-1600; analyzes changes in
       style. Includes examination of "the history of scholarship
       in...16th century prose literature." (Not seen; English
       summary in: English and American Studies in German: Sum-
       maries of Theses and Monographs, 1975. Edited by Werner
       Habicht. Tübingen: M. Niemeyer Verlag, 1976, pp. 61-62.)

*129   BOSSARD, RICHARD. "Die Liebe in der erzählenden Prosa Englands
       von Lyly bis Defoe." Ph.D. dissertation, University of
       Zurich, 1955.
            Abstract not available.

130   BOWERS, FREDSON THAYER. Elizabethan Revenge Tragedy, 1587-
       1642. Princeton: Princeton University Press, 1940, 296pp.
            Includes survey of collections of novelle and suggests
       that these stories "trained the audience to accept the plot
       and characterization [of revenge tragedy]...as dramatized
       truth" and "fostered prejudices concerning the general vil-
       lainy and treacherous revengefulness of foreigners" (pp. 57-
       61).

131   BOYCE, BENJAMIN. "The Effect of the Restoration on Prose Fic-
       tion." TSL, 6 (1961), 77-83.
            Characterizes kinds of prose fiction published between
       1640 and 1690; examines influence of Restoration on con-
       tinuing vogue of heroic romance.

132   BOYCE, BENJAMIN. "News from Hell: Satiritic Communications
       with the Nether World in English Writing of the Seventeenth
       and Eighteenth Centuries." PMLA, 58 (June 1943), 402-37.
       Surveys treatment in Elizabethan prose fiction finding
       few works on classical model of Lucian. Concludes that
       Elizabethan descriptions are devoid of humor and lack em-
       phasis on character of nether world. Includes chronological
       listing of treatments.

133   BRADISH, GAYNOR FRANCIS. "The Hard Pennyworth: A Study in
       Sixteenth Century Prose Fiction." Ph.D. dissertation,
       Harvard University, 1958, 194pp.
       Analyzes development of theme of "learning through ex-
       perience" in the works of Lyly, Greene, and Nashe, and in
       the jest books. Analyzes relationship of style and struc-
       ture to theme.

*134   BRENNAN, E. M. "The Concept of Revenge for Honour in English
       Fiction and Drama between 1580 and 1640." Ph.D. disserta-
       tion, University of London-Royal Holloway College, 1958.
       Abstract not available.

135   BRIE, FRIEDRICH. "Roman und Drama im Zeitalter Shakespeares."
       Shakespeare-Jahrbuch, 48 (1912), 125-47.
       Examines mutual influences of drama and prose fiction
       in Elizabethan age.

136   BROOKE, [C. F.] TUCKER. "The Renaissance," in A Literary His-
       tory of England. Edited by Albert C. Baugh. New York:
       Appleton-Century-Crofts, 1948, pp. 313-696.
       Includes overview of Renaissance prose fiction works;
       comments on style and influences (passim). Revised in 137.

137   BROOKE, [C. F.] TUCKER. "The Renaissance," in A Literary His-
       tory of England. Edited by Albert C. Baugh. 2d edition.
       New York: Appleton-Century-Crofts, 1967, pp. 312-696.
       Provides corrected reprint of 136 with supplementary
       notes by Matthias A. Shaaber.

138   BROWN, HUNTINGTON. "Introduction," in The Tale of Gargantua
       and King Arthur, by François Girault, c. 1534: The French
       Original of a Lost Elizabethan Translation. By François
       Girault. Edited by Huntington Brown. Cambridge: Harvard
       University Press, 1932, pp. xiii-xxxix.
       Discusses evidence for a lost Elizabethan prose transla-
       tion of Les Croniques admirables du Roy Gargantua.

*139   BRUSER, FREDELLE. "Concepts of Chastity in Literature, Chiefly
       Non-Dramatic, of the English Renaissance." Ph.D. disserta-
       tion, Radcliffe College, 1948.
       Abstract not available.

140   BURROWS, DOROTHY. "The Relation of Dryden's Serious Plays and
       Dramatic Criticism to Contemporary French Literature."
       Ph.D. dissertation, University of Illinois at Urbana-
       Champaign, 1933.
            Includes examination of influence of French heroic ro-
       mance (including English translations) on Dryden's plays.

141   BUSH, DOUGLAS. English Literature in the Earlier Seventeenth
       Century, 1600-1660. Oxford History of English Literature,
       5. Oxford: Clarendon Press, 1945, 629pp. [Revised edi-
       tion: Oxford: Clarendon Press, 1962, 688pp.]
            Includes overview of types of seventeenth-century prose
       fiction. Provides brief discussions of major works and in-
       fluences (passim). (No significant changes in discussion
       of prose fiction in revised edition.)

142   BUSH, DOUGLAS. Mythology and the Renaissance Tradition in
       English Poetry. Minneapolis: University of Minnesota
       Press, 1932, 370pp. [Revised edition: New York: W. W.
       Norton & Co., 1963, 384pp.]
            Includes overview of "Classical Tales in English Prose"
       to illustrate that the "Elizabethan reader found mythology
       and pseudo-mythology even in prose fiction" (pp. 35-39;
       33-37 in revised edition).

143   CAMP, CHARLES W[ELLNER]. The Artisan in Elizabethan Litera-
       ture. Columbia University Studies in English and Compara-
       tive Literature. New York: Columbia University Press,
       1924, 176pp.
            Examines changes in representation of and treatment of
       the artisan in literature (including prose fiction) from
       c. 1558 to 1642. Arranges discussion around various themes,
       e.g., "craftsman as heroic figure," "artisan as speculator
       and philanthropist," and "social aspirations of the artisan."

144   CANBY, HENRY SEIDEL. The Short Story in English. New York:
       Holt and Co., 1909, 400pp.
            Provides an overview of the development of the "short
       story" in the Elizabethan period. Analyzes influences--
       Italian novelle, euphuism, romance, vulgar literature,
       humanism, and "the English temperament"--on the development
       of short fiction. Emphasizes Elizabethans' concern for
       rhetorical embellishment rather than narrative art (passim).

145   CANBY, HENRY SEIDEL. A Study of the Short Story. New York:
       H. Holt and Co., 1913, 279pp.
            In Chapter III ("The Short Story of the Renaissance,"
       pp. 13-22) discusses the Elizabethan imitation of the
       Italian novella and the influence of the form on later
       Renaissance fiction.

146   CAREY, JOHN. "Sixteenth and Seventeenth Century Prose," in
      History of Literature in the English Language, Vol. II:
      English Poetry and Prose, 1540-1674. Edited by Christopher
      [B.] Ricks. London: Barrie & Jenkins, 1970, 339-431.
          In "Part II: Elizabethan Prose" (pp. 361-89) provides
      an overview of Elizabethan prose fiction. Focuses on style
      and argues that except for The Unfortunate Traveller Eliza-
      bethan prose fiction "is thoroughly and...deservedly dead...
      because it was meticulously superficial."

147   CARROLL, WILLIAM MEREDITH. Animal Conventions in English
      Renaissance Non-Religious Prose (1550-1600). New York:
      Bookman Associates, 1954, 166pp.
          Discusses the "conventional ideas about animals" in the
      jest books and in the prose fiction of Greene, Lodge,
      Grange, Lyly, Sidney, Rich, Deloney, Nashe, Painter, and
      Pettie. Includes Appendix listing references to various
      animals.

148   CAZAMIAN, LOUIS. The Development of English Humor. Durham:
      Duke University Press, 1952, 431pp.
          In the context of examining the development of humor
      during the Renaissance, characterizes the humor in the jest
      books and in the prose fiction of Greene, Lyly, Sidney,
      Nashe, Dekker, and Deloney (passim).

149   CHANDLER, FRANK WADLEIGH. The Literature of Roguery. 2 vols.
      Boston: Houghton, Mifflin, and Co., 1907, 602pp.
          Examines treatment and development of the rogue-type in
      various types of Renaissance prose fiction (jest books,
      popular tales, criminal biographies, picaresque tales, and
      translations) (passim).

150   CHARLANNE, LOUIS. L'Influence française en Angleterre au
      XVIIe siècle: La Vie sociale--la vie littéraire: Étude
      sur les relations sociales et littéraires de la France et
      de l'Angleterre surtout dans la seconde moité du XVIIe
      siècle. Paris: Société Française d'Imprimerie et de
      Librairie, 1906, 624pp.
          In Chapter VI ("Les Romans français en Angleterre,"
      pp. 387-404) discusses the popularity of the French romance
      in England: examines briefly the major translations and
      reasons for popularity.

151   CHICKERA, ERNST DE. "Palaces of Pleasure: The Theme of Re-
      venge in Elizabethan Translations of Novelle." RES, NS, 11
      (February 1960), 1-7.
          Examines attitudes toward revenge in translations and re-
      lationship to Elizabethan revenge tragedy. Distinguishes
      two types of revenge stories: one in which "the wrong or
      injury comes back to the wrongdoer in almost equal measure,"

the other "in which the wrongdoer is punished with a severity out of all proportion to the offence." Observes that
in the novelle emphasis is on private revenge and that the
action "is a basic impulse, natural and spontaneous."

152   CHURCH, RICHARD. The Growth of the English Novel. London:
      Methuen, 1951, 187pp.
          Provides an overview of the major developments in Renais-
      sance prose fiction as background for the development of the
      novel. Comments briefly on style and subject matter of the
      major works representative of the types of Renaissance prose
      fiction (pp. 15-46).

*153   CLARK, S. "English Renaissance Translations from Classical
      Latin." Ph.D. dissertation, Cambridge University, 1951.
      Abstract not available.

154   CLARK, WILLIAM S. "The Sources of the Restoration Heroic
      Play." RES, 4 (January 1928), 49-63.
          Argues that the development of the heroic play was in-
      fluenced primarily by the popularity of French romances
      (some in English translation), which provided sources for
      themes, plots, and characters.

155   CLEMENTS, ROBERT J. "Anatomy of the Novella." CLS, 9 (March
      1972), 3-16.
          In an attempt to provide for more precision in the use
      of the term novella, analyzes "four characteristic struc-
      tural elements": the framework, the "conscious unity of
      time," "the evolving length, and the thematic classification
      centering on the everyday dramas of men and women."

156   CLOUSTON, W[ILLIAM] A[LEXANDER]. The Book of Noodles: Stories
      of Simpletons; or, Fools and Their Follies. Book-Lover's
      Library. New York: A. C. Armstrong and Son, 1888, 248pp.
          Includes discussion of sources and analogues for various
      jests in Renaissance jest books.

157   COHEN, J[OHN] M[ICHAEL]. English Translators and Translations.
      Writers and Their Work, 142. London: Longmans, Green for
      the British Council and the National Book League, 1962,
      56pp.
          Discusses Elizabethan age as one of the two great periods
      of translation. Provides general overview of characteris-
      tics of translations and attitudes toward handling of text.

158   COLE, HOWARD C. A Quest of Inquirie: Some Contexts of Tudor
      Literature. Indianapolis: Pegasus, Bobbs-Merrill Co.,
      1973, 596pp.
          Includes discussion of influences (particularly that of
      the Court entertainment) on and characteristics of Eliza-
      bethan prose fiction (passim).

159   CONLEY, CAREY HERBERT. "Early Elizabethan Translations from
        the Classics." Ph.D. dissertation, Yale University, 1922.
        See 160.

160   CONLEY, C[AREY] H[ERBERT]. The First English Translators of
        the Classics. New Haven: Yale University Press, 1927,
        158pp.
            Provides detailed analysis of the characteristics of the
        "translation movement" 1550-1573.

161   COOLIDGE, JOHN S. "Martin Marprelate, Marvell, and Decorum
        Personae as a Satirical Theme." PMLA, 74 (December 1959),
        526-32.
            Argues that in developing the "device of using a theatri-
        cal, comic mask in non-dramatic writing" the anonymous
        Martin influenced the evolution of Elizabethan prose fic-
        tion.

*162 COOPER, ELIZABETH H. "The Medieval Background of English
        Renaissance Pastoral Literature." Ph.D. dissertation,
        Cambridge University, 1972.
            Abstract not available.

163   CORNER, HARRIET MARJORIE KRUSE. "Restoration Fiction: A
        Study of Structural Elements in Selected Works." Ph.D.
        dissertation, Washington State University, 1971, 173pp.
            Includes discussion of elements of structure ("use of
        details," "character motivation," "dialog," "suppression of
        minor characters," and "verisimilitude in plotting") in
        prose fiction 1600-1660.

164   CRANE, RONALD S[ALMON]. "The Vogue of Guy of Warwick from the
        Close of the Middle Ages to the Romantic Revival." PMLA,
        30 (June 1915), 125-94.
            Discusses, in general terms, the popularity of prose
        translations of medieval romances during latter part of
        sixteenth century because of a renewed interest in Middle
        Ages.

*165 CRANE, RONALD SALMON. "The Vogue of Medieval Chivalric Ro-
        mance During the English Renaissance." Ph.D. dissertation,
        University of Pennsylvania, 1911.
            Abstract not available. See 166.

166   CRANE, RONALD S[ALMON]. The Vogue of Medieval Chivalric Ro-
        mance During the English Renaissance. Menasha, Wisconsin:
        Collegiate Press, 1919, 57pp.
            Traces the publication of medieval chivalric romances in
        Renaissance England; examines the audience for and the re-
        action against the type; analyzes the influence on Eliza-
        bethan literature. Includes a chronological list of

"Editions of Romances Printed in England or for English
Readers between 1475 and 1640."

167   CRANE, WILLIAM G. "Introduction," in The Castle of Love
       (1549?). By Diego de San Pedro. Translated by John
       Bourchier, Lord Berners. Gainesville, Florida: Scholars'
       Facsimiles & Reprints, 1950, not paginated.
           Examines influence of the "highly wrought emotional ap-
       peals" of Spanish sentimental romances on the development
       of Elizabethan prose fiction.

168   CRANE, WILLIAM G. Wit and Rhetoric in the Renaissance: The
       Formal Basis of Elizabethan Prose Style. Columbia Univer-
       sity Studies in English and Comparative Literature, 129.
       New York: Columbia University Press, 1937, 293pp.
           In Chapter XI ("The Sentimental Novel and the Romance,"
       pp. 162–78) examines influence of the "highly wrought rhet-
       oric" of sentimental fiction translated during sixteenth
       century on development of English prose: provides an over-
       view of the translations and examines their sententious
       nature and use of rhetorical devices. In Chapter XII ("The
       Narrative Discourse," pp. 179–202) examines influence of
       moral discourse and sentimental romance on development of
       Renaissance prose fiction. Provides an overview of Eliza-
       bethan prose fiction, discussing characteristic rhetorical
       devices.

*169   CRANE, WILLIAM G. "Wit and Rhetoric in the Renaissance: The
       Formal Basis of Elizabethan Prose Style." Ph.D. disserta-
       tion, Columbia University, 1938, 285pp.
           See 168.

170   CRAWFORD, BARTHOLOW V. "The Use of Formal Dialogue in Narra-
       tive." PQ, 1 (July 1922), 179–91.
           Traces use of "instructive conversation" in prose fiction
       1500–1750, discussing the "relation of formal dialogue to
       narration" and its contribution to the development of the
       novel.

*171   CROCKETT, HAROLD KELLY. "The Picaresque Tradition in English
       Fiction to 1770: A Study of Popular Backgrounds, with Par-
       ticular Attention to Fielding and Smollett." Ph.D. disser-
       tation, University of Illinois at Urbana–Champaign, 1953,
       676pp.
           Abstract not available.

172   CROSS, WILBUR L. The Development of the English Novel. New
       York: Macmillan Co., 1899, 347pp.
           Includes brief overview of Elizabethan prose fiction and
       considers influence of French heroic romance on seventeenth-
       century fiction (pp. 10–18).

*172a DAGHISTANI, Y. "Mid-Seventeenth Century English Prose Fiction,
        1640-1660." Ph.D. dissertation, University of Leeds, 1968.
        Abstract not available.

173   DALZIEL, MARGARET. "Richardson and Romance." AUMLA, 33 (May
        1970), 5-24.
            Discusses Richardson's attitude toward romance and ex-
        amines the affinities between his novels and earlier romance
        (particularly seventeenth-century French romance).

174   DAVIS, WALTER R[ICHARDSON]. Idea and Act in Elizabethan Fic-
        tion. Princeton: Princeton University Press, 1969, 311pp.
            Defines "central endeavor" of Elizabethan prose fiction
        as "the testing of ideas of value by means of experience";
        analyzes interaction of ideals and action as conflict is
        manifested in structure, style, and characterization. Ex-
        amines works according to type (pastoral romance, courtly
        fiction, Greek romance, "realistic" fiction, and middle-
        class fiction) and analyzes, in particular, function of
        role-playing in works.

175   DAY, ROBERT ADAMS. Told in Letters: Epistolary Fiction before
        Richardson. Ann Arbor: University of Michigan Press, 1966,
        281pp.
            In Chapter 2 ("Letters as Ornament," pp. 10-26) traces
        use of letters in Renaissance prose fiction: examines use
        of letters for "motivation, plotting, and characterization"
        and assesses influence on development of later epistolary
        novel. Characterizes much of Renaissance prose fiction as
        influenced by the "'Ovidian wooing-story.'"

176   DE CATUR, LOUIS AUBREY. "Three Aspects of Folklore in Short
        Popular Fiction of the English Renaissance." Ph.D. disser-
        tation, University of Maryland, 1970, 245pp.
            Examines folk heroes, "folklore elements employed in
        tales dealing with the War between the Sexes," and "ten-
        dentious purposes" in jest books. Argues that these works
        provide "a body of serious materials which give a variety
        of insights into the life of the common man of the Renais-
        sance."

177   DE GRÈVE, MARCEL. "La Légende de Gargantua en Angleterre au
        XVIe siècle." RBPH, 38 (1960), 765-94.
            Examines allusions to Gargantua in sixteenth-century
        literature and argues that they do not point to the exis-
        tence of a translation of Rabelais's Gargantua and Panta-
        gruel before 1653.

*178   DIETERICH, ERICH. "Die Wurzel des englischen realistischen
        Romans im 16. und 17. Jahrhundert." Ph.D. dissertation,
        University of Göttingen, 1924.
        Abstract not available.

179   DOWDEN, EDWARD. "Elizabethan Romance," in Essays Modern and
       Elizabethan. By Edward Dowden. London: J. M. Dent &
       Sons; New York: E. P. Dutton & Co., 1910, pp. 351-80.
       Provides an overview of Elizabethan romance as an indi-
       cation of the taste of the sixteenth-century reading public.
       Discusses the influence of the Italian novella, noting the
       inability of English authors to imitate the form effective-
       ly. Argues that Elizabethan romances are of only antiquari-
       an interest.

180   DRAKE, NATHAN. Shakespeare and His Times. 2 vols. London:
       T. Cadell and W. Davies, 1817, 747, 683pp.
       Includes general overview of the Elizabethan prose fic-
       tion Shakespeare would have been familiar with (I, 518-93).

181   DUNLOP, JOHN [COLIN]. The History of Fiction: Being a Criti-
       cal Account of the Most Celebrated Prose Works of Fiction,
       from the Earliest Greek Romances to the Novels of the
       Present Age. 3 vols. Edinburgh: Longman, Hurst, Rees,
       Orme, and Browne, 1814, 436, 410, 436pp.
       Includes discussion of Sidney's Arcadia (see 2658) and
       Boyle's Parthenissa (see 592). See 182 and 183.

182   DUNLOP, JOHN [COLIN]. The History of Fiction: Being a Criti-
       cal Account of the Most Celebrated Prose Works of Fiction,
       from the Earliest Greek Romances to the Novels of the
       Present Age. Revised edition. 3 vols. Edinburgh: Long-
       man, Hurst, Rees, Orme, and Browne, 1816, 550, 303, 524pp.
       Reprints sections on Sidney and Boyle from 181; adds
       discussion of development of prose fiction from Lyly through
       Boyle (III, 422-54). See 183.

183   DUNLOP, JOHN COLIN. The History of Prose Fiction. Revised by
       Henry Wilson. 2 vols. London: G. Bell and Sons, 1896,
       615, 701pp.
       Reprints text of 182 and adds explanatory and biblio-
       graphical footnotes.

184   DUNN, ESTHER CLOUDMAN. The Literature of Shakespeare's Eng-
       land. New York: Charles Scribner's Sons, 1936, 336pp.
       Devotes section to discussion of change in style in
       Elizabethan prose fiction. Suggests that emphasis on moral
       didacticism encouraged development of simplicity in style
       (pp. 183-95).

185   DURHAM, CHARLES W. III. "Character and Characterization in
       Elizabethan Prose Fiction." Ph.D. dissertation, Ohio Uni-
       versity, 1969, 147pp.
       Examines methods of characterization in the prose fiction
       of Lyly, Sidney, Greene, Lodge, Nashe, and Deloney.
       "[D]emonstrates that there is a definite trend toward

introducing and romanticizing new kinds of characters...and
suggests that there is no progression from a romantic to a
realistic delineation of character during the period 1578-
1600."

186   EBEL, JULIA G[RACE]. "A Numerical Survey of Elizabethan
      Translations." Library, 5th Ser., 22 (June 1967), 104-27.
         Provides table listing (by STC number) translations from
      various languages for period 1560-1603. Comments on general
      trends in translations and notes that prose romances were
      the kind of works least translated.

187   EBEL, JULIA GRACE. "Studies in Elizabethan Translation."
      Ph.D. dissertation, Columbia University, 1964, 120pp.
         "[S]urveys all the translations composed between 1560 and
      1603"; examines "the identity of the Elizabethan reader of
      translations"; discusses "the involvement of the book trade
      in the output of translations"; and analyzes "the connection
      drawn by a significant number of translators between their
      own work and English cultural progress."

188   EBEL, JULIA G[RACE]. "Translation and Cultural Nationalism in
      the Reign of Elizabeth." JHI, 30, no. 4 (1969), 593-602.
         Examines effect of translation on the growth of national-
      ism. Examines ways in which translators "exemplify that
      quest for cultural and national identity which lies at the
      heart of Elizabethan literary activity."

189   EDWARDS, LEE ROSENBLUM. "Forces against Structure: Some
      Problems of Form in the Development of the English Novel."
      Ph.D. dissertation, University of California, San Diego,
      1969, 194pp.
         Examines "the problem of the development of narrative
      form in English prose fiction from the end of the sixteenth
      to the close of the eighteenth centuries." Observes that
      seventeenth-century novelists "were predominantly concerned
      with the moral utility and/or historical veracity of their
      works."

190   EINSTEIN, LEWIS. The Italian Renaissance in England. Columbia
      University Studies in English and Comparative Literature,
      6. New York: Columbia University Press, 1902, 438pp.
         Includes a discussion of the influence of Boccaccio,
      Sannazaro, and the novelle on Elizabethan fiction (pp. 362-
      66).

191   ESDAILE, ARUNDELL [JAMES KENNEDY]. "Introduction," in A List
      of English Tales and Prose Romances Printed before 1740.
      London: Blades, East, & Blades for the Bibliographical
      Society, 1912, pp. xi-xxxv.
         Provides chronological overview (1475-1739) of the vari-
      ous phases of and developments in English prose fiction.

192   FERRARA, FERNANDO. Jests e Merry Tales: Aspetti della narra-
      tiva popolaresca inglese del sedicesimo secolo. Nuovi
      Saggi, 27. Rome: Editrice dell'Ateneo, 1960, 257pp.
         Provides chronological overview of the development of
      the jest book during the sixteenth century: analyzes
      changes in style, structure, characterization, and narrative
      techniques. Examines the influence of the jest book on de-
      velopment of prose fiction and the integration of jest ma-
      terial into Elizabethan romance.

193   FIELD, BRADFORD S., JR. "The Use of Prose Fiction in English
      Drama, 1616-1642." Ph.D. dissertation, University of Mary-
      land, 1963, 513pp.
         "[S]urveys...plays...based upon prose fiction...[to ex-
      amine] the accommodations the dramatic discipline must make
      to adapt the narrative to the stage, the changes that may
      be forced upon tales in the narrative discipline, and...the
      methods or patterns of adaptations."

194   FISHER, HENRY C. "Realism and Morality in English Fiction
      before 1750." Ph.D. dissertation, University of Pennsyl-
      vania, 1938.
         Examines importance of Renaissance fiction to development
      of realism and moralism in novel. Finds that "Elizabethan
      fiction contributed to realistic fiction a sphere of life
      from the lower and middle classes and a definitely moralis-
      tic insistence that works of fiction be edifying while they
      were being amusing."

195   FITZMAURICE-KELLY, JAMES. The Relations between Spanish and
      English Literature. Liverpool: Liverpool University Press,
      1910, 32pp.
         Provides overview of translation of Spanish prose fiction
      and its influence on English fiction.

196   FLEMING, DAVID A., S.M. "Barclay's Satyricon: The First
      Satirical roman à clef." MP, 65 (November 1967), 95-102.
         Argues for importance of John Barclay's Euphormionis
      Lusinini Satyricon (1605-1607) to the development of realism
      in seventeenth-century novel. Considers especially the in-
      fluence on structure and characterization.

197   FLEMING, DAVID A. "John Barclay and the Rise of the Novel,"
      in Acta Conventus Neo-Latini Lovaniensis: Proceedings of
      the First International Congress of Neo-Latin Studies,
      Louvain, 23-28 August 1971. Edited by Jozef IJsewijn and
      Eckhard Kessler. Munich: Fink; Louvain: Leuven University
      Press, 1973, pp. 229-33.
         Discusses in general terms the influence of combination
      of satire and prose fiction in Barclay's Euphormionis
      Lusinini Satyricon on the development of seventeenth-century

fiction. Examines relationship between satiric intent and moralistic digressions in Renaissance fiction.

198 FORD, FORD MADOX. "The English Novel: From the Earliest Days to the Death of Joseph Conrad." Bookman, 68 (December 1928), 369-75; 68 (January 1929), 538-47; 68 (February 1929), 672-82; 69 (March 1929), 68-79. [Reprinted as: The English Novel: From the Earliest Days to the Death of Joseph Conrad. London: Constable & Co., 1930, 156pp.]
   Includes a brief discussion of the emphasis in Elizabethan prose fiction on the "cleverness" and "verbal juggleries" of the authors. Notes that he "cannot imagine anyone reading for pleasure" Elizabethan prose fiction.

199 FRIEDERICH, REINHARD H. "Myself Am Centre of My Circling Thought: Studies in Baroque Personae (Burton and Donne)." Ph.D. dissertation, University of Washington, 1971, 194pp.
   Includes examination of "standards for judging major works [of prose fiction] of the late sixteenth century." Argues that because of "character credibility and flexibility rather than plot manipulation" Gascoigne's Master F. J. and Nashe's Unfortunate Traveller "succeed, whereas Greene and Deloney fail since their static characters cannot generate more than didactic or simply cumulative structures."

200 FRIEDERICH, WERNER P., and DAVID HENRY MALONE. Outline of Comparative Literature from Dante Alighieri to Eugene O'Neill. UNCSCL, 11. Chapel Hill: University of North Carolina Press, 1954, 461pp.
   Discusses in very general terms the relationship of foreign prose fiction to that of Renaissance England (passim).

201 GALIGANI, GIUSEPPE. "Il Boccaccio nel Cinquecento inglese," in Il Boccaccio nella cultura inglese e anglo-americana. Edited by Giuseppe Galigani. Florence: L. S. Olschki, 1974, pp. 27-57.
   Provides overview of influence of Boccaccio on sixteenth-century prose fiction.

202 GARKE, ESTHER. The Use of Songs in Elizabethan Prose Fiction. Bern: Francke Verlag, 1972, 132pp.
   Analyzes types of songs, their relationships to plot and structure, and their functions (to complement or contrast setting, to present character relationships, to characterize singer and audience) in Elizabethan prose fiction. In Part II, provides detailed analysis of songs in Greene's Menaphon as illustration.

203   GAUNT, JOHN LANCASTER. "A Study of English Popular Fiction, 1660-1700." Ph.D. dissertation, University of Maryland, 1972, 189pp.
        Includes examination of "Restoration popular fiction... in the...context of the development of the genre since" 1475. Compares the earlier "essentially conservative fiction...with the polite fiction of the [Restoration] period."

204   GEROULD, GORDON HALL. The Patterns of English and American Fiction: A History. Boston: Little, Brown and Co., 1942, 536pp.
        Provides an overview of the development of prose fiction 1500-1660. Discusses in general terms major works (pp. 18-45).

205   GESNER, CAROL. "The Greek Romance Materials in the Plays of Shakespeare." Ph.D. dissertation, Louisiana State University and Agricultural and Mechanical College, 1956, 352pp. See 206.

206   GESNER, CAROL. Shakespeare & the Greek Romance. Lexington: University Press of Kentucky, 1970, 228pp.
        Discusses influence of Greek romance (including English translations of and Elizabethan prose fiction influenced by) on Shakespeare's plays. Includes examination of influence of Greek romance on Elizabethan prose fiction and an overview of English translations of Greek romances.

*207   GILES, E. L. "The Growth of Realism in the Fiction of the 16th and 17th Centuries, with Special Reference to the Development of the Picaresque Novel." Ph.D. dissertation, University of London-Birbeck College, 1943.
        Abstract not available.

208   GISELA, JUNKE. "Formen des Dialogs im frühen englischen Romans." Ph.D. dissertation, University of Köln, 1975, 150pp.
        Examines forms of dialogue and their uses in Renaissance prose fiction, especially that of Gascoigne, Lyly, Sidney, Greene, Nashe, and Deloney. Finds that dialogue was not used to create realistic character but as a vehicle for "extravagant style" or moral teaching. Concludes that late Elizabethan fiction "is a rational art aiming at grand effects rather than an art that wants to interpret empirical reality." (Abstract in: English and American Studies in German: Summaries of Theses and Monographs, 1975. Edited by Werner Habicht. Tübingen: M. Niemeyer Verlag, 1976, pp. 70-72.)

209   GOLDER, HAROLD. "Bunyan's Valley of the Shadow." MP, 27 (August 1929), 55-72.

Discusses influence of romances (especially Johnson's
Seven Champions of Christendom, Munday's Palmerin cycle,
and Mirror of Knighthood) on the narrative framework of
Pilgrim's Progress. Discusses, in particular, Bunyan's use
of conventional elements of the descent into cave or dark
valley in earlier romances.

210 GOLDER, HAROLD. "John Bunyan's Hypocrisy." North American
Review, 223 (June–August 1926), 323–32.
Examines Bunyan's reading of prose romances and their
influence on Pilgrim's Progress.

211 GÖLLER, KARL HEINZ. Romance und Novel: Die Anfänge des englischen Romans. Sprache und Literatur, Regensburger Arbeiten zur Anglistik und Amerikanistik, 1. Regensburg: Carl,
1972, 291pp.
Examines development of chivalric romance and picaresque
tale in Renaissance prose fiction. Analyzes use of journey
and fall as structural principles in some sixteenth-century
prose fiction works (passim).

212 GREENOUGH, CHESTER NOYES. A Bibliography of the Theophrastan
Character in English with Several Portrait Characters.
Edited by J. Milton French. HSCL, 18. Cambridge: Harvard
University Press, 1947, 359pp.
Provides chronological listing (by date of edition) of
works including characters; identifies character and loca-
tion. Includes several works of prose fiction.

*213 GREER, RICHARD ALLEN. "Adaptations of the Greek Romances in
the English Renaissance as Reflections of the Debate between
Fortune and Virtue." Ph.D. dissertation, Harvard University, 1972.
Abstract not available.

214 GREG, WALTER W[ILSON]. Pastoral Poetry & Pastoral Drama: A
Literary Inquiry, with Special Reference to the Pre-Restoration Stage in England. London: A. H. Bullen, 1906, 476pp.
Provides an overview of the characteristics (particularly
style and pastoral elements) of the pastoral romances of
Greene, Lodge, and Sidney. Finds that English prose romances do not exhibit genuine pastoralism. Discusses pastoral romances as sources for plays (pp. 141–54, 319–38,
passim).

215 GROSSMANN, RUDOLF. Spanien und das elisabethanische Drama.
Hamburgische Universität, Abhandlungen aus dem Gebiet der
Auslandskunde, 4. Hamburg: L. Friederichsen, 1920, 138pp.
Provides overview of influence of English translations
of Spanish prose fiction on Elizabethan drama.

216 GUBAR, SUSAN DAVID. "Tudor Romance and Eighteenth-Century
Fiction." Ph.D. dissertation, University of Iowa, 1972,
243pp.
Compares works from the two periods "to analyze the
movement toward realism"; finds "no historically continuous
or linear development." Examines structure and style of
works by Sidney, Greene, Lodge, Painter, Rich, and Pettie:
discusses reader response and how these works "call attention to their own literariness."

*217 GUILLEN, CLAUDIO. "The Anatomies of Roguery: A Comparative
Study in the Origins and the Nature of Picaresque Litera-
ture." Ph.D. dissertation, Harvard University, 1953, 336pp.
Abstract not available.

218 HATCHER, O. L. "Aims and Methods of Elizabethan Translators."
Englische Studien, 44, no. 2 (1912), 174-92.
Discusses the nationalistic, commercial, and literary
impulses behind translation; the defensiveness of most
translators; and the Elizabethan conception of translation.

219 HAVILAND, THOMAS PHILIP. The "Roman de Longue Haleine" on
English Soil. Ph.D. dissertation, University of Pennsylvania, 1929. Philadelphia: n.p., 1931, 183pp.
Examines conditions which led to the "growth and spread"
of French heroic romances in England. Provides overview of
English translations of heroic romances, surveys English
imitations, and examines influence on development of English
novel. Includes bibliography of English translations and
imitations.

220 HAZLITT, W[ILLIAM] CAREW. Studies in Jocular Literature: A
Popular Subject More Closely Considered. London: E. Stock,
1890, 238pp.
Examines the historical development of the jest (and
jest book); characterizes the types of jests and compila-
tions of jests; traces influences on jests as well as their
diffusion and affiliation; and discusses value for historical and literary study.

221 HELGERSON, RICHARD. The Elizabethan Prodigals. Berkeley:
University of California Press, 1976, 188pp.
Examines use of Prodigal Son motif and the "pattern of
rebellion, guilt, and repentance" in the prose fiction and
lives of Gascoigne, Lyly, Greene, Lodge, and Sidney. Examines works against humanist background to argue that a
"mixture of rebellion and submissiveness" characterizes the
writers.

222 HENDERSON, PHILIP. "Introduction," in Shorter Novels: Seventeenth Century. Edited by Philip Henderson. Everyman's

Library, 841. London: J. M. Dent & Sons; New York: E. P.
Dutton & Co., 1930, pp. vii-xiv.
Suggests that the decline, from the level reached by the
end of the previous century, of seventeenth-century prose
fiction can be partly attributed to the antagonistic divisions (court, Puritan, vulgar) of the reading audience.
Discusses briefly the popularity of French romance.

*223   HENNEBERGER, OLIVE P. "Proximate Sources for Italianate Ele-
ments in Shakespeare." Ph.D. dissertation, University of
Illinois at Urbana-Champaign, 1937.
Abstract not available.

224   HERFORD, CHARLES H. Studies in the Literary Relations of
England and Germany in the Sixteenth Century. Cambridge:
Cambridge University Press, 1886, 456pp.
Includes examination of influence of German Volksbücher
on sixteenth-century jest-biographies and jest books
(passim).

225   HIEATT, CHARLES W. "The Quality of Pastoral in As You Like
It." Genre, 7 (June 1974), 164-82.
Examines "how the pastoral tradition is manifest in
Renaissance romance." Discusses transformation of the
literary shepherd and relationship to romance hero.

226   HILL, ROWLAND MERLIN. "Realistic Descriptive Setting in English Fiction from 1550 through Fielding." Ph.D. dissertation, Boston University, 1941, 344pp.
Examines "the extent of...[realistic] setting as employed
by the authors of the period covered, the sources of that
setting, the techniques employed in using it as background
or as a device for characterization or furtherance of the
narrative action, and the extent to which it makes the
story of which it is a part more probable to the reader
than that story would otherwise be."

*227   HOLE, S. S. "A Critical Account of the Elizabethan Moralistic
Prose Pamphlet, 1580-1640, with Special Reference to Conventions of Subject and Style." Ph.D. dissertation, University of London-Westfield College, 1970.
Abstract not available.

228   HOLLIDAY, CARL. English Fiction from the Fifth to the Twentieth Century. New York: Century Co., 1912, 461pp.
In Chapter V ("The Fiction of the Sixteenth and Seventeenth Centuries," pp. 138-91) provides an overview, by
author, of major works of prose fiction; usually comments
on style.

229 HOLLINGSWORTH, HELEN. "A Kindle of Hybrids: A Study of Nar-
     rative Techniques in the Romance and Tale of the Early
     Seventeenth Century." Ph.D. dissertation, University of
     Tennessee, 1971, 326pp.
         "[E]xamines the narrative techniques--plot construction,
     mode of narration, setting, character depiction, and
     style--" in thirty-four seventeenth-century works.

230 HOOPS, REGINALD. Der Begriff "Romance" in der mittelenglischen
     und frühneuenglischen Literatur. AF, 68. Heidelberg: C.
     Winter, 1929, 106pp.
         Includes examination of meaning of term "romance" during
     Renaissance.

231 HORNÁT, JAROSLAV. Anglická renesanční próza: eufuistická
     beletrie od Pettieho Paláce Potěchy do Greenova Pandosta
     [Renaissance Prose in England: Euphuistic Fiction from
     Pettie's Palace of Pleasure to Greene's Pandosto]. Acta
     Universitatis Carolinae, Philologica, Monographia 33.
     Prague: Universita Karlova, 1970, 173pp.
         Traces development of euphuistic fiction from Painter
     through Greene. Examines characteristics of the type and
     analyzes its importance to development of Elizabethan prose
     fiction.

232 HORNÁT, JAROSLAV. "An Old Bohemian Legend in Elizabethan
     Literature." PP, 7 (1964), 345-52.
         Discusses references to Bohemia and Bohemian history in
     works of Lodge, Dekker, Deloney, Greene, and Forde.

233 HORNÁT, JAROSLAV. "Some Remarks on Fiction Style, Old and
     New." PP, 8 (1965), 204-11.
         In survey of "some syntactic features characteristic of
     various historical stages in the development of style in"
     English fiction, discusses Elizabethan prose style, charac-
     terizing it "as one with strong elements of rhetoric,...
     long sentence periods, [and] adorned with various rhetorical
     figures"--a stylistic pattern he characterizes as "mono-
     thematic with logical links."

*234 HORNE, CHARLES F. "The Historical Development of the Modern
     Novel out of Early Fiction." Ph.D. dissertation, New York
     University, 1905.
         Abstract not available.

235 HUDSON, HOYT HOPEWELL. The Epigram in the English Renaissance.
     Princeton: Princeton University Press, 1947, 188pp.
         In Chapter II ("The Epigrams of Sir Thomas More," pp. 23-
     79) discusses appearances of anecdotes from More's Epigram-
     mata in sixteenth-century jest books.

236   HUGHES, MERRITT Y. "Spenser's Debt to the Greek Romances."
      MP, 23 (August 1925), 67-76.
          Argues that there is "no evidence that Spenser derived
      any element of his poetry directly from any Greek romance";
      what resemblances there are had become literary common-
      places.

237   HUME, MARTIN [ANDREW SHARP]. "Some Spanish Influences in
      Elizabethan Literature." Transactions of the Royal Society
      of Literature of the United Kingdom, 2d Ser., 29 (1909),
      1-34.
          Traces the "Spanish origin of English narrative fiction."

238   HUME, MARTIN [ANDREW SHARP]. Spanish Influence on English
      Literature. London: E. Nash, 1905, 340pp.
          Provides an overview of the influence of Spanish litera-
      ture on Renaissance prose fiction.

239   HUNTER, G. K. "The Marking of Sententiae in Elizabethan
      Printed Plays, Poems, and Romances." Library, 5th Ser., 6
      (December 1951), 171-88.
          Examines reasons for and techniques of gnomic pointing
      in prose fiction (especially in 1655 edition of Sidney's
      Arcadia.)

*240 HURRELL, J[OHN] D[ENNIS]. "Themes and Conventions of Eliza-
      bethan Prose Fiction (1558-1603)." Ph.D. dissertation,
      University of Birmingham, 1955.
          Abstract not available.

241   JEWKES, W. T. "The Literature of Travel and the Mode of Ro-
      mance in the Renaissance." BNYPL, 67 (1963), 219-36.
      [Reprinted in: Literature as a Mode of Travel: Five Es-
      says. Edited by Warner G. Rice. New York: New York Public
      Library, 1963, pp. 13-30.]
          Examines influence of romance--particularly its idealiza-
      tion of self and experience--on travel literature. Draws
      upon Sidney's Arcadia, Lodge's Rosalynde, and Lyly's
      Euphues: The Anatomy of Wit for examples.

242   JOHNSON, R[EGINALD] BRIMLEY. "Introduction," in The Birth of
      Romance: From Euphues; Sidney's Arcadia; Romantics and
      Pastorals. Edited by R[eginald] Brimley Johnson. London:
      John Lane, 1928, pp. xiii-xxvii.
          Provides an overview of the development and characteris-
      tics of Elizabethan and seventeenth-century romance.

243   JOHNSTON, ARTHUR. Enchanted Ground: The Study of Medieval
      Romance in the Eighteenth Century. London: Athlone Press,
      University of London, 1964, 259pp.

Examines the knowledge of, growth of interest in, investigation of, and attitude toward medieval romance (including Renaissance editions of prose versions).

*244   JOHNSTON, A[RTHUR]. "Medieval Romance During the Seventeenth and Eighteenth Centuries." Ph.D. dissertation, Oxford University-Queen's College, 1957.
        Abstract not available.

245   JONES, FLORENCE NIGHTINGALE. Boccaccio and His Imitators in German, English, French, Spanish, and Italian Literature. Chicago: University of Chicago Press, 1910, 46pp.
        Provides listing (by tale) of translations and adaptations (including those by English Renaissance writers).

246   JUSSERAND, J[EAN] J[ULES]. The English Novel in the Time of Shakespeare. Translated by Elizabeth Lee. Revised edition. London: T. Fisher Unwin, 1890, 433pp.
        Examines development of and influences on prose fiction from Lyly through 1660. Focuses discussion on works of major authors (Lyly, Sidney, Greene, etc.). Sees Elizabethan fiction "chiefly intended for women." Revision of 248.

247   JUSSERAND, J[EAN] J[ULES]. The English Novel in the Time of Shakespeare. Translated by Elizabeth Lee. Introduction by Philip Brockbank. London: E. Benn; New York: Barnes & Noble, 1966, 446pp.
        Provides reprint of 246. In "Introduction to the New Edition," pp. v-x, discusses Jusserand's emphasis on "taste and manners."

248   JUSSERAND, J[EAN] J[ULES]. Le Roman au temps de Shakespeare. Paris: C. Delagrave, 1887, 210pp.
        Earlier version of 246. Provides overview of prose fiction from Lyly to 1660, with emphasis on Lyly, Greene, Sidney, and Nashe. See 247.

249   JUSSERAND, J[EAN JULES]. "Le Roman au temps de Shakespeare." RDM, 187 (1 February 1887), 573-612.
        Provides an overview of Elizabethan prose fiction from Lyly to end of century. Comments on style in individual works and authors' attempts to appeal to female audience.

250   KAHRL, STANLEY J[ADWIN]. "The Medieval Origins of the Sixteenth-Century English Jest-Books." Studies in the Renaissance, 13 (1966), 166-83.
        Discusses "the similarities in both style and content between the jests and their forbears the exempla."

251 KAPP, RUDOLF. "Die Volksbücher," in <u>Heilige und Heiligen-</u>
<u>legenden in England: Studien zum 16. und 17. Jahrhundert</u>,
Vol. I. Halle: Max Niemeyer Verlag, 1934, 242-58.
Provides overview of motifs of saints' legends in early
prose chivalric romances.

252 KETTLE, ARNOLD. "The Precursors of Defoe: Puritanism and the
Rise of the Novel," in <u>On the Novel: A Present for Walter</u>
<u>Allen on His 60th Birthday from His Friends and Colleagues</u>.
Edited by B[enedikt] S. Benedikz. London: Dent, 1971,
pp. 206-17.
Argues that "the development of Puritanism in the seventeenth century at first prevented but ultimately made possible the growth of the realistic novel." Examines
influence of Puritan allegories and spiritual autobiogra-
phies on development of the novel.

253 KINNEY, ARTHUR F[REDERICK]. "Introduction," in <u>Rogues, Vaga-</u>
<u>bonds, & Sturdy Beggars</u>. Edited by Arthur F[rederick]
Kinney. Barre, Massachusetts: Imprint Society, 1973,
pp. 11-57.
Includes discussion of importance of rogue literature in
the development of the novel.

254 KLEIN, KARL LUDWIG. <u>Vorformen des Romans in der englischen</u>
<u>erzählenden Prosa des 16. Jahrhunderts</u>. FAGAAS, 13.
Heidelberg: C. Winter, 1969, 260pp.
Analyzes characteristics of various types of prose nar-
ratives; discusses relationship to development of novel.

255 KNIGHT, GRANT C[OCHRAN]. <u>The Novel in English</u>. New York:
R. R. Smith, 1931, 403pp.
Provides brief overview of major works of Renaissance
prose fiction (pp. 12-20).

256 KNIGHTS, LIONEL CHARLES. "Aspects of the Economic and Social
Background of Comedy in the Early Seventeenth Century."
Ph.D. dissertation, Cambridge University, 1936.
Includes as appendix "Elizabethan Prose," which "is an
attempt to show how the qualities of the popular prose of
the period reflect the essential strength of contemporary
social life."

257 KNIGHTS, L[IONEL] C[HARLES]. "Elizabethan Prose." <u>Scrutiny</u>,
2 (March 1934), 427-38. [Reprinted in: L(ionel) C(harles)
Knights. <u>Drama & Society in the Age of Jonson</u>. New York:
George W. Stewart, 1937, pp. 301-14.]
Discusses characteristics of Elizabethan prose, especially those involving its close relationship to the spoken
word.

258   KOEPPEL, EMIL. Studien zur Geschichte der italienischen
      Novelle in der englischen Litteratur des sechzehnten Jahr-
      hunderts. Quellen und Forschungen, 70. Strassburg: K. J.
      Trübner, 1892, 106pp.
          Identifies translations of Italian novelle in Elizabethan
      fiction; examines influence of Italian works on their Eng-
      lish counterparts.

*259 KOIKE, SHIGERU. "17-Seiki no akuto-shosetsu" [Picaresque
      Novels in the 17th Century]. EigoS, 108 (1962), 372-73.
          Not seen. Listed in Kazuyoshi Enozawa and Sister Miyo
      Takano, "English Renaissance Studies in Japan, 1961-1963,"
      RenB, 1 (1974), 32.

260   KOLLER, KATHERINE. "The Puritan Preacher's Contribution to
      Fiction." HLQ, 11 (August 1948), 321-40.
          Discusses the influence on the development of prose fic-
      tion of "the use of dialogue, the attempts at realism and
      characterization, and the popularity of plain style" in the
      writings of Puritan preachers.

261   KOSZUL, A. "La Première traduction d'Arnalte et Lucenda et
      les débuts de la nouvelle sentimentale en Angleterre."
      PFLUS, 105. Paris: Belles Lettres, 1946, pp. 151-67.
          Examines introduction--through Clerc's translation and
      Bourchier's Castle of Love--of sentimental novel into Eng-
      land; describes characteristics of the type.

262   KRAPP, GEORGE PHILIP. The Rise of English Literary Prose.
      New York: Oxford University Press, 1915, 565pp.
          In Chapter VI ("The Courtly Writers," pp. 310-84) traces
      the development of the "courtly style" in Elizabethan fic-
      tion: discusses Spanish influence on the "high style" and
      examines the combination of "high style and morality" in
      sixteenth-century prose fiction. In Chapter VIII ("The
      Modernists," pp. 455-515) traces the development of a re-
      alistic style in Renaissance prose fiction.

263   KRIEGER, GOTTFRIED. Gedichteinlagen im englischen Roman.
      Ph.D. dissertation, University of Köln, Köln: n.p., 1969,
      274pp.
          Examines use of the verse inset in several Renaissance
      prose fiction works (by Gascoigne, Sidney, Lodge, Greene,
      and Deloney); discusses function and relation to theme and
      structure.

264   LANGFORD, GERALD. "John Barclay's Argenis: A Seminal Novel."
      University of Texas Studies in English, 1947, pp. 59-76.
          Examines the influence, both direct and through its in-
      fluence on French heroic romance, of Barclay's Argenis on
      the development of English fiction, particularly the roman

à clef. Traces influence on Brathwait's Panthalia, Cloria and Narcissus, Sales's Theophania, and Boyle's Parthenissa.

265 LANHAM, RICHARD [ALAN]. "Opaque Style in Elizabethan Fiction." PCP, 1 (1966), 25-31.
Using examples from Gascoigne, Lyly, Sidney, and Nashe, argues that heightened rhetorical style is frequently "the subject of the fiction," rather than mere ornamentation, in Elizabethan prose fiction.

266 LANHAM, RICHARD A[LAN]. "Theory of the Logoi: The Speeches in Classical and Renaissance Narrative," in To Tell a Story: Narrative Theory and Practice. Papers Read at a Clark Library Seminar, February 4, 1972. Los Angeles: William Andrews Clark Memorial Library, 1973, pp. 77-98.
Includes discussion of Elizabethan prose fiction in an examination of "how rhetorical narrative works best, most fully, and most like itself, precisely when it is most guilty of...[the] charges [of "no content only form, no thought only style, self-consciousness rather than sincerity, shallowness, deliberate unreality"], and how, given a dramatistic reality, these vices often become virtues."

267 LARKIN, GREGORY ALLAN. "The Four Ages of the English Pastoral Romance, 1580-1610." Ph.D. dissertation, Brigham Young University, 1975, 284pp.
"[A]nalyzes the art-nature conflict in the English Renaissance by tracing its manifestations in the English pastoral romance."

268 LATHROP, HENRY BURROWES. Translations from the Classics into English from Caxton to Chapman, 1477-1620. University of Wisconsin Studies in Language and Literature, 35. Madison: [University of Wisconsin], 1933, 350pp.
Includes discussion of Elizabethan translations of Greek and Latin prose fiction: provides overview of translations, discussing handling of text and style (pp. 158-68).

269 LATHROP, HENRY BURROWES. "Translations into English from Greek and Latin (to Boethius and Vincent of Lerins) from Caxton to Chapman: 1477-1620." PMLA, Appendix (1910), xxxii-xxxiii.
Abstract of paper read Central Division MLA meeting, 1909: Concludes that translations of "imaginative works... [were] mainly those famous in the Middle Ages."

270 LAWLIS, MERRITT [E.]. "Introduction," in Elizabethan Prose Fiction. Edited by Merritt [E.] Lawlis. Indianapolis: Odyssey Press, Bobbs-Merrill Co., 1967, pp. 1-12.
Discusses in general manner the characteristics of Elizabethan prose fiction and suggests kinds of adjustments required of modern reader.

*271   LEAVIS, QUEENIE DOROTHY. "Fiction and the Reading Public."
         Ph.D. dissertation, Cambridge University, 1932.
            See 272.

272   LEAVIS, Q[UEENIE] D[OROTHY]. Fiction and the Reading Public.
         London: Chatto & Windus, 1932, 364pp.
            Discusses the characteristics--particularly the restric-
         ted nature--of the Elizabethan reading public for fiction
         (passim).

273   LEE, A. C[OLLINGWOOD]. The Decameron: Its Sources and Ana-
         logues. London: David Nutt, 1909, 379pp.
            Traces analogues of tales in Renaissance prose fiction.

274   LEE, SIDNEY. The French Renaissance in England: An Account
         of the Literary Relations of England and France in the Six-
         teenth Century. Oxford: Clarendon Press, 1910, 518pp.
            In Book III ("French Influence on Elizabethan Prose,"
         pp. 131-79) points out that French influence on sixteenth-
         century prose fiction was minimal.

275   LEWIS, C[LIVE] S[TAPLES]. English Literature in the Sixteenth
         Century Excluding Drama. Oxford History of English Litera-
         ture, 3. Oxford: Clarendon Press, 1954, 704pp.
            Comments briefly on Painter, Pettie, and Fenton in dis-
         cussing the introduction of the novella into English litera-
         ture. Notes that the form had little influence on the
         development of English fiction (pp. 309-12). Surveys the
         growth of prose fiction in the latter part of the sixteenth
         century by dividing it into three classes: "the romantic,
         the realistic," and one which "subordinates narrative to
         rhetoric." Notes that "Elizabethan fiction points only
         rarely and uncertainly towards the novel properly so called"
         (pp. 394, 418-29, passim).

276   LIND, L. R. "'Tradduttore Traditore'--The Great Ages of
         Translation." CJ, 44 (March 1949), 371-77.
            Includes survey of prose fiction works translated during
         sixteenth and seventeenth centuries.

277   LINDSAY, JEAN STIRLING. "A Survey of the Town-Country and
         Court-Country Themes in Non-Dramatic Elizabethan Litera-
         ture." Ph.D. dissertation, Cornell University, 1943.
            Includes examination of the themes in prose fiction,
         1558-1603.

278   LONG, LITTLETON. "Tudor Jest-Books: A Study in Sixteenth-
         Century Humor." Ph.D. dissertation, Yale University, 1949.
            Analyzes types of humor in sixteenth-century jest books.
         Examines influences on the jest books, their social useful-
         ness, and their reflection of the period. Traces the evolu-
         tion of humor in the jest books.

279   LOVETT, ROBERT MORSS, and HELEN SARD HUGHES. The History of
          the Novel in England. Boston: Houghton Mifflin Co., 1932
          495pp.
              In Chapter 1 ("Elizabethan Fiction," pp. 7-16) survey
          prose fiction from Lyly to the end of the sixteenth century
          Divide Elizabethan prose fiction into three classes: "the
          idealistic romance," "the embryonic novel of manners," and
          "the picaresque novel." In Chapter 2 ("Seventeenth-Century
          Fiction," pp. 17-35), survey popularity of French romance.

*280   MacCARTHY, BRIDGET G. "Women's Share in the Development of
          the English Novel, 1621-1818." Ph.D. dissertation, Ire-
          land-National University, 1939.
              See 661, 3144, and 3221.

281   MACDONALD, HUGH. "Another Aspect of Seventeenth-Century
          Prose." RES, 19 (January 1943), 33-43.
              Notes that although prose of first half of seventeenth
          century was not homogeneous, the development of literary
          prose was generally characterized by "getting rid of exces-
          sive tropes, figures, and antitheses, and dropping part of
          the Elizabethan vocabulary."

*282   McGRATH, JULIET. "Pleasaunt Fable: English Fiction and His-
          toriography, 1485-1594." Ph.D. dissertation, University of
          Chicago, 1970.
              Abstract not available.

*283   McNEELY, SAMUEL SIDNEY, JR. "Popular Anecdotal Literature in
          Sixteenth Century England." Ph.D. dissertation, Louisiana
          State University and Agricultural and Mechanical College,
          1940, 366pp.
              Abstract not available.

284   McSHANE, [MOTHER] EDITH [ELIZABETH]. Tudor Opinions of the
          Chivalric Romance: An Essay in the History of Criticism.
          Washington: Catholic University of America Press, 1950,
          145pp. [Published on microcards.]
              Analyzes Tudor criticism of chivalric romance; examines
          writings on "function, matter, form, and authorship" of the
          romances.

285   MAGAW, BARBARA LOUISE. "The Female Characters in Prose
          Chivalric Romance in England, 1475-1603: Their Patterns
          and Their Influences." Ph.D. dissertation, University of
          Maryland, 1973, 298pp.
              Examines treatment of female characters "and their in-
          fluences on non-chivalric fiction, as well as their sources
          outside chivalric romance."

286 MAGOON, MARIAN WAITE. "Some Analogues to Elizabethan Jest
  Books in Medieval Ecclesiastical Literature." Ph.D. dissertation, University of Michigan, 1931.
    Traces analogues to various tales in Renaissance jest
  books in Medieval collections of exempla. Arranges sections
  by subject matter of tales.

*287 MALEH, G. "Early Seventeenth Century Prose Fiction." Ph.D.
  dissertation, University of Birmingham, 1962.
    Abstract not available.

288 MASSON, DAVID. British Novelists and Their Styles: Being a
  Critical Sketch of the History of British Prose Fiction.
  Boston: Gould and Lincoln; New York: Sheldon and Co.,
  1859, 312pp.
    Includes general overview of Renaissance prose fiction,
  Sidney through Boyle (pp. 63-80).

289 MATHEWS, ERNST GARLAND. "Studies in Anglo-Spanish Cultural
  and Literary Relations, 1598-1700." Ph.D. dissertation,
  Harvard University, 1938.
    Examines influence of translations of Spanish prose fic-
  tion and includes "list of translations published during
  the seventeenth century."

290 MATTHIESSEN, F[RANCIS] O[TTO]. "Introduction," in Translation
  an Elizabethan Art. By F[rancis] O[tto] Matthiessen. Cambridge: Harvard University Press, 1931, pp. 3-7.
    Discusses the "translator's work" as "an act of patriot-
  ism" and offers general observations on the style of Elizabethan translations.

291 MEYER, ARLIN GLENN. "Romance and Realism in the Novels of
  Aphra Behn and Previous Prose Fiction." Ph.D. dissertation,
  Ohio University, 1967, 194pp.
    Includes discussion of state of prose fiction in six-
  teenth and early seventeenth centuries (with emphasis on
  romance and realistic works) as background for analysis of
  Behn's place in the development of the novel.

292 MILLER, EDWIN HAVILAND. The Professional Writer in Elizabethan
  England: A Study of Nondramatic Literature. Cambridge:
  Harvard University Press, 1959, 296pp.
    Draws frequently upon prose fiction works for examples
  in analyzing the professional writer's attitude toward and
  awareness of the demands of his audience, and in examining
  his relationship with publishers and patrons. Emphasizes
  how the middle-class readers "imposed to a large extent
  their tastes upon" the products of the professional writers
  such as Greene, Dekker, Deloney, and Nashe.

293   MILLIGAN, BURTON ALVIERE. "Rogue Types and Roguery in Tudor
      and Stuart Literature." Ph.D. dissertation, Northwestern
      University, 1939.
         Includes discussion of rogues and roguery in Renaissance
      prose fiction.

294   MISH, CHARLES C[ARROLL]. "Best Sellers in Seventeenth-Century
      Fiction." PBSA, 47 (Fourth Quarter 1953), 356-73.
         Discusses criteria for determining best-seller and ex-
      amines the nineteen titles which had ten or more editions
      during the seventeenth century. Analyzes characteristics
      of these best-sellers.

295   MISH, CHARLES C[ARROLL]. "Black Letter as a Social Discrimin-
      ant in the Seventeenth Century." PMLA, 68 (June 1953),
      627-30.
         Observes that "[p]robably in no other category of Tudor-
      Stuart writing is the simultaneous existence of two reading
      publics, the upper-class and the middle-class, more evident
      than in the romances of the early seventeenth century."
      Notes that productions for the two audiences were sharply
      differentiated both artistically and typographically: those
      designed for the middle class were badly printed quartos
      set in black letter; those for the upper class were better
      printed folios set in Roman. Suggests that "black letter
      in the seventeenth century can be used as a determining
      criterion...to decide for which audience...a given work was
      produced."

296   MISH, CHARLES C[ARROLL]. "Comparative Popularity of Early Fic-
      tion and Drama." N&Q, 197 (21 June 1952), 269-70.
         Provides tabular comparison of "editions (not merely
      titles) published from the beginnings to 1642." Finds that
      during the period there were 260 pieces of fiction published
      in 717 editions, with "the average tale" having three edi-
      tions. Concludes "that, as reading material, fiction must
      be considered almost as popular as the drama."

297   MISH, CHARLES CARROLL. "English Prose Fiction, 1600-1642: A
      Survey." Ph.D. dissertation, University of Pennsylvania,
      1951, 474pp.
         Provides "a synoptic survey of all fiction printed (not
      merely written)" 1600-1642. Distinguishes types of fiction
      and finds development "in the direction of a more realistic
      setting and more probable action, together with better
      handled motivations, all conveyed through the medium of a
      more informal, rapid and natural prose."

298   MISH, CHARLES C[ARROLL]. "English Short Fiction in the Seven-
      teenth Century." SSF, 6 (Spring 1969), 233-330.

Surveys types (Tales of Sentiment, Collections of Tales,
Jest Books, Cautionary Tales, Miscellaneous Popular Fiction,
Picaresque) of prose fiction published 1600-1660. Examines
plot, character, and style of various examples in discussing
characteristics of each type. Also notes general lack of
quality in prose fiction of period.

299   MISH, CHARLES C[ARROLL]. "Introduction," in Short Fiction of
      the Seventeenth Century. Edited by Charles C[arroll] Mish.
      Stuart Editions. New York: New York University Press,
      1963, pp. vii-xvii.
          Divides seventeenth-century fiction into two kinds--
      romantic and realistic--and discusses the characteristics
      of various types of each to show the range of fiction of
      the period. See 60.

300   MISH, CHARLES C[ARROLL]. "Reynard the Fox in the Seventeenth
      Century." HLQ, 17 (August 1954), 327-44.
          Uses Reynard the Fox as example in analyzing the charac-
      teristics of the seventeenth-century best-seller. Also
      discusses revisions of Caxton's translation made by anony-
      mous editor in 1620 edition.

301   MODERSOHN, ANNA-BRUNHILDE. "Cicero im englischen Geistesleben
      des 16. Jahrhunderts." Archiv, 149 (1926), 33-51, 219-45.
          Includes lists of references to Cicero and his works in
      prose fiction.

*302 MORGAN, CHARLOTTE E. "The Beginnings of the Novel of Manners:
      A Study of English Prose Fiction between 1600 and 1740."
      Ph.D. dissertation, Columbia University, 1910.
      See 303.

303   MORGAN, CHARLOTTE E. The Rise of the Novel of Manners: A
      Study of English Prose Fiction between 1600 and 1740. New
      York: Columbia University Press, 1911, 281pp.
          Provides overview of the evolution of romance and the
      novel and discusses relationship to development of the novel
      of manners. Characterizes the style, structure, and con-
      tent of the various types of romances and novels written
      or translated 1500-1660 (pp. 3-66).

304   MORLEY, HENRY. Cassell's Library of English Literature, IV:
      Shorter Works in English Prose. London: Cassell & Co.,
      1889, 447pp.
          Provides general overview of Renaissance prose fiction
      along with several extracts from works plus the text of
      Greene's Pandosto.

305   MORTENSON, PETER. "Structure in Spenser's Faerie Queene,
      Book VI: Primitivism, Chivalry, and Greek Romance." Ph.D.
      dissertation, University of Oregon, 1966, 234pp.

Includes discussion of influence of tradition of "native
English pastoral romance" (Sidney, Greene, and Lodge) on
structure of Book VI.

306   NEELY, CAROL THOMAS. "Speaking True: Shakespeare's Use of
the Elements of Pastoral Romance." Ph.D. dissertation,
Yale University, 1969, 226pp.
"[E]xplores the nature and development of renaissance
pastoral romance."

307   NEILL, S. DIANA. A Short History of the English Novel. New
York: Macmillan, 1952, 340pp.
Discusses influences on Renaissance prose fiction and
provides overview of major types. Suggests that development of novel during sixteenth century was hindered by
"absence of a formal aesthetic."

308   NELSON, WILLIAM. "The Boundaries of Fiction in the Renais-
sance: A Treaty between Truth and Falsehood." ELH, 36
(March 1969), 30-58.
Examines "the way in which fiction comes to be recog-
nized, defined, and distinguished from history in the
Renaissance."

309   NELSON, WILLIAM. Fact or Fiction: The Dilemma of the Renaissance Storyteller. Cambridge: Harvard University Press,
1973, 129pp.
Traces "the history of...[the] defensive attitude
[against the charge that fiction was a lie],...examine[s]
the reasons for it, and...consider[s] its consequences for
the nature and tone of sixteenth- and seventeenth-century
fictitious narrative." Finds that sixteenth-century
writers "parodie[d] the role of historian rather than as-
sum[ing] it" and justified their work by stressing value
for entertainment and/or moral edification, and that seventeenth-century writers tended to "reject fiction by assert-
ing that their tales were not fiction but true as history
is true."

310   O'BRIEN, AVRIL SEARLE. "The Continuum of Prose Fiction: The
Beginnings, 1573-1607." Ph.D. dissertation, Rice University, 1968, 196pp.
Examines "selected works from the period 1573-1607 in
the light of realism, originality, characterization, use of
space and time, and structural unity, which are all factors
many critics consider to be the essential criteria for the
novel, [to show]...that aspects of the novelistic art were
developing long before the eighteenth century and that essentially the prose fiction of the late sixteenth century
differs from that of the eighteenth century no more than
that of the eighteenth century differs from the work of the
twentieth."

311   O'BRIEN, EDWARD J[OSEPH]. "Introduction," in <u>Elizabethan</u>
       <u>Tales</u>. Edited by Edward J[oseph] O'Brien. London: G.
       Allen & Unwin, 1937, pp. 11–33.
          Provides chronological overview of the development of
       the Elizabethan "short story." Examines influences on de-
       velopment and discusses the aristocratic and popular modes

312   O'CONNELL, LAURA STEVENSON. "Social Perceptions in Elizabe-
       than Best-Sellers and Popular Drama." Ph.D. dissertation
       Yale University, 1974, 303pp.
          Includes discussion of depiction of merchant in Eliza-
       bethan prose fiction.

313   O'CONNOR, JOHN J. Amadis de Gaule <u>and Its Influence on Eliza</u>
       <u>bethan Literature</u>. New Brunswick: Rutgers University
       Press, 1970, 318pp.
          In Chapter XI ("<u>Amadis</u> and Elizabethan Fiction," pp. 2(
       25) examines influence of <u>Amadis</u> on fiction; cautions, hov
       ever, that "the influence of <u>Amadis</u> is not...conspicuous
       and is only with great difficulty, if at all, to be diffei
       entiated from that of...other Spanish or French imports."

314   O'CONNOR, JOHN J. "Studies in the Theory and Practice of Pr
       Fiction, 1600–1640." Ph.D. dissertation, Harvard Univer-
       sity, 1951, 184pp.
          Consists of seven studies: (1) "the writer and his pul
       lic"; (2) "the epic poem in prose"; (3) "the common confu-
       sion between history and fiction"; (4) "attempts to make
       exotic fiction relevant by contemporary allusion"; (5) "ti
       dition and taste in fictional structures"; (6) "character:
       zation, the influence of the character books, and trends
       like the disappearance of the chivalric hero"; (7) "ideas
       of style." Examines "why fiction is in such a state of
       decline in the early 17th century." Includes discussions
       of works by Breton, Gainsford, Markham, Bettie, Wroth,
       Brathwait, and Godwin.

315   O'DELL, STERG. "Introduction," in <u>A Chronological List of</u>
       <u>Prose Fiction in English Printed in England and Other</u>
       <u>Countries, 1475–1640</u>. By Sterg O'Dell. Cambridge: Tech·
       nology Press of M. I. T., 1954, pp. 1–22.
          Discusses problems of classifying Renaissance prose fi
       tion and of establishing principles of selection.

*316   O'DELL, WILLIS H. S. "The Vogue of Prose Fiction in Elizabe
       than England." Ph.D. dissertation, Harvard University,
       1949, 169pp.
          Abstract not available.

317   ONG, WALTER J., S.J. "Oral Residue in Tudor Prose Style."
       <u>PMLA</u>, 80 (June 1965), 145–54.

Includes discussion of elements of oral residue--particularly "loose episodic structure"--in Elizabethan prose fiction.

318 OTT, ADÈLE. <u>Die italienische Novelle im englischen Drama von 1600 bis zur Restauration</u>. Zurich: Druck von Zürcher & Furrer, 1904, 124pp.
Provides overview of use of Italian novelle (frequently through English translation) as sources for late Renaissance drama.

319 OTTEN, KURT. <u>Der englische Roman vom 16. zum 19. Jahrhundert</u>. Grundlagen der Anglistik und Amerikanistik, 4. Berlin: E. Schmidt, 1971, 184pp.
Provides general critical estimate of major works of Renaissance prose fiction from Gascoigne to 1600. Includes discussion of works by Gascoigne, Lyly, Sidney, Nashe, and Deloney (pp. 19-43).

*320 OWEN, L. J. "Chivalric Friendship and Its Survival in the Sixteenth Century English Versions of Medieval Chivalric Romance." Ph.D. dissertation, University of London-University College, 1958.
Abstract not available.

321 PARKS, GEORGE B. "Before <u>Euphues</u>," in <u>Joseph Quincy Adams Memorial Studies</u>. Edited by James G. McManaway, Giles E. Dawson, and Edwin E. Willoughby. Washington: Folger Shakespeare Library, 1948, pp. 475-95.
Traces the development of psychological fiction in England, particularly as represented in translations of Italian novelle and Spanish romances. Finds that in the translated novelle, "almost any story has, or has added to it, a certain amount of subjective material, presumably in direct proportion to its psychological possibilities."

322 PARRILL, WILLIAM BRUCE. "The Elizabethan Background of Hell, the Devil, the Magician, and the Witch, and Their Use in Elizabethan Fiction." Ph.D. dissertation, University of Tennessee, 1964, 321pp.
"[E]xamines the background of ideas available to the writers of Elizabethan fiction about Hell, the Devil, the magician, and the witch, and studies the uses which Nashe, Greene, Dekker, Lodge, and the other fiction writers made of the wide variety of material available to them." Finds that use was largely satirical.

323 PARSONS, A. E. "The English Heroic Play." <u>MLR</u>, 33 (January 1938), 1-14.
Examines the relationship of heroic prose romance to epic theory and traces the influence of romance on the development of the heroic play.

324 PATCHELL, MARY [F.]. The Palmerin Romances in Elizabethan
     Prose Fiction. Columbia University Studies in English and
     Comparative Literature, 166. New York: Columbia Univer-
     sity Press, 1947, 171pp.
          Examines influence of Munday's Palmerin romances on
     Elizabethan prose fiction.

*325 PATCHELL, MARY F. "The Palmerin Romances in Elizabethan Prose
     Fiction." Ph.D. dissertation, Columbia University, 1948,
     157pp.
          See 324.

326 PIETZKER, ANNEMARIE. Der Kaufmann in der elisabethanischen
     Literatur. Quakenbrück: Handelsdruckerei C. Trute, 1931,
     82pp.
          Provides overview of depiction of merchant in several
     works of Elizabethan prose fiction.

327 [PROTHERO, ROWLAND EDMUND, BARON] ERNLE. The Light Reading of
     Our Ancestors. London: Hutchinson & Co., 1927, 336pp.
          Includes overview of English prose fiction 1500-1660.
     Discusses influence of Italian tales and Spanish fiction;
     traces themes, subject matter, and types of works. Stresses
     the experimental nature of Renaissance prose fiction.

328 [PROTHERO, ROWLAND EDMUND, BARON] ERNLE. "Light Reading of
     the Stuarts." Edinburgh Review, 238 (July 1923), 118-38.
          Examines the development of prose fiction during the
     seventeenth century and discusses causes of the stagnation
     in the production of original English fiction. Provides an
     overview of the types of works written or published during
     the period and concludes that "beneath the surface...is re-
     vealed a growing respect for truth to nature and for imita-
     tion of real life."

329 [PROTHERO, ROWLAND EDMUND, BARON] ERNLE. "Tudor Novels and
     Romances, I [II]." The Nineteenth Century and After, 92
     (October 1922), 566-75; (November 1922), 748-59.
          Traces "experiments" in sixteenth-century prose fiction
     through various influences (medieval romance, translations
     from Italian and Spanish, and pastoral), identifying con-
     tributions to growth of novel. Suggests early prose fic-
     tion works are primarily valuable as documents of social
     history.

330 PRUVOST, RENÉ. Matteo Bandello and Elizabethan Fiction.
     Bibliotèque de la Revue de Littérature Comparée, 113.
     Paris: H. Champion, 1937, 349pp.
          Examines the English translations and adaptations of
     Bandello's tales and analyzes the influence of Bandello on
     the development of Elizabethan prose fiction. Concludes

that "[w]hat the novels out of Bandello did was for a time
to lead the majority of Elizabethan novelists to provide
side by side, in the relations of somewhat flimsy stories,
ample and stereotyped rhetorical developments and long-
winded moral disquisitions, and to intersperse their prose
narratives with lyrical pieces."

331   PRUVOST, RENÉ. "Réflexions sur l'euphuisme a propos de deux
      romans élisabéthains." Revue Anglo-Américaine, 8 (1931),
      1–18.
            Argues for the importance of making a distinction between
      the influence of euphuism, which is defined more by subjects
      and topics than style, and that of arcadianism, the elements
      of which were established before the composition of Sidney's
      Arcadia.

332   Q., R. S. "Jest and Song Books." N&Q, 18 (20 October 1858),
      272–73.
            Provides list of jest books, including several from six-
      teenth and seventeenth century. Comments that early jest
      books are "not such as could with propriety be left open
      to general perusal."

333   RALEIGH, WALTER [ALEXANDER]. The English Novel: Being a
      Short Sketch of Its History from the Earliest Times to the
      Appearance of Waverly. London: J. Murray, 1894, 310pp.
            Provides overview of development of Renaissance prose
      fiction (pp. 25–100).

334   RANDALL, DALE B. J. The Golden Tapestry: A Critical Survey
      of Non-Chivalric Spanish Fiction in English Translation
      (1543–1657). Durham: Duke University Press, 1963, 272pp.
            Examines "the nature and extent of the Spanish fiction--
      especially the non-chivalric fiction--that was imported for
      Renaissance English readers." Discusses the theories and
      practices of the translators and the characteristics of the
      translations. Provides a generally chronological discussion
      of types of works translated and gives a brief critical es-
      timate of the translations.

335   RANDALL, DALE B. J. "Renaissance English Translations of Non-
      Chivalric Spanish Fiction (with Special Reference to the
      Period from 1620 to 1657)." Ph.D. dissertation, University
      of Pennsylvania, 1958, 670pp.
            Surveys translations of Spanish fiction. Devotes chap-
      ters to "novelas, non-chivalric romances, and satiric-
      realistic fiction," and examines English attitudes toward
      Spanish fiction. See 334.

336   RANSOME, ARTHUR. A History of Story-Telling: Studies in the
      Development of Narrative. London: T. C. & E. C. Jack,
      1909, 338pp.

> Includes overview of development of narrative in Eliza-
> bethan fiction: discusses influences on development of
> Elizabethan prose fiction, examines characteristics of
> narrative techniques, and discusses place in development
> of story-telling (pp. 67-90).

337   RICHARDS, MICHAEL REYNARD. "The Romantic Critics' Opinions of
        Elizabethan Non-Dramatic Literature." Ph.D. dissertation,
        University of Tennessee, 1972, 156pp.
            Includes discussion of prose fiction.

338   RICHMOND, VELMA E. BOURGEOIS. "The Development of the Rhetori-
        cal Death Lament from the Late Middle Ages to Marlowe."
        Ph.D. dissertation, University of North Carolina at Chapel
        Hill, 1959, 367pp.
            In Chapter IV examines the rhetorical death lament in
        Elizabethan novelle (Painter, Pettie, and Fenton) and ro-
        mances (Sidney and Greene). Finds a "constant attempt to
        develop the dramatic potentiality in laments within narra-
        tives."

339   RICHTER, TRAUGOTT LOUIS. "Anti-Feminism in English Literature
        from 1500 to 1660." Ph.D. dissertation, Northwestern Uni-
        versity, 1934.
            Devotes chapter to examination of treatment of topic in
        jest books, noting in particular "the close kinship between
        ...the jest-books and...the poems and tracts written solely
        for the purpose of attacking women."

340   RODAX, YVONNE R. "The Real and the Ideal in Novelle of Italy,
        France, and England." Ph.D. dissertation, New York Univer-
        sity, 1968, 221pp.
            See 341.

341   RODAX, YVONNE [R.]. The Real and the Ideal in the Novella of
        Italy, France, and England: Four Centuries of Change in
        the Boccaccian Tale. UNCSCL, 44. Chapel Hill: University
        of North Carolina Press, 1968, 144pp.
            In Chapter VII ("Borrowed Worlds: The Novella in Six-
        teenth-Century England," pp. 94-108) discusses the develop-
        ment of the novella; examines, in particular, relationships
        between style and content. Argues that the English novella
        is characterized by "the forcible application of an abstract
        system [through style and moralistic interpolations] to
        realistic material" which results in "a highly artificial
        representation of life" rather than idealism and sentimen-
        tality.

342   ROLFE, FRANKLIN PRESCOTT. "The Use of Verse in Elizabethan
        Prose Fiction and the Traditions Which Precede It." Ph.D.
        dissertation, Harvard University, 1931.

Finds that in comparison to other literatures (Classical, Oriental, Old Norse, French, etc.) "Elizabethan prose fiction...is of less importance intrinsically and in its use of verse than any other literature...examined, with the exception of the Greek romances." Finds that "[m]inor innovations indeed occur, and the types of verse used reveal certain predilections peculiarly English, but, compared with the changes in the form wrought by authors of other lands, these innovations seem insignificant."

343 ROSSI, SERGIO. "Goodly histories, tragicall matters, and other morall argument: La novella italiana nel Cinquecento inglese," in Contributi dell Istituto di filologia moderna. Edited by Sergio Rossi. Pubblicazioni della Università Cattolica del Sacro Cuore, Serie Inglese, 1. Milan: Vita e Pensiero, 1974, pp. 39-112.
   Discusses influence of the Italian novella, particularly through the translations of Painter and Fenton, on the development of Elizabethan prose fiction, especially that with a moral emphasis. Examines general moral emphasis in English fiction of 1566-1567.

344 ROUTH, HAROLD V. "London and the Development of Popular Literature," in The Cambridge History of English Literature, IV: Prose and Poetry, Sir Thomas North to Michael Drayton. Edited by A[dolphus] W[illiam] Ward and A[lfred] R[ayney] Waller. Cambridge: Cambridge University Press, 1910, 362-415.
   Includes general discussion of several prose fiction works which treat some aspect of London life or which are satirical.

345 ROUTH, HAROLD V. "The Progress of Social Literature in Tudor Times," in The Cambridge History of English Literature, III: Renascence and Reformation. Edited by A[dolphus] W[illiam] Ward and A[lfred] R[ayney] Waller. Cambridge: Cambridge University Press, 1909, 83-114.
   Includes general overview of sixteenth-century jest books--their development, general characteristics, and types of humor.

346 ROWSE, A[LFRED] L[ESLIE]. The Elizabethan Renaissance: The Cultural Achievement. New York: Scribner, 1972, 428pp.
   Provides overview of Elizabethan achievement in prose fiction; concludes that the works "are more readable today, for they have the salt of life in them, immature and inartistic as they are" (pp. 70-75).

347 SAINTSBURY, GEORGE. The English Novel. London: J. M. Dent & Sons; New York: E. P. Dutton & Co., 1913, 327pp.

In Chapter II ("From Lyly to Swift," pp. 32-76) provides brief overview of development of prose fiction during the Renaissance.

348 SAINTSBURY, GEORGE. A History of Elizabethan Literature. London: Macmillan and Co., 1887, 485pp.
Provides overview of major works of prose fiction; emphasizes style (passim).

349 SAINTSBURY, GEORGE. "Introduction," in Shorter Novels: Elizabethan and Jacobean. Introduction by George Saintsbury. Notes by Philip Henderson. Everyman's Library, 824. London: J. M. Dent & Sons; New York: E. P. Dutton & Co., 1929, pp. vii-xiv.
Discusses Elizabethan fiction writers' inability to "tell a story" and comments on the place of sixteenth-century fiction in the development of the novel. Slightly revised in 65 by R[obert] G[uy] Howarth.

*350 SALOMON, CARL EMANUEL. "The Genetic Evolution of the Novel." Ph.D. dissertation, University of Colorado, 1914.
Abstract not available.

351 SAMMUT, ALFONSO, La fortuna dell'Ariosto nell'Inghilterra elisabettiana. Milan: Vita e Pensiero, 1971, 158pp.
In Chapter 6 ("L'influsso sulla narrativa," pp. 128-41) provides overview of use of Ariosto's works as source in Elizabethan prose fiction (Gascoigne, Whetstone, Sidney, and Greene).

*352 SAVAGE, HOWARD JAMES. "Studies in English Prose Style, 1450-1616." Ph.D. dissertation, Harvard University, 1915.
Abstract not available.

*353 SCANLON, P[AUL] A. "Elizabethan Prose Fiction." Ph.D. dissertation, University of Dublin-Trinity College, 1967.
Abstract not available.

354 SCHLAUCH, MARGARET. Antecedents of the English Novel, 1400-1600 (from Chaucer to Deloney). Warsaw: PWN--Polish Scientific Publishers; London: Oxford University Press, 1963, 264pp.
Surveys development of sixteenth-century prose fiction, focusing on elements of realism and analysis of style. Organizes works by types, characterizing each and discussing contribution to development of prose fiction.

355 SCHLAUCH, MARGARET. "Early Tudor Colloquial English." PP, 1 (1958), 97-104.
Draws upon several works of prose fiction (including The Deceit of Women, Hundred Merry Tales, and Frederick of

<u>Jennen</u>) to analyze and illustrate the characteristics of
early Tudor colloquial English.

356 SCHLAUCH, MARGARET. "English Short Fiction in the 15th and
     16th Centuries." <u>SSF</u>, 3 (Summer 1966), 393–434.
        Surveys types of Renaissance short fiction: <u>exempla</u>
     and edifying tales, jests, anti-romantic novelle, single
     novelle, collected novelle, and framed novelle. Uses se-
     lected examples to illustrate characteristics of each type
     and suggests some topics for further study.

357 SCHLAUCH, MARGARET. "Themes of English Fiction, 1400–1600:
     Some Suggestions for Future Research." <u>KN</u>, 6 (1959),
     339–42.
        Suggests topics which need further research.

358 SCHULZ, ERNST. <u>Die englischen Schwankbücher bis herab zu</u>
     son's Drie Bobs (1607). Palaestra, 117. Berlin: Mayer &
     Müller, 1912, 238pp.
        Provides overview of jest books according to classifica-
     tion: detached jests, jest-biographies, comic novelle.
     Examines inter-relationships among various jests; includes
     bibliography. <u>See</u> 422.

359 SEIGEL, JULES PAUL. "Puritan Light Reading." <u>NEQ</u>, 37 (June
     1964), 185–99.
        Uses invoices and inventories of two Boston booksellers
     as a guide to New England middle-class taste in fiction.
     Surveys types of fiction on lists and concludes that despite
     the influence of Puritanism "the tastes of the middle-class
     reader in New England...were relatively the same as those
     of the middle-class reader in England."

360 SINGLETON, ROBERT R. "English Criminal Biography, 1651–1722."
     <u>HLB</u>, 18 (January 1970), 63–83.
        Surveys characteristics of genre and representative
     works; discusses fictional nature of works and affinities
     with jest book tradition. Includes "A Chronological Finding
     List of Criminal Biographies, 1651–1722" (pp. 80–82).

361 SLOANE, WILLIAM. <u>Children's Books in England & America in the</u>
     <u>Seventeenth Century: A History and a Checklist</u>. New York:
     King's Crown Press, Columbia University, 1955, 263pp.
        Includes general discussion of transformation of six-
     teenth-century prose fiction works into chapbooks for
     children (pp. 64–73).

362 SMITH, HALLETT. <u>Shakespeare's Romances: A Study of Some Ways</u>
     <u>of the Imagination</u>. San Marino: Huntington Library, 1972,
     258pp.

In portion of Chapter 1 ("The Romance Tradition as It Influenced Shakespeare," pp. 1-20), provides an overview of the development of Elizabethan prose romance.

363   SMITH, JOHN DALE. "Narrative Technique in the Realistic Prose Fiction of Greene, Nashe, and Deloney." Ph.D. dissertation, University of Wisconsin, 1968, 323pp.
      Includes overview of Elizabethan precursors of the realistic fiction of Deloney, Greene, and Nashe; divides works into two groups--the "popular tradition" and the "classical-formal."

*364 SMITH, SISTER MARGERY. "Reading Tastes in Early Tudor Times, 1475-1550." Ph.D. dissertation, University of Chicago, 1970.
      Abstract not available.

*365 SORIERI, LOUIS. "Boccaccio's Story of Tito e Gisippo in European Literature." Ph.D. dissertation, Columbia University, 1937, 268pp.
      See 366.

366   SORIERI, LOUIS. Boccaccio's Story of Tito e Gisippo in European Literature. Comparative Literature Series. New York: Institute of French Studies, 1937, 284pp.
      Discusses use in and influence on Elizabethan prose fiction (passim).

367   SPENCER, T[ERENCE] J. B. "Introduction," in Elizabethan Love Stories. Edited by T[erence] J. B. Spencer. Penguin Shakespeare Library. Harmondsworth: Penguin Books, 1968, pp. 7-31.
      Provides overview of the Elizabethan novella and discusses briefly the relationship of stories included (see 63) to Shakespeare's plays.

368   STATON, WALTER F., JR. "The Characters of Style in Elizabethan Prose." JEGP, 57, no. 2 (1958), 197-207.
      Discusses application of the three characters of style to subject matter by Sidney, Lyly, Greene, and Nashe. Argues that plain writing of last decade of sixteenth century was not due to change in taste but to attempt to make style consistent with subject.

369   STAUFFER, DONALD A. English Biography before 1700. Cambridge: Harvard University Press, 1930, 410pp.
      Includes discussion of influence of biography in transition from romance to novel. Examines "close connection between autobiography and romance" (pp. 223-28).

370   STEEVES, HARRISON R[OSS]. <u>Before Jane Austen: The Shaping of</u>
      <u>the English Novel in the Eighteenth Century</u>. New York:
      Holt, Rinehart, and Winston, 1965, 413pp.
          In Chapter II ("From <u>Arcadia</u> to Mount Zion," pp. 6-21)
      discusses in general terms the contribution of Elizabethan
      prose fiction to the development of the novel.

*371 STEVENSON, HAZEL A. "Herbal Lore as Reflected in the Works of
      the Major Elizabethans." Ph.D. dissertation, University of
      North Carolina at Chapel Hill, 1931.
          Abstract not available.

372   STEVENSON, LIONEL. <u>The English Novel: A Panorama</u>. Boston:
      Houghton Mifflin, 1960, 539pp.
          Includes overview of types of and development of Renais-
      sance prose fiction; comments on various influences. Con-
      cludes that during the last twenty years of the sixteenth
      century "prose fiction...had developed the several distinct
      species that were to prevail until the present day" (pp. 9-
      36).

*373 STRAUSS, LOUIS A. "The Ethical Character of the English Novel
      from Lilly to Richardson." Ph.D. dissertation, University
      of Michigan, 1901.
          Abstract not available.

374   SÜHNEL, RUDOLF. "What Modern Translators May Still Learn from
      the Old," in <u>English Studies Today, Second Series</u>. Edited
      by G. A. Bonnard. Bern: Francke Verlag, 1961, pp. 259-67.
          Discusses general characteristics of Elizabethan trans-
      lations and what Elizabethan attitudes toward handling of
      a text may teach modern translators.

375   SUTHERLAND, JAMES. <u>On English Prose</u>. The Alexander Lectures,
      1956-1957. Toronto: University of Toronto Press, 1957,
      133pp.
          In Chapter 2 ("Apes and Peacocks," pp. 31-56) examines
      the characteristics of the "artificial and periodic style"
      and the simpler, more colloquial style of Renaissance au-
      thors. Analyzes influence of Ciceronianism and rhetorical
      training on the former.

*376 TADA, KOZO. "Tudor-cho no hon-yaku [Tudor Translations]," in
      <u>Renaissance II: 1501-1625</u>. Edited by Rintaro Fukuhara and
      Masami Nishikawa. Tokyo: Kenkyusha, 1961, pp. 175-93.
          Not seen. Listed in Kazuyoshi Enozawa and Sister Miyo
      Takano, "English Renaissance Studies in Japan, 1961-1963,"
      <u>RenB</u>, 1 (1974), 23.

377   TEETS, BRUCE E. "Two Faces of Style in Renaissance Prose
      Fiction," in <u>Sweet Smoke of Rhetoric: A Collection of</u>

Renaissance Essays. Edited by Natalie Grimes Lawrence and
J. A. Reynolds. University of Miami Publications in English
and American Literature, 7. Coral Gables: University of
Miami Press, 1964, pp. 69-81.
    Discusses characteristics of the estilo culto (as repre-
sented in Lyly and Sidney) and the characteristics of the
"native, more realistic prose tradition existing in England
from medieval times" (as represented in Greene, Nashe,
Dekker, and Deloney). Also discusses inability of authors
of Renaissance prose fiction to "combine content and form
effectively."

378   THOMAS, HENRY. "English Translations of Portuguese Books before 1640." Library, 4th Ser., 7 (June 1926), 1-30.
    Notes only four Portuguese literary works were translated
into English before 1640: Diana, Amadis of Gaul, Palmerin
of England, and Palladine of England.

379   THOMAS, HENRY. "English Translations of Portuguese Books before 1640," in Miscelânea de estudos em honra de D. Carolina
Michaëlis de Vasconcellos. Revista da Universidade de Coimbra, 1. Coimbra, Portugal: Universidad de Coimbra, 1933,
pp. 690-711.
    Includes overview of English translations of Portuguese
prose fiction.

380   THOMAS, HENRY. Spanish and Portuguese Romances of Chivalry:
The Revival of the Romance of Chivalry in the Spanish Peninsula, and Its Extension and Influence Abroad. Cambridge:
Cambridge University Press, 1920, 343pp.
    In Chapter VII ("The New Chivalresque Romances in Eng-
land," pp. 242-301) provides overview of the translation,
reception, popularity, and influence of Spanish chivalric
romances.

381   THOMPSON, STITH. Motif-Index of Folk-Literature: A Classification of Narrative Elements in Folktales, Ballads, Myths,
Fables, Mediaeval Romances, Exempla, Fabliaux, Jest-Books,
and Local Legends. Indiana University Studies, 96-97, 100-
101, 105-106, 108-112. Bloomington: Indiana University,
1932-1936, 428, 435, 411, 501, 486, 647pp.
    Provides a classified index of motifs in jest books.
Revised in 382.

382   THOMPSON, STITH. Motif-Index of Folk-Literature: A Classification of Narrative Elements in Folktales, Ballads, Myths,
Fables, Mediaeval Romances, Exempla, Fabliaux, Jest-Books,
and Local Legends. Revised edition. 6 vols. Bloomington:
Indiana University Press, 1955-1958.
    Revision and expansion of 381. Provides expanded cover-
age of English jest books.

383   TIEJE, ARTHUR J[ERROLD]. "The Critical Heritage of Fiction in
      1579." Englische Studien, 47, no. 3 (1914), 415-48.
         Surveys critical commentary on theory of fiction in pref-
      atory matter or imbedded in text of prose fiction before
      1579. Finds that commentary is concerned with "the reason
      or reasons stated by an author for producing his composi-
      tion; with an aspect of realism which consists in an effort
      to make a reader believe a story which is told to him; with
      unity and coherence of structure; with style."

384   TIEJE, ARTHUR J[ERROLD]. "The Expressed Aim of the Long Prose
      Fiction from 1579 to 1740." JEGP, 11, no. 3 (1912), 402-32.
         Surveys critical prefaces to isolate five expressed aims
      or purposes of prose fiction writers: "the amusement of the
      reader; his edification; his instruction; the depicting of
      the life about him; the attempt to arouse his emotions."
      Discusses each aim in detail, analyzing effect on develop-
      ment of prose fiction.

385   TIEJE, ARTHUR JERROLD. "A Peculiar Phase of the Theory of
      Realism in Pre-Richardsonian Fiction." PMLA, 28 (June
      1913), 213-52.
         Surveys early prose fiction for examples to illustrate
      techniques ("assertions of veracity," use of "authorities,"
      and discovery of manuscript by reputable individual) used
      as "the conscious effort of an author to gain the implicit
      credence of the reader."

386   TIEJE, ARTHUR JERROLD. "The Problem of Setting in Pre-Richard-
      sonian Fiction." PMLA, 29, Appendix (1914), xxvi.
         Abstract of paper "read by title," MLA convention, 1913:
      "Term limited to accounts in fiction of scenery, objects,
      customs. Five uses consciusly discust before Richardson;
      setting to lend 'variety'--to impart information--to giv
      vividness--to express love for nature--to show influence of
      scenery upon man. Practically all setting apologized for
      as digression--a situation resulting from the antagonism of
      realists and romancers. Effort for geografical accuracy
      traceable from 1590, for temporal accuracy from 1620 [spell-
      ing, sic]."

387   TIEJE, ARTHUR JERROLD. The Theory of Characterization in
      Prose Fiction Prior to 1740. University of Minnesota
      Studies in Language and Literature, 5. Minneapolis: Uni-
      versity of Minnesota, 1916, 131pp.
         Analyzes "the expressed theory of characterization in
      the long prose fiction." Analyzes theories and practices
      of characterization in types of romantic and realistic prose
      fiction before 1660.

388   TING, NAI TUNG. "Studies in English Prose and Poetic Romances
      in the First Half of the Seventeenth Century." Ph.D. dis-
      sertation, Harvard University, 1941, 360pp.
         Provides "an historical, bibliographical and descriptive
      survey of the English romances written in both prose and
      verse and printed in the first half of the seventeenth
      century."

389   TREND, J[OHN] B[RAND]. "Introduction," in Spanish Short
      Stories of the Sixteenth Century in Contemporary Transla-
      tions. Edited by J[ohn] B[rand] Trend. World's Classics,
      326. Oxford: Oxford University Press, 1928, pp. v-xii.
         Suggests that in Elizabethan translations one finds "the
      perfect expression, in English, of the Spanish 'Golden Cen-
      tury.'" Discusses style and influence of translations re-
      printed (see 68) on English literature.

390   TRIENENS, ROGER J. "The Green-Eyed Monster: A Study of Sexual
      Jealousy in the Literature of the English Renaissance."
      Ph.D. dissertation, Northwestern University, 1949, 184pp.
         Includes survey of treatment of theme in prose fiction:
      includes discussion of Painter, Fenton, Gascoigne, Greene,
      and Sidney.

391   TSCHIPPER, MANFRED. "Lachen und Komik in England vom späten
      Mittelalter bis zur elisabethanischen Zeit: Studien zu
      Conduct Books, Mystery Plays und Jestbooks." Ph.D. disser-
      tation, University of Saarbrücken, 1969, 196pp.
         Analyzes motifs and techniques in early English jest
      books. Finds that early jest books "show a similarity with
      the mystery plays in the comic realism of certain figures
      ..., but [utilize] a much wider range of comic motifs."
      (Abstract in: English and American Studies in German:
      Summaries of Theses and Monographs, 1969. Edited by Werner
      Habicht. Tübingen: M. Niemeyer Verlag, 1970, pp. 29-30.)

392   TUCKERMAN, BAYARD. A History of English Prose Fiction from
      Sir Thomas Malory to George Eliot. New York: G. P. Put-
      nam's Sons, 1882, 339pp.
         Includes discussion of the development of prose fiction
      during the Renaissance in relation to social conditions of
      the times (pp. 74-90).

393   UNDERHILL, JOHN GARRETT. Spanish Literature in the England of
      the Tudors. Columbia University Studies in Literature.
      New York: Macmillan Co. for Columbia University Press,
      1899, 448pp.
         Provides general overview of sixteenth-century transla-
      tions of Spanish prose fiction; examines translations in
      cultural and historical context and discusses influence of
      translations on English prose fiction.

394   UNGERER, GUSTAV. <u>Anglo-Spanish Relations in Tudor Literature</u>.
        SAA, 8. Bern: Francke, 1956, 232pp.
            Includes overview of sixteenth-century English transla-
        tions of Spanish prose fiction.

*395   UPHAM, ALFRED HORATIO. "French Influence in English Literature
        from the Accession of Elizabeth to the Restoration." Ph.D.
        dissertation, Columbia University, 1908, 560pp.
            <u>See</u> 396.

396   UPHAM, ALFRED HORATIO. <u>The French Influence in English Litera-
        ture from the Accession of Elizabeth to the Restoration</u>.
        Columbia University Studies in Comparative Literature.
        New York: Columbia University Press, 1908, 570pp.
            Discusses reception, translation, and influence of French
        heroic romance in England. In Appendix A ("Translations,"
        pp. 471-505) provides a chronological list of English trans-
        lations from French.

*397   UTTER, ROBERT PALFREY. "Studies in the Origins of the English
        Novel: With Special Reference to the Influence of the
        Periodical Essay." Ph.D. dissertation, Harvard University,
        1906.
            Abstract not available.

398   VOCHT, HENRY DE. <u>De invloed van Erasmus op de engelsche
        tooneelliteratuur der XVIe en XVIIe eeuwen, eerste deel:
        Shakespeare Jest-Books, Lyly</u>. Gent: A. Siffer, 1908,
        303pp.
            Examines use of works of Erasmus as source of early jest
        books (pp. 30-91) and of Lyly's works.

399   WAGENKNECHT, EDWARD [CHARLES]. <u>Cavalcade of the English Novel</u>.
        New York: H. Holt and Co., 1943, 666pp.
            In Chapter 1 ("Fiction in Shakespeare's Time," pp. 1-15)
        surveys experimentation in types of Elizabethan prose fic-
        tion; discusses briefly theme, character types, and style
        of major works. In Chapter 2 ("The Seventeenth Century,"
        pp. 16-30), includes discussion of characteristics and
        popularity of French heroic romance. Includes bibliography.

400   WARD, B[ERNARD] M[ORDAUNT]. <u>The Seventeenth Earl of Oxford,
        1550-1604: From Contemporary Documents</u>. London: J.
        Murray, 1928, 424pp.
            In "Interlude: Lord Oxford's Euphuists, 1579-1588,"
        pp. 178-205, discusses Oxford as patron of prose fiction
        writers and translators.

401   WARDROPER, JOHN. "Introduction," in <u>Jest upon Jest: A Selec-
        tion from the Jestbooks and Collections of Merry Tales Pub-
        lished from the Reign of Richard III to George III</u>. Edited

by John Wardroper. London: Routledge & Kegan Paul, 1970,
pp. 1-25.
Provides a chronological overview of jest collections;
discusses subject matter and themes.

402 WARREN, F[REDERICK] M[ORRIS]. A History of the Novel Previous
to the Seventeenth Century. New York: H. Holt and Co.,
1895, 373pp.
Includes general overview of the achievement in English
Renaissance prose fiction (pp. 335-42).

403 WARTON, THOMAS. The History of English Poetry from the Close
of the Eleventh to the Commencement of the Eighteenth Century. 3 vols. London: Dodsley et al, 1774-1782, several
sections separately paginated.
In section 42 (III, 461-89) provides overview of Elizabethan translations from Italian prose fiction. See 404.

404 WARTON, THOMAS. History of English Poetry from the Twelfth to
the Close of the Sixteenth Century. Edited by W[illiam]
Carew Hazlitt. 4 vols. London: Reeves & Turner, 1871,
350, 384, 344, 479pp.
In section 60 (IV, 332-55) provides revision and expansion of Warton's overview of Elizabethan translations from
the Italian. See 403.

405 WASSERMAN, EARL R. Elizabethan Poetry in the Eighteenth Century. ISLL, 32, nos. 2-3. Urbana: University of Illinois
Press, 1947, 291pp.
In Appendix ("The Popularity of Elizabethan Prose Fiction
in the Eighteenth Century," pp. 253-59) points out that "the
popularity of many Elizabethan tales was unbroken throughout
the seventeenth and eighteenth centuries." Provides an
overview of the most popular works (particularly the chivalric tales) and discusses transformation into chapbooks or
"modernized" versions. Points out that although eighteenth-
century editions were not "neoclassicized" the stories were
abridged and the language modernized.

406 WATSON, HAROLD FRANCIS. The Sailor in English Fiction and
Drama, 1550-1800. Columbia University Studies in English
and Comparative Literature. New York: Columbia University
Press, 1931, 249pp.
In Chapter III ("The Sailor in Fiction and Drama, 1550-
1600," pp. 46-69) characterizes nautical elements and motifs
which appear in Elizabethan prose fiction; shows that sea
incidents and motifs are derived from Greek pastoral romances rather than contemporary accounts of voyages.

407 WATT, IAN. "Elizabethan Light Reading," in The Pelican Guide
to English Literature, Vol. II: The Age of Shakespeare.

62

Edited by Boris Ford. Harmondsworth: Penguin Books, 1955,
119-30.
Provides overview of Elizabethan prose fiction to illustrate how its characteristics differ from those of the
modern novel. Concludes that "Elizabethan culture was too
oral, too symbolic, and too traditional to entertain the
idea of that mainly representational prose genre--the novel."

408 WEAVER, CHARLES P. The Hermit in English Literature from the
Beginnings to 1660. George Peabody College for Teachers,
Contributions to Education, 11. Nashville: George Peabody
College for Teachers, 1924, 141pp.
Traces use of hermit in fiction, 1500-1660. Concludes
that rather than being a "Christian ascetic" the hermit in
Elizabethan prose fiction "is moral, and his chief function
is telling tales with moral intent" (pp. 107-15).

409 WEISS, ADRIAN. "The Rhetorical Concept of Narratio and Narrative Structure in Elizabethan Prose Fiction." Ph.D. dissertation, Ohio University, 1969, 222pp.
"[A]ttempts to illustrate the influence of the rhetorical
concept of narratio upon narrative structure in Elizabethan
prose fiction." Argues that the Elizabethan concept of
narratio "reveals how the Elizabethan author approached the
basic problems of characterization, plot development, development of theme, and finally, the attempt to achieve
organic unity."

410 WEITZMAN, ARTHUR JOSHUA. "The Influence of the Middle East on
English Prose Fiction, 1600-1725: An Eighteenth-Century
Perspective." Ph.D. dissertation, New York University,
1964.
Includes discussion of how in "the seventeenth century
the fables of Bidpai and French and English romances con-
tributed to the taste for Oriental tales."

411 WELD, JOHN SALTAR. "Studies in the Euphuistic Novel, 1576-
1640." Ph.D. dissertation, Harvard University, 1940, 304pp.
Analyzes pattern and typical components ("[s]peech, reply, soliloquy, letter, verse, and debate" with debate being
the main component) of the euphuistic novel. Illustrates
that the authors borrowed heavily from one another and examines reasons for decline of type.

412 WELLS, STANLEY [W.]. "Shakespeare and Romance," in Later
Shakespeare. Edited by John Russell Brown and Bernard
Harris. Stratford-upon-Avon Studies, 8. New York: St.
Martin's Press, 1967, pp. 48-79.
Examines influence of conventions of Elizabethan and
Greek romance on Shakespeare.

413 WHITE, HAROLD OGDEN. <u>Plagiarism and Imitation During the English Renaissance: A Study in Critical Distinctions</u>.
Harvard Studies in English, 12. Cambridge: Harvard University Press, 1935, 231pp.
Draws on several works of prose fiction for examples in
discussing Renaissance theory and practice involving imitation and originality. Suggests that in attempting to distinguish between an original work and a translation "[t]he
test of originality is the degree of reinterpretation, of
individualized transformation achieved by the author."

*414 WHITE, HAROLD O[GDEN]. "Plagiarism and Imitation in English
Literature, 1558-1625." Ph.D. dissertation, Harvard University, 1930.
<u>See</u> 413.

415 WHITE, R. S. "'Comedy' in Elizabethan Prose Romances." <u>YES</u>,
5 (1975), 46-51.
Examines use and meaning of term in Elizabethan prose
fiction. Finds that "to writers of Elizabethan prose romance, the word 'comedy' describes the completion of a
certain pattern, in which people are brought into relationships that have long been anticipated."

416 WHITEFORD, ROBERT NAYLOR. "Interdependence in English Fiction." <u>PMLA</u>, 29, Appendix (1914), xxii.
Abstract of paper read Central Division MLA Convention,
1913: Studies novels from Malory to Thomas De Morgan to
illustrate "the unconscious and conscious indetedness of
the English novelists to their English predecessors in atmosphere, motivation, dialog, and characterization [spell-
ing, sic]."

417 WHITEFORD, ROBERT NAYLOR. <u>Motives in English Fiction</u>. New
York: G. P. Putnam's Sons, 1918, 390pp.
In Chapter I ("From Sir Thomas Malory to Sir Francis
Bacon," pp. 1-51) surveys development of Renaissance prose
fiction. Discusses style and influence of major authors.

418 WICKS, ULRICH. "Metamorphoses of the Picaro: Picaresque Episodes." Ph.D. dissertation, University of Iowa, 1970,
345pp.
Attempts to define nature of picaresque fiction: surveys
scholarship on concept of picaresque; uses modal approach
in defining nature of picaresque narrative; provides bibliography of studies on picaresque.

419 WICKS, ULRICH. "The Nature of Picaresque Narrative: A Modal
Approach." <u>PMLA</u>, 89 (March 1974), 240-49.
Uses modal approach to delineate characteristics of
picaresque narrative: "[d]ominance of picaresque fictional

mode," "panoramic structure," "first-person point of view,"
"protagonist as picaro," "picaro-landscape relationship,"
"vast gallery of human types," "[i]mplied parody of other
fictional types," and "[c]ertain basic themes and motifs."

420 WICKS, ULRICH. "Picaro, Picaresque: The Picaresque in
Literary Scholarship." Genre, 5 (June 1972), 152-92.
Surveys trends in scholarship on picaresque fiction, in-
cluding that of the English Renaissance.

421 WILKINSON, C. H. "Introduction," in Two Tracts: Affrican and
Mensola, an Elizabethan Prose Version of Il ninfale Fieso-
lano by Giovanni Boccaccio and News and Strange Newes from
St. Christophers by John Taylor the Water Poet. Edited by
C. H. Wilkinson. Oxford: Roxburghe Club, 1946, pp. ix-
xxxi.
Provides detailed overview of Elizabethan translations
of works by Boccaccio.

422 WILSON, F[RANK] P[ERCY]. "The English Jestbooks of the Sixteenth and Early Seventeenth Centuries." HLQ, 2 (January
1939), 121-58.
Provides historical overview of jest books from Poggio
to c. 1640. Follows Schulz's classification (detached
jests, jest-biographies, and comic novelle), discussing
characteristics of and influences on each type. Supplies
addenda (annotated) to Schulz's bibliography (358). Revised in 423.

423 WILSON, F[RANK] P[ERCY]. "The English Jest-Books of the Sixteenth and Early Seventeenth Centuries," in Shakespearian
and Other Studies. By F[rank] P[ercy] Wilson. Edited by
Helen Gardner. Oxford: Clarendon Press, 1969, pp. 285-
324.
Reprints "with some additions and corrections" 422.

424 WILSON, F[RANK] P[ERCY]. Seventeenth Century Prose: Five
Lectures. Berkeley: University of California Press, 1960,
137pp.
In Lecture I ("A Survey," pp. 1-25) discusses lack of
significant contribution to the form of the novel in the
seventeenth century.

425 WINNY, JAMES. "Introduction," in Elizabethan Prose Translation. Edited by James Winny. Cambridge: Cambridge University Press, 1960, pp. ix-xxii.
Discusses relationship between rise of translation and
"intellectual outlook" of sixteenth-century England. Discusses contribution of translations to intellectual atmosphere and the "looseness" of translations.

*426 WOLFF, SAMUEL LEE. "The Greek Romances in Elizabethan Prose
Fiction." Ph.D. dissertation, Columbia University, 1912,
531pp.
See 427.

427 WOLFF, SAMUEL LEE. The Greek Romances in Elizabethan Prose
Fiction. Columbia University Studies in Comparative Literature. New York: Columbia University Press, 1912, 539pp.
Provides detailed examination of the influence of Greek
romance on development of Elizabethan fiction.

*428 WOODMAN, CHRISTOPHER S. "Polyphonic Narrative in Elizabethan
Literature." Ph.D. dissertation, Cambridge University,
1970.
Abstract not available.

*429 WORTHAM, JAMES LEMUEL, JR. "English Prose Style in Transla-
tions from the Classics, 1489-1580." Ph.D. dissertation,
Princeton University, 1939, 228pp.
Abstract not available.

430 WRIGHT, HERBERT G[LADSTONE]. Boccaccio in England from Chaucer
to Tennyson. London: Athlone Press, University of London,
1957, 509pp.
Provides overview of influence of works of Boccaccio on
Renaissance prose fiction; examines translations (with comments on sources and alterations of Boccaccio's text) and
influences.

431 WRIGHT, [JULIA] CELESTE TURNER. "The Amazons in Elizabethan
Literature." SP, 37 (July 1940), 433-56.
Surveys treatments of and attitudes toward the amazon in
Elizabethan literature (including prose fiction).

432 WRIGHT, LOUIS B. Middle-Class Culture in Elizabethan England.
Chapel Hill: University of North Carolina Press, 1935,
745pp.
Characterizes the popular literary taste in prose fiction
and examines the popularity of romance and other forms of
fiction among middle-class readers. Provides an overview of
the popular works, stressing in particular their didactic
element. Concludes that "the Elizabethan middle class had
an eager craving for stories, a craving which was satisfied
by a voluminous literature of fiction" (passim).

433 WRIGHT, LOUIS B. "The Purposeful Reading of Our Colonial An-
cestors." ELH, 4 (June 1937), 85-111.
Comments briefly on what fiction was read in seventeenth-
century America (Munday, Deloney, Sidney, Wroth).

434   WRIGHT, LOUIS B.   "The Reading of Renaissance English Women."
       SP, 28 (October 1931), 671-88.
            Discusses popularity of prose fiction (especially ro-
       mance) among women readers. Also examines attempts by au-
       thors to cater to taste of female audience.

*435   WRIGHT, MARGARET M.   "Shakespeare and the Italian Novellieri."
       Ph.D. dissertation, University of Manchester, 1951.
            Abstract not available.

436   WRIGHT, THOMAS EDWARD.   "The English Renaissance Prose Anatomy."
       Ph.D. dissertation, Washington University, 1963, 238pp.
            Examines the background (especially rhetorical) and the
       characteristics of the genre; distinguishes several types.

*437   WÜLLENWEBER, URSULA.   "Die spanische Romanze in England."
       Ph.D. dissertation, University of Bonn, 1958.
            Abstract not available.

438   ZALL, P. M.   "The Blending of Wit and Jest: An Introduction,"
       in A Nest of Ninnies and Other English Jestbooks of the
       Seventeenth Century.   Edited by P. M. Zall. Lincoln: Uni-
       versity of Nebraska Press, 1970, pp. ix-xviii.
            Examines characteristics of the medieval and the classi-
       cal jest traditions and discusses the blending of the two
       traditions in seventeenth-century jest books and jest-
       biographies.

439   ZALL, P. M.   "The Natural History of Jestbooks." PrS, 36
       (1963), 316-26.
            Traces development of jest book from Quintillian through
       sixteenth century. Discusses briefly types of sixteenth-
       century English jest books.

440   ZALL, P. M.   "The Natural History of Jestbooks: An Introduc-
       tion," in A Hundred Merry Tales and Other English Jestbooks
       of the Fifteenth and Sixteenth Centuries.   Edited by P. M.
       Zall. Lincoln: University of Nebraska Press, 1963, pp. 1-
       10.
            Traces the evolution of the jest and jest book from its
       beginnings through the sixteenth century. Comments on
       style, subject matter, and narrative techniques.

Authors/Translators/Titles

A., L.

Diego Ortuñez de Calahorra, The Seventh [Eighth] Books of the Myrrour of Knighthood. STC 18869-18870.

Studies

441   ATKINSON, DOROTHY F.   "The Authorship of The Mirror of Knighthood, Part Nine." MLQ, 6 (June 1945), 175-86.
       On basis of style, sentence structure, and vocabulary, argues that R. P. (not L. A.) translated the ninth part.

442   GILL, ROMA.   "Collaboration and Revision in Massinger's A Very Woman." RES, NS, 18 (May 1967), 136-48.
       Discusses Massinger's use of Mirror, Book VIII, as source.

443   GOLDER, HAROLD.   "Bunyan's Valley of the Shadow." MP, 27 (August 1929), 55-72.
       Uses examples from the Mirror to illustrate influence of earlier romances on narrative framework of Pilgrim's Progress. Discusses, in particular, the conventional elements of the descent into a cave or dark valley.

444   THOMAS, HENRY.   Spanish and Portuguese Romances of Chivalry: The Revival of the Romance of Chivalry in the Spanish Peninsula, and Its Extension and Influence Abroad.   Cambridge: Cambridge University Press, 1920, 343pp.
       Includes discussion of the translation of the various parts of the Mirror, allusions to the work in drama, and its use as a source in various plays (passim).

ADLINGTON, WILLIAM (fl. 1566)

Apuleius, The XI Bookes of the Golden Asse with the Marriage of Cupido and Psiches. STC 718-721.

Adlington

Editions

445 APULEIUS. The Golden Asse of Lucius Apuleius. Translated by
William Adlington. Introduction by E. B. Osborn. [London:]
Abbey Library, n.d., 318pp.
    Provides partly modernized reprint of 1639 edition. In
"Introduction," pp. v-xvii, comments briefly on Adlington's
handling of text.

446 APULEIUS. The Most Pleasant and Delectable Tale of the Marriage of Cupid and Psyche. Translated by William Adlington.
Edited by Andrew Lang. Bibliothèque de Carabas, 1. London:
Nutt, 1887, 153pp.
    Provides reprint from 1596 edition. In "Preface," pp.
xiii-xv, discusses briefly publishing history of Adlington's
translation.

447 APULEIUS. The Golden Ass of Apuleius. Translated by William
Adlington. Introduction by Charles Whibley. Tudor Translations, 1st Ser., 4. Edited by W. E. Henley. London:
David Nutt, 1893, 279pp.
    Provides reprint of 1639 edition. In "Introduction,"
pp. ix-xxx, discusses Adlington's treatment of the original
text, pointing out that although he had little Latin, was
misled by the French translation he consulted, and "aban-
doned the colour and variety of Apuleius," he nevertheless
produced a "masterpiece of prose." Examines Adlington's
style, particularly his vocabulary and rhythm. "Introduction" reprinted as: "Apuleius," in Studies in Frankness, by
Charles Whibley (New York: E. P. Dutton, 1912), pp. 115-41.

448 APULEIUS. The Excellent Narration of the Marriage of Cvpide
and Psyches. Translated by William Adlington. London:
Hacon & Ricketts, 1897, 57pp.
    Provides reprint from 1566 edition.

449 APULEIUS. The Excellent Narration of the Marriage of Cupide
and Psyches. Translated by William Adlington. London:
Ballantyne, 1897, 56pp.
    Provides reprint from 1566 edition.

450 APULEIUS. The Story of Cupid & Psyche. Translated by William
Adlington. Edited by R. J. Hughes. Temple Classics.
London: Dent, 1903, 112pp.
    Provides annotated reprint based on 1566 edition. In-
cludes Latin on facing page.

451 APULEIUS. The Most Pleasant and Delectable Tale of the Mar-
      riage of Cupid and Psyches. Translated by William Adling-
      ton. New Rochelle, New York: Elston Press, 1903, 50pp.
         Provides reprint from 1596 ediction.

*452 APULEIUS. The Golden Ass. Translated by William Adlington.
      London: Bell, 1904, 230pp.
         Not seen. Provides reprint of 1566 edition. Listed in
      NUC Pre-1956 Imprints, vol. 18, 690.

453 APULEIUS. Cupid and Psyche and Other Tales from the Golden Ass
      of Apuleius. Translated by William Adlington. Edited by
      W. H. D. Rouse. King's Classics. London: Moring, 1904,
      147pp.
         Provides modernized reprint based on 1566 edition; ex-
      purgates selections other than Cupid and Psyche.

454 APULEIUS. Cupid and Psyche. Translated by William Adlington.
      Photogravure and Colour Series. London: Routledge; New
      York: Dutton, 1905, 93pp.
         Provides modernized reprint of 1566 edition.

455 APULEIUS. The Golden Asse of Apuleius Done into English by
      William Adlington. Translated by William Adlington. Intro-
      duction by Thomas Seccombe. London: Richards, 1913, 327pp.
         Provides reprint of 1566 edition. In "Introduction,"
      pp. v-xxix, praises Adlington's style and his translation.

456 APULEIUS. The Most Pleasant and Delectable Tale of the Mar-
      riage of Cupid and Psyche. Translated by William Adlington.
      Introduction by W. H. D. Rouse. London: Chatto and Windus,
      1914, 58pp.
         Provides modernized reprint based on 1566 edition (?).

457 APULEIUS. The Golden Ass, Being the Metamorphoses of Lucius
      Apuleius. Translated by William Adlington. Revised by
      S[tephen] Gaselee. Loeb Classical Library. Cambridge:
      Harvard University Press; London: William Heinemann, 1915,
      631pp.
         Reprints text of 1566 edition with modernized punctuation
      and spelling and alterations designed to bring the text "in-
      to greater harmony with the Latin according to modern ideas
      of translation."

458 APULEIUS. The Golden Asse of Apuleius. Translated by William
      Adlington. Abbey Classics. London: Simpkin, 1922, 279pp.
         Provides reprint of 1639 edition. Anonymous "Introduc-
      tion," pp. ix-xxx, includes general discussion of Adling-
      ton's treatment of the text.

Adlington

459   APULEIUS. <u>The XI. Bookes of the Golden Asse</u>. Translated by
        William Adlington. Waltham Saint Lawrence, Berkshire:
        Golden Cockerel Press, 1923, 250pp.
            Provides reprint of 1639 edition.

*460   APULEIUS. <u>Cupid and Psyches: The Excellent Narration of
        Their Marriage</u>. Translated by William Adlington. London:
        Nonesuch Press, 1923, 60pp.
            Not seen. Provides slightly modernized reprint based on
        1639 edition. Listed in <u>NUC Pre-1956 Imprints</u>, vol. 19, 2.

*461   APULEIUS. <u>The Golden Ass of Lucius Apuleius</u>. Translated by
        William Adlington. Introduction by E. B. Osborn. London:
        Lane, 1923, 317pp.
            Not seen. Listed in <u>NUC Pre-1956 Imprints</u>, vol. 18,
        691. <u>See</u> 445.

462   APULEIUS. <u>The Golden Asse of Lucius Apuleius</u>. Translated by
        William Adlington. Watergate Library. London: Chapman,
        1924, 233pp.
            Provides modernized text based on 1639 edition.

463   APULEIUS. <u>The Story of Cupid and Psyches</u>. Translated by
        William Adlington. New York: Laurel Press, 1924, 62pp.
            Provides reprint from 1566 edition.

464   APULEIUS. <u>The Golden Ass of Lucius Apuleius</u>. Translated by
        William Adlington. Edited by F[rederick] J[oseph] Harvey
        Darton. London: Privately Printed for the Navarre Society,
        1924, 359pp.
            Provides modernized text based on 1566 edition, with some
        emendations from later editions. In "Introduction," pp. 25-
        40, discusses Adlington's style and the effect of his moral
        stance on his translation.

*465   APULEIUS. <u>The XI. Bookes of the Golden Asse</u>. Translated by
        William Adlington. Chelsea: Ashendene Press, 1924, 237pp.
            Not seen. Provides reprint of 1566 edition. Listed in
        <u>NUC Pre-1956 Imprints</u>, vol. 18, 691.

466   APULEIUS. <u>The Most Pleasant and Delectable Tale of the Mar-
        riage of Cupid and Psyche</u>. Translated by William Adlington.
        San Francisco: Windsor Press, 1926, 42pp.
            Provides reprint from 1566 edition.

467   APULEIUS. <u>Apuleius: The Golden Ass, Being the Metamorphoses
        of Lucius Apuleius</u>. Translated by William Adlington. In-
        troduction by Charles Whibley. Black and Gold Library.
        New York: Boni & Liveright, 1927, 288pp.

Provides modernized text based on the 1566 edition(?).
Includes reprint of "Introduction" in 447.

468 APULEIUS. Cupid and Psyches: The Excellent Narration of Their
Marriage Translated into English by William Adlington out of
the Latine Bookes of the Golden Asse. Translated by William
Adlington. London: Fortune Press, 1927, not paginated.
Provides partly modernized reprint from 1639 edition.

469 Entry cancelled.

470 APULEIUS. The Golden Ass. Translated by William Adlington.
Modern Library. New York: Modern Library, 1928, 319pp.
Provides modernized reprint based on unidentified edi-
tion.

471 APULEIUS. The Golden Ass. Translated by William Adlington.
New York: Marvin Press, 1931, 319pp.
Provides modernized reprint of unidentified edition.

472 APULEIUS. The Golden Asse, in The Golden Asse, Adlington's
Translation, 1566. The Satyricon, Burnaby's Translation,
1694. Daphnis and Chloe, Thornley's Translation, 1657.
London: Marshall, 1933, pp. v-xvi, 1-251 (separately
paginated).
Provides partly modernized text based on 1639 edition.

473 APULEIUS. Cupid & Psyches: The Most Pleasant & Delectable
Tale of Their Marriage. Translated by William Adlington.
London: Golden Cockerel Press, 1934, 48pp.
Provides reprint from 1639 edition.

*474 APULEIUS. The Golden Ass. Translated by William Adlington.
New York: Carlton House, 194-.
Not seen. Listed in NUC Pre-1956 Imprints, vol. 18, 692.

475 APULEIUS. The Golden Ass of Apuleius. Translated by William
Adlington. Introduction by Louis Macneice. Chiltern
Library. London: Lehmann, 1946, 239pp.
Provides reprint of 1639 edition. In "Introduction,"
pp. v-ix, comments on Adlington's style.

476 APULEIUS. The Golden Asse of Lucius Apuleius. Translated by
William Adlington. Introduction by Denis Saurat. London:
Westhouse, 1947, 220pp.
Provides partly modernized reprint of unidentified edi-
tion.

Adlington

477　APULEIUS. <u>The Golden Ass</u>. Translated by William Adlington.
　　　　Edited by Harry C. Schnur. New York: Collier, 1962, 286pp.
　　　　Provides modernized text based on unidentified edition.

Studies

478　BRZENK, EUGENE J. "Pater and Apuleius." <u>CL</u>, 10 (Winter 1958),
　　　　55-60.
　　　　　　Uses Adlington's translation as a source for comparison
　　　　to Pater's translation of the tale of Cupid and Psyche. In
　　　　comparing various passages, notes Adlington's "faithful ren-
　　　　dering" of the original: "[t]he Elizabethan version often
　　　　has the sound of a translation in its close following of
　　　　the Latin constructions."

479　GENEROSA, SISTER M. "Apuleius and <u>A Midsummer-Night's Dream</u>:
　　　　Analogue or Source, Which?" <u>SP</u>, 42 (April 1945), 198-204.
　　　　　　Argues that Shakespeare used Apuleius's <u>Golden Ass</u>, pos-
　　　　sibly in Adlington's translation, as a source for the play.

480　HAIGHT, ELIZABETH HAZELTON. <u>Apuleius and His Influence</u>. Our
　　　　Debt to Greece and Rome. New York: Longmans, Green, and
　　　　Co., 1927, 202pp.
　　　　　　Discusses Adlington's translation of the Cupid and Psyche
　　　　episode in the context of other English treatments and
　　　　translations of the tale; observes that Adlington's trans-
　　　　lation "still conveys to English readers more fully than
　　　　does any other prose version the winsome gladness of the
　　　　fairy-story" (passim).

481　HAIGHT, ELIZABETH HAZELTON. "On Certain Uses of Apuleius'
　　　　Story of Cupid and Psyche in English Literature." <u>Poet-
　　　　Lore</u>, 26 (1915), 744-62.
　　　　　　Includes discussion of Adlington's treatment of the tale
　　　　in a survey of adaptations and translations from the six-
　　　　teenth to the twentieth century. Notes Adlington's "de-
　　　　licious mingling of piety and humor in his approach."

482　HOFFMAN, ADOLF. <u>Das Psyche-Märchen des Apuleius in der eng-
　　　　lischen Literatur</u>. Strassburg: H. Huber, 1908, 120pp.
　　　　　　Includes discussion of Adlington's handling of text and
　　　　aspects of his style (pp. 3-10).

483　KAPLAN, JOEL H. "Apuleius as a Chapman Source." <u>N&Q</u>, NS, 22
　　　　(June 1975), 252.
　　　　　　Suggests that the story of Charite and Thrasylus (in Ad-
　　　　lington's translation ?) was a source of <u>The Widow's Tears</u>.

484　McPEEK, JAMES A. S.　"The Psyche Myth and A Midsummer Night's
　　　Dream."　SQ, 23 (Winter 1972), 69-79.
　　　　　Discusses Shakespeare's use of The Golden Ass, possibly
　　　in Adlington's translation, as the source for his refashion-
　　　ing of the Psyche myth.　Also discusses Shakespeare's prob-
　　　able use of Adlington's "To the Reader" in his translation.

485　MONTGOMERIE, W[ILLIA]M.　"Lucianus, Nephew to the King (Hamlet,
　　　III.ii.238)."　N&Q, NS, 3 (April 1956), 149-51.
　　　　　Suggests several echoes of Adlington's translation of
　　　The Golden Ass in Hamlet.

486　STARNES, D. T.　"Shakespeare and Apuleius."　PMLA, 60 (Decem-
　　　ber 1945), 1021-50.
　　　　　Discusses Shakespeare's use of Adlington's translation
　　　as source for several works.

487　TOBIN, J. J. M.　"Apuleius and Othello."　N&Q, NS, 24 (March-
　　　April 1977), 112.
　　　　　Suggests that Shakespeare used Adlington's translation
　　　as a source for Othello.

WILLIAM ALEXANDER, EARL OF STIRLING (1567?-1640)

[Supplement to] The Countesse of Pembrokes Arcadia.　By Philip Sidney.
　　STC 22544a.3-22550.　Wing S3768-3770.

Editions

488　SIDNEY, PHILIP.　The Countess of Pembroke's Arcadia.　Edited
　　　by Ernest A[lbert] Baker.　London:　G. Routledge and Sons;
　　　New York:　E. P. Dutton & Co., 1907, 718pp.
　　　　　Provides modernized reprint of 1739 London edition; in-
　　　cludes continuations by Alexander and Beling.

Studies

489　McGRAIL, T[HOMAS] H[ENRY].　Sir William Alexander, First Earl
　　　of Sterling:　A Biographical Study.　Edinburgh:　Oliver and
　　　Boyd, 1940, 287pp.
　　　　　Includes examination of Supplement to Arcadia in context
　　　of his other writings:　discusses date of composition and
　　　style.　Suggests that there are no "outstanding differences
　　　between Sidney's prose and Alexander's" (pp. 43-46).

490　MITCHELL, ALISON, and KATHARINE FOSTER.　"Sir William Alexan-
　　　der's Supplement to Book III of Sidney's Arcadia."　Library,
　　　5th Ser., 24 (September 1969), 234-41.

Alexander

Analyze the early printing history of the Supplement: identify William Stansby as the printer, discuss differences in the two states of the work, and suggest that it was printed after 31 August 1616.

491   WILES, AMERICUS GEORGE DAVID. "The Continuations of Sir Philip Sidney's Arcadia." Ph.D. dissertation, Princeton University, 1934.

Includes examination of Alexander's continuation; finds that with Johnstoun's it is the best of the continuations of the New Arcadia but that it has little merit as literature or as a continuation of Sidney's work.

492   WILES, A[MERICUS] G[EORGE] D[AVID]. "The Date of Publication and Composition of Sir William Alexander's Supplement to Sidney's Arcadia." PBSA, 50 (Fourth Quarter 1956), 387-92.

Establishes that "the first publication of Alexander's supplement, at least in an edition of the romance [i.e., Arcadia], was 1621" and suggests that the supplement was composed between 1613 and 31 August 1616.

493   WILES, A[MERICUS] G[EORGE] D[AVID]. "Sir William Alexander's Continuation of the Revised Version of Sir Philip Sidney's Arcadia." SSL, 3 (1966), 221-29.

Examines style, plot, and characterization in Alexander's continuation. Concludes that "[i]t lacks...a successful imitation of Sidney's style...; but it is highly successful in handling plot and character."

ALLEN, CHARLES

Enea Silvio Piccolomini, The Historie of Eurialus and Lucretia. STC 19973.

Editions

494   PICCOLOMINI, ENEA SILVIO. Eurialus and Lucretia. Translated by Charles Allen. In Short Fiction of the Seventeenth Century. Edited by Charles C[arroll] Mish. Stuart Editions. New York: New York University Press, 1963, pp. 285-337.

Provides modernized reprint of 1639 edition. In brief introductory note, considers the popularity of the work, the focus on Lucretia, and the nature of Allen's translation. See 60.

Studies

*495   GUINN, JOHN A.   "Aeneas Sylvius Piccolomini: His Relationship
        to Sixteenth-Century English Literature."   Ph.D. disserta-
        tion, University of Texas at Austin, 1939.
           Abstract not available.

THE ANCIENT, TRUE, AND ADMIRABLE HISTORY OF PATIENT GRISEL

   STC 12383, 12386.   Wing T2411-2413.

Editions

   495a The Ancient, True, and Admirable History of Patient Grisel, in
         The History of Patient Grisel: Two Early Tracts in Black-
         Letter.   Edited by J[ohn] Payne Collier.   Percy Society, 3.
         London: T. Richards for the Percy Society, 1842, pp. 1-42.
            Provides an annotated reprint of 1619 edition.   In "In-
         troduction," pp. vii-xi, discusses briefly the date of the
         work and relationship to early dramas on the subject.

   496   The History of Patient Grisel.   Edited by Henry B. Wheatley.
         Chap-Books and Folk-Lore Tracts, 1st Ser., 4.   London:
         Villon Society, 1885, 60pp.
            Provides reprint of 1619 edition.   In "Introduction,"
         pp. i-xiv, discusses publishing history of work.

   497   The Pleasant and Sweet History of Patient Grissell.   Bristol:
         High House Press, 1939, 24pp.
            Provides reprint of 1630? edition.

Studies

   498   JONES, W. MELVILLE.   "The Chapbook Treatment of the Griselda
         Tale."   SFQ, 17 (September 1953), 221-31.
            Surveys Renaissance treatments of the story and compares
         version in two eighteenth-century chapbooks with their
         source, The Ancient, True, and Admirable History.

ANTON, ROBERT (fl. 1616)

Moriomachia.   STC 685.

Anton

Editions

499   BECKER, GUSTAV. "Die erste englische Don Quijotiade." <u>Archiv</u>,
        122 (1909), 310-32.
            Provides reprint of 1613 edition of <u>Moriomachia</u>. Dis-
        cusses work as a satire in the tradition of <u>Don Quixote</u>.

500   ANTON, ROBERT. <u>Moriomachia</u>, in <u>Short Fiction of the Seven-
        teenth Century</u>. Edited by Charles C[arroll] Mish. Stuart
        Editions. New York: New York University Press, 1963,
        pp. 43-78.
            Provides modernized reprint of 1613 edition. In a brief
        introductory note, discusses the work as an anti-romance,
        "the first of its kind in English." <u>See</u> 60.

Studies

501   MISH, CHARLES C[ARROLL]. "Anton's <u>Moriomachia</u>." <u>SCN</u>, 11
        (1953), 24-25.
            Provides brief overview of contents and discusses work
        as satire on chivalric romances.

<u>ARMIN, ROBERT</u> (1565?-1610)

<u>Foole upon Foole: Or Six Sortes of Sottes</u> (revised as <u>A Nest of
    Ninnies</u>). <u>STC</u> 775.

Editions

502   ARMIN, ROBERT. <u>Nest of Ninnies</u>, in <u>Fools and Jesters: With
        a Reprint of Robert Armin's</u> Nest of Ninnies<u>, 1608</u>. Edited
        by J[ohn] Payne Collier. Shakespeare Society Publications,
        10. London: Shakespeare Society, 1842, pp. 1-67.
            Provides annotated reprint of 1608 edition.

503   ARMIN, ROBERT. <u>The Works of Robert Armin, Actor (1605-1609)</u>.
        Edited by Alexander B. Grosart. [Blackburn, England:]
        Printed for the Subscribers, 1880, 266pp.
            Provides annotated text of <u>Fool upon Fool</u>; in Appendix
        prints additions from 1608 edition of <u>A Nest of Ninnies</u>
        (pp. 1-59). In "Introduction," pp. v-xxxvii, discusses
        the printing and publication of <u>Fool upon Fool</u> and <u>A Nest
        of Ninnies</u> and asserts that <u>Fool upon Fool</u> is important for
        its historical matter on fools.

504   ARMIN, ROBERT. <u>A Nest of Ninnies</u>, in <u>A Nest of Ninnies and
        Other English Jestbooks of the Seventeenth Century</u>. Edited

by P. M. Zall. Lincoln: University of Nebraska Press,
1970, pp. 15-71.
Provides modernized reprint of 1608 edition with some
readings from Fool upon Fool (1600).

*505   ARMIN, ROBERT. "Robert Armin's Foole upon Foole (1600): A
Composite, Old-Spelling Edition, with Introduction." Edited
by Henry Frederick Lippincott, Jr. Ph.D. dissertation, University of Pennsylvania, 1972, 285pp.
See 507.

506   ARMIN, ROBERT. The Collected Works of Robert Armin. Introduc-
tions by J[ohn] P. Feather. 2 vols. New York: Johnson
Reprint Corporation, 1972, not paginated.
Provides facsimile reprints of: Tarlton's News Out of
Purgatory (1590), Fool upon Fool (1600), and A Nest of
Ninnies (1608). In "Introduction" to Tarlton's News presents evidence for Armin's authorship and discusses form of
work. In "Introduction" to Fool upon Fool comments briefly
on kinds of fools depicted. In "Introduction" to Nest of
Ninnies discusses ways in which changes affect "the whole
function of the book."

507   ARMIN, ROBERT. A Shakespeare Jestbook: Robert Armin's Foole
upon Foole (1600): A Critical, Old-Spelling Edition.
Edited by H[enry] F[rederick] Lippincott. Salzburg Studies
in English Literature, ElizS, 20. Salzburg: Institut für
Englische Sprache und Literatur, Universität Salzburg, 1973,
175pp.
Provides a critical, old-spelling edition based on 1600
edition. In "Introduction," pp. 1-40, analyzes the publishing history of the work, Armin's style, the historical background of the anecdotes, "the fool tradition in Armin," and
the relationship between Armin's fools and those of Shakespeare.

Studies

508   DAVIES, H. NEVILLE. "Introduction," in The Cobbler of Canterbury: Frederic Ouvry's Edition of 1862 with a New Introduction by H. Neville Davies. Cambridge, England: D. S.
Brewer; Totowa, New Jersey: Rowman and Littlefield, 1976,
pp. 1-55.
Examines similarity of structure between The Cobbler of
Canterbury and Armin's Fool upon Fool and A Nest of Ninnies
in discussing influence of The Cobbler of Canterbury on
Armin's two works.

Armin

509   FEATHER, JOHN [P.]. "A Check-List of the Works of Robert
       Armin." Library, 5th Ser., 26 (June 1971), 165-72.
            Provides check-list of extant editions: entry includes
       title-page transcription, collation, locations of copies,
       and miscellaneous notes. Ascribes Tarlton's News to Armin.
       See 515.

510   FELVER, CHARLES S[TANLEY]. Robert Armin, Shakespeare's Fool:
       A Biographical Essay. Kent State University Bulletin,
       Vol. 49, 1: Research Series, 5. Kent: Kent State Univer-
       sity, 1961, 82pp.
            Provides an overview of Armin's work, discussing in par-
       ticular his satire and his "philosophical" attitude toward
       folly. Examines his precision and eye for detail in charac-
       terization in Fool upon Fool and his "more sophisticated
       view of folly" in Nest of Ninnies.

511   FELVER, CHARLES STANLEY. "William Shakespeare and Robert
       Armin His Fool: A Working Partnership." Ph.D. disserta-
       tion, University of Michigan, 1956, 352pp.
            Examines "extent to which Shakespeare's Fools were in-
       fluenced by the writings...of Robert Armin."

512   GARDETTE, RAYMOND. "La Vie, le péché et la mort dans une ver-
       sion élisabéthaine de la 'nef des fous': la Suite des fous
       de Robert Armin (1568?-1615)." Caliban, 10 (1973), 3-17.
            Discusses Armin's castigation of worldly follies in Fool
       upon Fool; analyzes his emblematic method of characterizing
       various sins and follies under the guise of various kinds
       of fools.

513   GRAY, AUSTIN K. "Robert Armine, the Foole." PMLA, 42 (Septem-
       ber 1927), 673-85.
            Discusses Nest of Ninnies, noting the "sympathy and in-
       sight" with which Armin treats the characters and the "live-
       liness and local color" of the work.

514   LAKE, D. J. "The Canon of Robert Armin's Works: Some Diffi-
       culties." N&Q, NS, 24 (March-April 1977), 117-20.
            Argues that Armin's authorship of Tarlton's News is
       doubtful; affirms that Fool upon Fool and Nest of Ninnies
       is by Armin.

515   LIPPINCOTT, H[ENRY] F[REDERICK]. "Bibliographical Problems in
       the Works of Robert Armin." Library, 5th Ser., 30 (Decem-
       ber 1975), 330-31.
            Argues that printer's copy for Nest of Ninnies (1608)
       was 1605 edition of Fool upon Fool, not 1600 edition as

Feather (509) had suggested. Supports Feather's attribution of Tarlton's News Out of Purgatory to Armin.

516   LIPPINCOTT, H[ENRY] F[REDERICK]. "King Lear and the Fools of Robert Armin." SQ, 26 (Summer 1975), 243-53.
        Discusses characteristics of Armin's fools and examines differences between his fools and Shakespeare's. Suggests that the "moral view" of King Lear may have caused Armin to add the moral glosses to Nest of Ninnies.

517   M[URRY], J[OHN] M[IDDLETON]. "A 'Fellow' of Shakespeare: Robert Armin." New Adelphi, NS, 1 (March 1928), 251-53.
        Discusses reminiscences of Shakespeare's plays in Armin's works.

ARMSTRONG, ARCHIBALD (d. 1672)

A Choice Banquet of Witty Jests. Wing A3705-3707.

Editions

518   ARMSTRONG, ARCHIBALD. Archie Armstrong's Banquet of Jests. Preface by T. H. Jamieson. Edinburgh: W. Paterson, 1872, 423pp.
        Provides reprint of 1640 edition. Includes "List of the Editions," pp. xxvii-xxix.

519   ARMSTRONG, ARCHIBALD. A Banquet of Jests and Merry Tales. London: Hamilton, Adams; Glasgow: Thomas D. Morison, 1889, 236pp.
        Reprints text of unidentified seventeenth-century edition.

Studies

520   SHAWCROSS, JOHN T. "A Banquet of Jests and Archie Armstrong." LC, 29 (1963), 116-19.
        Argues against Armstrong's authorship; suggests that Richard Royston, the printer of the seventeenth-century editions of the work, attempted to capitalize on Armstrong's fame by including his portrait in some editions.

B., A.

Margaret of Angoulême, The Queene of Navarres Tales. STC 17323.

B., A.

Studies

521   BAWCUTT, N. W. "The Revenger's Tragedy and the Medici Family."
       N&Q, NS, 4 (May 1957), 192–93.
            Suggests that version of life of Alessandro de' Medici
       in The Queen of Navarre's Tales might have served as
       Tourneur's source.

B., W.

Certayne Conceyts & Jeasts, in The Philosophers Banquet. By Michael
    Scott. STC 22061.5-22063.

Editions

522   SCOTT, MICHAEL. Certayne Conceyts & Jeasts [from The Philoso-
       phers' Banquet]. Translated by W. B. In Shakespeare Jest-
       Books, Vol. III. Edited by W[illiam] Carew Hazlitt.
       London: Willis & Sotheran, 1864, 1–18 (separately pagin-
       ated).
            Provides annotated reprint from 1614 edition.

Studies

523   DUNN, THOMAS F. The Facetiae of the Mensa Philosophica.
       Washington University Studies in Language and Literature,
       NS, 5. St. Louis: Washington University, 1934, 55pp.
            Points out that Certain Conceits and Jests includes
       several tales translated from the Mensa Philosophica; notes
       borrowings.

524   MAGOON, MARIAN WAITE. "Some Analogues to Elizabethan Jest
       Books in Medieval Ecclesiastical Literature." Ph.D. disser-
       tation, University of Michigan, 1931.
            Traces analogues in Medieval collections of exempla to
       several tales in Certain Conceits and Jests.

BALDWIN, WILLIAM (c. 1515–1563)

A Marvelous Hystory Intitulede Beware the Cat. STC 1244-1245. Wing
    B547.

Editions

*525   BALDWIN, WILLIAM. Beware the Cat, 1570: An Exceedingly Rare
       and Curious Rhapsody Containing Matters Illustrative of the

History of the Stage and of the Writings of Shakespeare.
Edited by J[ames] O[rchard] Halliwell-Phillipps. London:
n.p., 1864, 99pp.
     Not seen. Only 10 copies issued. Listed in NUC Pre-
1956 Imprints, vol. 32, 166.

526   BALDWIN, WILLIAM. Beware the Cat, in Beware the Cat and The
       Funerals of King Edward the Sixth. Edited by William P.
       Holden. Connecticut College Monographs, 8. New London:
       Connecticut College, 1963, pp. 23-64.
           Provides annotated reprint of 1584 edition. In Appendix,
       pp. 90-95, reprints fragment of 1570 edition. In "Introduc-
       tion," pp. 6-22, traces publishing history and analyzes work
       as a prose satire.

Studies

527   BRIE, FRIEDRICH. "William Baldwin's Beware the Cat (1561)."
       Anglia, 37 (1913), 303-50.
           Analyzes work as a satire (provides running commentary
       on work). Traces publishing history.

528   FEASEY, EVELINE I. "William Baldwin." MLR, 20 (October 1925),
       407-18.
           Comments on satire and popularity of Beware the Cat in
       discussion of Baldwin's life and work.

529   HORE, HERBERT F. "Notice of a Rare Book, Entitled Beware the
       Cat." Journal of the Kilkenny and South-East of Ireland
       Archaeological Society, NS, 2, Part 2 (1859), 310-12.
           Comments on rarity of 1584 edition and provides extracts
       relating to Ireland.

530   H[ORE], H[ERBERT] F. "Old Irish Tales." N&Q, 5 (3 April
       1852), 318-19.
           Lists some of the "curious notices of Ireland and Irish-
       men" in Beware the Cat.

531   MALCOMSON, ROBERT. "Notice of a Book Entitled Beware the Cat."
       Journal of the Historical and Archaeological Association of
       Ireland, 3d Ser., 1 (1868), 187-92.
           Describes 1584 edition and transcribes portions relating
       to Ireland (with notes by James Graves).

532   N., F. "Beware the Cat, 1584." N&Q, 99 (10 June 1899), 446.
       Traces provenance of Heber copy.

Baldwin

533   TRENCH, WILBRAHAM F. "William Baldwin." <u>Modern Quarterly of</u>
      <u>Language and Literature</u>, 1 (1898), 259-67.
          Discusses <u>Beware the Cat</u> in context of Baldwin's life
      and works: traces publishing history and examines circum-
      stances of composition. Suggests that work was originally
      compiled by Streamer and that Baldwin re-issued it under
      his own name.

A BANQUET OF JESTS OR CHANGE OF CHEARE

    <u>STC</u> 1368-1373.

Studies

534   FRIEDMAN, ARTHUR. "Goldsmith and the Jest-Books." <u>MP</u>, 53
      (August 1955), 47-49.
          In discussion of sources of "four unexplained stories in
      his [Goldsmith's] writings" suggests jest of killing hog as
      analogue to incident in <u>She Stoops To Conquer</u>.

535   PARKER, WILLIAM R. "Milton's Hobson Poems: Some Neglected
      Early Texts." <u>MLR</u>, 31 (July 1936), 395-402.
          Calls attention to publication of one of the poems in
      1640 edition of <u>Banquet of Jests</u> and discusses text.

BARLEY, WILLIAM (fl. 1596)

<u>The Delightful History of Celestina the Faire, Daughter to the King</u>
    <u>of Thessalie</u> (translation of the French <u>Primaleon</u>). <u>STC</u> 4910.

Studies

536   BRAULT, GERARD J. "English Translations of the <u>Celestina</u> in
      the Sixteenth Century." <u>HR</u>, 28 (October 1960), 301-12.
          Examines in detail the publication history of Barley's
      <u>Delightful History of Celestina</u> and shows it to be a trans-
      lation of <u>Primaleon</u>, not <u>Calisto y Melibea</u>.

BARON, ROBERT (1630-1658)

[Greek: Erotŏpaignion]: Or the Cyprian Academy. Wing B889-890.

<u>An Apologie for Paris for Rejecting of Juno and Pallas</u>. Wing B888.

Studies

537   BECK, EDMUND. <u>Robert Barons Leben und Werke</u>. Strassburg:
         Druck von M. DuMont Schauberg, 1915, 42pp.
              Calls <u>Cyprian Academy</u> a "poetic novel": provides lengthy
         synopsis and lists parallels with Milton's works. Comments
         briefly on <u>Apology for Paris</u> (pp. 12-28).

538   BRIGGS, WILLIAM DINSMORE. "Robert Baron and Shakespeare."
         <u>N&Q</u>, 129 (13 June 1914), 467-68.
              Notes borrowings from Shakespeare and Sidney in <u>Cyprian
         Academy</u>.

539   FORKER, CHARLES R. "Robert Baron's Use of Webster, Shake-
         speare, and Other Elizabethans." <u>Anglia</u>, 83, no. 2 (1965),
         176-98.
              Indicates Baron's borrowings from Milton, Webster, and
         Shakespeare in his prose fiction. Suggests that Baron's
         method of composition was to write with his commonplace
         book open before him.

540   SMITH, G. C. MOORE. "Robert Baron, Author of <u>Mirza, a Trag-
         edie</u>." <u>N&Q</u>, 129 (3 January 1914), 1-3; (10 January 1914),
         22-24; (17 January 1914), 43-44; (24 January 1914), 61-63;
         (14 March 1914), 206.
              Comments on style in <u>Cyprian Academy</u>, discusses influence
         of Sidney's <u>Arcadia</u> on work, and points out "plagiarisms"
         from Milton and other seventeenth-century poets.

<u>THE BATCHELARS BANQUET: OR A BANQUET FOR BATCHELARS</u>
      (Sometimes ascribed to Thomas Dekker.)

      <u>STC</u> 6476-6479.

Editions

541   <u>The Batchelars Banquet</u>, in <u>The Non-Dramatic Works of Thomas
         Dekker</u>, Vol. I. By Thomas Dekker. Edited by Alexander B.
         Grosart. Huth Library. London: Printed for Private Cir-
         culation, 1884, 149-275.
              Provides reprint of 1603 edition.

*542   <u>Batchelars Banquet</u>. Edited by J[ohn] S[tephen] Farmer. Amer-
         sham, 1914.
              Not located. Listed in 769.

543   The Batchelars Banquet: <u>An Elizabethan Translation of Les</u>
         Quinze joyes de mariage. Edited by F[rank] P[ercy] Wilson.
         Oxford: Clarendon Press, 1929, 172pp.

The Batchelars Banquet

> Provides critical edition based on text of 1603 edition. In "Introduction," pp. vii-xlviii, traces publishing history and provides bibliographical analysis of seventeenth-century editions. Discusses anonymous translator's handling of text; argues against Dekker as translator and suggests instead Robert Tofte.

Studies

544 CROW, JOAN. "The Quinze joyes de mariage in France and England." MLR, 59 (October 1964), 571-77.
Places Bachelors' Banquet in context of publishing history and popularity of Les Quinze joyes. Notes that translation is based on 1595 French version edited by François Rosset.

545 ŁOBZOWSKA, MARIA. "Two English Translations of the XVth Century French Satire Les Quinze joyes de mariage." KN, 10, no. 1 (1963), 17-32.
Examines relationship of Bachelors' Banquet to the French original, discussing in particular the changes made by the translator to transfer the action of the work "to a middle-class milieu of 17th century London, with Puritanical atmosphere." Compares to earlier translation, The Fifteen Joys of Marriage, concluding that it had no influence on Bachelors' Banquet.

546 NEMO. "Thomas Dekker." N&Q, 75 (23 April 1887), 324-25.
Criticizes Swinburne (547) for praising Bachelors' Banquet at length but not giving the title.

547 SWINBURNE, ALGERNON CHARLES. "Thomas Dekker." Nineteenth Century, 21 (January 1887), 81-103.
Treats Bachelors' Banquet as Dekker's, praising the work. See 546.

548 WILLIAMSON, MARILYN L. "Blurt, Master Constable, III, iii, and The Batchelars Banquet." N&Q, NS, 4 (December 1957), 519-21.
Speculates that Middleton "had access to a copy of The Batchelars Banquet before it was published" and used it as a source for the scene. Suggests possibility that Dekker was the translator.

BELING, RICHARD (d. 1677)

A Sixth Booke to the Countesse of Pembrokes Arcadia. STC 1805. Wing S3768-3770.

Editions

549   SIDNEY, PHILIP. <u>The Countess of Pembroke's Arcadia</u>. Edited
      by Ernest Λ[lbert] Baker. London: G. Routledge and Sons;
      New York: E. P. Dutton & Co., 1907, 718pp.
         Provides modernized reprint of 1739 London edition; in-
      cludes continuations by Alexander and Beling.

Studies

550   WILES, AMERICUS G[EORGE] D[AVID]. "The Continuations of Sir
      Philip Sidney's <u>Arcadia</u>." Ph.D. dissertation, Princeton
      University, 1934.
         Includes examination of Beling's continuation; finds
      that his is the best of the continuations of the <u>Old Arcadia</u>
      but that it has little literary merit.

<u>BERNARD, RICHARD</u> (1567?-1641)

<u>The Isle of Man or the Legall Proceeding in Man-Shire against Sinne</u>.
   <u>STC</u> 1946-1952. Wing B2026-2031.

Bibliographies

551   DREDGE, JOHN INGLE. <u>The Writings of Richard Bernard, of Ep-
      worth, Worksop, and Batcombe: A Bibliography</u>. Horncastle:
      W. K. Morton, 1890, 25pp.
         Provides chronological annotated bibliography of works
      by Bernard.

Editions

552   BERNARD, RICHARD. <u>The Isle of Man</u>. Introduction by Richard
      Edwards. Bristol: R. Edwards, 1803, 211pp.
         Provides partly modernized reprint based on unidentified
      edition. In "To the Reader," pp. 3-8, notes that Bunyan
      used work as a source for <u>Pilgrim's Progress</u> and discusses
      allegorical nature of work. Thomas Roberts, in "Letter to
      the Publisher," pp. 9-21, discusses Bunyan's knowledge of
      the work and its allegorical nature.

553   BERNARD, RICHARD. <u>The Isle of Man; or, Legal Proceedings in
      Manshire against Sin</u>. London: T. Tegg and Son, 1834,
      178pp.
         Provides modernized text based on unidentified edition.

Bernard

Studies

554 MÜLLER, MAX. Richard Bernard: The Isle of Man (1626): Eine
     literargeschichtliche Untersuchung. Markneukirchen: J.
     Schmidt, 1933, 96pp.
        Provides general critical examination of Isle of Man:
     traces publication history; compares editions of 1626, 1627,
     and 1628; analyzes work as an allegory and as a Puritan
     book of edification; discusses work in context of background
     of Puritan ideas; analyzes relationship with Bunyan's works
     (particularly Pilgrim's Progress).

*555 WHAREY, JAMES BLANTON. "A Study of the Sources of Bunyan's
     Allegories: With Special Reference to Deguileville's Pil-
     grimage of Man." Ph.D. dissertation, The Johns Hopkins
     University, 1904, 136pp.
        See 556.

556 WHAREY, JAMES BLANTON. A Study of the Sources of Bunyan's
     Allegories: With Special Reference to Deguileville's Pil-
     grimage of Man. Baltimore: J. H. Furst Co., 1904, 137pp.
        In Chapter IV ("Richard Bernard: The Isle of Man,"
     pp. 78-91) examines Bunyan's knowledge of Bernard's work:
     concludes that Isle of Man possibly influenced Pilgrim's
     Progress and "contain[s] the germ of" the Holy War. Pro-
     vides synopsis of Isle of Man. Notes influence on other
     works (passim).

BETTIE, WILLIAM

The Historie of Titana and Theseus. STC 1980-1981.

Studies

557 WELD, JOHN SALTAR. "Studies in the Euphuistic Novel, 1576-
     1640." Ph.D. dissertation, Harvard University, 1940, 304pp.
        Traces sources of Titana and Theseus.

558 WELD, JOHN S[ALTAR]. "W. Bettie's Titana and Theseus." PQ,
     26 (January 1947), 36-44.
        Notes tendency of "euphuistic novelists" to borrow
     heavily from other works and traces Bettie's extensive bor-
     rowings from Greene's Pandosto and Arthur Golding's trans-
     lation of Ovid's Metamorphoses.

BORDE, ANDREW (1490?-1549)

The Merry Tales of the Mad Men of Gottam. STC 1021. Wing B3749.

Editions

559   [BORDE, ANDREW.] The Merry Tales of the Wise Men of Gotham.
       Edited by James Orchard Halliwell[-Phillipps]. London:
       J. R. Smith, 1840, 24pp.
          Provides reprint based on unidentified early nineteenth-
       century edition. In "Introduction," pp. 3-8, discusses the
       legendary background of the tales.

560   BORDE, ANDREW. Mery Tales of the Mad Men of Gotham, in
       Shakespeare Jest-Books, Vol. III. Edited by W[illiam] Carew
       Hazlitt. London: Willis & Sotheran, 1864, 1-26.
          Provides annotated reprint of 1630 edition. In brief
       introductory note discusses the bibliographical history of
       the work.

*561   [BORDE, ANDREW.] "The Merry Tales of the Mad Men of Gotham:
       An Edition and Commentary." Edited by Stanley Jadwin Kahrl.
       Ph.D. dissertation, Harvard University, 1962.
          See 562.

562   B[ORDE], A[NDREW] OF PHISIKE DOCTOUR. Merie Tales of the Mad
       Men of Gotam. Edited by Stanley J[adwin] Kahrl. [With
       R. I. The History of Tom Thumbe. Edited by Curt F. Bühler.]
       RETS. Evanston: Northwestern University Press for the
       Renaissance English Text Society, 1965, 47pp. (separately
       paginated).
          Reprints text of unique Harvard copy of c. 1565 edition
       printed by Thomas Colwell. In "Introduction," pp. ix-xxii,
       discusses bibliographical history of work, claims for
       Borde's authorship, and date of composition.

Studies

563   CLOUSTON, W[ILLIAM] A[LEXANDER]. The Book of Noodles: Stories
       of Simpletons; or, Fools and Their Follies. Book-Lover's
       Library. New York: A. C. Armstrong and Son, 1888, 248pp.
          Provides detailed discussion of sources and analogues
       for tales in Mad Men of Gotham (pp. 16-55).

564   FERRARA, FERNANDO. Jests e Merry Tales: Aspetti della narra-
       tiva popolaresca inglese del sedicesimo secolo. Nuovi
       Saggi, 27. Rome: Edizioni dell'Ateneo, 1960, 257pp.

Borde

> Examines importance of <u>Mad Men of Gotham</u> to the develop-
> ment of sixteenth-century jest books. Discusses sources of
> work (passim).

565   FIELD, JOHN EDWARD. <u>The Myth of the Pent Cuckoo: A Study in</u>
> <u>Folklore</u>. London: E. Stock, 1913, 227pp.
> Provides "a scientific enquiry into the meaning and
> value of the widespread story of the men who pent, or hedged
> in, the Cuckoo, which appears in the old <u>Tales of the Wise</u>
> <u>Men of Gotham</u>." Examines antiquarian and folklore value of
> work.

566   STAPLETON, ALFRED. <u>All about the Merry Tales of Gotham</u>.
> Nottingham: Pearson, 1900, 198pp.
> Includes modernized reprint based on 560. Provides ex-
> tensive notes on local history and literary allusions,
> traces analogues of tales, examines question of authorship,
> and examines publishing history of work.

567   WARDROPER, JOHN. "Borde and Scoggin," in <u>Jest upon Jest: A</u>
> <u>Selection from the Jestbooks and Collections of Merry Tales</u>
> <u>Published from the Reign of Richard III to George III</u>.
> Edited by John Wardroper. London: Routledge & Kegan Paul,
> 1970, pp. 198-99.
> Examines evidence in favor of Borde as compiler of
> <u>Scoggin's Jests</u>.

<u>BOURCHIER, JOHN, BARON BERNERS</u> (1467-1533)

<u>Arthur of Lytell Brytayne</u>. <u>STC</u> 807-808.

<u>The Ancient Historie of Huon of Bourdeaux</u>. <u>STC</u> 13999.

Diego de San Pedro, <u>The Castell of Love</u>. <u>STC</u> 21739.5-21742.

Editions

568   <u>The History of the Valiant Knight Arthur of Little Britain</u>.
> Translated by John Bourchier, Baron Berners. Edited by
> E[dward] V[ernon] Utterson. London: White, Cochrane and
> Co., 1814, 588pp.
> Provides reprint of 1555(?) edition. In "The Editor's
> Preface" discusses Bourchier's style and the publishing
> history of the work.

569   <u>The Boke of Duke Huon of Burdeux</u>. Translated by John Bourchier,
> Baron Berners. Edited by S[idney] L. Lee. EETS, Extra

Series, 40, 41, 43, 50. London: N. Trübner for the Early
English Text Society, 1882-1887, 907pp.
Provides critical edition based on 1534 edition. In
"Introduction," pp. vii-lix, discusses the popularity of
Bourchier's translation, the influence of the work on
Shakespeare, and the publishing history of the work.

570 SAN PEDRO, DIEGO DE. The Castle of Love (1549?). Translated
by John Bourchier, Baron Berners. Introduction by William
G. Crane. Gainesville, Florida: Scholars' Facsimiles &
Reprints, 1950, not paginated.
Provides facsimile reprint of 1549? edition. In "Introduction" considers briefly text from which Bourchier translated, his style, and the extant editions of the translation.

571 "A Textual Edition on Modern Principles of Arthur of Little
Britain, a Romance of the Sixteenth Century Translated by
John Bourchier, Lord Berners." Edited by George Emile
Mitchell. Ph.D. dissertation, University of Notre Dame,
1969, 1051pp.
Provides critical edition based on text of 1555 edition.

Studies

572 BAKER, ERNEST A[LBERT]. The History of the English Novel,
Vol. I. London: H. F. & G. Witherby, 1924, 336pp.
Discusses Bourchier's translations, in particular his
style and treatment of the text in Huon of Bordeaux
(pp. 219-28, 255-58, passim).

573 BLAKE, N. F. "Lord Berners: A Survey." M&H, NS, 2 (1971),
119-32.
Surveys problems connected with dating editions of
Bourchier's translations and offers suggestions for further
study.

574 COTTRELL, G. W. "Carcel de Amor." TLS, 27 April 1933,
p. 295.
Points out that Bourchier translated from a French version of 1526. See 575 and 576.

575 CRANE, WILLIAM G. "Carcel de Amor." TLS, 9 March 1933,
p. 167.
Discusses dates of editions of Bourchier's translation.
Suggests that it is the "first translation directly from
Spanish which was published in England." See 574 and 576.

Bourchier

576 CRANE, WILLIAM G. "Carcel de Amor." TLS, 1 June 1933, p. 380.
     In reply to 574, suggests that Bourchier used a Spanish
     edition as well as the 1526 French version.

577 CRANE, WILLIAM G. "Lord Berners's Translation of Diego de San
     Pedro's Cárcel de Amor." PMLA, 49 (December 1934), 1032-35.
     Poses question of source for Bourchier's translation,
     noting that "Prologe" is translated from the French edition
     while Nicolas Nunez's continuation, usually omitted from
     French and Italian translations, is included. Suggests that
     Bourchier learned Spanish as he translated work, using
     French translation as aid.

578 DRAPER, JOHN W. "A Reference to Huon in Ben Jonson." MLN, 35
     (November 1920), 439-40.
     Notes allusion to Huon of Bordeaux--possibly through
     Jonson's use of Bourchier's translation--in Magnetic Lady.

579 EBERT, WILHELM. Vergleich der beiden Versionen von Lord
     Berners' Huon of Burdeux. Halle: Hohmann, 1917, 92pp.
     Compares 1534 edition with that of 1601 to illustrate
     how Catholic references were expurgated in later edition
     and how the language changed; examines alterations in prepo-
     sitional phrases, tenses, verb forms, pronouns, and sub-
     stantives.

580 FLETCHER, JEFFERSON B. "Huon of Burdeux and The Fairie Queene."
     JEGP, 2, no. 2 (1899), 203-12.
     Discusses parallels between Book I of Spenser's poem and
     first 85 chapters of Bourchier's translation to illustrate
     Spenser's indebtedness to the latter. Concludes that Huon
     is source for "chief outlines and characters of...[Spenser's]
     romantic fairy world" and the development of plot in Book I.
     See 583.

581 GREENLAW, EDWIN [A.]. "Britomart at the House of Busirane."
     SP, 26 (April 1929), 117-30.
     Discusses Arthur of Little Britain as source of Faerie
     Queene, III, xi-xii. Suggests that the romance is "probably
     the greatest single influence to be traced in Spenser's
     poem."

582 KINNEY, MURIEL. "Possible Traces of Huon de Bordeaux in the
     English Ballad of Sir Aldingar." RR, 1 (July-September
     1910), 314-21.
     Examines possible influence of Bourchier's translation
     on ballad and notes in passing indebtedness of Robin Good-
     Fellow His Mad Pranks to Huon of Bordeaux.

583   MacARTHUR, JOHN R.   "The Influence of Huon of Burdeux upon The
      Fairie Queene."   JEGP, 4, no. 2 (1902), 215-38.
            Refutes point-by-point Fletcher's argument (580) for in-
      fluence of Huon on Spenser's poem. Instead, suggests that
      influence is limited to isolated details; points out paral-
      lels between Bourchier's translation and Red Cross's fight
      with dragon and Guyon's voyage.

584   McNEIR, WALDO F.   "Traditional Elements in the Character of
      Greene's Friar Bacon."   SP, 45 (April 1948), 172-79.
            Draws upon Huon of Bordeaux in discussion of conventional
      elements in the treatment of benevolent magicians in early
      romances.

585   MICHIE, SARAH.   "The Faerie Queene and Arthur of Little
      Britain."   SP, 36 (April 1939), 105-23.
            Examines Spenser's extensive use of Bourchier's transla-
      tion as source for The Faerie Queene.

586   MITCHELL, G. E.   "The Sixteenth Century Editions of Arthur of
      Little Britain."   RBPH, 50, no. 3 (1972), 793-95.
            Argues against possibility of an edition prior to that
      of 1555. Suggests speculation about an earlier edition is
      due to Joseph Ames's carelessness in his Typographical An-
      tiquities.

587   OBEREMBT, KENNETH JOSEPH.   "Sir John Bourchier's Arthur of
      Lytell Brytayne: Its Relation to the French Artus de la
      Petite Bretagne."   Ph.D. dissertation, University of Iowa,
      1972, 249pp.
            Examines Bourchier's treatment of the original text,
      particularly his expansions and the effects of his change
      of the "casual style" of the original into "English formal
      style."

588   SCHLEICH, GUSTAV.   "Lesefrüchte aus Übersetzungen von Lord
      Berners."   Archiv, 160 (1931), 34-50.
            Examines influence of Purfoot's protestantism on changes
      in his 1601 edition of Huon, discusses Bourchier's use of
      proverbs, and provides notes on his vocabulary.

589   SEATON, ETHEL.   "Marlowe's Light Reading," in Elizabethan and
      Jacobean Studies Presented to Frank Percy Wilson. Edited
      by Herbert Davis and Helen Gardner. Oxford: Clarendon
      Press, 1959, pp. 17-35.
            Discusses reminiscences of Bourchier's Huon of Bordeaux
      in a general discussion of influence of medieval romance on
      Marlowe's works.

Bourchier

590   TAYLOR, ANNE ROBB. "Grant translateur: The Life and Translations of John Bourchier, Second Baron Berners." Ph.D. dissertation, Brown University, 1968, 171pp.
Provides overview of Bourchier as translator.

BOYLE, ROGER, EARL OF ORRERY (1621–1679)

Parthenissa. Wing 0488–494.

Studies

591   DAVIES, CHARLES. "Introduction," in Prefaces to Four Seventeenth-Century Romances. ARS, 42. Los Angeles: William
Andrews Clark Memorial Library, University of California,
1953, pp. i–vi.
Discusses Boyle's "Preface" to Parthenissa in the context of an overview of the issues and concerns of "the long
argument about Romance" in the seventeenth century.

592   DUNLOP, JOHN [COLIN]. The History of Fiction: Being a Critical Account of the Most Celebrated Prose Works of Fiction,
from the Earliest Greek Romances to the Novels of the
Present Age, Vol. III. Edinburgh: Longman, Hurst, Rees,
Orme, and Browne, 1814, 436pp.
Provides synopsis of Parthenissa and discusses influence
of French heroic romance on the work (pp. 363–69). See
182 and 183.

593   HAVILAND, THOMAS P[HILIP]. "Chief of the English Heroic Romances." LC, 6 (October 1938), 40–45.
Discusses Parthenissa as an example of the heroic romance. Finds that "it excels its English brethren in lofty
sentiment, in rich description, in details of tournament
and armed conflict," noting in particular Boyle's depiction
of battle scenes.

594   HAVILAND, THOMAS PHILIP. The "Roman de Longue Haleine" on
English Soil. Ph.D. dissertation, University of Pennsylvania, 1929. Philadelphia: n.p., 1931, 183pp.
Examines influence of French heroic romance on Parthenissa; discusses general characteristics (style, structure, etc.) of the work (pp. 116–24).

595   KAGAN, DAVID. "Roger Boyle's Parthenissa." Serif, 7 (March
1970), 30–31.
Notes variants from Miller's description (598) in some
copies of 1676 edition.

596 LANGFORD, GERALD. "John Barclay and His <u>Argenis</u>." Ph.D.
dissertation, University of Virginia, 1940, 199pp.
Includes discussion of influence of <u>Argenis</u> on
<u>Parthenissa</u>.

597 LYNCH, KATHLEEN M. <u>Roger Boyle, First Earl of Orrery</u>. Knox-
ville: University of Tennessee Press, 1965, 320pp.
Provides overview of characteristics of <u>Parthenissa</u>:
discusses Boyle's treatment of Platonic love and the auto
biographical elements in work (pp. 187-94).

598 MILLER, C[LARENCE] WILLIAM. "A Bibliographical Study of
<u>Parthenissa</u> by Roger Boyle Earl of Orrery." <u>SB</u>, 2 (1949-
1950), 115-37.
Provides an "intensive study of the various editions and
issues": establishes that Henry Bradshaw's 1654-1655 dating
of first edition is incorrect; argues that first edition was
printed in 1651. Provides analytical description of editions and issues. <u>See</u> 595.

599 MILLER, CLARENCE WILLIAM. "The Influence of the French
Heroico-Historical Romance on Seventeenth Century English
Prose Fiction." Ph.D. dissertation, University of Virginia,
1940.
Provides detailed analysis of influence of French romances on <u>Parthenissa</u>; argues that La Calprenède's <u>Cassandre</u>
served as Boyle's "prototype." Provides bibliographical
analysis of early editions.

600 MILLER, C[LARENCE] WILLIAM. "A Source Note on Boyle's <u>The</u>
<u>General</u>." <u>MLQ</u>, 8 (June 1947), 146-50.
Discusses influence of <u>Romeo and Juliet</u> on <u>Parthenissa</u>,
and the influence of the romance on Boyle's <u>The General</u>.
Attempts to reconstruct Boyle's plan for conclusion of
<u>Parthenissa</u>.

601 MORGAN, CHARLOTTE E. <u>The Rise of the Novel of Manners: A</u>
<u>Study of English Prose Fiction between 1600 and 1740</u>. New
York: Columbia University Press, 1911, 281pp.
Provides in Appendix A a "Summary of <u>Parthenissa</u>" (pp.
138-42) as an example of "the content and structure of...
folio romances."

<u>BRATHWAIT, RICHARD</u> (1588?-1673)

<u>Ar't Asleepe Husband? A Boulster Lecture</u>. STC 3555.

<u>Panthalia: Or the Royal Romance</u>. Wing B4273.

Brathwait

The Penitent Pilgrim. Wing B4275.

The Two Lancashire Lovers; or the Excellent History of Philocles and
    Doriclea. STC 3590-3590a.

Mariano Silesio, The Arcadian Princesse: Or, the Triumph of Justice.
    STC 22553.

Editions

602   BRATHWAIT, RICHARD. The Penitent Pilgrim. London: William
        Pickering, 1847, 273pp.
            Provides modernized reprint of 1641 edition.

Studies

*603   BLACK, MATTHEW W. "Richard Brathwait: An Account of His Life
        and Works." Ph.D. dissertation, University of Pennsylvania,
        1927.
            Abstract not available.

604   BOYCE, BENJAMIN. "History and Fiction in Panthalia: Or the
        Royal Romance." JEGP, 57, no. 3 (1958), 477-91.
            Discusses blend of fiction and interpretation of histori-
        cal events (1580-1658), arguing for importance of work in
        development of historical romance. Examines general charac-
        teristics of book (style, plot, narrative techniques, and
        especially characterization). Provides key to characters.

605   HAVILAND, THOMAS P[HILIP]. "The Heroic Panthalia." LC, 3
        (1935), 14-15.
            Reports the acquisition of copy of 1659 edition and
        comments briefly on the thinly concealed treatment of con-
        temporary affairs.

606   LANGFORD, GERALD. "John Barclay and His Argenis." Ph.D.
        dissertation, University of Virginia, 1940, 199pp.
            Includes discussion of influence of Argenis on Panthalia.

607   MILLER, CLARENCE WILLIAM. "The Influence of the French
        Heroico-Historical Romance on Seventeenth Century English
        Prose Fiction." Ph.D. dissertation, University of Virginia,
        1940.
            Finds that influence of French romance on Panthalia "is
        almost negligible." Calls Brathwait's work "a poor imita-
        tion of Argenis."

BRETON, NICHOLAS (1545?-1626?)

Choice, Chance, and Change, or Conceits in Their Colours. STC 3636.

Grimellos Fortunes. STC 3657.

A Merrie Dialoge betwixt the Taker and Mistaker (a later edition as A Mad World My Masters). STC 3667-3668.

The Miseries of Mavillia, in The Will of Wit, Wits Wil, or Wils Wit. STC 3705-3707.

A Poste with a Madde Packet of Letters. STC 3684-3694. Wing B4387-4390.

The Strange Fortune of Two Excellent Princes. STC 3702.

Bibliographies

608   TANNENBAUM, SAMUEL A., and DOROTHY R. TANNENBAUM. Nicholas Breton (A Concise Bibliography). Elizabethan Bibliographies, 39. New York: Samuel A. Tannenbaum, 1946, 33pp. Provide classified list of editions and criticism.

Editions

609   BRETON, NICHOLAS. The Miseries of Mavillia, in The Will of Wit, Otherwise Called, Wit's Will, or Will's Wit. By Nicholas Breton. Edited by James O[rchard] Halliwell[-Phillipps]. London: T. Richards, 1860, pp. 91-154.
      Provides reprint of text of 1599 edition. In "Preface," pp. v-viii, traces bibliographical history of the work.

610   BRETON, NICHOLAS. The Works in Verse and Prose of Nicholas Breton. Edited by Alexander B. Grosart. Chertsey Worthies' Library. 2 vols. Edinburgh: Printed for Private Circulation, 1879, pagination not continuous.
      Provides annotated, old spelling texts based on early editions of The Miseries of Mavillia, The Strange Fortunes of Two Excellent Princes, A Post with a Mad Packet of Letters, and Grimello's Fortunes. In the "Memorial-Introduction," pp. ix-lxxvi, discusses the publication and dating of Breton's works, the Protestant bias and melancholy of his works, his style (and other characteristic traits of his works), and his originality. Provides a brief critical estimate of each work.

Breton

611   BRETON, NICHOLAS. Choice, Chance, and Change (1606) or
      Glimpses of Merry England in the Olden Time. Edited by
      Alexander B. Grosart. Manchester: Printed for the Sub-
      scribers, 1881, 92pp.
          Provides reprint of 1606 edition. In prefatory remarks
      discusses evidence for Breton's authorship and value of
      work for its depiction of early customs.

612   BRETON, NICHOLAS. A Mad World My Masters and Other Prose Works
      by Nicholas Breton. Edited by Ursula Kentish-Wright. 2
      vols. London: Cresset Press, 1929, 508pp.
          Provides slightly modernized, unannotated reprints based
      on "the originals" of A Mad World My Masters, The Miseries
      ⸤f Mavillia, and A Post with a Mad Packet of Letters. In
      "Introduction," pp. vii-xxx, discusses Breton's works in
      the context of his life and times.

613   BRETON, NICHOLAS. Grimellos Fortunes, in Two Pamphlets of
      Nicholas Breton: Grimellos Fortunes (1604), An Olde Mans
      Lesson (1605). By Nicholas Breton. Edited by E. G. Morice.
      University of Bristol Studies, 4. Bristol: University of
      Bristol, 1936, pp. 21-63.
          Provides annotated text based on 1604 edition. In "In-
      troduction," pp. 9-19, discusses sources, theme, and style
      of work.

614   BRETON, NICHOLAS. "A Critical Edition of Part I of Nicholas
      Breton's A Poste with a Madde Packet of Letters." Edited
      by Timothy Reed Howlett. Ph.D. dissertation, Northern
      Illinois University, 1972, 364pp.
          Provides critical edition of Part I. Analyzes printing
      history of work and provides bibliographical analysis of
      seventeenth-century editions.

Studies

615   CRUPI, CHARLES. "The Date of Breton's Mavillia." N&Q, NS, 16
      (January 1969), 27-28.
          Suggests that Mavillia "should...be dated around 1580."

616   CUTTS, JOHN P. "The Strange Fortunes of Two Excellent Princes
      and The Arbor of Amorous Deuises." Renaissance News, 15
      (Spring 1962), 2-11.
          Transcribes setting of "I would thou wert not faire"--a
      song in Strange Fortunes--from John Bartlet's A Booke of
      Ayres; also notes variants.

*617   FLOURNOY, FITZGERALD. "Nicholas Breton: Biography, Bibli-
        ography, and Census." Ph.D. dissertation, Yale University,
        1936.
             Abstract not available.

618   FLOURNOY, FITZGERALD. "William Breton, Nicholas Breton, and
        George Gascoigne." RES, 16 (July 1940), 262-73.
             Suggests, in passing, that Breton's complaints of poverty
        and cynicism about money in his works have a biographical
        basis.

619   HARTER, BETSY WELLER. "Nicholas Breton's Prose: A Study of
        Sub-Genres and Techniques Contributing to the Development
        of the Eighteenth-Century English Novel." Ph.D. disserta-
        tion, University of Rochester, 1966, 396pp.
             Analyzes "the wide variety of forms and techniques"
        Breton used in his prose fiction and their influence on the
        development of the eighteenth-century novel.

620   KENTISH-WRIGHT, URSULA. "Shakespeare and Nicholas Breton."
        Cornhill Magazine, 159 (June 1939), 815-26.
             Points out passages in Shakespeare's works which bear
        similarity to passages in Breton's prose fiction as "cir-
        cumstantial evidence" of a friendship between the two
        writers.

*621   KUSKOP, THEODOR F[RIEDRICH KARL]. Nicholas Breton und seine
        Prosaschriften. Leipzig: Seele, 1902, 100pp.
             Not seen. Listed in NUC Pre-1956 Imprints, vol. 309,
        286.

622   McCLOSKEY, FRANK HOWLAND. "Studies in the Works of Nicholas
        Breton." Ph.D. dissertation, Harvard University, 1929.
             Examines Breton's prose fiction in relation to "prede-
        cessors and contemporaries in its kind." Finds that for
        Mavillia "Breton's models were Lazarillo and Jack Wilton"
        and that Strange Fortunes of Two Excellent Princes is "a
        successor to the later and maturer tales by Greene." Con-
        cludes that "Breton had no gift for sustained narration."

623   MONROE, NELLIE ELIZABETH. Nicholas Breton as a Pamphleteer.
        Ph.D. dissertation, University of Pennsylvania, 1929.
        Philadelphia: n.p., 1929, 98pp.
             Provides brief critical assessment of each of Breton's
        prose fiction works. Examines his style, his variety in
        form and subject matter, and his ability to adapt his work
        to popular taste.

Breton

624   ROBERTSON, JEAN. "Introduction," in <u>Poems by Nicholas Breton</u>
      <u>(not Hitherto Reprinted)</u>. By Nicholas Breton. Edited by
      Jean Robertson. Liverpool English Texts & Studies. Liver-
      pool: Liverpool University Press, 1952, pp. XI-CLIX.
          Includes short-title list of Breton's work with a de-
      tailed discussion establishing his canon.

625   SINGER, GODFREY FRANK. <u>The Epistolary Novel: Its Origin,</u>
      <u>Development, Decline, and Residuary Influence</u>. Philadel-
      phia: University of Pennsylvania Press, 1933, 276pp.
          Includes discussion of Breton's style, didacticism, and
      philosophy in <u>A Post with a Mad Packet</u>. Argues that work
      "helped largely to forward the general popularity of the
      letter-writer" and that Breton "is the direct precursor of
      Richardson and the 'familiar' letter-writer" (pp. 27-33).

626   SULLIVAN, FRANK. "Breton, Nicholas (?1545-?1626): <u>A Poste</u>
      <u>with a Packet of Madde Letters</u>." <u>PBSA</u>, 37, no. 3 (1943),
      233.
          Suggests that "1607 issue...seems to have been printed
      before the 1606 edition." Identifies printers of both.

627   WHITING, MARY BRADFORD. "Nicholas Breton, Gentleman: A Ter-
      centenary." <u>Fortnightly Review</u>, NS, 125 (May 1929), 618-32.
          Provides survey and general discussion of Breton's works;
      finds his prose fiction "distinctly dull."

628   WRIGHT, THOMAS EDWARD. "The English Renaissance Prose Anatomy."
      Ph.D. dissertation, Washington University, 1963, 238pp.
          Examines <u>A Post with a Mad Packet</u> as an example of the
      "use of the letter collection form."

<u>BREWER, THOMAS</u> (fl. 1624)

<u>The Life and Death of the Merry Devill of Edmonton, with the Pleasant</u>
   <u>Prancks of Smug the Smith</u>. <u>STC</u> 3719.

Editions

629   B[REWER], T[HOMAS]. <u>The Life and Death of the Merry Deuill of</u>
      <u>Edmonton</u>. London: J. Nichols and Son, 1819, 54pp.
          Provides reprint of 1631 edition.

630   [BREWER, THOMAS]. <u>The Life and Death of the Merry Devil of</u>
      <u>Edmonton</u>, in The Merry Devil of Edmonton, 1608: <u>Edited</u>
      <u>with an Introduction and Notes, and a Reprint of</u> The Life
      and Death of the Merry Devil of Edmonton, by T. B., 1631.

Edited by William Amos Abrams. Durham: Duke University
Press, 1942, pp. 224-67.
    Provides a reprint of 1631 edition. In "Introduction,"
pp. 3-103, examines relationship between play and prose
work: argues that prose work includes episodes based on
play as it was originally performed and uses 1631 edition
to reconstruct scenes not retained in printed version of
play. Identifies author as Tony Brewer.

Studies

631   GREG, W[ALTER] W[ILSON]. "The Merry Devil of Edmonton."
       Library, 4th Ser., 25, nos. 3-4 (1945), 122-39.
           Examines relationship of Life and Death of the Merry
       Devil of Edmonton to the play. Suggests that the two works
       developed independently from a common body of traditional
       materials.

BROWNE, WILLIAM, OF TAVISTOCK (1590?-1645?)

Marin le Roy, Sieur de Gomberville, The History of Polexander. Wing
    G1025-1026.

Studies

632   Entry cancelled.

633   CLARK, WILLIAM S. "The Sources of the Restoration Heroic
       Play." RES, 4 (January 1928), 49-63.
           Points out that Browne's History of Polexander was the
       main source for Dryden and Howard's The Indian Queen.

BURTON, WILLIAM (1575-1645)

Achilles Tatius, The Most Delectable History of Clitiphon and Leu-
    cippe. STC 90.

Editions

634   ACHILLES TATIUS. The Loves of Clitophon and Leucippe. Trans-
       lated by William Burton. Edited by Stephen Gaselee and
       H[erbert] F[rancis] B[rett] Brett-Smith. Oxford: Black-
       well, 1923, 183pp.
           Provides reprint of 1597 edition. In "Introduction,"
       pp. xiii-xxii, Gaselee discusses discovery of unique copy
       and the source of Burton's translation. In "William

Burton

> Burton Translator," pp. xxiii–xxxi, Brett–Smith examines reasons for inaccuracies in translation and discusses Burton's style.

Studies

635   GESNER, CAROL. "Cymbeline and the Greek Romance: A Study in Genre," in Studies in English Renaissance Literature. Edited by Waldo F. McNeir. LSUSHS, 12. Baton Rouge: Louisiana State University Press, 1962, pp. 105–31.
       Argues for Shakespeare's use of Clitophon and Leucippe, probably in Burton's translation, as a source for the play.

636   PEDDIE, R. A. "An Elizabethan Discovery." TLS, 10 February 1905, pp. 50–51.
       Announces discovery of a copy of Burton's translation of Clitophon and Leucippe. Reprinted in 427.

C., R. (possibly Raffe Carr)

The Troublesome and Hard Adventures in Love. Wing C1781.

Studies

637   RANDALL, DALE B. J. "The Troublesome and Hard Adventures in Love: An English Addition to the Bibliography of Diana." BHS, 38 (April 1961), 154–58.
       Points out use of Montemayor's Diana and Gil Polo's Diana enamorada as sources for the work and suggests that the translator is Raffe Carr.

C., W.

The First [Second] Part of the Renowned Historie of Fragosa King of Aragon. STC 4319–4320.

Studies

638   WELD, JOHN SALTAR. "Studies in the Euphuistic Novel, 1576–1640." Ph.D. dissertation, Harvard University, 1940, 304pp.
       Discusses influences on Fragosa.

A C. MERY TALYS

   STC 23663–23664.5.

A C. Mery Talys

Editions

639   Shakespeare's Jest Book [A C. Mery Talys]. Edited by S. W.
       Singer. Chiswick: Whittingham, 1815, 150pp.
          Provides reprint of 1526 edition. In "Advertisement,"
       pp. vii-xii, corrects earlier assumption, noting that this
       is the work alluded to in Much Ado about Nothing (see 2977).
       Notes analogue of one story in an "ancient MS. Art of speak-
       ing French" (pp. xv-xviii).

640   A C Merry Tales, in Shakespeare's Merry Tales. London: G.
       Routledge, 1845, pp. 1-104.
          Provides modernized text based upon 639. In "Preface,"
       pp. iii-xiv, anonymous writer discusses popularity of work
       and paraphrases "Advertisement" in 639.

641   A Hundred Mery Talys, in Shakespeare Jest-Books, Vol. I.
       Edited by W[illiam] Carew Hazlitt. London: Willis &
       Sotheran, 1864, v-xii, 11-129 (separately paginated).
          Provides annotated reprint of 1526 edition. In "Intro-
       duction," pp. i-x, discusses the bibliographical history of
       the work and allusions to it.

642   Shakespeare's Jest Book: A Hundred Mery Talys, from the Only
       Perfect Copy Known. Edited by Herman Oesterley. London:
       J. R. Smith, 1866, 181pp. [Reprinted: with "Introduction"
       by Leonard R. N. Ashley. Gainesville, Florida: Scholars'
       Facsimiles & Reprints, 1970, 188pp.]
          Reprints Göttingen copy of 1526 edition. Discusses
       sources and analogues in notes. In "Introduction," pp. iii-
       xiv, describes 1526 edition and compares it with later ones.

643   A Hundred Merry Tales: The Earliest English Jest-Book. Edited
       by W[illiam] Carew Hazlitt. London: J. W. Jarvis, 1887,
       not paginated.
          Provides facsimile of Göttingen copy of 1526 edition:
       includes annotations on sources. In "Editor's Preface,"
       pp. i-xiii, argues that collection was made by John Heywood
       "with the assistance, possibly at the instigation, of Sir
       Thomas More."

644   A Hundred Merry Tales, in A Hundred Merry Tales and Other Eng-
       lish Jestbooks of the Fifteenth and Sixteenth Centuries.
       Edited by P. M. Zall. Lincoln: University of Nebraska
       Press, 1963, pp. 57-150.
          Provides modernized reprint of Göttingen copy of 1526
       edition. In "The Natural History of Jestbooks: An Intro-
       duction," pp. 1-10, calls work "the closest thing we have

A C. Mery Talys

    to a distinctively native English jestbook." Comments on
    style and realism.

645   A Hundred Merry Tales. Edited by Franklin S. Klaf and Bern-
       hardt J. Hurwood. New York: Citadel Press, 1964, 126pp.
         Provide modernized text based upon unidentified edition.
       In "Introduction," pp. 9-16, discuss Shakespeare's use of
       work and suggest that tale 60 was used by Rabelais as a
       source in Gargantua and Pantagruel.

Studies

646   A., S. "Samuel Rowlands Anticipated by Luther." N&Q, 53
       (17 June 1876), 490-91.
         Relates nineteenth-century version of a tale from A
       Hundred Merry Tales.

647   COLLIER, J[OHN] PAYNE. "Verification of a Jest." N&Q, 29
       (18 June 1864), 491.
         Suggests historical source for "Of the Woman that Said
       Her Wooer Came too Late" and relates tradition that A Hun-
       dred Merry Tales "was the last book that Elizabeth, just
       before her death, was gratified by hearing read."

648   FERRARA, FERNANDO. Jests e Merry Tales: Aspetti della narra-
       tiva popolaresca inglese del sedicesimo secolo. Nuovi
       Saggi, 27. Rome: Edizioni dell'Ateneo, 1960, 257pp.
         Analyzes place of Hundred Merry Tales in development of
       sixteenth-century jest book. Examines realism (in charac-
       terization, details, and language), style, narrative tech-
       niques, and satire. Discusses types of tales and influences
       of medieval models on work (pp. 94-100, passim).

649   HAZLITT, W[ILLIAM] CAREW. Studies in Jocular Literature: A
       Popular Subject More Closely Considered. London: E. Stock,
       1890, 238pp.
         Discusses the lack of original matter in Hundred Merry
       Tales and suggests that Thomas More and/or John Heywood
       were contributors to the collection (pp. 117-20, 153-61,
       passim).

650   KLEIN, KARL LUDWIG. Vorformen des Romans in der englischen
       erzählenden Prosa des 16. Jahrhunderts. FAGAAS, 13.
       Heidelberg: C. Winter, 1969, 260pp.
         Examines influence of Hundred Merry Tales on rogue pam-
       phlets; compares to Boccaccio's narrative technique (pp. 86-
       98).

651 LIPKING, JOANNA BRIZDLE. "Traditions of the Facetiae and Their
Influence in Tudor England." Ph.D. dissertation, Columbia
University, 1970, 477pp.
Examines influence of facetiae on the jest book. Suggests that A Hundred Merry Tales and Tales and Quick Answers
"are best understood as imitations of the books of facetiae,
showing the same organization, conception of the joke, and
comic resources."

652 M., T. H. "The Hundred Merry Tales." N&Q, 31 (21 January
1865), 51.
Describes briefly a copy of the 1526 edition recently
discovered in Royal Library at Göttingen.

653 MAGOON, MARIAN WAITE. "Some Analogues to Elizabethan Jest
Books in Medieval Ecclesiastical Literature." Ph.D. dissertation, University of Michigan, 1931.
Traces analogues in Medieval collections of exempla to
several tales in Hundred Merry Tales.

654 SCHULZ, ERNST. Die englischen Schwankbücher bis herab zu
Dobson's Drie Bobs (1607). Palaestra, 117. Berlin: Mayer
& Müller, 1912, 238pp.
Includes discussion of sources, style, and subject mat-
ter of Hundred Merry Tales (pp. 23-30).

655 UNGER, F. W. "Zur Shakespeare-Litteratur." Serapeum, 25,
no. 9 (1864), 142-44.
Describes Göttingen University copy of 1526 edition of
Hundred Merry Tales.

CAREW, RICHARD, OF ANTHONY (1555-1620)

Henri Estienne, A World of Wonders. STC 10553-10554.

Studies

656 CROSSLEY, JA[ME]S. "Hen. Stephens's Apology for Herodotus,
English Translation." N&Q, 56 (29 September 1877), 246-47.
Suggests that Richard Carew was translator of World of
Wonders. Queries existence of a 1608 Edinburgh edition.

657 WOOD, D. N. C. "Ralph Cudworth the Elder and Henry Estienne's
World of Wonders." ELN, 11 (December 1973), 93-100.
Argues against Richard Carew as translator; suggests
Ralph Cudworth the Elder.

Cavendish

CAVENDISH, MARGARET, DUCHESS OF NEWCASTLE (1623-1673)

Natures Pictures. Wing N855-856.

Studies

658   GAGEN, JEAN. "Honor and Fame in the Works of the Duchess of
      Newcastle." SP, 56 (July 1959), 519-38.
            Includes discussion of Cavendish's treatment of honor
      and fame in Nature's Pictures. Finds that her conception
      of the ideals was shaped by the "influence of the Renais-
      sance concept of honor."

659   GRANT, DOUGLAS. "The 'Fantastical' Margaret Cavendish." The
      Listener, 30 October 1952, pp. 726-27.
            Discusses in general terms the characteristics of her
      writing--especially her lack of concern for order.

660   GRANT, DOUGLAS. Margaret the First: A Biography of Margaret
      Cavendish, Duchess of Newcastle, 1623-1673. London: Hart-
      Davis, 1957, 253pp.
            Discusses the variety in Nature's Pictures and finds all
      of the tales "essentially autobiographical." Identifies
      narrative and characterization as her two weaknesses
      (passim).

661   MacCARTHY, B[RIDGET] G. Women Writers: Their Contribution to
      the English Novel, 1621-1744. Cork: Cork University Press,
      1944, 288pp.
            Examines Cavendish's expression of own opinions and cre-
      ation of herself as "her favourite heroine" in Nature's
      Pictures. Discusses her style and the intrusion of pseudo-
      philosophy into tales, but asserts that she is "a very good
      story-teller" (passim).

662   PERRY, HENRY TEN EYCK. The First Duchess of Newcastle and
      Her Husband as Figures in Literary History. Harvard Studies
      in English, 4. Boston: Ginn and Co., 1918, 335pp.
            Provides overview of the contents of Nature's Pictures,
      examines subject matter (especially treatment of love), and
      discusses structure of work (pp. 203-13).

CHARLETON, WALTER (1619-1707)

The Ephesian Matron. Wing C3670-3671.

Editions

663   CHARLETON, WALTER. The Ephesian Matron (1668). Introduction
      by Achsah Guibbory. ARS, 172-73. Los Angeles: William
      Andrews Clark Memorial Library, University of California,
      1975, not paginated.
         Provides facsimile reprint of 1668 edition. In "Intro-
      duction," pp. i-xii, discusses Charleton's handling of
      Widow of Ephesus tale, the influence of Hobbes and Epicurus
      on work, the discussion of love, and the attitude toward the
      matron. Argues that work is an "expose" of "the general
      human nature defined by Hobbes" in Human Nature.

Studies

664   URE, PETER. "The Widow of Ephesus: Some Reflections on an
      International Comic Theme." DUJ, 49 (December 1956), 1-9.
         Points out that in The Ephesian Matron, Charleton "is
      really defining love and making an attack on the current
      fashionable cult of 'Platonic' love."

665   WILLIAMSON, GEORGE. "The Ephesian Matron Versus the Platonic
      Lady." RES, 12 (October 1936), 445-49.
         Provides an account of the work as a naturalistic, sa-
      tiric attack on the Platonic cult.

CHETTLE, HENRY (1560?-1607?)

Kind Harts Dreame. STC 5123.

Piers Plainnes Seaven Yeres Prentiship. STC 5124.

Editions

666   CHETTLE, HENRY. Kind-Heart's Dream: Containing Five Appari-
      tions with Their Invectives against Abuses Reigning. Edited
      by Edward F. Rimbault. Percy Society, 5. London: C.
      Richards for the Percy Society, 1841, 104pp.
         Provides an annotated text based on a transcript of the
      1592 edition.

667   CHETTLE, HENRY. Kind-Harts Dreame, in Shakspere Allusion-
      Books, Part I. Edited by C[lement] M[ansfield] Ingleby.
      New Shakspere Society Publications, Series 4, no. 1. Lon-
      don: N. Trübner for New Shakspere Society, 1874, pp. 35-76.
         Provides partly modernized reprint of 1593 edition. In
      "General Introduction," pp. i-xxxv, discusses allusions to

Chettle

playwrights in work. Reprints 688 as "Supplement," pp. xxxvii-xlviii.

*668   CHETTLE, HENRY. Piers Plainnes Seven Yeres Prentiship. Edited by Herman Varnhagen. Erlangen: n.p., 1900.
        Not seen. Listed in NUC Pre-1956 Imprints, vol. 105, 682.

669   CHETTLE, HENRY. Kind-Hartes Dreame, in Henrie Chettle, Kind-Hartes Dreame, 1592; William Kemp, Nine Daies Wonder, 1600. Edited by G[eorge] B[agshawe] Harrison. Bodley Head Quartos, 4. London: John Lane, Bodley Head, 1923, 67pp. (separately paginated).
        Provides slightly corrected reprint of 1592 edition.

670   CHETTLE, HENRY. Piers Plainness: Seven Years' Prenticeship, in The Descent of Euphues: Three Elizabethan Romance Stories: Euphues, Pandosto, Piers Plainness. Edited by James Winny. Cambridge: Cambridge University Press, 1957, pp. 122-74.
        Provides slightly modernized text based on 1595 edition. In "Introduction" (pp. ix-xxv) discusses work as an amalgamation of elements from romance and rogue literature, characterizes Chettle's style, and examines the influence of Euphues on the work.

671   CHETTLE, HENRY. Kind-Heart's Dream Containing Five Apparitions, with Their Invectives against Abuses, in Kind-Heart's Dream Containing Five Apparitions with Their Invectives against Abuses by Henry Chettle, 1593. A Mirror of Monsters by William Rankins, 1587. Introduction by Peter Davison. New York: Johnson Reprint Corporation, 1972, not paginated.
        Provides facsimile reprint of 1593 edition. In "Introduction," discusses objects of attack and tone. Argues that Tarlton's defense is meant to be ironic.

Studies

672   AUSTIN, WARREN B. "The Authorship of Certain Renaissance English Pamphlets: An Informal Account of Work in Progress," in Proceedings: Computer Applications to Problems in the Humanities: A Conversation in the Disciplines. Edited by Frederick M. Burelbach, Jr. Brockport: State University of New York, Brockport, 1970, pp. 93-99.
        Provides preliminary report on 673.

673   AUSTIN, WARREN B. A Computer-Aided Technique for Stylistic Discrimination: The Authorship of Greene's Groatsworth of

Wit. Project 7-G-036. Grant No. OEG-1-7-070036-4593.
U. S. Department of Health, Education, and Welfare. Washington: U. S. Office of Education, 1969, 155pp.
   Analyzes "patterns of word-choice" and other linguistic
variables (syntax, lexis, morphology) in works of Greene
and Chettle to determine authorship of Groatsworth. Finds
that the "frequency patterns [of the linguistic variables]
found in the questioned work [i.e., Groatsworth] differed
in every case from those that had been established as char-
acteristic of Greene; and in every case they matched those
established as typical of Chettle."

674   AUSTIN, WARREN B. "The Posthumous Greene Pamphlets: A Com-
      puterized Study." ShN, 16 (November-December 1966), 45.
         Reports on computer study of prose style of Robert Greene
      and Henry Chettle to determine authorship of Groatsworth of
      Wit and The Repentance of Robert Greene. See 673.

675   AUSTIN, WARREN B. "Technique of the Chettle-Greene Forgery:
      Supplementary Material on the Authorship of the Groatsworth
      of Wit." ShN, 20 (December 1970), 43.
         Supplements his earlier study (673) by noting how
      Chettle used passages from Greene's own works (particularly
      Greene's Never Too Late and Francesco's Fortunes) to fabri-
      cate the Groatsworth of Wit. See 686.

676   BROWN, ELAINE V. BEILIN. "The Uses of Mythology in Elizabethan
      Romance." Ph.D. dissertation, Princeton University, 1973,
      336pp.
         Analyzes Chettle's use of the Venus-Diana myth in Piers
      Plainness.

677   DAVIS, WALTER R[ICHARDSON]. Idea and Act in Elizabethan Fic-
      tion. Princeton: Princeton University Press, 1969, 311pp.
         Analyzes Chettle's "satiric interpolations" in romance
      form and examines narrative technique, plot, and style in
      Piers Plainness (pp. 202-10).

678   EVERITT, E. B. The Young Shakespeare: Studies in Documentary
      Evidence. Anglistica, 2. Copenhagen: Rosenkilde and
      Bagger, 1954, 188pp.
         Explains allusions in Chettle's preface to Kind-Heart's
      Dream and explores relationship of preface to others writ-
      ten about the same time (pp. 14-19, passim).

679   FELDMAN, ABRAHAM. "Shakspere and the Scholars." N&Q, 194
      (24 December 1949), 556.

Chettle

> Argues that Chettle's Kind-Heart's Dream "does not con-
> tain a word that can be reasonably construed as a reference
> to Shakspere." See: Howard Parsons, "Shakespeare and the
> Scholars," N&Q, 195 (24 June 1950), 283-84; and J[ames]
> C[loutts] Maxwell, "Shakespeare and the Scholars," N&Q, 195
> (5 August 1950), 349.

680   HILL, ROWLAND MERLIN. "Realistic Descriptive Setting in Eng-
       lish Fiction from 1550 through Fielding." Ph.D. disserta-
       tion, Boston University, 1941, 344pp.
          Discusses Chettle's use of "stage property" setting and
       setting as background in his prose fiction.

681   JENKINS, HAROLD. The Life and Work of Henry Chettle. London:
       Sidgwick and Jackson, 1934, 284pp.
          In Chapter II ("Non-Dramatic Works," pp. 30-53) discusses
       Kind-Heart's Dream as satire and "exposure of current
       abuses," examines influences on Piers Plainness, and argues
       for Chettle's authorship.

682   KRIEFELTS, BARBARA. "Eine statistische Stilanalyse zur
       Klarung von Autorenschaftsfragen, durchgefuhrt am Beispiel
       von Greens Groatsworth of Wit." Ph.D. dissertation, Uni-
       versity of Köln, 1972, 128pp.
          Through computer analysis of style of Chettle and Greene
       argues that Chettle was author of Groatsworth.

683   M[ARDER], L[OUIS]. "Chettle's Forgery of the Groatsworth of
       Wit and the 'Shake-scene' Passage." ShN, 20 (December
       1970), 42.
          Summarizes findings in 673.

684   M[ARDER], L[OUIS]. "Greene's Attack on Shakespeare: A Post-
       humous Hoax?" ShN, 16 (September 1966), 29-30.
          Reports on Austin's investigation of authorship of
       Groatsworth of Wit (see 673).

685   O'CONNOR, JOHN J. "On the Authorship of the Ratsey Pamphlets."
       PQ, 30 (October 1951), 381-86.
          Points out borrowings in Ratsey's Ghost from Kind-Heart's
       Dream.

686   PEARCE, T. M. "On the Chettle-Greene Question." ShN, 21
       (February 1971), 4.
          Comments on 675, suggesting that Chettle might have re-
       written passages while editing the manuscript of Greene's
       Groatsworth of Wit. In appended reply, Austin reasserts
       evidence pointing to Chettle's authorship.

687 SCHLAUCH, MARGARET. <u>Antecedents of the English Novel, 1400–1600 (from Chaucer to Deloney)</u>. Warsaw: PWN--Polish Scientific Publishers; London: Oxford University Press, 1963, 264pp.

Examines interweaving of "pastoral motifs with acrid satire" in <u>Piers Plainness</u> (pp. 200–205).

688 SIMPSON, R[ICHARD]. "Shakspere Allusion-Books." <u>The Academy</u>, 5 (11 April 1874), 400–401.

Argues that Shakespeare and Marlowe were the dramatists to whom Chettle's apology was directed in the "Epistle" to <u>Kind-Heart's Dream</u>. <u>See</u> 689. Reprinted in 667.

689 STAUNTON, H[OWARD]. "A Mistaken Allusion to Shakespeare." <u>The Athenaeum</u>, No. 2415 (7 February 1874), pp. 193–94.

Argues that Shakespeare is not one of the dramatists to whom the apology is directed in the Epistle to <u>Kind-Heart's Dream</u>. <u>See</u> 688.

690 THOMAS, SIDNEY. "The Printing of <u>Greenes Groatsworth of Witte</u> and <u>Kind-Harts Dreame</u>." <u>SB</u>, 19 (1966), 196–97.

Establishes that the copy for <u>Kind-Heart's Dream</u> was divided between two printers, John Wolfe and John Danter.

CLERC, JOHN

Diego de San Pedro, <u>A Certayn Treatyse Moste Wyttely Devysed</u> [i.e., <u>Arnalt and Lucenda</u>].

Editions

691 SAN PEDRO, DIEGO DE. Tractado de amores de Arnalte e Lucenda <u>nella traduzione inglese di John Clerk</u>. Translated by John Clerc. Edited by Clara Fazzari. Accademia Toscana di Scienze e Lettere "La Colombaria," Studi 29. Florence: Leo S. Olschki Editore, 1974, 126pp.

Provides partly modernized, annotated text based on 1543 edition. In "Introduzione," pp. 5–30, discusses Clerc's style, compares his translation with that by Desainliens, and describes unique copy of work.

Studies

692 KOSZUL, A. "La Première traduction d'<u>Arnalte et Lucenda</u> et les débuts de la nouvelle sentimentale en Angleterre." PFLUS, 105. Paris: Belles Lettres, 1946, pp. 151–67.

Examines Clerc's handling of text (especially his literalism and mistranslations) and compares his translation with that of Desainliens, which he finds better.

Cloria and Narcissus

CLORIA AND NARCISSUS

 Wing C4725-4726.

Studies

693   HAVILAND, THOMAS PHILIP. The "Roman de Longue Haleine" on
      English Soil. Ph.D. dissertation, University of Pennsyl-
      vania, 1929. Philadelphia: n.p., 1931, 183pp.
          Examines influence of French heroic romance on Cloria
      and Narcissus and reproduces an early key to the characters
      and places (pp. 106-10).

694   LANGFORD, GERALD. "John Barclay and His Argenis." Ph.D. dis-
      sertation, University of Virginia, 1940, 199pp.
          Includes discussion of influence of Argenis on Cloria
      and Narcissus.

THE COBLER OF CAUNTERBURIE
    As The Tincker of Turvey, 1630.

 STC 4579-4581.

Editions

*695 The Cobler of Canterburie. Edited by Frederic Ouvry. London:
      J. E. Taylor, 1862, 86pp.
          Not seen. Listed in NUC Pre-1956 Imprints, vol. 113,
      391. See 697.

696   The Tinker of Turvey, in Short Fiction of the Seventeenth
      Century. Edited by Charles C[arroll] Mish. Stuart Edi-
      tions. New York: New York University Press, 1963, pp.
      115-91.
          Provides modernized reprint of 1630 edition. In brief
      introductory note, discusses relationship of Tinker of Tur-
      vey with the original version, Cobbler of Canterbury.
      See 60.

697   The Cobbler of Canterbury: Frederic Ouvry's Edition of 1862
      with a New Introduction by H. Neville Davies. Cambridge,
      England: D. S. Brewer; Totowa, New Jersey: Rowman and
      Littlefield, 1976, 145pp.
          Reproduces text of 695 (omitting Preface) with an Appen-
      dix listing substantive errors in Ouvry's edition. In
      "Introduction" (pp. 1-55), analyzes the work as an "invec-
      tive against" Tarlton's News, examines the structure,

112

The Cobler of Caunterburie

assesses the influence of Chaucer on the work, and traces
its influence on later works (including Dryden's Of Drama-
tick Poesie). Finds that Tinker of Turvey is an inferior
adaptation of Cobbler.

Studies

698   DAVIES, H. NEVILLE. "Dryden's Rahmenerzählung: The Form of
      An Essay of Dramatick Poesie," in Fair Forms: Essays in
      English Literature from Spenser to Jane Austen. Edited by
      Maren-Sofie Røstvig. Totowa, New Jersey: Rowman and
      Littlefield, 1975, pp. 119–46.
         Argues that Dryden used Cobbler of Canterbury as source
      for the form of his Essay. Examines influence of Chaucer
      on Cobbler of Canterbury and analyzes the structure of the
      work.

699   EVERITT, E. B. The Young Shakespeare: Studies in Documentary
      Evidence. Anglistica, 2. Copenhagen: Rosenkilde and
      Bagger, 1954, 188pp.
         Explains allusions in Preface to Cobbler of Canterbury;
      assesses the evidence for Greene's authorship; and discusses
      relationships between the work and Tarlton's News (passim).

700   GALIGANI, GUISEPPE. "Il Boccaccio nel Cinquecento inglese,"
      in Il Boccaccio nella cultura inglese e anglo-americana.
      Edited by Giuseppe Galigani. Florence: L. S. Olschki,
      1974, pp. 27–57.
         Discusses use of Decameron as source for Cobbler of
      Canterbury.

701   GASSNER, HEINRICH. "The Cobler of Caunterburie." Englische
      Studien, 19 (1894), 453–55.
         Points out sources in Decameron for some of the tales in
      Cobbler of Canterbury.

702   HURRELL, JOHN DENNIS. "Loues Load-Starre: A Study in Eliza-
      bethan Literary Craftsmanship." Boston University Studies
      in English, 1, no. 4 (1955–1956), 197–209.
         Analyzes changes anonymous author made in translating
      one of the tales from the Decameron; examines Kittowe's use
      of Cobbler of Canterbury as source for Love's Load-Star.

703   M., J. "The Cobbler of Canterbury." N&Q, 30 (30 July 1864),
      86.
         Reports existence of a 1681 edition.

The Cobler of Caunterburie

704 McMILLAN, MARY EVELYN. "An Edition of Greenes Vision and A
     Maidens Dreame by Robert Greene." Ph.D. dissertation, Uni-
     versity of Alabama, 1960, 188pp.
        Examines relationship between Greene's Vision and Cobbler
     of Canterbury and Tarlton's News.

705 MARCO, SERGIO DE. "Il Boccaccio nel Settecento inglese," in
     Il Boccaccio nella cultura inglese e anglo-americana.
     Edited by Giuseppe Galigani. Florence: L. S. Olschki,
     1974, pp. 93–111.
        Discusses influence of Decameron on Cobbler of Canterbury
     and the relationship of the work to Tarlton's News.

706 SCHLAUCH, MARGARET. Antecedents of the English Novel, 1400–
     1600 (from Chaucer to Deloney). Warsaw: PWN--Polish Scien-
     tific Publishers; London: Oxford University Press, 1963,
     264pp.
        Discusses Cobbler of Canterbury as an example of "framed
     novelle," calling it "a minor anonymous masterpiece." Dis-
     cusses author's use of sources and his originality in "his
     negative attitude to inherited romance" and in his "effort
     to create a new type of non-courtly novelle centered on
     craftsmen and villagers" (pp. 157-63).

707 WHITMAN, JAMES DALTON, JR. "The Lyric Poetry of Robert
     Greene." Ph.D. dissertation, Florida State University,
     1966, 164pp.
        Argues that Greene was author of Cobbler of Canterbury.

CODRINGTON, ROBERT (d. 1665)

Marguerite de Navarre. Heptameron: Or the History of the Fortunate
     Lovers. Wing M593.

Studies

708 THOMAS, HENRY. "A Forgotten Translation of Cervantes." Revue
     Hispanique, 45 (1919), 1–11.
        Points out that in his The Spanish Decameron (1697),
     L'Estrange plagiarized his interpolated stories from the
     Heptameron from Codrington's translation.

COGAN, HENRY

Madeleine de Scudéry. Ibrahim: Or the Illustrious Bassa. Wing
     S2160-2161.

Copland, Robert

Studies

709   ALLEN, NED B. "The Sources of Dryden's The Mock Astrologer."
       PQ, 36 (October 1957), 453–64.
           Discusses Dryden's use of Scudéry's Ibrahim, probably in
       Cogan's translation.

710   HAVILAND, THOMAS P[HILIP]. "Elkanah Settle and the Least
       Heroic Romance." MLQ, 15 (June 1954), 118–24.
           Discusses Settle's use of Ibrahim as source for his play
       Ibrahim, the Illustrious Bassa.

COPLAND, ROBERT (fl. 1508–1533)

Helyas Knight of the Swan. STC 7571–7572.

The Romance of Kynge Apollyn of Thyre.

Editions

711   The History of Helyas, Knight of the Swan. Translated by
       Robert Copland. In A Collection of Early Prose Romances,
       Vol. III. Edited by William J. Thoms. London: William
       Pickering, 1828, 145pp. (separately paginated). [Also
       published separately.]
           Provides reprint of 1550? edition. In introductory
       notes (pp. i–xi) discusses various other treatments of the
       story.

*712   The Romance of Kynge Apollyn of Thyre. Translated by Robert
       Copland. Edited by Edmund William Ashbee. London: For
       Private Circulation, 1870, not paginated.
           Not seen; only 21 copies issued. Listed in NUC Pre–1956
       Imprints, vol. 18, 415.

713   The History of Helyas, Knight of the Swan. Translated by
       Robert Copland. Edited by Robert Hoe. New York: Grolier
       Club, 1901, not paginated.
           Provides type facsimile of 1512 edition printed on vellum
       by De Worde.

714   The Knight of the Swanne. Translated by Robert Copland. In
       Early English Prose Romances. Edited by William J. Thoms.
       Revised and enlarged edition. London: G. Routledge and
       Sons; New York: E. P. Dutton & Co. [1907], pp. 691–784.
           Reprint of 711.

Copland, Robert

Studies

715   FLOEGEL, WERNER. "Het Nederlandsche volksboek Historie van
          den Ridder Metter Swane: oorsprong en navolgingen." RBPH,
          24 (1945), 73-90.
             Includes comparison of Copland's Helyas with the German
          and French versions.

716   FRANCIS, F[RANK] C[HALTON]. Robert Copland: Sixteenth-Century
          Printer and Translator. Glasgow University Publications,
          David Murray Lectures, 24. Glasgow: Jackson, 1961, 44pp.
             Provides general overview of Copland's career as a trans-
          lator.

717   MOORE, W. G. "Robert Copland and His Hye Way." RES, 7 (Octo-
          ber 1931), 406-18.
             Surveys Copland's career. Suggests that although his
          works do not merit extended study, he is important as a
          pioneer among Tudor translators of French literature.

COPLAND, WILLIAM

Here Beginneht a Merye Jest of a Man that Was Called Howleglas.   STC
    10564-10565.

Editions

718   Howleglas. [Translated by William Copland.] Edited by
          Frederic Ouvry. London: Privately Printed, 1867, 105pp.
             Provides reprint of 1528? edition. In "Preface," pp.
          iii-viii, discusses publishing history of work and attempts
          to date various editions.

719   Howleglas. [Translated by William Copland.] In A Hundred
          Merry Tales and Other English Jestbooks of the Fifteenth
          and Sixteenth Centuries. Edited by P. M. Zall. Lincoln:
          University of Nebraska Press, 1963, pp. 151-237.
             Provides modernized, expurgated reprint of 1528? edition.
          In "The Natural History of Jestbooks: An Introduction,"
          pp. 1-10, comments on characterization and structure.

720   A Merye Jest. Translated by William Copland. English Experi-
          ence, 311. Amsterdam: Theatrvm Orbis Terrarvm; New York:
          Da Capo Press, 1971, not paginated.
             Provides facsimile reprint made up from two copies of
          1528? edition.

Studies

721 A., S. "Samuel Rowlands Anticipated by Luther." N&Q, 53
     (17 June 1876), 490–91.
        Relates nineteenth-century version of "Howleglas His
     Journey to Bremen."

722 BRIE, FRIEDRICH. Die englischen Ausgaben des Eulenspiegel und
     ihre Stellung in der Geschichte des Volksbuches. Weimar:
     R. Wagner Sohn Buchdruckerei, 1902, 68pp.
        Describes extant English editions and establishes rela-
     tionships among them. Traces origin of English version to
     a lost Low German version.

723 BRIE, FRIEDRICH. Eulenspiegel in England. Palaestra, 27.
     Berlin: Mayer & Müller, 1903, 160pp.
        Includes discussion of editions by Doesborgh and Copland:
     their relationship, sources, and influence upon the jest
     book tradition. Provides reprint of the extant fragment of
     Doesborgh's edition (pp. 126–38).

724 CLOUSTON, W[ILLIAM] A[LEXANDER]. "Eastern Origin of a Jest
     of Scogin." N&Q, 59 (17 May 1879), 382–83.
        Suggests that a jest in A Merry Jest of Howleglas served
     as source for one in Scoggin's Jests.

725 S. "Count Lucanor and Howleglas." N&Q, 60 (26 July 1879),
     62–63.
        Points out analogue to "How Howleglas Took upon Him to
     Be a Painter" in Don Juan Manuel's Count Lucanor.

726 S., A. "Howleglas and Knolle's Historie of the Turks." N&Q,
     74 (31 July 1886), 81–82.
        Points out analogue in Knolle's Historie to "How that
     Howleglas Would Flee from...Mewbrough."

COTTERELL, SIR CHARLES (1612?–1701)

Gautier de Costes de la Calprenède. Cassandra the Fam'd, Now Rendred
   into English. Wing L106–110.

Editions

727 KUEHN, EDWIN. "A Reorientation to the Heroic Romance: La
     Calprenède's Cassandre." Ph.D. dissertation, University of
     North Carolina, Chapel Hill, 1973, 472pp.

D., T.

"[I]ncludes a retyped copy of the first three books of
the <u>Cassandra</u> in Sir Charles Cotterell's English translation."

D., T.

Jean Bonaventure des Périers. <u>The Mirrour of Mirth</u>. <u>STC</u> 6784.5.

Editions

728 DES PÉRIERS, JEAN BONAVENTURE. <u>The Mirror of Mirth and Pleasant Conceits</u>. Translated by T. D. Edited by James Woodrow
Hassell, Jr. Columbia: University of South Carolina Press,
1959, 221pp.
    Provides an annotated facsimile reprint of 1583 edition;
includes list of variants from 1592 edition. In "Introduction," pp. 1-20, provides a highly condensed version of 730.

Studies

729 HASSELL, J[AMES] WOODROW, JR. "Bonaventure des Périers
Abroad," in <u>Renaissance and Other Studies in Honor of Wil-
liam Leon Wiley</u>. Edited by George Bernard Daniel, Jr.
UNCSRLL, 72. Chapel Hill: University of North Carolina
Press, 1968, pp. 123-31.
    Includes discussion of <u>Mirror of Mirth</u> in examination of
Des Périer's popularity in England.

730 HASSELL, J[AMES] WOODROW, JR. "An Elizabethan Translation of
the Tales of Des Périers: <u>The Mirrour of Mirth</u>, 1583 and
1592." <u>SP</u>, 52 (April 1955), 172-85.
    Provides bibliographical description of both editions,
discusses relationship between the two editions, compares
the translation with the original, and suggests candidates
(especially Deloney) for translator.

731 HASSELL, J[AMES] WOODROW, JR. "On the Influence in England
of Henri Estienne and Bonaventure des Périers: The Sources
of <u>Scoggins Jestes</u> (1613)," in <u>Mediaeval Studies in Honor
of Urban Tigner Holmes, Jr.</u> Edited by John Mahoney and
John Esten. UNCSRLL, 56. Chapel Hill: University of
North Carolina Press, 1965, pp. 79-88.
    Discusses use of <u>Mirror of Mirth</u> as source for <u>Scoggin's
Jests</u>.

DALLINGTON, SIR ROBERT (1561-1637)

Francesco Colonna. Hypnerotomachia: The Strife of Love in a Dreame.
   STC 5577-5578.

Editions

732   COLONNA, FRANCESCO. The Strife of Love in a Dream: Being the
      Elizabethan Version of the First Book of the Hypnerotomachia
      of Francesco Colonna. Translated by Robert Dallington.
      Edited by Andrew Lang. Tudor Library. London: D. Nutt,
      1890, 274pp.
         Provides reprint of 1592 edition. In "Introduction,"
      pp. v-xvii, discusses the rarity of copies of the work and
      Dallington's style; calls the translation "ignorant and un-
      intelligible."

733   COLONNA, FRANCESCO. Hypnerotomachia. Translated by Robert
      Dallington. English Experience, 87. Amsterdam: Theatrvm
      Orbis Terrarvm; New York: Da Capo Press, 1969, not pagi-
      nated.
         Provides facsimile reprint of 1592 edition.

734   COLONNA, FRANCESCO. Hypnerotomachia: The Strife of Love in
      a Dreame (1592). Translated by Robert Dallington. Intro-
      duction by Lucy Gent. Delmar, New York: Scholars' Fac-
      similes & Reprints, 1973, 227pp.
         Provides facsimile reprint of 1592 edition. In "Intro-
      duction," pp. v-xix, discusses the translation as an "epi-
      tome" of the "Elizabethans' attitude to art." Examines
      influence of translation on Elizabethan literature of the
      1590s and discusses claims of Dallington as translator.

*735 COLONNA, FRANCESCO. Hypnerotomachia: The Strife of Love in
      a Dream. Translated by Robert Dallington. Renaissance and
      the Gods. New York: Garland Publishing Co., 1976.
         Not seen. Facsimile reprint of 1592 edition. Cited in
      "Renaissance Books," RenQ, 29 (Winter 1976), 754.

Studies

736   URE, PETER. "Some Notes on the Vocabulary of the Translation
      of Colonna's Hypnerotomachia." N&Q, 197 (20 December 1952),
      552-54.
         Lists several OED additions and antedatings from Dalling-
      ton's translation, which "is rich in obsolete and rare
      words, many of them technical terms."

119

Davies

DAVIES, JOHN, OF KIDWELLY (1627?-1693)

Francisco de Quevedo y Villegas, The Life and Adventures of Buscon
the Witty Spaniard; To Which Is Added the Provident Knight. Wing
Q190-191A.

Charles Sorel, The Extravagant Shepherd: The Anti-Romance; or the
History of the Shepherd Lysis. Wing S4703-4704A.

Madeleine de Scudéry, Clelia (with George Havers). Wing S2151-2156.

Gautier de Costes de la Calprenède, Cleopatra (Parts 11-12). Wing
L120-124.

Honoré d'Urfé, Astrea: A Romance. Wing U132.

Studies

737   THOMAS, H[ENRY]. "The English Translations of Quevedo's La
      Vida del Buscón." Revue Hispanique, 81 (1933), 282-99.
          Provides bibliographical description of the 1657 edition
      of The Life and Adventures of Buscon; establishes that John
      Davies of Kidwelly was the translator and that he translated
      from a 1633 French version by the Sieur de la Geneste.

738   TUCKER, JOSEPH E. "John Davies of Kidwelly (1627?-1693),
      Translator from the French: With an Annotated Bibliography
      of His Translations." PBSA, 44, no. 2 (1950), 119-52.
          Discusses Davies's translations of French prose fiction
      in context of examination of the range and selectivity of
      his translations. Discusses characteristics of his style.
      Argues for his importance as representative of "the impor-
      tant place occupied by English translators and their trans-
      lations in the later seventeenth-century world of letters."
      Provides annotated chronological listing of translations.

DAY, ANGEL (fl. 1575-1595)

Longus, Daphnis and Chloe. STC 6400.

Editions

739   LONGUS. Daphnis and Chloe. Translated by Angel Day. Edited
      by Joseph Jacobs. Tudor Library, 2. London: D. Nutt,
      1890, 187pp.
          Provides reprint of 1587 edition. In "Introduction,"
      pp. ix-xxxi, discusses Day's closeness in following Amyot's
      translation and comments on his undistinguished style.

740   LONGUS. Daphnis and Chloe. Translated by Angel Day. New
        Rochelle, New York: Elston Press, 1904, 101pp.
            Provides reprint of 1587 edition.

Studies

741   DOYLE, CHARLES CLAY. "Daphnis and Chloe and the Faunus Episode
        in Spenser's Mutability." NM, 74 (1973), 163–68.
            Discusses Dorcon's attempted rape of Chloe as source for
        Faunus-Diana episode (VII. vi. 37–55).

742   GESNER, CAROL. "The Tempest as Pastoral Romance." SQ, 10
        (Autumn 1959), 531–39.
            Examines probability of influence of Day's Daphnis and
        Chloe on the pastoral element of The Tempest.

743   PRUVOST, RENÉ. "Le Daphnis and Chloe d'Angel Day, 1587."
        Revue Anglo-Américaine, 10 (August 1933), 481–89.
            Discusses the kinds and significance of changes, particu-
        larly those done on moral grounds, made by Day in translat-
        ing from Amyot. Finds that the alterations cause the work
        to tend toward the "usual form" of the sixteenth-century
        novel.

744   WOLFF, SAMUEL LEE. The Greek Romances in Elizabethan Prose
        Fiction. Columbia University Studies in Comparative Liter-
        ature. New York: Columbia University Press, 1912, 539pp.
            Examines Day's expansions of Amyot's text in translating
        Daphnis and Chloe and discusses his style (pp. 240–45). In
        Appendix A provides "Textual Notes on the Relations between
        Day's and Amyot's Versions of Daphnis and Chloe" (pp. 465–
        69).

745   WOLFF, SAMUEL LEE. "The Winter's Tale, Greene's Pandosto, and
        the Greek Romances." PMLA, 25, Appendix (1910), xxii–xxiii.
            Abstract of paper read at 1909 MLA meeting. Notes that
        Day's Daphnis and Chloe was one of Greene's sources for
        Pandosto.

THE DECAMERON, CONTAINING AN HUNDRED PLEASANT NOVELS
    Anonymous translation of Giovanni Boccaccio's Decameron.

    STC 3172–3174. Wing B3378–3379.

Editions

746   BOCCACCIO, GIOVANNI. The Decameron. Introduction by Edward
        Hutton. 4 vols. Tudor Translations, 1st Ser., 41–44.

The Decameron

Edited by W. E. Henley. London: David Nutt, 1909, 359,
255, 268, 332pp.
Provides reprint of first five days from 1625 edition and
last five days from 1620 edition. In "Introduction," I,
ix-cxxv, comments briefly on 1620 translation.

*747 BOCCACCIO, GIOVANNI. Decameron. 2 vols. Oxford: Shakespeare
Head Press, 1934-1935.
Not seen. Provides text based on 1625 edition compared
with 1620 edition. Listed in NUC Pre-1956 Imprints, vol.
62, 454.

748 BOCCACCIO, GIOVANNI. The Decameron. Introduction by Edward
Hutton. New York: Heritage Club, 1940, 558pp.
Provides reprint of 1620 translation; omits the two
added stories, replacing them with later translations of
the two original ones. Includes reprint of introduction
to 746.

749 "The Story of Bernardo and Generva," in Elizabethan Love
Stories. Edited by T[erence] J. B. Spencer. Penguin
Shakespeare Library. Harmondsworth: Penguin Books, 1968,
pp. 161-75.
Provides modernized text from 1620 edition.

Studies

750 BUSK, R. H. "An English Translation of the Decameron." N&Q,
73 (3 April 1886), 262-65.
Lists several errors in 1620 translation. See R. H.
Busk, "English Translation of the Decameron," N&Q, 73 (24
April 1886), 333, for correction.

751 BUSK, R. H. "English Translation of the Decameron." N&Q, 74
(21 August 1886), 150.
Calls 1620 translation a "'paraphrase'" that does not
adequately represent the original.

752 M., A. J. "English Translation of the Decameron." N&Q, 73
(24 April 1886), 333.
Comments on the 1620 translation calling it "a book right
profitable and delectable to read; a storehouse of fine old
English."

753 MUNSTERBERG, MARGARET. "The Decameron in English." More
Books: The Bulletin of the Boston Public Library, 19
(April 1944), 127-31.
Discusses briefly the anonymous translator's style and
treatment of his source, the French translation by Le Maçon.

754 R., R. "Decameron." N&Q, 74 (11 December 1886), 470-71.
Suggests that "the reason the folio is dated 1625-20 is
that when the book was printed in 1620 there was found to
be a difficulty about the licensing"; when published in
1625, a new title was substituted in the first volume but
the "title to the second volume, dated 1620, was not cancelled." Also objects to obscenity of work.

755 R., R. "The Decameron in English." N&Q, 73 (13 February
1886), 131.
Notes existence of 1643 and 1647 editions of translation
"which appear to be totally unknown to...bibliographers."

756 STILLINGER, JACK. "Keats and Romance." SEL, 8 (Autumn 1968),
593-605.
Discusses Keats's use of 1684 edition of 1620 translation
of Decameron as source for "Isabella," noting how he expands
and makes "more realistic" some details.

757 WRIGHT, HERBERT G[LADSTONE]. "The First English Translation
of the Decameron." MLR, 31 (October 1936), 500-12.
Argues that anonymous translator used Le Maçon's translation and Lionardo Salviati's edition. Discusses translator's inaccuracy, "diffuseness," and alterations made as
"concessions to decency and morality."

758 WRIGHT, HERBERT G[LADSTONE]. The First English Translation
of the Decameron (1620). Essays and Studies on English
Language and Literature, 13. Upsala: Lundequistska Bok-
handeln, 1963, 278pp.
Provides detailed analysis of "personality," techniques,
and style of translator to argue that John Florio probably
translated work. Examines translator's use of Lionardo
Salviati's Italian edition and of Le Maçon's French translation. In Appendix 3 discusses "The History of the Wood-
cuts in the English Translation of 1620" (pp. 271-75).

759 WRIGHT, HERBERT G[LADSTONE]. "Keats's Isabella." TLS, 17
April 1943, p. 192.
Discusses changes made by anonymous translator in Boccaccio's version and Keats's use of the 1684 edition as a
source for the poem. See 760.

760 WRIGHT, HERBERT G[LADSTONE]. "Possible Indebtedness of
Keats's Isabella to the Decameron." RES, NS, 2 (July
1951), 248-54.
Supplements earlier article (759), suggesting Keats's
use of fifth edition (1684) of 1620 translation as source
for the "description of the scene of Lorenzo's murder."

The Deceyte of Women

THE DECEYTE OF WOMEN

  STC 6451-6452.

Editions

761   BRIE, FRIEDRICH. "The Deceyte of Women: Älteste englische
        Novellensammlung (1547)." Archiv, 156 (1929), 17-52.
          Provides transcript of 1560? edition. Discusses the
        erotic nature of the work and traces sources. Revised ver-
        sion of 762.

Studies

762   BRIE, FRIEDRICH. "Die erste englische Novellensammlung (The
        Deceyte of Women)," in Stephaniskos (Ernst Fabricius zum
        VI. IX. MDCCCCXXVII). Freiburg: Himmer, 1927, pp. 5-10.
          Discusses work as a combination of humorous-erotic and
        moralistic tales; reprinted in slightly revised form in
        761.

763   SCHLAUCH, MARGARET. Antecedents of the English Novel, 1400-
        1600 (from Chaucer to Deloney). Warsaw: PWN--Polish Scien-
        tific Publishers; London: Oxford University Press, 1963,
        264pp.
          Discusses work as example of anti-romantic novelle. Ex-
        amines relation of several tales to source, particularly
        Number 18, suggesting that the writer's "work on it was of
        some importance in the history of native fiction" (pp. 101-
        108, passim).

764   SCHLAUCH, MARGARET. "A Sixteenth-Century English Satirical
        Tale About Gdańsk." KN, 4 (1957), 95-120.
          Discusses "A New Deceit Done of Late at Dansk." Provides
        detailed analysis of linguistic features of tale, stressing
        "its colloquial, idiomatic style." Compares with Frederyke
        of Jennen, suggesting that Deceit of Women is a translation
        of a lost Flemish work and that the same person translated
        both works.

765   STEIN, HAROLD. "Six Tracts about Women: A Volume in the
        British Museum." Library, 4th Ser., 15 (June 1934), 38-48.
          Provides bibliographical description of 1560? edition
        and discusses briefly style and contents.

DEKKER, THOMAS (1572?-1632)

The Wonderfull Yeare, 1603. STC 6534-6535.

Newes from Hell; Brought by the Divell's Carrier. STC 6514. (Revised as A Knights Conjuring, Done in Earnest: Discovered in Jest.
STC 6508.)

Penny-Wise Pound Foolish. STC 6516.

The Ravevens Almanacke, Foretelling of a Plague, Famine and Civile
Warre. STC 6519.

Jests to Make You Merie (with George Wilkins). STC 6541.

Bibliographies

766 ALLISON, A[NTONY] F[RANCIS]. Thomas Dekker, c. 1572-1632: A
     Bibliographical Catalogue of the Early Editions (To the End
     of the 17th Century). Pall Mall Bibliographies, 1. Folke-
     stone: Dawsons of Pall Mall, 1972, 143pp.
         Provides bibliography (arranged alphabetically by title)
     of Dekker's works; includes photographic facsimiles of
     title pages and annotated descriptions (collation and list
     of contents).

767 DONOVAN, DENNIS. "Thomas Dekker, 1945-1965," in Elizabethan
     Bibliographies Supplements, II: Thomas Dekker, 1945-1965;
     Thomas Heywood, 1938-1965; Cyril Tourneur, 1945-1965. Com-
     piled by Dennis Donovan. London: Nether Press, 1967,
     17-28.
         Provides chronological list of editions and studies;
     continues 768.

768 TANNENBAUM, SAMUEL A., and DOROTHY R. TANNENBAUM. Supplement
     to Thomas Dekker, a Concise Bibliography. Elizabethan
     Bibliographies. New York: Samuel A. Tannenbaum, 1945,
     17pp.
         Supplements 769. Continued by 767.

769 TANNENBAUM, SAMUEL A. Thomas Dekker (A Concise Bibliography).
     Elizabethan Bibliographies, 7. New York: Samuel A. Tannen-
     baum, 1939, 52pp.
         Provides classified listing of editions and criticism.
     Continued in 767-68.

Dekker

Editions

770   DEKKER, THOMAS. A Knight's Conjuring: Done in Earnest, Dis-
      covered in Jest. Edited by Edward F. Rimbault. Percy
      Society, 5. London: T. Richards for the Percy Society,
      1842, 116pp.
            Provides an annotated reprint of 1607 edition. In "In-
      troduction," pp. vii-xvi, discusses briefly the work as an
      answer to Nashe's Pierce Penniless and points out how the
      present work is "an alteration and improvement" of News from
      Hell.

771   DEKKER, THOMAS. The Non-Dramatic Works of Thomas Dekker.
      Edited by Alexander B. Grosart. 5 vols. Huth Library.
      London: Printed for Private Circulation, 1884-1886. 285,
      359, 378, 310, 304pp.
            Includes reprints of: The Wonderful Year, 1603 (I, 71-
      148); News from Hell, 1606 (II, 83-153); Jests to Make You
      Merry, 1607 (II, 267-359); The Raven's Almanac, 1609 (IV,
      167-266). Also includes The Bachelors' Banquet, 1603 (I,
      149-275) as Dekker's.

772   DEKKER, THOMAS. Penny-Wise, Pound-Foolish, in John Fordes
      dramatische Werke. By John Forde. Edited by W. Bang.
      Materialien zur Kunde des Älteren Englischen Dramas, 23.
      Louvain: A. Uystpruyst, 1908, pp. 179-210.
            Provides reprint of 1631 edition in Appendix.

773   DEKKER, THOMAS. The VVonderfull Yeare. Edited by G[eorge]
      B[agshawe] Harrison. Bodley Head Quartos, 8. London:
      John Lane, The Bodley Head; New York: E. P. Dutton, 1924,
      88pp.
            Provides a corrected reprint of 1603 edition.

774   DEKKER, THOMAS. The Wonderfull Yeare, in The Plague Pamphlets
      of Thomas Dekker. By Thomas Dekker. Edited by F[rank]
      P[ercy] Wilson. Oxford: Clarendon Press, 1925, pp. 1-61.
            Provides annotated text based on 1603 edition collated
      with other seventeenth-century editions. In "Introduction,"
      pp. xi-xxvii, discusses evidence for Dekker's authorship
      and similarities in subject matter, style, and vocabulary
      with News from Gravesend. In "Bibliography," pp. xxix-
      xxxix, discusses relationship among the three seventeenth-
      century editions.

775   DEKKER, THOMAS. The Wonderful Year, in Three Elizabethan
      Pamphlets. Edited by G[eorge] R. Hibbard. London: Harrap,
      1951, pp. 160-207.

Provides modernized, annotated reprint of 1603 edition.
In "Introduction," pp. 11-34, provides an overview of the
development of the pamphlet as a form and examines briefly
how Dekker "found in the pamphlet form...a means of self-
expression and a field for experiment."

776 DEKKER, THOMAS. Thomas Dekker: The Wonderful Year, The Gull's
     Horn-Book, Penny-Wise, Pound-Foolish, English Villainies
     Discovered by Lantern and Candlelight, and Selected Writ-
     ings. Edited by E. D. Pendry. Stratford-upon-Avon Library,
     4. London: Edward Arnold, 1967, 374pp.
        Provides modernized text of Wonderful Year based on 1603
     edition and of Penny-Wise, Pound-Foolish based on 1631 edi-
     tion. In "Introduction," pp. 1-22, provides an overview of
     Dekker's life and works: discusses style, subject matter,
     structure, and themes of his work. Emphasizes, in particu-
     lar, his "toughness and bitterness." In notes section,
     discusses the sources and bibliographical history of The
     Wonderful Year (pp. 310-13) and Penny-Wise, Pound-Foolish
     (pp. 317-20).

777 DEKKER, THOMAS. "An Edition of A Knights Conjuring (1607) by
     Thomas Dekker." Edited by Larry Michael Robbins. Ph.D.
     dissertation, University of California, Berkeley, 1969,
     312pp.
        Provides critical old-spelling edition based on 1607
     edition. Provides bibliographical analysis of early edi-
     tions and discusses publishing history and structure of
     work. Examines relationship with News from Hell and Nashe's
     Pierce Penniless.

Studies

778 ADKINS, MARY GRACE MUSE. "Puritanism in the Plays and Pam-
     phlets of Thomas Dekker." University of Texas Studies in
     English, 1939, pp. 86-113.
        Finds that Dekker's attitude toward Puritanism is incon-
     sistent, ranging from "vilification" to "actual sympathy."
     Classifies references in pamphlets to show that Dekker's
     satire is directed at the social aspects (especially hypo-
     crisy) of Puritanism.

779 BAKER, ERNEST A[LBERT]. The History of the English Novel,
     Vol. II. London: H. F. & G. Witherby, 1929, 303pp.
        In Chapter XIII ("Thomas Dekker," pp. 209-21), provides
     a survey of Dekker's prose fiction; comments on the con-
     tents and characteristics of each work.

Dekker

780   BOYCE, BENJAMIN. "News from Hell: Satiritic Communications
        with the Nether World in English Writing of the Seventeenth
        and Eighteenth Centuries." PMLA, 58 (June 1943), 402-37.
            Surveys treatment in Elizabethan prose fiction, discuss-
        ing the "Lucianic account of the dead" in News from Hell.
        Finds "less satire than outspoken inveighing against vices;
        and humor, such as it is, tends to be supplanted by reli-
        gious preachment."

781   BOYCE, BENJAMIN. "A Restoration 'Improvement' of Thomas Dek-
        ker." MLN, 50 (November 1935), 460-61.
            Points out that News from Hell was revised as Poor
        Robin's Visions in 1677 by unknown author attempting to
        capitalize on the popularity of Roger L'Estrange's Visions:
        Or Hell's Kingdom. Compares revision with original.

782   BULLEN, A[RTHUR] H[ENRY]. "Thomas Dekker," in Elizabethans.
        By A[rthur] H[enry] Bullen. New York: E. P. Dutton & Co.,
        1924, pp. 71-94.
            Includes an indication of the contents and a brief criti-
        cal assessment of each of Dekker's works of prose fiction.

783   [CHILD, HAROLD H.] "Thomas Dekker and the Underdog: The Com-
        passionate Realist from Pamphlet Prose to Lyric Beauty."
        TLS, 31 May 1941, pp. 262, 264. [Reprinted as: "Thomas
        Dekker and the Underdog," in Essays and Reflections. By
        Harold H. Child. Edited by S. C. Roberts. Cambridge:
        Cambridge University Press, 1948, pp. 95-104.]
            Discusses combination of love for London, realism, and
        compassion for downtrodden in Dekker's prose works.

*784 GREGG, KATE LELIA. "Thomas Dekker: A Study in Economic and
        Social Backgrounds." Ph.D. dissertation, University of
        Washington, 1916, 52pp.
            See 785.

785   GREGG, KATE L[ELIA]. "Thomas Dekker: A Study in Economic and
        Social Backgrounds." University of Washington Publications,
        Language and Literature, 2, no. 2.(1924), 55-112.
            Examines how Dekker's pamphlets reflect economic and so-
        cial concerns (particularly those involving enclosure, re-
        ligion, and government) of the age and how Dekker's work
        was shaped by those concerns.

786   HARDER, KELSIE B. "The Names of Thomas Dekker's Devils."
        Names, 3 (December 1955), 210-18.
            Analyzes Dekker's synonyms for the devil in News from
        Hell and their relationship to "the religious, political,
        and social satire" in the work.

*787   HARTMEYER, KÄTHE. "Die Sozial- und Kulturverhältnisse Englands
        in der elizabethanischen Zeit gesehen mit den Dichtern Th.
        Deloney, Th. Dekker und Ben Jonson." Ph.D. dissertation,
        University of Münster, 1950.
            Abstract not available.

788   HILL, ROWLAND MERLIN. "Realistic Descriptive Setting in Eng-
        lish Fiction from 1550 through Fielding." Ph.D. disserta-
        tion, Boston University, 1941, 344pp.
            Examines Dekker's use of setting, noting that "he only
        rarely used setting organically to influence action or
        character directly, employing it primarily as background."
        Discusses his combination of "mock-heroic" with "realistic"
        setting and his use of "Gothic graveyard detail."

*789   HUNT, MARY LELAND. "Thomas Dekker: A Study." Ph.D. disser-
        tation, Columbia University, 1911, 213pp.
            See 790.

790   HUNT, MARY L[ELAND]. Thomas Dekker: A Study. Columbia Uni-
        versity Studies in English. New York: Columbia University
        Press, 1911, 226pp.
            Includes chronological overview of Dekker's prose works;
        discusses his style and subject matter, and provides brief
        critical estimate of each work.

791   JONES-DAVIES, M[ARIE]-T[HÉRÈSE]. Un Peintre de la vie lon-
        donienne: Thomas Dekker (Circa 1572-1632). 2 vols. Études
        Anglaises, 6. Paris: Didier, 1958, 415, 478pp.
            Provides detailed analysis of form and thought in Dek-
        ker's prose fiction: examines sources and influences; ana-
        lyzes in detail his depiction of London and his use of the
        city as a central motif; discusses his realism, satire,
        humor, morality; describes forms utilized; analyzes narra-
        tive techniques and style; traces popularity and influence;
        provides annotated bibliography.

792   JUSSERAND, J[EAN] J[ULES]. The English Novel in the Time of
        Shakespeare. Translated by Elizabeth Lee. Revised edition.
        London: T. Fisher Unwin, 1890, 433pp.
            Examines characteristics of Dekker's style and influence
        of Nashe upon him (pp. 330-46).

793   KOPPENFELS, WERNER VON. "Zur zeitgenössischen Aufnahme des
        elisabethanischen 'Romans': Nashes Unfortunate Traveller
        in der Literatur der Shakespeare-Epoche." Anglia, 94,
        nos. 3-4 (1976), 361-87.
            Includes discussion of influence of Unfortunate Travel-
        ler on Wonderful Year.

Dekker

794   ŁOBZOWSKA, MARIA. "Conventional and Original Elements in
      Thomas Dekker's Non-Dramatic Prose Satire." <u>KN</u>, 13, no. 2
      (1966), 171-81.
          Analyzes themes used by Dekker, and compares his works
      with those by Greene, Lodge, and Nashe to ascertain "atti-
      tudes to the problems treated in their pamphlets and their
      approach to the social conditions of their times." Finds
      ability to transpose "real events and living people into
      literature in a form corresponding to reality" Dekker's
      most important contribution to prose literature.

*795 MOSELEY, EDWIN M. "The Bourgeoise Consciousness of Thomas
      Dekker: A Study in Attitudes." Ph.D. dissertation, Syra-
      cuse University, 1948.
          Abstract not available.

796   NEMO. "Thomas Dekker." <u>N&Q</u>, 75 (23 April 1887), 324-25.
          Criticizes Swinburne (805) for praising <u>The Bachelors'</u>
      <u>Banquet</u> at length but not giving the title.

797   OSBORN, JAMES M. "Edmund Malone and the Dryden Almanac Story."
      <u>PQ</u>, 16 (October 1937), 412-14.
          Transcribes note by Malone in his copy of <u>The Critical</u>
      <u>and Miscellaneous Prose Works of John Dryden</u>, in which he
      discusses version of the anecdote found in <u>Jests to Make</u>
      <u>You Merry</u>. See 798.

798   OSBORN, JAMES M. "Edmund Malone and the Dryden Almanac Story."
      <u>PQ</u>, 17 (January 1938), 84-86.
          Reprints text of earlier note (797), omitting transcrip-
      tion of one jest.

799   PARRILL, WILLIAM BRUCE. "The Elizabethan Background of Hell,
      the Devil, the Magician, and the Witch, and Their Use in
      Elizabethan Fiction." Ph.D. dissertation, University of
      Tennessee, 1964, 321pp.
          "[S]tudies the uses which Nashe, Greene, Dekker, Lodge
      and the other fiction writers made of the wide variety of
      material available" on the topics. Finds that use was
      largely satirical.

800   PAYLOR, W. J. "Thomas Dekker and the 'Overburian' Characters."
      <u>MLR</u>, 31 (April 1936), 155-60.
          Discusses characteristics of Dekker's thought, style,
      and subject matter in his prose works in suggesting his
      authorship of six prison characters added to 1616 edition
      of <u>Sir Thomas Overbury His Wife</u>.

801 PRICE, GEORGE R. Thomas Dekker. TEAS, 71. New York: Twayne
      Publishers, 1969, 189pp.
          In Chapter 4 ("Dekker's Non-Dramatic Work," pp. 112-32)
      provides an overview of Dekker's prose pamphlets: discusses
      influences on works, style, didacticism, and lack of tight
      structure.

802 SERONSY, CECIL C. "Dekker and Falstaff." SQ, 4 (July 1953),
      365-66.
          Suggests possible influence of robbery scene in I Henry
      IV on description of the "gorbelly Host" in The Wonderful
      Year.

803 SHAW, PHILLIP [B.]. "The Position of Thomas Dekker in Jacobean
      Prison Literature." PMLA, 62 (June 1947), 366-91.
          Discusses Dekker's portion of Jests to Make You Merry in
      context of his other prison literature, noting that he re-
      iterated his earlier complaint about the neglect of poor
      debtors and that he anticipated the prison character, which
      was soon to become an important literary type in prison
      literature.

*804 SHAW, PHILLIP B. "Social Aspects of Thomas Dekker." Ph.D.
      dissertation, New York University, 1944, 240pp.
          Abstract not available.

805 SWINBURNE, ALGERNON CHARLES. "Thomas Dekker." Nineteenth
      Century, 21 (January 1887), 81-103.
          Surveys Dekker's pamphlets, discussing style and content
      and providing a brief critical assessment of each. See
      796.

806 THORNTON, GEORGE E. "The Social and Moral Philosophy of
      Thomas Dekker." ESRS, 4 (December 1955), 1-36.
          In discussion of Dekker's "stern moral code" manifested
      in his pamphlets, analyzes his economic and social philos-
      ophy in The Wonderful Year.

807 WAAGE, FREDERICK OSWIN, JR. "Thomas Dekker's Career as a
      Pamphleteer, 1603-1609: Preliminary Studies of Five Major
      Works and Their Background." Ph.D. dissertation, Princeton
      University, 1971, 588pp.
          Analyzes Dekker's "use of literary conventions and...
      discussion of contemporary social, political and religious
      issues" in The Wonderful Year.

808 WILSON, F[RANK] P[ERCY]. "Introduction," in The Batchelars
      Banquet: An Elizabethan Translation of Les Quinze joyes

Dekker

de mariage. Edited by F[rank] P[ercy] Wilson. Oxford:
Clarendon Press, 1929, pp. vii–xlviii.
    Argues that Dekker was not the translator.

809   WILSON, F[RANK] P[ERCY]. "Some English Mock–Prognostications."
       <u>Library</u>, 4th Ser., 19 (June 1938), 6–43.
           Discusses <u>Raven's Almanac</u> in examining "comic parodies
       of astrological prognostications."

810   WILSON, F[RANK] P[ERCY]. "Some English Mock–Prognostications,"
       in <u>Shakespearian and Other Studies</u>. By F[rank] P[ercy]
       Wilson. Edited by Helen Gardner. Oxford: Clarendon Press,
       1969, pp. 251–84.
           Reprint, "with minor additions and corrections," of 810.

<u>DELONEY, THOMAS</u> (1543?–1607?)

<u>The Gentle Craft</u>. <u>STC</u> 6555–6556. Wing D944–945, D953–955, D960–962.

<u>The Pleasant History of John Winchcomb, Called Jack of Newberie</u>. <u>STC</u>
    6559–6563. Wing D958, D963–965.

<u>Thomas of Reading</u>. <u>STC</u> 6569–6572. Wing D966.

Editions

811   DELONEY, THOMAS. <u>Thomas of Reading: Or the Sixe Worthie</u>
       <u>Yeomen of the West</u>. Edinburgh: J. Ballantyne and Co.,
       [1812], not paginated.
           Provides reprint of 1632 edition.

812   DELONEY, THOMAS. <u>The History of Thomas of Reading; or the Six</u>
       <u>Worthy Yeomen of the West</u>, in <u>A Collection of Early Prose</u>
       <u>Romances</u>, Vol. I. Edited by William J. Thoms. London:
       W. Pickering, 1828, 116pp. (separately paginated). [Also
       published separately.]
           Provides reprint of 1632 edition. In "Preface," pp. i–
       vi, comments on the "many curious allusions to manners and
       customs now obsolete."

*813   DELONEY, THOMAS. <u>The Pleasant History of John Winchcomb</u>.
       Speenhamland: n.p., 184–, 75pp.
           Not seen. Apparently a reprint of 1680 edition. Listed
       in <u>NUC Pre-1956 Imprints</u>, vol. 138, 297.

814   DELONEY, THOMAS. <u>The History of John Winchcomb, Usually</u>
       <u>Called Jack of Newbury, the Famous Clothier</u>. Edited by

James O[rchard] Halliwell[-Phillipps]. London: T.
Richards, 1859, 133pp.
Provides reprint of 1633 edition. In "Preface," pp. v-
viii, discusses Deloney's use of traditional biographical
and historical material.

815   DELONEY, THOMAS. Thomas of Reading, in Thomas Deloney His
Thomas of Reading and Three Ballads on the Spanish Armada.
Edited by Charles Roberts Aldrich and Lucian Swift Kirtland.
New York: J. F. Taylor, 1903, pp. 1-178.
Provide modernized annotated reprint based on 1632 edi-
tion(?). In "Introduction to Thomas of Reading," pp. iii-
xvi, discuss Deloney's appeal to a middle-class audience,
his style, and the place of the work in the development of
English fiction.

816   DELONEY, THOMAS. The Gentle Craft. Edited by Alexis
F[rederick] Lange. 2 vols. Palaestra, 18. Berlin:
Mayer & Müller, 1903, 272pp.
Provides reprint of 1648 edition of Part I and 1639 edi-
tion of Part II. In "Introduction," pp. V-XLIV, discusses
literary influences (jest book, ballad, and drama) on De-
loney's prose fiction, traces the publishing history of The
Gentle Craft, and identifies Deloney's sources for the work.

817   DELONEY, THOMAS. Jack of Newbury, in Thomas Deloney: Eine
Studie über Balladenlitteratur der Shakespere-Zeit. Nebst
Neudruck von Deloney's Jack of Newberry. By Richard
Sievers. Palaestra, 36. Berlin: Mayer & Müller, 1904,
pp. 147-244.
Provides reprint of 1630 edition with notes on readings
from later editions.

818   DELONEY, THOMAS. The Pleasant Historie of Thomas of Reading,
in Early English Prose Romances. Edited by William J.
Thoms. Revised and enlarged edition. London: G. Routledge
and Sons; New York: E. P. Dutton and Co., [1907], pp. 441-
519.
Reprint of 812.

819   DELONEY, THOMAS. The Works of Thomas Deloney. Edited by
Francis Oscar Mann. Oxford: Clarendon Press, 1912, 634pp.
Provides reprint of 1626 edition of Jack of Newbury,
1648 edition of The Gentle Craft, and 1623 edition of
Thomas of Reading (all annotated). In section of "Introduction" ("Deloney and the Elizabethan Novel," pp. xiv-
xxxi) discusses influence of the jest book and the realistic tradition in prose fiction on Deloney's novels.

Deloney

820   DELONEY, THOMAS. The History of Thomas of Reading, in Some
       Old English Worthies. Edited by Dorothy Senior. London:
       S. Swift and Co., 1912, pp. 27-122.
           Provides annotated, modernized reprint of 1632 edition.
       In "Introduction," pp. 9-26, discusses "allusions to manners
       and customs now obsolete" and praises character of Margaret.

821   DELONEY, THOMAS. Jack de Newbury. Thomas de Reading. Trans-
       lated by Abel Chevalley. Paris: Gallimard, 1926, 249pp.
           Provides French translation of Jack of Newbury and
       Thomas of Reading. In "Avant-propos," pp. 11-15, comments
       briefly on importance of Deloney's depiction of working-
       class life.

822   DELONEY, THOMAS. Le Noble métier. Translated by Abel Che-
       valley. Paris: Gallimard, 1927, 251pp.
           Provides French translation of The Gentle Craft. In
       "Avant-propos," pp. 7-11, traces sources and comments on
       publication history. Calls work the most realistic and
       most characteristic of Deloney's fiction.

823   DELONEY, THOMAS. Deloney's Gentle Craft: The First Part.
       Edited by Wilfrid J. Halliday. Oxford: Clarendon Press,
       1928, 96pp.
           Provides "a modernized version of the edition of 1648,
       corrected by comparison with the edition of 1637." In
       "Introduction," pp. 4-16, provides a brief critical esti-
       mate of Deloney's prose fiction and its place in the de-
       velopment of the novel. Examines publishing history and
       sources of Gentle Craft, and discusses Deloney's depiction
       of the shoemakers.

824   DELONEY, THOMAS. Jacke of Newberie and Thomas of Reading, in
       Shorter Novels: Elizabethan and Jacobean. Introduction by
       George Saintsbury. Notes by Philip Henderson. Everyman's
       Library, 824. London: J. M. Dent & Sons; New York: E. P.
       Dutton & Co., 1929, pp. 1-155.
           Provides partly modernized reprints of 1626 edition of
       Jack of Newbury and of 1623 edition of Thomas of Reading.
       In "Notes," pp. xv-xvii, Henderson comments on Deloney's
       middle-class subject matter, his realism, and his "subtle
       sense of drama." In 1969 reprint (65), the "Notes" are
       slightly revised by R[obert] G[uy] Howarth.

825   DELONEY, THOMAS. The Most Pleasant and Delectable History of
       John Winchcombe, Otherwise Called Jack of Newbury: And
       First of His Love and Pleasant Life, in Elizabethan Fiction.
       Edited by Robert Ashley and Edwin M. Moseley. San Francis-
       co: Rinehart Press, 1953, pp. 309-402.

Provide partly modernized text based on 819. In "Introduction" (pp. xvii-xx) relate the work to the middle-class
concerns ignored by Sidney, Lyly, and Gascoigne.

826 DELONEY, THOMAS. The Novels of Thomas Deloney. Edited by
     Merritt E. Lawlis. Bloomington: Indiana University Press,
     1961, 494pp.
          Provides critical edition of Deloney's prose fiction
     works. In "Introduction," pp. xi-xxxii, discusses Deloney's
     prose fiction in the context of his life and works. Ana-
     lyzes influence of drama and jest book on his works, dis-
     cusses the naturalness of his dialogue, and examines his
     characterization (especially his depiction of women charac-
     ters and his creation of effective "flat" characters). In
     "Explanatory Notes" analyzes the printing and publication
     of each work and provides a bibliographical description of
     early editions. For corrections, see 827.

827 DELONEY, THOMAS. Thomas of Reading: Or, the Six Worthy Yeo-
     men of the West, in Elizabethan Prose Fiction. Edited by
     Merritt [E.] Lawlis. Indianapolis: Odyssey Press, Bobbs-
     Merrill Co., 1967, pp. 548-624.
          Provides partly modernized, emended text based on 1612
     edition. (See pp. 637-39 for discussion of the relationship
     among extant editions and a list of substantive emendations.
     Also lists two corrections to his earlier edition [826].)
     In introductory note, discusses eclectic nature of the work,
     suggesting that it might be called a "'novel-romance,'" and
     notes Deloney's reversal of conventions of romance.

828 DELONEY, THOMAS. Thomas of Reading. Menston, England:
     Scolar Press, 1969, 72pp.
          Provides facsimile reprint of the British Library copy
     of the 1612 edition.

Studies

829 ATKINS, J[OHN] W[ILLIAM] H[EY]. "Elizabethan Prose Fiction,"
     in The Cambridge History of English Literature, III: Renas-
     cence and Reformation. Edited by A[dolphus] W[illiam] Ward
     and A[lfred] R[ayney] Waller. Cambridge: Cambridge Univer-
     sity Press, 1909, 339-73.
          Includes discussion of structure of, depiction of con-
     temporary life in, style of, and influences on Deloney's
     prose fiction (pp. 367-72).

830 BACHE, WILLIAM B. "'The Murder of Old Cole': A Possible
     Source for Macbeth." SQ, 6 (Summer 1955), 358-59.

Deloney

Examines murder of Cole in <u>Thomas of Reading</u> as source
for murder of Duncan.

831   BACHE, WILLIAM B. "Spenser and Deloney." <u>N&Q</u>, NS, 1 (June
       1954), 232-33.
          Points out similarity between Deloney's story of the
       murder of Cole and "Spenser's episode of the attempted mur-
       der of Britomart by Dolon."

832   BAKER, ERNEST A[LBERT]. <u>The History of the English Novel</u>,
       Vol. II. London: H. F. & G. Witherby, 1929, 303pp.
          Includes examination of Deloney's place in the develop-
       ment of realistic fiction. Examines the naturalness of his
       dialogue, the dramatic qualities of his style, the influen-
       ces of earlier tales on his works, his humor, and his effec-
       tive characterizations (pp. 170-92, passim).

833   BLOOR, R[OBERT] H[ENRY] U[NDERWOOD]. <u>The English Novel from
       Chaucer to Galsworthy</u>. University Extension Library.
       London: I. Nicholson and Watson, 1935, 248pp.
          Examines Deloney's novels as the "most realistic of the"
       Elizabethan age. Provides summaries of the three works
       (pp. 100-109).

834   BLUESTONE, MAX. <u>From Story to Stage: The Dramatic Adaptation
       of Prose Fiction in the Period of Shakespeare and His Con-
       temporaries</u>. SEngL, 70, The Hague: Mouton, 1974, 341pp.
          Includes examination of transformation and adaptation of
       <u>The Gentle Craft, Part I</u> by Dekker in <u>The Shoemaker's Holi-
       day</u> and by Rowley in <u>A Shoemaker, A Gentleman</u> (passim).

835   BOWERS, FRED. "An Evaluative Study of the Transformational-
       Generative Approach to the Syntactic Description of Thomas
       Deloney's Prose." Ph.D. dissertation, University of
       British Columbia, 1967.
          Uses the "Transformational-Generative Model, as revised
       in 1965," to describe "the syntax of Thomas Deloney's
       novels."

836   BOWERS, FREDERICK. "A Transformational Description of the
       Elizabethan <u>be</u> + V-<u>ing</u>." <u>Orbis</u>, 17 (1968), 23-33.
          Utilizes "the Transformational-Generative model of syn-
       tactic description" to examine "the <u>be</u> + V-<u>ing</u> structures
       in the novels of Thomas Deloney." Suggests that "it is the
       popular and colloquial level of Deloney's writing that ac-
       counts for the unexpected high frequency" of the <u>be</u> + V-<u>ing</u>
       structures.

837 CAMP, CHARLES W[ELLNER]. The Artisan in Elizabethan Literature. Columbia University Studies in English and Comparative Literature. New York: Columbia University Press,
1924, 176pp.
Analyzes the characteristics of Deloney's representation
of the craftsman and themes in his prose fiction. Discusses
influence of Deloney's works on later literary treatments of
the artisan (pp. 12-16, 25-34, passim).

838 CHANDLER, W. K. "The Sources of the Characters in The Shoemaker's Holiday." MP, 27 (November 1929), 175-82.
Discusses changes Dekker made in characters drawn from
The Gentle Craft. Provides table listing facts about Eyre
as presented by Deloney, Dekker, and chronicles.

839 CHEVALLEY, ABEL. "Le Roman corporatif au temps de Shakespeare."
Le Navire d'Argent, 1 February 1926, pp. 64-74.
Sees Deloney's fiction as a mirror of the life of the
worker and as documents on the relations between the history
of art and that of the proletariat. Forms Chapter I of 840.

840 CHEVALLEY, ABEL. Thomas Deloney: Le Roman des métiers au
temps de Shakespeare. Paris: Librairie Gallimard, 1926,
254pp.
Examines Deloney's novels in context of social and economic changes during latter part of sixteenth century.
Sees Deloney's prose fiction as a novelistic mirror of the
life of the worker. Discusses structure, style, realism,
place in development of English novel, and influence on
later drama and prose fiction.

841 CROSSE, G. "A Shakespeare Allusion." TLS, 1 August 1929,
p. 608.
Points out allusion to Venus and Adonis in Jack of Newbury.

842 DAHL, TORSTEN. Linguistic Studies in Some Elizabethan Writ-
ings, I: An Inquiry into Aspects of the Language of Thomas
Deloney. Acta Jutlandica, 23, no. 2: Humanistisk Serie,
36. Copenhagen: E. Munksgaard, 1951, 215pp.
Includes discussion of style and characterization in
Deloney's prose fiction. Provides philological analysis
arranged under headings: "Case and Number in Substantives,"
"Number," "Pronouns of Address," "Other Pronouns," "Ar-
ticles, Adjectives, and Adverbs," "Shall and Will," and
"Should and Would."

137

Deloney

843   DAHL, TORSTEN. <u>Linguistic Studies in Some Elizabethan Writ-</u>
      <u>ings, II: The Auxiliary "Do."</u> Acta Jutlandica, 28, no. 1:
      Humanistisk Serie, 42. Copenhagen: E. Munksgaard, 1956,
      104pp.
         Examines "the various uses to which the auxiliary <u>do</u> was
      put" by Deloney. Attempts "to understand and explain De-
      loney's reasons for periphrasis and non-periphrasis"; finds
      that Deloney's use "is largely (entirely ?) governed by
      structural considerations."

844   DAVIS, WALTER R[ICHARDSON]. <u>Idea and Act in Elizabethan Fic-</u>
      <u>tion</u>. Princeton: Princeton University Press, 1969, 311pp.
         Provides detailed analysis of the structure of the three
      novels; examines relationship of structure to presentation
      of conflict between the ideal and the actual (pp. 238-80).

845   DONOW, HERBERT S. "Thomas Deloney and Thomas Heywood: Two
      Views of the Elizabethan Merchant." Ph.D. dissertation,
      University of Iowa, 1966, 205pp.
         Analyzes characteristics of Deloney's portrayal of mer-
      chants "against a background of contemporary thought"; finds
      that Deloney's merchant is "an heroic figure of sorts com-
      bining the best characteristics of the medieval guildsman
      with the Elizabethan entrepreneur" and that "Deloney...
      sought to present the merchant as a modern hero, a fully
      secular man."

846   DORSINVILLE, MAX. "Design in Deloney's <u>Jack of Newbury</u>."
      <u>PMLA</u>, 88 (March 1973), 233-39.
         Argues that Deloney inverts Greco-Roman "aristocratic
      tradition [which] sees the state in the analogue of an
      inter-related family...headed by a benevolent, but ethically
      rigorous, father figure" and uses motifs of state (Jack's
      household), prince (Jack), and his education (middle-class
      upbringing) to structure novel. Suggests that Deloney's
      representation of the middle class is less realistic than
      usually thought and that his purpose is to instruct and
      delight a middle-class readership.

847   DUNN, CHARLES W. "Weaver of Silk, Spinner of Tales: A Study
      of Thomas Deloney, Novelist." <u>McMaster University Quarter-</u>
      <u>ly</u>, April (1946), pp. 49-55.
         Surveys Deloney's three prose fiction works, discussing
      contents, offering appreciative commentary, and examining
      realistic elements.

848   DURHAM, CHARLES W. III. "Character and Characterization in
      Elizabethan Prose Fiction." Ph.D. dissertation, Ohio Uni-
      versity, 1969, 147pp.
      Examines Deloney's methods of characterization.

849   EIN, RONALD BORIS. "The Serpent's Voice: Commentary and
      Readers' Beliefs in Elizabethan Fiction." Ph.D. disserta-
      tion, Indiana University, 1974, 273pp.
      "[E]xamines the opening chapter of Jack of Newbury from
      the successive perspectives of narrator commentary...,
      character commentary..., and implied author commentary."

850   FRIEDERICH, REINHARD H. "Myself Am Centre of My Circling
      Thought: Studies in Baroque Personae (Burton and Donne)."
      Ph.D. dissertation, University of Washington, 1971, 194pp.
      Argues that because of "character credibility and flexi-
      bility rather than plot manipulation" Nashe's Unfortunate
      Traveller and Gascoigne's Master F. J. "succeed, whereas
      Greene and Deloney fail since their static characters can-
      not generate more than didactic or simply cumulative struc-
      tures."

851   GARKE, ESTHER. The Use of Songs in Elizabethan Prose Fiction.
      Bern: Francke Verlag, 1972, 132pp.
      Draws frequently on Deloney's novels for examples in
      analysis of types of songs, their relationships to plot and
      structure, and their functions (to complement or contrast
      setting, to present character relationships, to characterize
      singer and audience) in middle-class fiction.

852   GAVIGAN, WALTER V. "Nuns in Novels." Catholic World, 140
      (November 1934), 186-95.
      In an overview of representation of nuns in English
      novels, discusses Deloney's use in Thomas of Reading of the
      theme of "the woman thwarted in love who turns for solace
      to the convent." Points out that Deloney's Margaret is ap-
      parently "the first nun to be immortalized in English fic-
      tion."

853   GISELA, JUNKE. "Formen des Dialogs im frühen englischen Ro-
      man." Ph.D. dissertation, University of Köln, 1975, 150pp.
      Examines form and use of dialogue in Deloney's prose
      fiction. See 208.

854   HABLÜTZEL, MARGRIT ELISABETH. Die Bildwelt Thomas Deloneys:
      Ein Beitrag zur Erkenntnis von Zeitgeist und Gattungs-
      geschichte der englischen Renaissance. SAA, 16. Bern: A.
      Francke, 1946, 119pp.

Deloney

Analyzes and classifies imagery in Deloney's prose fiction and discusses relationship of his use of imagery to that of his contemporaries. Analyzes Deloney's style (calls him conservative).

*855 HARTMEYER, KÄTHE. "Die Sozial- und Kulturverhältnisse Englands in der elizabethanischen Zeit gesehen mit den Dichtern Th. Deloney, Th. Dekker und Ben Jonson." Ph.D. dissertation, University of Münster, 1950.
Abstract not available.

856 HILL, ROWLAND MERLIN. "Realistic Descriptive Setting in English Fiction from 1550 through Fielding." Ph.D. dissertation, Boston University, 1941, 344pp.
Examines Deloney's use of "local color" elements in his settings. Notes that he was "the first to employ successfully Gothic 'grave yard' detail as a means of intensifying realistic dramatic episodes." Observes that Deloney "revealed the inherent value of setting as a means of motivating plot and producing changes in character attitudes."

857 HOWARTH, R[OBERT] G[UY]. Two Elizabethan Writers of Fiction: Thomas Nashe and Thomas Deloney. Cape Town: University of Cape Town Editorial Board, 1956, 60pp.
Discusses Deloney's "glorification of the English artisan and of common life," his characterization, his "talent for myth-making," his style, his "mastery of the art of dialogue," and his structural techniques. Provides running commentary on his three prose fiction works (pp. 33-60).

858 KAPP, RUDOLF. "Thomas Deloney, The Gentle Craft: Eine hagiologische Untersuchung." Anglia, 62 (1938), 263-85.
Examines Deloney's use of the St. Crispin and St. Crispianus legend.

859 KATONA, ANNA. "A Shakespeare-korabeli angol irodalom a munkásságról," FK, 8 (June 1962), 123-32.
Includes examination of Deloney's idealized and unrealistic portraits of the master/journeyman/apprentice relationships; focuses on Jack of Newbury.

860 KENDLE, BURTON. "Elizabethan Bootstraps: The Social Ethics of Thomas Deloney's Shoemakers and Other Artisans," in Proceedings of the Sixth National Convention of the Popular Culture Association, Chicago, Illinois, April 22-24, 1976. Compiled by Michael T. Marsden. [Bowling Green, Ohio: Bowling Green Popular Press, 1976,] pp. 283-91.

Discusses Deloney's treatment of the theme of "the power and dignity of hard work," his style, and his ability to translate "mythic and romance motifs to the homely terms that suit the ethical goals and the experience and taste of his audience."

861 KING, T. J. "The 1623 Reprint of Thomas of Reading: A Computer Analysis." ShN, 15 (December 1965), 54.
Reports on progress of computer collation of 1612 and 1623 editions in an attempt to "gain additional evidence concerning the accuracy with which Jaggard's compositors set type from printed copy now extant."

862 KRIEGER, GOTTFRIED. Gedichteinlagen im englischen Roman. Ph.D. dissertation, University of Köln, Köln: n.p., 1969, 274pp.
Includes discussion of function and relation to theme and structure of verse insets in Deloney's prose fiction (passim).

863 KUEHN, GEORGE W. "Deloney and Gilds." TLS, 19 December 1936, p. 1052.
Points out passages in Deloney's prose fiction to illustrate his "use of historical or legendary backgrounds to disguise current controversy" over matters relating to guilds in late sixteenth-century England.

864 KUEHN, GEORGE W. "The Novels of Thomas Deloney as Source for 'Climate of Opinion' in Sixteenth-Century Economic History." Journal of Political Economy, 48 (December 1940), 865-75.
Suggests that in his novels "Deloney advocated consistently the Tudor 'very and true commonweal' theory of society as his general social ideal." Argues that Jack of Newbury is a veiled account of an actual protest in 1595 by weavers against foreign workmen illegally practicing the craft.

865 KUEHN, G[EORGE] W. "Thomas Deloney: Two Notes." MLN, 52 (February 1937), 103-105.
(I) Suggests similarity between the Wolsey-Henry VIII episode in Jack of Newbury and a pamphlet Complaint of the Yeoman Weavers against the Immigrant Weavers (1595). (II) Provides notes on editions earlier than ones reprinted in Mann's edition (819).

866 LAPART, CHRISTIAN. "Une Histoire policière à la manière élisabéthaine: Le meurtre de Thomas Cole." Caliban, 6 (January 1969), 7-13.

Deloney

Examines Deloney's creation of suspense in handling the
murder of Cole (<u>Thomas of Reading</u>). Analyzes Deloney's
juxtaposition of Cole's irrational premonitions of his im-
pending death to the realism in the description of prosaic
events. Finds that the tale of Cole possesses all the in-
tensity of a tragic action.

867   LAPART, CHRISTIAN. "La Promotion du travail à l'époque élisa-
      béthaine, vue à travers les romans de Thomas Deloney."
      <u>Caliban</u>, 2, no. 1 (1966), 85-95.
         Analyzes Deloney's emphasis on social advancement as the
      reward for honest labor in his three works of prose fiction.

868   LAWLIS, MERRITT E. <u>Apology for the Middle Class: The Dramatic
      Novels of Thomas Deloney</u>. IUHS, 46. Bloomington: Indiana
      University Press, 1960, 175pp.
         Analyzes Deloney's indebtedness to dramatic technique,
      his styles (realistic, euphuistic, and jest book), the in-
      fluence of the jest book on plot structure, and techniques
      of characterization. Includes section on the unity of
      <u>Thomas of Reading</u> and provides detailed synopsis of each
      work.

*869 LAWLIS, MERRITT E. "The Prose Fiction of Thomas Deloney."
      Ph.D. dissertation, Harvard University, 1951, 184pp.
         <u>See</u> 868.

870   LAWLIS, MERRITT E. "Thomas Deloney and Richard Casteler."
      <u>N&Q</u>, 198 (January 1953), 4-7.
         Traces biography of Casteler to illustrate Deloney's
      handling of historical material; finds that Deloney (in
      <u>Gentle Craft</u>, Part II) used only selected details available
      to him, relying mainly on his imagination.

871   MACKERNESS, E. D. "Thomas Deloney and the Virtuous Proletari-
      at." <u>Cambridge Journal</u>, 5 (October 1951), 34-50.
         Examines how Deloney's prose fiction (particularly <u>Jack
      of Newbury</u>) does not mirror actual social conditions but
      instead presents "an industrious and contented proletariat
      trusting in the value of work to obtain favour from the
      Almighty." Argues that while Deloney glorifies tradesmen
      and portrays the dignity of work, he also teaches "a doc-
      trine of acquiescence and passivity so as to avoid the fear
      of social disturbance." Also discusses Deloney's prose
      style.

872   McNEIR, WALDO F. "The Source of Simon Eyre's Catch-Phrase."
      <u>MLN</u>, 53 (April 1938), 275-76.

Points out that direct source of Eyre's "Prince am I
none, yet am I princely borne" (Dekker, The Shoemaker's
Holiday) is Greene's Orlando Furioso; however, notes that
"the idea that a shoemaker is a prince born" comes from
Deloney's The Gentle Craft.

873 MATTERN, TERRENCE JOHN. "Ballad Elements in the Prose Fiction
of Thomas Deloney." Ph.D. dissertation, University of Texas
at Austin, 1966, 318pp.
Analyzes characteristics of Deloney's fiction which "stem
from habits of ballad composition."

*874 MAUGERI, ALDO. "Storia e leggenda nella commedia The Shoe-
maker's Holiday di Thomas Dekker." Pubblicazioni della
Facoltà di Lettere e Filosofia dell' Università di Messina,
4 (1956), 181-92.
Not seen. Listed in MHRA Annual Bibliography, 32 (1955-
1956), #3815.

875 MAUGERI, ALDO. Studi su Thomas Dekker. Messina: Grafiche La
Sicilia, 1958, 117pp.
Includes discussion of Dekker's use of Gentle Craft as
source for The Shoemaker's Holiday (pp. 65-78).

*876 OKAMOTO, SAIKEI. "Realism e no sekkin--Thomas Deloney no
sakuhin ni tsuite [Approach to Realism--On the Works of
Thomas Deloney]." Eibungaku-shi (Hosei-daigaku), No. 4
(March 1961), pp. 4-13.
Not seen. Listed in Kazuyoshi Enozawa and Sister Miyo
Takano, "English Renaissance Studies in Japan, 1961-1963,"
RenB, 1 (1974), 24.

877 PARKER, DAVID. "Jack of Newbury: A New Source." ELN, 10
(March 1973), 173-80.
Argues against assumption that "Deloney was original in
championing the middle class." Points out several correspondences between Jack of Newbury and ballad "A Gest of
Robin Hood," arguing that Deloney was "continuing the tradition of middle-class social protest."

878 PÄTZOLD, KURT-MICHAEL. Historischer Roman und Realismus: Das
Erzählwerk Thomas Deloneys. Sprache und Literatur, Regensburger Arbeiten zur Anglistik und Amerikanistik, 6. Regensburg: Carl, 1972, 174pp.
Analyzes Deloney's novels as realistic historical fiction. Examines realism, transformation of elements of
chivalric romances, use of dialogue, treatment of theme of
social ascent, characterization, setting, handling of time,
and uses of narrative voice.

Deloney

879 PÄTZOLD, KURT-MICHAEL. "Thomas Deloney and the English Jest-
     Book Tradition." ES, 53 (August 1972), 313-28.
         Analyzes Deloney's use of "celebrated figures," inci-
     dents, and motifs from jest book and/or oral tradition.
     Examines "how Deloney assimilates in his Thomas of Reading
     several details from the popular tradition and transforms
     them to suit his own purpose."

880 PÄTZOLD, KURT-MICHAEL. "Thomas Deloneys Thomas of Reading und
     das Jest-Book The Pinder of Wakefield: Eine vergleichende
     Interpretation." NM, 72 (1971), 113-26.
         Examines Deloney's use of the jest book as source for
     portions of Thomas of Reading.

881 PIETZKER, ANNEMARIE. Der Kaufmann in der elisabethanischen
     Literatur. Quakenbrück: Handelsdruckerei C. Trute, 1931,
     82pp.
         Includes discussion of Deloney's depiction of merchant
     in his prose fiction (pp. 25-35).

882 POWYS, LLEWELYN. "Thomas Deloney." VQR, 9 (October 1933),
     578-94.
         Provides general appreciation of Deloney's prose fiction:
     discusses his realism, style, and subject matter, and pro-
     vides a synopsis of each of the three novels.

883 PRATT, SAMUEL MAXON. "Thomas Deloney: A Biographical and
     Critical Study." Ph.D. dissertation, Cornell University,
     1951.
         Examines style, use of dialect, "economic" themes, struc-
     ture, and realism in the three novels. Includes "A Check-
     List of the Works of Thomas Deloney" (arranged by work)
     with a chronological list of editions.

884 REUTER, OLE. "Some Aspects of Thomas Deloney's Prose Style."
     NM, 40 (1939), 23-72.
         Discusses popularity, structure, sources, didacticism,
     and themes of works. Analyzes characteristics of Deloney's
     style, emphasizing the influence of his middle-class back-
     ground on his style and topics.

885 REUTER, OLE. "Thomas Deloney's Use of Richard Eden's History
     of Trauayle in the West and East Indies," in Language and
     Society: Essays Presented to Arthur M. Jensen. Copenhagen:
     Berlingske Bogtrykkeri, 1961, pp. 141-46.
         Discusses Deloney's use of Eden's work as a source for
     a passage in The Gentle Craft.

886   ROBERTS, WARREN E. "Folklore in the Novels of Thomas Deloney,"
      in Studies in Folklore in Honor of Distinguished Service
      Professor Stith Thompson. Edited by W. Edson Richmond.
      Indiana University Publications, Folklore Series, 9.
      Bloomington: Indiana University Press, 1957, pp. 119-29.
        Analyzes Deloney's use of legends, folktales, ballads,
      proverbs, and superstitions. Demonstrates "that Deloney
      used a considerable amount of folklore, most of which he
      knew as part of the immense stock of Elizabethan oral tradi-
      tion."

887   ROLLINS, HYDER E. "Deloney's Sources for Euphuistic Learning."
      PMLA, 51 (June 1936), 399-406.
        Examines Deloney's use of Stephen Batman's The Doom Warn-
      ing All Men to the Judgment and Thomas Johnson's Cornuco-
      piae, Or Divers Secrets as sources for natural history
      references and "erudite-looking anecdotes" in his novels.
      Argues that use of Johnson's work suggests that Jack of
      Newbury, Thomas of Reading, and Gentle Craft, Part I, were
      composed in 1597; and that Gentle Craft, Part II, was com-
      posed late 1597 or in 1598.

888   ROLLINS, HYDER E. "Notes on Thomas Deloney." MLN, 32 (Febru-
      ary 1917), 121-23.
        Identifies allusion to The Gentle Craft in one of Sir
      John Harington's epigrams.

889   ROLLINS, HYDER E. "Thomas Deloney and Brian Melbancke: Notes
      on Sources." Harvard Studies and Notes in Philology and
      Literature, 19 (1937), 219-29.
        Discusses Deloney's use of Shakespeare's Lucrece as a
      source for passages in his novels.

890   ROLLINS, HYDER E. "Thomas Deloney's Euphuistic Learning and
      The Forest." PMLA, 50 (September 1935), 679-86.
        Discusses Deloney's use of Fortescue's The Forest as a
      source of his learning and euphuistic style, showing that
      portions of Jack of Newbury are copied verbatim from The
      Forest.

891   SANNA, VITTORIA. "Introduzione," in The Shoemaker's Holiday
      or The Gentle Craft. By Thomas Dekker. Edited by Vittoria
      Sanna. Biblioteca Italiana di Testi Inglesi, 13. Bari:
      Adriatica Editrice, 1968, pp. 5-38.
        Includes discussion of Dekker's use of The Gentle Craft
      as a source.

Deloney

892   SCHALL, LARRYETTA M.   "The Proletarian Tradition and Thomas
       Deloney." Ph.D. dissertation, University of Nevada, Reno,
       1972, 175pp.
            Analyzes Deloney's "novels as examples of popular, so-
       cial protest literature" and his contribution to the "exist-
       ing proletarian tradition." Argues that "[t]hrough his
       major theme, the commonwealth, Deloney criticized then-
       existing conditions and attitudes and suggested a christian,
       social-contract form of government."

893   SCHLAUCH, MARGARET. Antecedents of the English Novel, 1400-
       1600 (from Chaucer to Deloney). Warsaw: PWN--Polish
       Scientific Publishers; London: Oxford University Press,
       1963, 264pp.
            Discusses Deloney as an author of middle-class fiction,
       stressing the "effectiveness of his dialogues and comic
       situations" (pp. 237-45).

894   SMITH, JOHN DALE. "Narrative Technique in the Realistic Prose
       Fiction of Greene, Nashe, and Deloney." Ph.D. dissertation,
       University of Wisconsin, 1968, 323pp.
            Examines Deloney's "use of dialogue, dramatic confronta-
       tion, and low comedy." Argues that Deloney's works "de-
       serve the [n]ame novel" and discusses his place in the
       development of the novel.

895   STEANE, J. B. "A Note on The Gentle Craft, St. Hugh's Bones,
       and Simon Eyre," in The Shoemaker's Holiday. By Thomas
       Dekker. Edited by J. B. Steane. Cambridge: Cambridge
       University Press, 1965, pp. 135-40.
            Discusses Dekker's use of The Gentle Craft as a source.

896   TRNKA, BOHUMIL. "Bohemia in English Literature (Sir John
       Fortescue and Thomas Deloney)." Yearbook of the Anglo-
       American Club Union of Czechoslovakia, 1928, pp. 55-57.
            Notes that Deloney retells the story of the Czech prince
       Přemysl the Plowman in Jack of Newbury. Suggests that De-
       loney was relying on oral tradition for the story.

897   WOLFF, HERMANN. "Das Charakterbild Heinrichs VIII. in der
       Englischen Literatur bis Shakespeare." Ph.D. dissertation,
       University of Freiburg, 1972, 238pp.
            Includes examination of Deloney's characterization of
       Henry VIII in Jack of Newbury and The Gentle Craft. (Ab-
       stract in: English and American Studies in German: Sum-
       maries of Theses and Monographs, 1974. Edited by Werner
       Habicht. Tübingen: M. Niemeyer Verlag, 1975, pp. 53-54.)

898 WOLTER, JÜRGEN. <u>Das Prosawerk Thomas Deloneys: Studien zu</u>
     <u>Erzählkunst, Weltbild und Geschichtlichkeit</u>. Gesamthoch-
     schule Wuppertal, Schriftenreihe Literatur, 3. Bonn:
     Bouvier Verlag H. Grundmann, 1976, 157pp.
         Analyzes structure--especially in relationship to the
     motif of social ascent--of each of Deloney's works of prose
     fiction. Traces progressive darkening of Deloney's <u>weltan-</u>
     <u>schauung</u>, relating changes to developments in Elizabethan
     life and literature.

*899 YOSHIDA, TETSUO. "On Thomas Deloney's Fiction." <u>SELL</u>, No.
     22 (1972), pp. 113-35.
         Not located. Listed in <u>1972 MLA International Bibliog-</u>
     <u>raphy</u>, I, #2893. In Japanese; English summary, p. 181.

<u>DESAINLIENS, CLAUDE (CLAUDIUS HOLYBAND)</u>

Diego de San Pedro, <u>The Pretie and Wittie Historie of Arnalt & Lu-</u>
     <u>cenda</u>. <u>STC</u> 6758-6760.

Studies

900 FAZZARI, CLARA. "Introduzione," in Tractado de amores de
     Arnalte e Lucenda <u>nella traduzione inglese di John Clerk</u>.
     By Diego de San Pedro. Edited by Clara Fazzari. Accademia
     Toscana di Scienze e Lettere "La Colombaria," Studi, 29.
     Florence: Leo S. Olschki Editore, 1974, pp. 5-30.
         Provides comparison of Desainliens's translation with
     that by Clerc.

901 KOSZUL, A. "La Première traduction d'<u>Arnalte et Lucende</u> et
     les débuts de la nouvelle sentimentale en Angleterre."
     PFLUS, 105. Paris: Belles Lettres, 1946, pp. 151-67.
         Compares Desainliens's translation with that by Clerc;
     finds that Desainliens's is the better.

902 KRAUSE, ANNA. "Apunte bibliographico sobre Diego de San
     Pedro." <u>RFE</u>, 35 (1952), 126-30.
         Includes discussion of Desainliens's translation, where
     the tragic catastrophe is converted into a happy ending.

903 SIMONINI, R. C., JR. "The Italian Pedagogy of Claudius Holly-
     band." <u>SP</u>, 49 (April 1952), 144-54.
         Discusses <u>Arnalt and Lucenda</u> in the context of Desain-
     liens's "place...in the history of the teaching of the
     Italian language in England and...his contributions in
     methods and materials to that tradition."

The Dialoges of Creatures Moralysed

THE DIALOGES OF CREATURES MORALYSED

STC 6815.

Editions

*904   The Dialogues of Creatures Moralized. Edited by Joseph Hasle-
       wood. London: R. Triphook, 1816.
              Not seen. Listed in NUC Pre-1956 Imprints, vol. 142,
       292.

Studies

905   R., R. "Eastern Origin of a Jest of Scogin." N&Q, 60 (25
      October 1879), 331-32.
             Cites analogue in Dialogues of Creatures Moralized to
      jest in Scoggin's Jests.

DICKENSON, JOHN (fl. 1594-1598)

Arisbas, Euphues Amidst His Slumbers; or Cupids Journey to Hell. STC
    6817.

Greene in Conceipt: New Raised from His Graue to Write the Tragique
    Historie of Faire Valeria of London. STC 6819.

Editions

906   DICKENSON, JOHN. Prose and Verse by John Dickenson. Edited
      by Alexander B. Grosart. Manchester: Printed for the
      Subscribers, 1878, 192pp.
             Provides annotated reprints of 1594 ediction of Arisbas
      and 1598 edition of Greene in Conceit.

907   HENDRICKS, WALTER. "John Dickenson: The Man and His Works."
      Ph.D. dissertation, Northwestern University, 1941, 279pp.
             Provides old-spelling texts of Arisbas (1594) and Greene
      in Conceit (1598). Examines "nature of Dickenson's works
      and discuss[es] problems of sources, style, diction, order
      of composition, and influence."

Studies

908   DAVIS, WALTER R[ICHARDSON]. "The Plagiarisms of John Hynd."
      N&Q, NS, 16 (March 1969), 90-92.
             Traces Hind's borrowings from Arisbas in Lysimachus and
      Varrona.

909   GARKE, ESTHER. The Use of Songs in Elizabethan Prose Fiction.
      Bern: Francke Verlag, 1972, 132pp.
         Draws frequently on Arisbas for examples in analysis of
      types of songs, their relationships to plot and structure,
      and their functions (to complement or contrast setting, to
      present character relationships, to characterize singer
      and audience).

910   SVOB, MICHAEL JOSEPH. "The Scholar's Aliquid of John Dickin-
      son." Ph.D. dissertation, University of Illinois at Ur-
      bana-Champaign, 1966, 463pp.
         Provides a critical estimate of Arisbas and examines in-
      fluence of Arcadia on work. Discusses Greene in Conceit as
      a "realistic novel in the manner of Robert Greene...[and]
      fully euphuistic in style."

DIGGES, LEONARD (d. 1571?)

Gonzalo Cespedes y Maneses. Gerardo, the Unfortunate Spaniard. STC
   4919. Wing C1783.

Studies

911   FITZMAURICE-KELLY, JAMES. "Un hispanófilo inglés del siglo
      XVII," in Homenaje á Menéndez y Pelayo, Vol. I. Madrid:
      V. Suárez, 1899, 47-56.
         Discusses Digges's handling of text in his translation
      of Gerardo.

912   KLEIN, EMMO [OSWALD]. Fletchers The Spanish Curate und seine
      Quelle. Halle: Buchdruckerei von H. John, 1905, 64pp.
         Provides scene-by-scene analysis of Fletcher's use of
      Gerardo as source.

913   LLOYD, BERTRAM. "A Minor Source of The Changeling." MLR, 19
      (January 1924), 101-102.
         Suggests Gerardo as Middleton and Rowley's source for
      three incidents in the play.

914   MARTIN, RILEY TELFORD III. "A Critical Introduction to the
      Digges' Translation of Poema trágico del español Gerardo."
      Ph.D. dissertation, Wayne State University, 1973, 228pp.
         Analyzes Digges's handling of style and themes in his
      translation. Suggests that "English preoccupation with
      [the]...themes [of Fortuna and desengaño] (as evidenced in
      the works of Gascoigne, Lyly, Nashe, Greene, etc.) may have
      helped to insure the success of Gerardo in England."

Digges

915 MATHEWS, ERNST G[ARLAND]. "The Murdered Substitute Tale."
    MLQ, 6 (June 1945), 187-95.
        Discusses influence of tale of Roberto (from Digges's
    Gerardo) on drama, particularly Middleton and Rowley's
    treatment of De Flores in The Changeling.

916 MATHEWS, ERNST GARLAND. "Studies in Anglo-Spanish Cultural
    and Literary Relations, 1598-1700." Ph.D. dissertation,
    Harvard University, 1938.
        Includes discussion of Gerardo; comments on Digges's
    handling of text and style.

917 RANDALL, DALE B. J. The Golden Tapestry: A Critical Survey
    of Non-Chivalric Spanish Fiction in English Translation
    (1543-1657). Durham: Duke University Press, 1963, 272pp.
        Includes discussion of Digges's handling of the original
    text--especially his alterations--in his translation of
    Gerardo (pp. 112-18).

DOBSONS DRIE BOBBES
    Sometimes ascribed to George Dobson.

    STC 6930.

Editions

918 Dobsons Drie Bobbes, in Die englischen Schwankbücher bis herab
    zu Dobson's Drie Bobs (1607). By Ernst Schulz. Palaestra,
    117. Berlin: Mayer & Müller, 1912, pp. 89-223.
        Provides reprint of 1607 edition. Includes discussion
    of style, historical background, and sources.

919 Dobsons Drie Bobbes: A Story of Sixteenth Century Durham.
    Edited by E. A. Horsman. University of Durham Publications.
    London: Oxford University Press, 1955, 134pp.
        Provides annotated critical text of 1607 edition. In
    "Introduction" (pp. vii-xxiii) examines the relationship
    of work to the jest book tradition, the use of Durham local
    detail and historical characters, the continuity of plot,
    the style and language of the work, and the author's atti-
    tude toward his subject.

Studies

920 COLGRAVE, BERTRAM. "Dobson's Drie Bobs." DUJ, NS, 12 (June
    1951), 77-85.

Discusses work in context of Durham local history, identifying characters and allusions.

921   O'BRIEN, AVRIL S[EARLE]. "Dobsons Drie Bobbes: A Significant
       Contribution to the Development of Prose Fiction." SEL, 12
       (Winter 1972), 55-70.
          Discusses characterization, description, "psychological
       realism," and structural unity in arguing for value of work
       in studying development of Renaissance prose fiction.

922   WILSON, F[RANK] P[ERCY]. "The English Jestbooks of the Six-
       teenth and Early Seventeenth Centuries." HLQ, 2 (January
       1939), 121-58.
          In general overview of jest books, singles out Dobson's
       Dry Bobs for special notice because of its affinity with the
       form of the novel. Notes that it "applies to the jest-
       biography the technique of the novella." Reprinted as 423.

DU VERGER, SUSAN, AND T. BRUGIS

Jean Pierre Camus, Admirable Events; Selected Out of Foure Bookes.
   STC 4549-4550.

Studies

923   MISH, CHARLES C[ARROLL]. "The Waking Mans Dreame." TLS, 28
       December 1951, p. 837.
          Identifies this tale, supposedly from a lost collection
       of prose tales by Richard Edwards (1570), as part of Du
       Verger and Brugis's Admirable Events.

ELYOT, SIR THOMAS (1499?-1546)

The Boke Named The Gouernour (includes translation of the tale of
   Titus and Gisippus from Giovanni Boccaccio's Decameron). STC 7635-
   7642.

Editions

924   ELYOT, THOMAS. The Book Named the Governour. Edited by
       Arthur Turberville Eliot. Newcastle-upon-Tyne: J. Hernaman;
       London: Ridgway and Sons, 1834, 333pp.
          Provides reprint of unidentified early edition.

Elyot

925   ELYOT, THOMAS. <u>The Boke Named the Gouernour</u>. Edited by Henry
      H[erbert] S[tephen] Croft. 2 vols. London: C. K. Paul &
      Co., 1880, 870pp.
          Provides annotated text based on 1531 edition.

926   ELYOT, THOMAS. <u>The Boke Named the Governour</u>. Introduction by
      Foster Watson. Everyman's Library, 227. London: J. M.
      Dent & Co.; New York: E. P. Dutton & Co., 1907, 340pp.
          Provides modernized text based on unidentified edition.

927   ELYOT, THOMAS. <u>The Book Named the Governor</u>. Edited by S[tan-
      ford] E. Lehmberg. Everyman's Library, 227. London: Dent;
      New York: Dutton, 1962, 255pp.
          Provides modernized text based on unidentified edition.

Studies

928   GALIGANI, GIUSEPPE. "Il Boccaccio nel Cinquecento inglese,"
      in <u>Il Boccaccio nella cultura inglese e anglo-americana</u>.
      Edited by Giuseppe Galigani. Florence: L. S. Olschki,
      1974, pp. 27-57.
          Discusses Elyot's use of <u>Decameron</u> as source for story
      of Titus and Gisippus; examines Elyot's handling of text,
      especially his amplifications.

929   GOODE, CLEMENT TYSON. "Sir Thomas Elyot's <u>Titus and Gysippus</u>."
      <u>MLN</u>, 37 (January 1922), 1-11.
          Argues Elyot's source is the version by Petrus Alphonsus
      in <u>Disciplina Clericalis</u>, not that by Boccaccio or Philip
      Beroaldo. Suggests Elyot's version was one of influences
      on the structure of Lyly's <u>Euphues</u>.

930   RAITH, JOSEF. <u>Boccaccio in der englischen Literatur von
      Chaucer bis Painters Palace of Pleasure: Ein Beitrag zur
      Geschichte der italienischen Novelle in England</u>. Aus
      Schrifttum und Sprache der Angelsachsen, 3. Leipzig:
      Robert Noske, 1936, 173pp.
          Examines Elyot's translation of Boccaccio's story of
      Titus and Gisippus: discusses his handling of the text and
      his treatment of the theme of friendship (pp. 101-12).

931   SARGENT, RALPH M. "Sir Thomas Elyot and the Integrity of <u>The
      Two Gentlemen of Verona</u>." <u>PMLA</u>, 65 (December 1950), 1166-
      80.
          Discusses Shakespeare's use of Elyot's version of the
      Titus and Gisippus story as a source. Notes that Elyot's
      treatment emphasizes "devotion to friendship as an ideal."

F., P.

932   SORIERI, LOUIS. Boccaccio's Story of Tito e Gisippo in Euro-
       pean Literature. Comparative Literature Series. New York:
       Institute of French Studies, 1937, 284pp.
            Includes examination of Elyot's alterations in tale and
       speculation about his sources (pp. 152-57).

F., P.

The Historie of the Damnable Life and Deserued Death of Dr. John
    Faustus. STC 10711-10714. Wing H2151-2156.

Bibliographies

933   HENNING, HANS. Faust Bibliographie, I: Allgemeines, Grund-
       lagen, Gesamtdarstellungen. Das Faust-Thema vom 16. Jahr-
       hundert bis 1790. Berlin: Aufbau-Verlag, 1966, 530pp.
            Includes list of editions of (pp. 127-33) and works
       about (pp. 144-54) History of Doctor John Faustus.

Editions

934   The History of the Life and Death of Dr. John Faustus. Trans-
       lated by P. F. In A Collection of Early Prose Romances,
       Vol. III. Edited by William J. Thoms. London: William
       Pickering, 1828, 146pp. (separately paginated). [Also
       published separately.]
            Provides reprint of 1700 edition. In introductory note
       (pp. iii-viii) comments on other treatments of the legend.

*935   The Historie of the Damnable Life and Deserved Death of Doctor
       John Faustus. Translated by P. F. London: E. Mallett,
       1887, 64pp.
            Not seen. Facsimile reprint of 1592 edition. Listed in
       NUC Pre-1956 Imprints, vol. 247, 563.

936   The English Faust-Book of 1592. Edited by H[enri] Logeman.
       Université de Gand, Recueil de Travaux, Faculté de Philoso-
       phie et Lettres, 24. Gand: Librairie H. Engelcke; Amster-
       dam: Schröder, 1900, 197pp.
            Provides annotated, corrected reprint of 1592 edition.
       In "Introduction," pp. V-XVI, discusses clues to transla-
       tor's identity and his handling of the German text. Argues
       that an edition preceded that of 1592.

937   The History of the Damnable Life and Deserved Death of Dr. John
       Faustus. Translated by P. F. In Early English Prose Ro-
       mances. Edited by William J. Thoms. Revised and enlarged

edition. London: G. Routledge and Sons; New York: E. P.
Dutton and Co., [1907], pp. 785-884.
Reprint of 934.

938   The History of the Damnable Life and Deserved Death of Doctor
John Faustus, in The History of the Damnable Life and De-
served Death of Doctor John Faustus, 1592. Together with
The Second Report of Faustus, Containing His Appearances
and the Deeds of Wagner, 1594. Edited by William Rose.
Broadway Translations. London: G. Routledge; New York:
E. P. Dutton, 1925, pp. 59-208.
Provides modernized text based on 936. In "Introduction,"
pp. 1-58, discusses work in context of Faust legend in Eng-
land. Reprinted as 941.

939   The Historie of the Damnable Life and Deserved Death of Doctor
John Faustus. Translated by P. F. In The Sources of the
Faust Tradition from Simon Magus to Lessing. By Philip
Mason Palmer and Robert Pattison More. New York: Oxford
University Press, 1936, pp. 132-236.
Provide annotated reprint of 1592 edition. Briefly
comment on relationship to the 1587 Spies Faustbuch and on
the importance of the work in the development of the Faust
legend.

940   The Historie of the Damnable Life and Deserved Death of Doctor
John Faustus. Translated by P. F. In The Tragical History
of Doctor Faustus. By Christopher Marlowe. Revised by
Basil Ashmore. London: Blandford Press, 1948, pp. 103-215.
Provides modernized reprint of 1592 edition.

941   The Historie of the Damnable Life and Deserved Death of Doctor
John Faustus, 1592. Translated by P. F. Edited by William
Rose. Foreword by William Karl Pfeiler. South Bend: Uni-
versity of Notre Dame Press, 1963, 226pp.
Reprints History of Doctor John Faustus from 938 along
with Rose's "Introduction."

942   The Damnable Life and Deserved Death of Doctor John Faustus.
Translated by P. F. English Experience, 173. Amsterdam:
Theatrvm Orbis Terrarvm; New York: Da Capo Press, 1969,
89pp.
Provides facsimile reprint of 1592 edition.

Studies

943   BAKELESS, JOHN E[DWIN]. The Tragicall History of Christopher
Marlowe. 2 vols. Cambridge: Harvard University Press,
1942, 825pp.

Includes discussion of Marlowe's use of the History of Doctor John Faustus as source for Doctor Faustus (passim).

944 BEACH, SARAH MOREHOUSE. "The 'Julius Caesar Obelisk' in the English Faust Book and Elsewhere." MLN, 35 (January 1920), 27-31.
Explains allusion to "the Pyramide that Julius Caesar brought out of Africa" in the History of Doctor John Faustus.

945 BLUESTONE, MAX. From Story to Stage: The Dramatic Adaptation of Prose Fiction in the Period of Shakespeare and His Contemporaries. SEngL, 70. The Hague: Mouton, 1974, 341pp.
Includes examination of the transformation and adaptation of The History of Doctor John Faustus in Marlowe's Dr. Faustus (passim).

946 BOAS, FREDERICK S. "Introduction," in The Tragical History of Doctor Faustus. By Christopher Marlowe. Edited by Frederick S. Boas. New York: Dial Press, 1932, pp. 1-52.
Discusses date of the History of Doctor John Faustus and its use as a source for both 1604 and 1616 texts. Reprints extracts in Appendix I ("Source Passages for the English Faust Book," pp. 177-95).

947 BROWN, BEATRICE DAW. "Marlowe, Faustus, and Simon Magus." PMLA, 54 (March 1939), 82-121.
Argues that in History of Doctor John Faustus Faustus is little more than a mountebank and sensualist with little of the heroic and tragic personality of Marlowe's character. Suggests that patristic writings influenced story as it is preserved in the History and that its readers would call to mind the Simon Magus legend.

948 BUTLER, E[LIZA] M[ARIAN]. The Fortunes of Faust. Cambridge: Cambridge University Press, 1952, 383pp.
Discusses dating of History of Doctor John Faustus, speculates about the characteristics and personality of P. F., and analyzes his style. Compares English version to the German Faustbuch to illustrate how the translator's "omissions and alterations contribute to a total effect of greater spiritual proportions" (pp. 31-41, passim).

949 CAMPBELL, LILY B[ESS]. "Doctor Faustus: A Case of Conscience." PMLA, 67 (March 1952), 219-39.
Analyzes difference in impression left by Marlowe's play and its source, the History of Doctor John Faustus.

F., P.

950   DEATS, SARA MUNSON. "Marlowe's Doctor Faustus: From Chapbook
       to Tragedy." Ph.D. dissertation, University of California,
       Los Angeles, 1970, 399pp.
            Examines Marlowe's use of the History of Doctor John
       Faustus as source; discusses "date, relationship to German
       Faustbook, [and] genre" of the History.

951   DÉDÉYAN, CHARLES. Le Thème de Faust dans la littérature euro-
       péenne, Vol. I. Les Cahiers des Lettres Modernes. Paris:
       Lettres Modernes, 1954, 290pp.
            Examines the anonymous translator's humor, knowledge of
       Germany, language, and changes in the German text (pp. 33-
       40).

952   DELIUS, THEODOR. Marlowe's Faustus und seine Quelle: Ein
       Beitrag zur Kritik des Dramas. Bielefeld: Druck von Vel-
       hagen & Klasing, 1881, 31pp.
            Provides detailed analysis of Marlowe's use of the His-
       tory of Doctor Faustus as source.

953   DÜNTZER, HEINRICH. "Zu Marlowe's Faust." Anglia, 1 (1878),
       44-54.
            Includes examination of Marlowe's knowledge of the His-
       tory of Doctor John Faustus. (See W. Wagner, "Zu Marlowe's
       Faust," Anglia, 2 [1879], 309-13.)

954   FALIGAN, ERNEST. Histoire de le légende de Faust. Paris:
       Hachette et Cie, 1888, 506pp.
            Includes discussion of date of History of Doctor John
       Faustus and the translator's handling of text of Spies's
       edition. Misreads "Gent" as name of translator (pp. 241-
       46).

955   FRITZ, JOSEF. "Ein Unbekannter englischer Faustbuchdruck."
       MLN, 28 (November 1913), 230-31.
            Provides bibliographical description of a copy of 1634
       edition of the History of Doctor John Faustus in the Biblio-
       thèque Nationale.

956   GREG, W[ALTER] W[ILSON]. "Introduction," in Marlowe's Doctor
       Faustus, 1604-1616: Parallel Texts. By Christopher
       Marlowe. Edited by W[alter] W[ilson] Greg. Oxford:
       Clarendon Press, 1950, pp. 1-139.
            Discusses publishing history of History of Doctor John
       Faustus, its date of publication ("about May 1592"), and
       its use as source for the play.

957   HAWKINS, SHERMAN. "The Education of Faustus." <u>SEL</u>, 6
       (Spring 1966), 193-209.
          Discusses relationship between <u>History of Doctor John
       Faustus</u> and middle portion of Marlowe's <u>Doctor Faustus</u>.
       Suggests that Marlowe "selected the <u>Faust Book</u> episodes
       which his collaborators dramatized."

958   IIOUK, RAYMOND A. "<u>Doctor Faustus</u> and <u>A Shrew</u>." <u>PMLA</u>, 62
       (December 1947), 950-57.
          Argues that <u>History of Doctor John Faustus</u> was used for
       additions to 1616 edition of Marlowe's <u>Doctor Faustus</u> and
       as source by author of <u>The Taming of a Shrew</u>.

959   HUGHES, WALTER. "The Early Development of the Faust Legend."
       <u>Papers of the Manchester Literary Club</u>, 1 (April 1882),
       101-24.
          Discusses Marlowe's use of the <u>History of Doctor John
       Faustus</u> as a source.

960   JUMP, JOHN D. "Introduction," in <u>Doctor Faustus</u>. By Christo-
       pher Marlowe. Edited by John D. Jump. Revels Plays.
       Cambridge: Harvard University Press, 1962, pp. xix-lxv.
          Includes discussion of importance of date of first pub-
       lication of <u>History of Doctor John Faustus</u> to dating Mar-
       lowe's play and examines use of work as source for play.
       Observes that P. F.'s "departures from his original involve
       the ascription to Faustus of a genuine intellectual ardour."
       Reprints extracts from <u>History</u> in Appendix II (pp. 123-40).

961   KOCHER, PAUL H. "The Early Date for Marlowe's <u>Faustus</u>." <u>MLN</u>,
       58 (November 1943), 539-42.
          Argues source of Harvey's reference to Faustus in <u>An
       Advertisement for Papp-Hatchet</u> is the <u>History of Doctor
       John Faustus</u>, providing further evidence of existence of
       an edition of the work by 1589 (<u>see</u> 962).

962   KOCHER, PAUL H. "The English <u>Faust Book</u> and the Date of Mar-
       lowe's <u>Faustus</u>." <u>MLN</u>, 55 (February 1940), 95-101.
          Argues for existence of a 1590 edition (printed at Cam-
       bridge) of <u>History of Doctor John Faustus</u>. Suggests P. F.
       was a Cambridge man, possibly Peter Frenche. <u>See</u> 961.

963   LOGEMAN, H[ENRI]. <u>Faustus-Notes: A Supplement to the Com-
       mentaries on Marlowe's</u> Tragicall History of D. Faustus.
       Université de Gand, Recueil de Travaux, Faculté de Philoso-
       phie et Lettres, 21. Gand: H. Engelcke, 1898, 165pp.
          Includes discussion of Marlowe's use of <u>History of Doc-
       tor John Faustus</u> as source; argues that he used only the
       English version and not the German <u>Faustbuch</u> (pp. 133-48).

F., P.

964 LOGEMAN, H[ENRI]. "'Morte Caval' in the English Faustbook."
    MLN, 13 (April 1898), 103-105.
        Observes that the phrase "morte caval" in History of
    Doctor John Faustus has no equivalent in the original and
    suggests that the correct reading is "monte caval," a refer-
    ence to the Monte Cavallo.

965 McKILLOP, ALAN D. "A Victorian Faust." PMLA, 40 (September
    1925), 743-68.
        Discusses Philip James Bailey's use of History of Doctor
    John Faustus as source for his Festus.

*966 MÜNCH, W. "Die innere Stellung Marlowes zum Volksbuch von
    Faust," in Festschrift zur Begrussüng der XXXIV Versammlung
    deutscher Philologen und Schulmänner zu Trier. Trier:
    Lintz, 1879, pp. 107-38.
        Not seen. Cited in 943.

967 NOSWORTHY, J. M. "Some Textual Anomalies in the 1604 Doctor
    Faustus." MLR, 41 (January 1946), 1-8.
        Discusses History of Doctor John Faustus as source for
    1604 and 1616 versions of Marlowe's play.

968 PANTIN, W. E. P. "The Sources of Marlowe's Dr. Faustus." The
    Academy, 31 (25 June 1887), 449.
        Analyzes Marlowe's use of the History of Doctor John
    Faustus as a source.

969 REED, ROBERT R., JR. "Nick Bottom, Dr. Faustus, and the Ass's
    Head." N&Q, NS, 6 (July-August 1959), 252-54.
        Suggests that History of Doctor John Faustus was Shake-
    speare's source for the incident in A Midsummer Night's
    Dream.

970 REYNOLDS, JAMES A. "Marlowe's Dr. Faustus: 'be a divine in
    show' and 'When all is done, divinity is best.'" AN&Q, 13
    (May 1975), 131-33.
        Suggests inconsistency created by "be a divine in show"
    is the result of Marlowe's incomplete assimilation of a de-
    tail in the History of Doctor John Faustus, where Faustus
    uses the various arts as a cover for his necromancy.

971 RICHARDS, ALFRED E. "Marlowe, Faustus, Scene 14." MLN, 22
    (April 1907), 126-27.
        Identifies the History of Doctor John Faustus as the
    source of some lines in 1604 edition of Marlowe's play.

972 ROHDE, RICHARD. Das englische Faustbuch und Marlowes Tragödie. Studien zur Englischen Philologie, 43. Halle: Niemeyer, 1910, 70pp.
Argues that John Dee was translator; points out details that only an eye witness could have known. Examines Marlowe's use of the History of Doctor John Faustus as a source.

973 SCHMID, E. "Marlowes Faust und sein Verhältnis zu den deutschen und englischen Faustbüchern." Jahrbuch für Romanische und Englische Sprache und Literatur, NS, 2 (1875), 42-62.
Discusses Marlowe's use of the History of Doctor John Faustus as a source.

*974 SCHRÖDER, KURT RUDOLF. Textverhaltnisse und Entstehungsgeschichte von Marlowes Faust. Ph.D. dissertation, University of Berlin. Berlin, 1909, 87pp.
Attempts to use reliance on History of Doctor John Faustus as test for Marlowe's authorship of passages in both versions of Doctor Faustus. Not located: annotation from review by Robert K. Root, Englische Studien, 43, no. 1 (1910), 117-34.

975 SINKO, GRZEGORZ. "Dr. Faustus' Travels in Silesia and Poland," in Studies in Language and Literature in Honour of Margaret Schlauch. Edited by Mieczysław Brahmer, Stanisław Helsztyński, and Julian Krzyzanowski. Warsaw: Polish Scientific Publishers, 1966, pp. 397-411.
Examines descriptions of towns in Silesia and Poland in History of Doctor John Faustus and speculates that P. F.'s source of information was "travel relations gathered first- or second-hand" and that investigating early travellers to area might provide some clue to identify of author. Identifies first 1587 edition of German Volksbuch as basis of the translation.

*976 VENZLAFF, GUNTHER. Textüberlieferung und Enstehungsgeschichte von Marlowes Doctor Faustus. Ph.D. dissertation, University of Greifswalder. Berlin, 1909, 80pp.
Provides detailed comparison between both versions of Marlowe's play and History of Doctor John Faustus: "[t]his comparison shows that, though the readings given by A [1605 and 1609 editions] are in general nearer in their wording to the language of the Faust Book than those of B [1616-1663 editions], in some cases the reverse is true." Not located: annotation from review by Robert K. Root, Englische Studien, 43, no. 1 (1910), 117-34.

F., P.

977   WAUGH, BUTLER. "Deep and Surface Structure in Traditional and Sophisticated Literature: Faust." <u>SAB</u>, 33, no. 3 (May 1968), 14-17.
        Characterizes the narrative of the <u>History of Doctor John Faustus</u> as "surface structure" and examines Marlowe's transformation of materials from the prose version into "deep structure" in <u>Doctor Faustus</u>.

978   ZARNCKE, FR[IEDRICH]. "Das englische Volksbuch vom Doctor Faust." <u>Anglia</u>, 9 (1886), 610-12.
        Examines evidence for existence of edition of the <u>History of Doctor John Faustus</u> prior to that of 1592; discusses date of earliest edition.

THE FAMOUS & RENOWNED HISTORY OF MORINDOS

    <u>STC</u> 18108.

Editions

979   <u>The Famous and Renowned History of Morindos</u>, in <u>Short Fiction of the Seventeenth Century</u>. Edited by Charles C[arroll] Mish. Stuart Editions. New York: New York University Press, 1963, pp. 1-42.
        Provides modernized reprint of 1609 edition. In short introductory note, calls attention to the author's narrative skill. <u>See</u> 60.

Studies

980   BOORMAN, S. C. "Some Elizabethan Notes (1)." <u>Trivium</u>, 1 (1966), 184-87.
        In second note ("A Possible Allusion in Donne's 'A Tale of a Citizen and His Wife'") suggests that lines 62-66 contain an allusion to "Avarice her tragedy" in <u>Morindos</u>.

THE FAMOUS HISTORIE OF FRYER BACON, ALSO THE MANNER OF HIS DEATH

    <u>STC</u> 1183-1184. Wing F371-374.

Editions

981   <u>The Famous Historie of Fryer Bacon</u>, in <u>Miscellanea Antiqua Anglicana; or, a Select Collection of Curious Tracts Illustrative of the History, Literature, Manners, and Biography</u>

The Famous Historie of Fryer Bacon

of the English Nation. London: R. Triphook, 1816, 48pp.
(separately paginated).
    Provides reprint of 1629 edition.

982   The History of Friar Bacon, in A Collection of Early Prose
    Romances, Vol. I. Edited by William J. Thoms. London:
    William Pickering, 1828, 70pp. (separately paginated).
    [Also published separately.]
        Provides reprint of 1629 edition. In introductory com-
    ments discusses work in context of Bacon legend. Reprinted
    in 984 and 985.

983   The Famous Historie of Fryer Bacon. Edited by Edmund Goldsmid.
    2 vols. Edinburgh: Privately Printed, 1886, 96pp.
        Provides reprint of "early copy" (i.e., 1629 edition ?).

984   The Famous Historie of Fryer Bacon, in Early Prose Romances.
    Edited by Henry Morley. Carisbrooke Library, 4. London:
    G. Routledge, 1889, pp. 285-328.
        Reprints text from 982. In "Introduction" discusses
    briefly the development of the legend (pp. 23-27). Re-
    printed in 985.

985   The Famous Historie of Fryer Bacon, in Early English Prose Ro-
    mances. Edited by William J. Thoms. Revised and enlarged
    edition. London: G. Routledge and Sons; New York: E. P.
    Dutton & Co., [1907], pp. 285-328.
        Reprint of 984.

986   The Famous History of Friar Bacon, in Some Old English Worthies.
    Edited by Dorothy Senior. London: S. Swift and Co., 1912,
    pp. 177-235.
        Provides annotated, modernized reprint of 1661 edition.
    In "Introduction," pp. 9-26, traces historical and legendary
    background of Roger Bacon.

987   The Famous Historie of Fryer Bacon, in Friar Bacon and Friar
    Bungay. John of Bordeaux; or, the Second Part of Friar
    Bacon. By Robert Greene. Edited by Benevenuto Cellini.
    Biblioteca di Classici Stranieri, Serie Inglese, 1.
    Florence: La Nuova Italia, 1952, pp. 183-214.
        Provides reprint of unidentified edition. In "Introduzi-
    one," pp. VII-XXX, discusses Greene's use of work as a
    source.

The Famous Historie of Fryer Bacon

Studies

988   ASSARSSON-RIZZI, KERSTIN. Friar Bacon and Friar Bungay: A
        Structural and Thematic Analysis of Robert Greene's Play.
        LSE, 44. Lund: C. W. K. Gleerup, 1972, 164pp.
            In chapter "Relationship to Sources" (pp. 24-43) dis-
        cusses dating, structure, and moralizing tone of Friar Bacon
        and examines Greene's use as source for incident, character,
        and spectacle.

989   LAW, ROBERT ADGER. "Two Parallels to Greene and Lodge's
        Looking-Glass." MLN, 26 (May 1911), 146-48.
            Suggests episode in Friar Bacon as source of portion of
        the play.

990   McNEIR, WALDO F. "Robert Greene and John of Bordeaux." PMLA,
        64 (September 1949), 781-801.
            Discusses Friar Bacon as source for John of Bordeaux and
        Greene's Friar Bacon and Friar Bungay.

991   McNEIR, WALDO F. "Traditional Elements in the Character of
        Greene's Friar Bacon." SP, 45 (April 1948), 172-79.
            Discusses Friar Bacon in context of examination of con-
        ventional elements in the presentation of the benevolent
        magician in early romances. Examines Greene's use of the
        prose work as a source for his characterization of Bacon.

992   RITTER, OTTO. De Roberti Greeni Fabula: Friar Bacon and Friar
        Bungay. Thoruni: E. Lambeck, 1866, 38pp.
            Examines Greene's use of Friar Bacon as a source; com-
        pares play and prose tract. Shows "that the stories of...
        [the] prose-tract are not original productions that dated
        from Bacon, but were in the course of time attributed to
        him."

993   SANDYS, JOHN EDWIN. "Roger Bacon in English Literature," in
        Roger Bacon: Essays Contributed by Various Writers on the
        Occasion of the Commemoration of the Seventh Centenary of
        His Birth. Edited by A[ndrew] G[eorge] Little. Oxford:
        Clarendon Press, 1914, pp. 359-72.
            Discusses Friar Bacon in context of examination of de-
        piction of Bacon in English literature; provides liberal
        extracts from work.

994   SENN, WERNER. "Robert Greene's Handling of Source Material in
        Friar Bacon and Friar Bungay." ES, 54 (December 1973),
        544-53.
            Discusses Greene's selection and expansion of details
        from Friar Bacon.

The Famous History of George a Green

THE FAMOUS HISTORY OF GEORGE A GREEN, PINDAR OF THE TOWN OF WAKEFIELD

In manuscript; first published 1706.

Editions

995   The History of George a Green, Pindar of the Town of Wakefield,
      in A Collection of Early Prose Romances, Vol. II. Edited
      by William J. Thoms. London: William Pickering, 1828,
      69pp. (separately paginated). [Also published separately.]
          Provides reprint of unidentified edition (probably that
      of 1706). In introductory notes (pp. iii-xi) lists allu-
      sions to and treatments of the George a Green story.

996   History of George a Greene, Pindar of the Town of Wakefield,
      in Early English Prose Romances. Edited by William J.
      Thoms. Revised and enlarged edition. London: G. Routledge
      and Sons; New York: E. P. Dutton & Co., [1907], pp. 557-99.
      Reprint of 995.

997   The History of George a Green, in Some Old English Worthies.
      Edited by Dorothy Senior. London: S. Swift and Co., 1912,
      pp. 123-75.
          Provides annotated, modernized reprint of 1706 edition.

Studies

998   ALBRIGHT, EVELYN MAY. "Eating a Citation." MLN, 30 (November
      1915), 201-206.
          Discusses Famous History of George a Greene, which was
      probably written before 1593, as source for the eating of
      seals in George a Greene, the Pinner of Wakefield and Sir
      John Oldcastle.

999   HORSMAN, E. A. "Introduction," in The Pinder of Wakefield.
      Edited by E. A. Horsman. English Reprints Series, 12.
      Liverpool: Liverpool University Press, 1956, pp. vii-xii.
          Discusses relationship between The Famous History of
      George a Greene, The Pindar of Wakefield, and the play
      George a Greene.

1000 NELSON, MALCOLM ANTHONY. "The Robin Hood Tradition in English
      Literature in the Sixteenth and Seventeenth Centuries."
      Ph.D. dissertation, Northwestern University, 1961, 274pp.
      See 1001.

1001 NELSON, MALCOLM A[NTHONY]. The Robin Hood Tradition in the
      English Renaissance. Salzburg Studies in English

The Famous History of George a Green

>Literature, ElizS, 14. Salzburg: Institut für Englische
>Sprache und Literatur, Universität Salzburg, 1973, 269pp.
>   Discusses The Famous History of George a Greene as "a
>representation of the state of the [Robin Hood] tradition
>at the beginning of the seventeenth century." Argues that
>the prose work is not the source of the play George a
>Greene; examines anonymous author's use of Munday and
>Chettle's The Downfall of Robert, Earl of Huntington and
>The Death of Robert, Earl of Huntington as sources for the
>Famous History (pp. 98-112, 168-71).

1002   NELSON, MALCOLM A[NTHONY]. "The Sources of George A Greene,
>the Pinner of Wakefield." PQ, 42 (April 1963), 159-65.
>   Argues that The Famous History of George a Greene is not
>the source of the play. Discusses possible sources of the
>romance and its relationship to Robin Hood legend.

1003   PENNEL, CHARLES ALEXANDER. "A Critical Edition of George a
>Greene, the Pinner of Wakefield." Ph.D. dissertation, Uni-
>versity of Illinois at Urbana-Champaign, 1962, 265pp.
>   Discusses use of Famous History of George a Greene as a
>source for the play.

FENTON, SIR GEOFFREY (1539?-1608)

Matteo Bandello, Certaine Tragicall Discourses. STC 10791-10792.

Editions

1004   BANDELLO, MATTEO. Certain Tragical Discourses of Bandello.
>Translated by Geoffrey Fenton. Introduction by Robert
>Langton Douglas. 2 vols. Tudor Translations, 19-20.
>Edited by W. E. Henley. London: David Nutt, 1898, 333,
>317pp.
>   Reprints text of 1567 edition. In "Introduction," (I,
>vii-lviii) discusses Fenton's handling of Belleforest's
>version, the autobiographical elements in the interpola-
>tions, the influence of Fenton's "nascent Puritanism" on
>his additions, his didacticism, and his style (especially
>its euphuistic qualities). Also argues that Fenton's trans-
>lation is the object of Ascham's attack on Italian tales.
>"Introduction" reprinted in 1005.

1005   BANDELLO, MATTEO. Bandello: Tragical Tales. Translated by
>Geoffrey Fenton. Edited by Hugh Harris. Introduction by
>Robert Langton Douglas. Broadway Translations. London:
>G. Routledge & Sons; New York: E. P. Dutton & Co., [1923?],
>572pp.

Provides modernized text based on 1567 edition. Reprints "Introduction" to 1004 (pp. 1-37).

Studies

1006   BASKERVILL, C. R. "Bandello and The Broken Heart." MLN, 28
        (February 1913), 51-52.
             Suggests Fenton's translation of the story of Livio and
        Camilla (Discourse 11) might have influenced Ford.

1007   BOOTHE, BERT E. "The Contributions of the Italian Novella to
        the Formation and Development of Elizabethan Prose Fiction,
        1566-1582." Ph.D. dissertation, University of Michigan,
        1936.
             Provides detailed analysis of Fenton's translations of
        Italian tales in Certain Tragical Discourses: examines his
        handling of the originals (especially his variations), his
        style, his themes, and the "Puritanical outlook" of the
        tales.

1008   BULLOUGH, GEOFFREY. "Introduction [to Othello]," in Narrative
        and Dramatic Sources of Shakespeare, Vol. VII. Edited by
        Geoffrey Bullough. London: Routledge and Kegan Paul;
        New York: Columbia University Press, 1973, 193-238.
             Discusses tale of "Albanoys Captain" as possible source
        for Othello. Notes that Fenton expanded "Bandello's 2,200
        words to 10,500" and in contrast to Bandello "tried to enter
        the minds of the characters, and described in detail the
        symptom of melancholy and the needless turmoil of jealousy."

1009   FELLHEIMER, JEANETTE. "Geoffrey Fenton: A Study in Elizabe-
        than Translation." Ph.D. dissertation, Yale University,
        1941, 335pp.
             Examines Fenton's treatment of Belleforest's text, his
        didacticism, his interpolation of personal attitudes toward
        religion and women, and his euphuistic style. Also examines
        influence of Certain Tragical Discourses on Elizabethan
        prose fiction.

1010   FELLHEIMER, JEANETTE. "Some Words in Geoffrey Fenton's Cer-
        taine Tragicall Discourses." MLN, 61 (December 1946),
        538-40.
             Provides antedatings and additions to OED. Calls vo-
        cabulary "richer than in any of his later translations."

1011   GOTTLIEB, STEPHEN A. "Fenton's Novelle." RLC, 40, no. 1
        (1966), 121-28.

Fenton

Discusses relationships between Fenton's "heavy moralizing tendencies" and his rhetorical techniques, characterization, political bias, narrative techniques, and "the
Elizabethan world view."

1012   HOOK, FRANK S.   "Introduction," in The French Bandello: A
       Selection.   The Original Texts of Four of Belleforest's
       Histoires tragiques Translated by Geoffrey Fenton and Wil-
       liam Painter, Anno 1567.   Edited by Frank S. Hook.   Univer-
       sity of Missouri Studies, 22, no. 1.   Columbia: University
       of Missouri, 1948, pp. 9-51.
            Examines Fenton's handling of Belleforest's text (par-
       ticularly his expansions), his style, his treatment of love,
       and the influence of his Puritanism on his treatment of the
       text.

1013   KOEPPEL, EMIL.   Studien zur Geschichte der italienischen
       Novelle in der englischen Litteratur des sechzehnten Jahr-
       hunderts.   Quellen und Forschungen, 70.   Strassburg: K. J.
       Trübner, 1892, 106pp.
            Identifies Italian sources of Certain Tragical Discourses
       (pp. 13-17).

1014   McCARRON, WILLIAM E.   "Othello and Fenton: An Addendum."
       N&Q, NS, 13 (April 1966), 137-38.
            Adds to Siegel's evidence (1018) that Shakespeare used
       Certain Tragical Discourses as a source.

1015   MILLS, LAURENS J.   One Soul in Bodies Twain: Friendship in
       Tudor Literature and Stuart Drama.   Bloomington, Indiana:
       Principia Press, 1937, 480pp.
            Discusses Fenton's treatment of friendship theme in Cer-
       tain Tragical Discourses (pp. 175-82).

1016   PRESSON, ROBERT K.   "Marston's Dutch Courtezan: The Study of
       an Attitude in Adaptation."   JEGP, 55, no. 3 (1956), 406-13.
            Focuses on differences between play and story of Countess
       of Celant, Marston's probable source.

1017   PRUVOST, RENÉ.   Matteo Bandello and Elizabethan Fiction.
       Bibliothèque de la Revue de Littérature Comparée, 113.
       Paris: H. Champion, 1937, 349pp.
            Analyzes Fenton's language, "rhetorical amplifications,"
       and added moral emphasis in his adaptations of Bellefor-
       est's translations of Bandello.   Compares his adaptation of
       several tales with other translations/adaptations (passim).

1017a ROSSI, SERGIO. "Goodly histories, tragicall matters, and
       other morall argument: La novella italiana nel Cinquecento
       inglese," in <u>Contributi dell'Istituto di filologia moderna</u>.
       Edited by Sergio Rossi. Pubblicazioni della Università
       Cattolica del Sacro Cuore, Serie Inglese, 1. Milan: Vita
       e Pensiero, 1974, pp. 39-112.
            Surveys publications of 1566-1567 to place <u>Certain Tragi-
       cal Discourses</u> and Painter's <u>Palace of Pleasure</u> in context
       of continuing development of literature with a moral empha-
       sis. Discusses Fenton's moral intent, his handling of the
       texts, his style, and the dramatic qualities of the tales.

1018   SIEGEL, PAUL N. "A New Source for <u>Othello</u>?" <u>PMLA</u>, 75 (Sep-
       tember 1960), 480.
            Suggests story of "Albanoys Captain" as possible source.
       <u>See</u> 1014.

1019   STARNES, D. T. "Geoffrey Fenton, Seneca, and Shakespeare's
       <u>Lucrece</u>." <u>PQ</u>, 43 (April 1964), 280-83.
            Points out analogue to passage in <u>Lucrece</u> in story of
       Bishop Loys Gonsaga's rape of Julia.

<u>FIDGE, GEORGE</u>

<u>Hind's Ramble</u>. Wing F854.

<u>The English Gusman: or the History of That Unparallel'd Thief James
    Hind</u>. Wing F852.

Studies

1020   FALLER, LINCOLN B. "The Myth of Captain James Hind: A Type
       of Primitive Fiction before Defoe." <u>BNYPL</u>, 79 (Winter
       1976), 139-66.
            Discusses <u>Hind's Ramble</u> and <u>The English Gusman</u> in the
       context of the narratives of Hind's adventures. Discusses
       the use of <u>Hind's Ramble</u> as a source of later narratives
       and argues that the work is "offered up as nothing more
       than aids to wish fulfillment." Discusses the relationship
       of the Hind narratives to later pamphlets on highwaymen.

<u>FORDE, EMANUEL</u> (fl. 1607)

<u>The Famous Historie of Montelyon, Knight of the Oracle</u>. <u>STC</u> 11167.
    Wing F1523-1531.

Forde

The Most Pleasant Historie of Ornatus and Artesia. STC 11168–11170.
Wing F1531A, F1541–1543.

Parismus, the Renowned Prince of Bohemia. STC 11171–11175. Wing
F1521–1522, F1532–1540, F1544–1545.

Editions

1021   FORDE, EMANUEL. The Most Pleasant History of Ornatus and Artesia, in Shorter Novels: Seventeenth Century. Edited by
Philip Henderson. Everyman's Library, 841. London: J. M.
Dent & Sons; New York: E. P. Dutton & Co., 1930, pp. 1–143.
Provides modernized reprint of 1634 edition. In "Introduction," pp. x–xii, discusses briefly the setting, which
provides the "chief pleasure" for today's readers.

Studies

1022   BONHEIM, HELMUT. "Emanuel Forde: Ornatus and Artesia."
Anglia, 90, nos. 1–2 (1972), 43–59.
Points out popularity of Forde's prose fiction in seventeenth century. Suggests that Ornatus and Artesia is the
best and "most readable" of Forde's works, and examines the
textual history of the work, its structure, Forde's use of
conventional "novel" elements, and his style.

1023   FALKE, AMELIA ANNE. "Medieval and Popular Elements in the
Romances of Emanuel Forde." Ph.D. dissertation, Michigan
State University, 1974, 305pp.
Analyzes the interlace structure of Forde's prose fic-
tion, his style, and his treatment of love and female
characters.

1024   LOISEAU, JEAN. "Le Récit dans le roman d'Emmanuel Ford:
Ornatus and Artesia," in Récit et roman: Formes du roman
anglais du XVIe au XXe siècle. Études Anglaises, 42.
Paris: Didier, 1972, pp. 16–21.
Argues that although Forde made use of the conventions
of Greek and chivalric romance, his frequent prosaic or
ironic treatment of events and characters suggests a dis-
creet protest against these conventions. Examines plot,
character, and style in his prose fiction.

FORTESCUE, THOMAS

Pedro Mexía, The Foreste or Collection of Histories, Dooen Out of
Frenche. STC 17849–17850.

Studies

1025 BATTENHOUSE, ROY W[ESLEY]. Marlowe's Tamburlaine: A Study in
Renaissance Moral Philosophy. Nashville: Vanderbilt Uni-
versity Press, 1941, 283pp.
Includes discussion of Marlowe's use of Fortescue's The
Forest as a source for his play (passim).

1026 BROOKE, C. F. TUCKER. "'Figging'--Fortescue's Foreste." MLN,
25 (March 1910), 95-96.
Discusses occurrence of word in Fortescue's translation.

1027 BROOKE, C. F. TUCKER. "Marlowe's Tamburlaine." MLN, 25
(March 1910), 93-94.
Discusses briefly The Forest as a source for Tamburlaine.

1028 IZARD, THOMAS C. "The Principal Source for Marlowe's Tamburlaine." MLN, 58 (June 1943), 411-17.
Argues that The Forest is not Marlowe's source.

1029 ROLLINS, HYDER E. "Notes on the Sources of Melbancke's
Philotimus." Harvard Studies and Notes in Philology and
Literature, 18 (1936), 177-98.
Points out Melbancke's extensive borrowings from The
Forest.

1030 ROLLINS, HYDER E. "Thomas Deloney's Euphuistic Learning and
The Forest." PMLA, 50 (September 1935), 679-86.
Discusses The Forest as source of Deloney's learning and
euphuistic style. Observes that The Forest "is largely
fiction, but it is not a novel or a series of tales."

1031 SPENCE, LESLIE. "The Influence of Marlowe's Sources on Tamburlaine I." MP, 24 (November 1926), 181-99.
Discusses Marlowe's use of details from The Forest and
argues that it and the other sources gave "the play most of
its so-called Marlowesque features."

1032 SPENCE, LESLIE. "Tamburlaine and Marlowe." PMLA, 42 (September 1927), 604-22.
Discusses Marlowe's use of The Forest in his conception
of Tamburlaine's character. Observes that Fortescue's
translation stresses "Tamburlaine's ability, the glory of
his career, his courtesy, the love and awe of his follow-
ers" and presents him as above both human and moral law.

G., T.

G., T.

The Right Pleasant and Variable Tragicall Historie of Fortunatus.
  (Translation from Dutch.) Wing R1509-1510.

Studies

1033   COLLIER, J[OHN] PAYNE. "Thomas Churchyard and the Romance of
       Fortunatus." N&Q, 37 (4 January 1868), 2-3.
          Describes and prints portion of Churchyard's verse ab-
       stract of work. Also describes 1676 edition. See 1036.

1034   HERFORD, CHARLES H. Studies in the Literary Relations of
       England and Germany in the Sixteenth Century. Cambridge:
       Cambridge University Press, 1886, 456pp.
          In Appendix III ("The English Prose Versions of Fortuna-
       tus," pp. 405-407) compares 1650? version with the 1676
       version.

1035   LANGE, ALEXIS F[REDERICK]. "On the Relation of Old Fortunatus
       to the Volksbuch." MLN, 18 (May 1903), 141-44.
          Compares the translation with the German original and
       argues that the English version was the source of the
       earlier version of Dekker's Old Fortunatus.

1036   M., J. "Fortunatus: Thomas Churchyard." N&Q, 37 (28 March
       1868), 295.
          Notes that 1682 edition also includes Churchyard's verse
       abstract of the romance. See 1033.

1037   MAUGERI, ALDO. Studi su Thomas Dekker. Messina: Grafiche La
       Sicilia, 1958, 117pp.
          Includes discussion of Dekker's use of Fortunatus as
       source for Old Fortunatus (pp. 38-61).

GAINSFORD, THOMAS (d. 1624?)

The Historie of Trebizond. STC 11521.

Studies

1038   ERATH, JOHN FRANCIS. "The Life and Works of Thomas Gainsford:
       A Jacobean Hack Writer." Ph.D. dissertation, Rutgers Uni-
       versity, 1968, 213pp.
          Discusses History of Trebizond, calling it Gainsford's
       "greatest literary achievement...and the most successful
       romance in imitation of Sidney's Arcadia in the first half
       of the seventeenth century."

1039   TING, NAI TUNG. "Studies in English Prose and Poetic Romances in the First Half of the Seventeenth Century." Ph.D. dissertation, Harvard University, 1941, 360pp.
        Finds that Trebizond "owed little to Sidney in plot, but was Arcadian in its style, structure, and components." Concludes that work "overdid the worst features of the Arcadian style and was entirely lacking in artistic merit."

GASCOIGNE, GEORGE (1542?-1577)

A Pleasant Discourse of the Adventures of Master F. I., in A Hundreth Sundrie Flowres. STC 11635. (Revised as The Pleasant Fable of Ferdinando Ieronimi and Leonora de Valasco, in The Posies of G. Gascoigne. STC 11636-11639.)

The Pleasant Tale of Hemetes the Hermite. British Library MS. Royal 18.A.48. STC 7596.

Bibliographies

1040   JOHNSON, ROBERT C. "George Gascoigne, 1941-1966," in Elizabethan Bibliographies Supplements, IX: Minor Elizabethans: Roger Ascham, 1946-1966; George Gascoigne, 1941-1966; John Heywood, 1944-1966; Thomas Kyd, 1940-1966; Anthony Munday, 1941-1966. Compiled by Robert C. Johnson. London: Nether Press, 1968, 19-25.
        Provides chronological list of editions and criticism, 1941-1966; supplements 1043.

1041   MILLS, JERRY LEATH. "Recent Studies in Gascoigne." ELR, 3 (Spring 1973), 322-27.
        Provides commentary on selected critical studies arranged under various headings. Notes that only Gascoigne's prose fiction has been the subject of detailed study. Includes selective list of studies.

1042   PRICE, JOHN EDWARD. "A Secondary Bibliography of George Gascoigne with an Introduction Summarizing the Trend of Gascoigne Scholarship." BB, 25 (May-August 1968), 138-40.
        Lists nine items chronologically in section headed "Prose." Concludes that after early neglect, current interest in Gascoigne studies is on Master F. J.

1043   TANNENBAUM, SAMUEL A. George Gascoigne (A Concise Bibliography). Elizabethan Bibliographies, 26. New York: Samuel A. Tannenbaum, 1942, 22pp.
        Provides classified listing of editions and studies. Continued by 1040.

Gascoigne

Editions

1044   GASCOIGNE, GEORGE. The Hermit's Tale at Woodstock, in The
        Progresses and Public Processions of Queen Elizabeth, Vol.
        I. Edited by John Nichols. London: J. Nichols and Son,
        1823, 553-84.
            Reprints British Library MS. Royal 18.A.48.

1045   GASCOIGNE, GEORGE. The Complete Poems of George Gascoigne.
        Edited by William Carew Hazlitt. 2 vols. London: Rox-
        burghe Library, 1869-1870, 552, 360pp.
            Provides reprint of The Pleasant Fable of Ferdinando
        Jeronimi and Leonora de Valasco from 1575 edition (I, 415-
        86). Also includes reprint of The Hermit's Tale from
        British Library MS. Royal 18.A.48. (II, 135-70). In "Pre-
        face" (I, v-xxx) discusses bibliographical problems of A
        Hundred Sundry Flowers and argues that 1575 edition should
        be preferred over the "spurious" one of 1573.

1046   [The Tale of Hemetes the Hermit,] in The Queen's Majesty's
        Entertainment at Woodstock, 1575. Edited by A[lfred] W[il-
        liam] Pollard. Oxford: H. Daniel and H. Hart, 1903, pp.
        xvi-xxii.
            Reprints text from unique fragment of 1575 edition. In
        "Preface," pp. v-xv, discusses publication of work and
        points out that Gascoigne was not author.

1047   GASCOIGNE, GEORGE. The Complete Works of George Gascoigne.
        Edited by John W. Cunliffe. 2 vols. Cambridge English
        Classics. Cambridge: Cambridge University Press, 1907-
        1910, 506, 600pp.
            Reprints text of The Pleasant Fable of Ferdinando
        Jeronimi and Leonora de Valasco from 1575 edition (I, 383-
        453) and Hemetes the Hermit from British Library MS. Royal
        18.A.48 (II, 473-510).

1048   CUNLIFFE, J[OHN] W. "The Queenes Majesties Entertainment at
        Woodstocke." PMLA, 26 (March 1911), 92-141.
            Reprints text of 1585 edition, which includes Hemetes
        the Hermit. Points out that Gascoigne was not author of
        tale but used it as vehicle to exhibit his skills as a
        translator. Identifies the hermit as Sir Henry Lee, Queen's
        Champion.

*1049   GASCOIGNE, GEORGE. "An Edition, with Introduction, Notes, and
        Glossary, of George Gascoigne's A Hundreth Sundrie Flowres."
        Edited by C[harles] T[yler] Prouty. Ph.D. dissertation,
        Cambridge University, 1939.
            See 1050.

1050   GASCOIGNE, GEORGE. George Gascoigne's A Hundreth Sundrie
        Flowres. Edited by C[harles] T[yler] Prouty. University
        of Missouri Studies, 17, no. 2. Columbia: University of
        Missouri, 1942, 305pp.
            Provides critical edition based on 1573 edition. In
        "Introduction," pp. 9-43, discusses the bibliographical his-
        tory of the work, the date of publication, and the problem
        of authorship (argues that Gascoigne was sole author).

1051   GASCOIGNE, GEORGE. The Pleasant Fable of Ferdinando Jeronimi
        and Leonora de Valasco, Translated out of the Italian Riding
        Tales of Bartello, in Elizabethan Fiction. Edited by Robert
        Ashley and Edwin M. Moseley. San Francisco: Rinehart
        Press, 1953, pp. 1-81.
            Provide partly modernized text based on 1047. In "In-
        troduction" (pp. ix-x) note differences from the conventions
        of medieval romance and suggest that Gascoigne's major con-
        tribution to the development of the novel is his "presenta-
        tion of a specific and real situation rather than an ideal
        one."

1052   GASCOIGNE, GEORGE. The Adventures of Master F. J., in Eliza-
        bethan Prose Fiction. Edited by Merritt [E.] Lawlis.
        Indianapolis: Odyssey Press, Bobbs-Merrill Co., 1967,
        pp. 31-111.
            Provides partly modernized text based on 1573 edition.
        In introductory note argues that Master F. J. is a novel if
        judged by Henry James's criteria. Suggests that the most
        striking aspect of the work is Gascoigne's "consistent at-
        tempt to suggest, without the aid of omniscience, the inner
        life of his characters."

1053   GASCOIGNE, GEORGE. A Hundred Sundry Flowers, 1573. Menston,
        England: Scolar Press, 1970, 469pp.
            Provides facsimile reprint of British Library copy of
        1573 edition.

Studies

1054   ADAMS, ROBERT P. "Gascoigne's Master F. J. as Original Fic-
        tion." PMLA, 73 (September 1958), 315-26.
            Through an examination of the place of Master F. J. in
        the context of A Hundred Sundry Flowers and of the complex
        role of G. T. as the author/narrator who maintains the
        comic focus, argues that Gascoigne created a piece of ori-
        ginal imaginative fiction--one' which creates an impression
        of reality--not an autobiographical work or a roman à clef.

Gascoigne

1055   AMBROSE, GENEVIEVE. Review of <u>A Hundreth Sundrie Flowres</u>,
        edited by B[ernard] M[ordaunt] Ward. <u>MLR</u>, 22 (April 1927),
        214-20.
           Takes issue with several of Ward's conclusions (1107).
        Notes that "each of the original hundred 'sundrie flowres'
        ...is mentioned by title or theme" in <u>Master F. J.</u> Suggests
        that there were two issues of the 1573 edition (<u>see</u> 1073).

1056   ANDERAU, ALFRED. <u>George Gascoignes</u> The Adventures of Master
        F. J.<u>: Analyse und Interpretation</u>. SAA, 57. Bern:
        Francke, 1966, 160pp.
           Analyzes character, setting, structure, narrative tech-
        niques, and role of narrator.

1057   ANON. "A Pioneer Novel." <u>TLS</u>, 19 September 1942, p. 463.
           Discusses <u>Master F. J.</u> as the "first English psychologi-
        cal novel."

1058   ARDOLINO, FRANK. "The Fictionalization of Master F.J.: An
        Analysis of Gascoigne's <u>The Pleasant Fable</u>...." <u>Essays in</u>
        <u>Literature: A Journal of Graduate Scholarship</u>, 1, no. 2
        (June 1973), 1-16.
           Denies that Gascoigne revised <u>Master F. J.</u> "merely to
        obviate charges of slander." Argues that because audience
        misunderstood his moral intentions in <u>Master F. J.</u>, Gas-
        coigne changed his narrative techniques and expurgated the
        text in the <u>Pleasant Fable</u> "in order to clarify his strong
        moral purpose."

1059   BOWERS, FREDSON THAYER. "Notes on Gascoigne's <u>A Hundreth</u>
        <u>Sundrie Flowres</u> and <u>The Posies</u>." <u>Harvard Studies and Notes</u>
        <u>in Philology and Literature</u>, 16 (1934), 13-35.
           Argues that Bartello is an Italianized form of "Batte,"
        the nickname of Gascoigne's close friend Bartholmew Withi-
        poll--Gascoigne attributed the revision of <u>Master F. J.</u> to
        the fictitious Bartello as a "pleasant joke" on his friend.
        Also discusses the publication of <u>A Hundred Sundry Flowers</u>.

1060   BRADNER, LEICESTER. "The First English Novel: A Study of
        George Gascoigne's <u>Adventures of Master F. J.</u>" <u>PMLA</u>, 45
        (June 1930), 543-52.
           Sees the work as a "realistic portrayal of English upper
        class life" based on an actual incident. Argues that Gas-
        coigne's development of plot and character and his integra-
        tion of poems, letters, and <u>questioni d'amore</u> result in a
        fully developed picture of life.

1061   BRADNER, LEICESTER. "Point of View in George Gascoigne's
       Fiction." SSF, 3 (Fall 1965), 16-22.
           Analyzes the role of G. T. and Gascoigne's artistry in
       the creation of the consistent point of view of the editor/
       narrator.

1062   BROOKS, E. ST. JOHN. "Gascoigne and Hatton." TLS, 16 January
       1937, p. 44.
           Points out parallels between incidents in Master F. J.
       and life of Christopher Hatton to support Ward's identifi-
       cation of F. J. with Hatton (1107). Suggests that Elinor
       was Elizabeth Cavendish.

1063   CUNLIFFE, JOHN W. "George Gascoigne," in The Cambridge History
       of English Literature, III: Renascence and Reformation.
       Edited by A[dolphus] W[illiam] Ward and A[lfred] R[ayney]
       Waller. Cambridge: Cambridge University Press, 1909,
       201-10.
           Discusses Master F. J. in context of Gascoigne's other
       writings; calls work "the first prose tale of modern life"
       and offers evidence identifying Bartello with Gascoigne.

1064   DAVIS, WALTER R[ICHARDSON]. Idea and Act in Elizabethan Fic-
       tion. Princeton: Princeton University Press, 1969, 311pp.
           Examines Master F. J. (both versions) as example of
       "courtly fiction." Interprets work as a testing of an ideal
       (courtly love) against the actual. Discusses function of
       narrator as "comic realist" (pp. 97-109).

1065   EIN, RONALD BORIS. "The Serpent's Voice: Commentary and
       Readers' Beliefs in Elizabethan Fiction." Ph.D. disserta-
       tion, Indiana University, 1974, 273pp.
           Analyzes implied narrator commentary in "the narrator
       summary" at the beginning of Master F. J.

1066   FIELER, FRANK B. "Gascoigne's Use of Courtly Love Conventions
       in The Adventures Passed by Master F. J." SSF, 1 (Fall
       1963), 26-32.
           Examines Gascoigne's use of courtly love conventions to
       achieve comic effect.

1067   FRIEDERICH, REINHARD H. "Myself Am Centre of My Circling
       Thought: Studies in Baroque Personae (Burton and Donne)."
       Ph.D. dissertation, University of Washington, 1971, 194pp.
           Argues that because of "character credibility and flexi-
       bility rather than plot manipulation" Master F. J. and
       Nashe's Unfortunate Traveller "succeed, whereas Greene and
       Deloney fail since their static characters cannot generate
       more than didactic or simply cumulative structures."

175

Gascoigne

1068   GARKE, ESTHER. The Use of Songs in Elizabethan Prose Fiction. Bern: Francke Verlag, 1972, 132pp.
     Draws frequently on Master F. J. for examples in analysis of types of songs, their relationships to plot and structure, and their functions (to complement or contrast setting, to present character relationships, to characterize singer and audience).

1069   GASCOIGNE, GEORGE. A Hundreth Sundrie Flowres: From the Original Edition of 1573. Edited by B[ernard] M[ordaunt] Ward. 2d edition. Edited by Ruth Loyd Miller. Port Washington, New York: Kennikat Press for Minos Publishing Co., 1975, 412pp.
     Provides facsimile reprint of 1107 and reprint of 1106 with additional notes by editor.

1070   GISELA, JUNKE. "Formen des Dialogs im frühen englischen Roman." Ph.D. dissertation, University of Köln, 1975, 150pp.
     Examines form and use of dialogue in Master F. J. See 208.

1071   GOING, WILLIAM T. "Gascoigne and the Term 'Sonnet Sequence.'" N&Q, NS, 1 (May 1954), 189-91.
     Discusses use of the term in Master F. J.

1072   GOTTFRIED, RUDOLF. "Autobiography and Art: An Elizabethan Borderland," in Literary Criticism and Historical Understanding: Selected Papers from the English Institute. Edited by Phillip Damon. New York: Columbia University Press, 1967, pp. 109-34.
     Includes discussion of Gascoigne's use of G. T. to fuse "elements which he implies to be autobiographical and elements which he draws from literary tradition."

1073   GREG, W[ALTER] W[ILSON]. "A Hundreth Sundrie Flowres." MLR, 22 (October 1927), 441-42.
     Corrects Ambrose's theory that there were two issues of the 1573 edition of A Hundred Sundry Flowers (1055).

1074   GREG, W[ALTER] W[ILSON]. "A Hundreth Sundry Flowers." Library, 4th Ser., 7 (December 1926), 267-82.
     Argues against several of Ward's conclusions (1107), especially the identification of F. J. as Christopher Hatton. Suggests that A Hundred Sundry Flowers was published March 1572/3.

1075   HELGERSON, RICHARD. The Elizabethan Prodigals. Berkeley: University of California Press, 1976, 188pp.

Includes discussion of Gascoigne's use of the Prodigal
Son motif in Master F. J. (passim).

1076 HENNING, RICHARD. George Gascoigne als Übersetzer italien-
ischer Dichtungen. Königsberg: Gutenberg-Druckerei, 1913,
121pp.
Assumes that Gascoigne means "Bandello" rather than
"Bartello" in indentfying source of revision and proceeds
to trace sources of revised version of Master F. J. in Bandello's novels. Comments on style (pp. 70-78).

1077 JOHNSON, RONALD C[ONANT]. George Gascoigne. TEAS, 133. New
York: Twayne Publishers, 1972, 167pp.
In chapter on Master F. J. (pp. 119-36) discusses narrative technique, characterization, satire, poetry criticism,
and style (particularly Gascoigne's bawdy). Emphasizes
critical treatment of courtly love tradition.

1078 JORDAN, JOHN CLARK. "Greene and Gascoigne." MLN, 30 (February
1915), 61-62.
Points out that The Pleasant Fable is Greene's source for
a portion of A Disputation between a He and a She Conny-
Catcher.

1079 KITTLE, WILLIAM. Edward de Vere, Seventeenth Earl of Oxford,
1550-1604. Washington, D. C.: Buchanan Co., 1935, 252pp.
Argues that Oxford was author of Hemetes the Hermit and
was figured in the Hermit and Hemetes, and that he was the
author of works assigned to Gascoigne (passim).

1080 KITTLE, WILLIAM. Edward de Vere, 17th Earl of Oxford, and
Shakespeare. Baltimore: Monumental Printing Co., 1942,
223pp.
In Chapter X ("A Study of the Name of George Gascoigne,"
pp. 64-68), identifies Oxford as the author of Master F. J.
and Hemetes the Hermit; also identifies Oxford as the Hermit
in the latter work.

1081 KITTLE, WILLIAM. G. Gascoigne, April 1562 to January 1, 1578,
or Edward de Vere Seventeenth Earl of Oxford, 1550-1604.
Washington, D. C.: W. F. Roberts Co., 1930, 217pp.
In attempting to prove that Gascoigne's works are by Oxford, argues that Hemetes the Hermit was delivered orally
by Oxford to Elizabeth at Woodstock; that the work is "in
defense of his relations with his wife and her father, William Cecil, and also in defense of his then recent escape
into Holland"; and that he wrote the four-language version
in 1575. Points out some differences in text between 1585
edition of Hemetes the Hermit and MS. Royal 18.A.48 (passim).

Gascoigne

1082   KRIEGER, GOTTFRIED. <u>Gedichteinlagen im englischen Roman</u>.
        Ph.D. dissertation, University of Köln. Köln: n.p., 1969,
        274pp.
            Includes discussion of function and relation to theme and
        structure of verse insets in <u>Master F. J.</u> (passim).

1083   LANHAM, RICHARD A[LAN]. "Narrative Structure in Gascoigne's
        <u>F. J.</u>" <u>SSF</u>, 4 (Fall 1966), 42–50.
            Argues that the structure of <u>Master F. J.</u> is that of a
        sonnet sequence, thus the work should not be read as a
        novel.

1084   LANHAM, RICHARD [ALAN]. "Opaque Style in Elizabethan Prose
        Fiction." <u>PCP</u>, 1 (1966), 25–31.
            Examines tension between language and plot in <u>Master F.
        J.</u> by analyzing how Gascoigne provides an ironic context
        for F. J.'s rhetoric. Argues that rhetoric is "the subject
        of the fiction."

1085   LONG, PERCY WALDRON. "From <u>Troilus</u> to <u>Euphues</u>," in <u>Anniversary
        Papers by Colleagues and Pupils of George Lyman Kittredge</u>.
        Edited by F. N. Robinson. Boston: Ginn and Co., 1913,
        pp. 367–76.
            Discusses <u>Master F. J.</u> as a novel and examines its place
        in the development of early prose fiction. Traces influence
        on character, phrasing, and incident in Grange's <u>Golden
        Aphroditis</u>.

1086   McGRATH, LYNETTE F[AY]. "George Gascoigne's Moral Satire:
        The Didactic Use of Convention in <u>The Adventures Passed by
        Master F. J.</u>" <u>JEGP</u>, 70, no. 3 (1971), 432–50.
            Discusses F. J. as "negative moral example" and argues
        that Gascoigne has "a moral, Christian purpose of dissuasion
        from promiscuity and irresponsibility, and persuasion to
        proper charitable love" whose end is marriage. Argues that
        Gascoigne relies heavily on Andreas Capellanus's <u>Art of
        Courtly Love</u> and discusses ironic use to which he puts bor-
        rowings from the treatise. Also considers how Gascoigne
        ironically juxtaposes "the sensual consequences of the
        courtly love convention with the Platonic idealizations of
        the Italianate poetic conventions."

1087   McGRATH, LYNETTE FAY. "Studies in the Norms and Techniques of
        Sixteenth-Century English Satire from Skelton to Donne."
        Ph.D. dissertation, University of Illinois at Urbana-Cham-
        paign, 1968, 625pp.
            Includes examination of irony in <u>Master F. J.</u>

1088   McNEIR, WALDO F.   "Ariosto's Sospetto, Gascoigne's Suspicion,
        and Spenser's Malbecco," in Festschrift für Walther Fischer.
        Heidelberg: Carl Winter, 1959, pp. 34-48.
            Argues against Nelson's conclusion (1090) that Spenser
        used Master F. J. as source. Examines Gascoigne's use of
        Ariosto as a source, particularly his additions which create
        "psychological vividness" and his changes in the characteri-
        zation "to illustrate the doubts that perturb the hero
        [F. J.] when he begins to fear" that Elinor had returned to
        the secretary.

1089   McNEIR, WALDO F.   "Heywood's Sources for the Main Plot of A
        Woman Killed with Kindness," in Studies in the English
        Renaissance Drama in Memory of Karl Julius Holzknecht.
        Edited by Josephine W[aters] Bennett, Oscar Cargill, and
        Vernon Hall, Jr.   New York: New York University Press,
        1959, pp. 189-211.
            Compares Frances's story of the gentleman "married to a
        very fair gentlewoman" with Greene's "improvement" of the
        story in A Disputation between a He Conny-Catcher and a She
        Conny-Catcher and Heywood's use of it in A Woman Killed with
        Kindness, which emphasized the characterization of the hus-
        band.

1090   NELSON, WILLIAM.   "A Source for Spenser's Malbecco." MLN, 68
        (April 1953), 226-29.
            Suggests that from the "unpromising materials" of Master
        F. J., Spenser constructed the tale of Malbecco and Helle-
        nore (Faerie Queene, III. ix-x.). Cites close parallels
        between the fable of Suspicion and the description of Mal-
        becco; suggests Hellenore is modelled on F. J.'s "Helen-
        Elinor." See 1088.

*1091   OKUMA, SAKAE.   "George Gascoigne." Oberon, 15, no. 2 (1974),
        66-76.
            Not located. In Japanese. Listed in MLA International
        Bibliography for 1975, I:#3170.

1092   PARRISH, PAUL A.   "The Multiple Perspectives of Gascoigne's
        The Adventures of Master F. J." SSF, 10 (Winter 1973),
        75-84.
            Reacts against popular "romantic" view of F. J. and "re-
        alistic" view of G. T. by analyzing the complexity of the
        points-of-view of F. J., G. T., and Frances. Argues that
        "Gascoigne creates multiple perspectives toward the basic
        action of the narrative, perspectives that only the reader,
        as the final participant in this creative process, can
        judge."

Gascoigne

1093   PHILMUS, M. R. ROHR. "Gascoigne's Fable of the Artist as a
        Young Man." JEGP, 73, no. 1 (1974), 13-31.
            Argues that Master F. J. is a "version of the 'novel of
        the artist,'" a Künstlerroman. Analyzes poems, finding that
        F. J. rejects the Petrarchan mode in favor of a plain style,
        and that the poems "are arranged, carefully and critically,
        to trace the ideal story of F. I.'s growth as a poet." Dis-
        cusses how Gascoigne uses narrative links to further theme
        by having "the language of G. T. represent...the standards
        of a plain prose style, thus establishing a norm against
        which F. I.'s changing uses of language gain prominence and
        are critically defined."

1094   PROUTY, CHARLES T[YLER]. "Elizabethan Fiction: Whetstone's
        'The Discourse of Rinaldo and Giletta' and Grange's The
        Golden Aphroditis," in Studies in Honor of A. H. R. Fair-
        child. Edited by Charles T[yler] Prouty. University of
        Missouri Studies, 21, no. 1. Columbia: University of
        Missouri, 1946, pp. 133-50.
            Examines influence of Master F. J. on "Rinaldo and
        Giletta" and Golden Aphroditis.

1095   PROUTY, C[HARLES] T[YLER]. "Gascoigne in the Low Countries
        and the Publication of A Hundreth Sundrie Flowres." RES,
        12 (April 1936), 139-46.
            Dates publication of A Hundred Sundry Flowers after 19
        March 1572/3; suggests that work was published in April.

1096   PROUTY, C[HARLES] T[YLER]. George Gascoigne: Elizabethan
        Courtier, Soldier, and Poet. New York: Columbia University
        Press, 1942, 351pp.
            Argues that "a true understanding of the merits" of Mas-
        ter F. J. requires awareness of autobiographical nature of
        work. Analyzes work as "the first psychological novel,"
        stressing Gascoigne's narrative techniques of "revelation
        by implication" and "psychological point of view." Also
        discusses structure, characterization, and realism (pp. 188-
        212, passim). Examines translations of Hemetes the Hermit
        and shows that only the French is a literal translation;
        the Italian and Latin are more idiomatic and freer (pp. 221-
        28, passim).

1097   ROHR, M. R. "Gascoigne and 'My Master Chaucer.'" JEGP, 67
        (January 1968), 20-31.
            Discusses influence of Chaucer's Troilus and Criseyde on
        character, incident, and point of view in Master F. J.

1098   SCANLON, PAUL A. "Whetstone's 'Rinaldo and Giletta': The
       First Elizabethan Prose Romance." WP, 2 (1973), 195-206.
          Includes discussion of Whetstone's use of Master F. J.
       as source: examines how Whetstone idealizes story.

1099   SCHELLING, FELIX E[MMANUEL]. The Life and Writings of George
       Gascoigne with Three Poems Heretofore not Reprinted. Pub-
       lications of the University of Pennsylvania: Series in
       Philology, Literature, and Archaeology, 2, no. 4. Boston:
       Ginn & Co.; Halle: M. Niemeyer, 1893, 131pp.
          Includes discussion of Master F. J. in context of Gas-
       coigne's life and writings. Suggests that work is autobi-
       ographical; discusses, in general terms, style and changes
       in 1575 edition (passim).

1100   SCHLAUCH, MARGARET. Antecedents of the English Novel, 1400-
       1600 (from Chaucer to Deloney). Warsaw: PWN--Polish Scien-
       tific Publishers; London: Oxford University Press, 1963,
       264pp.
          Discusses Master F. J. (both versions) as "social come-
       dy," pointing out traditional and innovative elements (pp.
       228-34).

1101   SCHOTT, PENELOPE SCAMBLY. "The Narrative Stance in The Adven-
       tures of Master F. J.: Gascoigne as Critic of His Own
       Poems." RenQ, 29 (Autumn 1976), 368-77.
          Argues that Gascoigne's attitudes in Certain Notes of
       Instruction provide "the best insight into G. T.'s narrative
       tone" since "G. T., as narrator, is akin to Gascoigne as
       literary critic." Discusses G. T.'s tolerant, charitable,
       and appreciative attitude toward the poems.

1102   SIERACKI, CHARLES ALFRED. "The Narrator in Elizabethan Prose
       Fiction: Gascoigne and Nashe." Ph.D. dissertation, Uni-
       versity of Illinois at Urbana-Champaign, 1971, 185pp.
          Analyzes "how...[Gascoigne] shapes the identity of the
       narrator and manipulates this persona to expose the comic
       nature of the other characters and, thereby, to shape the
       satiric theme" of Master F. J. Examines how "Gascoigne
       ridicules the behavior of many of his contemporaries for
       whom the courtly love ideals had become a debased excuse
       for adultery."

1103   SMITH, CHARLES W. "Structural and Thematic Unity in Gas-
       coigne's The Adventures of Master F. J." PLL, 2 (1966),
       99-108.
          Argues that rather than writing a roman à clef, Gascoigne
       has a moral purpose; suggests that the revision was

Gascoigne

occasioned by the readers' failure to comprehend the moral purpose. Analyzes how the inset tales reveal the moral theme which is "the destruction of moral perception by untempered passion."

1104 VELZ, JOHN W. "Gascoigne, Lyly, and the Wooing of Bianca." N&Q, NS, 20 (April 1973), 130-33.
Suggests that Shakespeare used Master F. J. as source of the wooing scene in Taming of the Shrew.

1105 VOYTOVICH, EDWARD R. "The Poems of Master F. J.: A Narrator's Windfall." Thoth, 13, no. 3 (1974), 17-25.
Examines the interdependence of the prose sections and the poems and letters, suggesting that they "work together to create a sophisticated portrait of F. J." Analyzes how poems and letters reveal F. J.'s subjective reaction to events and how the two devices "afford G. T. a greater degree of omniscience than would otherwise be possible for a first-person minor-character narrator."

1106 WARD, B[ERNARD] M[ORDAUNT]. "Further Research on A Hundreth Sundrie Flowres." RES, 4 (January 1928), 35-48.
Argues that F. J. is Christopher Hatton and G. T. is George Turberville. Reprinted in 1069.

1107 WARD, B[ERNARD] M[ORDAUNT]. "Introduction," in A Hundreth Sundrie Flowres from the Original Edition. By George Gascoigne. Edited by B[ernard] M[ordaunt] Ward. Haslewood Books. London: Frederick Etchells and Hugh Macdonald, 1926, pp. vii-xxxix.
Identifies F. J. as Christopher Hatton and G. T. as Edward DeVere, Earl of Oxford, and identifies the latter as the editor of the work. Argues that Gascoigne claimed Master F. J., revised it, and attempted to pass it off as a translation from Bartello to clear Hatton from its stigma. Includes as appendix "A Comparison between the Adventures of Master F. I. (1573) and the Fable of Ferdinando Jeronimi (1575-6)," pp. 187-89. Reprints only enough of the prose of Master F. J. to provide a context for the poems (pp. 7-31). See 1055, 1062, and 1074; reprinted in 1069.

1108 WARD, B[ERNARD] M[ORDAUNT]. The Seventeenth Earl of Oxford, 1550-1604: From Contemporary Documents. London: J. Murray, 1928, 424pp.
In "Interlude: 'The Crown of Bays,'" pp. 130-44, discusses relationship of Master F. J. to Oxford; identifies F. J. as Christopher Hatton and G. T. as George Turberville.

1109   WATERS, GREGORY LEO. "G. T.'s 'Worthles Enterprise': A Study
        of the Narrator in Gascoigne's The Adventures of Master F.
        J.," in "I. Conrad Aiken: A Basis for Criticism. II.
        G. T.'s 'Worthles Enterprise': A Study of the Narrator in
        Gascoigne's The Adventures of Master F. J. III. Blake and
        Rossetti." Ph.D. dissertation, Rutgers University, 1974,
        668pp.
            Argues that Gascoigne comments "rather subtly on the am-
        biguous moral character of his narrator" and that G. T. "be-
        comes himself an object of satire."

1110   WILLIAMS, GORDON. "Gascoigne's Master F. J. and the Develop-
        ment of the Novel." Trivium, 10 (May 1975), 137-50.
            Examines ways in which Master F. J. anticipates later
        development of the novel; discusses Gascoigne's narrative
        techniques, characterization, and bawdy.

1111   YATES, FRANCES A. "Elizabethan Chivalry: The Romance of the
        Accession Day Tilts." JWCI, 20 (1957), 4-25.
            Suggests that Sir Henry Lee was the author of Hemetes
        the Hermit.

GESTA ROMANORUM

    STC 21286.2-21287. Wing R631-640.

Editions

1112   Wynkyn de Worde's Gesta Romanorum. Introductory Note by
        Ronald Tamplin. Exeter Medieval English Texts. Exeter:
        University of Exeter, 1974, 166pp.
            Provides facsimile reprint of 1510 edition.

Studies

1113   ANON. "Gesta Romanorum." Retrospective Review, 2, Part 2
        (1820), Article 9, 327-29.
            Provides bibliographical description of undated De Worde
        edition and transcribes one tale as a specimen of contents.

1114   HERRTAGE, SIDNEY J. H. "Introduction," in The Early English
        Versions of the Gesta Romanorum. Edited by Sidney J. H.
        Herrtage. EETS, Extra Series, 33. London: Oxford Univer-
        sity Press for the Early English Text Society, 1879, pp.
        vii-xxxi.
            Includes discussion of relationship of text of De Worde's
        edition to manuscript versions. Reprints text of eight
        tales not in extant manuscripts (pp. 429-44).

Gesta Romanorum

1115   MADDEN, FREDERIC. "Introduction," in <u>The Old English Versions</u>
        of the <u>Gesta Romanorum</u>. Edited by Frederic Madden. London:
        Shakespeare Press for the Roxburghe Club, 1838, pp. iii-xxi.
             Describes sixteenth-century translations and discusses
        relationship of manuscript translations to printed ones.
        Reprints portions of De Worde's edition (pp. 486-503).

1116   SCHWARTZ, HERBERT F. "John Fletcher and the <u>Gesta Romanorum</u>."
        <u>MLN</u>, 34 (March 1919), 146-49.
             Suggests "Emperor Titus" as a source for <u>Loyal Subject</u>
        and "Dolfinus" as a source for <u>A King and No King</u>.

1117   SCHWARTZ, HERBERT F. "One of the Sources of the <u>Queen of</u>
        <u>Corinth</u>." <u>MLN</u>, 24 (March 1909), 76-77.
             Cites portion of tale of Edfenne from De Worde's edition
        as source for denouement of <u>Queen of Corinth</u>.

<u>GIFFORD, HUMFREY</u> (fl. 1580)

<u>A Posie of Gilloflowers</u>. <u>STC</u> 11872.

Editions

1118   GIFFORD, HUMFREY. <u>The Complete Poems and Translations in</u>
        <u>Prose of Humfrey Gifford, Gentleman (1580)</u>. Edited by
        Alexander B. Grosart. Manchester: Printed for the Sub-
        scribers, 1875, 195pp.
             Provides annotated reprint of 1580 edition of <u>Posy of</u>
        <u>Gilloflowers</u>.

1119   GIFFORD, HUMFREY. <u>A Posie of Gilloflowers</u>. Edited by
        F[rederick] J[oseph] Harvey Darton. London: Hawthornden
        Press, 1933, 198pp.
             Provides modernized reprint of 1580 edition. In "Intro-
        duction," pp. v-xxii, discusses the diversity of subject
        matter.

<u>GODWIN, FRANCIS, BISHOP OF HEREFORD</u> (1562-1633)

<u>The Man in the Moon or a Discourse of a Voyage Thither by D. Gonsales</u>.
    <u>STC</u> 11943. Wing G970.

Editions

1120   GODWIN, FRANCIS. [<u>The Man in the Moon</u>], in <u>The Harleian Mis-</u>
        <u>cellany</u>, Vol. VIII. Edited by William Oldys. Revised by
        Thomas Park. London: J. White and Cochrane, 1811, 344-61.

Reprints abridged version from Nathaniel Crouch's <u>A View of the English Acquisitions in Guinea and the East</u> (1686).

1121 GODWIN, FRANCIS. "The Voyage of Domingo Gonzales to the World of the Moon." Edited by E. Hönncher. <u>Anglia</u>, 10 (1887), 428–56.

Provides reprint of 1120. In "Bemerkungen," pp. 452–56, points out parallels with Swift's <u>Gulliver's Travels</u> and Cyrano de Bergerac's <u>Histoire comique</u>.

1122 GODWIN, FRANCIS. <u>The Man in the Moone</u>, in The Man in the Moone and Nuncius Inanimatus. By Francis Godwin. Edited by Grant McColley. Smith College Studies in Modern Languages, 19, no. 1. Northampton, Massachusetts: Smith College, 1937, pp. 1–48.

Provides annotated, corrected reprint of 1638 edition. In "Introduction," pp. vii–xiv, reviews evidence for Godwin's authorship and date of composition.

1123 GODWIN, FRANCIS. <u>The Man in the Moone</u>. Foreword by F. C. M. Hereford: Nagrom, 1959, 54pp.

Provides text reprinted from 1122. In "Foreword," comments briefly on popularity of work.

1124 GODWIN, FRANCIS. <u>The Man in the Moone: Or a Discourse of a Voyage Thither</u>. Edited by Ivan Volkoff. [San Marino, California(?):] n.p., 1961, 112pp.

Provides annotated reprint of 1657 edition.

1125 GODWIN, FRANCIS. <u>The Man in the Moon</u>, in <u>Short Fiction of the Seventeenth Century</u>. Edited by Charles C[arroll] Mish. Stuart Editions. New York: New York University Press, 1963, pp. 235–83.

Provides modernized reprint of 1657 edition. In a brief introductory note, discusses the work as a combination of utopian fiction and <u>voyage imaginaire</u>. <u>See</u> 60.

*1126 GODWIN, FRANCIS. <u>The Man in the Moone</u>. London: Albion Press, 1969.

Not located. Facsimile reprint of 1638 edition. Listed in <u>MHRA Annual Bibliography</u>, 45 (1970), #4507.

1127 GODWIN, FRANCIS. <u>The Man in the Moone</u>. Menston, England: Scolar Press, 1971, not paginated.

Provides facsimile reprint of 1638 edition.

Godwin

1128   GODWIN, FRANCIS. The Man in the Moone. English Experience,
        459. Amsterdam: Theatrvm Orbis Terrarvm; New York: Da
        Capo Press, 1972, 137pp.
           Provides facsimile reprint of 1638 edition.

Studies

1129   BAILEY, J[AMES] O[SLER]. Pilgrims Through Space and Time:
        Trends and Patterns in Scientific and Utopian Fiction. New
        York: Argus Books, 1947, 341pp.
           Examines various techniques used by Godwin in context of
        broad examination of scientific romances (passim).

1130   COPELAND, THOMAS A. "Francis Godwin's The Man in the Moone:
        A Picaresque Satire." Extrapolation, 16 (May 1975), 156-63.
           Argues that work "is not primarily science fiction at
        all but a picaresque satire incorporating a utopian voyage."
        Concludes that reader is "left with a typically seventeenth-
        century contradiction, a belief in the decay of the world
        and confidence in the existence of natural principles of
        order and harmony."

1131   CORNELIUS, PAUL EDWIN. "Languages in Seventeenth- and Early
        Eighteenth-Century Imaginary Voyages." Ph.D. dissertation,
        Columbia University, 1962, 279pp.
           Examines influence of Chinese on Godwin's lunar language.

1132   CORNELIUS, PAUL EDWIN. Languages in Seventeenth- and Early
        Eighteenth-Century Imaginary Voyages. Geneva: Librairie
        Droz, 1965, 177pp.
           In Chapter III ("Francis Godwin's The Man in the Moone
        and Its Influence," pp. 39-64) provides a synopsis of God-
        win's work, discusses the Chinese influence behind his lunar
        language, and examines influence of the language on works
        by John Wilkins, Andreas Müller, and Cyrano de Bergerac.

1133   CROUCH, LAURA ERNESTINE. "The Scientist in English Literature:
        Domingo Gonsales (1638) to Victor Frankenstein (1817)."
        Ph.D. dissertation, University of Oklahoma, 1975, 275pp.
           Includes discussion of Man in the Moon in examination of
        the evolution of the scientist figure in English literature.

1134   DAVIES, H. NEVILLE. "Bishop Godwin's 'Lunatique Language.'"
        JWCI, 30 (1967), 296-316.
           Places Godwin's lunar language in the context of the
        "tradition of invented languages," identifies Godwin's
        source for its main features, and provides the key to God-
        win's musical cipher system.

1135 DAVIES, H. NEVILLE. "Symzonia and The Man in the Moone." N&Q,
NS, 15 (September 1968), 342-44.
Discusses influence of Godwin's work on Adam Seaborn's
Symzonia.

1136 DUPONT, V[ICTOR]. L'Utopie et le roman utopique dans la littérature anglaise. Paris: M. Didier, 1941, 835pp.
Discusses characteristics of Godwin's lunar society and
the place of Man in the Moon in English utopian fiction
(pp. 164-69, passim).

1137 EFFINGER, JOHN R. "The Sources of Cyrano's Trip to the Moon."
PMLA, 17, Appendix II (1902), lxxxiii.
Abstract of paper delivered at 1901 Central Division
meeting: notes that influence of Man in the Moon on Cyrano
was slight.

1138 GREEN, ROGER LANCELYN. Into Other Worlds: Space-Flight in
Fiction from Lucian to Lewis. London and New York:
Abelard-Schuman, 1958, 190pp.
In Chapter 3 ("How Gonsales Visited the Moon," pp. 32-44)
provides detailed synopsis of moon journey and calls the
work "the most important journey into other worlds before
the nineteenth century."

1139 HARRISON, THOMAS P. "Birds in the Moon." Isis, 45 (December
1954), 323-30.
Points out Charles Morton's use of Man in the Moon as
source for his "hypothesis that birds migrate to the moon"
(Compendium Physicae).

1140 KNOWLSON, JAMES R. "A Note on Bishop Godwin's Man in the
Moone: The East Indies Trade Route and a 'Language' of
Musical Notes." MP, 65 (May 1968), 357-61.
Identifies route Gonsales takes in returning home as
East Indies trade route and suggests various travel accounts
as sources of places and names of characters. Identifies
musical language as cipher based on assigning "each letter
of the Latin alphabet to a place on the musical scale" and
traces idea to several early books on cryptography.

1141 KNOWLSON, JAMES [R.]. Universal Language Schemes in England
and France, 1600-1800. University of Toronto Romance
Series, 29. Toronto: University of Toronto Press, 1975,
311pp.
Points out influence of knowledge of Chinese language
and of "sixteenth- and early seventeenth-century works on
cryptography and signalling" on Godwin's lunar language.

Godwin

Notes that the language "is not...a language at all, but
simply a cipher in which the letters of an existing alphabet
may be transcribed" (pp. 117-22).

1142   KNOWLSON, JAMES [R.]. "Voyages to the Moon." The Listener,
       69 (7 February 1963), 242-43.
            Compares Man in the Moon to other seventeenth-century
       works about moon-voyages; notes parallels to modern talk of
       space flight.

1143   LAWTON, H[AROLD] W. "Bishop Godwin's Man in the Moone." RES,
       7 (January 1931), 23-55.
            Examines possible sources, including Godwin's use of
       current scientific discoveries, and influence on John Wil-
       kins, Cyrano de Bergerac (via Jean Baudoin's translation),
       and Swift. Dates composition 1625-1629; describes published
       editions and translations in a "Bibliographical Note" (pp.
       52-54).

1144   LAWTON, HAROLD W. "Notes sur Jean Baudoin et sur ses traduc-
       tions de l'Anglais (1619; 1624-1625; 1626; 1648)." RLC, 6
       (1926), 673-81.
            Discusses Baudoin's translation of Godwin's Man in the
       Moon and its influence on Cyrano de Bergerac.

1145   LEIGHTON, PETER. Moon Travellers: A Dream that Is Becoming
       a Reality. London: Oldbourne, 1960, 240pp.
            Suggests that Man in the Moon was written in "the pica-
       resque tradition" and provides a lengthy extract from the
       work (pp. 61-71).

1146   McCOLLEY, GRANT. "The Date of Godwin's Domingo Gonsales."
       MP, 35 (August 1937), 47-60.
            Examines sources to argue that date of composition is
       definitely after 1615 and that work was probably written
       1627-28.

1147   McCOLLEY, GRANT. "The Pseudonyms of Francis Godwin." PQ, 16
       (January 1937), 78-80.
            Identifies E. M. and Edward Mahon as Godwin's pseudonyms.

1148   McCOLLEY, GRANT. "The Third Edition of Francis Godwin's The
       Man in the Moone." Library, 4th Ser., 17 (March 1937),
       472-75.
            Points out that the third edition is not London, 1768,
       but that which appeared in Nathaniel Crouch's A View of the
       English Acquisitions in Guinea and the East (1686). Dis-
       cusses Crouch's alterations in the text and the influence
       of his text on later editions.

1149   MERCHANT, W. M[OELWYN]. "Bishop Francis Godwin, Historian and
       Novelist." Journal of the Historical Society of the Church
       in Wales, 5 (1955), 45-51.
          Analyzes complexity of tone and narrative structure of
       Man in the Moon: finds that work "falls into three well de-
       fined movements with a corresponding change in narrative
       style" and examines Godwin's use of narrative voice.

1150   MOORE, PATRICK. Science and Fiction. London: G. G. Harrap,
       1957, 192pp.
          Includes discussion of popularity of Man in the Moon and
       of Godwin's "lively imagination" and "sense of humour" (pp.
       31-38).

1151   NICOLSON, MARJORIE [HOPE]. "Cosmic Voyages." ELH, 7 (June
       1940), 83-107.
          Discusses Man in the Moon in the context of the develop-
       ment of the cosmic voyage genre and examines its "importance
       in both the history of science and the history of litera-
       ture."

1152   NICOLSON, MARJORIE H[OPE]. "Early Space-Travellers." CLC, 9
       (1959), 9-15.
          Discusses Man in the Moon in the context of other early
       treatments of cosmic voyages.

1153   NICOLSON, MARJORIE HOPE. Voyages to the Moon. New York:
       Macmillan Co., 1948, 315pp.
          Includes discussion of Man in the Moon as an example of
       the lunar voyage: examines work as a romance and an utopia,
       provides lengthy synopsis, and traces influence on later
       works (pp. 71-85).

1154   PHILMUS, ROBERT M. "Into the Unknown: The Evolution of Sci-
       ence Fiction in England from Francis Godwin to H. G. Wells."
       Ph.D. dissertation, University of California, San Diego,
       1968, 208pp.
          See 1155.

1155   PHILMUS, ROBERT M. Into the Unknown: The Evolution of Science
       Fiction from Francis Godwin to H. G. Wells. Berkeley: Uni-
       versity of California Press, 1970, 186pp.
          Analyzes Godwin's attempt to convince reader through
       "empirical observations." Examines Man in the Moon in con-
       text of lunar voyages (pp. 40-47).

1167   TIEJE, RALPH EARLE. "The Prose Voyage Imaginaire before 1800:
       An Historical and Critical Study." Ph.D. dissertation, Uni-
       versity of Illinois at Urbana-Champaign, 1917, 288pp.

Godwin

> Discusses <u>Man in the Moon</u> in context of development of
> <u>voyage imaginaire</u>. Notes that work "is a picaresque ro-
> mance, a Robinsonade, and a <u>voyage imaginaire</u> in one" and
> discusses Gonsales as "a rounded character."

1157   WILLIAMS, SPARKS HENDERSON. "Domingo Gonsales." <u>N&Q</u>, 50
         (12 September 1874), 209-10.
         Traces publication of editions of <u>Man in the Moon</u> and
         provides overview of critical comment on work.

1158   WRIGHT, THOMAS EDWARD. "The English Renaissance Prose Anatomy."
         Ph.D. dissertation, Washington University, 1963, 238pp.
         Examines <u>Man in the Moon</u> as an example of the fantastic
         journey form.

<u>THE GOODLI HISTORY OF THE MOSTE NOBLE AND BEAUTYFULL LADYE LUCRES OF
SCENE IN TUSKANE</u>
By Enea Silvio Piccolomini.

<u>STC</u> 19969.8-19972.

Editions

1159   The Goodli History of the Most Noble & Beautifull Ladye Lucres,
         in The Hystorie of the Most Noble Knight Plasidas and Other
         Rare Pieces: Collected into One Book by Samuel Pepys and
         Forming Part of the Pepysian Library. Edited by Henry
         Hucks Gibbs. London: J. B. Nichols & Sons for the Rox-
         burghe Club, 1873, pp. 111-61.
         Provides corrected text based on 1567 edition. In "Pre-
         face," pp. i-xxiii, discusses publishing history of English
         translations. In "Notes," pp. xxiv-xxx, provides compari-
         sons with Latin original and other English translations.

Studies

1160   BORINSKI, LUDWIG. "The Origin of the Euphuistic Novel and Its
         Significance for Shakespeare," in <u>Studies in Honor of T. W.
         Baldwin</u>. Edited by Don Cameron Allen. Urbana: University
         of Illinois Press, 1958, pp. 38-52.
         Suggests that <u>The Goodly History of the Lady Lucrece</u>
         "apparently created the fashion of the dramatic novel which
         Painter" and others attempted to capitalize upon. Analyzes
         characteristics of the form.

*1161   GUINN, JOHN A. "Aeneas Sylvius Piccolomini: His Relationship
        to Sixteenth-Century English Literature." Ph.D. disserta-
        tion, University of Texas at Austin, 1939.
        Abstract not available.

1162   GUINN, JOHN A. "The Letter Device in the First Act of The Two
       Gentlemen of Verona." University of Texas Studies in Eng-
       lish, 20 (1940), 72-81.
       Suggests that in his treatment of the episode Shakespeare
       is indebted to the Goodly History of the Lady Lucrece.

1163   SAVAGE, HOWARD J[AMES]. "The Beginning of Italian Influence
       in English Prose Fiction." PMLA, 32 (March 1917), 1-21.
       Focuses discussion on Goodly History of the Lady Lucrece,
       the beginning of Italian influence on English prose fiction.
       Examines historical basis of work and compares Latin orig-
       inal with translation, noting that latter was altered in
       important ways to adapt work to new audience. Discusses
       importance of work to development of epistolary technique
       of Elizabethan prose fiction, noting that it is the "first
       story in Tudor England in which the plot is organically de-
       pendent for its advancement upon the instrument of the
       letter."

1164   SCHLAUCH, MARGARET. Antecedents of the English Novel, 1400-
       1600 (from Chaucer to Deloney). Warsaw: PWN--Polish Scien-
       tific Publishers; London: Oxford University Press, 1963,
       264pp.
       Discusses The Goodly History of the Lady Lucrece as an
       example of the "new successors of the society romance," ex-
       amining how "the matters of daily life...penetrate the ac-
       tion of a plot originally aristocratic" (pp. 120-27, passim).

GOODMAN, NICHOLAS

Hollands Leaguer: or an Historical Discourse of the Life of Dona
    Britanica Hollandia. STC 12027.

Editions

1165   GOODMAN, NICHOLAS. "Hollands Leaguer by Nicholas Goodman: A
       Critical Edition." Edited by Dean Stanton Barnard, Jr.
       Ph.D. dissertation, University of Michigan, 1963, 162pp.
       See 1166.

1166   GOODMAN, NICHOLAS. Hollands Leaguer by Nicholas Goodman: A
       Critical Edition. Edited by Dean Stanton Barnard, Jr.
       SEngL, 47. The Hague: Mouton, 1970, 149pp.

Goodman

       Provides both an annotated old-spelling and a modernized
text based on the 1632 edition. In "Introduction" (pp. 7-
47) analyzes work as "a parable of the Church of England
from a Protestant point of view," assesses the influence of
various forms on the work, analyzes Goodman's style, speculates about his intended audience, and describes the topical
background.

Studies

1167   KATANKA, MARGARET C. "Goodman's Holland's Leaguer (1632)--
       Further Examples of the Plagiarism of Richard Head." N&Q,
       NS, 21 (November 1974), 415-17.
         Points out Head's use of Holland's Leaguer in The Miss
       Display'd.

GOODWINE, THOMAS POPE

The Moste Pleasaunt Historye of Blanchardine and the Faire Eglantine
   (paraphrased from French). STC 3125-3126.

Studies

1168   F., F. J. "Blanchardine and Eglantine, 1597." N&Q, 50 (12
       December 1874), 464-65.
         Gives bibliographical description of Hamburg Library
       copy of 1597 edition.

GOODYEAR, WILLIAM (fl. 1581)

Jean de Cartigny, The Voyage of the Wandering Knight. STC 4700-4703.
   Wing C681-682.

Editions

1169   CARTIGNY, JEAN DE. The Wandering Knight: Reprinted from the
       Copy of the First English Edition in the Henry E. Huntington
       Library. Translated by William Goodyear. Edited by Dorothy
       Atkinson Evans. Seattle: University of Washington Press,
       1951, 215pp.
         Provides an annotated text based on the 1581 edition.
       In "Introduction," pp. xi-xlvii, discusses the publishing
       history of the work, the nature of Robert Norman's editor-
       ship, the literary qualities of the work, the allegory, and
       the influence on English literature (especially Spenser's
       Faerie Queene).

Studies

1170 ATKINSON, DOROTHY F. "The Wandering Knight, the Red Cross
Knight, and 'Miles Dei.'" HLQ, 7 (February 1944), 109-34.
[Reprinted in: The Sword, 11 (1947), 3-26.]
Points out "the remarkable episodic and structural re-
semblances" between Goodyear's Voyage of the Wandering
Knight and Book I of The Faerie Queene. Examines in detail
the Prodigal Son motif in Goodyear's work, arguing that the
same motif underlies Book I of Spenser's poem.

1171 [FORDE, RICHARD]. "The Voyage of the Wandering Knight." Retrospective Review, 1, Part 2 (1820), Article 5, 250-58.
Lists contents and transcribes several passages from
Goodyear's translation for the purpose of suggesting that
the work "may have furnished some of the materials, if not
the basis, of Bunyan's admirable superstructure" of Pilgrim's Progress.

1172 WHAREY, JAMES BLANTON. A Study of the Sources of Bunyan's
Allegories: With Special Reference to Deguileville's Pil-
grimage of Man. Baltimore: J. H. Furst Co., 1904, 137pp.
In Chapter III ("Jean de Cartheny: The Voyage of the
Wandering Knight," pp. 69-77) investigates Bunyan's possible
use of Goodyear's translation as source of Pilgrim's Progress; concludes that there are no "distinct traces" of
Bunyan's use of the work. Provides a synopsis of Goodyear's
translation.

GOSSON, STEPHEN (1555-1624)

The Ephemerides of Phialo. STC 12093-12094.

Editions

1173 GOSSON, STEPHEN. The Ephemerides of Phialo. Preface by
Arthur Freeman. The English Stage: Attack and Defense,
1577-1739. New York: Garland Publishing Co., 1973, not
paginated.
Provides facsimile reprint of 1579 edition. In "Preface," pp. 5-6, provides brief note on publishing history.

Studies

1174 ALLEN, DON CAMERON. "Melbancke and Gosson." MLN, 54 (February 1939), 111-14.

Gosson

> Provides evidence of borrowings in Melbancke's <u>Philotimus</u>
> from <u>The Ephemerides of Phialo</u>. (<u>See also</u> Allen's letter:
> <u>MLN</u>, 54 [May 1939], 398.)

1175 RINGLER, WILLIAM [A.]. "The Immediate Source of Euphuism."
      <u>PMLA</u>, 53 (September 1938), 678-86.
      Argues that euphuism was developed and perfected by John
      Rainolds in his Latin lectures, which provided the model
      for the euphuistic style of Lyly, Pettie, Gosson, and Lodge.

*1176 RINGLER, WILLIAM A., JR. "Stephen Gosson, 1554-1624: A Bi-
      ographical and Critical Study." Ph.D. dissertation, Prince-
      ton University, 1937.
      <u>See</u> 1177.

1177 RINGLER, WILLIAM [A.]. <u>Stephen Gosson: A Biographical and
      Critical Study</u>. Princeton Studies in English, 25. Prince-
      ton: Princeton University Press, 1942, 155pp.
      Examines how Gosson "designed...<u>Ephemerides</u> as a reply"
      to Lyly's <u>Euphues: The Anatomy of Wit</u>; discusses stylistic
      and structural similarities between the two works. Dis-
      cusses Gosson's euphuistic style, the autobiographical basis
      of the work, and its influence on later writers. Analyzes
      influence of form and manner of academic orations on struc-
      ture and style. Provides bibliographical analysis of 1579
      edition (passim).

GOUBOURNE, JOHN

Giovanni Boccaccio, <u>A Famous Tragicall Discourse of Two Lovers, Affrican and Mensola</u>.

Editions

1178 BOCCACCIO, GIOVANNI. <u>A Famous Tragicall Discourse of Two
      Lovers, Affrican and Mensola</u>. Translated by John Goubourne.
      In <u>Two Tracts: Affrican and Mensola, an Elizabethan Prose
      Version of Il ninfale Fiesolano by Giovanni Boccaccio and
      Newes and Strange Newes from St. Christophers by John Tay-
      lor the Water Poet</u>. Edited by C. H. Wilkinson. Oxford:
      Roxburghe Club, 1946, not paginated.
      Provides reprint of 1597 edition. In "Introduction,"
      pp. ix-xxxi, discusses Goubourne's handling of text, traces
      publishing history, provides bibliographical analysis, and
      discusses work in context of Elizabethan translations of
      Boccaccio.

*1179   BOCCACCIO, GIOVANNI. The Nymphs of Fiesole. Translated by
        John Goubourne. Verona: Editiones Officinae Bodoni, 1952,
        138pp.
            Not seen. Listed in NUC Pre-1956 Imprints, vol. 62, 477.

Studies

1180   WRIGHT, HERBERT G[LADSTONE]. Boccaccio in England from Chaucer
        to Tennyson. London: Athlone Press, University of London,
        1957, 509pp.
            Includes discussion of Goubourne's style and his "slavish
        fidelity" to the translation by Antoine Guercin (pp. 108-12).

GRANGE, JOHN (fl. 1577)

The Golden Aphroditis. STC 12174.

Editions

1181   GRANGE, JOHN. The Golden Aphroditis, 1577. New York:
        Scholars' Facsimiles & Reprints, [1936], not paginated.
            Provides facsimile reprint of 1577 edition.

1182   GRANGE, JOHN. The Golden Aphroditis and Grange's Garden. In-
        troduction by Hyder E. Rollins. New York: Scholars' Fac-
        similes & Reprints, 1939, not paginated.
            Provides facsimile reprint of 1577 edition. In "Intro-
        duction," pp. iii-viii, discusses style and subject matter
        and traces some sources.

Studies

1183   BROWN, ELAINE V. BEILIN. "The Uses of Mythology in Elizabethan
        Romance." Ph.D. dissertation, Princeton University, 1973,
        336pp.
            Analyzes mythological references in Golden Aphroditis.

1184   GARKE, ESTHER. The Use of Songs in Elizabethan Prose Fiction.
        Bern: Francke Verlag, 1972, 132pp.
            Draws frequently on Golden Aphroditis for examples in
        analysis of types of songs, their relationships to plot and
        structure, and their functions (to complement or contrast
        setting, to present character relationships, to characterize
        singer and audience).

1185   LONG, PERCY WALDRON. "From Troilus to Euphues," in Anniversary
        Papers by Colleagues and Pupils of George Lyman Kittredge.

Grange

Edited by F. N. Robinson. Boston: Ginn and Co., 1913, pp. 367-76.
   Discusses importance of Golden Aphroditis in development of sixteenth-century prose fiction, particularly as "a direct link between Gascoigne and Lyly." Points out parallels in character, phrasing, and incident with Gascoigne's Master F. J. and argues that "The Golden Aphroditis, far more closely than any book hitherto adduced, anticipates Lyly's euphuism."

1186   PROUTY, CHARLES T[YLER]. "Elizabethan Fiction: Whetstone's 'The Discourse of Rinaldo and Giletta' and Grange's The Golden Aphroditis," in Studies in Honor of A. H. R. Fairchild. Edited by Charles T[yler] Prouty. University of Missouri Studies, 21, no. 1. Columbia: University of Missouri, 1946, pp. 133-50.
   Examines influence of Gascoigne's Master F. J. upon Golden Aphroditis and discusses Grange's "complete reversal of the general tone of" Master F. J. Finds that Grange's interest is in "the subtleties of love language and love behavior." Argues that Golden Aphroditis is a roman à clef.

1187   ROLLINS, HYDER E. "John Grange's The Golden Aphroditis." Harvard Studies and Notes in Philology and Literature, 16 (1934), 177-98.
   Provides synopsis of plot, discusses Grange's style, and points out several of his sources. Argues for importance of work in development of Renaissance prose fiction.

1188   TILLEY, M[ORRIS] P[ALMER]. "Borrowings in Grange's Golden Aphroditis." MLN, 53 (June 1938), 407-12.
   Points out Grange's borrowings from James Sanford's The Garden of Pleasure, noting that most are anecdotes treating love.

GRANTHAM, HENRY (fl. 1571-1587)

Giovanni Boccaccio, A Pleasaunt Disport of Diuers Noble Personages Entitled Philocopo. STC 3180-3182.

Editions

*1189   BOCCACCIO, GIOVANNI. Thirteene Most Pleasaunt and Delectable Questions Entituled a Disport of Diverse Noble Personages. Translated by Henry Grantham. Introduction by Edward Hutton. London: P. Davies, 1927, 125pp.
   Not seen. Listed in NUC Pre-1956 Imprints, vol. 62, 473.

1190   BOCCACCIO, GIOVANNI. <u>The Most Pleasant and Delectable Ques-
        tions of Love</u>. Translated by Henry Grantham. Introduction
        by Thomas Bell. New York: Illustrated Editions, 1931,
        133pp. [Another edition: New York: Three Sirens Press,
        1931.]
            Provides modernized reprint of 1566 edition.

1191   BOCCACCIO, GIOVANNI. "An Edition of <u>A Pleasaunt Disport of
        Diuers Noble Personages. Written in Italian by M. Iohn
        Bocace Florentine and Poet Laureat in His Boke which Is
        Entituled Philocopo. And Nowe Englished by H. G.</u>" Edited
        by John A. Allen. Ph.D. dissertation, University of North
        Carolina at Chapel Hill, 1954, 930pp.
            Provides critical edition based on 1567 edition collated
        with those of 1571 and 1587. Examines influence on develop-
        ment of Elizabethan prose fiction, especially Gascoigne's
        <u>Adventures of Master F. J.</u> and Grange's <u>Golden Aphroditis</u>.

1192   BOCCACCIO, GIOVANNI. <u>Filocopo</u>. Translated by Henry Grantham.
        English Experience, 277. Amsterdam: Theatrvm Orbis Ter-
        rarvm; New York: Da Capo Press, 1970, not paginated.
            Provides facsimile reprint of 1567 edition.

1193   BOCCACCIO, GIOVANNI. <u>Thirteen Most Pleasant and Delectable
        Questions of Love</u>. Translated by Henry Grantham. Edited
        by Harry Carter. New York: Clarkson N. Potter, 1974,
        186pp.
            Provides a "reworking" of the text of 1189. Although
        "[n]othing from the original translation has been omitted,"
        some "[w]ords have been changed or added, and structure re-
        arranged only when cadence and flow of language required
        it."

Studies

1194   SHERBO, ARTHUR. "<u>The Knight of Malta</u> and Boccaccio's <u>Filo-
        colo</u>." <u>ES</u>, 33 (1952), 254-57.
            Argues that the source of the play is not Painter's
        <u>Palace of Pleasure</u>, but Boccaccio's <u>Filocolo</u>, probably in
        Grantham's translation. Compares Painter's version with
        that by Grantham.

1195   WRIGHT, HERBERT G[LADSTONE]. "The Elizabethan Translation of
        the <u>Questioni d'Amore</u> in the <u>Filocolo</u>." <u>MLR</u>, 36 (July
        1941), 289-303.
            Discusses sources of the translation, variants among the
        three English editions, and style of translator. Decides
        in favor of Grantham as translator.

Greene

GREENE, ROBERT (1558-1592)

Alcida: Greenes Metamorphosis. STC 12216.

Arbasto, the Anatomie of Fortune. STC 12217-12222.

The Blacke Bookes Messenger. STC 12223.

Ciceronis Amor, Tullies Loue: Wherein Is Discoursed the Prime of Ciceroes Youth. STC 12224-12232.

Euphues His Censure to Philautus. STC 12239-12240.

Greenes Farewell to Folly. STC 12241-12242.

Greenes Groats-Worth of Witte. STC 12245-12250.

Greenes Mourning Garment. STC 12251-12252.

Greenes Neuer Too Late: Or, a Powder of Experience Sent to All Youthfull Gentlemen. STC 12253-12258.

Greenes Orpharion. STC 12260.

Gwydonius; the Carde of Fancie. STC 12262-12264.

Mamillia; a Looking Glass for the Ladies of England. STC 12269-12270.

Menaphon: Camillas Alarum to Slumbering Euphues. STC 12272-12275.

Morando: The Tritameron of Loue. STC 12276-12277.

The Myrrour of Modestie. STC 12278.

Pandosto: The Triumph of Time. STC 12285-12292. Wing G1827A, G1832-1838.

Penelopes Web. STC 12293-12294.

Perimedes the Blacke-Smith, a Golden Methode, How to Vse the Minde in Pleasant and Profitable Exercise. STC 12295.

Philomela: The Lady Fitzwaters Nightingale. STC 12296-12298.

Planetomachia. STC 12299.

The Spanish Masquerado. STC 12309-12310.

Jean de Flores, <u>A Paire of Turtle Doves, or the Tragicall History of</u>
<u>Bellora and Fidelio</u> (translation ascribed to Greene). <u>STC</u> 11094.

Bibliographies

1196   ALLISON, A[NTONY] F[RANCIS]. <u>Robert Greene, 1558-1592: A</u>
<u>Bibliographical Catalogue of the Early Editions in English</u>
<u>(to 1640)</u>. Pall Mall Bibliographies, 4. Folkestone:
Dawson, 1975, 75pp., 2 microfiche.
Provides analytical bibliography of editions of Greene's
works: notes include short-title, collation, and list of
contents. Includes "Chronology of the Publications of
Greene's Works to 1640," pp. 9-14. Title page of each edition reproduced on microfiche.

1197   DEAN, J[AMES] S., JR. "Robert Greene: An Addendum and Supple-
mentary Bibliography of Editions, Biography, and Criticism,
1945-1969." <u>RORD</u>, 13-14 (1972), 181-86.
Provides supplement to 1199.

1198   HAYASHI, TETSUMARO. <u>Robert Greene Criticism: A Comprehensive</u>
<u>Bibliography</u>. Introduction by Louis Marder. Scarecrow
Author Bibliographies Series, 6. Metuchen, New Jersey:
Scarecrow Press, 1971, 146pp.
Provides classified listing of editions and criticism,
as well as listing of locations of copies of early editions.

1199   JOHNSON, ROBERT C. "Robert Greene, 1945-1965," in <u>Elizabethan</u>
<u>Bibliographies Supplements, V: Robert Greene, 1945-1965;</u>
<u>Thomas Lodge, 1939-1965; John Lyly, 1939-1965; Thomas Nashe,</u>
<u>1941-1965; George Peele, 1939-1965</u>. Compiled by Robert C.
Johnson. London: Nether Press, 1968, pp. 15-26.
Provides chronological list of criticism and editions,
1945-1965; supplements 1202 and 1203. <u>See</u> 1197.

1200   NESTRICK, WILLIAM. "Robert Greene," in <u>The Predecessors of</u>
<u>Shakespeare: A Survey and Bibliography of Recent Studies</u>
<u>in English Renaissance Drama</u>. Edited by Terence P. Logan
and Denzell S. Smith. Lincoln: University of Nebraska
Press, 1973, pp. 56-92.
Includes section on prose fiction in overview of scholarship on Greene; provides selective bibliography.

1201   PARR, JOHNSTONE, I. A. SHAPIRO, and NORMAN J. SANDERS. <u>List</u>
<u>of Editions, Copies, and Locations of the Works of Robert</u>
<u>Greene (Including Apocrypha): Compiled in Preparation for</u>
<u>an Edition Sponsored by the Shakespeare Institute (Univer-</u>
<u>sity of Birmingham) and the University of Alabama</u>.

Greene

> Stratford-upon-Avon: Shakespeare Institute, University of
> Birmingham, 1958, 15pp.
> Provide listing arranged by <u>STC</u> number of location of
> copies.

1202 TANNENBAUM, SAMUEL A. <u>Robert Greene (A Concise Bibliography)</u>.
Elizabethan Bibliographies, 8. New York: Samuel A. Tannenbaum, 1939, 66pp.
Provides classified list of editions and criticism. <u>See</u>
1203 and 1199.

1203 TANNENBAUM, SAMUEL A., and DOROTHY R. TANNENBAUM. <u>Supplement</u>
<u>to a Bibliography of Robert Greene</u>. Elizabethan Bibliog-
raphies. New York: Elizabethan Bibliographies, 1950, 23pp.
Supplement to 1202.

Editions

1204 GREENE, ROBERT. <u>Greene's Groats-Worth of Wit Bought with a</u>
<u>Million of Repentance</u>. Edited by [S.] Egerton Brydges.
Lee Priory: Johnson and Warwick, 1813, 78pp.
Provides reprint of 1621 edition. In "Preface, Biographical and Critical," pp. 1-22, discusses publication
of work and Chettle's editorship.

1205 GREENE, ROBERT. <u>Greene's Arcadia; or, Menaphon: Camilla's</u>
<u>Alarum to Slumbering Euphues in His Melancholy Cell at</u>
<u>Silexedra</u>, in <u>Archaica: Containing a Reprint of Scarce Old</u>
<u>English Prose Tracts</u>, Vol. I, no. 2. Edited by S. Egerton
Brydges. London: Private Press of Longman, Hurst, Rees,
Orme, and Browne, 1815, 111pp. (separately paginated).
[Also published separately.]
Provides reprint of 1616 edition. In "Preface," pp.
vii-xvii, discusses style.

1206 GREENE, ROBERT. <u>Philomela, the Lady Fitzwater's Nightingale</u>,
in <u>Archaica: Containing a Reprint of Scarce Old English</u>
<u>Prose Tracts</u>, Vol. I, no. 1. Edited by S. Egerton Brydges.
London: Private Press of Longman, Hurst, Rees, Orme, and
Browne, 1815, 80pp. (separately paginated). [Also published
separately.]
Provides reprint of 1615 edition.

1207 GREENE, ROBERT. <u>Pandosto</u>, in <u>Shakespeare's Library: A Collec-</u>
<u>tion of the Romances, Novels, Poems, and Histories Used by</u>
<u>Shakespeare as the Foundation of His Dramas</u>, Vol. I. Edited
by J[ohn] Payne Collier. London: T. Rodd, 1843, 68pp.
(separately paginated).

Provides annotated reprint of 1588 edition. In "Introduction to R. Greene's Pandosto," pp. i-vii, discusses the
popularity of Greene's work and criticizes the lameness of
his conclusion.

1208   GREENE, ROBERT. Pandosto: The Triumph of Time, in The Works
        of William Shakespeare, Vol. VIII. By William Shakespeare.
        Edited by James O[rchard] Halliwell[-Phillipps]. London:
        C. & J. Adlard for the Editor, 1859, 8-36.
            Provides reprint of 1588 edition. In "Introduction [to
        The Winter's Tale]," pp. 3-46, discusses popularity of
        Greene's work and provides a brief publication history.

1209   GREENE, ROBERT. The Myrrour of Modestie, in Illustrations of
        Old English Literature, Vol. III. Edited by J[ohn] Payne
        Collier. London: Privately Printed, 1866, 32pp. (sepa-
        rately paginated).
            Provides reprint of 1584 edition.

1210   GREENE, ROBERT. Greene's Groats-Worth of Wit Bought with a
        Million of Repentance. Edited by J[ames] O[rchard] H[alli-
        well-Phillipps]. London: Chiswick Press, 1870, 61pp.
            Provides reprint of 1596 edition.

1211   GREENE, ROBERT. Perimedes the Blacke-Smith. Edited by J[ohn]
        Payne Collier. Miscellaneous Tracts. Temp. Eliz. & Jac.
        I, 1. London: n.p., 1870, 71pp.
            Provides reprint of 1588 edition. In "Introduction,"
        pp. i-ii, calls Perimedes "a hasty production."

1212   GREENE, ROBERT. Greens Groats-Worth of Wit, in Shakspere
        Allusion-Books, Part I. Edited by C[lement] M[ansfield]
        Ingleby. New Shakspere Society Publications, Series 4,
        no. 1. London: N. Trübner for New Shakspere Society, 1874,
        pp. 1-34.
            Provides reprint of 1596 edition. In "General Introduc-
        tion," pp. i-xxxv, discusses allusions in Greene's attack
        on the stage and playwrights. Reprints 1449 as "Supple-
        ment," pp. xxxvii-xlviii.

1213   GREENE, ROBERT. Pandosto, in Shakespeare's Library: A Collec-
        tion of the Plays, Romances, Novels, Poems, and Histories
        Employed by Shakespeare in the Composition of His Works,
        Vol. IV. Edited by John Payne Collier. 2d edition revised.
        Edited by W[illiam] Carew Hazlitt. London: Reeves and
        Turner, 1875, 10-83.
            Provides reprint of 1207. See 1408.

Greene

1214   GREENE, ROBERT. <u>Menaphon: Camila's Alarm to Slumbering</u>
       <u>Euphues in His Melancholy Cell at Silexedra, etc.</u> Edited
       by Edward Arber. English Scholar's Library of Old and
       Modern Works, 12. London: Privately Printed, 1880, 108pp.
            Provides reprint of 1589 edition. Includes a chrono-
       logical list of "The English Works of Robert Greene, Gabriel
       Harvey, and Thomas Nash" (pp. vi–x). In "Introduction,"
       pp. xi–xvi, discusses date of publication, the importance
       of Nashe's "Preface," and (briefly) the "virility" of
       Greene's prose.

1215   GREENE, ROBERT. <u>The Life and Complete Works in Prose and</u>
       <u>Verse of Robert Greene.</u> Edited by Alexander B. Grosart.
       Huth Library. 15 vols. London: Printed for Private Cir-
       culation, 1881–1886, 440, 364, 282, 356, 320, 316, 352,
       266, 391, 321, 344, 311, 425, 317, 244pp.
            Provides annotated reprints (from early editions) of
       Greene's prose fiction. In "General Preface," II, ix–xvi,
       comments on style. Includes 1461.

*1216 GREENE, ROBERT. <u>Groats-Worth of Wit Bought with a Million of</u>
       <u>Repentance.</u> Edited by [S.] Egerton Brydges. Bookworm's
       Garner, 6. Edinburgh: E. & G. Goldsmid, 1889, 86pp.
            Not seen. Listed in <u>NUC Pre-1956 Imprints</u>, vol. 217, 53.

1217   GREENE, ROBERT. <u>Pandosto; or, the Triumph of Time</u>, in <u>Cas-</u>
       <u>sell's Library of English Literature, IV: Shorter Works in</u>
       <u>English Prose</u>. By Henry Morley. London: Cassell & Co.,
       1889, 50–65.
            Provides modernized reprint based on unidentified edi-
       tion.

1218   GREENE, ROBERT. <u>Greens Groats-Worth of Wit</u>, in <u>Elizabethan &</u>
       <u>Jacobean Pamphlets</u>. Edited by George Saintsbury. London:
       Percival, 1892, pp. 115–63.
            Provides reprint of 1596 edition.

1219   GREENE, ROBERT. <u>Pandosto</u>, in <u>The Winter's Tale</u>. By William
       Shakespeare. Edited by Horace Howard Furness. New Vario-
       rum. Philadelphia: J. B. Lippincott and Co., 1898, pp.
       324–52.
            Provides text based on 1213. Includes extracts from
       scholarship on <u>Pandosto</u> as source of play (pp. 321–24).

1220   GREENE, ROBERT. <u>Pandosto; or, the Historie of Dorastus and</u>
       <u>Fawnia</u>. New Rochelle, New York: Elston Press, 1902, 58pp.
            Provides reprint of 1588 edition.

1221   GREENE, ROBERT. Greene's Pandosto or Dorastus and Fawnia, Be-
        ing the Original of Shakespeare's Winter's Tale. Edited by
        P[ercy] G[oronwy] Thomas. Shakespeare Classics, 2. New
        York: Duffield and Co.; London: Chatto & Windus, 1907,
        177pp.
            Provides modernized text based on 1588 edition. In "In-
        troduction" (pp. ix-xxii) examines Shakespeare's use of
        work as source for Winter's Tale, the sources of Pandosto,
        and other forms of the story. In Appendix, reprints Second
        Day of Puget de la Serre's Pandoste ou la princesse mal-
        heureuse, a prose tragedy based on Pandosto.

1222   GREENE, ROBERT. Greene's Groats-Worth of Wit. Sheldonian
        Series, 4. Oxford: B. H. Blackwell, 1919, 84pp.
            Provides modernized text based on 1592 edition.

1223   GREENE, ROBERT. Greenes Groats-VVorth of Witte, in Robert
        Greene, M. A., Groats-VVorth of Witte, Bought with a Million
        of Repentance; The Repentance of Robert Greene, 1592. Edit-
        ed by G[eorge B[agshawe] Harrison. Bodley Head Quartos, 6.
        London: John Lane, The Bodley Head; New York: E. P. Dutton
        & Co., 1923, pp. 3-52.
            Provides a corrected reprint of 1592 edition.

1224   GREENE, ROBERT. The Blacke Bookes Messenger, in Robert Greene,
        M. A., The Blacke Bookes Messenger, 1592; "Cuthbert Conny-
        Catcher," The Defence of Conny-Catching, 1592. Edited by
        G[eorge] B[agshawe] Harrison. Bodley Head Quartos, 10.
        London: John Lane, 1924, pp. v-viii, 1-33.
            Reprints text of 1592 edition. In "Introduction," pp.
        v-viii, briefly discusses work in context of Greene's ex-
        posés of the London underworld.

1225   GREENE, ROBERT. Greene's Groatsworth of Wit, in A Miscellany
        of Tracts and Pamphlets. Edited by A. C. Ward. World's
        Classics, 304. Oxford: Oxford University Press, 1927,
        pp. 89-129.
            Provides modernized reprint of unidentified edition.

1226   GREENE, ROBERT. Menaphon, in Menaphon by Robert Greene and A
        Margarite of America by Thomas Lodge. Edited by G[eorge]
        B[agshawe] Harrison. Oxford: Basil Blackwell, 1927,
        pp. 1-108.
            Provides an annotated reprint of 1589 edition. In "In-
        troduction," pp. v-xii, discusses work as a pastoral romance
        and points out that it should be read aloud to capture its
        "very real charm."

Greene

1227 GREENE, ROBERT. The Carde of Fancie, in Shorter Novels:
      Elizabethan and Jacobean. Introduction by George Saints-
      bury. Notes by Philip Henderson. Everyman's Library, 824.
      London: J. M. Dent & Sons; New York: E. P. Dutton & Co.,
      1929, pp. 157-260.
          Provides partly modernized reprint of 1587 edition. In
      "Notes," pp. xvii-xx, comments on style and characteriza-
      tion. Reprinted in 65.

1228 GREENE, ROBERT. The Black Book's Messenger, in The Elizabethan
      Underworld: A Collection of Tudor and Early Stuart Tracts
      and Ballads Telling of the Lives and Misdoings of Vagabonds,
      Thieves, Rogues, and Cozeners, and Giving Some Account of
      the Operation of the Criminal Law. Edited by A[rthur]
      V[alentine] Judges. London: Routledge & Kegan Paul, 1930,
      pp. 248-64.
          Provides modernized reprint of 1592 edition.

1229 GREENE, ROBERT. Ciceronis Amor: Tullies Love, in Ciceronis
      Amor: Tullies Love (1589) and A Quip for an Upstart
      Courtier (1592). By Robert Greene. Introduction by Edwin
      Haviland Miller. Gainesville, Florida: Scholars' Fac-
      similes & Reprints, 1954, not paginated.
          Provides facsimile reprint of 1589 edition. In "Intro-
      duction" (pp. 5-9) briefly discusses Ciceronis Amor as "an
      excellent example of Greene's skill in writing romance."

*1230 GREENE, ROBERT. "An Edition of the Planetomachia and Pene-
      lope's Web of Robert Green." Edited by D. F. Bratchell.
      Ph.D. dissertation, University of Birmingham, 1956.
          Abstract not available.

1231 GREENE, ROBERT. Pandosto: The Triumph of Time, in The Descent
      of Euphues: Three Elizabethan Romance Stories: Euphues,
      Pandosto, Piers Plainness. Edited by James Winny. Cam-
      bridge: Cambridge University Press, 1957, pp. 67-121.
          Provides slightly modernized text based on 1607 edition.
      In "Introduction" (pp. ix-xxv) discusses Greene's prose
      style, the preëminence of the plot in the work, and the in-
      fluence of Euphues.

*1232 GREENE, ROBERT. "An Edition of Greene's Farewell to Folly and
      Alphonsus, King of Aragon." Edited by N[orman] J. Sanders.
      Ph.D. dissertation, University of Birmingham, 1958.
          Abstract not available.

1233 GREENE, ROBERT. Due romanzi (Gwydonius; The Mourning Garment).
      Edited by Fernando Ferrara. Collana di Letterature Moderne,
      10. Naples: Edizioni Scientifiche Italiane, 1960, 356pp.

Provides critical editions of the two works, with Gwydonius based on text of 1584 edition and The Mourning Garment on 1590 edition. In "Introduzione," pp. 1-32,
discusses two works in context of Greene's evolution as
prose fiction writer. In discussion of Gwydonius examines
influences on and sources of work, narrative techniques,
use of Prodigal motif, characterization, style, and structure. In discussion of The Mourning Garment examines influences on and sources of work, style, use of Prodigal
motif, and themes.

*1234   GREENE, ROBERT. "Editions of Perymedes the Blacksmith and
Pandosto by Robert Greene." Edited by S[tanley] W. Wells.
Ph.D. dissertation, University of Birmingham, 1962.
Abstract not available.

*1235   GREENE, ROBERT. "An Edition of Greene's Euphues His Censure
to Philautus and Philomela." Edited by J[ames] S. Dean.
Ph.D. dissertation, University of Birmingham, 1963.
Abstract not available.

1236   GREENE, ROBERT. Pandosto, in The Winter's Tale. By William
Shakespeare. Edited by J[ohn] H[enry] P[yle] Pafford.
Arden Shakespeare. London: Methuen; Cambridge: Harvard
University Press, 1963, pp. 181-225.
Provides modernized text based on 1595 edition collated
with the editions of 1588 and 1592. In "Introduction,"
pp. xv-lxxxix, discusses the closeness with which Shake-
speare followed Pandosto as source.

*1237   GREENE, ROBERT. "An Edition of Robert Greene's Alcida (1588)."
Edited by J. A. Lavin. Ph.D. dissertation, University of
Birmingham, 1964.
Abstract not available.

1238   GREENE, ROBERT. Pandosto: The Triumph of Time, in Elizabethan
Prose Fiction. Edited by Merritt [E.] Lawlis. Indianapolis:
Odyssey Press, Bobbs-Merrill Co., 1967, pp. 226-77.
Provides partly modernized text based on 1588 edition
supplemented with readings from the 1592 edition. (See
pp. 630-31 for a list of substantive emendations and a discussion of the relationship among early editions.) In introductory note, characterizes the work as a "romance-
anatomy" and compares it with Euphues: The Anatomy of Wit.
Suggests that the frequent shifts in point of view result
from Greene's attempt "to enable the reader to understand
the situation as a whole in all its complexity."

Greene

1239   GREENE, ROBERT. Greene's Groats-Worth of Wit, 1592. Menston,
        England: Scolar Press, 1969, 50pp.
            Provides facsimile reprint of the British Library copy
        of the 1592 edition.

1240   GREENE, ROBERT. "A Critical Old-Spelling Edition of Robert
        Greene's Morando: The Tritameron of Loue." Edited by
        Thelma Marie Anderson. Ph.D. dissertation, Kent State Uni-
        versity, 1969, 406pp.
            Provides critical old-spelling edition based on 1584 edi-
        tion of Part I and 1587 edition of Part II. Examines date
        of composition, discusses sources, and provides biblio-
        graphical analysis of early editions.

1241   GREENE, ROBERT. "A Critical Edition of Robert Greene's
        Ciceronis Amor: Tullies Love." Edited by Charles Howard
        Larson. Ph.D. dissertation, Indiana University, 1970,
        219pp.
            See 1244.

*1242   GREENE, ROBERT. "An Edition of Greene's Ciceronis Amor."
        Edited by G. T. Allman. Ph.D. dissertation, University of
        Birmingham, 1972.
            Abstract not available.

1243   GREENE, ROBERT. The Black Book's Messenger, in Rogues, Vaga-
        bonds, & Sturdy Beggars. Edited by Arthur F[rederick]
        Kinney. Barre, Massachusetts: Imprint Society, 1973,
        pp. 187-205.
            Provides modernized, annotated reprint based on 1592
        edition. In brief introductory note (pp. 189-90) comments
        on the "singular vision of the meaninglessness of life" in
        the work.

1244   GREENE, ROBERT. A Critical Edition of Robert Greene's Cice-
        ronis Amor: Tullies Love. Edited by Charles Howard Larson.
        Salzburg Studies in English Literature, ElizS, 36. Salz-
        burg: Institut für Englische Sprache und Literatur, Uni-
        versität Salzburg, 1974, 217pp.
            Provides a critical old-spelling edition based on 1589
        edition. In "Critical Introduction," pp. vi-xli, discusses
        date of composition, sources, popularity and audience,
        genre (romance), characterization, plot structure, and
        style. In "Textual Introduction," pp. xlii-lxi, examines
        the textual history of the work.

1245   GREENE, ROBERT. Pandosto: The Triumph of Time, in Narrative
        and Dramatic Sources of Shakespeare, Vol. VIII. Edited by

Geoffrey Bullough. London: Routledge & Kegan Paul; New York: Columbia University Press, 1975, 156-99.
    Reprints text of 1588 edition (with signature B from 1592 edition). In "Introduction [to The Winter's Tale]" (pp. 115-55), examines Shakespeare's use of Greene's romance as the source of the play.

Studies

1246   ACHESON, ARTHUR. Shakespeare, Chapman and Sir Thomas More. London: B. Quaritch, 1931, 280pp.
    Identifies objects of attacks on actors and dramatists in Greene's prose works (pp. 27-41, passim).

1247   ADAMS, JOSEPH QUINCY, JR. "Greene's Menaphon and The Thracian Wonder." MP, 3 (January 1906), 317-25.
    Identifies source of Menaphon as story of Curan and Argentile in William Warner's Albion's England, and analyzes use of Greene's novel as a source of The Thracian Wonder.

1248   ADAMS, JOSEPH QUINCY. "Thomas Forde's Love's Labyrinth," in Studies in Language and Literature in Celebration of the Seventieth Birthday of James Morgan Hart, November 2, 1909. New York: H. Holt and Co., 1910, pp. 1-42.
    Analyzes Forde's use of Menaphon as a source. Traces development of the Menaphon story and suggests William Warner's Albion's England as Greene's source.

1249   ALEXANDER, PETER. Shakespeare's Henry VI and Richard III. Shakespeare Problems, 3. Cambridge: Cambridge University Press, 1929, 237pp.
    In "Greene's Quotation from 3 Henry VI" (pp. 39-50) argues that Greene is not accusing Shakespeare of plagiarism; suggests that by parodying one of Shakespeare's lines "Greene invites his reader to laugh at the style of the upstart crow."

1250   ALLEN, DON CAMERON. "Science and Invention in Greene's Prose." PMLA, 53 (December 1938), 1006-18.
    Illustrates that Greene invented a majority of his references to natural history but that the source of his astrological learning in Planetomachia was Melanchthon's edition of Ptolemy.

1251   ANON. "Suppositions about Shakespeare." New Monthly Magazine, 60 (November 1840), 297-304.
    Suggests causes of Greene's attack on Shakespeare in Groatsworth of Wit.

Greene

1252   APPLEGATE, JAMES E. "Classical Allusions in the Prose Work
        of Robert Greene." Ph.D. dissertation, Johns Hopkins Uni-
        versity, 1954, 262pp.
            Provides alphabetical index to classical and pseudo-
        classical allusions in Greene's work; provides identifica-
        tion of sources in classical works and/or Renaissance
        compendia.

1253   APPLEGATE, JAMES [E.]. "The Classical Learning of Robert
        Greene." BHR, 28 (1966), 354-68.
            Analyzes the sources of Greene's classical allusions and
        the extent of his classical learning. Suggests that Greene
        relied on memory, not phrase books, for his material. Con-
        cludes that Greene's purpose in using classical references
        was to reinforce the moral purpose he claimed for his works;
        however, the characteristic inaccuracy, distortion, or in-
        completeness of his allusions controvert his purpose.

1254   AUSTIN, WARREN B. "The Authorship of Certain Renaissance Eng-
        lish Pamphlets: An Informal Account of Work in Progress,"
        in Proceedings: Computer Applications to Problems in the
        Humanities: A Conversation in the Disciplines. Edited by
        Frederick M. Burelbach, Jr. Brockport: State University
        of New York, Brockport, 1970, pp. 93-99.
            Provides preliminary report on 1255.

1255   AUSTIN, WARREN B. A Computer-Aided Technique for Stylistic
        Discrimination: The Authorship of Greene's Groatsworth of
        Wit. Project 7-G-036. Grant No. OEG-1-7-070036-4593,
        U. S. Department of Health, Education, and Welfare. Wash-
        ington: U. S. Office of Education, 1969, 155pp.
            Analyzes "patterns of word-choice" and other linguistic
        variables (syntax, lexis, morphology) in works of Greene
        and Chettle to determine authorship of Groatsworth. Finds
        that the "frequency patterns [of the linguistic variables]
        found in the questioned work [i.e., Groatsworth] differed
        in every case from those that had been established as char-
        acteristic of Greene; and in every case they matched those
        established as typical of Chettle." See 1254, 1256, and
        1258.

1256   AUSTIN, WARREN B. "The Posthumous Greene Pamphlets: A Com-
        puterized Study." ShN, 16 (November-December 1966), 45.
            Reports on computer study of prose style of Robert Greene
        and Henry Chettle to determine authorship of Groatsworth of
        Wit and The Repentance of Robert Greene (see 1255).

1257 AUSTIN, WARREN B. "A Supposed Contemporary Allusion to
      Shakespeare as a Plagiarist." SQ, 6 (Autumn 1955), 373-80.
      Argues attack on Shakespeare in Groatsworth of Wit is
      not alluded to in Greene's Funeralls by R. B.

1258 AUSTIN, WARREN B. "Technique of the Chettle-Greene Forgery:
      Supplementary Material on the Authorship of the Groatsworth
      of Wit." SltN, 20 (December 1970), 43.
      Supplements earlier study (1255) by noting how Chettle
      used passages from Greene's own works (particularly Greene's
      Never Too Late and Francesco's Fortunes) to fabricate the
      Groatsworth of Wit. See 1420.

1259 BACON, WALLACE A. "Introduction," in William Warner's Syrinx
      or a Sevenfold History. By William Warner. Edited by
      Wallace A. Bacon. Northwestern University Studies, Humani-
      ties Series, 26. Evanston: Northwestern University Press,
      1950, pp. xi-lxxxv.
      Examines Greene's debts in his prose fiction to Syrinx.

1260 BAKER, ERNEST A[LBERT]. The History of the English Novel,
      Vol. II. London: H. F. & G. Witherby, 1929, 303pp.
      Devotes Chapter VI ("Euphuism and Arcadianism--Robert
      Greene" pp. 90-113) to a survey of Greene's prose fiction.
      Examines influence of Sidney and Lyly on Greene's works,
      Greene's use of the frame story, his didacticism, and his
      characterization.

1261 BALDWIN, T[HOMAS] W. On the Literary Genetics of Shakspere's
      Plays. Urbana: University of Illinois Press, 1959, 574pp.
      In Chapter I ("The Literary Genetics of Robert Greene's
      Shake-scene Passage," pp. 1-55) examines Greene's castiga-
      tion of opponents in his earlier works as a context for
      interpreting the passage in Groatsworth of Wit. Argues
      that in the passage "the real object of Greene's attack is
      the company of players. Shakspere is berated because the
      company is alleged to prefer him to all others as a drama-
      tist." In Chapter II ("The Chronology of Robert Greene's
      Plays," pp. 56-104) examines interconnections between
      Greene's plays and prose works.

1262 BASS, EBEN. "Swinburne, Greene, and 'The Triumph of Time.'"
      VP, 4 (Winter 1966), 56-61.
      Examines the influence of Greene's Pandosto on Swin-
      burne's poem "The Triumph of Time."

1263 BELL, ROBERT. "Robert Greene, 1560-1592," in Poems of Robert
      Greene and Christopher Marlowe. By Robert Greene and

Greene

Christopher Marlowe. Edited by Robert Bell. London:
J. W. Parker and Son, 1856, pp. 7-30.
   Provides overview of Greene's fiction in the context of
his life and works; stresses autobiographical nature of his
fiction.

*1264   BENYEI, P. S.   "Robert Greene and The Anatomy of Roguery."
        Ph.D. dissertation, Columbia University, 1948.
        Abstract not available.

1265   BERNHARDI, WOLFGANG.   Robert Greene's Leben und Schriften.
       Leipzig: Verlag der Volksbuchhandlung, 1874, 50pp.
          Provides chronological overview of Greene's prose fiction
       (in context of life and works).   Points out autobiographical
       elements.

1266   BIGGS, M. A.   "The Origin of The Winter's Tale."   N&Q, 135
       (3 March 1917), 164-65.
          Discusses correspondences between Pandosto and story of
       Ziemowit and suggests that the story, perhaps in ballad
       form, was Greene's source.

1267   BISWAS, DINESH CHANDRA.   Shakespeare's Treatment of His Sources
       in the Comedies.   Calcutta: Jadavpur University, 1971,
       299pp.
          Examines Shakespeare's use of Pandosto as the source for
       The Winter's Tale (pp. 155-69).

1268   BLUESTONE, MAX.   From Story to Stage: The Dramatic Adaptation
       of Prose Fiction in the Period of Shakespeare and His Con-
       temporaries.   SEngL, 70.   The Hague: Mouton, 1974, 341pp.
          Includes examination of Shakespeare's adaptation and
       transformation of Pandosto in The Winter's Tale and of the
       anonymous author's use of Menaphon in The Thracian Wonder
       (passim).

1269   BOAS, F[REDERICK] S.   "Greene, Marlowe, and Machiavelli."   TLS,
       3 August 1940, p. 375.
          Identifies allusion to Machiavelli in Groatsworth of Wit.

1270   BOUCHIER, JONATHAN.   "Literary Parallel."   N&Q, 82 (30 August
       1890), 165-66.
          Notes similarity of passage in Walter Scott's Ivanhoe to
       passage in Greene's Menaphon.

1271   BRADBROOK, MURIEL C.   "Beasts and Gods: Greene's Groats-Worth
       of Witte and the Social Purpose of Venus and Adonis."   ShS,
       15 (1962), 62-72.

Analyzes Greene's work as "a disparagement, or rhetorical invective, against the common player" and suggests that "while not a direct reply to Greene's Groats-Worth of Witte, [Shakespeare's Venus and Adonis] may be regarded as a response provoked by this piece of vilification." Analyzes structure of Greene's pamphlet.

1272   BRADISH, GAYNOR FRANCIS. "The Hard Pennyworth: A Study in Sixteenth Century Prose Fiction." Ph.D. dissertation, Harvard University, 1958, 194pp.
Analyzes Greene's use of theme of "learning through experience" and his development of it through the use of "autobiographical narrative" in Black Book's Messenger and Groatsworth of Wit. Analyzes relationships of style and structure to theme.

1273   BRERETON, J[OHN] LE GAY. "The Relation of The Thracian Wonder to Greene's Menaphon." MLR, 2 (October 1906), 34–38.
Examines anonymous author's use of Menaphon as source and explains Greene's allusion to "Senesse."

1274   BRIE, FRIEDRICH. "Lyly und Greene." Englische Studien, 42 (1910), 217–22.
Suggests that Lyly used Alcida as source for his Love's Metamorphosis.

1275   BRION, MARCEL. "Robert Greene." Correspondant, 10 March 1930, pp. 734–45.
Draws comparisons between Greene's life and treatment of Roberto in Groatsworth of Wit; sees Roberto as an autobiographical character.

1276   BROOKE, [C. F.] TUCKER. "The Renaissance," in A Literary History of England. Edited by Albert C. Baugh. New York: Appleton-Century-Crofts, 1948, pp. 313–696.
Provides overview of Greene's prose fiction: discusses influences on Greene and his influence on later writers, his style, and his movement from romance to realism (pp. 421–28). See 137.

1277   BROWN, ELAINE V. BEILIN. "The Uses of Mythology in Elizabethan Romance." Ph.D. dissertation, Princeton University, 1973, 336pp.
Analyzes Greene's use of the Judgment of Paris myth in Menaphon and Ciceronis Amor, and of the Venus myth in his prose fiction generally.

Greene

1278   BROWN, J. M. "An Early Rival of Shakespere." New Zealand
        Magazine, No. 6 (April 1877), pp. 97-133.
            Examines attack on Shakespeare in Groatsworth. Sections
        reprinted in 1461.

1279   BROWNE, C. ELLIOT. "The Date of Greene's Menaphon." N&Q, 49
        (25 April 1874), 334.
            Replies to 1460, affirming that first edition was pub-
        lished in 1589.

1280   BROWNE, C. ELLIOT. "Greene's 'Upstart crow.'" N&Q, 50 (25
        July 1874), 64.
            Points out use of "crow" to refer to Greene's detractors
        in commendatory sonnet to Perimedes.

1281   BROWNE, C. ELLIOT. "Marlowe and Machiavelli." N&Q, 52 (14
        August 1875), 141-42.
            Discusses reference to Machiavelli in Groatsworth of Wit;
        suggests allusion is to Marlowe.

1282   BROWNE, C. ELLIOT. "On Shakespeare's Pastoral Names." N&Q,
        48 (27 December 1873), 509-10.
            Suggests that Chettle took the name of Melicert (Eng-
        land's Mourning Garment) from Greene's Menaphon.

1283   C., P. A. "A Study of Shakespeare's Winter's Tale: Considered
        in Connection with Greene's Pandosto and the Alkestis of
        Euripides." Poet-Lore, 4, no. 10 (1892), 516-21.
            Provides an "outline for a comparative study" of Pandosto
        and The Winter's Tale along with "suggestions of subjects
        for papers" and "propositions for discussion."

1284   CAMDEN, CARROLL, JR. "Chaucer and Greene." RES, 6 (January
        1930), 73-74.
            Notes parallel in Greene's Farewell to Folly to Chaucer's
        use of a proverb comparing old men to leeks; suggests Greene
        might have taken it from Chaucer.

1285   C[ARO], J. "Über die eigentliche Quelle des Wintermärchens von
        Shakspeare." Magazin für die Literatur des Auslandes, 64,
        no. 32 (1863), 392-94.
            Examines story of Ziemowit as source for Pandosto. See
        1365.

1286   CARO, J. "Die historischen Elemente in Shakespeare's Sturm und
        Wintermärchen." Englische Studien, 2 (1879), 141-85.
            Suggests possibility that European tale of Ziemowit might
        have formed the basis for Pandosto.

*1287   CAWLEY, ROBERT RALSTON. "The Influence of the Voyagers in
         Non-Dramatic English Literature between 1550 and 1560."
         Ph.D. dissertation, Harvard University, 1921.
              See 1288.

1288   CAWLEY, ROBERT RALSTON. Unpathed Waters: Studies in the In-
         fluence of the Voyagers on Elizabethan Literature. Prince-
         ton: Princeton University Press, 1940, 295pp.
              Examines Greene's use of geographic detail in his prose
         fiction. Points out that he used classical sources more
         than contemporary geographic knowledge and that although he
         invents details much of his inaccuracy is due to the common
         misinformation of the age (pp. 215-20, passim).

1289   CHAPMAN, WILLIAM H[ALL]. William Shakspere and Robert Greene:
         The Evidence. Oakland, California: Tribune Publishing
         Co., 1912, 190pp.
              Argues that Will Kemp, not Shakespeare, is the object of
         Greene's censure in Groatsworth.

1290   CHAPMAN, WILLIAM HALL. Shakespeare the Personal Phase. [Los
         Angeles: United Printing Co.], 1920, 425pp.
              In "Who Was Shake-Scene? (The Object of Robert Greene's
         Censure)," pp. 281-372, discusses references in Groatsworth:
         identifies Shakescene as Will Kemp or Robert Wilson and
         "young Juvenal" as Lodge. Points out similarities between
         Black Book's Messenger and Repentance of Robert Greene.

1291   COLE, HOWARD C. A Quest of Inquirie: Some Contexts of Tudor
         Literature. Indianapolis: Pegasus, Bobbs-Merrill Co.,
         1973, 596pp.
              Includes discussion of influences on Greene's prose fic-
         tion and the relationships between his prose fiction and
         his plays (passim).

1292   COLLIER, J[OHN] PAYNE. "Old Ballad upon the Winter's Tale."
         N&Q, 3 (4 January 1851), 1-3.
              Notes particulars of a ballad "The Royal Courtly Garland,
         or Joy after Sorrow," which was possibly based on Pandosto.

1293   COLLINS, J[OHN] CHURTON. "General Introduction," in The Plays
         & Poems of Robert Greene, Vol. I. By Robert Greene. Edited
         by J[ohn] Churton Collins. Oxford: Clarendon Press, 1905,
         1-69.
              Attempts to ascertain "in what way and to what extent
         the novels which are assumed to be autobiographical really
         are so." Provides overview of Greene's prose fiction.

Greene

1294 COLLINS, JOHN CHURTON. "The Predecessors of Shakespeare," in
Essays and Studies. By John Churton Collins. London: Macmillan, 1895, pp. 91-192.
Includes general appreciative discussion of Greene's
prose fiction. Discusses "Greene's favourite theme"--"the
contrast between the purity and long-suffering of woman,
and the follies and selfishness of man" (pp. 162-70).

1295 COLLINS, ROBERT ARNOLD. "The Christian Significance of the
Astrological Tradition: A Study in the Literary Use of
Astral Symbolism in English Literature from Chaucer to
Spenser." Ph.D. dissertation, University of Kentucky, 1968,
261pp.
Examines how Greene in Planetomachia "develops a personi-
fication of the planet Saturn into a symbol of Christian as-
ceticism, opposing it, in a kind of astrological debate,
with a portrait of Venus suggestive of the new Humanism."

1296 CORSER, THOMAS. "Greene's Groatsworth of Witte." N&Q, 3 (14
June 1851), 479.
Comments briefly on differences in preliminary matter of
1596 edition and that of 1617 and of 1621.

1297 CRANE, THOMAS FREDERICK. Italian Social Customs of the Sixteenth Century and Their Influence on the Literatures of
Europe. Cornell Studies in English. New Haven: Yale University Press, 1920, 705pp.
Includes a synoptic overview of Greene's prose fiction
to illustrate the influence of Italian culture and literature on his works; asserts that "[n]o writer of this period
[i.e., the sixteenth century]...shows more markedly the influence of Italy than Robert Greene" (pp. 521-28).

1298 CURTIS, G. B. "A Study in Elizabethan Typography." Baconiana,
3rd Ser., 24 (1939), 6-21.
Identifies two states of Lodge's commendatory sonnet in
Spanish Masquerado (A2^v) and applies Bacon's bi-lateral
cipher to poem. Argues against Ewen's conclusions (1321).

1299 D., C. "Robert Greene's Arbasto." N&Q, 61 (12 June 1880),
472.
Gives bibliographical description of 1584 edition "hitherto unknown." See 1300 for correction.

1300 D., C. "Robert Greene's Arbasto." N&Q, 61 (19 June 1880),
493.
Corrects previous note (1299), indicating that an imper-
fect copy of 1584 edition is listed in Hazlitt's Handbook
(17).

1301   DAVIS, C. A. C. "The Upstart Crow." TLS, 17 August 1951,
        p. 517.
            Suggests that Edward Alleyn "was the real target for
        Greene's malice."

1302   DAVIS, WALTER R[ICHARDSON]. Idea and Act in Elizabethan Fic-
        tion. Princeton: Princeton University Press, 1969, 311pp.
            Analyzes phases of development and changes of style in
        Greene's prose fiction; discusses influences on his prose
        fiction; examines function of role-playing and disguise in
        the works. Finds a "radical disjunction of moral value and
        real action" in examining relationship between ideal and
        actual in Greene's fiction (passim).

1303   DAVIS, WALTER R[ICHARDSON]. "The Plagiarisms of John Hynd."
        N&Q, NS, 16 (March 1969), 90-92.
            Traces Hind's borrowings from Penelope's Web in Eliosto
        Libidinoso.

1304   DEAN, JAMES S., JR. "Antedatings from Robert Greene." N&Q,
        NS, 10 (August 1963), 296-98.
            Lists OED antedatings from Euphues His Censure to Phi-
        lautus and Philomela.

1305   DEAN, JAMES S., JR. "Antedatings from Robert Greene." N&Q,
        NS, 16 (April 1969), 126-28.
            Lists OED antedatings from Greene's prose fiction.

1306   DEAN, JAMES S., JR. "Borrowings from Robert Greene's Philomela
        in Robert Davenport's The City-Night-Cap." N&Q, NS, 13
        (August 1966), 302-303.
            Adds to Jordan's list of borrowings (1353).

1306a   DEAN, J[AMES] S. "Greek to the Popular Elizabethan Printer:
        Some Examples from Robert Greene's Romances." Analytical &
        Enumerative Bibliography, 1 (Summer 1977), 189-202.
            Examines errors in Greek in Planetomachia, Euphues His
        Censure to Philautus, and Greene's Never too Late, suggest-
        ing that errors were typical of those made by Elizabethan
        compositors setting Greek. Credits compositors rather than
        Greene with the errors.

1307   DEAN, J[AMES] S., JR. "Robert Greene's Romantic Heroines:
        Caught up in Knowledge and Power?" BSUF, 4, no. 4 (Autumn
        1973), 3-12.
            Analyzes how Fawnia and Sephestia "are important in that
        they share in the knowledge of Fate and the power of Love,
        and become romantic instruments of comic resolution."

Greene

Examines Greene's conception of his heroines: how they re-
act to fate and how through love they "instinctively bring
about both personal and political order." Argues against
common view that Greene's women are one-dimensional.

1308   DÉDÉYAN, CHARLES. "Dante en Angleterre: Dante et les poètes
        élisabéthains: Churchyard, Harvey, Greene, et Spenser."
        LR, 15 (1961), 235-60.
            Examines two of Greene's references to Dante: identifies
        passage from Mamillia as a translation of Louise Labé's
        Debat de folie et d'amour; notes that passage ostensibly
        translated from Dante in Farewell to Folly is not from
        Dante's works.

1309   DELIUS, N[IKOLAUS]. "Greene's Pandosto und Shakespeare's
        Winter's Tale." Shakespeare-Jahrbuch, 15 (1880), 22-43.
            Analyzes Shakespeare's use of Pandosto as source.

1310   DENT, ROBERT W. "Greene's Gwydonius: A Study in Elizabethan
        Plagiarism." HLQ, 24 (February 1961), 151-62.
            Points out extent of Greene's plagiarism from Pettie's
        Petite Palace and discusses his techniques of adapting what
        he copied.

*1311   DEWAR, R. "Robert Greene." Reading University College Review,
        6 (1914), 115-38.
            Not located. Listed in 1202.

1312   DOHERTY, PAUL COLMAN. "The Prose Works of Robert Greene."
        Ph.D. dissertation, University of Missouri, Columbia, 1964,
        295pp.
            Devotes chapters to study of "style, narrative, and
        rhetoric" of Greene's prose fiction. Examines Repentance
        of Robert Greene "in the context of his [Greene's] time and
        of his fiction."

1313   DREW, PHILIP. "Was Greene's 'Young Juvenal' Nashe or Lodge?"
        SEL, 7 (Winter 1967), 55-66.
            Reviews evidence for and against both as subject of allu-
        sion in Groatsworth of Wit.

1314   DUNLOP, JOHN [COLIN]. The History of Fiction: Being a Criti-
        cal Account of the Most Celebrated Prose Works of Fiction,
        from the Earliest Greek Romances to the Novels of the
        Present Age, Vol. III. Revised edition. Edinburgh: Long-
        man, Hurst, Rees, Orme, and Browne, 1816, 524pp.
            Includes discussion of Shakespeare's use of Pandosto and
        provides a synopsis of Philomela, "the most beautiful" of
        Greene's prose works (pp. 436-47). See 183.

1315   DURHAM, CHARLES W. III.   "Character and Characterization in
       Elizabethan Prose Fiction." Ph.D. dissertation, Ohio Uni-
       versity, 1969, 147pp.
           Examines Greene's methods of characterization.

1316   DYCE, ALEXANDER. "Some Account of Robert Greene and His Writ-
       ings," in <u>The Dramatic and Poetical Works of Robert Greene</u>
       & George Peele, Vol. I. By Robert Greene and George Peele.
       Edited by Alexander Dyce. London: William Pickering, 1831,
       i-cxii.
           Discusses several of Greene's prose fiction works in the
       context of his life and times and provides lengthy extracts
       from <u>Pandosto</u>, <u>Greene's Never too Late</u>, and <u>Groatsworth of
       Wit</u>. Includes a "List of Greene's Prose-Works" and reprints
       the poems from the prose fiction works in the body of the
       edition. <u>See</u> 1438.

1317   EIN, RONALD BORIS. "The Serpent's Voice: Commentary and
       Readers' Beliefs in Elizabethan Fiction." Ph.D. disserta-
       tion, Indiana University, 1974, 273pp.
           Examines implied narrator commentary in "the narrator
       summary" at the beginning of <u>Pandosto</u>.

1318   ENNIS, LAMBERT. "Anthony Nixon: Jacobean Plagiarist and
       Hack." <u>HLQ</u>, 3 (July 1940), 377-401.
           Points out Nixon's plagiarism of <u>Greene's Mourning Gar-
       ment</u> in his <u>A Strange Foot-Post</u>.

1319   ESLER, ANTHONY. "Robert Greene and the Spanish Armada." <u>ELH</u>,
       32 (September 1965), 314-32.
           Examines Greene's use of "cultural symbolism" in <u>The
       Spanish Masquerado</u> to argue that the work mirrors the Eliza-
       bethan attitude toward the Spanish war.

1320   EVERITT, E. B. <u>The Young Shakespeare: Studies in Documentary
       Evidence</u>. Anglistica, 2. Copenhagen: Rosenkilde and
       Bagger, 1954, 188pp.
           Explains allusions in Nashe's Preface to <u>Menaphon</u> and in
       Greene's <u>Groatsworth of Wit</u>; discusses relationship of these
       works with other pamphlets written about the same time.
       Examines evidence for Greene's authorship of <u>Cobbler of
       Canterbury</u> (passim).

1321   EWEN, C. L'ESTRANGE. "The Gallup Decipher." <u>Baconiana</u>, 22
       (October 1935), 66-77; (January 1937), 253-58.
           Criticizes Elizabeth Gallup's application of Bacon's bi-
       lateral cipher to Greene's <u>Spanish Masquerado</u>. <u>See also</u>:
       Henry Seymour, "A Note on the Foregoing," <u>Baconiana</u>, 22.

Greene

(October 1935), 77–79; and B. G. Theobald, "Mrs. Gallup's
Competence," <u>Baconiana</u>, 22 (June 1936), 125–27. <u>See</u> 1298.

1322   FERRARA, FERNANDO. <u>L'opera narrativa di Robert Greene</u>. Col-
lana Ca' Foscari, Facoltà di Lingue e Letterature Straniere.
Venice: La Goliardica Editrice, 1957, 383pp.
Analyzes evolution of Greene's narrative art. Examines
sources and influences on individual works, Greene's style,
his narrative techniques, his characterization, his themes,
and relationships of his prose fiction to his plays.

1323   FORSYTHE, ROBERT S. "Notes on <u>The Spanish Tragedy</u>." <u>PQ</u>, 5
(January 1926), 78–84.
Suggests Kyd's probable indebtedness to <u>Planetomachia</u>.

1324   FREEMAN, ARTHUR. "Notes on the Text of <u>2 Henry VI</u> and the
'Upstart Crow.'" <u>N&Q</u>, NS, 15 (April 1968), 128–30.
Adds support to Wilson's argument (1489) that Greene is
attacking Shakespeare for plagiarism.

1325   FRIEDERICH, REINHARD H. "Myself Am Centre of My Circling
Thought: Studies in Baroque Personae (Burton and Donne)."
Ph.D. dissertation, University of Washington, 1971, 194pp.
Argues that because of "character credibility and flexi-
bility rather than plot manipulation" Nashe's <u>Unfortunate</u>
<u>Traveller</u> and Gascoigne's <u>Master F. J.</u> "succeed, whereas
Greene and Deloney fail since their static characters cannot
generate more than didactic or simply cumulative structures."

1326   GARKE, ESTHER. <u>The Use of Songs in Elizabethan Prose Fiction</u>.
Bern: Francke Verlag, 1972, 132pp.
Draws frequently on Greene's works of prose fiction for
examples in analysis of types of songs, their relationships
to plot and structure, and their functions (to complement
or contrast setting, to present character relationships, to
characterize singer and audience). In Part II, provides a
detailed analysis of Greene's use of songs in <u>Menaphon</u>, particularly their contributions to atmosphere, characterization, and structure.

1327   GEREVINI, SILVANA. "Shakespeare 'Corvo Rifatto.'" <u>Letterature</u>
<u>Moderne</u>, 7, no. 2 (1957), 195–205.
Argues that interpretation of "upstart crow" passage in
<u>Groatsworth of Wit</u> must be divorced from the problems sur-
rounding the <u>Henry VI</u> plays and <u>The True Tragedy of Richard</u>
<u>Duke of York</u>.

1328 GISELA, JUNKE. "Formen des Dialogs im frühen englischen Roman." Ph.D. dissertation, University of Köln, 1975, 150pp.
Examines form and use of dialogue in Mamillia, Card of Fancy, and Pandosto. See 208.

1329 GOEPP, PHILIP H. II. "The Narrative Material of Apollonius of Tyre." ELH, 5 (June 1938), 150-72.
Suggests relationship between the Constance cycle in Apollonius and plot of Pandosto, arguing that "there is sufficient similarity to make very unlikely the notion that Greene himself invented the story."

1330 GOREE, ROSELLE GOULD. "Concerning Repetitions in Greene's Romances." PQ, 3 (January 1924), 69-75.
Discusses deliberate nature of Greene's repetition of passages from his own work. Adds to Hart's lists of repetitions (1334). See 1471.

1331 GREENE, ROBERT. Green Pastures: Being Choice Extracts from the Works of Robert Greene, M. A., of both Universities, 1560(?)-1592. Compiled by Alexander B. Grosart. Elizabethan Library. Chicago: A. C. McClurg, [1894], 189pp.
Provides extracts (arranged alphabetically by subject heading, e.g., "Abominable," "Idleness," "Perseverence Wins") from Greene's works.

1332 GRUBB, MARION. "Lodge's Borrowing from Ronsard." MLN, 45 (June 1930), 357-60.
Identifies sources in Ronsard's poetry for Lodge's complimentary verse prefixed to Spanish Masquerado.

1333 GUBAR, SUSAN DAVID. "Tudor Romance and Eighteenth-Century Fiction." Ph.D. dissertation, University of Iowa, 1972, 243pp.
Includes examination of structure and style of Greene's prose fiction: discusses reader response and how the works "call attention to their own literariness."

1334 HART, H[ENRY] C[HICHESTER]. "Robert Greene's Prose Works." N&Q, 112 (1 July 1905), 1-5; (29 July 1905), 81-84; (26 August 1905), 162-64; (16 September 1905), 224-27; (16 December 1905), 483-85; 113 (3 February 1906), 84-85; (17 March 1906), 202-204; (5 May 1906), 343-44; (2 June 1906), 424-25; (9 June 1906), 442-45; (16 June 1906), 463-65; (23 June 1906), 484-87; (30 June 1906), 504-506. [Reprinted as: H(enry) Chichester Hart. Some Remarks on Robert Greene's Prose Works: Chiefly with Reference to the Use He Has Made of Other Writers. London: Athenaeum Press, n.d., 83pp.]

Greene

Discusses characteristics of Greene's borrowings from
other writers and traces his use of his own works and those
of Lyly and Pierre de la Primaudaye as sources. Discusses
the influence of Greene on Lodge's Rosalynde, suggesting
that "it is hard to believe that...[Greene] did not touch
it up for the press." See 1330, 1445, and 1471.

1335 HATCHER, O. L. "The Sources and Authorship of The Thracian
Wonder." MLN, 23 (January 1908), 16-20.
Discusses Menaphon as one of the sources of the play.

1336 HELGERSON, RICHARD. The Elizabethan Prodigals. Berkeley:
University of California Press, 1976, 188pp.
Provides detailed examination of Greene's uses of the
Prodigal Son motif in his prose fiction, particularly the
relationships between Greene himself and his prodigal characters. Analyzes Greene's movement from didactic to romantic fiction and his seeming repudiation of the latter.
Examines his departure "from the humanistic moral tradition"
in his use of the repentance motif (passim).

1337 HELGERSON, RICHARD. "Lyly, Greene, Sidney, and Barnaby Rich's
Brusanus." HLQ, 36 (February 1973), 105-18.
Discusses influence of Gwydonius on plot and euphuistic
style of Brusanus. Points out that Rich carries on process
begun by Greene of diluting "euphuistic rhetoric with action."

1338 HELGERSON, RICHARD. "The Prodigal Son in Elizabethan Fiction."
Ph.D. dissertation, Johns Hopkins University, 1970, 197pp.
Examines Greene's use of Prodigal Son motif. See 1336.

1339 HENDERSON, ARCHIBALD, JR. "Family of Mercutio." Ph.D. dissertation, Columbia University, 1954, 270pp.
Examines ways in which Peratio (Morando) "display[s] the
traits of the mocker at love and at women."

1340 HERFORD, C[HARLES] H. "A Few Suggestions on Greene's Romances
and Shakspere." New Shakspere Society Transactions, 1888,
pp. 181-90.
Discusses influence of Farewell to Folly, Greene's Mourning Garment, and Euphues His Censure to Philautus on
Shakespeare.

1341 HILL, N. W. "Greene's Menaphon." N&Q, 118 (1 August 1908),
85-86.
Identifies characters in Menaphon with contemporary playwrights.

1342   HILL, ROWLAND MERLIN. "Realistic Descriptive Setting in Eng-
       lish Fiction from 1550 through Fielding." Ph.D. disserta-
       tion, Boston University, 1941, 344pp.
          Finds that "Greene made a...circumstantial use of the
       stage-property type of setting, providing a rather minutely
       worked-out locale employed in and essential to the action,
       and so affording narrative probability." Suggests that
       "[t]he most exceptional use of setting by the early pam-
       phleteers was probably Greene's perhaps accidental use of
       it to create a mood productive of change in character."

1343   HOLLIDAY, CARL. English Fiction from the Fifth to the Twenti-
       eth Century. New York: Century Co., 1912, 461pp.
          Includes discussion of Lyly's influence on Greene and
       his style (pp. 152-60).

1344   HONIGMAN, E. A. J. "Shakespeare's 'Lost Source-Plays.'" MLR,
       49 (July 1954), 293-307.
          Argues reference in Groatsworth of Wit to the "upstart
       crow" "was not meant to suggest that Shakespeare had revised
       plays by...other writers, but that he had pilfered senten-
       tiae and examples." Suggests parallels between Groatsworth
       of Wit and Nashe's Epistle to Menaphon.

1345   HORNÁT, JAROSLAV. Anglická renesanční próza: eufuistická
       beletrie od Pettieho Paláce Potěchy do Greenova Pandosta
       [Renaissance Prose in England: Euphuistic Fiction from
       Pettie's Palace of Pleasure to Greene's Pandosto]. Acta
       Universitatis Carolinae, Philologica, Monographia, 33.
       Prague: Universita Karlova, 1970, 173pp.
          Examines influence of Lyly on Greene's prose fiction,
       Greene's place in the development of euphuistic fiction,
       the development of his prose fiction, his sources, and the
       structure of his works (pp. 105-54).

1346   HORNÁT, JAROSLAV. "Mamillia: Robert Greene's Controversy with
       Euphues." PP, 5 (1962), 210-18.
          Analyzes Greene's attempt to establish thematic and
       structural parallels with Euphues. Argues that Greene, in
       his favorable treatment of women and his creation of "posi-
       tive heroines," deliberately offered a contrast to the atti-
       tude toward women in Euphues: The Anatomy of Wit.

1347   HORNÁT, JAROSLAV. "Two Euphuistic Stories of Robert Greene:
       The Carde of Fancie and Pandosto." PP, 6 (1963), 21-35.
          Discusses works in the context of the development of
       euphuistic fiction. Analyzes symmetrical parallelism of
       style, structure, episodes, characters, and action in

Greene

Gwydonius. Discusses sources, analogies with Greene's earlier works, and structure of Pandosto. Analyzes Greene's combination of two types of fiction in Pandosto: the tragic novella (story of Pandosto) and the pastoral tale (story of Dorastus and Fawnia).

1348   HUNTER, G. K. "Isocrates' Precepts and Polonius' Character." SQ, 8 (Autumn 1957), 501-506.
      Uses extracts from Gwydonius and Greene's Mourning Garment to illustrate the popularity and conventionality of Polonius's advice to Laertes.

1349   INGLEBY, C[LEMENT] M[ANSFIELD]. "Greene's 'Young Juvenal.'" Athenaeum, No. 2418 (28 February 1874), p. 292.
      Argues against Staunton's conclusion (1459) that the reference is to Nashe; argues for Lodge. See 1458.

1350   JEAFFRESON, J[OHN] CORDY. "Robert Greene," in Novels and Novelists from Elizabeth to Victoria, Vol. I. London: Hurst and Blackett, 1858, 7-27.
      Asserts that Greene's "works give the reader the most agreeable idea of what a novel at the end of the sixteenth century was." Provides lengthy extract from Greene's Never Too Late.

1351   JENKINS, HAROLD. "On the Authenticity of Greene's Groatsworth of Wit and The Repentance of Robert Greene." RES, 11 (January 1935), 28-41.
      Offers refutations of Sanders's arguments against authenticity of Groatsworth of Wit (1442). Argues work was written before 1592.

1352   JONES, FREDERIC L. "Another Source for The Trial of Chivalry." PMLA, 47 (September 1932), 668-70.
      Argues that Gwydonius was source of "enveloping action" and conclusion of play. Notes set of parallel characters.

1353   JORDAN, JOHN CLARK. "Davenport's The City Nightcap and Greene's Philomela." MLN, 36 (May 1921), 281-84.
      Discusses Greene's work as source of the play. Concludes that the speeches in Philomela "have more of genuine emotion." See 1306.

*1354   JORDAN, JOHN CLARK. "Robert Greene." Ph.D. dissertation, Columbia University, 1915, 231pp.
      See 1355.

1355   JORDAN, JOHN CLARK. Robert Greene. New York: Columbia Uni-
        versity Press, 1915, 243pp.
            Traces development of Greene's prose fiction: discusses
        influence of Lyly on early works; examines "frame-work
        tales" and romances; discusses characterization; analyzes
        use of Prodigal Son motif and other themes. Provides anno-
        tated chronology of Greene's works.

1356   JUNG, FRITZ. Greene, Nash, und die Schauspieler. Freiburg:
        Hochreuther, 1911, 62pp.
            Examines Greene's criticism of actors in his prose fic-
        tion.

1357   JUSSERAND, J[EAN] J[ULES]. The English Novel in the Time of
        Shakespeare. Translated by Elizabeth Lee. Revised edition.
        London: T. Fisher Unwin, 1890, 433pp.
            Provides overview of Greene's prose fiction (arranged by
        type). Discusses autobiographical elements, didacticism,
        characterization, style (and Lyly's influence upon it), and
        influence on later writers (pp. 150-92).

1358   KAHIN, HELEN ANDREWS. "Jane Anger and John Lyly." MLQ, 8
        (March 1947), 31-35.
            Suggests that Jane Anger's Jane Anger Her Protection for
        Women was written in reply to Greene's Euphues His Censure
        to Philautus.

*1359   KENDALL, JACK L. "The Relation between the Plays and the Ro-
        mances of Robert Greene." Ph.D. dissertation, Yale Univer-
        sity, 1955, 930pp.
            Abstract not available.

1360   KENYON, F. G. "Greene's Planetomachia." TLS, 21 December
        1916, p. 625.
            Discusses omission of leaves following prefatory matter
        in some copies of 1585 edition.

1361   KLEIN, KARL LUDWIG. Vorformen des Romans in der englischen
        erzählenden Prosa des 16. Jahrhunderts. FAGAAS, 13.
        Heidelberg: C. Winter, 1969, 260pp.
            Includes discussion of style and characterization of Ned
        Browne in Black Book's Messenger (pp. 99-126).

1362   KNAPP, MARY. "A Note on Nash's Preface to Greene's Menaphon."
        N&Q, 164 (11 February 1933), 98.
            Explains phrase "thrust Elisium into Hell" and suggests
        that Marlowe is "the object of this allusion."

Greene

1363 KOEPPEL, EMIL. "Beiträge zur Geschichte des elisabethanischen
      Dramas." Englische Studien, 16 (1892), 357-74.
          Includes notes on Greene's prose fiction as source for
      various Elizabethan plays.

1364 KOEPPEL, EMIL. Studien zur Geschichte der italienischen
      Novelle in der englischen Litteratur des sechzehnten Jahr-
      hunderts. Quellen und Forschungen, 70. Strassburg: K. J.
      Trübner, 1892, 106pp.
          Identifies Italian sources of and influences on Greene's
      prose fiction; discusses his style and influence of Pettie
      on his works (pp. 51-58).

1365 KOZMIAN, STANISLAUS. "'A Winter's Tale.'" Athenaeum, No.
      2506 (6 November 1875), p. 609.
          Relates Caro's account (1285) of the history of Ziemowit,
      which served as the "original source" of Pandosto.

1366 KRAPP, GEORGE PHILIP. The Rise of English Literary Prose.
      New York: Oxford University Press, 1915, 565pp.
          Includes an overview of Greene's prose fiction to illus-
      trate his tendency to adopt different forms and his inabil-
      ity to exploit possibilities for realism (pp. 492-502,
      passim).

1367 KRIEFELTS, BARBARA. "Eine statistische Stilanalyse zur
      Klarung von Autorenschaftsfragen, durchgefuhrt am Beispiel
      von Greens Groatsworth of Wit." Ph.D. dissertation, Uni-
      versity of Köln, 1972, 128pp.
          Through computer analysis of style of Greene and Chettle
      argues that Chettle was author of Groatsworth of Wit.

1368 KRIEGER, GOTTFRIED. Gedichteinlagen im englischen Roman.
      Ph.D. dissertation, University of Köln. Köln: n.p., 1969,
      274pp.
          Includes discussion of function and relation to theme
      and structure of verse insets in Greene's prose fiction
      (passim).

1369 KÜNSTLER, ERNST. "Böhmen am Meer." Shakespeare-Jahrbuch, 91
      (1955), 212-16.
          Suggests that Greene's depiction of Bohemia having a
      seacoast was the result of humanist transmission of Enea
      Silvio Piccolomini's description of Bohemia as situated on
      the Baltic.

1370 LARSON, CHARLES H[OWARD]. "Robert Greene's Ciceronis Amor:
      Fictional Biography in the Romance Genre." SNNTS, 6 (Fall
      1974), 256-67.

224

In examining work as prose romance, discusses reasons
for its popularity, its plot, Greene's development of the
principal characters as representational types, and his
"revelation of theme through character."

1371   LAUCHERT, FRIEDRICH. "Der Einfluss des Physiologus auf den
        Euphuismus." Englische Studien, 14 (1890), 188-210.
        Examines influence of works about natural history on
euphuism. Provides listings of references to animals in
the works of Lyly, Greene, and Lodge.

1372   LAWLOR, JOHN. "Pandosto and the Nature of Dramatic Romance."
        PQ, 41 (January 1962), 96-113.
        Analyzes "differences of plot and characterisation" be-
tween Pandosto and Shakespeare's The Winter's Tale to assess
"the characteristics of romance as a dramatic form."

1373   LEE, A. COLLINGWOOD. "Nash's Menaphon: 'Eternisht.'" N&Q,
        84 (8 August 1891), 116.
        Replies to earlier query (James T. Foard, "Nash's Mena-
phon," N&Q, 84 [11 July 1891], 28-29), explaining Nashe's
allusion in Preface to "tale of John a Brainford's will"
and suggesting that "eternisht" means "eternized."

1374   LIEVSAY, JOHN LEON. "Greene's Panther." PQ, 20 (July 1941),
        296-303.
        Discusses the "mixture...of tradition and invention" in
allusions to panther in Greene's prose works.

1375   LIEVSAY, JOHN LEON. "Robert Greene, Master of Arts, and
        'Mayster Steeven Guazzo.'" SP, 36 (October 1939), 577-96.
        Details Greene's borrowings from George Pettie's trans-
lation of Stefano Guazzo's La Civil conversation in Mamillia, Penelope's Web, and Farewell to Folly.

1376   LIEVSAY, JOHN LEON. Stefano Guazzo and the English Renais-
        sance, 1575-1675. Chapel Hill: University of North Caro-
        lina Press, 1961, 358pp.
        Suggests that Greene used Guazzo's La Civil conversation
as source in his prose fiction (pp. 99-107).

1377   LINDHEIM, NANCY R[OTHWAX]. "Lyly's Golden Legacy: Rosalynde
        and Pandosto." SEL, 15 (Winter 1975), 1-20.
        Discusses Greene's adaptation and modification of the
elements of euphuism. Concludes that "Greene employed the
soliloquy of moral choice as the main vehicle of character
delineation and as the structural principle for his general
world view"; the result was not "Lyly's world of inevitable

Greene

> paradox...but a world of moral anarchy, where choice is
> balanced against choice but there is no stable criterion
> for making decisions."

1378   McCOY, DOROTHY SCHUCHMAN. Tradition and Convention: A Study
of Periphrasis in English Pastoral Poetry from 1557-1715.
SEngL, 5. The Hague: Mouton, 1965, 289pp.
Includes examination of characteristics of style in
Menaphon. Finds that Greene's "language [is] more ornamental and less witty than that of Sidney" and that Greene's
"intention to create the appearance of brilliant play of
intellect...supersedes all other intentions" (pp. 176-85).

1379   McDONALD, EDWARD D. "An Example of Plagiarism among Elizabe-
than Pamphleteers: Samuel Rowlands' Greenes Ghost Haunting
Conie-Catchers." Indiana University Studies, 1, no. 11.
Bloomington: Indiana University, 1913, pp. 143-70.
Traces Rowlands's extensive borrowings from Black Book's
Messenger.

1380   MacLAINE, ALLAN H. "Greene's Borrowings from His Own Prose
Fiction in Bacon and Bungay and James the Fourth." PQ, 30
(January 1951), 22-29.
Discusses relationship of "incidentals, plot ideas, and
character types" between prose works and the two plays.

1381   McNEAL, THOMAS H. "The Clerk's Tale as a Possible Source for
Pandosto." PMLA, 47 (June 1932), 453-60.
Discusses similarities "in characters, in situations,
and in general plot-structure" between the two works as support for the possibility that Greene might have used Chaucer's work as a source.

*1382   McNEAL, THOMAS H. "The Influence of Chaucer on the Works of
Robert Greene." Ph.D. dissertation, University of Texas
at Austin, 1937.
Abstract not available.

1383   McNEAL, THOMAS H. "The Literary Origins of Robert Greene."
Shakespeare Association Bulletin, 14 (July 1939), 176-81.
Summarizes critical commentary on Greene's sources (Lyly,
Sidney, Boccaccio, Greek romances, Italian novelle).

1384   McNEAL, THOMAS H. "Who Is Silvia?--And Other Problems in the
Greene-Shakspere Relationship." Shakespeare Association
Bulletin, 13 (October 1938), 240-54.
Discusses motif of "a lady, adorned by nature with much
beauty and many virtues, who receives a host of suitors,

usually men of rank from foreign parts" in <u>Mamillia</u>; suggests that Shakespeare (in <u>The Two Gentlemen of Verona</u> and
<u>The Merchant of Venice</u>) was influenced by Greene's use of
this motif.

1385 McNEIR, WALDO F. "The Date of <u>A Looking Glass for London</u>."
<u>N&Q</u>, NS, 2 (July 1955), 282-83.
Discusses relationship of theme of repentance in play to
Greene's prose fiction of 1589-1590.

1386 McNEIR, W[ALDO] F. "Greene's 'Tomliuclin': <u>Tamburlaine</u>, or
<u>Tom a Lincoln</u>?" <u>MLN</u>, 58 (May 1943), 380-82.
Argues that "life of Tomliuclin" in prefatory epistle to
<u>Greene's Farewell to Folly</u> is an allusion to the story of
Tom a Lincoln, not Marlowe's <u>Tamburlaine</u>.

1387 McNEIR, WALDO F. "A Proverb of Greene's Emended." <u>N&Q</u>, 197
(15 March 1952), 117.
Suggests that "Achilles" should be "a child's" in "Her-
cules shoo on Achilles foote" (<u>Penelope's Web</u>).

1388 McNEIR, WALDO F. "Robert Greene and <u>John of Bordeaux</u>." <u>PMLA</u>,
64 (September 1949), 781-801.
Discusses parallels between <u>John of Bordeaux</u> and Greene's
prose fiction, suggesting that tale of Calamus and Cratyna
in <u>Penelope's Web</u> was possible source of Ferdinand-Rossalin
relationship in play.

1389 MAGENDIE, MAURICE. <u>Le Roman français au XVIIe siècle: De
l'Astrée au Grand Cyrus</u>. Paris: E. Droz, 1932, 457pp.
Includes discussion of influence of Regnault's translation of <u>Pandosto</u> upon Du Bail's <u>Roman d'Albanie et Sicile</u>
(pp. 67-71).

1390 M[ARDER], L[OUIS]. "Chettle's Forgery of the <u>Groatsworth of
Wit</u> and the 'Shake-scene' Passage." <u>ShN</u>, 20 (December
1970), 42.
Summarizes findings in 1255.

1391 M[ARDER], L[OUIS]. "Greene's Attack on Shakespeare: A Posthumous Hoax?" <u>ShN</u>, 16 (September 1966), 29-30.
Reports on Austin's investigation of authorship of
<u>Groatsworth of Wit</u> (<u>see</u> 1255).

1392 MATULKA, BARBARA. <u>The Novels of Juan de Flores and Their European Diffusion: A Study in Comparative Literature</u>. Comparative Literature Series. New York: Institute of French
Studies, 1931, 493pp.

Greene

Shows that <u>A Pair of Turtle Doves</u> is not a translation
of De Flores's <u>Grisel y Mirabella</u> but that it is based upon
<u>Aurelio and Isabel</u>. Provides comparison with earlier trans-
lation and discusses translator's "exaggerated euphuistic
style" (pp. 212-19).

1393   MAVEETY, S. R. "What Shakespeare Did with <u>Pandosto</u>: An Interpretation of <u>The Winter's Tale</u>," in <u>Pacific Coast Studies</u>
<u>in Shakespeare</u>. Edited by Waldo F. McNeir and Thelma N.
Greenfield. Eugene: University of Oregon, 1966, pp. 263-
79.
Analyzes how "Shakespeare deliberately manipulated his
source (Greene's <u>Pandosto</u>) in the first three acts to create
a framework for his action that gives no hope of the grace
of God." Contrasts treatment of Leonates's/Pandosto's
jealousy in the two works.

1394   MILLER, EDWIN H[AVILAND]. "The Pamphlets of Robert Greene."
Ph.D. dissertation, Harvard University, 1951, 184pp.
Includes examination of <u>Groatsworth of Wit</u> and provides
brief overview of Greene's prose fiction, noting his lack
of effective characterization and his style.

1395   MILLER, EDWIN HAVILAND. <u>The Professional Writer in Elizabethan</u>
<u>England: A Study of Nondramatic Literature</u>. Cambridge:
Harvard University Press, 1959, 296pp.
Discusses Greene as an example of "how exploitative
Elizabethan professionals were" of patrons and examines his
ability to appeal to popular taste (passim).

1396   MILLER, EDWIN HAVILAND. "The Relationship of Robert Greene
and Thomas Nashe (1588-1592)." <u>PQ</u>, 33 (October 1954),
353-67.
Suggests that reference in <u>Groatsworth of Wit</u> to joint
authorship of a "Comedie" is to a prose work, not a play.
Suggests collaboration on <u>Defense of Cony-Catching</u>.

1397   MILLER, EDWIN H[AVILAND]. "Samuel Rid's Borrowings from
Robert Greene." <u>N&Q</u>, NS, 1 (June 1954), 236-38.
Identifies Rid's use of <u>Black Book's Messenger</u> as source
for his <u>Martin Mark-All</u>.

1398   MILLS, LAURENS J. <u>One Soul in Bodies Twain: Friendship in</u>
<u>Tudor Literature and Stuart Drama</u>. Bloomington, Indiana:
Principia Press, 1937, 480pp.
Examines Greene's use of friendship theme in his prose
fiction, particularly "the use he makes of it in connection
with love, of a court-of-love type, silvered over with
Platonism" (pp. 196-214).

1399   MITHAL, H. S. D.   "The Authorship of <u>Fair Em</u> and <u>Martin Mar-</u>
       <u>Sixtus</u>."   <u>N&Q</u>, NS, 7 (January 1960), 8-10.
          Discusses Greene's attack in <u>Mourning Garment</u> on the
       author of <u>Fair Em</u> and R. W.'s reference in <u>Martin Mar-Sixtus</u>
       to Greene's attack.

1400   MONTGOMERIE, WILLIAM.   "Sporting Kid (The Solution of the
       'Kidde in Aesop' Problem)."   <u>Life and Letters To-Day</u>, 36
       (January 1943), 18-24.
          Suggests that Nashe (in Preface to <u>Menaphon</u>) used refer-
       ence because he recognized parallels between Spenser's
       <u>Shepheards Calender</u> ("May") and <u>Hamlet</u>.

1401   MOORMAN, F[REDERIC] W[ILLIAM].   "Introduction," in <u>The Winter's</u>
       <u>Tale</u>.   By William Shakespeare.   Edited by F[rederic] W[il-
       liam] Moorman.   Arden Shakespeare.   London: Methuen, 1912,
       pp. ix-xxxiii.
          Discusses influence of Greek romance on <u>Pandosto</u> and
       Shakespeare's use of Greene's work as source.

1402   MORLEY, HENRY.   <u>English Writers, IX: Spenser and His Time</u>.
       London: Cassell & Co., 1892, 472pp.
          Provides a general overview of Greene's prose fiction
       (pp. 215-26, 268-79).

1403   MOWAT, BARBARA ADAMS.   "A Tale of Sprights and Goblins."   <u>SQ</u>,
       20 (Winter 1969), 37-46.
          Examines differences between <u>Winter's Tale</u> and <u>Pandosto</u>.

1404   MUIR, KENNETH.   "Greene and <u>Troilus and Cressida</u>."   <u>N&Q</u>, NS, 2
       (April 1955), 141-42.
          Points out "resemblances" between <u>Euphues His Censure to</u>
       <u>Philautus</u> and <u>Troilus and Cressida</u>, and suggests that
       Shakespeare "took a great deal of atmospheric detail from
       Greene's book."

1405   MUIR, KENNETH.   <u>Shakespeare's Sources, I: Comedies and Trag-</u>
       <u>edies</u>.   London: Methuen & Co., 1957, 279pp.
          Includes discussion of Shakespeare's use of <u>Pandosto</u> as
       source for <u>The Winter's Tale</u> (pp. 240-51).

1406   N., E. L.   "The <u>Winter's Tale</u>."   <u>N&Q</u>, 3 (8 February 1851), 101.
          Calls attention to an inaccurate reference in edition of
       <u>Pandosto</u> in 1207.

1407   NICHOLSON, BRINSLEY.   "Jottings in By-Ways, II: <u>Euphues' Sha-</u>
       <u>dow</u>, Lodge's or Greene's?"   <u>N&Q</u>, 49 (10 January 1874), 21-23.
          Argues that Lodge, not Greene, was author.

Greene

1408   NICHOLSON, WATSON. "Pandosto and The Winter's Tale." MLN, 21
       (November 1906), 219-20.
          Discusses how Shakespeare's changes in geography and
       plot have caused confusion in identifying characters in the
       play with their originals in Pandosto. Also offers a cor-
       rection to 1213.

1409   NILLSSON, P. G. "The Upstart Crow and Henry VI." MSpr, 58
       (1964), 293-303.
          Argues that Greene's attack on Shakespeare in Groatsworth
       of Wit was caused by Greene's jealousy and bitterness over
       Shakespeare's revisions of The Contention and The True Tra-
       gedy of Richard Duke of York, plays on which Greene had
       collaborated.

1410   O'CONNOR, JOHN J. "On the Authorship of the Ratsey Pamphlets."
       PQ, 30 (October 1951), 381-86.
          Points out borrowings in Ratsey's Ghost from Greene's
       Menaphon and Groatsworth of Wit.

*1411 OKUBO, JUNICHIRO. "Romantic Motives in The Winter's Tale--
       From Greene's Romance to Shakespeare." Kanazawa Daigaku
       Hobungakubu Ronshu, No., 12 (1965), pp. 1-22.
          Not located. Listed in Walter E. Habenicht, "Shakespeare:
       An Annotated World Bibliography for 1965," SQ, 17 (1966),
       270.

1412   OLIVE, W. J. "Davenport's Debt to Shakespeare in The City-
       Night-Cap." JEGP, 49, no. 3 (1950), 333-44.
          In footnotes, points out several "hitherto unlisted"
       parallels between play and Philomela.

1413   OLIVER, LESLIE MAHIN. "The Spanish Masquerado: A Problem in
       Double Edition." Library, 5th Ser., 2 (June 1947), 14-19.
          Analyzes the bibliographical problems in and printing of
       the two states of the 1589 edition.

1414   ØSTERBERG, V[ALDEMAR]. "Nashe's 'Kid in Aesop': A Danish
       Interpretation." Translated by J[ohn] Dover Wilson. RES,
       18 (October 1942), 385-94.
          Provides paraphrase of portion of 1415 discussing allu-
       sion in Nashe's "Epistle" to Greene's Menaphon.

1415   ØSTERBERG, V[ALDEMAR]. Studier over Hamlet-teksterne. Copen-
       hagen: Gyldendalske, 1920, 75pp.
          Examines Nashe's allusion to "Kid in Aesop" (Preface to
       Menaphon); argues that allusion is to Kyd. See 1414.

1416   PARR, JOHNSTONE. "Robert Greene and His Classmates at Cam-
          bridge." PMLA, 77 (December 1962), 536-43.
              Suggests that the "few verbal similarities" between
          Mamillia and Melbancke's Philotimus might be due to fact
          that the two were classmates at St. John's. That Lyly was
          incorporated M.A. in 1579 at Cambridge might explain
          Greene's imitation of Euphues in Mamillia. Suggests that
          G. B. who composed prefatory verses for Mamillia, Alcida,
          and Ciceronis Amor was William Boston.

1417   PARR, JOHSTONE. "Sources of the Astrological Prefaces in
          Robert Greene's Planetomachia." SP, 46 (July 1949), 400-
          410.
              Shows that first preface is "an almost direct translation
          of Lucian's De Astrologia plagiarized under the guise of
          his [Greene's] own essay"; the second is a translation of a
          portion of Joannis Joviani Pontano's "Aegidius Dialogus."
          Also shows that Greene's citations from authorites must be
          viewed with suspicion.

1418   PARR, JOHNSTONE, and I. A. SHAPIRO. Instructions to Editors
          of the Works of Robert Greene: Compiled in Preparation for
          an Edition Sponsored by the Shakespeare Institute (Univer-
          sity of Birmingham) and the University of Alabama. Strat-
          ford-upon-Avon: Shakespeare Institute, University of
          Birmingham, 1959, 35pp.
              Provide instructions for handling text and commentary
          and presenting results of bibliographical analysis and col-
          laboration of editions.

1419   PARRILL, WILLIAM BRUCE. "The Elizabethan Background of Hell,
          the Devil, the Magician, and the Witch, and Their Use in
          Elizabethan Fiction." Ph.D. dissertation, University of
          Tennessee, 1964, 321pp.
              "[S]tudies the uses which Nashe, Greene, Dekker, Lodge
          and the other fiction writers made of the wide variety of
          material available" on the topics. Finds that use was
          largely satirical.

1420   PEARCE, T. M. "On the Chettle-Greene Question." ShN, 21
          (February 1971), 4.
              Comments on 1258, suggesting that Chettle might have re-
          written passages while editing the manuscript of Greene's
          Groatsworth of Wit. In following reply, Austin reasserts
          evidence pointing to Chettle's authorship.

1421   PENNEL, CHARLES A[LEXANDER]. "Robert Greene and 'King or
          Kaisar.'" ELN, 3 (September 1965), 24-26.

Greene

Notes that phrase, which occurs in <u>Greene's Mourning Garment</u>, is not as common as usually thought.

1422   PEROTT, JOSEPH DE. "Robert Greene and the Italian Translation of <u>Achilles Tatius</u>." <u>MLN</u>, 29 (February 1914), 63.
Identifies Italian translation of <u>Clitophon and Leucippe</u> used by Greene as source in his prose fiction.

1423   PEROTT, JOSEPH DE. "Robert Greenes Entlehnung aus dem <u>Ritterspiegel</u>." <u>Englische Studien</u>, 39 (1908), 308-309.
Points out Greene's use of <u>Le Chevalier du soleil</u> as source for passage in <u>Pandosto</u>.

1424   PIERCE, SYDNEY JANE. "Borrowings and Originality in the Works of Robert Greene." Ph.D. dissertation, University of Rochester, 1972, 272pp.
Examines characteristics of Greene's prose fiction and the nature and use of his borrowings from other works to argue that "the influence of his sources upon his works is negligible in most cases."

1425   PORTER, CHARLOTTE, and HELEN A. CLARKE. "Sources," in <u>The Winter's Tale</u>. By William Shakespeare. Edited by Charlotte Porter and Helen A. Clarke. New York: T. Y. Crowell, 1908, pp. 118-25.
Discuss Shakespeare's use of <u>Pandosto</u> as source.

1426   POSTON, MARIANNE SHEARS. "Robert Greene's Satire." Ph.D. dissertation, University of Illinois at Urbana-Champaign, 1969, 304pp.
Examines characteristics--satiric personae, subjects, style--of Greene's satiric technique in <u>Never Too Late</u>, <u>Francesco's Fortunes</u>, and <u>Groatsworth of Wit</u>.

1427   POTEZ, HENRI. "Le Premier roman anglais traduit en Francais." <u>RHL</u>, 11 (1904), 42-55.
Discusses Regnault's translation (1615) of <u>Pandosto</u>; examines his handling of Greene's text.

1428   PRUVOST, R[ENÉ]. "Greene's <u>Gwydonius</u>." <u>TLS</u>, 6 August 1925, p. 521.
Questions whether the "Debate between Folly and Love" was included in 1584 edition, of which no copy can be located. <u>See</u> 1440.

1429   PRUVOST, RENÉ. <u>Matteo Bandello and Elizabethan Fiction</u>. Bibliothèque de la Revue de Littérature Comparée, 113. Paris: H. Champion, 1937, 349pp.

Traces the influence of Bandello on Greene's prose fiction; examines the sentimental rhetoric and the psychological element in the characterization in analyzing Mamillia
as an imitation of Euphues (passim).

1430   PRUVOST, RENÉ. "Réflexions sur l'euphuisme a propos de deux
        romans élisabéthains." Revue Anglo-Américaine, 8 (1931),
        1-18.
            Analyzes tone, style, theme, and characterization in
        Greene's Menaphon to argue that, while Greene was influenced
        by Lyly, the term "euphuistic" is insufficient to charac-
        terize the nature of the work. Argues that the influence
        of arcadianism must also be recognized.

1431   PRUVOST, RENÉ. "Robert Greene a-t-il accusé Shakespeare de
        plagiat?" EA, 12, no. 3 (1959), 198-204.
            Refutes Wilson's arguments (1489) and reaffirms his
        earlier conclusion (1432) that Greene in Groatsworth of Wit
        did not accuse Shakespeare of plagiarism.

1432   PRUVOST, RENÉ. Robert Greene et ses romans (1558-1592): Con-
        tribution à l'histoire de la Renaissance en Angleterre.
        Publications de la Faculté des Lettres d'Alger, 2d ser.,
        2. Paris: Belles Lettres, 1938, 650pp.
            Analyzes influence of Lyly on style and subject matter
        of Greene's fiction; examines characteristics of Greene's
        style; traces sources of each work. Analyzes themes and
        techniques in, and form of, each work. Examines Greene's
        place in development of Elizabethan prose fiction. In-
        cludes bibliography of Greene's works.

1433   PYLE, FITZROY. The Winter's Tale: A Commentary on the Struc-
        ture. New York: Barnes & Noble, 1969, 211pp.
            Includes discussion of Shakespeare's use of Pandosto as
        source (passim).

1434   QUAINTANCE, RICHARD E., JR. "The French Source of Greene's
        'What Thing Is Love?'" N&Q, NS, 10 (August 1963), 295-96.
            Traces source of poem in Menaphon to poem by Saint-
        Gelais; argues that "Dorons Eclogue joynd with Carmelas"
        "is more mock pastoral than mock blazon."

1435   Q[UILLER-COUCH, ARTHUR]. "Introduction," in The Winter's Tale.
        By William Shakespeare. Edited by Arthur Quiller-Couch and
        John Dover Wilson. Cambridge: Cambridge University Press,
        1931, pp. vii-xxvi.
            Includes discussion of Shakespeare's use of Pandosto as
        source (pp. xiii-xviii).

Greene

1436   RANSON, DAVID NICHOLAS. "Tarletons Newes Out of Purgatorie:
        A Critical Edition with Introduction and Commentary."
        Ph.D. dissertation, Case Western Reserve University, 1974,
        233pp.
            Argues that Greene was author.

1437   RE, ARUNDELL DEL. "Two Elizabethan Realists: Robert Greene
        and Thomas Nashe," in The Secret of the Renaissance and
        Other Essays and Studies. By Arundell del Re. Tokyo:
        Kaitakusha, 1930, pp. 72-112.
            Discusses Greene's style and examines in general terms
        his contribution to "the evolution of realistic prose fic-
        tion."

1438   REARDON, JAMES P. "The Maiden's Dream by Robert Greene: An
        Unknown Poetical Tract," in The Shakespeare Society's
        Papers, Vol. II. London: Shakespeare Society, 1845, 127-
        29.
            Provides additions and corrections to catalogue of
        Greene's works in 1316.

1439   RIBNER, IRVING. "Greene's Attack on Marlowe: Some Light on
        Alphonsus and Selimus." SP, 52 (April 1955), 162-71.
            Discusses reasons for Greene's attack on Marlowe in
        "Address to the Gentlemen Readers" which prefaces Perimedes.

1440   ROBERTS, W. "Greene's Gwydonius." TLS, 20 August 1925,
        p. 545.
            Answers 1428; traces provenance of Huntington copy of
        1584 edition.

1441   SANDERS, CHAUNCEY ELWOOD. "Greene's Last Years." Ph.D. dis-
        sertation, University of Chicago, 1929.
            Evaluates biographical detail drawn from Greene's own
        work. Discusses allusions in Groatsworth of Wit and ana-
        lyzes "the suspicious circumstances surrounding the publi-
        cation of Greene's posthumous works." Suggests that Groats-
        worth of Wit was subjected to "a violent process of edit-
        ing."

1442   SANDERS, CHAUNCEY ELWOOD. "Robert Greene and His 'Editors.'"
        PMLA, 48 (June 1933), 392-417.
            Examines evidence for Greene's authorship of Groatsworth
        of Wit and events surrounding publication of work. Con-
        siders it unlikely that work is by Greene alone; suggests
        it is partly Greene's work but was "edited" before publica-
        tion. See 1351.

1443   SANDERS, CHAUNCEY [ELWOOD], and WILLIAM A. JACKSON. "A Note
        on Greene's <u>Planetomachia</u> (1585)." <u>Library</u>, 4th Ser., 16
        (March 1936), 444-47.
            Points out that confusion in make-up of most copies is
        due to division of copy between two compositors. Describes
        one Bodleian copy (Tanner 253) as complete and correct.

1444   SANDERS, NORMAN. "Greene's 'Tomliuolin.'" <u>N&Q</u>, NS, 9 (June
        1962), 229-30.
            Explains how misreading "Tomliuclin" in <u>Farewell to Folly</u>
        arose; suggests that Greene is referring to a well-known
        piece of ephemeral literature, possibly a lost ballad of
        "Thomalyn."

1445   SANDERS, NORMAN. "Robert Greene's Way with a Source." <u>N&Q</u>,
        NS, 14 (March 1967), 89-91.
            Supplements Hart's list (1334) of Greene's borrowings
        from Pierre de la Primaudaye's <u>French Academy</u>.

1446   SCHELLING, FELIX E[MMANUEL]. "<u>A Groatsworth of Wit</u>," in <u>The</u>
        <u>Queen's Progress and Other Elizabethan Sketches</u>. By Felix
        E[mmanuel] Schelling. London: Laurie, 1904, pp. 129-47.
            Transcribes portions of work and identifies playwrights
        alluded to in prefatory remarks.

1447   ŠEŠPLAUKIS, ALFONSAS. "Early Theories on East European Sources
        of Shakespeare's <u>The Tempest</u> and <u>The Winter's Tale</u>."
        <u>Lituanus</u>, 12 (1965), 45-62.
            Surveys scholarship on source of Greene's <u>Pandosto</u>. Con-
        cludes that possibility of an Eastern European source is
        still open to question.

1448   SHINDLER, JOHN HARRISON. "New Meaning for an Old Tale: The
        Literary Background of Shakespeare's <u>The Winter's Tale</u>," in
        "I. New Meaning for an Old Tale: The Literary Background
        of Shakespeare's <u>The Winter's Tale</u>. II. Active Longing:
        A Reading of Henry Vaughan's 1650 <u>Silex Scintillans</u>. III.
        The Writer-Narrator's Struggle in Laurence Sterne and Samuel
        Beckett." Ph.D. dissertation, Rutgers University, 1975,
        165pp.
            Examines "how Shakespeare's use of Lodge's <u>Rosalynde</u> [as
        a source] for <u>As You Like It</u> affects his later use of
        Greene's <u>Pandosto</u> [as a source] for <u>The Winter's Tale</u>."
        Finds that "Shakespeare transforms <u>Pandosto</u> by bringing a
        restorative pastoral structure to it."

1449   SIMPSON, R[ICHARD]. "Shakspere Allusion-Books." <u>The Academy</u>,
        5 (11 April 1874), 400-401.

Greene

> Argues that Greene's "young Juvenal" (<u>Groatsworth of
> Wit</u>) is a reference to Nashe, not Lodge. <u>See</u> 1458-59. Re-
> printed in 1212.

1450 SMART, JOHN SEMPLE. <u>Shakespeare: Truth and Tradition</u>. London: E. Arnold & Co., 1928, 224pp.
> Includes explication of passage on Shakespeare in <u>Groats-</u>
> <u>worth of Wit</u>; argues that it is evidence of Shakespeare's
> authorship of <u>III Henry VI</u> (pp. 191-98).

1451 SMITH, G. C. MOORE. "Lyly, Greene, and Shakespeare." <u>N&Q</u>,
116 (14 December 1907), 461.
> Points out Greene's use of Lyly's <u>Campaspe</u> and <u>Euphues</u>
> as a source for <u>Pandosto</u>.

1452 SMITH, HALLETT. <u>Shakespeare's Romances: A Study of Some Ways</u>
<u>of the Imagination</u>. San Marino: Huntington Library, 1972,
258pp.
> In Chapter 6 ("<u>The Winter's Tale</u> and <u>Pandosto</u>," pp. 95-
> 120) discusses Shakespeare's transformation of Greene's
> romance, illustrating how Shakespeare "underlines or forti-
> fies the convention[s]" of the Greek romance.

1453 SMITH, JOHN DALE. "Narrative Technique in the Realistic Prose
Fiction of Greene, Nashe, and Deloney." Ph.D. dissertation,
University of Wisconsin, 1968, 323pp.
> "[T]races Greene's development as a realistic story-
> teller." Finds that <u>Groatsworth of Wit</u> "clearly foreshadows
> the autobiographical fiction of the nineteenth and twentieth
> centuries." Examines Greene's place in the development of
> the novel.

1454 SOUTH, HELEN PENNOCK. "The Upstart Crow." <u>MP</u>, 25 (August
1927), 83-86.
> Traces tradition of classical and medieval antecedents
> of fable of crow dressed in feathers from another bird and
> suggests Greene's possible sources.

1455 SPENCER, TERENCE. "Shakespeare's Isle of Delphos." <u>MLR</u>, 47
(April 1952), 199-202.
> Explains Greene's allusion to Apollo's oracle at Delphos
> (<u>Pandosto</u>) by noting that in the seventeenth century the
> island of Delos "was commonly known as Delphos."

1456 SPERONI, CHARLES. "Did Greene Have Shakespeare in Mind?" <u>MLN</u>,
87 (January 1972), 139-41.
> Cites evidence from Greene's <u>The Royal Exchange</u> which
> points to disenchantment with players expressed in <u>Groats-</u>
> <u>worth of Wit</u>.

1457   STANFORD, ANN. "Shakespeare and Francis Sabie." SQ, 15
        (Autumn 1964), 454-55.
            Compares briefly the treatment of Mepsa/Mopsa in Sabie's
        The Fisher-Man's Tale with Greene's Pandosto, the source of
        Sabie's poem.

1458   STAUNTON, H[OWARD]. "Greene's Young Juvenal." Athenaeum,
        No. 2421 (21 March 1874), p. 391.
            Answers 1349, reiterating evidence that Nashe is the ob-
        ject of the reference in Groatsworth of Wit (see 1459 and
        1449).

1459   STAUNTON, H[OWARD]. "A Mistaken Allusion to Shakespeare."
        Athenaeum, No. 2415 (7 February 1874), pp. 193-94.
            Identifies references to playwrights in Groatsworth of
        Wit; argues that the "young Juvenal" is Nashe. See 1349,
        1458, and 1449.

1460   STOROJENKO, NICHOLAS. "The Date of Greene's Menaphon." N&Q,
        48 (6 December 1873), 441-42.
            Shows that 1587 edition is a ghost which was created out
        of a misunderstanding of a passage in Euphues His Censure
        to Philautus; argues that 1589 edition was the first edi-
        tion. See 1279.

1461   STOROJENKO, NICHOLAS. Robert Greene: His Life and Works. A
        Critical Investigation. Translated by E. A. Brayley
        Hodgetts. In The Life and Complete Works in Prose and Verse
        of Robert Greene, Vol. I. By Robert Greene. Edited by
        Alexander B. Grosart. Huth Library. London: Printed for
        Private Circulation, 1881, 440pp.
            Includes chronological overview of Greene's prose fic-
        tion: provides brief synopsis of each work, comments on
        sources and/or influences. Discusses style, autobiographi-
        cal elements, and Shakespeare's use of Pandosto as source
        for Winter's Tale. Finds that "the majority of Greene's
        works are so-called love-pamphlets, of almost every vari-
        ety." In "Introduction to Professor Storojenko's Life of
        Greene," pp. ix-lxxxvii, Grosart provides running commentary
        on work and reproduces "substantially" 1278. Also argues
        that "young Juvenal" in Groatsworth of Wit refers to Nashe.

1462   THOMAS, SIDNEY. "The Meaning of Greene's Attack on Shake-
        speare." MLN, 66 (November 1951), 483-84.
            Suggests that phrase in Groatsworth of Wit likely would
        have been read as an accusation of plagiarism because of
        the Elizabethan association of "the concept of borrowed
        plumage with literary theft."

Greene

1463 THOMAS, SIDNEY. "The Printing of Greenes Groatsworth of Witte
and Kind-Harts Dreame." SB, 19 (1966), 196-97.
Establishes that the copy for Groatsworth of Wit was divided between two printers, John Wolfe and John Danter.

1464 THORNTON, RICHARD H. "Notes on Words for the N.E.D." N&Q,
130 (28 November 1914), 424-26.
Draws several examples from Greene's prose fiction.

*1465 TIMMERMAN, JOHN R. "Robert Greene, Prose Fictionist and
Dramatist." Ph.D. dissertation, University of Texas at
Austin, 1952, 199pp.
Abstract not available.

1466 TOYNBEE, PAGET. "Two Alleged Quotations from Dante by Robert
Greene." Athenaeum, No. 3877 (15 February 1902), p. 210.
Points out misquotations from Dante in Mamillia and
Farewell to Folly. Suggests Greene was quoting from memory
and requests sources. (See Paget Toynbee, "References to
Dante by Robert Greene," Athenaeum, No. 3878 [22 February
1902], p. 243).

1467 TRIENENS, ROGER J. "The Green-Eyed Monster: A Study of
Sexual Jealousy in the Literature of the English Renaissance." Ph.D. dissertation, Northwestern University, 1949,
184pp.
Finds that "[t]he Italianate manner of presenting jealous
characters both for the sake of entertainment and as a basis
for common-sense moralizing is best exemplified in Elizabethan prose by...Pandosto...[and] Philomela."

1468 TUCKERMAN, BAYARD. A History of English Prose Fiction from
Sir Thomas Malory to George Eliot. New York: G. P. Putnam's Sons, 1882, 339pp.
Includes discussion of Lyly's influence on Greene's style
and brief critical estimates of his major prose fiction
works (pp. 82-90).

1469 VELZ, JOHN W. "Robert Greene and Philip of Macedon." N&Q,
NS, 12 (May 1965), 195.
Traces source of references to Philip in Pandosto and
Morando to Plutarch's Moralia.

1470 VETTER, THEODOR. ["Robert Greene und seine Prosa,"] in Ver-
handlungen der vierundvierzigsten Versammlung deutscher
Philologen und Schulmänner in Dresden. Edited by Reinhard
Albrecht. Leipzig: Teubner, 1897, pp. 147-51.

Report of a talk by Vetter: provides brief overview of
Greene's autobiographical pamphlets and questions the authenticity of Groatsworth.

1471 VINCENT, C[HARLES] J[ACKSON]. "Further Repetitions in the
Works of Robert Greene." PQ, 18 (January 1939), 73-77.
Adds to lists by Hart (1334) and Goree (1330).

1472 VINCENT, CHARLES JACKSON. "Natural History in the Works of
Robert Greene." Ph.D. dissertation, Harvard University,
1938.
Provides detailed investigation of Greene's sources for
his references to natural history.

1473 VINCENT, C[HARLES] J[ACKSON]. "Pettie and Greene." MLN, 54
(February 1939), 105-11.
Provides evidence of Greene's borrowings from Pettie,
arguing that A Petite Palace, rather than Lyly's Euphues,
is the main source of Greene's prose style.

1474 WALKER, ROY. "'The Upstart Crow.'" TLS, 10 August 1951,
p. 501.
Suggests possible borrowings from Greene by Shakespeare
that caused the diatribe.

1475 WALSH, WILLIAM PATRICK. "Robert Greene, Moralist: A Study of
the Renaissance Ideals of Love and Courtship in His Prose
and Drama, 1580-1592." Ph.D. dissertation, University of
California, Riverside, 1971, 417pp.
Analyzes how Greene in his prose fiction "portray[s] a
moral ideal of romantic love which is related to the notion
of romantic marriage emerging in the Renaissance."

1476 WELD, JOHN S[ALTAR]. "Some Problems of Euphuistic Narrative:
Robert Greene and Henry Wotton." SP, 45 (April 1948),
165-71.
Examines Greene's borrowings from Wotton's Courtly Controversy in Mamillia not "for the sake of explaining motivation or supporting argument" but for providing ornamentation.
Suggests that while Greene is moving away from a medieval
assumption that a "generalized argument...must apply to all
individuals of a species" he does not achieve "the fully
developed position that the individual is of dominating
interest."

1477 WELD, JOHN SALTAR. "Studies in the Euphuistic Novel, 1576-
1640." Ph.D. dissertation, Harvard University, 1940, 304pp.

Greene

Shows that Greene used Jacques d'Yver's <u>Le Printemps d'Yver</u> as source in several works; illustrates other euphuistic writers' use of Greene as source.

1478 WELD, JOHN S'[ALTAR]. "W. Bettie's <u>Titana and Theseus</u>." <u>PQ</u>, 26 (January 1947), 36-44.
Traces Bettie's extensive borrowings from <u>Pandosto</u>.

1479 WELLS, STANLEY [W.]. "Greene and Pliny." <u>N&Q</u>, NS, 8 (November 1961), 422-24.
Examines natural history allusions in <u>Planetomachia</u> which Greene borrowed from <u>A Summary of the Antiquities and Wonders of the World Abstracted out of...Pliny</u>.

1480 WELLS, STANLEY W. "Impartial." <u>N&Q</u>, NS, 6 (October 1959), 353-54.
Explains meaning of "impartial" in <u>Perimedes</u>.

1481 WELLS, STANLEY [W.]. "Shakespeare and Romance," in <u>Later Shakespeare</u>. Edited by John Russell Brown and Bernard Harris. Stratford-upon-Avon Studies, 8. New York: St. Martin's Press, 1967, pp. 48-79.
Includes discussion of romance elements in <u>Pandosto</u> and Shakespeare's alteration of them in his use of Greene's work as source for <u>The Winter's Tale</u>.

1482 WELLS, STANLEY [W.]. "A Shakespearean Droll?" <u>TN</u>, 15 (1961), 116-17.
Argues that the eighteenth-century droll <u>The Famous History of Dorastus and Fawnia</u> was an adaptation of Shakespeare's <u>The Winter's Tale</u> rather than <u>Pandosto</u>.

1483 WELLS, STANLEY [W.]. "Some Words in 1588." <u>N&Q</u>, NS, 9 (June 1962), 205-207.
Lists <u>OED</u> antedatings and new meanings from <u>Perimedes</u> and <u>Pandosto</u>.

1484 WHITAKER, VIRGIL K. "Still Another Source for <u>Troilus and Cressida</u>," in <u>English Renaissance Drama: Essays in Honor of Madeleine Doran & Mark Eccles</u>. Edited by Standish Henning, Robert Kimbrough, and Richard Knowles. Carbondale, Illinois: Southern Illinois University Press; London: Feffer & Simons, 1976, pp. 100-107.
Discusses parallels between <u>Euphues His Censure to Philautus</u> and <u>Troilus and Cressida</u> in examining possibility of Shakespeare's use of Greene's work as a source for various aspects of the play, including "the cynical...treatment of the Trojan War itself."

1485 WHITE, MARGARET IMOGINE ZECHIEL. "The Influence of John Lyly's
Euphues upon Selected Pieces of Elizabethan Prose Fiction."
Ph.D. dissertation, University of Illinois at Urbana-Cham-
paign, 1971, 332pp.
Examines influence of Lyly's style, themes, didacticism,
and narrative techniques and devices on Mamillia.

1486 WHITE, R. S. "'Comedy' in Elizabethan Prose Romances." YES,
5 (1975), 46-51.
Includes examination of meaning of Greene's use of term
in his romances.

1487 WHITEFORD, ROBERT NAYLOR. Motives in English Fiction. New
York: G. P. Putnam's Sons, 1918, 390pp.
Discusses influence of euphuism on Greene's prose fiction
and examines the autobiographical element in his works
(pp. 23-31).

1488 WHITMAN, JAMES DALTON, JR. "The Lyric Poetry of Robert
Greene." Ph.D. dissertation, Florida State University,
1966, 164pp.
Includes discussion of relationships between poetry and
prose in Greene's prose fiction: points out how Greene frequently used poems to describe characters in the works.
Argues that Greene was author of Cobbler of Canterbury.

1489 WILSON, J[OHN] DOVER. "Malone and the Upstart Crow." ShS, 4
(1951), 56-68.
In arguing that Greene was accusing Shakespeare of plagiarism in Groatsworth of Wit, examines the classical background of the "upstart crow" allusion and speculates on
Greene's reasons for attacking Shakespeare. See 1324 and
1431.

1490 WOLFF, SAMUEL LEE. The Greek Romances in Elizabethan Prose
Fiction. Columbia University Studies in Comparative Literature. New York: Columbia University Press, 1912, 539pp.
Discusses Greene's use of Boccaccio as a source in his
prose fiction and examines influence of Greek romances on
his works. Discusses in detail Greene's treatment of fortune (pp. 367-458).

1491 WOLFF, S[AMUEL] L[EE]. "Robert Greene and the Italian Renaissance." Englische Studien, 37, no. 3 (1907), 321-74.
Examines influence of culture, thought, and literature
of Italy, and the influence of Greene's "underlying Puritanism" on his literary work. Praises Greene for his talent at
narrative, but argues that his Puritanism "prevents his

Greene

imagination from ever acquiring power enough to weld together narrative and moralistic elements."

1492   WOLFF, SAMUEL LEE.   "The Winter's Tale, Greene's Pandosto, and
       the Greek Romances."   PMLA, 25, Appendix (1910), xxii-xxiii.
           Abstract of paper read at 1909 MLA meeting: points out
       Greene's use of Greek romance, especially Heliodorus's
       Aethiopica and Daphnis and Chloe in Day's translation.

1493   WOODWARD, PARKER.   Euphues the Peripatician.   London: Gay and
       Bird, 1907, 208pp.
           In Chapter III ("The Red-Nosed Minister," pp. 54-70)
       argues that Bacon was author of Greene's prose fiction.

1494   WRIGHT, [JULIA] CELESTE TURNER.   "Mundy and Chettle in Grub
       Street."   Boston University Studies in English, 5 (Autumn
       1961), 129-38.
           Discusses circumstances surrounding publication of
       Groatsworth of Wit.

1495   ZEITLER, WILLIAM IRVING.   "The Life, Works, and Literary In-
       fluence of William Warner."   Ph.D. dissertation, Harvard
       University, 1928.
           Includes examination of Greene's use of Warner's works
       as sources.

GRIMESTON, EDWARD

Simon Goulart, Admirable and Memorable Histories.   STC 12135.

Studies

1496   BOAS, F[REDERICK] S.   "Edward Grimeston, Translator and Ser-
       geant-at-Arms."   MP, 3 (April 1906), 395-409.
           Discusses briefly Admirable Histories in the context of
       Grimeston's life and other translations.

1497   BOKLUND, GUNNAR.   The Duchess of Malfi: Sources, Themes,
       Characters.   Cambridge: Harvard University Press, 1962,
       199pp.
           Includes examination of Webster's use of Admirable His-
       tories as source (passim).

1498   CLARK, G. N.   "Edward Grimeston, the Translator."   EHR, 43
       (October 1928), 585-98.
           Discusses background and general characteristics of
       Grimeston's translations; provides list of his works.

H., L.

Gratiae Ludentes: Jests from the Universities.

Studies

1499   DESCONOCIDO. "Note on a Passage in Hudibras." N&Q, 2 (29
        June 1850), 68-69.
            Suggests the jest "One that Wore but One Spur" (Gratiae
        Ludentes) as source of a passage in Hudibras.

HART, ALEXANDER (fl. 1640)

The Tragi-Comicall History of Alexto and Angelica. STC 12885.

Editions

1500   Alexto and Angelica. Translated by Alexander Hart. In Short
        Fiction of the Seventeenth Century. Edited by Charles
        C[arroll] Mish. Stuart Editions. New York: New York Uni-
        versity Press, 1963, pp. 365-421.
            Reprints modernized text of 1640 edition. In brief in-
        troductory note, discusses Hart's stylistic excesses and
        bookishness. See 60.

Studies

1501   WELD, JOHN SALTAR. "Studies in the Euphuistic Novel, 1576-
        1640." Ph.D. dissertation, Harvard University, 1940, 304pp.
            Traces sources of Alexto and Angelica.

HEALEY, JOHN (d. 1610)

Joseph Hall, The Discovery of a New World. STC 12686.

Editions

1502   HALL, JOSEPH. The Discovery of a New World (Mundus Alter et
        Idem). Translated by John Healey. Edited by Huntington
        Brown. Cambridge: Harvard University Press, 1937, 266pp.
            Provides annotated, emended text of 1609 edition. In
        "Introduction," pp. xv-xxv, discusses Healey's treatment of
        Hall's Latin text; finds that Healey's translation has "the
        integrity of an independent work."

Healey

1503   HALL, JOSEPH. The Discovery of a New World. Translated by
          John Healey. English Experience, 119. Amsterdam: Theatrvm
          Orbis Terrarvm; New York: Da Capo Press, 1969, 278pp.
          Provides facsimile reprint of 1609 edition.

Studies

1504   DAVENPORT, A. "Samuel Rowlands." N&Q, NS, 2 (April 1955),
          150.
              Points out Rowlands's use of Healey's Discovery as a
          source for Martin Markall.

1505   LACASSAGNE, C[LAUDE]. "La Satire religieuse dans Mundus Alter
          et Idem de Joseph Hall." RANAM, 4 (1971), 141-56.
              Uses Healey's translation to analyze the subjects and
          techniques used by Hall in his religious satire.

1506   PETHERICK, EDWARD A. "Mundus Alter et Idem." Gentleman's
          Magazine, 281 (July 1896), 66-87.
              Discusses differences in preliminary matter in two copies
          of Healey's translation and the light the differences throw
          on the question of Hall's authorship of work.

HERE AFTER FOLOWETH A TREATYSE TAKEN OUT OF A BOKE WHICHE THEODOSIUS
FOUNDE IN IHERÙSALEM IN THE PRETORYE OF PYLATE OF JOSEPH OF
ARIMATHY

   STC 14806.

Editions

1507   The Life of Joseph of Armathy, in Joseph of Arimathie: Other-
          wise Called the Romance of the Seint Graal, or Holy Grail.
          Edited by Walter W. Skeat. EETS, Original Ser., 44. Lon-
          don: Oxford University Press for the Early English Text
          Society, 1871, pp. 25-32.
              Provides annotated reprint of De Worde edition. In
          "Preface," pp. vii-xlvii, briefly discusses sources.

HERE BEGINNETH THE LYF OF THE MOSTE MYSCHEVOUST ROBERT THE DEVYLL

   STC 21070-21071.

Editions

1508   The Lyfe of Robert the Deuyll: A Romance, in A Collection of
          Early Prose Romances, Vol. I. Edited by William J. Thoms.

Here Begynneth...Mary of Nemmegen

London: William Pickering, 1828, 62pp. (separately paginated). [Also published separately.]
    Provides reprint of unidentified edition. In introduc-
tory note (pp. iii–vi), comments on publishing history.
Reprinted 1509–10.

1509   Robert the Deuyll, in Early Prose Romances. Edited by Henry
       Morley. Carisbrooke Library, 4. London: G. Routledge,
       1889, pp. 167–206.
           Reprints text from 1508. In "Introduction" traces de-
       velopment of the legend (pp. 14–17). Reprinted 1510.

1510   Robert the Deuyll, in Early English Prose Romances. Edited by
       William J. Thoms. Revised and enlarged edition. London:
       G. Routledge and Sons; New York: E. P. Dutton and Co.,
       [1907], pp. 167–206.
           Reprints 1509.

Studies

1511   HAMILTON, DONNA B. "Some Romance Sources for King Lear:
       Robert of Sicily and Robert the Devil." SP, 71 (April
       1974), 173–91.
           Summarizes contents of De Worde edition and compares
       story with Lodge's treatment in Robert Second Duke of Nor-
       mandy.

1512   SAJAVAARA, KARI. "The Two English Prose Texts of Robert the
       Devil Printed by Wynkyn de Worde." NM, 63 (1962), 62–68.
           Compares Cambridge and British Library copies of the
       two editions with 1496 edition of Vie du terrible Robert le
       Diable and suggests that, although both English versions are
       based on the same translation, the Cambridge copy "is an
       earlier and more original edition."

HERE BEGYNNETH A LYTTELL STORY THAT WAS OF A TRWETHE DONE IN THE LANDE
OF GELDERS OF A MAYDE THAT WAS NAMED MARY OF NEMMEGEN

    STC 17557.

Editions

1513   Mary of Nimmegen: A Facsimile Reproduction of the English Ver-
       sion in the Huntington Library. Introduction by Harry Mor-
       gan Ayres and Adriaan Jacob Barnouw. Cambridge: Harvard
       University Press, 1932, not paginated.

Here Begynneth...Mary of Nemmegen

> Provide facsimile reprint of c. 1518 edition. In "Intro-
> duction," pp. 3-5, discuss briefly the dating and bibliog-
> raphical history of work.

Studies

1514   BARNOUW, A[DRIAAN] J[ACOB]. "Mary of Nimmegen." GR, 6 (Janu-
        ary 1931), 69-84.
        Argues against Kronenberg's theory (1516) that English
        translation is based on a lost Dutch prose tale; instead,
        supports "the traditional view that the English prose book
        is based on the play as we know it in Vorsterman's edition,"
        but on an earlier printing not extant.

1515   KRONENBERG, M. E. "De Houtsneden in Mariken van Nieumeghen en
        het Engelsche volksboek." Het Boek, 18 (June 1929), 177-86.
        Examines woodcuts in Doesborgh's edition and their rela-
        tionship to the cuts in Vorsterman's Dutch edition.

1516   KRONENBERG, M. E. "Het Mirakelspel van Mariken van Nieumeghen
        en het Engelsche volksboek." De Nieuwe Taalgids, 23, no. 1
        (1929), 24-43.
        Argues that English version is a translation of a lost
        Dutch prose tale. See 1514; 1519; C. P. B[urger], Jr.,
        "Een Nieuwe studie over Mariken van Nieumeghen," Het Boek,
        18 (March 1929), 104-10; and W. H. Beuken, "Mariken's eer-
        herstel," Tijdschrift voor Taal en Letteren, 19 (1931),
        111-22.

1517   PROCTOR, ROBERT. Jan van Doesborgh, Printer at Antwerp: An
        Essay in Bibliography. Illustrated Monographs, 2. London:
        Chiswick Press for the Bibliographical Society, 1894, 132pp.
        Includes bibliographical description of Doesborgh's edi-
        tion; suggests that work was "doubtless translated from the
        Dutch" and was printed 1518-1519. Suggests that Lawrence
        Andrewe was translator. Provides notes on illustrations
        (passim).

1518   SCHLAUCH, MARGARET. "Mary of Nijmeghen (The Female Faust) in
        an English Prose Version of the Early Tudor Period." PP, 6
        (1963), 4-11.
        Examines theme of work, analyzes translator's modifica-
        tion of the story, and discusses characteristics of the
        anonymous translator's style.

1519   WOLTHUIS, G. W. Review of Mary of Nemmegen, edited by Harry
        Morgan Ayres and Adriaan Jacob Barnouw. ES, 16 (1934),
        183-89.

Here Begynneth...VII Wyse Maysters of Rome

Argues against Kronenberg's hypothesis (1516) that the
English version is a translation of a lost Middle-Dutch
prose story. Suggests a closer relationship between the
English version and the Middle-Dutch miracle play <u>Mariken
van Nieumeghen</u>.

<u>HERE BEGYNNETH THYSTORYE OF YE VII WYSE MAYSTERS OF ROME</u>

<u>STC</u> 21297-21300.

Editions

1520   <u>The History of the Seven Wise Masters of Rome</u>. Edited by
       George Laurence Gomme. Chap-Books and Folk-Lore Tracts,
       1st Ser., 2. London: Villon Society, 1885, 198pp.
          Provides reprint of 1520 edition with some additions from
       1671 edition. In "Introduction," pp. i-xvii, discusses pub-
       lishing history, provides an overview of the contents, and
       traces some sources and analogues.

Studies

1521   BOND, D. F. "Two Chap-Book Versions of <u>The Seven Sages of
       Rome</u>." <u>MLN</u>, 52 (November 1937), 494-98.
          Describes two chapbook versions derived from De Worde's
       edition.

1522   CAMPBELL, KILLIS. "Introduction," in The Seven Sages of Rome:
       <u>Edited from the Manuscripts</u>. Edited by Killis Campbell.
       Albion Series of Anglo-Saxon and Middle English Poetry.
       Boston: Ginn & Co., 1907.
          Includes overview of the sixteenth-century editions
       (pp. lx-lxvi).

1523   CAMPBELL, KILLIS. "A Study of the Romance of the Seven Sages
       with Special Reference to the Middle English Versions."
       <u>PMLA</u>, 14, no. 1 (1899), 1-107.
          Discusses briefly the sixteenth-century versions, noting
       that the De Worde edition bears little relationship to sur-
       viving Middle English versions and was probably translated
       from a Latin version.

1524   MISH, CHARLES C[ARROLL]. "Thomas Howard's <u>Seven Wise Mis-
       tresses</u>." <u>N&Q</u>, NS, 7 (April 1960), 140-42.
          Shows that Howard's work is a continuation of <u>The History
       of the Seven Wise Masters of Rome</u>; examines how <u>Mistresses</u>
       "parallels <u>Masters</u> closely."

Here Begynneth...VII Wyse Maysters of Rome

1525   ROBERTS, WARREN E.   "Spenser's Fable of the Oak and the
        Briar." SFQ, 14 (September 1950), 150-54.
            Discusses parallels between February eclogue of Spenser's
        Shepheardes Calendar and first story in De Worde's edition
        of The History of the Seven Wise Masters; suggests that
        Spenser used the De Worde version as source.

HIND, JOHN (fl. 1606)

Eliosto Libidinoso: Described in Two Books. STC 13509.

The Most Excellent Historie of Lysimachus and Varrona. STC 13510.

Studies

1526   DAVIS, WALTER R[ICHARDSON].   "The Plagiarisms of John Hynd."
        N&Q, NS, 16 (March 1969), 90-92.
            Traces Hind's borrowings from Lodge's Rosalynde and
        Dickenson's Arisbas in Lysimachus and Varrona and from
        Greene's Penelope's Web in Eliosto Libidinoso.

1527   WELD, JOHN S[ALTAR].   "Notes on the Novels of John Hind." PQ,
        21 (April 1942), 171-78.
            Points out Hind's borrowings in Lysimachus and Varrona
        and Eliosto Libidinoso.

1528   WELD, JOHN SALTAR.   "Studies in the Euphuistic Novel, 1576-
        1640." Ph.D. dissertation, Harvard University, 1940, 304pp.
            Traces Hind's plagiarisms in Lysimachus and Varrona and
        Eliosto Libidinoso.

THE HISTORIE OF AURELIO AND OF ISABELL
    By Jean de Flores

    STC 11092-11093.

Studies

1529   B., W. C.   "Aurelio and Isabell." N&Q, 46 (13 July 1872), 29.
            Notes existence of polyglot (French, Italian, Spanish,
        and English) edition published at Antwerp in 1607.

*1530 MATULKA, BARBARA.   "The Novels of Juan de Flores and Their
        European Diffusion: A Study in Comparative Literature."
        Ph.D. dissertation, Columbia University, 1931, 475pp.
            See 1531.

The Historie of Frier Rush

1531   MATULKA, BARBARA. The Novels of Juan de Flores and Their
        European Diffusion: A Study in Comparative Literature.
        Comparative Literature Series. New York: Institute of
        French Studies, 1931, 493pp.
              Shows that A Pair of Turtle Doves is based on Aurelio
        and Isabel; compares two works (pp. 212-19).

THE HISTORIE OF FRIER RUSH

    STC 21451-21452.5. Wing H2121.

Editions

1532   The Historie of Frier Rush. London: R. Triphook, 1810, 39pp.
              Provides reprint of 1620 edition.

1533   The Pleasant History of Frier Rush, in A Collection of Early
        Prose Romances, Vol. I. Edited by William J. Thoms. Lon-
        don: William Pickering, 1828, 48pp. (separately paginated).
        [Also published separately.]
              Provides reprint of 1620 edition. Reprinted 1534-35.

1534   The History of Friar Rush, in Early Prose Romances. Edited by
        Henry Morley. Carisbrooke Library, 4. London: G. Rout-
        ledge, 1889, pp. 409-46.
              Reprints text from 1533. In "Introduction" discusses
        briefly the development of the legend (pp. 28-29).

1535   The History of Friar Rush, in Early English Prose Romances.
        Edited by William J. Thoms. Revised and enlarged edition.
        London: G. Routledge and Sons; New York: E. P. Dutton and
        Co., [1907], pp. 409-40.
              Reprint of 1534.

1536   The History of Friar Rush, in Some Old English Worthies. Edi-
        ted by Dorothy Senior. London: S. Swift and Co., 1912,
        pp. 237-68.
              Provides annotated, modernized reprint of 1620 edition.

Studies

1537   HERFORD, CHARLES H. Studies in the Literary Relations of Eng-
        land and Germany in the Sixteenth Century. Cambridge:
        Cambridge University Press, 1886, 456pp.
              Includes discussion of the background of the Rush legend
        and Dekker's use of the History of Friar Rush as a source
        for If This Be not a Good Play the Devil Is in It (pp. 293-
        318).

The History of Guy of Warwick

THE HISTORY OF GUY OF WARWICK

   <u>STC</u> 12540-12542. Wing F375-376.

Editions

1538   The History of Guy Earl of Warwick, in <u>Early Prose Romances</u>.
       Edited by Henry Morley. Carisbrooke Library, 4. London:
       G. Routledge, 1889, pp. 329-408.
         Provides modernized reprint of unidentified edition.

1539   The History of Guy Earl of Warwick, in <u>Early English Prose</u>
       <u>Romances</u>. Edited by William J. Thoms. Revised and enlarged
       edition. London: G. Routledge and Sons; New York: E. P.
       Dutton and Co., [1907], pp. 329-408.
         Reprint of 1538.

THE HISTORY OF THE BIRTH, TRAVELS, STRANGE ADVENTURES, AND DEATH OF
   FORTUNATUS
   Translation from Dutch

   Wing H2145.

Studies

1540   HERFORD, CHARLES H. <u>Studies in the Literary Relations of Eng-</u>
       <u>land and Germany in the Sixteenth Century</u>. Cambridge:
       Cambridge University Press, 1886, 456pp.
         In Appendix III ("The English Prose Versions of Fortuna-
       tus," pp. 405-407) points out that the 1650? version is
       based on a German edition published at Frankfurt in 1550.
       Compares the 1650? version with that of 1676, characterizing
       the former as "a free and conventional paraphrase by a man
       of letters and of the world."

THE HISTORY OF TITUS ANDRONICUS

Editions

1541   The History of Titus Andronicus, in <u>The Tragedy of Titus An-</u>
       <u>dronicus</u>. By William Shakespeare. Edited by Sylvan Barnet.
       Signet Classic Shakespeare. New York: New American
       Library, 1964, pp. 135-48.
         Provides modernized text of eighteenth-century edition.
       In introductory note, suggests that this edition is a re-
       print of a sixteenth-century one, which was possibly
       Shakespeare's source.

[Howe Howleglas Served a Taylor]

1542   The History of Titus Andronicus, in Narrative and Dramatic
        Sources of Shakespeare, Vol. VI. Edited by Geoffrey Bul-
        lough. London: Routledge and Kegan Paul; New York:
        Columbia University Press, 1966, 34-48.
            Provides reprint of text of eighteenth-century chapbook
        version which derives from a sixteenth-century edition. In
        "Introduction [to Titus Andronicus]," pp. 3-33, discusses
        Shakespeare's use of History of Titus Andronicus as a source
        for the play and examines the relationship between the prose
        version and an early ballad about Titus Andronicus. Traces
        sources of prose work to Ovid's Metamorphoses and Seneca's
        Thyestes.

Studies

1543   METZ, G. HAROLD. "The History of Titus Andronicus and Shake-
        speare's Play." N&Q, NS, 22 (April 1975), 163-66.
            Argues against Mincoff's contention (1544) that the His-
        tory of Titus Andronicus was derived from the play.

1544   MINCOFF, M[ARCO]. "The Source of Titus Andronicus." N&Q, NS,
        18 (April 1971), 131-34.
            Argues that the prose history was derived from Shake-
        speare's play and the Titus ballad. See 1543.

1545   SARGENT, RALPH M. "The Source of Titus Andronicus." SP, 46
        (April 1949), 167-83.
            Suggests that an eighteenth-century chapbook The History
        of Titus Andronicus, the Renowned Roman General is possibly
        a reprint of a sixteenth-century work of prose fiction which
        served as Shakespeare's source. Provides a detailed com-
        parison of chapbook version and play.

[HOWE HOWLEGLAS SERVED A TAYLOR]

STC 10563.

Editions

1546   BRIE, FRIEDRICH. Eulenspiegel in England. Palaestra, 27.
        Berlin: Mayer & Müller, 1903, 160pp.
            Includes discussion of editions printed by Doesborgh and
        Copland: their relationship, sources, and influence upon
        jest book tradition. Includes reprint of the extant frag-
        ment of Doesborgh's edition (pp. 126-38).

[Howe Howleglas Served a Taylor]

Studies

1547   BRIE, FRIEDRICH. Die englischen Ausgaben des Eulenspiegel und
        ihre Stellung in der Geschichte des Volksbuches. Weimar:
        R. Wagner Sohn Buchdruckerei, 1902, 68pp.
            Describes extant English editions and establishes rela-
        tionships among them. Traces origin of English version to
        a lost Low German version.

1548   PROCTER, ROBERT. Jan van Doesborgh, Printer at Antwerp: An
        Essay in Bibliography. Illustrated Monographs, 2. London:
        Chiswick Press for The Bibliographical Society, 1894, 132pp.
            Provides bibliographical description of Doesborgh's edi-
        tion of Howleglas; suggests that work was translated from
        the Dutch and that Lawrence Andrewe was possibly the trans-
        lator. Provides notes on illustrations (passim).

HOWELL, JAMES (1594?-1666)

[Dendrologia:] Dodona's Grove, or the Vocall Forrest. STC 13872.
    Wing H3059-3062.

Studies

*1549   CLEVELAND, EDWARD D. "James Howell, Bourgeois Cavalier."
        Ph.D. dissertation, Johns Hopkins University, 1950, 199pp.
            Abstract not available.

1550   COLE, DAVID LAWRENCE. "James Howell and the Speech of the
        Commonwealth: Seventeenth-Century Prose Style in Transi-
        tion." Ph.D. dissertation, Texas Tech University, 1974,
        526pp.
            Includes discussion of Dodona's Grove in analysis of
        characteristics of Howell's prose style.

1551   LANGFORD, GERALD. "John Barclay and His Argenis." Ph.D. dis-
        sertation, University of Virginia, 1940, 199pp.
            Includes discussion of influence of Argenis on Dodona's
        Grove.

1552   VANN, WILLIAM HARVEY. Notes on the Writings of James Howell.
        [Waco, Texas: Baylor University Press, 1924], 71pp.
            Includes bibliographical descriptions of editions of
        Dodona's Grove.

1553   WILSON, GRAHAM CUNNINGHAM. "James Howell: Man and Writer."
        Ph.D. dissertation, Stanford University, 1952.

The Hystorie of Hamblet

Includes discussion of Dodona's Grove in context of
Howell's life and works.

1554 WINSHIP, GEORGE PARKER. "Notes on Certain Peculiarities in
Early Editions of James Howell." Grolier Club Gazette, 1
(April 1926), 182-85.
Suggests that gap in pagination in 1644 edition of Do-
dona's Grove is the result of "a miscalculation in dividing
the copy between two printers."

THE HYSTORIE OF HAMBLET
By Francois de Belleforest.

Editions

1555 The History of Hamlet, Prince of Denmark, in Shakespeare's
Library: A Collection of the Romances, Novels, Poems, and
Histories Used by Shakespeare as the Foundation of His
Dramas, Vol. I. Edited by J[ohn] Payne Collier. London:
T. Rodd, 1843, i-xvi, 134-82.
Provides reprint of 1608 edition. In "Introduction,"
pp. iii-vii, suggests 1585 as date of first edition. Re-
printed in 1556-57.

1556 The Hystorie of Hamblet, in The Works of William Shakespeare,
Vol. XIV. By William Shakespeare. Edited by James O[r-
chard] Halliwell[-Phillipps]. London: C. & J. Adlard for
the Editor, 1865, 122-50.
Provides reprint of 1555.

1557 The History of Hamlet, in Shakespeare's Library: A Collection
of the Plays, Romances, Novels, Poems, and Histories Em-
ployed by Shakespeare in the Composition of His Works,
Vol. II. Edited by John Payne Collier. 2d edition revised.
Edited by W[illiam] Carew Hazlitt. London: Reeves and
Turner, 1875, 213-79.
Provides reprint of 1555.

1558 The Hystorie of Hamblet, in Shakespeare's Hamlet-Quellen: Saxo
Grammaticus (lateinisch und deutsch), Belleforest und The
Hystorie of Hamblet. Zusammengestellt und mit Vorwort,
Einleitung und Nachträgen. By Robert Gericke. Edited by
Max Moltke. Leipzig: J. A. Barth, 1881, pp. XXXVII-C.
Provides reprint based on 1555.

1559 The History of Hamlet, in Early Prose Romances. Edited by
Henry Morley. Carisbrooke Library, 4. London: G. Routledge, 1889, pp. 237-84.

The Hystorie of Hamblet

             Provides modernized reprint of 1608 edition. In "Intro-
duction" traces development of the legend (pp. 20-23).

1560   The Hystorie of Hamblet, in The True Story of Hamlet and
       Ophelia. By Fredericka Beardsley Gilchrist. Boston:
       Little, Brown, and Co., 1889, pp. 275-339.
           Provides reprint based on 1557. Argues that some form
       of The History of Hamlet was used as a source by Shakespeare
       (passim).

1561   The History of Hamlet, Prince of Denmark, in Early English
       Prose Romances. Edited by William J. Thoms. Revised and
       enlarged edition. London: G. Routledge and Sons; New York:
       E. P. Dutton and Co., [1907], pp. 237-84.
           Provides reprint of 1559.

1562   The Hystorie of Hamblet, in The Sources of Hamlet: With Essay
       on the Legend. Edited by Israel Gollancz. Shakespeare
       Classics. London: Oxford University Press, 1926, pp. 165-
       321.
           Reprints text of 1608 edition with text from Bellefor-
       est's Histoires tragiques on facing page.

1563   The Hystorie of Hamblet, in Narrative and Dramatic Sources of
       Shakespeare, Vol. VII. Edited by Geoffrey Bullough. Lon-
       don: Routledge and Kegan Paul; New York: Columbia Univer-
       sity Press, 1973, 81-124.
           Reprints text of 1608 edition (in footnotes traces im-
       portant differences from Belleforest). In "Introduction
       [to Hamlet]," pp. 3-59, points out that treatment of the
       closet scene in History of Hamlet suggests that the anony-
       mous translator had seen a performance of Hamlet. Notes
       that translator used 1582 Paris edition of Histoires tra-
       giques.

Studies

1564   CAIRNCROSS, ANDREW S. "A Source for Antony." ELN, 13 (Septem-
       ber 1975), 4-6.
           Argues that History of Hamlet is the "main source of
       Hamlet" and "must have appeared in an earlier edition" than
       that of 1608. Finds parallels between Hamlet's speech on
       his father and Antony's funeral oration.

1565   CORBIN, JOHN. The Elizabethan Hamlet: A Study of the Sources,
       and of Shakespere's Environment, to Show that the Mad Scenes
       Had a Comic Aspect Now Ignored. London: E. Mathews; New
       York: Scribner's, 1895, 99pp.

Jacke of Dover His Quest of Inquirie

Argues that History of Hamlet was source and examines
Shakespeare's use of it. Suggests that work was translated
from Belleforest c. 1570 (passim).

1566   DEROCQUIGNY, J. "Shakespeare et Belleforest." Revue Anglo-
        Américaine, 1 (August 1924), 527-28.
            Compares episode of Polonius's death in History of Hamlet
        with episode in Belleforest's Histoires tragiques to argue
        that Shakespeare used the English version (in an edition
        earlier than that of 1608) rather than Belleforest as a
        source for Hamlet.

1567   FITZGERALD, JAMES D. "The Sources of the Hamlet Tragedy."
        Proceedings of the Royal Philosophical Society of Glasgow,
        40 (1908-1909), 177-206.
            Argues that History of Hamlet was Shakespeare's source;
        lists several "verbal correspondences" between the two
        works.

1568   GREENWOOD, G[RANVILLE] G. Is There a Shakespeare Problem?
        London: John Lane, 1916, 639pp.
            In section "Shakespeare and The Hystorie of Hamblet"
        (pp. 175-80) argues that Shakespeare did not use the work
        as a source.

1569   [HERAUD, JOHN ABRAHAM.] "Re-Touching the Lord Hamlet."
        Household Words, 16 (5 December 1857), 545-48.
            Compares History of Hamlet with other versions of the
        Hamlet story. Notes how anonymous translator altered his
        version, particularly "for the sake of moral application."

JACKE OF DOVER HIS QUEST OF INQUIRIE

    STC 14291-14292, 19307-19307.5.

Editions

1570   Jack of Dover, His Quest of Inquirie, or His Privy Search for
        the Veriest Foole in England: A Collection of Merry Tales
        Published at the Beginning of the Sixteenth Century. Edited
        by T[homas] Wright. Percy Society, 7. London: T. Richards
        for the Percy Society, 1842, 65pp.
            Reprints text of first part from 1604 edition, text of
        second part from 1608 edition.

1571   Jack of Dover, in Shakespeare Jest-Books, Vol. II. Edited by
        W[illiam] Carew Hazlitt. London: Willis & Sotheran, 1864,
        311-54.

255

Jennings

Provides an annotated reprint of 1604 edition. In brief
introductory note discusses bibliographical history of the
work.

JENNINGS, JOHN

Jean Pierre Camus, Elise, or Innocencie Guilty. Wing C413.

Studies

1572   UPHAM, A[LFRED] H[ORATIO]. "Another Translation from Camus."
       MLN, 28 (March 1913), 94.
          Notes Jennings's translation provides further evidence
       of popularity of the "quasi-tragic and highly moralized
       novel" before Richardson.

JOHNSON, RICHARD (1573-1659?)

The Most Famous History of the Seaven Champions of Christendome.
    STC 14677-14683. Wing J796-804, J805-806, J811.

The Most Pleasant History of Tom a Lincolne. STC 14684-14685. Wing
    J807-810.

The Pleasant Conceits of Old Hobson the Merry Londoner. STC 14688-
    14689.7.

The History of Tom Thumbe, the Little. STC 14056. (Possibly by
    Johnson.)

Editions

1573   JOHNSON, RICHARD. The Seven Champions of Christendom. London:
       Knight, n.d., 416pp.
          Provides modernized reprint of unidentified edition.

1574   [JOHNSON, RICHARD.] The Renowned History of the Seven Champi-
       ons of Christendom. London: W. Baynes et al, 1824, 450pp.
          Provides modernized reprint of unidentified edition.

1575   JOHNSON, RICHARD. The Renowned History of the Seven Champions
       of Christendom. London: C. and J. Rivington et al, 1824,
       528pp.
          Provides text based on 1755 edition. In "Preface," pp.
       xv-xvii, anonymous author comments on popularity and style
       of work.

1576   JOHNSON, RICHARD. The History of Tom a Lincoln, the Red Rose
       Knight, in A Collection of Early Prose Romances, Vol. II.
       Edited by William J. Thoms. London: William Pickering,
       1828, 141pp. (separately paginated). [Also published
       separately.]
          Provides reprint of 1635 edition. In introductory note
       (pp. i-viii) comments on Johnson's knowledge of chivalric
       romances.

1577   [JOHNSON, RICHARD.] The Pleasant Conceits of Old Hobson, the
       Merry Londoner. Edited by James Orchard Halliwell[-Phil-
       lipps]. Percy Society, 9. London: T. Richards for the
       Percy Society, 1843, 42pp.
          Provides annotated reprint of 1607 edition.

1578   JOHNSON, RICHARD. The Renowned History of the Seven Champions
       of Christendom. London: J. S. Pratt, 1845, 480pp.
          Provides modernized reprint of unidentified edition.

*1579 JOHNSON, RICHARD. The Extraordinary Adventures of the Seven
       Champions of Christendom. London: Griffin, Bohn, 1861.
          Not seen. Listed in NUC Pre-1956 Imprints, vol. 282,
       341.

*1580 JOHNSON, RICHARD. The Renowned History of the Seven Champions
       of Christendom. Halifax: Milner and Sowerby, 1862, 382pp.
          Not seen. Listed in NUC Pre-1956 Imprints, vol. 282,
       345.

1581   JOHNSON, RICHARD. The Conceits of Old Hobson, in Shakespeare
       Jest-Books, Vol. III. Edited by W[illiam] Carew Hazlitt.
       London: Willis & Sotheran, 1864, 1-52 (separately pagi-
       nated).
          Provides a slightly modernized, annotated reprint of
       1607 edition. In "Introduction," pp. 2-6, discusses the
       bibliographical history of the work.

1582   JOHNSON, RICHARD. The Seven Champions of Christendom. London:
       William Tegg, 1867, 416pp.
          Provides modernized reprint of unidentified edition.

1583   JOHNSON, RICHARD. The Pleasant Historie of Tom a Lincoln, the
       Red Rose Knight, in Early English Prose Romances. Edited
       by William J. Thoms. Revised and enlarged edition. London:
       G. Routledge and Sons; New York: E. P. Dutton and Co.,
       [1907], pp. 601-90.
          Reprint of 1576.

Johnson

*1584   JOHNSON, RICHARD. The Seven Champions of Christendom. Edited
         by F[rederick] J[oseph] Harvey Darton. London: W. Gardner,
         Darton & Co.; New York: F. A. Stokes Co., 1913, 429pp.
             Not seen. Listed in NUC Pre-1956 Imprints, vol. 282,
         346.

*1585   JOHNSON, RICHARD. "Richard Johnson and The Seven Champions of
         Christendom (1596 and 1597): Materials for an Edition of
         His Works. Vol. II, The Seven Champions of Christendom,
         Part I. By Richard Johnson. Transcribed from the Edition
         of 1626?" Edited by David Allan Robertson, Jr. Ph.D. dis-
         sertation, Princeton University, 1940, 588pp.
             Abstract not available.

 1586   [JOHNSON, RICHARD.] R. I. The History of Tom Thumbe. Edited
         by Curt F. Bühler. [With A. B. of Phisike Doctour. Merie
         Tales of the Mad Men of Gotam. Edited by Stanley J(adwin)
         Kahrl.] RETS. Evanston: Northwestern University Press
         for The Renaissance English Text Society, 1965, 42pp.
         (separately paginated).
             Reprints text of 1621 edition. In "Introduction," pp.
         v-xvii, discusses folklore and literary background, allu-
         sions to Tom Thumb, and evidence for Johnson's authorship.

 1587   JOHNSON, RICHARD. "A Critical Edition of Richard Johnson's
         Tom a Lincolne." Edited by Richard Stephen Marcus Hirsch.
         Ph.D. dissertation, Brown University, 1972, 260pp.
             Provides critical old-spelling edition based on 1631 edi-
         tion. Analyzes relationship between Johnson's "moral posi-
         tion" and structure of work, his treatment of Arthur, his
         style, and his sources.

Studies

 1588   ANON. "Preface," in The Seven Champions of Christendom. By
         Richard Johnson. London: Blackwood, 1861, pp. iii-iv.
             Asserts that Seven Champions "undoubtedly inspired"
         Spenser. Provides expurgated, "slightly condensed" text
         based on unidentified edition.

 1589   APP, AUGUST J[OSEPH]. Lancelot in English Literature: His
         Rôle and Character. Washington: Catholic University of
         America, 1929, 268pp.
             Discusses treatment of Lancelot in Tom a Lincoln, par-
         ticularly how he serves as a foil for Tom (passim).

 1590   BRIE, FRIEDRICH. "Eine neue Quelle zu Cymbeline?" Shakespeare-
         Jahrbuch, 44 (1908), 167-70.

Examines possibility that Seven Champions was one of
Shakespeare's sources.

1591   BROWNE, C. ELLIOT. "The Seven Champions." N&Q, 52 (9 October
        1875), 287-88.
        Speculates on basis of internal evidence that work was
        "considerably later than Shakespeare's time." Requests in-
        formation on date of earliest extant copy. See 1600 and
        1601.

1592   CHAMBERS, E[DMUND] K[ERCHEVER]. The English Folk-Play. Ox-
        ford: Clarendon Press, 1933, 256pp.
        Argues that Seven Champions is the source (possibly
        through some intermediary version) of an early Mummers'
        Play (pp. 174-85, passim).

1593   DAWSON, GILES E. "[Introduction]," in The Seven Champions of
        Christendome. By John Kirke. Edited by Giles E. Dawson.
        Western Reserve University Bulletin, NS, Vol. 32, no. 16.
        Cleveland: Western Reserve University, 1929, pp. vii-xxii.
        Discusses the popularity of Johnson's Seven Champions and
        Kirke's use of it as a source for the play.

1594   DICKSON, ARTHUR. "'Fat' (Hamlet, V.ii.298)." SQ, 2 (April
        1951), 171-72.
        Notes use of "fat" meaning "sweating" in Seven Champions
        in support of interpretation of word in Hamlet.

1595   EIRIONNACH. "Seven Champions of Christendom." N&Q, 17 (23
        January 1858), 76-77.
        Provides notes on various editions of the work.

1596   GOLDER, HAROLD. "Browning's Childe Roland." PMLA, 39 (Decem-
        ber 1924), 963-78.
        Includes discussion of possible influence of Seven Cham-
        pions on poem.

1597   GOLDER, HAROLD. "Bunyan's Valley of the Shadow." MP, 27
        (August 1929), 55-72.
        Uses examples from Seven Champions to illustrate influ-
        ence of earlier romances on narrative framework of Pilgrim's
        Progress. Discusses, in particular, the conventional ele-
        ments of the descent into a cave or dark valley.

1598   GOLDER, HAROLD. "The Chivalric Background of Pilgrim's
        Progress." Ph.D. dissertation, Harvard University, 1925.
        Includes discussion of Bunyan's use of Seven Champions.

Johnson

1599   HALLIWELL[-PHILLIPPS], J[AMES] O[RCHARD]. "The Seven Champions
        and Shakespeare." N&Q, 18 (31 July 1858), 94.
            Notes that he had pointed out Shakespeare's acquaintance
        with Seven Champions before Keightley (1600).

1600   KEIGHTLEY, THOMAS. "The Seven Champions and Shakspeare."
        N&Q, 18 (17 July 1858), 46.
            Suggests that Seven Champions was source for some of
        Shakespeare's imagery. See 1591 and 1599.

1601   KEIGHTLEY, THO[MA]S. "The Seven Champions and Shakspeare."
        N&Q, 18 (18 September 1858), 236-37.
            Suggests possible dates for publication of various parts
        of Seven Champions. Notes that the first part of the Faerie
        Queene is "founded" upon first part of Seven Champions.

1602   L. "Richard Johnson and the Seven Champions of Christendom."
        N&Q, 15 (25 April 1857), 339.
            In response to earlier query (15 [4 April 1857], 267)
        notes that work "was in print but a few years ago, as a
        book for boys."

1603   McNEIR, W[ALDO] F. "Greene's 'Tomliuclin': Tamburlaine or
        Tom a Lincoln?" MLN, 58 (May 1943), 380-82.
            Notes early references to Tom a Lincoln, suggesting story
        was current before Johnson wrote Tom a Lincoln.

1604   MAHL, MARY ROBERTA. "The Authorship of Fowler MS. V.a.139,
        'The Famous History of St. George England's Brave Champion,'
        by G. B." Ph.D. dissertation, New York University, 1961,
        320pp.
            Discusses author's use of Johnson's Seven Champions as
        source.

1605   MATZKE, JOHN E. "The Legend of Saint George: Its Development
        into a Roman d'Aventure." PMLA, 19 (September 1904),
        449-78.
            Analyzes the Seven Champions as example of fusion of the
        story of Bevis of Hampton and the legend of St. George.
        Notes that Johnson followed version unknown at present.
        Considers influence of Seven Champions on later St. George
        ballads.

1606   MAXWELL, J[AMES] C[LOUTTS]. "'Fat and Scant of Breath' Again."
        ES, 32 (1951), 29-30.
            Notes use of "fat" meaning "sweating" in Seven Champions
        in support of interpretation of term in Hamlet.

1607   SMITH, ROLAND M. "King Lear and the Merlin Tradition." MLQ,
       7 (June 1946), 153-74.
            Cites several passages from Tom a Lincoln "which bear a
       resemblance to Shakespeare's King Lear" but does not argue
       for Johnson's influence on play.

1608   WILLKOMM, HANS WERNER. Über Richard Johnsons Seven Champions
       of Christendom (1596). Berlin: Mayer & Müller, 1911.
            Traces publishing history of work; examines subject mat-
       ter, structure, sources, style, and influence on later
       works.

JOHNSTOUN, JAMES

[Supplement to] The Countess of Pembroke's Arcadia. By Philip Sidney.
    STC 22550.

Studies

1609   WILES, AMERICUS GEORGE DAVID. "The Continuations of Sir
       Philip Sidney's Arcadia." Ph.D. dissertation, Princeton
       University, 1934.
            Includes examination of Johnstoun's continuation; finds
       that with Alexander's it is the best of the continuations
       of the New Arcadia but that it has little literary merit.

KEMP, WILLIAM (fl. 1600)

Kemps Nine Daies Wonder: Performed in a Daunce from London to Nor-
    wich. STC 14923.

Editions

1610   KEMP, WILLIAM. Kemps Nine Daies Wonder: Performed in a Daunce
       from London to Norwich. Edited by Alexander Dyce. Camden
       Society Publications, 11. London: Camden Society, 1840,
       63pp.
            Provides annotated reprint of 1600 edition.

1611   KEMP, WILLIAM. Kemps Nine Daies Wonder: Performed in a Daunce
       from London to Norwich. [Edited by Edmund William Ashbee.
       London: Privately Printed, 187-,] not paginated.
            Provides facsimile reprint of 1600 edition.

1612   KEMP, WILLIAM. Kempes Nine Daies Wonder, Performed in a Jour-
       ney from London to Norwich. Edited by Edmund Goldsmid.

Kemp

> Collectanea Adamantea, 2. Edinburgh: Privately Printed,
> 1884, 50pp.
> Provides annotated reprint of 1600 edition(?).

1613   KEMP, WILLIAM. Kemp's Nine Days' Wonder: Performed in a
        Dance from London to Norwich, in An English Garner, VI:
        Social England. Edited by Edward Arber. Introduction by
        Andrew Lang. London: Constable, 1909, 139-62.
        Provides reprint of 1600 edition.

1614   KEMP, WILLIAM. Kemps Nine Daies Wonder, in Henrie Chettle,
        Kind-Hartes Dreame, 1592; William Kemp, Nine Daies Wonder,
        1600. Edited by G[eorge] B[agshawe] Harrison. Bodley Head
        Quartos, 4. London: John Lane, Bodley Head, 1923, 35pp.
        Reprints slightly corrected text of 1600 edition.

1615   KEMP, WILLIAM. Kemp's Nine Days' Wonder Performed in a Dance
        from London to Norwich, in A Miscellany of Tracts and Pam-
        phlets. Edited by A. C. Ward. World's Classics, 304.
        Oxford: Oxford University Press, 1927, pp. 131-59.
        Provides modernized reprint based on unidentified edi-
        tion.

1616   KEMP, WILLIAM. Kemp's Nine Days Wonder, Performed in a Dance
        from London to Norwich, 1600, in Kemp's Nine Days Wonder by
        William Kemp; Tarlton's Jests; with A Pretty New Ballad,
        Entitled the Crow Sits upon the Wall. Introduction by
        J[ohn] P. Feather. New York: Johnson Reprint, 1972, not
        paginated.
        Provides facsimile reprint of 1600 edition. In brief
        "Introduction" discusses literary allusions in work.

Studies

1617   HOBBINS, J. H. "Odd Corners of Elizabethan Literature."
        Papers of the Manchester Literary Club, 50 (1924), 253-69.
        Includes discussion of Kemp's Nine Days Wonder as it re-
        veals "the wholehearted kindliness and bluff good humour of
        the times."

1618   KOEPPEL, E[MIL]. "'The prince of the burning crowne' and
        Palmerin d'Oliva." Archiv, 100 (1898), 23-30.
        Explains allusion in phrase from Kemp's Nine Days Wonder.

KIRKMAN, FRANCIS (1632-c.1680)

The Famous and Renowned History of Amadis de Gaula, Part IV. Wing
    F358.

The Loves and Adventures of Clerio and Lozia. Wing L3260.

Bibliographies

1619   GIBSON, STRICKLAND. "A Bibliography of Francis Kirkman: With
       His Prefaces, Dedications, and Commendations (1652–80)."
       Oxford Bibliographical Society Publications, NS, 1, part 2
       (1949), 47–148.
           Provides bibliographical descriptions of editions of
       Kirkman's prose fiction translations and discusses his
       literalness in translating works.

Studies

1620   BALD, R. C. "Francis Kirkman, Bookseller and Author." MP, 41
       (August 1943), 17–32.
           Drawing on Kirkman's autobiography The Unlucky Citizen,
       discusses circumstances surrounding translation and publi-
       cation of Amadis and Clerio and Lozia.

1621   FORMAN, GAIL I. "The Life and Works of Francis Kirkman: A
       Study in Restoration Publishing." Ph.D. dissertation,
       University of Maryland, 1972, 216pp.
           Examines Kirkman's prose fiction translations in the
       context of his life and other works.

KITTOWE, ROBERT

Loves Load-Starre: Lively Deciphered in a Historie. STC 15026.

Studies

1622   HURRELL, JOHN DENNIS. "Loues Load-Starre: A Study in Eliza-
       bethan Literary Craftsmanship." Boston University Studies
       in English, 1, no. 4 (1955–1956), 197–209.
           Examines Kittowe's expansions of his source The Cobbler
       of Canterbury; analyzes Kittowe's use of conventions of ro-
       mance in his work.

LE GRYS, SIR ROBERT (d. 1635)

John Barclay, John Barclay His Argenis. STC 1393–1394.

Studies

1623   G., M. A. E. "Sir Robert le Gris." N&Q, 19 (22 October 1859),
       335.

Le Grys

In answer to earlier query for information on Le Grys,
notes references to him in Public Record Office documents,
including letter of 26 February 1628 to Earl of Montgomery,
Lord Chamberlain, regarding licensing of his translation,
and letter of 28 February 1628 from Lord Conway to Station-
ers' Company granting license.

1624   SCHMID, KARL FRIEDRICH. John Barclays Argenis: Eine litterar-
       historische Untersuchung. Literarhistorische Forschungen,
       31. Berlin: E. Felber, 1903, 183pp.
          Provides bibliographical description of 1629 edition of
       Le Grys' translation; comments briefly on style and handling
       of text (pp. 91-96).

L'ESTRANGE, SIR NICHOLAS (d. 1655)

"Merry Passages and Jeasts" (manuscript jest book, Harleian MS. 6395).

Editions

1625   L'ESTRANGE, NICHOLAS. "Merry Passages and Jeasts": A Manu-
       script Jestbook of Sir Nicholas Le Strange (1603-1655).
       Edited by H[enry] F[rederick] Lippincott. ElizS, 29.
       Salzburg: Institut für Englische Sprache und Literatur,
       Universität Salzburg, 1974, 266pp.
          Provides annotated, partly modernized transcript of
       Harleian MS. 6395. In "Introduction," pp. 1-16, describes
       manuscript, discusses date of composition, characterizes
       style, and examines "verisimilitude and range of subjects
       in the jests." See 1626 for addenda.

Studies

1626   LIPPINCOTT, H[ENRY] F[REDERICK]. "'Merry Passages and Jeasts'
       and Sir Nicholas L'Estrange." LC, 41 (Winter 1977),
       149-62.
          Revision of portions of introduction to 1625. Confirms
       L'Estrange's compilation of work; discusses style, range
       of subject matter, degree of "historical truth" and "psy-
       chological truth," and nature of the bawdy. Includes "Ad-
       ditional Explanatory Notes for L'Estrange's 'Merry Passages
       and Jeasts'" (see 1625).

1627   NICHOLS, J. G. "Notices of Sir Nicholas Lestrange and His
       Family Connexions," in Anecdotes and Traditions Illustrative
       of Early English History and Literature: Derived from MS
       Sources. Edited by William J. Thoms. Camden Society, 5.

The Life and Death of Gamaliell Ratsey

London: John Bowyer Nichols and Son for the Camden Society,
1839, pp. xi-xxviii.
Identifies L'Estrange as compiler of "Merry Jests" and
identifies several of his sources. Thoms transcribes
several of the tales, "of which the greater portion are
unfit for publication."

1628   RACE, SYDNEY. "Harleian MS. 6395 and Its Editor." <u>N&Q</u>, NS, 4
(February 1957), 77-79.
Examines shortcomings of W. J. Thoms's transcription of
a selection from L'Estrange's "Merry Jests" (1627).

1629   WILLETTS, PAMELA. "Nicholas Le Strange and John Jenkins."
<u>M&L</u>, 42 (January 1961), 30-43.
Assesses evidence for identity of compiler of Harleian
MS. 6395; suggests it was L'Estrange. Discusses references
to music in "Merry Jests."

THE LIFE AND DEATH OF GAMALIELL RATSEY

<u>STC</u> 20753.

Editions

1630   The Life and Death of Gamaliel Ratsey, in <u>Illustrations of Old
English Literature</u>, Vol. III. Edited by J[ohn] Payne
Collier. London: Privately Printed, 1866, 48pp. (separately paginated).
Provides reprint of 1605 edition. In brief introductory
note, discusses bibliographical history of the work and
seventeenth-century references to Ratsey.

1631   The Life and Death of Gamaliel Ratsey, 1605. Introduction by
S. H. Atkins. Shakespeare Association Facsimiles, 10.
London: Oxford University Press for the Shakespeare Association, 1935, not paginated.
Provides facsimile reprint of 1605 edition. In "Introduction," pp. v-xii, discusses the notoriety of Ratsey and
popularity of works about him. Examines style and characterization in work.

Studies

1632   LIEVSAY, JOHN LEON. "Newgate Penitents: Further Aspects of
Elizabethan Pamphlet Sensationalism." <u>HLQ</u>, 7 (November
1943), 47-69.
Traces use of Greene's works as sources for <u>Life and
Death</u>. Argues Samuel Rowlands was the author. <u>See</u> 1633.

The Life and Death of Gamaliell Ratsey

1633   O'CONNOR, JOHN J.   "On the Authorship of the Ratsey Pamphlets."
       PQ, 30 (October 1951), 381-86.
           Argues against Lievsay's identification of Samuel Row-
       lands as author (1632).   Traces sources of Life and Death
       of Gamaliel Ratsey.

THE LIFE AND PRANKS OF LONG MEG OF WESTMINSTER

   STC 17782-17783.3.

Editions

1634   The Life of Long Meg of Westminster, in Miscellanea Antiqua
        Anglicana; or, a Select Collection of Curious Tracts Illus-
        trative of the History, Literature, Manners, and Biography
        of the English Nation.   London: R. Triphook, 1816, 38pp.
        (separately paginated).
            Provides reprint of 1635 edition.

1635   The Life of Long Meg of Westminster, in The Old Book Collec-
        tor's Miscellany: Or a Collection of Readable Reprints of
        Literary Rarities, Illustrative of the History, Literature,
        Manners, and Biography of the English Nation During the
        Sixteenth and Seventeenth Centuries, Vol. II.   Edited by
        Charles Hindley.   London: Reeves and Turner, 1872, 82pp.
        (separately paginated).
            Provides modernized reprint of 1635 edition.   In "Intro-
        duction," pp. iii-xxix, reprints text of an eighteenth-
        century chapbook version and lists allusions to Long Meg in
        sixteenth- and seventeenth-century works.

1636   The Life of Long Meg of Westminster, in Short Fiction of the
        Seventeenth Century.   Edited by Charles C[arroll] Mish.
        Stuart Editions.   New York: New York University Press,
        1963, pp. 79-113.
            Provides modernized reprint of 1635 edition.   In brief
        introductory note discusses work as a jest-biography.   See
        60.

LODGE, THOMAS (1558-1625)

An Alarum against Usurers (includes The Delectable Historie of For-
    bonius and Prisceria).   STC 16653.

Euphues Shadow, the Battle of the Sences.   STC 16656.

The Famous, True, and Historicall Life of Robert Second Duke of Normandy, Surnamed Robin the Divell. STC 16657.

The Life and Death of William Long Beard. STC 16659.

A Margarite of America. STC 16660.

Rosalynde: Euphues Golden Legacie. STC 16664-16673.5. Wing L2810.

Wits Miserie, and the Worlds Madnesse. STC 16677.

Bibliographies

1637   ALLISON, A[NTONY] F[RANCIS]. Thomas Lodge, 1558-1625: A Bibliographical Catalogue of the Early Editions (To the End of the 17th Century). Pall Mall Bibliographies, 2. Folkestone and London: Dawsons, 1973, 98pp.
        Provides analytical bibliography (arranged alphabetically by title) of editions, issues, and variant states. Includes photographic facsimiles of title-pages in place of transcription of title.

1638   COLLIER, J[OHN] PAYNE. "On Thomas Lodge and His Works." Gentleman's Magazine, 189 (December 1850), 605-11.
        Provides an annotated chronological list of Lodge's works; frequently notes location of copies.

1639   HOUPPERT, JOSEPH W. "Thomas Lodge," in The Predecessors of Shakespeare: A Survey and Bibliography of Recent Studies in English Renaissance Drama. Edited by Terence P. Logan and Denzell S. Smith. Lincoln: University of Nebraska Press, 1973, pp. 153-60.
        Comments on recent scholarship on some of Lodge's prose fiction (mainly Rosalynde) and provides a selective bibliography.

1640   JOHNSON, ROBERT C. "Thomas Lodge, 1939-1965," in Elizabethan Bibliographies Supplements, V: Robert Greene, 1945-1965; Thomas Lodge, 1939-1965; John Lyly, 1939-1965; Thomas Nashe, 1941-1965; George Peele, 1939-1965. Compiled by Robert C. Johnson. London: Nether Press, 1968, 27-34.
        Provides chronological list of editions and criticism, 1939-1965; supplements 1642.

1641   ROBERTS, W. "Thomas Lodge's Rosalynde." Athenaeum, No. 3883 (29 March 1902), pp. 404-405.
        Provides bibliographical descriptions of and notes on early editions.

Lodge

1642 TANNENBAUM, SAMUEL A. Thomas Lodge (A Concise Bibliography).
      Elizabethan Bibliographies, 11. New York: Samuel A.
      Tannenbaum, 1940, 38pp.
         Provides classified list of editions and scholarship.
      Continued by 1640.

Editions

*1643 LODGE, THOMAS. Rosalynde: Euphues' Golden Legacie Found after
      His Death in His Cell at Silexedra. London: Rodd, 1841,
      130pp.
         Not seen. Listed in NUC Pre-1956 Imprints, vol. 338, 98.

1644 LODGE, THOMAS. Rosalynde, in Shakespeare's Library: A Collec-
      tion of the Romances, Novels, Poems, and Histories Used by
      Shakespeare as the Foundation of His Dramas, Vol. I. Edited
      by J[ohn] Payne Collier. London: T. Rodd, 1843, 134pp.
      (separately paginated).
         Provides annotated reprint of 1592 edition. In "Intro-
      duction," pp. i-iv, discusses Rosalynde in context of
      Lodge's life and works and comments on popularity.

1645 LODGE, THOMAS. An Alarum against Usurers and The Delectable
      History of Forbonius and Prisceria, in A Defence of Poetry,
      Music, and Stage Plays...to Which Are Added...An Alarum
      against Usurers and The Delectable History of Forbonius and
      Prisceria. By Thomas Lodge. Edited by David Laing.
      Shakespeare Society Publications, 48. London: Shakespeare
      Society, 1853, 206pp.
         Provides reprint of 1584 edition of Alarum and Forbonius
      and Prisceria (pp. 33-113). In "Some Account of Thomas
      Lodge and His Writings," pp. xi-lxv, discusses Lodge's
      prose fiction in context of his life and other writings.
      Provides a "Catalogue of Thomas Lodge's Works," pp. lvi-
      lxxvii.

1646 LODGE, THOMAS. Rosalynde, in The Works of William Shakespeare,
      Vol. VI. By William Shakespeare. Edited by James O[rchard]
      Halliwell[-Phillipps]. London: C. & J. Adlard for the
      Editor, 1856, 5-68.
         Provides reprint of 1590 edition with some readings from
      1592 edition.

1647 LODGE, THOMAS. The Margarite of America. Edited by James
      O[rchard] Halliwell[-Phillipps]. London: Thomas Richards,
      1859, 139pp.
         Provides reprint of 1596 edition.

1648   LODGE, THOMAS. <u>The Life and Death of William Long Beard</u>, in
        <u>Illustrations of Old English Literature</u>, Vol. II. Edited
        by J[ohn] Payne Collier. London: Privately Printed, 1866,
        i-ii, 1-83 (separately paginated).
        Reprints text of 1593 edition.

1649   LODGE, THOMAS. <u>Rosalynde</u>, in <u>Shakespeare's Library: A Collec-
        tion of the Plays, Romances, Novels, Poems, and Histories
        Employed by Shakespeare in the Composition of His Works</u>,
        Vol. II. Edited by John Payne Collier. 2d edition revised.
        Edited by W[illiam] Carew Hazlitt. London: Reeves and
        Turner, 1875, 3-144.
        Provides reprint of 1644.

1650   LODGE, THOMAS. <u>The Complete Works of Thomas Lodge</u>. Introduc-
        tion by Edmund [W.] Gosse. 4 vols. Hunterian Club Re-
        prints. Glasgow: Hunterian Club, 1883, separately
        paginated. [Each work also published separately.]
            Provides reprints of early editions of Lodge's prose
        fiction. In "Memoir of Thomas Lodge" (I, 46pp.) provides
        overview of Lodge's prose fiction in context of his life
        and works. Includes "Bibliographical Index" (I, 27pp.)
        which provides description of early editions. ("Memoir of
        Thomas Lodge" reprinted as: "Thomas Lodge," in <u>Seventeenth-
        Century Studies: A Contribution to the History of English
        Poetry</u>. By Edmund W. Gosse. London: Kegan Paul, Trench,
        & Co., 1883, pp. 1-40.)

*1651   LODGE, THOMAS. <u>Rosalind</u>. Cassell's National Library. New
        York: Cassell & Co., 1887, 192pp.
            Not seen. Listed in <u>NUC Pre-1956 Imprints</u>, vol. 338, 97.

1652   LODGE, THOMAS. <u>Rosalynde</u>, in <u>As You Like It</u>. By William
        Shakespeare. Edited by Horace Howard Furness. New Vari-
        orum. Philadelphia: J. B. Lippincott Co., 1890, pp. 316-
        87.
            Provides reprint from 1650. Includes overview of schol-
        arship on Shakespeare's use of <u>Rosalynde</u> as a source (pp.
        305-10).

1653   LODGE, THOMAS. <u>Rosalynde, a Novel</u>. Photogravure and Colour
        Series. London: G. Routledge & Sons, [19--], 150pp.
            Provides modernized text based on unidentified edition.

1654   LODGE, THOMAS. <u>Rosalynde: Euphues Golden Legacie Found after
        His Death in His Cell at Silexedra</u>. Caxton Series. London:
        G. Newnes, 1902, 187pp.
            Provides reprint of unidentified edition.

Lodge

1655   LODGE, THOMAS. Rosalynde, or Euphues Golden Legacie. New
        Rochelle, New York: Elston Press, 1902, 126pp.
        Reprints text of 1592 edition.

1656   LODGE, THOMAS. Lodge's Rosalynde: Being the Original of
        Shakespeare's As You Like It. Edited by W[alter] W[ilson]
        Greg. Shakespeare Library. London: Oxford University
        Press, 1907, 239pp.
            Provides annotated, modernized text based on 1650. In
        "Introduction," pp. ix-xxiii, discusses merit of work as a
        pastoral romance, Lodge's sources, and the relationship of
        Rosalynde to As You Like It. Reprints 1748 in Appendix,
        pp. 187-209.

1657   LODGE, THOMAS. Rosalynde; or, Euphues' Golden Legacy. Edited
        by Edward Chauncey Baldwin. Boston: Ginn and Co., 1910,
        161pp.
            Provides modernized reprint of 1592 edition. In "Intro-
        duction," pp. vii-xxi, discusses Lodge's use of Tale of
        Gamelyn as source, his euphuistic style, and his narrative
        skill; examines Rosalynde as a pastoral romance and its use
        by Shakespeare as a source for As You Like It.

1658   LODGE, THOMAS. Rosalynde, in Noble English, II: From Thomas
        Lodge to John Milton. Edited by Henry Newbolt. London:
        T. Nelson & Sons, 1925, 15-81.
            Provide modernized text based on unidentified edition.

1659   LODGE, THOMAS. A Margarite of America, in Menaphon by Robert
        Greene and A Margarite of America by Thomas Lodge. Edited
        by G[eorge] B[agshawe] Harrison. Oxford: Blackwell, 1927,
        pp. 109-226.
            Provides an annotated reprint of 1595 edition. In "In-
        troduction," pp. v-xii, points out that work should be read
        aloud to capture its "very real charm."

1660   LODGE, THOMAS. Rosalynde, in Malory to Mrs. Behn: Specimens
        of Early Prose Fiction. Edited by Albert Morton Turner and
        Percie Hopkins Turner. Nelson's English Series. New York:
        T. Nelson and Sons, 1930, pp. 105-243.
            Provides modernized text based on unidentified edition.

1661   LODGE, THOMAS. "Thomas Lodge's Wits Miserie and the Worlds
        Madnesse: Edited with Introduction and Notes. (Volume I:
        Introduction and Text. Volume II: Notes and Bibliography).
        Edited by Robert John Kearns. Ph.D. dissertation, Univer-
        sity of Michigan, 1959, 452pp.

Provides critical edition based on text of 1596 edition.
In "Introduction" examines structure, sources, and influence
of Theophrastan character on work.

1662   LODGE, THOMAS. <u>Rosalind: Euphues' Golden Legacy Found after</u>
        <u>His Death in His Cell at Silexedra</u>, in <u>Elizabethan Prose</u>
        <u>Fiction</u>. Edited by Merritt [E.] Lawlis. Indianapolis:
        Odyssey Press, Bobbs-Merrill Co., 1967, pp. 278-394.
            Provides partly modernized text based on 1590 edition.
        (<u>See</u> pp. 631-33 for a list of substantive emendations and
        a discussion of the relationship among early editions.) In
        introductory note, discusses Lodge's style, finding that
        its strength lies in its appropriateness to subject matter,
        and his refashioning of the materials of romance, concluding
        that the "essential genius" of the work is the assimilation
        of the elements and traditions he drew upon.

1663   LODGE, THOMAS. <u>Wits Miserie and the Worlds Madnesse</u>. English
        Experience, 198. Amsterdam: Theatrvm Orbis Terrarvm; New
        York: Da Capo Press, 1969, 121pp.
            Provides facsimile reprint of 1596 edition.

1664   LODGE, THOMAS. <u>Wits' Misery, 1596</u>. Menston, England: Scolar
        Press, 1971, 124pp.
            Provides facsimile reprint of 1596 edition.

1665   LODGE, THOMAS. <u>Rosalynde, 1592</u>. Introduction by L. M. Rob-
        bins. Menston, England: Scolar Press, 1972, 124pp.
            Provides facsimile reprint of 1592 edition. In introduc-
        tory "Note" comments briefly on plot, style, and theme.

Studies

1666   AOYAMA, SEIKO. "A Study of <u>As You Like It</u>: Shakespeare's Di-
        vergence from His Original." <u>Collected Essays by the Mem-</u>
        <u>bers of the Faculty (Kyoritsu Women's Junior College)</u>,
        No. 6 (December 1962), pp. 89-108.
            Discusses Shakespeare's use of <u>Rosalynde</u> as a source;
        examines in particular Shakespeare's alterations in plot
        and character.

1667   BAIRD, RUTH CATES. "<u>As You Like It</u> and Its Source," in <u>Essays</u>
        <u>in Honor of Walter Clyde Curry</u>. Vanderbilt Studies in the
        Humanities, 2. Nashville: Vanderbilt University Press,
        1954, pp. 143-59.
            Analyzes plot structure of <u>Rosalynde</u>; discusses charac-
        terization, especially how environment determines character;
        examines Lodge's conception of love as "a fashionable atti-
        tude" rather than "an emotion to be felt and experienced."

Lodge

1668   BAKER, ERNEST A[LBERT]. <u>The History of the English Novel</u>,
       Vol. II. London: H. F. & G. Witherby, 1929, 303pp.
            Includes a survey of Lodge's prose fiction, discussing
       in particular the influence of Lyly (pp. 114-20, passim).

1669   BEATY, FREDERICK L. "Lodge's <u>Forbonius and Prisceria</u> and
       Sidney's <u>Arcadia</u>." <u>ES</u>, 49 (February 1968), 38-45.
            Argues that Lodge had access to a manuscript of Sidney's
       <u>Old Arcadia</u> and was deliberately imitating it in <u>Forbonius
       and Prisceria</u>. Points out similarities in plot, style, and
       poetry between the two works.

1670   BEATY, FREDERICK L. "The Novels of Thomas Lodge." Ph.D. dis-
       sertation, Harvard University, 1952, 199pp.
            Examines Lodge's prose fiction in order "to trace the
       development of his talents, point out possible sources, and
       evaluate his achievement." Examines influences on the
       works and discusses Lodge's style.

1671   BERG, KENT TALBOT VAN DEN. "Theatrical Fiction and the Reality
       of Love in <u>As You Like It</u>." <u>PMLA</u>, 90 (October 1975), 885-
       93.
            Notes that Lodge envisions forest as a theater, which
       suggests an isolated, "self-enclosing and protected charac-
       ter" and that Rosalynde in disguise "dramatizes herself for
       her lover" by becoming an actor.

1672   BISWAS, DINESH CHANDRA. <u>Shakespeare's Treatment of His Sources
       in the Comedies</u>. Calcutta: Jadavpur University, 1971,
       299pp.
            Examines Shakespeare's use of <u>Rosalynde</u> as a source for
       <u>As You Like It</u> (pp. 75-89).

1673   BLUESTONE, MAX. <u>From Story to Stage: The Dramatic Adaptation
       of Prose Fiction in the Period of Shakespeare and His Con-
       temporaries</u>. SEngL, 70. The Hague: Mouton, 1974, 341pp.
            Includes examination of Shakespeare's adaptation and
       transformation of <u>Rosalynde</u> in <u>As You Like It</u> (passim).

1674   BRÉGY, KATHERINE. "Lodge and His <u>Rosalynde</u> (A Shakespearean
       Precursor)." <u>Catholic World</u>, 105 (June 1917), 311-20.
       [Reprinted in: Katherine Brégy. <u>Poets and Pilgrims from
       Geoffrey Chaucer to Paul Claudel</u>. New York: Benziger
       Brothers, 1925, pp. 24-41.]
            Discusses Lodge's style and relationship of <u>Rosalynde</u>
       with <u>As You Like It</u>. Provides synopsis of work, which she
       describes as a "picturesque, pedantic and leisurely" ro-
       mance.

1675　BROWN, ELAINE V. BEILIN. "The Uses of Mythology in Elizabethan
　　　　Romance." Ph.D. dissertation, Princeton University, 1973,
　　　　336pp.
　　　　　Analyzes Lodge's use of Venus-Diana myth in Rosalynde
　　　　and A Margarite of America.

1676　BYRD, DAVID G. "Shakespeare's Familiaritie between Sir Rowland
　　　　and Duke Senior in As You Like It." SQ, 26 (Spring 1975),
　　　　205-206.
　　　　　Traces Shakespeare's source for friendship to passage in
　　　　Rosalynde.

1677　CARL, R. "Über Lodge's Leben und Werke: Eine kritische Unter-
　　　　suchung im Anschluss an David Laing." Anglia, 10 (1887),
　　　　234-88.
　　　　　Provides chronological overview of Lodge's prose fiction;
　　　　synthesizes scholarship on sources and influences. Includes
　　　　list of works with notes on locations of copies and on mod-
　　　　ern editions.

1678　CLARK, CUMBERLAND. A Study of As You Like It. London:
　　　　Golden Vista Press, 1931, 118pp.
　　　　　In Chapter IV ("The Sources of the Plot," pp. 28-34)
　　　　discusses Shakespeare's use of Rosalynde as source.

1679　CLUETT, ROBERT. "Arcadia Wired: Preliminaries to an Elec-
　　　　tronic Investigation of the Prose Style of Philip Sidney."
　　　　Lang&S, 7 (Spring 1974), 119-37.
　　　　　Presents "a partial quantitative account of Sidney's
　　　　style in prose fiction measured against those of Lodge,
　　　　Lyly, and Nashe." Concentrates analysis on syntax and word
　　　　classes.

1680　COLBY, ELBRIDGE. English Catholic Poets: Chaucer to Dryden.
　　　　Milwaukee: Bruce Publishing Co., 1936, 228pp.
　　　　　Includes overview of Lodge's works; comments on Catholic
　　　　influence in his later writings (pp. 72-84).

1681　CONDEE, RALPH WATERBURY. "Lodge and a Lucan Passage from
　　　　Mirandula." MLN, 63 (April 1948), 254-56.
　　　　　Notes that in Wit's Misery Lodge uses Octavianus Mirandu-
　　　　la's Illustrium Poetarum Flores as source for Latin quota-
　　　　tion from Lucan but does not translate from it. Postulates
　　　　Lodge either made his own translation at earlier date or is
　　　　using unknown English translation.

1682　CRANE, THOMAS FREDERICK. Italian Social Customs of the Six-
　　　　teenth Century and Their Influence on the Literatures of

Lodge

Europe. Cornell Studies in English. New Haven: Yale
University Press, 1920, 705pp.
Provides a detailed synopsis of A Margarite of America
to illustrate the Italian influence on the work (pp. 545-
51).

1683 CUVELIER, ELAINE. "La Raison et l'imaginaire dans Rosalynde,
ou la therapeutique du desordre," in La Raison et l'imaginaire: Actes du congrès de Rennes (1970). Société des
Anglicistes de l'Enseignement Supérieur. Études Anglaises,
45. Paris: M. Didier, [1973], pp. 59-67.
Analyzes three phases of the work--disorder, movement
into imaginary world, return to order--to examine how re-
generation of characters in Arden makes possible the return
to a rational, ordered world.

1684 DAVENPORT, A[RNOLD]. "Samuel Rowlands and Thomas Lodge."
N&Q, 184 (2 January 1943), 13-16.
Examines Rowlands's use of Wit's Misery as source for
his The Letting of Humour's Blood in the Head Vein.

1685 DAVIS, WALTER R[ICHARDSON]. Idea and Act in Elizabethan Fiction. Princeton: Princeton University Press, 1969, 311pp.
Examines development of Lodge's fiction, especially the
manner in which he juxtaposes the ideal and the real. Examines use of role-playing and disguises in his works and
argues that Lodge, unlike Sidney, emphasizes "the action of
pastoral, the means of coming into contact with ideals
rather than the ideals themselves" (passim).

1686 DAVIS, WALTER R[ICHARDSON]. "Masking in Arden: The Histronics
[sic] of Lodge's Rosalynde." SEL, 5 (Winter 1965), 151-63.
[Reprinted in: Pastoral and Romance: Modern Essays in
Criticism. Edited by Eleanor Terry Lincoln. Englewood
Cliffs, New Jersey: Prentice-Hall, 1969, pp. 71-82.]
Discusses integral relationship of disguise to plot and
theme, and examines relationship between role-playing and
the ideal, concluding that each character "finds his proper
nature by acting it out dramatically." (Errata slip in
Spring issue.)

1687 DAVIS, WALTER R[ICHARDSON]. "The Plagiarisms of John Hynd."
N&Q, NS, 16 (March 1969), 90-92.
Traces Hind's borrowings from Rosalynde in Lysimachus
and Varrona.

1688 DELIUS, N[IKOLAUS]. "Lodge's Rosalynde und Shakespeare's As
You Like It." Shakespeare-Jahrbuch, 6 (1871), 226-49.
Analyzes Shakespeare's use of Rosalynde as a source.

1689 DER, DON W. "Imitation and Imagery in Shakespeare: Factors of Originality in Romeo and Juliet, As You Like It, and Twelfth Night." Ph.D. dissertation, University of Florida, 1968, 223pp.
Includes examination of Shakespeare's use of Rosalynde as a source.

1690 DURHAM, CHARLES W. III. "Character and Characterization in Elizabethan Prose Fiction." Ph.D. dissertation, Ohio University, 1969, 147pp.
Examines Lodge's methods of characterization.

1691 EIN, RONALD BORIS. "The Serpent's Voice: Commentary and Readers' Beliefs in Elizabethan Fiction." Ph.D. dissertation, Indiana University, 1974, 273pp.
Analyzes implied narrator commentary in "the narrator summary" at the beginning of Rosalynde.

1692 FADER, DANIEL NELSON. "Apthonius and Elizabethan Prose Romance." Ph.D. dissertation, Stanford University, 1963, 265pp.
Analyzes influences of "the formal prescriptions for one or another of the exercises in Apthonius's Progymnasmata" on Euphues, Arcadia, and Rosalynde. Finds that the "relationship between the exercises and the romances is one important source of the lack of vital movement which characterizes all three of the narratives; the more eclectic the author's use of the rhetorical schemes, the more lively his story."

1693 FLEISSNER, ROBERT F. "Richard's Phaëthon Image." AN&Q, 10 (December 1971), 52-53.
Suggests that Lodge's Rosalynde is the source of the image in Shakespeare's Richard II (3.3.178).

1694 FOX, CHARLES A. O. "Thomas Lodge and Shakespeare." N&Q, NS, 3 (May 1956), 190.
Suggests passage in Rosalynde as source for Shakespeare's sonnet 129.

1695 GARKE, ESTHER. The Use of Songs in Elizabethan Prose Fiction. Bern: Francke Verlag, 1972, 132pp.
Draws frequently on Lodge's novels for examples in analysis of types of songs, their relationships to plot and structure, and their functions (to complement or contrast setting, to present character relationships, to characterize singer and audience).

Lodge

1696   GUBAR, SUSAN DAVID. "Tudor Romance and Eighteenth-Century
        Fiction." Ph.D. dissertation, University of Iowa, 1972,
        243pp.
             Includes examination of structure and style of Lodge's
        prose fiction: discusses reader response and how the works
        "call attention to their own literariness."

1697   HAMILTON, DONNA B. "Some Romance Sources for King Lear:
        Robert of Sicily and Robert the Devil." SP, 71 (April
        1974), 173-91.
             Argues for Lodge's Robert Second Duke of Normandy as a
        direct source of Lear. Compares Lodge's romance to the
        anonymous Robert the Devil and to Lear. Analyzes in detail
        the following in Lodge's work: "(1) the pattern of confes-
        sion, trial, and reward, (2) the interest in defining the
        source of the wickedness in life, and (3) the tension cre-
        ated when the God-fearing Christians and the atheists are
        in opposition to each other."

1698   HARMAN, EDWARD GEORGE. The Countesse of Pembrokes Arcadia
        (With a Chapter on Thomas Lodge). London: Cecil Palmer,
        1924, 243pp.
             Argues that Rosalynde, Euphues's Shadow, Robert Second
        Duke of Normandy, A Margarite of America, and Forbonius and
        Prisceria were written by someone else (apparently Francis
        Bacon).

1699   HART, H[ENRY] C[HICHESTER]. "Robert Greene's Prose Works."
        N&Q, 113 (17 March 1906), 202-204.
             Discusses influence of Greene on Lodge's Rosalynde, sug-
        gesting that "it is hard to believe that...[Greene] did not
        touch it up for the press."

1700   [HEATH, MEYRICK. "Lodge's Rosalynde."] Academy, 50 (7 Novem-
        ber 1896), 355-56.
             Discusses Lodge's style and Shakespeare's use of Rosa-
        lynde as a source. (Report of paper read before the Clifton
        Shakespeare Society, 24 October 1896.)

1701   HELGERSON, RICHARD. The Elizabethan Prodigals. Berkeley:
        University of California Press, 1976, 188pp.
             Provides detailed examination of Lodge's use of the
        Prodigal Son motif in his prose fiction, particularly the
        relationships between Lodge himself and his characters.
        Traces evolution in Lodge's work from the "harmonious reso-
        lution of Rosalind" to the "bleaker world, a world of sharp,
        and finally irreconcilable conflict" in the later prose fic-
        tion (pp. 105-23).

1702 HELGERSON, RICHARD. "The Prodigal Son in Elizabethan Fiction."
Ph.D. dissertation, Johns Hopkins University, 1970, 197pp.
Examines Lodge's use of Prodigal Son motif.

1703 HERPICH, CHA[RLE]S A. "The Source of the 'Seven Ages.'" N&Q,
105 (18 January 1902), 46-47.
Suggests passage in A Margarite of America as source of
Jaques's speech.

1704 HIEATT, CHARLES W. "The Quality of Pastoral in As You Like
It." Genre, 7 (June 1974), 164-82.
Discusses "how pastoral tradition is manifest" in Rosalynde and "how Shakespeare altered...[Rosalynde] within its
generic context."

*1705 HIRAOKA, TOMOKAZU. "From Rosalynde to As You Like It." Toyama
Daigaku Bungaku Kiyo, March, 1956.
Not located. In Japanese. Listed in Paul A. Jorgensen,
"Shakespeare: An Annotated Bibliography for 1956," SQ, 8
(1957), 270.

1706 HORNÁT, JAROSLAV. Anglická renesanční próza: eufuistická
beletrie od Pettieho Paláce Potěchy do Greenova Pandosta
[Renaissance Prose in England: Euphuistic Fiction from
Pettie's Palace of Pleasure to Greene's Pandosto]. Acta
Universitatis Carolinae, Philologica, Monographia 33.
Prague: Universita Karlova, 1970, 173pp.
Examines influence of Lyly on Lodge, especially in Forbonius. Examines Lodge's place in the development of
euphuistic fiction and discusses his "relatively sensitive
approach to the sentiments and psychological traits of his
characters" (pp. 83-104).

1707 HORNÁT, JAROSLAV. "An Old Bohemian Legend in Elizabethan
Literature." PP, 7 (1964), 345-52.
Discusses Lodge's use of Enea Silvio Piccolomini's
Historia Bohemica as source for William Longbeard. Suggests
that Lodge "tried to develop a new type of novel by basing
his narrative on...historical sources."

1708 HORNÁT, JAROSLAV. "Spisovatelské počátky Thomase Lodge [The
Literary Beginnings of Thomas Lodge]." ČMF, 43, no. 4
(1961), 193-207.
Discusses Forbonius and Prisceria as "a typical euphuistic romance" in which Lodge follows "the unwritten laws of
the newly developed literary type." Includes summary in
English (pp. 206-207).

Lodge

1709   HUNTER, G. K. "Isocrates' Precepts and Polonius' Character."
       ShQ, 8 (Autumn 1957), 501-506.
           Uses extracts from Rosalynde and A Margarite of America
       to illustrate the popularity and conventionality of
       Polonius's advice to Laertes.

1710   [JENKINSON, J. A. "As You Like It and Rosalynde."] Academy,
       45 (19 May 1894), 420-21.
           Discusses Shakespeare's use of Rosalynde as a source.
       (Report of paper read before the Elizabethan Society, 2 May
       1894).

1711   JONES, DEBORAH CHAMPION. "Sources of the Natural History in
       the Literary Works of Thomas Lodge." Ph.D. dissertation,
       Radcliffe College, 1932.
           Identifies sources of Lodge's references to natural his-
       tory in his prose fiction.

1712   JUSSERAND, J[EAN] J[ULES]. The English Novel in the Time of
       Shakespeare. Translated by Elizabeth Lee. Revised edition.
       London: T. Fisher Unwin, 1890, 433pp.
           Discusses influence of Lyly on Lodge and examines some
       of his narrative techniques (pp. 202-15).

1713   KAPLOWITZ, KAREN M. "The Function of the Poetry in the Prose
       Fiction of Thomas Lodge." Ph.D. dissertation, New York
       University, 1974, 376pp.
           Examines structural and thematic relationships of poems
       to prose to trace the "development of Lodge's attitude to-
       ward eloquence" and to argue that the "poems are the actual
       subject of his fiction."

1714   KASTNER, L. E. "Thomas Lodge as an Imitator of the French
       Poets." Athenaeum, No. 4017 (22 October 1904), pp. 552-53;
       No. 4018 (29 October 1904), p. 591.
           Identifies sources of some of poems in Lodge's prose
       fiction.

1715   KAUL, R. K. "Lodge, Shakespeare and the Olde Daunce." LCrit,
       6 (1963), 19-28.
           Discusses "the characteristics of Ovidian love discern-
       ible in Rosalynde."

1716   KRIEGER, GOTTFRIED. Gedichteinlagen im englischen Roman.
       Ph.D. dissertation, University of Köln. Köln: n.p., 1969,
       274pp.
           Includes discussion of function and relation to theme
       and structure of verse insets in Lodge's prose fiction
       (passim).

1716a LARSON, CHARLES [HOWARD]. "Lodge's Rosalind: Decorum in
Arden." SSF, 14 (Spring 1977), 117-27.
Argues "that decorum is a vital concept for all of the
characters in the story and that Lodge's plot is designed
to bring about an eventual revelation of this value of
decorum to everyone." Examines setting and place of work
in pastoral literature, and suggests that "[t]he book can
be seen as a kind of guide to literary, social, and sexual
decorum."

1717 LATHAM, AGNES [MARY CHRISTABEL]. "Introduction," in As You
Like It. By William Shakespeare. Edited by Agnes [Mary
Christabel] Latham. Arden Shakespeare. London: Methuen,
1975, pp. ix-xci.
Includes examination of Shakespeare's use of Rosalynde
as a source.

1718 LAUCHERT, FRIEDRICH. "Der Einfluss des Physiologus auf den
Euphuismus." Englische Studien, 14 (1890), 188-210.
Examines influence of works about natural history on
euphuism. Provides listings of references to animals in
the works of Lyly, Greene, and Lodge.

1719 LINDHEIM, NANCY R[OTHWAX]. "Lyly's Golden Legacy: Rosalynde
and Pandosto." SEL, 15 (Winter 1975), 1-20.
Discusses Lodge's selection, modification, and pattern-
ing of elements of euphuism (especially the soliloquy) "to
turn the philosophical import of Lyly's style away from its
warning of the discrepancy between appearance and reality,
and towards an affirmation that in the romance world the
forces of Nature combine to harmonize the two halves of
this antithesis."

1720 LONG, W. H. "Thomas Lodge, Poet, Author, Physician, &c."
Antiquarian Magazine & Bibliographer, 3, no. 16 (1883),
189-95.
Includes comments on Lodge's prose fiction (particularly
his gibes at critics) in general overview of life and works.

1721 McALEER, JOHN J. "Thomas Lodge's Verse Interludes." CLAJ, 6
(December 1962), 83-89.
Examines use of verse interludes in Forbonius and Prisceria and Rosalynde, suggesting that through such Lodge gave
"full vent to his lyric impulse" while retaining his euphuistic style. Also discusses influence of Lyly, Sidney,
and Greene, and Lodge's inability to break away from his
models.

Lodge

1722   MILLS, LAURENS J. <u>One Soul in Bodies Twain: Friendship in</u>
        <u>Tudor Literature and Stuart Drama</u>. Bloomington, Indiana:
        Principia Press, 1937, 480pp.
            Examines Lodge's use of friendship theme in his prose
        fiction (pp. 220-25).

1723   MINCOFF, MARCO. "What Shakespeare Did to <u>Rosalynde</u>."
        <u>Shakespeare-Jahrbuch</u>, 96 (1960), 78-89. [Reprinted in:
        <u>Twentieth Century Interpretations of</u> As You Like It. Edited
        by Jay L. Halio. Englewood Cliffs, New Jersey: Prentice-
        Hall, 1968, pp. 98-106.]
            Includes discussion of structure of <u>Rosalynde</u> and Lodge's
        treatment of love in examining Shakespeare's transformation
        of the work.

1724   MUIR, KENNETH. <u>Shakespeare's Sources, I: Comedies and Tra-</u>
        <u>gedies</u>. London: Methuen & Co., 1957, 279pp.
            Includes examination of Shakespeare's use of <u>Rosalynde</u>
        as source for <u>As You Like It</u> (pp. 55-66).

1725   NICHOLSON, BRINSLEY. "Jottings in By-Ways, II: <u>Euphues'</u>
        <u>Shadow</u>, Lodge's or Greene's?" <u>N&Q</u>, 49 (10 January 1874),
        21-23.
            Argues that Lodge, not Greene, was author.

*1726   PARADISE, NATHANIEL BURTON. "Thomas Lodge: The History of an
        Elizabethan." Ph.D. dissertation, Yale University, 1925,
        254pp.
            <u>See</u> 1727.

1727   PARADISE, N[ATHANIEL] BURTON. <u>Thomas Lodge: The History of</u>
        <u>an Elizabethan</u>. New Haven: Yale University Press, 1931,
        264pp.
            Includes chronological overview of Lodge's prose fiction:
        provides critical estimate of each work and discusses style
        and influences. In Appendix B ("Lodge's Borrowings," pp.
        215-30) notes Lodge's use of French and Italian sonneteers;
        in Appendix C ("A Chronological List of the Writings of
        Thomas Lodge," pp. 231-43) provides transcription of title
        pages and notes on modern editions.

1728   PARRILL, WILLIAM BRUCE. "The Elizabethan Background of Hell,
        the Devil, the Magician, and the Witch, and Their Use in
        Elizabethan Fiction." Ph.D. dissertation, University of
        Tennessee, 1964, 321pp.
            "[S]tudies the uses which Nashe, Greene, Dekker, Lodge
        and the other fiction writers made of the wide variety of
        material available" on the topics. Finds that use was
        largely satirical.·

1729   PIERCE, ROBERT B. "The Moral Languages of Rosalynde and As
        You Like It." SP, 68 (April 1971), 167-76.
            Argues that although "full of moral talk" Lodge's romance
        is lacking in "moral significance"; examines relationship
        of style to character to illustrate how Lodge "uses didac-
        ticism as a kind of literary decoration."

1730   POLLACK, CLAUDETTE [HOOVER]. "Lodge's A Margarite of America:
        An Elizabethan Medley." Ren&R, 12, no. 1 (1976), 1-11.
            Examines "the way Lodge assimilated the most popular
        modes of Renaissance prose and poetry" in the work. Ex-
        amines his use of sources and the influence of types of
        prose fiction on the work. Suggests that the contrast be-
        tween "the pastoral setting and the harsh brutality of the
        story itself" is indicative of the movement away from pas-
        toral romance to more realistic fiction.

1731   POLLACK, CLAUDETTE [HOOVER]. "Romance and Realism in Lodge's
        Robin the Devil." SSF, 13 (Fall 1976), 491-97.
            Examines Lodge's sources and analyzes his depiction of
        Robert's conversion to argue that Lodge "was consciously
        working toward a compromise between romance and realism,
        with emphasis on the latter." Argues that Robert Second
        Duke of Normandy is important in the "transition from ro-
        mance to realism" in the 1590s.

1732   POLLACK, CLAUDETTE HOOVER. "Studies of the Novels of Thomas
        Lodge." Ph.D. dissertation, Yale University, 1969, 221pp.
            Examines Lodge's eclecticism in using sources and his
        experimentation in forms and styles to investigate his con-
        tributions to the development of English prose fiction.
        Provides detailed analysis of Forbonius and Prisceria,
        Euphues's Shadow, and A Margarite of America.

1733   PROUTY, CHARLES TYLER. "Some Observations on Shakespeare's
        Sources." Shakespeare-Jahrbuch, 96 (1960), 64-77.
            Includes discussion of Shakespeare's use of Rosalynde.

1734   PRUVOST, RENÉ. "Réflexions sur l'euphuisme a propos de deux
        romans élisabéthains." Revue Anglo-Américaine, 8 (1931),
        1-18.
            Notes the similarities of Lodge's A Margarite of America
        with Lyly's Euphues but argues that the term "euphuistic"
        is insufficient to characterize the nature of Lodge's work.
        Suggests that the influence of arcadianism must also be
        considered.

Lodge

1735   RAE, WESLEY D. <u>Thomas Lodge</u>. TEAS, 59. New York: Twayne,
        1967, 128pp.
            Provides synopsis and brief critical assessment of each
        of Lodge's prose fiction works. Traces changes in prose
        style and outlines influences on each work.

1736   RINGLER, WILLIAM [A.]. "The Immediate Source of Euphuism."
        <u>PMLA</u>, 53 (September 1938), 678-86.
            Argues that euphuism was developed and perfected by John
        Rainolds in his Latin lectures, which provided the model
        for the euphuistic style of Lyly, Pettie, Gosson, and Lodge.

1737   ROMIG, EDNA DAVIS. "<u>As You Like It</u>: Shakespeare's Use of His
        Source, Lodge's <u>Rosalynde</u>." <u>University of Colorado Studies</u>,
        16 (1929), 300-22.
            In examining Shakespeare's treatment of Lodge's <u>Rosa-
        lynde</u>, analyzes contrasts in style, plot structure, and
        characterization.

1738   RUTHROF, H[ORST G.]. "The Dialectic of Aggression and Recon-
        ciliation in <u>The Tale of Gamelyn</u>, Thomas Lodge's <u>Rosalynde</u>,
        and Shakespeare's <u>As You Like It</u>." UCTSE, 4 (1973), 1-15.
            Examines Lodge's failure to reconcile the "dialectical
        structure" which he took over from <u>The Tale of Gamelyn</u> with
        the elements of pastoral romance; argues that this lack of
        reconciliation results in "a <u>recurrent bathos</u>" and in
        Lodge's failure to attain his intention of illustrating the
        moral, "concord is the sweetest conclusion." In Appendix,
        provides diagram of "dialectical structure" of <u>Rosalynde</u>.

1739   RYAN, PAT M., JR. <u>Thomas Lodge, Gentleman</u>. Hamden, Connecti-
        cut: Shoe String Press, 1958, 158pp.
            Places Lodge's prose fiction in the context of his life
        and other writings; provides a brief assessment of each
        work. Includes "A Selective Bibliography" of works about
        Lodge, 1625-1958.

1740   SCHLEINER, WINFRIED. "'That virtue is not measured by birth
        but by action': Reality versus Intention in Lodge's <u>Rosa-
        lynde</u>." <u>ZAA</u>, 23, no. 1 (1975), 12-15.
            Examines how characters think and act according to
        Renaissance ideas of rank and station despite Lodge's em-
        phasis of the contrary. Discusses, in particular, the
        Saladyne-Aliena relationship.

1741   SERONSY, CECIL C. "The Seven Ages of Man Again." <u>SQ</u>, 4 (July
        1953), 364-65.

Suggests A Margarite of America as a possible source for
Jaques's speech. Notes Lodge's conception of "life as a
stage play without decorum" in the work.

1742   SHINDLER, JOHN HARRISON. "New Meaning for an Old Tale: The
       Literary Background of Shakespeare's The Winter's Tale,"
       in "I. New Meaning for an Old Tale: The Literary Back-
       ground of Shakespeare's The Winter's Tale. II: Active
       Longing: A Reading of Henry Vaughan's 1650 Silex Scintil-
       lans. III. The Writer-Narrator's Struggle in Laurence
       Sterne and Samuel Beckett." Ph.D. dissertation, Rutgers
       University, 1975, 165pp.
            Examines "how Shakespeare's use of Lodge's Rosalynde
       [as a source] for As You Like It affects his later use of
       Greene's Pandosto [as a source] for The Winter's Tale."

1743   SISSON, CHARLES J. "Thomas Lodge and His Family," in Thomas
       Lodge and Other Elizabethans. Edited by Charles J. Sisson.
       Cambridge: Harvard University Press, 1933, pp. 1-163.
            Includes discussion of autobiographical elements in his
       prose fiction.

1744   SMITH, HALLETT. Shakespeare's Romances: A Study of Some Ways
       of the Imagination. San Marino: Huntington Library, 1972,
       258pp.
            In Chapter 5 ("As You Like It and Rosalynde," pp. 71-94)
       compares Lodge's work with the play in order to illustrate
       "Shakespeare's imagination at work." Discusses Shake-
       speare's transformation of elements (particularly the re-
       duction of the pastoral element) borrowed from Rosalynde.

1745   SMITH, HOMER. "Pastoral Influence in the English Drama."
       PMLA, 12, no. 3 (1897), 355-460.
            Observes that Lodge added the pastoral and court elements
       to Tale of Gamelyn and that the characters in Rosalynde "be-
       came purely conventional pastoral characters from the moment
       they entered the forest." Discusses Shakespeare's use of
       Rosalynde as source for As You Like It.

1746   STATON, WALTER F., JR. "A Lodge Borrowing from Watson."
       Renaissance News, 14 (Spring 1961), 3-6.
            Concludes that "Lodge's sonnet [beginning "In how con-
       trarious forms have I conversed"] in Robert Duke of Normandy
       is an expansion of Watson's number 10 of The First Sett [of
       Italian Madrigals]."

1747   STONE, JOSEPH. "Shakespeare's As You Like It as Part of the
       Courtly Love Tradition." Humanities Magazine, 24, no. 2
       (1967), 32-45.

Lodge

Examines Lodge's use of the courtly love and Petrarchan
traditions in presenting love relationships in Rosalynde;
compares with Shakespeare's treatment of love in As You
Like It.

1748   STONE, W. G. "Shakspere's As You Like It and Lodge's Rosalynde
        Compared." New Shakspere Society Transactions, 1880-1886,
        pp. 277-93.
        Examines differences in treatment of plot and characters.
        Reprinted in 1656.

*1749   TENNEY, EDWARD ANDREWS. "A Life of Thomas Lodge, 1558-1625."
        Ph.D. dissertation, Cornell University, 1932.
        See 1750.

1750   TENNEY, EDWARD ANDREWS. Thomas Lodge. Cornell Studies in
        English, 26. Ithaca: Cornell University Press, 1935,
        216pp.
        Places Lodge's prose fiction in the context of his life
        and other works.

1751   THORNTON, RICHARD H. "Words Used in Thomas Lodge's Wits
        Miserie, 1596." N&Q, 130 (14 November 1914), 385.
        Provides list of antedatings and words not in the OED.
        For comment see: G. C. Moore Smith (28 November 1914),
        435; H. H. Johnson (28 November 1914), 435; St. Swithin
        (28 November 1914), 435; Edward Bensley (12 December 1914),
        473; and Tho[ma]s Ratcliffe (12 December 1914), 473.

1752   TOLMAN, ALBERT H. "Shakespeare's Manipulation of His Sources
        in As You Like It." MLN, 37 (February 1922), 65-76.
        Discusses similarities and differences between Rosalynde
        and As You Like It to illustrate Shakespeare's transforma-
        tion of a source. See 1753.

1753   TOLMAN, ALBERT H. "Shakespeare's Manipulation of His Sources
        in As You Like It," in Falstaff and Other Shakespearean
        Topics. By Albert H. Tolman. New York: Macmillan Co.,
        1925, pp. 65-80.
        Reprint "with additions" of 1752.

*1754   VAGANAY, H. Lodge and Desportes. Maĉon: Privately Printed,
        1922.
        Not located. Listed in "New Publications," MLR, 17
        (October 1922), 447.

1755   VARGO, EDWARD P., S.V.D. "Rosalynde! Heavenly Rosalind!"
        FJS, No. 7 (1974), pp. 39-48.

284

Discusses Shakespeare's transformation of <u>Rosalynde</u>,
particularly his compression of details not directly related to the Rosalind-Orlando love story and his "tendency
to soften violence and to humanize the characters and incidents that are treated crudely and harshly" by Lodge. Compares the rhetoric and structuredness of <u>Rosalynde</u> with the
"vitality and variety" of <u>As You Like It</u>.

1756   WALKER, ALICE. "Italian Sources of Lyrics of Thomas Lodge."
        <u>MLR</u>, 22 (January 1927), 75-79.
            Notes that Ludovico Paschale's <u>Rime volgari</u> is the source
        for seven poems (four of which Lodge had ascribed to Dolce)
        in <u>A Margarite of America</u> and for one sonnet in <u>William
        Longbeard</u>.

1757   WALKER, ALICE. "The Life of Thomas Lodge." <u>RES</u>, 9 (October
        1933), 410-32; 10 (January 1934), 46-54.
            Discusses publication of some of Lodge's works in con-
        text of his life. Illustrates that "the facts of Lodge's
        life show that <u>An Alarum against Usurers</u> has a firm basis
        in personal experience."

1758   WALKER, ALICE. "The Reading of an Elizabethan: Some Sources
        for the Prose Pamphlets of Thomas Lodge." <u>RES</u>, 8 (July
        1932), 264-81.
            Examines Lodge's borrowings from English and foreign
        sources, especially in <u>Wit's Misery</u> ("the most interesting,
        the most vigorous and the most successful of Lodge's pam-
        phlets"). Observes that Lodge was familiar with several
        medieval works and many theological treatises but that
        "evidence of a first-hand knowledge of the classics is
        rare" in his works.

1759   WEISS, ADRIAN. "The Rhetorical Concept of <u>Narratio</u> and Narra-
        tive Structure in Elizabethan Prose Fiction." Ph.D. disser-
        tation, Ohio University, 1969, 222pp.
            In investigation of "the influence of the rhetorical con-
        cept of <u>narratio</u> upon narrative structure" finds that
        Lodge's <u>Rosalynde</u> and <u>Robert Second Duke of Normandy</u> "are
        indebted to <u>narratio</u>, and that, indeed, <u>narratio</u> determined
        the very nature of" the works.

1760   WHITWORTH, CHARLES [W.], JR. "<u>Rosalynde</u>: As You Like It and
        as Lodge Wrote It." <u>ES</u>, 58 (April 1977), 114-17.
            Discusses how scholars have been misled by Shakespeare's
        play into assuming that Gerismond and Torismond were
        brothers; points out erroneous conclusions based on assump-
        tion of a fraternal relationship.

Lodge

1761   WHITWORTH, CHARLES W. "Thomas Lodge: Elizabethan Pioneer."
        CahiersE, 3 (1973), 5-15.
            Discusses Lodge's prose fiction--particularly in terms
        of his experimentation and innovation--in the context of
        his life and times.

1762   WOLK, ANTHONY. "The Extra Jaques in As You Like It." SQ, 23
        (Winter 1972), 101-105.
            Argues that the three brothers in Rosalynde "appear to
        exemplify the three temptations of the world." Suggests
        that Lodge's characterization of Fernandyne is "possibly a
        commentary on what Shakespeare did in As You Like It."

1763   WOODWARD, PARKER. "Thomas Lodge." Baconiana, 15 (January-
        April 1917), 100-109.
            Argues that Lodge's works were "written by young Francis
        Bacon."

1764   WURTZBURG, C. A. "Die Handlung in Wie es Euch gefällt: Eine
        induktive Studie." Shakespeare-Jahrbuch, 27 (1892), 230-37.
            Includes discussion of Shakespeare's use of Rosalynde as
        a source for As You Like It.

LONG, KINGSMILL

John Barclay, Barclay His Argenis. STC 1395.

Studies

1765   SCHMID, KARL FRIEDRICH. John Barclays Argenis: Eine litterar-
        historische Untersuchung. Literarhistorische Forschungen,
        31. Berlin: E. Felber, 1903, 183pp.
            Provides bibliographical description of 1625 and 1636
        editions of Long's translation; discusses briefly his style
        and treatment of text (pp. 91-96).

LOVEDAY, ROBERT (1621?-1657?)

Gautier de Costes de la Calprenède, Hymen's Praeludia: Or Love's
    Masterpiece, Being the First Part of Cleopatra (Loveday translated
    Parts I-III). Wing L111-114, L122-124.

Studies

1766   HUNTLEY, FRANK LIVINGSTONE. "Robert Loveday: Commonwealth
        Man of Letters." RES, NS, 2 (July 1951), 262-67.

Discusses Hymen's Praeludia in context of Loveday's life
and works, especially in relation to his celibate life.

LYLY, JOHN (1554-1606)

Euphues: The Anatomy of Wyt. STC 17051-17067.

Euphues and His England: Containing His Voyage and Adventures. STC
    17068-17079.

Bibliographies

1767 HOUPPERT, JOSEPH W. "John Lyly," in The Predecessors of
      Shakespeare: A Survey and Bibliography of Recent Studies
      in English Renaissance Drama. Edited by Terence P. Logan
      and Denzell S. Smith. Lincoln: University of Nebraska
      Press, 1973, pp. 125-42.
          Provides overview of recent scholarship on Euphues and
      selective bibliography.

1768 JOHNSON, ROBERT C. "John Lyly, 1939-1965," in Elizabethan
      Bibliographies Supplements, V: Robert Greene, 1945-1965;
      Thomas Lodge, 1939-1965; John Lyly, 1939-1965; Thomas
      Nashe, 1941-1965; George Peele, 1939-1965. Compiled by
      Robert C. Johnson. London: Nether Press, 1968, pp. 35-43.
          Provides chronological list of editions and criticism,
      1939-1965; supplements 1769.

1769 TANNENBAUM, SAMUEL A. John Lyly (A Concise Bibliography).
      Elizabethan Bibliographies, 12. New York: Samuel A.
      Tannenbaum, 1940, 46pp.
          Provides classified list of editions and criticism.
      Continued by 1768.

Editions

1770 LYLY, JOHN. Euphues: The Anatomy of Wit. Euphues and His
      England. Edited by Edward Arber. English Reprints, 9.
      London: A. Murray & Son, 1869, 478pp.
          Provides edited texts based on collation of "early" edi-
      tions. In "Introduction," pp. 11-30, discusses rarity of
      early editions and transcribes notices of works from 1586-
      1861. Includes bibliography.

1771 LYLY, JOHN. Evphves: The Anatomy of Wit: To Which Is Added
      the First Chapter of Sir Philip Sidney's Arcadia. Edited

287

Lyly

by Friedrich Landmann. Englische Sprach- und Literaturdenkmale, 4. Heilbronn: Verlag von Gebr. Henninger, 1887,
182pp.
Provides annotated text (omitting dialogue between Euphues and Atheos) based on 1579 edition. In "Introduction"
(pp. III-XXXII) discusses bibliographical history of work
and qualities of euphuistic style. Traces origin of euphuism to Antonio de Guevara and discusses the influence of
Thomas North's translation The Dial of Princes on the contents and style of Euphues.

1772   LYLY, JOHN. The Complete Works of John Lyly. Edited by
R[ichard] Warwick Bond. 3 vols. Oxford: Clarendon Press,
1902, 559, 578, 624pp.
Provides critical editions of Euphues: The Anatomy of
Wit and Euphues and His England. In "Life of John Lyly"
(I, 1-82) discusses the works in context of his life and
times. In "Euphues: The Text and Bibliography" (I, 83-
118) provides bibliographical analysis of editions, discusses relationships among them, and establishes order of
editions. In "Euphues and Euphuism" (I, 119-75) attempts
"to summarize and condense" previous discussions of the
style. Examines origins and characteristics of euphuism,
and its influence on development of English prose. Describes the two parts as the "first English novel," traces
Lyly's sources, and analyzes Shakespeare's debt to Lyly's
prose fiction.

*1773 LYLY, JOHN. Euphues: The Anatomy of Wit. N.p.: n.p.:
1906?, 157pp.
Not seen. Listed in NUC Pre-1956 Imprints, vol. 347,
206.

1774   LYLY, JOHN. Euphues: The Anatomy of Wit. Euphues & His England. Edited by Morris William Croll and [W.] Harry Clemons. London: George Routledge & Sons; New York: E. P.
Dutton & Co., 1916, 537pp.
Provide critical edition of the 1578 edition of Euphues:
The Anatomy of Wit and the 1580 edition of Euphues and His
England. In "Introduction: The Sources of the Euphuistic
Rhetoric," pp. v-lxiv, Croll argues that "[e]uphuism is not
the product of humanistic imitation of the ancients" but
rather developed out of the schemata of Medieval Latin
prose. Discusses influence of later humanistic thought on
contents of Euphues, noting in particular the work's bourgeois character. "Introduction" reprinted in 1826.

1775　LYLY, JOHN. <u>Euphues: The Anatomy of Wit</u>, in <u>Elizabethan Fic-</u>
<u>tion</u>. Edited by Robert Ashley and Edwin M. Moseley. San
Francisco: Rinehart Press, 1953, pp. 83-156.
　　Provide partly modernized text (omitting concluding letters) based on 1772. In "Introduction," pp. x-xiii, suggest
that Lyly's style both reflects and ridicules the concerns
of "the remnant feudal aristocracy."

1776　LYLY, JOHN. <u>Euphues: The Anatomy of Wit</u>, in <u>The Descent of</u>
<u>Euphues: Three Elizabethan Romance Stories:</u> Euphues, Pan-
dosto, Piers Plainness. Edited by James Winny. Cambridge:
Cambridge University Press, 1957, pp. 1-66.
　　Provides slightly modernized text based on 1578 edition;
omits concluding letters. In "Introduction" (pp. ix-xxv)
provides an overview of the characteristics of Lyly's style
and examines the influence of the work on later Elizabethan
prose fiction.

1777　LYLY, JOHN. <u>Euphues: The Anatomy of Wit</u>, in <u>Elizabethan Prose</u>
<u>Fiction</u>. Edited by Merritt [E.] Lawlis. Indianapolis:
Odyssey Press, Bobbs-Merrill Co., 1967, pp. 112-88.
　　Provides partly modernized text based on the second edition, 1579 (omits the concluding letters). (See pp. 627-29
for a list of substantive emendations and a discussion of
the importance of the second edition.) In introductory
note, examines the characteristics of Lyly's style, suggesting that his primary interest is in the expression and
manipulation of ideas.

Studies

1778　ACKERMAN, CATHERINE A. "John Lyly and Fashionable Platonism
in Caroline Poetry." <u>Lock Haven Bulletin</u>, No. 3 (1961),
pp. 19-23.
　　Suggests that through the Euphues-Philautus debate "Lyly
made <u>discussion</u> of Platonic love popular" and thus influenced the popularity of discussions of and writings on
Platonic love at Queen Henrietta Maria's court.

1779　ADDIS, JOHN, JR. "Lyly's <u>Euphues</u>." <u>N&Q</u>, 39 (20 March 1869),
276.
　　Cites more parallels to proverbs in <u>Euphues</u> (<u>see</u> 1780).

1780　ADDIS, JOHN, JR. "Lyly's <u>Euphues</u> (ed. Arber)." <u>N&Q</u>, 39
(23 January 1869), 76-77.
　　Points out proverbs in <u>Euphues</u> and suggests parallels in
other writers. Also queries meaning of some passages (<u>see</u>
1779, 1824, and 1899).

Lyly

1781   AINGER, ALFRED. "Euphuism--Past and Present," in <u>Lectures and</u>
       <u>Essays</u>, Vol. I. By Alfred Ainger. Edited by H[enry]
       C[harles] Beeching. London: Macmillan and Co.; New York:
       Macmillan Co., 1905, pp. 156-87.
           Examines development, characteristics, and influence of
       euphuism; traces euphuistic tendencies in prose from six-
       teenth through nineteenth century. Discusses Lyly's sig-
       nificance to literature.

1782   ANDERS, H[EINRICH] R. D. <u>Shakespeare's Books: A Dissertation</u>
       <u>on Shakespeare's Reading and the Immediate Sources of His</u>
       <u>Works</u>. Berlin: Georg Reimer, 1904, 316pp.
           Reviews scholarship on influence of Lyly on Shakespeare
       and cites parallels between <u>Euphues</u> and the plays (passim).

1783   ANON. "John Lyly and the Euphuists." <u>Chamber's Journal</u>, 68
       (17 October 1891), 667-69.
           Provides general comments on Lyly's style and his in-
       fluence.

1784   ARBER, EDWARD. "'Euphues and His Ephoebus.'" <u>N&Q</u>, 38 (7 No-
       vember 1868), 437.
           Notes that "Euphues and His Ephoebus" "is almost entirely
       a literal translation from Plutarch on 'Education.'"

1785   ARMES, WILLIAM D. "A Forgotten Poet." <u>The Californian: A</u>
       <u>Western Monthly Magazine</u>, 3 (February 1881), 180-83.
           Provides general discussion of Lyly's style, the morality
       in <u>Euphues</u>, and the popularity and influence of the work.

1786   ATKINS, J[OHN] W[ILLIAM] H[EY]. "Elizabethan Prose Fiction,"
       in <u>The Cambridge History of English Literature, III: Renas-</u>
       <u>cence and Reformation</u>. Edited by A[dolphus] W[illiam] Ward
       and A[lfred] R[ayney] Waller. Cambridge: Cambridge Univer-
       sity Press, 1909, 339-73.
           Includes examination of <u>Euphues</u> as the "first English
       novel" and as a moral treatise. Discusses sources, influ-
       ences on later writers, and style (which is "the outcome of
       a desire to write with clearness and precision") (pp. 344-
       50).

1787   AURNER, ROBERT RAY. "The History of Certain Aspects of the
       Structure of the English Sentence." <u>PQ</u>, 2 (July 1923),
       187-208.
           Analyzes frequency of Lyly's use of various sentence ele-
       ments in <u>Euphues</u> and notes that his style represents the
       "first deliberate attempt to organize the English sentence."

1788   B., C. C. "Euphues: Parallel Passages." N&Q, 87 (13 May
        1893), 366.
            Notes parallels between passages in Euphues: The Anatomy
        of Wit and poems by Burns and Cowper. (See R. R., "Euphues:
        Parallel Passages," N&Q, 87 [10 June 1893], 454).

1789   B., C. C. "Lyly's Euphues and His England." N&Q, 76 (27 Au-
        gust 1887), 173.
            In response to earlier query, explains meaning of two
        words in work. See 1907.

1790   B., W. C. "Proverbs and Phrases." N&Q, 38 (14 November 1868),
        459-60.
            Lists several proverbs from Euphues.

1791   BACON, WALLACE A. "Introduction," in William Warner's Syrinx
        or a Sevenfold History. By William Warner. Edited by Wal-
        lace A. Bacon. Northwestern University Studies, Humanities
        Series, 26. Evanston: Northwestern University Press, 1950,
        pp. xi-lxxxv.
            Examines influence of Euphues on Warner's style (pp.
        xlvii-lii).

1792   BAILY, JOHNSON. "Lyly's Euphues." N&Q, 39 (13 February 1869),
        160.
            Discusses meaning of words and phrases in Euphues.

1793   BAKER, ERNEST A[LBERT]. The History of the English Novel,
        Vol. II. London: H. F. & G. Witherby, 1929, 303pp.
            In Chapter IV ("Lyly's Euphues," pp. 57-66), argues that
        the two Euphues works are not rudimentary novels but form
        "a treatise on education and manners." Examines the charac-
        teristics and influence of Lyly's style, the place of his
        work in the development of the novel, and his influence on
        later Elizabethan fiction.

1794   BANG, W., and H[ENRY] DE VOCHT. "Klassiker und Humanisten als
        Quelle älterer Dramatiker." Englische Studien, 36 (1906),
        383-93.
            Points out possible sources in work of Erasmus for
        Euphues.

1795   BARISH, JONAS A. "The Prose Style of John Lyly." ELH, 23
        (March 1956), 14-35.
            Correlates "certain categories of Lyly's style with cate-
        gories of meaning" and argues that "the plays and the
        novels...[are] part of a single stylistic system." Consid-
        ers in detail Lyly's use of antithesis to support

Lyly

contention that "logicality is...the basic principle of Lyly's style."

1796 BARLEY, ALFRED H. "Euphues and Bacon's Thought." Baconiana, 17 (September 1924), 276-89.
Argues that Euphues was written by Bacon and that in Euphues (the character) "we have a very good picture of the young Francis Bacon in the first flush of youth and high spirits."

1797 BASSE, MAURITS. Stijlaffectatie bij Shakespeare, vooral uit het oogpunt van het euphuisme. Université de Gand, Recueil de Travaux, Faculté de Philosophie et Lettres, 14. Gand: Van Goethem; The Hague: Nijhoff, 1895, 222pp.
Discusses characteristics of euphuism and analyzes its effect on Shakespeare's style.

1798 BAYNE, THOMAS. "Euphuism." N&Q, 93 (25 January 1896), 66-67.
Compares two "droll" and erroneous accounts of euphuism in trots for University examinations.

1799 BELJAME, ALEXANDRE. "John Lyly et l'euphuisme." Revue des Cours et Conférences, 8 (1 February 1900), 490-94; (22 March 1900), 18-23; (3 May 1900), 297-300.
Provides synopsis of Euphues, examines the characteristics of Lyly's style, and comments on dramatic techniques used in work.

1800 BENHAM, ALLEN R. "A Note on Lyly's Euphues." PQ, 7 (April 1928), 201-202.
Notes possible allusion to "A New Ballad of the Marigold."

1801 BENNETT, JOSEPHINE WATERS. "Characterization in Polonius' Advice to Laertes." SQ, 4 (January 1953), 3-9.
Argues that in Polonius's speech Shakespeare is not attempting to suggest Euphues to his audience since he echoes only precepts, not style. Suggests that Shakespeare is using Isocrates's Ad Demonicum as source, the same work Lyly drew on for moral precepts.

1802 BEST, MICHAEL R. "Nashe, Lyly, and Summers Last Will and Testament." PQ, 48 (January 1969), 1-11.
Discusses Nashe's criticism of Lyly's euphuism.

1803 BEUM, ROBERT. "The Scientific Affinities of English Baroque Prose." EM, 13 (1962), 59-80.
Argues that euphuism and Ciceronianism "possess a common, twofold quality...: repose and balance."

1804   BLOOR, R[OBERT] H[ENRY] U[NDERWOOD]. The English Novel from
        Chaucer to Galsworthy. University Extension Library. Lon-
        don: I. Nicholson and Watson, 1935, 248pp.
           Discusses Lyly's style and argues that popularity of
        Euphues was due to its conduct book form and to its "tone
        and spirit" rather than to the style (pp. 63-72).

1805   [BOND, RICHARD WARWICK.] "John Lyly: Novelist and Dramatist."
        Quarterly Review, 183, no. 365 (1896), 110-38.
           Provides extended analysis of ornamental and structural
        characteristics of Lyly's style. Discusses original aspects
        of Euphues. Essay review of 1770.

1806   BORINSKI, LUDWIG. "The Origin of the Euphuistic Novel and Its
        Significance for Shakespeare," in Studies in Honor of T. W.
        Baldwin. Edited by Don Cameron Allen. Urbana: University
        of Illinois Press, 1958, pp. 38-52.
           Examines the place of Lyly in the development of the
        euphuistic novel and analyzes the characteristics of the
        form.

1807   BRADISH, GAYNOR FRANCIS. "The Hard Pennyworth: A Study in
        Sixteenth Century Prose Fiction." Ph.D. dissertation, Har-
        vard University, 1958, 194pp.
           Analyzes Lyly's use of theme of "learning through ex-
        perience"; discusses relationships of style and structure
        to theme, and influence of Euphues upon subsequent treat-
        ments of theme in Greene and Nashe.

*1808   BRONSEN, DAVID. "Weltanschauung, Ästhetik und Alltagsbild der
        englischen Renaissance und deren Widerspiegelung in den
        Werken John Lylys." Ph.D. dissertation, University of Wien,
        1956, 302pp.
           Abstract not available.

1809   BROWN, HUNTINGTON. Prose Styles: Five Primary Types. Minne-
        sota Monographs in the Humanities, 1. Minneapolis: Univer-
        sity of Minnesota Press, 1966, 159pp.
           Classifies euphuism as a "scientific-didactic style,"
        one best-suited to exposition. Asserts that euphuism was
        the "prevailing style of...[Elizabethan] prose." Finds
        euphuistic style completely inappropriate to Lyly's Euphues
        because it is fiction (pp. 44-52).

1810   BROWN, J. T. T. "On the Influence of John Lyly." Scottish
        Historical Review, 1 (October 1903), 70-73.
           Argues that Lyly's influence on the development of Eng-
        lish prose is not as important and pervasive as Bond claims
        (1772).

Lyly

1811   CATEL, JEAN. "John Lyly, immoraliste." Cahiers du Sud, 10
        (June 1933), 145-53.
            Finds Lyly the most curious of a line of immoralists and
        esthetes which populate English literature. Identifies
        Lyly with Euphues and discusses the incongruity between the
        character and Lyly's own life. Argues that Lyly's works
        are a romanticized version of his life as he wished to
        live it.

1812   CAZAMIAN, LOUIS. The Development of English Humor. Durham:
        Duke University Press, 1952, 431pp.
            Examines possibility that a humorous intent underlies
        Lyly's euphuistic style (pp. 131-36).

1813   CHILD, CLARENCE GRIFFIN. John Lyly and Euphuism. Münchener
        Beiträge zur Romanischen und Englischen Philologie, 7.
        Erlangen and Leipzig: Deichert, 1894, 135pp.
            Provides detailed review of research on origin, develop-
        ment, and characteristics of euphuism. Analyzes structural
        and ornamental characteristics (particularly "Lyly's purely
        euphonic use of alliteration") of style. Argues that eu-
        phuists were concerned with form, not content, and that the
        style developed naturally during the period, not through
        some foreign influence. Examines influence of style on
        writers after Lyly.

1814   CLEMEN, WOLFGANG. Shakespeares Bilder: Ihre Entwicklung und
        ihre Funktionem im dramatischen Werk. Bonner Studien zur
        Englischen Philologie, 27. Bonn: P. Hanstein, 1936, 347pp.
            Includes discussion of Lyly's imagery and influence of
        euphuism on Shakespeare (pp. 312-17).

1815   CLEMONS, W. HARRY. "'The Foolish Eiesse.'" MLN, 25 (June
        1910), 200.
            Identifies "ciesse" in Euphues: The Anatomy of Wit as
        "eyas."

1816   CLUETT, ROBERT. "Arcadia Wired: Preliminaries to an Electron-
        ic Investigation of the Prose Style of Philip Sidney."
        Lang&S, 7 (Spring 1974), 119-37.
            Presents "a partial quantitative account of Sidney's
        style in prose fiction measured against those of Lodge,
        Lyly, and Nashe." Concentrates analysis on syntax and word
        classes.

1817   COLVILE, KENNETH NEWTON. "John Lyly," in Fame's Twilight:
        Studies of Nine Men of Letters. By Kenneth Newton Colvile.
        London: P. Allan & Co., 1923, pp. 65-101.
            Discusses in general terms Lyly's prose style.

1818   COOK, ALBERT S. "Euphuistic Natural History in Plutarch."
       MLN, 18 (May 1903), 160-61.
       Suggests that Plutarch and other classical authors be
       searched for sources of euphuistic references to natural
       history.

1819   COOKSEY, CHARLES F. "Annotated Copy of Euphues." N&Q, 80
       (6 July 1889), 6.
       Reports his possession of a copy of 1581 edition with
       "some very remarkable annotations in a contemporary hand of
       almost microscopial characters." Requests someone to de-
       cipher notes and report results in N&Q.

1820   COURTHOPE, W[ILLIAM] J[OHN]. A History of English Poetry, II:
       The Renaissance and the Reformation. London: Macmillan
       and Co., 1897, 457pp.
       Includes examination of influence of Lyly's euphuism on
       the language of the court; discusses the development of eu-
       phuism, the characteristics of Lyly's style, and its im-
       portance to the development of English prose (pp. 179-202).

1821   CRANE, THOMAS FREDERICK. Italian Social Customs of the Six-
       teenth Century and Their Influence on the Literatures of
       Europe. Cornell Studies in English. New Haven: Yale Uni-
       versity Press, 1920, 705pp.
       Includes a discussion of Italian influences on Lyly's
       prose fiction (pp. 528-32).

1822   CRANE, WILLIAM G. Wit and Rhetoric in the Renaissance: The
       Formal Basis of Elizabethan Prose Style. Columbia Univer-
       sity Studies in English and Comparative Literature, 129.
       New York: Columbia University Press, 1937, 293pp.
       Examines Lyly's prose fiction as the culmination of vari-
       ous influences--moral discourses, courtesy books, sentimen-
       tal novels, "processes of rhetorical amplification and
       ornamentation practiced in schools"--on development of
       Elizabethan fiction (pp. 194-202).

1823   CRAWFORD, D. A. E. L. "John Lyly." BJRL, 8 (July 1924),
       312-44.
       Discusses characteristics of Lyly's style and its influ-
       ence on English prose; examines influences on Lyly and his
       effect on later writers. Characterizes Euphues as "a genu-
       ine example of psycho-analysis--a studied picture of the
       cultivated Elizabethan mind."

Lyly

1824   CREDE. "Lyly's Euphues." N&Q, 39 (20 March 1869), 275-76.
       Argues against Morris's explanation (1899) of meaning
       of "chips" and cites various examples of use of word in
       proverbs.

1825   CROLL, MORRIS W[ILLIAM]. "The Origin of the Euphuistic
       Rhetoric." PMLA, 29 Appendix (1914), xxii-xxiii.
       Abstract of paper "read by title," MLA convention, 1913:
       argues stylistic characteristics "ar chiefly medieval sur-
       vivals, and that their increast use in England in the six-
       teenth century, tho ultimately due to the new literary
       impetus of humanism, was contrary to humanistic ideals and
       precepts [spelling, sic]."

1826   CROLL, MORRIS W[ILLIAM]. "The Sources of the Euphuistic
       Rhetoric," edited by R. J. Schoeck and J. Max Patrick, in
       Style, Rhetoric, and Rhythm: Essays by Morris W. Croll.
       By Morris W[illiam] Croll. Edited by J. Max Patrick and
       Robert O. Evans. Princeton: Princeton University Press,
       1966, pp. 235-95.
       Provide reprint of "Introduction" to 1774, with addi-
       tional notes by editors. In "Foreword to Essay Six," pp.
       237-40, Schoeck and Patrick assess Croll's contribution to
       question of origin of euphuism, note other works which sup-
       plement his essay, and suggest other areas for investiga-
       tion.

1827   DA CREMA, JOSEPH J. "The Neoplatonic Element in John Lyly."
       Ph.D. dissertation, Temple University, 1968, 179pp.
       Examines how Euphues reflects Lyly's "considerable knowl-
       edge of Renaissance neoplatonism." Finds that in his prose
       fiction "much of the neoplatonism is 'literary,' a kind
       often dependent on fashionable and polite formulas for love
       discussions."

1828   DANNENBERG, FRIEDRICH. Das Erbe Platons in England bis zur
       Bildung Lyly: Stufen einer Spiegelung. Arbeiten zur Geist-
       esgeschichte der Germanischen und Romanischen Völker, NS,
       13. Berlin: Junker und Dünnhaupt Verlag, 1932, 260pp.
       In Book VI ("Die platonische Bedingtheit und Sendung von
       Lylys Euphues," pp. 156-91) examines influence of Platonism
       on work. Traces influences on content and style, and dis-
       cusses Euphues as a Puritan work.

1829   DAVIS, WALTER R[ICHARDSON]. Idea and Act in Elizabethan Fic-
       tion. Princeton: Princeton University Press, 1969, 311pp.
       Discusses Euphues as a type of "courtly fiction." Ex-
       amines ways in which Lyly uses ideas and "his vivid

histrionic sense": notes, in particular, his tendency "to present...[ideas] from a variety of viewpoints in order to show a spectrum of possible attitudes." Analyzes function of role-playing in work (and the relationship of style-- particularly antithesis--to the role-playing). In Euphues and His England examines "the relation between ideas and experience" (passim).

1830 DUHAMEL, P[IERRE] ALBERT. "Sidney's Arcadia and Elizabethan Rhetoric." SP, 45 (April 1948), 134-50.
Applies method suggested by John Brinsely (Ludus Liter-arius) for analysis of rhetoric to passage from Euphues. Analyzes "Lyly's conception of inventio and dispositio," concluding that he emphasizes the ornamental, rather than the probative, value of rhetoric. Analyzes passage from Sidney as point of contrast. See 1869.

1831 DUNLOP, JOHN [COLIN]. The History of Fiction: Being a Criti-cal Account of the Most Celebrated Prose Works of Fiction, from the Earliest Greek Romances to the Novels of the Pres-ent Age, Vol. III. Revised edition. Edinburgh: Longman, Hurst, Rees, Orme, and Browne, 1816, 524pp.
Provides a brief synopsis of Euphues and details the faults of the work: "constant antithesis," "absurd affec-tation of learning," and "ridiculous superabundance of similitudes." Discusses popularity and influence of the work (pp. 427-33). See 183.

1832 DURHAM, CHARLES W. III. "Character and Characterization in Elizabethan Prose Fiction." Ph.D. dissertation, Ohio Uni-versity, 1969, 147pp.
Examines Lyly's methods of characterization.

1833 EIN, RONALD BORIS. "The Serpent's Voice: Commentary and Readers' Beliefs in Elizabethan Fiction." Ph.D. disserta-tion, Indiana University, 1974, 273pp.
Analyzes implied narrator commentary in "the narrator summary" at the beginning of Euphues.

1834 ENNIS, LAMBERT. "Anthony Nixon: Jacobean Plagiarist and Hack." HLQ, 3 (July 1940), 377-401.
Points out plagiarism of Euphues in Nixon's A Strange Foot-Post.

1835 ESPINER-SCOTT, JANET. "Seneque dans la prose anglaise de More a Lyly (1500-1580)." RLC, 34, no. 2 (1960), 177-95.
Includes examination of Lyly's knowledge of Seneca's works as revealed in Euphues; finds his knowledge rather superficial.

Lyly

1836 EVANS, ROBERT O. "Aphorism--An Aspect of Euphuism." N&Q, NS,
      3 (July 1956), 278-79.
          Discusses "the frequent use of aphorism or cliché as
      part of a euphuistic simile"--points out that aphorism is
      a "characteristic of the style [that] has been neglected by
      the critics."

1837 FADER, DANIEL NELSON. "Apthonius and Elizabethan Prose Ro-
      mance." Ph.D. dissertation, Stanford University, 1963,
      265pp.
          Analyzes influences of "the formal prescriptions for one
      or another of the exercises in Apthonius's Progymnasmata"
      upon Euphues, Arcadia, and Rosalynde. Finds that the "re-
      lationship between the exercises and the romances is one
      important source of the lack of vital movement which charac-
      terizes all three of the narratives; the more eclectic the
      author's use of the rhetorical schemes, the more lively his
      story."

1838 FEUILLERAT, ALBERT. John Lyly: Contribution a l'histoire de
      la Renaissance en Angleterre. Cambridge: Cambridge Univer-
      sity Press, 1910, 673pp.
          Examines both parts of Lyly's Euphues in the context of
      his life and times, and discusses the influence of the works
      on subsequent literature. Analyzes the influence of Protes-
      tant humanism and Ascham's Schoolmaster on Euphues: The
      Anatomy of Wit; examines Lyly's didactic intent, his anti-
      Italianism, and his imitation of Classical sources in the
      work. Discusses Euphues and His England as a reflection of
      the state of England; examines Lyly's attempt to appeal to
      female readers in the work; and discusses his characteriza-
      tion. Analyzes the characteristics of his style, its ori-
      gin, and its influence.

1839 GARNETT, JAMES M. "Notes on Elizabethan Prose." PMLA, 4,
      no. 1 (1889), 41-61.
          Criticizes earlier writers for concentrating too much on
      the excesses of euphuism; argues that in many places Lyly's
      style is clear, simple, natural, and forceful. Notes
      Shakespeare's parody in Romeo and Juliet of phrase from
      "Epistle Dedicatory" to Euphues.

1840 GIBBS, HENRY H[UCKS]. "Euphuism." N&Q, 62 (27 November 1880),
      436.
          Distinguishes euphemism from euphuism, providing a brief
      definition of the latter.

1841   GISELA, JUNKE. "Formen des Dialogs im frühen englischen Ro-
        man." Ph.D. dissertation, University of Köln, 1975, 150pp.
        Examines form and use of dialogues in Euphues. See 208.

1842   GOHLKE, MADELON [SPRENGNETHER]. "Reading Euphues." Criticism,
        19 (Spring 1977), 103–17.
           Analyzes effect of Lyly's euphuistic language on reader.
        Argues that "Lyly's euphuism is based on two levels of dis-
        course, one of which is latent or implicit" and that the
        style is "obstructive." Analyzes "the discrepancy between
        words and intentions" in work. Examines treatment of love/
        lust and the role of Lucilla; argues that "[t]he plot is
        constructed in such a way as to present Euphues with a
        choice between heterosexual passion and homosexual love."

1843   GOODE, CLEMENT TYSON. "Sir Thomas Elyot's Titus and Gysippus."
        MLN, 37 (January 1922), 1–11.
           Notes similarity of Lyly's treatment of story to that of
        Elyot and argues that Elyot's version (along with that by
        Boccaccio and/or Philip Beroaldo) was source of structure
        of Euphues.

1844   GRANJOUX, GEORGES. "La Raison et l'imaginaire dans l'Euphues
        de John Lyly," in La Raison et l'imaginaire: Actes du
        Congrès de Rennes (1970). Société des Anglicistes de l'En-
        seignement Supérieur. Études Anglaises, 45. Paris: M.
        Didier, [1973], pp. 43–58.
           Analyzes subject matter and imagery of dialogues and
        monologues in Euphues: The Anatomy of Wit. Examines Lyly's
        imagery and his use of it to indicate the wisdom or foolish-
        ness of the speaker.

1845   GUSKAR, H. "Fletchers Monsieur Thomas und seine Quellen."
        Anglia, 28 (1905), 397–420; 29 (1906), 1–54.
           Examines Fletcher's use of Euphues as a source. (See
        also: Arthur Ludwig Stiefel, "Zur Quellenfrage von John
        Fletcher's Monsieur Thomas," Englische Studien, 36 [1906],
        238–43; and O. L. Hatcher, "On the Sources of Fletcher's
        Monsieur Thomas," Anglia, 30 [1907], 89–102.)

1846   HART, H[ENRY] C[HICHESTER]. "Robert Greene's Prose Works."
        N&Q, 112 (1 July 1905), 1–5; (29 July 1905), 81–84; (26
        August 1905), 162–64; (16 September 1905), 224–27; (16 De-
        cember 1905), 483–85; 113 (3 February 1906), 84–85; (17
        March 1906), 202–204; (5 May 1906), 343–44; (2 June 1906),
        424–25; (9 June 1906), 463–65; (23 June 1906), 484–87; (30
        June 1906), 504–506. [Reprinted as: H(enry) Chichester
        Hart. Some Remarks on Robert Greene's Prose Works: Chiefly

with Reference to the Use He Has Made of Other Writers.
London: Athenaeum Press, n.d., 83pp.]
   Includes discussion of influence of Euphues on Greene's
prose fiction.

1847   HART, J[AMES] M[ORGAN]. "Euphuism." Transactions of the
   Association of Ohio Colleges, 21 (1889), 30–53. [Also
   separately published: Oberlin, Ohio: Oberlin News Press,
   1890, 24pp.]
      Summarizes current state of research on origin of eu-
   phuism. Discusses characteristics of Lyly's style and examines misconceptions about euphuism. Also discusses Sir
   Walter Scott's knowledge of euphuism.

1848   HAZLITT, W[ILLIAM] CAREW. "Lyly's Euphues and Euphues and His
   England." N&Q, 32 (26 August 1865), 165.
      Provides bibliographical particulars on 1579 and 1580
   editions.

*1849 HEIMANN, ANNELIESE. "Studien zur Analyse der Verbalform in
   John Lylys erzählender und dramatischer Prosa." Ph.D.
   dissertation, University of Wien, 1958, 185pp.
      Abstract not available.

1850   HELGERSON, RICHARD. The Elizabethan Prodigals. Berkeley:
   University of California Press, 1976, 188pp.
      Provides detailed examination of Lyly's use of the Prodi-
   gal Son motif in Euphues, particularly in terms of the relationship between Lyly himself and Euphues. Analyzes
   reasons for popularity of the work and its influence on
   later writers. Examines relationship of Euphues: The
   Anatomy of Wit to its humanist background, arguing that it
   "covertly and perhaps unconsciously undermines" "the content
   of the humanist curriculum...and the humanist didactic method" and that Lyly's "didactic pretensions" are at odds with
   his "creation of character." Examines why character of
   Euphues––"one of the most consistently unsympathetic figures
   in English literature"––was "so attractive to the younger
   Elizabethans." Analyzes differences in "drift" between
   Euphues: The Anatomy of Wit and Euphues and His England
   (passim).

1851   HELGERSON, RICHARD. "The Prodigal Son in Elizabethan Fiction."
   Ph.D. dissertation, Johns Hopkins University, 1970, 197pp.
      Examines Lyly's use of Prodigal Son motif. Argues that
   Lyly's "failure [in Euphues: The Anatomy of Wit] to make
   credible his supposed satire of all the things that make
   the book so popular, his satire of women, of love, of wit,

led him in Euphues and His England to show the inadequacy
of conventional wisdom while turning his attention toward
romantic love."

1852   HELTZEL, VIRGIL B. "Haly Heron: Elizabethan Essayist and
        Euphuist." HLQ, 16 (November 1952), 1-21.
            Discusses Heron's euphuistic style and suggests "that
        experimentation with the new style, as he and Lyly practiced
        it, may have been more prevalent in the 1570's than has
        hitherto been supposed, and that...it is futile to point to
        a specific source, influence, or stimulus to account for
        the 'new English' of either author."

1853   HENSE, C. C. "John Lilly und Shakespeare." Shakespeare-Jahr-
        buch, 7 (1872), 238-300; 8 (1873), 224-79.
            Includes examination of influence of Lyly's euphuism on
        Shakespeare's works.

1854   HOLLIDAY, CARL. English Fiction from the Fifth to the Twenti-
        eth Century. New York: Century Co., 1912, 461pp.
            Includes discussion of Lyly's moralizing and style in
        Euphues and the effect of the work on later writers (pp.
        145-52).

1855   HORNÁT, JAROSLAV. Anglická renesanční próza: eufuistická
        beletrie od Pettieho Paláce Potěchy do Greenova Pandosta
        [Renaissance Prose in England: Euphuistic Fiction from
        Pettie's Palace of Pleasure to Greene's Pandosto]. Acta
        Universitatis Carolinae, Philologica, Monographia 33.
        Prague: Universita Karlova, 1970, 173pp.
            Discusses influence of Ascham's Schoolmaster on Euphues:
        The Anatomy of Wit (noting that Lyly differs from Ascham in
        his emphasis on "experience of life") and the influences on
        and sources of Euphues and His England. Finds that in
        Euphues and His England Lyly repeats themes of earlier work
        but emphasizes the fictional element "in the form of stories
        whose texture...is strongly rhetorical and dialectic...,
        yet with an epic structure." Examines Lyly's influence on
        later writers. Surveys scholarship on origin and immediate
        source of euphuism. Argues that "not only Euphues but eu-
        phuism in the broad sense of the term was an offshoot of
        the humanistic trend in English prose...and a typical prod-
        uct of the English Renaissance period" (pp. 37-82).

*1856   HORNÁT, JAROSLAV. "Lyly's Anatomy of Wit and Ascham's Schole-
        master." Acta Universitatis Carolinae, 1961.
            Not located. According to 1767 "emphasizes Lyly's de-
        pendence on humanistic works devoted to pedagogy and courtly
        conduct, and, particularly, on Ascham's Scholemaster."

Lyly

1857   HORNÁT, JAROSLAV. "Mamillia: Robert Greene's Controversy with
        Euphues." PP, 5 (1962), 210-18.
            Analyzes Greene's deliberate thematic and structural
        parallels with Euphues and contrasts Greene's favorable
        treatment of women and "positive heroines" with the negative
        attitude toward women in Euphues.

1858   HOUPPERT, JOSEPH W. John Lyly. TEAS, 177. Boston: Twayne,
        1975, 169pp.
            Includes analysis of style, narrative technique, struc-
        ture, and themes. Provides running commentary on narrative
        of Euphues: The Anatomy of Wit and Euphues and His England.
        Stresses "the complexity of Lyly's ironic vision of reality"
        (passim).

1859   HUNT, T. W. "Euphuism in Literature and Style." New Englander
        and Yale Review, 14 (March 1889), 189-99.
            Traces source of euphuism to Italy and examines charac-
        teristics of Lyly's style in attempting to define euphuism.

1860   HUNTER, G. K. "Isocrates' Precepts and Polonius' Character."
        ShQ, 8 (Autumn, 1957), 501-506.
            Uses extracts from both parts of Euphues to illustrate
        the popularity and conventionality of Polonius's advice to
        Laertes.

1861   HUNTER, G. K. John Lyly: The Humanist as Courtier. Cam-
        bridge: Harvard University Press, 1962, 386pp.
            Argues that, rather than being original, Lyly is a syn-
        thesizer, both of stylistic elements and of attitudes and
        ideas. In approaching Euphues: The Anatomy of Wit
        "through the society for which...[Lyly] wrote," analyzes
        the influence of humanist thought on the work (seeing Eu-
        phues as a "Humanist Prodigal"); argues that the work is a
        "treatise on wit"; and analyzes the Terentian five-act
        dramatic structure of the work. Examines the themes of
        Euphues and His England and its relationship to the earlier
        work. Discusses the characteristic elements of euphuism
        and examines the origin, development, and influence of the
        style (passim).

1862   HUNTER, G. K. Lyly and Peele. Writers and Their Work, 206.
        London: Longmans, Green for the British Council and the
        National Book League, 1968, 52pp.
            Examines theme of wit versus experience and analyzes re-
        lationship between style and structure in Euphues. Sees
        Lyly's style as "a functional expression of the kind of
        world that...Lyly was trying to create."

1863 HUPPÉ, BERNARD F. "Allegory of Love in Lyly's Court Comedies."
      ELH, 14 (June 1947), 93-113.
          Discusses conception of love in both parts of Euphues;
      compares to treatment of love in Lyly's plays.

1864 JEFFERY, VIOLET M[AY]. John Lyly and the Italian Renaissance.
      Bibliothèque de la Revue de Littérature Comparée, 53.
      Paris: H. Champion, 1928, 155pp.
          Argues for Lyly's indebtedness "to Italian literary tra-
      ditions and conventions" in Euphues. Examines Lyly's knowl-
      edge of Italian authors; his use of questioni d'amore; his
      attitude toward love, woman, and beauty; his treatment of
      the themes of friendship and magic; and his use of Italian
      social customs. Also argues for Italian influence on the
      formation of euphuism.

1865 JUSSERAND, J[EAN] J[ULES]. The English Novel in the Time of
      Shakespeare. Translated by Elizabeth Lee. Revised edition.
      London: T. Fisher Unwin, 1890, 433pp.
          Examines Euphues as novel of manners "written expressly
      for women." Discusses characteristics of euphuistic style,
      Lyly's didacticism, and the popularity and influence of the
      work (pp. 103-50, passim).

1866 KAHIN, HELEN ANDREWS. "Jane Anger and John Lyly." MLQ, 8
      (March 1947), 31-35.
          Suggests that Jane Anger's Jane Anger Her Protection for
      Women was written in reply to Greene's Euphues His Censure
      to Philautus. Discusses Lyly as "a participant in the
      literary quarrel about women."

1867 KIMMELMAN, ELAINE. "A Forerunner of Euphuism." Boston Public
      Library Quarterly, 2 (1950), 189-91.
          Comments on Bourchier's influence on development of eu-
      phuism in his translation of Guevara's Golden Book of Marcus
      Aurelius.

1868 KING, WALTER N. "John Lyly: A Critical Study." Ph.D. dis-
      sertation, Yale University, 1952, 199pp.
          Analyzes "Lyly's employment of the two Renaissance tra-
      ditions of love" in Euphues. Finds that structure of Eu-
      phues: The Anatomy of Wit is "akin to that of the sermon
      and exemplum, yet modified by a consistent technique of de-
      bate"; the structure of Euphues and His England is "akin to
      that of the frame-story, also transformed by Lylian debate."

1869 KING, WALTER N. "John Lyly and Elizabethan Rhetoric." SP, 52
      (April 1955), 149-61.

Lyly

Argues against Duhamel's conclusion that Lyly ignores
demands of logic (1830). Argues that in rhetorical set-
pieces "Lyly concentrates not only upon the logic, or lack
of logic, of the arguments, but upon the dramatic situation
and the characterization of the participants." Analyzes
Euphues's reply to Eubulus to illustrate that Lyly can
utilize logical development. Argues that Lyly, in "adapting
the rhetorical set-piece to narrative purposes," is an in-
novator.

1870 KITTLE, WILLIAM. Edward de Vere, Seventeenth Earl of Oxford,
1550-1604. Washington, D. C.: Buchanan Co., 1935, 252pp.
Identifies Euphues as Oxford (pp. 99-102).

1871 KNEILE, KARL. Die Formenlehre bei John Lyly. Heidelberg: C.
Winter, 1914, 101pp.
Examines Lyly's use of the parts of speech in his prose
style.

1872 KNIGHT, G. WILSON. "Lyly." RES, 15 (April 1939), 146-63.
[Reprinted in abridged form in: Shakespeare's Contemporaries. Edited by Max Bluestone and Norman Rabkin. Englewood Cliffs, New Jersey: Prentice-Hall, 1961, pp. 12-21.]
Discusses Lyly's style, noting that it "plays constantly
round psychological contradictions" and that it "reflects
that balancing of contradictions that is also the core of
Elizabethan drama." Considers relationship of style and
subject matter of Euphues to that of Lyly's plays.

1873 KOLIN, PHILIP C. "Possible Source for Lyly's Eubulus." AN&Q,
10 (February 1972), 83-84.
Suggests "an Athenian statesman named Eubulus" as possible model.

1874 KRAPP, GEORGE PHILIP. The Rise of English Literary Prose.
New York: Oxford University Press, 1915, 565pp.
Includes discussion of Lyly's didacticism, scholarship,
and style in Euphues. Examines his change in moral stance
and style from Euphues: The Anatomy of Wit to Euphues and
His England. Compares his style to that of Sidney (pp. 347-
62, passim).

1875 LACEY, H. "John Lyly and His Euphues." Gentleman's Magazine,
278 (March 1895), 292-303.
Provides a synopsis of Euphues and discusses the development and influence of euphuism, and the characteristics of
Lyly's style. Sees Lyly as a "curious fossil."

1876   LANDMANN, FRIEDRICH. <u>Der Euphuismus, sein Wesen, seine Quelle,</u>
       <u>seine Geschichte: Beitrag zur Geschichte der englischen</u>
       <u>Literatur des sechzehnten Jahrhunderts</u>. Giessen: Druck
       von Wilhelm Keller, 1881, 111pp.
            Traces influences on development of euphuism, arguing
       that Guevara is the immediate source of Lyly's style. Ex-
       amines characteristics (especially alliteration) of euphuism
       and traces its influence on writers after Lyly.

1877   LANDMANN, F[RIEDRICH]. "Shakspere and Euphuism: <u>Euphues</u> an
       Adaptation from Guevara." <u>New Shakspere Society Transac-</u>
       <u>tions</u>, 1880-1886, pp. 241-76.
            Traces source of euphuism to Guevara's style and argues
       that his <u>Dial of Princes</u> is Lyly's source for the content
       of <u>Euphues</u>; discusses characteristics of euphuism and
       Shakespeare's parody of the style. Discusses displacement
       of euphuism by other styles.

1878   LANHAM, RICHARD [ALAN]. "Opaque Style in Elizabethan Prose
       Fiction." <u>PCP</u>, 1 (1966), 25-31.
            Discusses contrast between rhetoric and plot in <u>Euphues</u>,
       pointing out that Lyly's use of rhetorical embellishment
       has been misunderstood because "no one has been willing to
       consider the rhetorical style in its context." Argues that
       "[t]he style is the <u>object</u> of the work, a demonstration of
       what the work is <u>about</u>."

1879   LAUCHERT, FRIEDRICH. "Der Einfluss des Physiologus auf den
       Euphuismus." <u>Englische Studien</u>, 14 (1890), 188-210.
            Examines influence of works about natural history on
       euphuism. Provides listings of references to animals in
       the works of Lyly, Greene, and Lodge.

1880   LEE, S. L. "Euphuism." <u>Athenaeum</u>, No. 2907 (14 July 1883),
       pp. 49-50.
            Argues that Bourchier and Francis Bryan are two of the
       "progenitors" of euphuism. (<u>See</u> Mary A. Ward, "Euphuism,"
       <u>Athenaeum</u>, No. 2912 [18 August 1883], pp. 205-206.)

1881   LEGOUIS, ÉMILE. "John Lyly." <u>Revue des Cours et Conférences</u>,
       22 (5 July 1914), 598-603.
            Comments on: anti-Italianism, didacticism, allegory,
       attitudes toward women, treatment of love, style, and auto-
       biographical nature of <u>Euphues</u>.

1882   LEWIS, C[LIVE] S[TAPLES]. <u>English Literature in the Sixteenth</u>
       <u>Century Excluding Drama</u>. Oxford History of English Litera-
       ture, 3. Oxford: Clarendon Press, 1954, 704pp.

Lyly

Discusses qualities of euphuism, the lack of effective
narrative structure, and the "intolerable" didacticism in
Euphues. Sees Euphues as "a temporary aberration" from
Lyly's work as a dramatist and finds that it "marks...[no]
advance in the art of fiction." Finds the narrative ele-
ments more effective and the didacticism less severe in
Euphues and His England than in Euphues: The Anatomy of
Wit (pp. 312-17, passim).

1883 LIEVSAY, JOHN LEON. Stefano Guazzo and the English Renaissance, 1575-1675. Chapel Hill: University of North Carolina Press, 1961, 358pp.
Suggests that Lyly used Guazzo's La Civil conversation
as source for Euphues (pp. 78-83).

1884 LINDHEIM, NANCY R[OTHWAX]. "Lyly's Golden Legacy: Rosalynde
and Pandosto." SEL, 15 (Winter 1975), 1-20.
Concludes that "euphuism proved a useful legacy to the
Elizabethan romance writer. It conferred neatness, form
and the gloss of elegance..., and also supplied certain
motifs and situations that could help shape a romance narrative."

1885 LOISEAU, JEAN. "Deux attitudes élisabéthaines devant le
voyage: Lyly (Euphues) et Nashe (Jack Wilton)," in Le
Voyage dans la littérature anglo-saxonne. Actes du Congrès
de Nice (1971). Société des Anglicistes de l'Enseignement
Supérieur. Paris: M. Didier, 1972, pp. 13-19.
Examines treatment of and attitude toward travel and
foreign countries in Euphues.

1886 LONG, PERCY WALDRON. "From Troilus to Euphues," in Anniversary
Papers by Colleagues and Pupils of George Lyman Kittredge.
Edited by F. N. Robinson. Boston: Ginn and Co., 1913,
pp. 367-76.
Argues against frequent contention that Euphues is the
first English novel. Suggests Lyly was anticipated by Gascoigne and Grange ("The Golden Aphroditis, far more closely
than any book hitherto adduced, anticipates Lyly's euphuism"). Discusses importance of Ascham's Schoolmaster as
Lyly's source.

1887 MACAULAY, ROSE. "Lyly and Sidney," in The English Novelists:
A Survey of the Novel by Twenty Contemporary Novelists.
Edited by Derek Verschoyle. London: Chatto & Windus, 1936,
pp. 29-47.
Calls Euphues the "first long novel in English narrative
prose about pseudo-contemporary life." Discusses popularity

of work, its sources, and Lyly's style. Concludes that it
is "the remarkable virtuosity shown in the artful development and consistent maintenance of the...manner...that is
the pride of Euphues, and its claim on our admiration as a
brilliant and elegant tour de force."

1888   McKERROW, R[ONALD] B[RUNLEES]. "Euphues and the Colloquies of
       Erasmus." Modern Language Quarterly, 7 (October 1904),
       99–100.
          Identifies Erasmus' Puerpera as source of passage in
       "Euphues and His Ephoebus."

1889   MARCHAM, F. "Lyly's Euphues and His England." N&Q, 111 (13
       May 1905), 366.
          Traces source of passage to Merry Tales and Quick
       Answers.

1890   MARINO, JAMES ARTHUR. "The Cult of Ideal Friendship in Three
       Elizabethan Novels." Ph.D. dissertation, Louisiana State
       University and Agricultural and Mechanical College, 1972,
       226pp.
          Examines Lyly's use of friendship "for narrative content,
       thematic unity, and character development."

1891   MASSINGHAM, H[AROLD] J[OHN]. "John Lyly, 1553?-1606," in The
       Great Tudors. Edited by Katharine Garvin. London: I.
       Nicholson & Watson, 1935, pp. 565–80.
          Discusses popularity of Euphues and comments generally
       on nature of Lyly's prose style. Concludes that Lyly "be-
       came a best-seller simply as an ambassador of the fashion-
       able code."

1892   MÉZIÈRES, A[LFRED JEAN FRANÇOIS]. Prédécesseurs et contempo-
       rains de Shakespeare. Paris: Charpentier, 1863, 419pp.
          In Chapter III discusses influence of Florentine Neo-
       Platonism on Euphues; examines characteristics of euphuism,
       Italian influences on its development, and its influence
       on Shakespeare (pp. 59–98).

*1893 MICHELS, WILHELM. Barockstil bei Shakespeare und Calderón.
       Paris: n.p., 1929, 89pp.
          Not seen. Listed in NUC Pre-1956 Imprints, vol. 382, 15.
       According to 1955 "[t]he author presents the thesis that,
       in common with the Spanish poet Góngora, Lyly has an in-
       clination to verbalism, an urge to fullness and amplifica-
       tion of diction."

Lyly

1894 MILLS, LAURENS J. <u>One Soul in Bodies Twain: Friendship in</u>
<u>Tudor Literature and Stuart Drama</u>. Bloomington, Indiana:
Principia Press, 1937, 480pp.
Discusses Lyly's treatment of friendship theme in <u>Eu-</u>
<u>phues</u> (pp. 182-92).

1895 MOORE, J. MURRAY. "A Study of Euphuism." <u>Proceedings of the</u>
<u>Liverpool Literary and Philosophical Society</u>, 50 (1896),
125-51.
Examines the "historic interest and intrinsic literary
merit" of <u>Euphues</u>. Suggests that Lyly "invented" his style
so that "a didactic style...might be relieved of its heavi-
ness." Provides a synopsis of both parts, discusses Lyly's
didacticism, and comments on influence on later writers.

1896 MORLEY, HENRY. <u>English Writers, VIII: From Surrey to Spenser</u>.
London: Cassell & Co., 1892, 432pp.
Provides lengthy synopsis of <u>Euphues</u>, examines didacticism in work, and discusses characteristics of euphuism
(pp. 305-22).

1897 [MORLEY, JOHN.] Review of <u>The Dramatic Works of John Lilly</u>
<u>(the Euphuist): With Notes, and Some Account of His Life</u>
<u>and Writings</u>, by F. W. Fairholt. <u>Quarterly Review</u>, 109,
no. 218 (1861), 350-83.
Attempts to exonerate Lyly of charge that he corrupted
language and taste by showing that <u>Euphues</u> "was popular,
because it followed, not because it set, a fashion." Traces
origin of euphuism to influence of Italian literature and
manners and to writings of early humanists; examines Lyly's
use of Ascham's <u>Schoolmaster</u> as source; examines influence
of euphuism on later writers. Argues that <u>Euphues</u> is a
work on moral education and on religion.

*1898 MORRIS, J. B. <u>John Lyly and English Euphuism</u>. Bath: n.p.,
1879, 28pp.
Not located. Listed in 1769.

1899 MORRIS, J. P. "Lyly's <u>Euphues</u>." <u>N&Q</u>, 39 (13 February 1869),
160.
Explains meaning of "chips" in passage from <u>Euphues</u> in
answer to one of Addis's queries (1780). <u>See</u> 1824.

1900 MORSBACH, LORENZ. "Shakespeare und der Euphuismus." <u>Nachrich-</u>
<u>ten von der Königlichen Gesellschaft der Wissenschaften zu</u>
<u>Göttingen, philologische-historische Klasse</u>. Berlin:
Weidmann, 1908, pp. 660-69.
Analyzes elements of Lyly's euphuism and illustrates its
influence on Shakespeare.

1901   MUSTARD, W. P. "'Hippocrates' Twins.'" <u>MLN</u>, 38 (May 1923),
313.
        Suggests that the phrase in <u>Euphues and His England</u> re-
fers to "some traditional statement of the famous Greek
physician about the life history of twins." <u>See</u> 1902.

1902   MUSTARD, W. P. "'Hippocrates' Twins.'" <u>MLN</u>, 41 (January
1926), 50.
        Adds another allusion to those noted in 1901.

1903   MUSTARD, W. P. "Note on Lyly's <u>Euphues</u>." <u>MLN</u>, 43 (December
1928), 537.
        Identifies Plutarch's <u>Marcus Cato</u> as source of reference
to Cato removing Manilius from the Senate in <u>Euphues and
His England</u>.

1904   MUSTARD, W. P. "Notes on Lyly's <u>Euphues</u>." <u>MLN</u>, 33 (June
1918), 334-42.
        Suggests several sources of passages. <u>See</u> 1905 and 1906.

1905   MUSTARD, W. P. "Notes on Lyly's <u>Euphues</u>." <u>MLN</u>, 34 (February
1919), 121-22.
        Offers additional notes on sources. <u>See</u> 1904 and 1906.

1906   MUSTARD, W. P. "Notes on Lyly's <u>Euphues</u>." <u>MLN</u>, 40 (February
1925), 120-21.
        Offers additional notes on sources. <u>See</u> 1904 and 1905.

1907   NICHOLSON, BR[INSLEY]. "Lyly's <u>Euphues and His England</u>." <u>N&Q</u>,
76 (27 August 1887), 172-73.
        In response to earlier query, explains meaning of five
allusions and terms in work. <u>See</u> 1789.

1908   NORDEN, EDUARD. <u>Die antike Kunstprosa vom VI. Jahrhundert v.
Chr. bis in die Zeit der Renaissance</u>. 2 vols. Leipzig:
B. G. Teubner, 1898, 988pp.
        Argues that euphuism arose out of imitation of schemes
of Cicero and Isocrates (pp. 773-809).

1909   O'HARA, JAMES EUGENE, JR. "The Rhetoric of Love in Lyly's
<u>Euphues and His England</u> and Sidney's <u>Arcadia</u>." Ph.D. dis-
sertation, University of Michigan, 1974, 210pp.
        Analyzes characteristics of style in Lyly's work and at-
tempts to differentiate between euphuism and arcadianism.

1910   ONALED. "<u>Euphues and Lucilla</u>." <u>N&Q</u>, 38 (31 October 1868),
418.

Lyly

In answer to Onaled's query on eighteenth-century novel founded on Euphues, editor supplies title and publication information for two editions of work.

1911 OTTEN, KURT. Der englische Roman vom 16. zum 19. Jahrhundert. Grundlagen der Anglistik und Amerikanistik, 4. Berlin: E. Schmidt, 1971, 184pp.
Includes general critical estimate of Euphues in context of discussion of development of English novel (pp. 21-26).

1912 PALMER, J. FOSTER. "Euphues." N&Q, 89 (13 January 1894), 37.
Provides brief description of copy of 1617 edition of Euphues and His England.

1913 PARKS, GEORGE B. "Before Euphues," in Joseph Quincy Adams Memorial Studies. Edited by James G. McManaway, Giles E. Dawson, and Edwin E. Willoughby. Washington: Folger Shakespeare Library, 1948, pp. 475-95.
Discusses Euphues: The Anatomy of Wit and Euphues and His England as psychological novels but argues that, rather than representing an innovation, they come "near the end of a tradition of [psychological] prose fiction." Traces the development of psychological fiction which culminated with Euphues.

1914 PEROTT, JOSEPH DE. "The Mirrour of Knighthood." RR, 4 (October-December 1913), 397-402.
Explains allusion in Euphues to "Artimedorus or Lisimandro," characters in The Mirror.

1915 PRUVOST, RENÉ. Matteo Bandello and Elizabethan Fiction. Bibliothèque de la Revue de Littérature Comparée, 113. Paris: H. Champion, 1937, 349pp.
Examines the influence of Bandello on Lyly's fiction; discusses rhetorical embellishment and didacticism in analyzing Euphues as a moral treatise; traces the influence of Euphues on Elizabethan fiction (passim).

1916 PRUVOST, RENÉ. "Réflexions sur l'euphuisme a propos de deux romans élisabéthains." Revue Anglo-Américaine, 8 (1931), 1-18.
Points out that euphuism is more a matter of subjects and topics than of style, and argues for the need to distinguish between the influence of euphuism and arcadianism. Examines affinities of Greene's Menaphon and Lodge's A Margarite of America with Lyly's Euphues but concludes that the term "euphuistic" is insufficient to characterize the two works.

310

1917 PRUVOST, RENÉ. Robert Greene et ses romans (1558-1592): Con-
tribution à l'histoire de la Renaissance en Angleterre.
Publications de la Faculté des Lettres d'Alger, 2d Ser., 2.
Paris: Belles Lettres, 1938, 650pp.
Analyzes influence of style, form, and subject matter of
Lyly's Euphues on Greene's prose fiction (especially Mamil-
lia). Discusses characteristics of euphuism and reviews
scholarship on sources and development of style (pp. 77-95).

1918 PRUVOST, RENÉ. "Variations élisabéthaines sur wit et will,"
in Mélanges de linguistique et philologie: Fernand Mossé
in memoriam. Paris: Didier, 1959, pp. 423-36.
Includes discussion of Lyly's use of terms in Euphues.

1919 QUIMBY, ERNEST S. "The Indebtedness of Lyly's Euphues to Certain of Its Predecessors." Colonnade, 14 (1922), 231-54.
Discusses Lyly's probable use of Castiglione's Courtier
and North's translation of The Dial of Princes, and points
out elements of euphuism in the style of earlier writers.
Suggests that "an attempt to express English national spirit, to elevate the ideals of the courtier, and to pay homage
to the English gentlewoman, are characteristics of Lyly's
euphuism."

1920 R., R. "Another Old Joke." N&Q, 62 (17 July 1880), 45.
Points out analogue to story in Euphues and His England
in Plutarch's Morals, Rich's Honesty of This Age, and joke
told by Dr. Keate of Eton.

1921 RALEIGH, WALTER [ALEXANDER]. The English Novel: Being A Short
Sketch of Its History from the Earliest Times to the Appearance of Waverley. London: J. Murray, 1894, 310pp.
Examines characteristics of Lyly's style, his didactic
moralism, and his imposition of form on prose. Calls Euphues "the first original prose novel written in English"
(pp. 29-48).

1922 RINGLER, WILLIAM [A.]. "The Immediate Source of Euphuism."
PMLA, 53 (September 1938), 678-86.
Argues that euphuism was developed and perfected by John
Rainolds in his Latin lectures, which provided the model for
the euphuistic style of Lyly, Pettie, Gosson, and Lodge.

1923 ROBIN, P[ERCY] ANSELL. Animal Lore in English Literature.
London: Murray, 1932, 206pp.
Draws heavily on Euphues for examples in analysis of
animal references in English literature.

Lyly

1924   ROBINSON, RUTH WINIFRED. "An Anatomy of <u>Euphues</u>." <u>Vassar</u>
       <u>Miscellany</u>, 4 (April 1912), 473-77.
             Provides brief overview of Lyly's style, narrative tech-
       niques, didacticism, and influence on Elizabethan litera-
       ture. Calls <u>Euphues</u> "the first English novel to deal with
       contemporary life."

1925   RUSHTON, W[ILLIAM] L[OWES]. "The Death of Count Melun." <u>N&Q</u>,
       46 (13 July 1872), 29.
             Suggests influence of <u>Euphues</u> on passage in Shakespeare's
       <u>King John</u>.

1926   RUSHTON, W[ILLIAM] L[OWES]. "'Heart cannot conceive.'" <u>N&Q</u>,
       46 (12 October 1872), 292.
             Suggests <u>Euphues</u> as Shakespeare's source for the phrase
       in <u>Macbeth</u>.

1927   RUSHTON, WILLIAM LOWES. <u>Shakespeare's Euphuism</u>. London:
       Longmans, Green, and Co., 1871, 107pp.
             Provides list of parallels between <u>Euphues</u> and Shake-
       speare's plays to illustrate Shakespeare's use of Lyly as
       a source.

1928   RUSHTON, W[ILLIAM] L[OWES]. "'Tongue far from Heart.'" <u>N&Q</u>,
       46 (7 September 1872), 183.
             Suggests that <u>Euphues</u> is Shakespeare's source for the
       phrase in <u>Measure for Measure</u>.

1929   SAINTSBURY, GEORGE. <u>A History of English Prose Rhythm</u>. Lon-
       don: Macmillan and Co., 1912, 505pp.
             Discusses Lyly briefly, noting that except in the plays
       he "contributes little directly to the advancement of Eng-
       lish prose rhythm" (pp. 129-34).

1930   SANDBANK, SHIMON. "Euphuistic Symmetry and the Image." <u>SEL</u>,
       11 (Winter 1971), 1-13.
             Argues that "it is Lyly's urge to write rhythmically--
       not his analytic mind--that gives rise to his balanced
       structures" and discusses relationship of emphasis on rhythm
       to-imagery. Suggests that Lyly's preference for simile over
       metaphor and his habit of utilizing strings of similes is
       the result of his desire for rhythm and symmetry. Finds
       that Lyly totally eliminates "the physical attributes of the
       image," suggesting that this characteristic "may prove to be
       the main difference between Euphuistic imagery and other
       sixteenth-century imagery."

1931   SCHELLING, FELIX [EMMANUEL]. <u>English Literature During the</u>
        <u>Lifetime of Shakespeare</u>. New York: H. Holt and Co., 1927,
        501pp.
            Includes discussion of the characteristics, development,
        and influence of euphuism. Distinguishes between Lyly's
        style and that of Sidney (pp. 34-44).

1932   SMITH, G. C. MOORE. "Lyly, Green, and Shakespeare." <u>N&Q</u>, 116
        (14 December 1907), 461.
            Points out Greene's use of <u>Euphues</u> as a source for <u>Pan-</u>
        <u>dosto</u>.

1933   SMITH, JOHN HAZEL. "Sempronia, John Lyly, and John Foxe's
        Comedy of <u>Titus and Gesippus</u>." <u>PQ</u>, 48 (October 1969),
        554-61.
            Discusses source of Lyly's knowledge of Titus-Gisippus
        story, suggesting his possible familiarity with Foxe's play.

1934   SOELLNER, ROLF. "Shakespeare and the <u>Consolatio</u>." <u>N&Q</u>, NS, 1
        (March 1954), 108-109.
            Argues that <u>Euphues</u> is not Shakespeare's source for <u>Romeo</u>
        <u>and Juliet</u>, 3.3.54-56.

*1935   SPECK, RUDOLF. "Die formale und inhaltliche Verwendung des
        Sprichworkes in Lylys <u>Euphues</u>." Ph.D. dissertation, Uni-
        versity of Kiel, 1955.
            Abstract not available.

1936   SPINGARN, J. E. "<u>Euphues</u>." <u>N&Q</u>, 88 (11 November 1893), 385-
        86.
            Describes Columbia University copy of 1592 edition of
        <u>Euphues and His England</u>, an edition unrecorded by bibliog-
        raphers.

1937   [SQUIRE, JOHN COLLINGS.] SOLOMON EAGLE [pseudonym]. "The
        Worst Style in the World," in <u>Books in General</u>. By Solomon
        Eagle [i.e., John Collings Squire]. New York: Alfred A.
        Knopf, 1919, pp. 214-20.
            Comments on style of <u>Euphues</u>, concluding that "[w]hat a
        really judicious critic would do would be to ridicule the
        style and admire the book."

1937a   STEINBERG, THEODORE L. "The Anatomy of <u>Euphues</u>." <u>SEL</u>, 17
        (Winter 1977), 27-38.
            Examines narrative and structure to argue that <u>Euphues:</u>
        <u>The Anatomy of Wit</u> is "not a straightforward didactic work"
        but a parody of courtesy books--an "'anti-courtesy book.'"
        Concludes that "<u>Euphues</u> is essentially a comic work."

313

Lyly

1938   STENBERG, THEODORE. "Elizabeth as Euphuist before Euphues."
        University of Texas Studies in English, 8 (1928), 65-78.
            Argues that Elizabeth's letters "must have been one of
        the main influences in the development of Euphuism." Sug-
        gests that Lyly was influenced by Elizabeth's style rather
        than vice versa. See 1939.

1939   STENBERG, THEODORE. "More about Queen Elizabeth's Euphuism."
        University of Texas Studies in English, 13 (1933), 64-77.
            Provides further evidence of Elizabeth's euphuistic style
        (see 1938).

1940   STEVENSON, DAVID LLOYD. The Love-Game Comedy. Columbia Uni-
        versity Studies in English and Comparative Literature, 164.
        Morningside Heights, New York: Columbia University Press,
        1946, 271pp.
            In Chapter 9 ("Lyly's Quarreling Lovers," pp. 148-73),
        analyzes conceptions of love embodied in Euphues, Philautus,
        and Fidus to demonstrate how "Lyly suggests some of the dif-
        ficulties which beset young men seeking the ideals of ro-
        mance in the real world." Suggests that "[t]he characters
        in Euphues dramatize the gulf between the effects of an
        actual love affair and the supposed effects prescribed by
        genteel tradition" and "illustrate no dramatic and concerted
        reconciliation."

1941   STŘÍBRNÝ, ZDENĚK. "John Lyly a dvorské drama [John Lyly and
        the Court Drama]." PP, 6 (1963), 100-12.
            Analyzes how Lyly "adapted the main features of euphuism"
        to his dramatic works. (Includes English summary.)

1942   STUEBER, SISTER M. STEPHANIE, C.S.J. "The Balanced Diction of
        Hooker's Polity." PMLA, 71 (September 1956), 808-826.
            Contrasts Hooker's emphasis on "use of words to express
        the natures of things" with the "purely ornamental and ca-
        pricious diction characteristic of...Euphuism," where words
        are used ornamentally for stylistic effect.

1943   SWART, J. "Lyly and Pettie." ES, 23 (1941), 9-18.
            Provides a statistical analysis of sentence structure,
        alliteration, and sound patterns in comparing the styles of
        the two writers. Finds Lyly's style more "systematic."

1944   SYMONDS, JOHN ADDINGTON. Shakspere's Predecessors in the Eng-
        lish Drama. London: Smith, Elder, & Co., 1884, 687pp.
            Includes discussion of popularity of Euphues, its themes,
        and Lyly's purpose in the work. Examines development and
        characteristics of euphuism (passim).

1945   TERRY, F. C. BIRBECK.   "'To Make Love.'"   N&Q, 64 (29 October
       1881), 347.
          Suggests that passage in Euphues and His England illus-
       trates "the origin of the phrase."

1946   TILLEY, MORRIS PALMER.   Elizabethan Proverb Lore in Lyly's
       Euphues and in Pettie's Petite Pallace with Parallels from
       Shakespeare.   University of Michigan Publications, Language
       and Literature, 2.   New York: Macmillan Co., 1926, 471pp.
          Provides list of proverbs in Euphues.   Discusses Lyly's
       borrowings from Pettie's proverbs, the importance of the
       proverb as a component of Lyly's style, and the use of
       Euphues as a source for proverbs.   In Appendix A (pp. 357-
       82) traces passages from Euphues in the Maxwell Younger
       Manuscript (1586); in Appendix B (pp. 383-93) traces pas-
       sages from Euphues in Wit's Commonwealth.   (Proverbs from
       Euphues subsumed in: Morris Palmer Tilley, A Dictionary of
       the Proverbs in England in the Sixteenth and Seventeenth
       Centuries: A Collection of Proverbs Found in English Liter-
       ature and Dictionaries of the Period [Ann Arbor: University
       of Michigan Press, 1950], 866pp.)

1947   TILLEY, M[ORRIS] P[ALMER].   "Euphues and Ovid's Heroical
       Epistles."   MLN, 45 (May 1930), 301-308.
          Shows that the first half of Lucilla's reply to Euphues's
       marriage proposal is a paraphrase of Helen's epistle to
       Paris.

1948   TILLEY, M[ORRIS] T[i.e., P(almer)].   "Much Ado about Nothing
       (V.i.178)."   MLN, 40 (March 1925), 186-88.
          Traces history of proverb "women either love entirely or
       hate deadly" which appears in Euphues, suggesting that Lyly
       might have drawn it from Pettie's Petite Palace.

1949   TILLEY, MORRIS P[ALMER].   "A Parody of Euphues in Romeo and
       Juliet."   MLN, 41 (January 1926), 1-8.
          Argues that 1.2.34-61 is a parody of euphuism: the Ser-
       vant's "It is written...the painter with his nets" is an un-
       mistakable misquotation from the "Epistle Dedicatory" to
       Euphues.

1950   TILLOTSON, GEOFFREY.   "The Prose of Lyly's Comedies," in Essays
       in Criticism and Research.   By Geoffrey Tillotson.   Cam-
       bridge: Cambridge University Press, 1942, pp. 17-30.
          Analyzes differences in the prose style of Euphues and
       that of the comedies.   Discusses changes "in the quality and
       applications of...imagery" and rhythm.

Lyly

1951   TOOR, DAVID SYDNEY. "Euphuism in England before John Lyly."
        Ph.D. dissertation, University of Oregon, 1965, 197pp.
            Traces development of euphuism in English prose from Old
        English to Lyly. Argues "that euphuism was not imported
        into England during the Renaissance from Continental models,
        but that it made its first appearance in the earliest liter-
        ary prose in the language based on classical rhetorical
        models."

1952   TORRETTA, LAURA. "L'Italofobia di John Lyly e i rapporti
        dell'Euphues col rinascimento italiano." Giornale Storico
        della Letteratura Italiana, 103 (June 1934), 205-53.
            Analyzes anti-Italian sentiment in Euphues and the in-
        fluence of Italian literature on the work and on euphuism.

1953   TUCKERMAN, BAYARD. A History of English Prose Fiction from
        Sir Thomas Malory to George Eliot. New York: G. P. Put-
        nam's Sons, 1882, 339pp.
            Includes discussion of Lyly's style and his didacticism
        in Euphues (pp. 74-82).

1954   VANČURA, ZDENĚK. "An American 'Euphuist': Nathaniel Ward
        (1558-1652?)," in Charisteria Guilelmo Mathesio Quinqua-
        genario a Discipulis et Circuli Linguistici Pragensis
        Sodalibus Oblata. Prague: Pražský Linguistický Kroužck,
        1932, pp. 135-38.
            Argues that in style and syntax Ward was influenced more
        by "the unbroken tradition of Latin devotional prose than
        the ephemeral courtly fashion introduced by Lyly's Euphues."

1955   VANČURA, ZDENĚK. "Euphuism and Baroque Prose." ČMF, 18
        (1932), 291-96.
            Argues against contention by Michels (1893) that Lyly's
        style is Baroque.

1956   VANČURA, ZDENĚK. "Teorie o původu eufuismu." ČMF, 17 (1931),
        207-14.
            Provides overview of scholarship on origin and charac-
        teristics of euphuism.

1957   VINCENT, LEON H. "An Elizabethan Novelist." Poet-Lore, 9,
        no. 1 (1897), 47-63. [Reprinted in: Leon H. Vincent.
        The Bibliotaph and Other People. Boston: Houghton Mifflin,
        1899, pp. 137-64.]
            Discusses plot, style, and didacticism in both parts of
        Euphues, and examines the reasons for the popularity of the
        two works.

1958   VOCHT, HENRY DE. *De invloed van Erasmus op de engelsche*
       tooneelliteratuur der XVIe en XVIIe eeuwen, eerste deel:
       Shakespeare Jest-Books, Lyly. Gent: A. Siffer, 1908, 303pp.
          Examines Lyly's use of works of Erasmus as source for
       Euphues (pp. 92-256).

1959   VREELAND, PHILIP THOMAS. "A Quantitative Analysis of the Style
       of John Lyly." Ph.D. dissertation, University of Northern
       Colorado, 1971, 211pp.
          Attempts "to determine the contribution of John Lyly to
       the development of...'Euphuism.'" Examines influence of
       syntax of classical authors, theories of Erasmus, classical
       rhetorical principles, and contemporary "rhetorical textbook
       materials" on Lyly's style. Provides quantitative analysis
       of the components of Lyly's style.

*1960 WAKAMEDA, TAKEJI. "John Lyly." *SELit*, 8 (1928), 567-83.
          Not seen. Cited in 1767.

1961   WARBURG, JEREMY. "Idiosyncratic Style." *Review of English*
       Literature, 6 (April 1965), 56-65.
          Includes discussion of Lyly in overview of idiosyncratic
       styles in literature. Relates Lyly's use of schemata to
       Elizabethans' "desire to hear fine speech" and to an "at-
       tempt to enrich and to display the riches of the language."

1962   WEISE, GEORG. "Manierismo e letteratura, II: Il gusto delle
       antitesi astratte e delle metafore concettose nella lettera-
       tura inglese del Rinascimento." *RLMC*, 19 (December 1966),
       253-78.
          Examines differences in use of antithesis in Elizabethan
       Petrarchan poetry and in Lyly's style; examines the differ-
       ent origins of the two distinct styles.

1963   WENDELSTEIN, LUDWIG. *Beitrag zur Vorgeschichte des Euphuismus.*
       Halle: Hofbuchdruckerei von C. A. Kämmerer, 1902, 89pp.
          Traces influences on development of elements of euphuism,
       particularly those involving sound. Examines influence of
       native writings, study of rhetoric, and reading matter.

1964   WEYMOUTH, RICHARD F. "On Euphuism." *TPS*, 1870-1872, Part 3,
       pp. 1-17.
          Analyzes elements (antithesis, alliteration, consonance,
       and figures of speech) of Lyly's style to arrive at defini-
       tion of euphuism: "a combination of well-balanced antithe-
       sis with...transverse alliteration...; while a euphuistic
       style...[is] one which abounds not only in such euphuisms,
       but also in classical and mythological allusions and multi-
       farious illustrations."

Lyly

1965   WHIPPLE, T. K. "Isocrates and Euphuism." MLR, 11 (January
        1916), 15-27; (April 1916), 129-35.
            Argues against Isocrates as source for Lyly's style,
        noting that the schemes of formal rhetoric were common
        knowledge during sixteenth century.

1966   WHITE, MARGARET IMOGINE ZECHIEL. "The Influence of John Lyly's
        Euphues upon Selected Pieces of Elizabethan Prose Fiction."·
        Ph.D. dissertation, University of Illinois at Urbana-Cham-
        paign, 1971, 332pp.
            Analyzes Lyly's style, themes, didacticism, and narrative
        techniques and devices; traces influences of these traits
        on Munday's Zelauto, Greene's Mamillia, Melbancke's Philoti-
        mus, and Warner's Pan His Syrinx.

1967   WHITEFORD, ROBERT NAYLOR. Motives in English Fiction. New
        York: G. P. Putnam's Sons, 1918, 390pp.
            Discusses Lyly's style and its influence on later writ-
        ers, particularly Greene (pp. 18-23).

1968   WILLIAMSON, GEORGE. The Senecan Amble: A Study in Prose Form
        from Bacon to Collier. Chicago: University of Chicago
        Press, 1951, 377pp.
            Provides analysis of elements of Lyly's euphuistic style
        and examines its relationship to Ciceronian, Isocratean,
        and Senecan styles. Analyzes Lyly's contribution to the
        development of prose style, concluding that he "simplified
        the sentence structure of...[his] time" and "first taught
        English prose to manoeuvre with precision" (passim).

1969   WILSON, JOHN DOVER. "Euphues and the Prodigal Son." Library,
        2d Ser., 10 (October 1909), 337-61.
            Refutes assumption that Euphues is a reordering of Gue-
        vara's Dial of Princes; argues that Lyly's work is "a direct
        adaptation of the Prodigal Son story as developed by the
        Dutch dramatists." Discusses dramatic characteristics of
        Euphues.

1970   WILSON, JOHN DOVER. John Lyly. Cambridge: Macmillan and
        Bowes, 1905, 156pp.
            Examines the characteristics of Lyly's style; examines
        influences on development of euphuism, arguing against
        theory that Guevara was originator; traces influence of
        style on later writers. Traces influences on Euphues: The
        Anatomy of Wit, comments on the moral atmosphere of the
        work, and discusses its place in the development of prose
        fiction. Argues that Euphues and His England is "the first
        English novel" and discusses its structure, subject matter,

and Lyly's characterization. Examines differences between two parts of Euphues.

1971   WOLFF, SAMUEL LEE. The Greek Romances in Elizabethan Prose
        Fiction. Columbia University Studies in Comparative Litera-
        ture. New York: Columbia University Press, 1912, 539pp.
            Examines the influence of Greek romance--as it was fil-
        tered through Boccaccio--on Euphues (pp. 248-61).

1972   WOLFF, SAMUEL LEE. "The Humanist as Man of Letters: John
        Lyly." SR, 31 (January 1923), 8-35.
            Discusses state of research on Lyly and, in particular,
        takes issue with several of Feuillerat's arguments (1838).
        Analyzes influence of Prodigal Son story and Boccaccio's
        tale of Titus and Gisippus on Euphues: The Anatomy of Wit,
        and discusses Lyly's style. Argues for Lyly's importance
        as influence on later writers.

1973   WOLFF, SAMUEL LEE. "A Source of Euphues: The Anatomy of Wyt."
        MP, 7 (April 1910), 577-85.
            Examines Lyly's use of Boccaccio's tale of Titus and
        Gisippus as a source for the plot.

1974   WOODWARD, PARKER. Euphues the Peripatician. London: Gay and
        Bird, 1907, 208pp.
            In Chapter I ("Euphues," pp. 1-24) argues that Bacon was
        author of Euphues.

1975   WURTH, LEOPOLD. Das Wortspiel bei Shakspere. WBEP, 1. Wien
        and Leipzig: W. Braumüller, 1895, 271pp.
            Includes discussion of characteristics of euphuism and
        the influence of the style on Shakespeare (pp. 157-72).

*1976   YACOWAR, M. "John Lyly and the Uses of Irony." Ph.D. disser-
        tation, University of Birmingham, 1968.
            Abstract not available.

*1977   YAMADA, TAIJI. "Euphuism," in Renaissance II: 1501-1625.
        Edited by Rintaro Fukuhara and Masami Nishikawa. Tokyo:
        Kenkyusha, 1961, pp. 209-18.
            Not seen. In Japanese. Listed in Kazuyoshi Enozawa and
        Sister Miyo Takano, "English Renaissance Studies in Japan,
        1961-1963," RenB, 1 (1974), 23.

1978   YATES, FRANCES A. "Italian Teachers in Elizabethan England."
        JWCI, 1 (1937), 103-16.
            Suggests that John Florio's use of Guevara in his First
        Fruits "may have contributed something towards the formation
        of euphuism" in England.

Lyly

1979   ZANDVOORT, R[EINARD] W. "Brutus's Forum Speech in <u>Julius</u>
        <u>Caesar</u>." <u>RES</u>, 16 (January 1940), 62-66. [Reprinted in:
        R(einard) W. Zandvoort. <u>Collected Papers: A Selection of</u>
        <u>Notes and Articles Originally Published in English</u> Studies
        <u>and Other Journals</u>. Groningen Studies in English, 5.
        Groningen: Wolters, 1954, pp. 50-57.]
           Discusses characteristics of euphuism to argue that
        Shakespeare assigned euphuistic prose to Brutus to provide
        dramatic contrast with the "Arcadia" style of Antony's
        speech which follows.

1980   ZANDVOORT, R[EINARD] W. "What Is Euphuism?," in <u>Mélanges de</u>
        <u>linguistique et philologie: Fernand Mossé in memoriam</u>.
        Paris: Didier, 1959, pp. 508-17. [Reprinted in R(einard)
        W. Zandvoort. <u>Collected Papers II: Articles in English</u>
        <u>Published between 1955 and 1970</u>. Groningen Studies in Eng-
        lish, 10. Groningen: Wolters-Noordhoff, 1970, pp. 12-21.]
           Seeks to define euphuism and to differentiate it from
        arcadianism: finds that while Sidney occasionally uses
        euphuistic "patterns" for ornamentation, Lyly uses such as
        the "groundwork" of his style. Provides an overview of
        scholarship on euphuism and discusses treatment of the
        style in "handbooks and works of reference" for the non-
        Renaissance specialist.

<u>A LYTTLE TREATYSE CALLED THE IMAGE OF IDLENESSE: MATTERS MOVED</u>
<u>BETWENE WALTER WEDLOCKE AND BAWDIN BACHELER</u>

    <u>STC</u> 25196-25197.5.

Studies

1981   ROLLINS, HYDER E. "An Elizabethan Ballad of Malmerophus and
        Sillera." <u>MLN</u>, 49 (December 1934), 498-500.
           Suggests that anonymous author of ballad used the <u>Image</u>
        <u>of Idleness</u> as source for story of the two lovers.

<u>MABBE, JAMES</u> (1572-1642?)

Mateo Alemán, <u>The Rogue, or the Life of Guzman de Alfarache</u>. <u>STC</u> 288-
    291. Wing A903-904.

Cervantes Saavedra, Miguel de. <u>Exemplarie Novells</u>. <u>STC</u> 4914. Wing
    C1770.

Editions

1982   CERVANTES SAAVEDRA, MIGUEL DE. Exemplary Novels. Translated
       by James Mabbe. Edited by S. W. Orson. 2 vols. London:
       Gibbings & Co.; Philadelphia: J. B. Lippincott Co., 1900,
       244, 211pp.
           Provides modernized reprint based on 1654 edition(?).
       In "Introduction," I, v-xi, comments briefly on publishing
       history of work.

*1983   CERVANTES SAAVEDRA, MIGUEL DE. The Examplary Novels. Trans-
       lated by James Mabbe. 2 vols. London: Society of English
       Bibliophilists, 1900.
           Not seen. Listed in NUC Pre-1956 Imprints, vol. 101,
       495.

1984   CERVANTES SAAVEDRA, MIGUEL DE. "The Spanish Ladie" and Other
       Stories. Translated by James Mabbe. Edited by Arthur
       Ransome. World's Story Tellers. London and Edinburgh:
       T. C. & E. C. Jack, 1909, 214pp.
           Includes reprints (from 1640 edition) of Mabbe's trans-
       lations of "The Spanish Lady," "The Force of Blood," and
       "The Liberal Lover."

1985   ALEMÁN, MATEO. The Rogue; or, the Life of Guzman de Alfarache.
       Translated by James Mabbe. Introduction by James Fitz-
       maurice-Kelly. 4 vols. Tudor Translations, 2d Ser., 2-5.
       Edited by W. E. Henley. London: Constable and Co., 1924,
       205, 291, 358, 353pp.
           Provides reprint of 1623 edition. In "Introduction,"
       I, ix-xxxvi, praises quality of Mabbe's translation and
       discusses his qualifications as a translator. Examines
       Mabbe's vocabulary and style and discusses his use of
       Spanish, French, and Italian editions.

1986   CERVANTES SAAVEDRA, MIGUEL DE. "The Spanish Ladie" and Two
       Other Stories from Cervantes. Translated by James Mabbe.
       London: Oxford University Press, 1928, 197pp.
           Provides reprints of "The Spanish Lady," "The Jealous
       Husband," and "The Liberal Lover" from 1640 edition.

1987   CERVANTES SAAVEDRA, MIGUEL DE. "The Jealous Husband" from the
       Exemplary Novels of Miguel de Cervantes. Translated by
       James Mabbe. Prologue by Walter Starkie. Valencia del Cid:
       Editorial Castalia, 1945, 123pp.
           Provides modernized text based on 1982. In "Prologue,"
       pp. 11-15, comments briefly on Mabbe's style.

Mabbe

Studies

1988   BROWNE, C. ELLIOT. "Shakspeare Illustrations." N&Q, 53
       (19 February 1876), 143–44.
          Cites parallel from Mabbe's Rogue to Falstaff's comments
       on honor.

1989   CORNEY, BOLTON. "Ben. Jonson and James Mabbe." N&Q, 33
       (21 April 1866), 315.
          Calls attention to Jonson's prefatory poem to the Rogue
       and observes that Mabbe's translation provides "illustra-
       tions of the assumed peculiarities in the diction of"
       Shakespeare.

*1990 GUARDIA MASSO, P. "James Mabbe, eminente hispanista oxoniense
       del siglo XVII: Su personalidad literaria. Estudio de
       varios MSS inéditos y del The Spanish Bawd, London, 1631."
       Ph.D. dissertation, University of Barcelona, 1971.
          Abstract not available. Cited in 1992.

1991   KNOWLES, EDWIN B. "Cervantes y la literatura inglesa."
       Realidad, 2 (1947), 268–97.
          Includes discussion of Mabbe's Exemplary Novels; charac-
       terizes his translation as excellent.

1992   MARTINEZ LACALLE, GUADALUPE. "Introduction," in Celestine or
       the Tragick-Comedie of Calisto and Melibea. By Fernando de
       Rojas. Translated by James Mabbe. Edited by Guadalupe
       Martinez Lacalle. Collećión Támesis, Serie B, 14. London:
       Tamesis Books, 1972, pp. 1–92.
          Includes overview of Mabbe's translation of Spanish prose
       fiction; discusses style and techniques of translation.

1993   MONCADA, ERNEST JOSEPH. "An Analysis of James Mabbe's Trans-
       lation of Mateo Alemán's Guzmán de Alfarache." Ph.D. dis-
       sertation, University of Maryland, 1966, 217pp.
          Examines Mabbe's handling of text and analyzes his "use
       of figurative language,...his penchant for amplification,...
       his inclusion of Spanish and Latin words..., his handling
       of Spanish proverbs and...his own copious use of English
       proverb lore and his mistranslations, changes and indebted-
       ness to others."

1994   PIE[R]CE, FRANK. "James Mabbe and La Española Inglesa." RLC,
       23 (1949), 80–85.
          Examines Mabbe's omission in his translation of all ref-
       ences to England, to Elizabeth I and her court, and to
       Catholics and Catholicism. Attributes Mabbe's bowdlerizing

of the text in his Exemplary Novels to the "explosive atmosphere of the England of Charles I."

1995 RANDALL, DALE B. J. The Golden Tapestry: A Critical Survey
of Non-Chivalric Spanish Fiction in English Translation
(1543–1657). Durham: Duke University Press, 1963, 272pp.
Includes examination of Mabbe's style and alterations in
the original texts in his translations (passim).

1996 RUSSELL, P. E. "A Stuart Hispanist: James Mabbe." BHS, 30,
no. 118 (1953), 75–84.
Discusses Mabbe's translations in context of his life
and work. Comments on Mabbe's criticism of works he translated and suggests that this criticism, along with "his
scholarly approach to the authors with whom he concerned
himself," sets him apart from other translators.

1997 SALAZAR CHAPELA, ESTEBAN. "Clasicos espanoles en Inglaterra."
CA, 11, no. 1 (1952), 256–61.
Includes discussion of influence of Mabbe's translations
on English literature.

1998 SECORD, ARTHUR W. "I. M. of the First Folio Shakespeare and
Other Mabbe Problems." JEGP, 47, no. 4 (1948), 374–81.
Discusses Mabbe as translator and traces some common
phrasing between the Rogue and the commendatory poem as internal evidence that Mabbe is I. M.

1999 STEPHENSON, PETER S. "Congreve's Incognita: The Popular
Spanish Novela Form Burlesqued." SSF, 9 (Fall 1972), 333–
42.
Uses Mabbe's Exemplary Novels to illustrate the characteristics of the Spanish novella, a form which was popular
in English translation during the latter part of the seventeenth century and which Congreve satirized in Incognita.

2000 THOMAS, HENRY. "A Forgotten Translation of Cervantes." Revue
Hispanique, 45 (1919), 1–11.
Points out that for five of the novels in his The Spanish
Decameron (1687) L'Estrange merely paraphrased Mabbe's
Exemplary Novels.

MARKHAM, GERVASE (1568?–1637)

The English Arcadia, Alluding His Beginning from Sir Philip Sydneys
Ending. STC 17350.5–17351.

Markham

The Second and Last Part of the First Booke of the English Arcadia.
STC 17352.

The Most Famous and Renowned Historie of that Woorthie Knight Mervine
(translation ascribed to Markham). STC 17844.

Bibliographies

2001   POYNTER, F[REDERICH] N[OEL] L[AWRENCE]. A Bibliography of
       Gervase Markham, 1568?-1637. Oxford Bibliographical Society
       Publications, NS, 11. Oxford: Oxford Bibliographical So-
       ciety, 1962, 226pp.
           Provides bibliographical descriptions of Markham's works
       of prose fiction. Discusses briefly the relationship of
       English Arcadia to Sidney's Arcadia and comments on the
       "literary quality" of Mervine (pp. 69-74).

Studies

2002   POYNTER, F[REDERICH] N[OEL] L[AWRENCE]. "Gervase Markham."
       E&S, NS, 15 (1962), 27-39.
           Discusses briefly Markham's prose fiction in general
       overview of life and works.

*2003 POYNTER, F[REDERICH] N[OEL] L[AWRENCE]. "The Life and Work of
       Gervase Markham (1568-1637)." Ph.D. dissertation, Univer-
       sity of London-Westfield College, 1956.
           Abstract not available.

*2004 WALSHE, ELYN. "Gervase Markham: The First English Hack
       Writer." Bookman, 81 (October 1931), 52-53.
           Not located. Listed in MHRA Annual Bibliography, 12
       (1931), #1630.

2005   WILES, AMERICUS G[EORGE] D[AVID]. "The Continuations of Sir
       Philip Sidney's Arcadia." Ph.D. dissertation, Princeton
       University, 1934.
           Includes examination of Markham's continuation; finds
       that it is inferior to Beling's continuation and that it
       has little literary merit.

MELBANCKE, BRIAN (fl. 1583)

Philotimus: The Warre betwixt Nature and Fortune. STC 17800.5-17801.

Editions

2006 MELBANCKE, BRIAN. "Brian Melbancke's Philotimus (1583): A
Critical Edition." Edited by Arthur Leroy Colby. Ph.D.
dissertation, University of North Carolina, Chapel Hill,
1969, 477pp.
Provides a largely diplomatic text based on Huntington
copy of 1583 edition. Examines date, sources, style, and
content.

Studies

2007 ALLEN, DON CAMERON. "Melbancke and Gosson." MLN, 54 (February
1939), 111-14.
Provides evidence of borrowings in Philotimus from Gosson's The Ephemerides of Phialo. (See also Allen's letter,
MLN, 54 [May 1939], 398.)

2008 BROWN, ELAINE V. BEILIN. "The Uses of Mythology in Elizabethan
Romance." Ph.D. dissertation, Princeton University, 1973,
336pp.
Analyzes Melbancke's use of Judgment of Paris myth in
Philotimus.

2009 MAUD, RALPH. "The Date of Brian Melbancke's Philotimus."
Library, 5th Ser., 11 (June 1956), 118-20.
Argues that, based on biographical evidence, the preface
was written November, 1582, and that, based on Melbancke's
borrowings from Stephen Batman's Batman upon Bartholome,
"most of the novel must have been written after the middle
of March 1581/82." Establishes December 1582 as date of
printing.

2010 PARR, JOHNSTONE. "Robert Greene and His Classmates at Cambridge." PMLA, 77 (December 1962), 536-43.
Suggests that the "few verbal similarities" between
Philotimus and Greene's Mamillia might be due to the fact
that the two were classmates at St. John's.

2011 ROLLINS, HYDER E. "Notes on Brian Melbancke's Philotimus."
SP, Extra Ser., 1 (May 1929), 40-57.
Describes contents, notes examples of proverbs and
"curious" diction, lists literary allusions, and identifies
several of Melbancke's borrowings from Elizabethan poetry.
See 2012 and 2013.

2012 ROLLINS, HYDER E. "Notes on the Sources of Melbancke's
Philotimus." Harvard Studies and Notes in Philology and
Literature, 18 (1936), 177-98.

325

Melbancke

> Adds to his previous note on Melbancke's borrowings from poets and authors of prose fiction (Lyly, Pettie, Underdowne, Fortescue, and Gosson). See 2011 and 2013.

2013 ROLLINS, HYDER E. "Thomas Deloney and Brian Melbancke: Notes on Sources." Harvard Studies and Notes in Philology and Literature, 19 (1937), 219-29.
> Adds to his earlier lists of borrowings in Philotimus (2011-12).

2014 TILLEY, M[ORRIS] P[ALMER]. "Further Borrowings from Poems in Philotimus." SP, 27 (April 1930), 186-214.
> Adds to Rollins's list of sources (2011). Observes that "Melbancke...illustrates the inherent weakness of the euphuistic writers who viewed the ornamentation of a sentence, or of an argument, as of greater importance than the thought it expressed."

2015 WHITE, MARGARET IMOGINE ZECHIEL. "The Influence of John Lyly's Euphues upon Selected Pieces of Elizabethan Prose Fiction." Ph.D. dissertation, University of Illinois at Urbana-Champaign, 1971, 332pp.
> Examines influence of Lyly's style, themes, didacticism, and narrative techniques and devices on Philotimus.

MERIE TALES NEWLY IMPRINTED AND MADE BY MASTER SKELTON

STC 22618.

Editions

2016 Merie Tales of Skelton, in The Poetical Works of John Skelton, Vol. I. By John Skelton. Edited by Alexander Dyce. London: Thomas Rodd, 1843, liii-lxxiii.
> Reprints text of 1567 edition.

2017 Merie Tales of Skelton, in Shakespeare Jest-Books, Vol. II. Edited by W[illiam] Carew Hazlitt. London: Willis & Sotheran, 1864, 1-36.
> Provides annotated reprint of 1567 edition. In brief introductory note, discusses bibliographical history of the work.

2018 Merry Tales Made by Master Skelton, in A Hundred Merry Tales and Other English Jestbooks of the Fifteenth and Sixteenth Centuries. Edited by P. M. Zall. Lincoln: University of Nebraska Press, 1963, pp. 323-48.
> Provides modernized reprint of 1567 edition.

Middleton, Christopher

Studies

2019 NELSON, WILLIAM. <u>John Skelton, Laureate</u>. Columbia University
Studies in English and Comparative Literature, 139. New
York: Columbia University Press, 1939, 276pp.
Argues that the <u>Merry Tales</u> "is not altogether worthless
as a source of biographical information" about Skelton
(pp. 108-13, passim).

<u>MIDDLETON, CHRISTOPHER</u> (1560?-1628)

<u>The Famous Historie of Chinon of England</u>. STC 17866.

Editions

2020 MIDDLETON, CHRISTOPHER. <u>The Famous Historie of Chinon of Eng-
land</u>, in The Famous Historie of Chinon of England<u>, by Christopher Middleton; to Which Is Added</u> The Assertion of King
Arthur<u>, Translated by Richard Robinson from Leland's Asser-
tio Inclytissimi Arturii</u>. Edited by William Edward Mead.
EETS, Original Ser., 165. London: Oxford University Press
for the Early English Text Society, 1925, pp. 1-85 (separately paginated).
Provides annotated reprint based on 1597 edition. In
"Introduction," pp. i-lxviii, discusses work in context of
Arthurian literature and examines sources, structure, style,
and use of supernatural.

Studies

2021 APP, AUGUST, J[OSEPH]. <u>Lancelot in English Literature: His
Rôle and Character</u>. Washington: Catholic University of
America, 1929, 268pp.
Discusses treatment of Lancelot in <u>Chinon of England</u>,
particularly how his love of Laura rather than Guinevere
"differs essentially from his traditional rôle" (pp. 106-
112).

2022 BRIE, FRIEDRICH. "Das Märchen von Childe Rowland und sein
Nachleben (Christopher Middleton's <u>Chinon of England</u>,
Peele's <u>Old Wife's Tale</u> und Milton's <u>Comus</u>)," in <u>Anglica:
Untersuchungen zur englischen Philologie: Alois Brandl zum
siebzigsten Geburtstage überreicht</u>, II. Palaestra, 148.
Leipzig: Mayer & Müller, 1925, pp. 118-43.
Examines Middleton's handling of the Childe Roland tale
and compares his treatment with that by Peele.

Middleton, Thomas

MIDDLETON, THOMAS (1580-1627)

The Ant and the Nightingale: Or Father Hubburds Tales. STC 17874.3-
17874.7.

Bibliographies

2023   DONOVAN, DENNIS G. "Thomas Middleton, 1939-1965," in Elizabe-
       than Bibliographies Supplements, I: Thomas Middleton,
       1939-1965; John Webster, 1940-1965. Compiled by Dennis G.
       Donovan. London: Nether Press, 1967, 15-36.
          Provides chronological list of editions and criticism,
       1939-1965; supplements 2024.

2024   TANNENBAUM, SAMUEL A. Thomas Middleton (A Concise Bibliog-
       raphy). Elizabethan Bibliographies, 13. New York: Samuel
       A. Tannenbaum, 1940, 45pp.
          Provides classified list of editions and criticism.
       Continued by 2023.

Editions

2025   MIDDLETON, THOMAS. Father Hubburd's Tales; or, the Ant and
       the Nightingale, in The Works of Thomas Middleton, Vol. V.
       By Thomas Middleton. Edited by Alexander Dyce. London:
       E. Lumley, 1840, 547-603.
          Provides partly modernized, annotated reprint of 1604
       edition.

2026   MIDDLETON, THOMAS. Father Hubburd's Tales; or, The Ant and
       the Nightingale, in The Works of Thomas Middleton, Vol.
       VIII. By Thomas Middleton. Edited by A[rthur] H[enry]
       Bullen. Boston: Houghton Mifflin, 1886, 47-109.
          Provides modernized reprint of 1604 edition with notes
       on readings from earlier edition.

2027   MIDDLETON, THOMAS. "A Critical Edition of Thomas Middleton's
       Micro-Cynicon, Father Hubburds Tales, and The Blacke Booke."
       Edited by Larry Wayne Irwin. Ph.D. dissertation, University
       of Wisconsin, 1969, 243pp.
          Provides a critical old-spelling edition of Father Hub-
       burd's Tales based on 1604 edition. Discusses evidence for
       Middleton's authorship, the work as a Menippean satire, and
       parallels between the work and his plays.

Studies

2028   ADAMS, JOSEPH QUINCY. "Introduction," in The Ghost of Lucrece.
       By Thomas Middleton. Edited by Joseph Quincy Adams. New

328

York: Scribner's for Trustees of Amherst College, 1937,
pp. xi-xxxiii.
Discusses publishing history of The Ant and the Nightingale and its autobiographical basis.

2029   BARKER, RICHARD HINDRY. Thomas Middleton. New York: Columbia
University Press, 1958, 228pp.
Includes discussion of Middleton's treatment of the
"foibles of contemporary society" in The Ant and the Nightingale (pp. 36-40, passim).

2030   FERRARA, FERNANDO. Jests e Merry Tales: Aspetti della narrativa popolaresca inglese del sedicesimo secolo. Nuovi
Saggi, 27. Rome: Editrice dell'Ateneo, 1960, 257pp.
Examines place of Father Hubburd's Tales in development
of jest book: discusses satire, style, and characterization
(pp. 229-34).

*2031   GEORGE, D. F. "A Critical Study of Thomas Middleton's Borrow-
ings and of His Imitations of Other Authors in His Prose,
Poetry, and Dramatic Works." Ph.D. dissertation, University
of London-King's College, 1966.
Abstract not available.

2032   PRICE, GEORGE R. "The Early Editions of The Ant and the Nightingale." PBSA, 43, no. 2 (1949), 179-90.
Examines printing and publication of Middleton's pamphlet
to show that edition with title The Ant and the Nightingale
preceded that with title Father Hubburd's Tales. Examines
relationship of two editions and suggests that second edition was printed because of Middleton's demand for a corrected edition.

2033   SHAABER, M[ATTHIAS] A. "The Ant and the Nightingale and
Father Hubburds Tales." LC, 14, no. 2 (April 1947), 13-16.
Corrects listings in STC, provides full bibliographical
descriptions of both editions, and discusses the printing
and publication of the work.

2034   SYKES, H. DUGDALE. "Thomas Middleton's Early Non-Dramatic
Work." N&Q, 148 (20 June 1925), 435-38.
Argues on basis of internal evidence that Father Hub-
burd's Tales is by Middleton.

MUNDAY, ANTHONY (1560-1633)

Zelauto: The Fountaine of Fame. STC 18283.

Munday

Amadis of Gaule. STC 541-544.

Claude Colet, The Famous Historie of Palladine of England. STC 5541.
Wing C5090-5090A.

Étienne de Maisonneuve, Gerileon of England: The Second Part. STC
17206.

Francisco de Moraes, The Honorable, Pleasant, and Rare Conceited Historie of Palmendos. STC 18064. Wing F377-378.

Francisco de Moraes, Palmerin of England. STC 19161-19165. Wing
F979.

Palmerin d'Oliva. STC 19157-19160.

Primaleon of Greece. STC 20366-20367.

Bibliographies

2035   JOHNSON, ROBERT C. "Anthony Munday, 1941-1966," in Elizabethan
        Bibliographies Supplements, IX: Minor Elizabethans: Roger
        Ascham, 1946-1966; George Gascoigne, 1941-1966; John Hey-
        wood, 1944-1966; Thomas Kyd, 1940-1966; Anthony Munday,
        1941-1966. Compiled by Robert C. Johnson. London: Nether
        Press, 1968, 43-48.
            Provides chronological list of editions and criticism,
        1941-1966; supplements 2036.

2036   TANNENBAUM, SAMUEL A. Anthony Mundy, Including the Play of
        "Sir Thomas Moore" (A Concise Bibliography). Elizabethan
        Bibliographies, 27. New York: Samuel A. Tannenbaum, 1942,
        46pp.
            Provides classified list of editions and criticism.
        Continued by 2035.

Editions

2037   MUNDAY, ANTHONY. Anthony Munday's Zelauto: The Fountaine of
        Fame, 1580. Edited by Jack Stillinger. Carbondale:
        Southern Illinois University Press, 1963, 234pp.
            Provides critical edition of the 1580 edition. In "In-
        troduction," pp. vii-xxix, discusses structure, narrative
        technique, style, and characterization. Analyzes literary
        and cultural influences on content.

*2038   MUNDAY, ANTHONY. "A Critical Edition of Anthony Munday's
        Zelavto." Edited by G[eoffrey] Creigh. Ph.D. dissertation,
        University of Birmingham, 1963.
           Abstract not available.

Studies

2039   BRIE, FRIEDRICH. "Zur Entstehung des Kaufmann von Venedig."
       Shakespeare-Jahrbuch, 49 (1913), 97–121.
          Identifies Zelauto as a source of Merchant of Venice;
       traces Munday's source.

2040   BULLOUGH, GEOFFREY. "Introduction [to Merchant of Venice],"
       in Narrative and Dramatic Sources of Shakespeare, Vol. I.
       Edited by Geoffrey Bullough. London: Routledge and Kegan
       Paul; New York: Columbia University Press, 1957, 445–62.
          Compares treatment of flesh-bond story in Book III of
       Zelauto with that in Merchant of Venice, suggesting possi-
       bility that "Shakespeare remembered Zelauto in drafting his
       Court Scene."

2041   BYRNE, M. ST. CLARE. "Anthony Munday and His Books." Library,
       4th Ser., 1 (March 1921), 225–56.
          Considers question of Munday's authorship of Amadis de
       Gaule, Book II, and discusses his place in the development
       of Elizabethan prose fiction.

2042   BYRNE, M. ST. CLARE. "Anthony Munday's Spelling as a Literary
       Clue." Library, 4th Ser., 4 (June 1923), 9–23.
          Identifies characteristics of Munday's spelling and ex-
       amines printed texts to ascertain how consistently composi-
       tor followed his idiosyncrasies.

2043   CORNEY, BOLTON. "Munday, Drayton, and Chettle." N&Q, 15
       (4 April 1857), 261.
          Identifies Michael Drayton as author of commendatory
       verse to second part of Primaleon and Henry Chettle as au-
       thor of commendatory verse to third part.

2044   CREIGH, GEOFFREY. "Zelauto and Italian Comedy: A Study in
       Sources." MLQ, 29 (March 1968), 161–67.
          Argues that "the structure and tone of [the third part
       of Zelauto]...clearly suggest a general indebtedness to six-
       teenth-century Italian comedy" and that Shakespeare used
       Zelauto as source in Merchant of Venice.

2045   GALIGANI, GIUSEPPE. "La versione inglese del Palmerín de
       Olivia," in Studi sul Palmerín de Olivia, III: Saggi e

331

Munday

ricerche. Istituto di Letteratura Spagnola e Ispano-Americana, 13. Pisa: Università di Pisa, 1966, pp. 239-88.
Argues that Munday used an Italian as well as a French version as source for his translation of Palmerin. Provides detailed examination of Munday's handling of the text (especially his amplifications and his expurgations of erotic or religious passages) and of his competence as a translator.

2046   GOLDER, HAROLD. "Bunyan's Valley of the Shadow." MP, 27 (August 1929), 55-72.
Uses examples from Palmerin romances to illustrate influence of earlier romances on narrative framework of Pilgrim's Progress. Discusses, in particular, the conventional elements of the descent into a cave or dark valley.

2047   GREBANIER, BERNARD. The Truth about Shylock. New York: Random House, 1962, 381pp.
Discusses Munday's use of the pound of flesh story in Zelauto as an interesting variant of the motif. Doubts that Shakespeare used Zelauto as a source for The Merchant of Venice (pp. 108-13).

2048   HAYES, GERALD R. "Anthony Munday's Romances: A Postscript." Library, 4th Ser., 7 (June 1926), 31-38.
Notes that prefatory matter in recently recovered copy of 1596 edition of The Second Book of Primaleon of Greece supports Southey's suggestion that Munday employed other translators (see 2059). Offers some corrections to 2049.

2049   HAYES, GERALD R. "Anthony Munday's Romances of Chivalry." Library, 4th Ser., 6 (June 1925), 57-81.
Discusses the sequence of the works and provides a publication history from 1580 to 1664. Argues that it is practically possible that Munday is the translator of all the works. See 2048.

2050   HAYES, GERALD R. "Melzi's Dating of Palmerino di Inghilterra, Part III." Library, 4th Ser., 7 (March 1927), 409-13.
Notes that if Palmerino di Inghilterra, Part III, was published in 1584, then first edition of Munday's Palmerin of England, Parts I and II, can be dated between 1584 and 1587.

2051   IOTA RHO. "Palmerin of England." N&Q, 27 (14 February 1863), 136.
Gives contents of 1616 edition of first part of Palmerin of England. See also: J[ohn] Payne Collier, "Palmerin of England," N&Q, 27 ·(28 February 1863), 178.

2052   KITTLE, WILLIAM. Edward de Vere, Seventeenth Earl of Oxford,
        1550-1604. Washington, D. C.: Buchanan Co., 1935, 252pp.
           Argues for possibility that Gascoigne (i.e., Oxford)
        wrote "some part of Zelauto [sic] three years prior to its
        publication in 1581" (pp. 104-109).

2053   KITTLE, WILLIAM. Edward de Vere, 17th Earl of Oxford, and
        Shakespeare. Baltimore: Monumental Printing Co., 1942,
        223pp.
           In Chapter VII ("Zelauto the Fountaine of Fame," pp. 47-
        49), identifies Zelauto as Oxford, the Soldane as Elizabeth
        I, and the episode describing Zelauto's escape from the
        Soldane as a "realistic description of London, its Garden
        and the escape through the Traitor's Gate."

2054   O'CONNOR, JOHN J. Amadis de Gaule and Its Influence on Eliza-
        bethan Literature. New Brunswick: Rutgers University
        Press, 1970, 318pp.
           In Chapter VII ("The Translations of Herberay and Mun-
        day," pp. 131-47) examines the closeness with which Munday
        follows Nicholas de Herberay's French version and compares
        Munday's translation with the French and Spanish versions.

2055   O'CONNOR, JOHN J. "Another Human Footstool." N&Q, NS, 2
        (August 1955), 332.
           Notes parallel to "Tamburlaine's use of Bajazet as a
        footstool" in Munday's Gerileon.

2056   PATCHELL, MARY [F.]. The Palmerin Romances in Elizabethan
        Prose Fiction. Columbia University Studies in English and
        Comparative Literature, 166. New York: Columbia University
        Press, 1947, 171pp.
           Discusses Munday's style and treatment of text; analyzes
        themes and motifs, the treatment of love and marriage,
        structure, characterization, popularity, and influence on
        Elizabethan prose fiction. Includes summaries of Munday's
        Palmerin translations.

2057   PRUVOST, RENÉ. "La Trame romanesque du Marchand de Venise."
        LanM, 45 (March-April 1951), 99-109.
           Examines Munday's third part of Zelauto as part of a
        tradition in which the suspicious, avaricious father is
        cast as a villain.

2058   SCANLON, PAUL A. "Munday's Zelauto: Form and Function." WP,
        2 (1973), 184-94.
           Finds that the four episodes take "the form of, respec-
        tively, a biblical parable, a court panegyric, a medieval

      sermon, and a romantic-comic <u>novella</u>"; examines how "each episode centres on a particular kind of writing and is directed toward a specific end." Discusses problems that arise from Munday's structure.

2059   [SOUTHEY, ROBERT.] "Preface," in <u>Palmerin of England</u>, Vol. I. By Francisco de Moraes. Translated by Anthony Munday and Robert Southey. Edited by Robert Southey. London: Longman, Hurst, Rees, and Orme, 1807, vii-xlv.
        Includes discussion of Munday's carelessness as a translator.

2060   SPENS, JANET. <u>An Essay on Shakespeare's Relation to Tradition</u>. Oxford: B. H. Blackwell, 1916, 112pp.
        Includes discussion of relationship of <u>Merchant of Venice</u> to <u>Zelauto</u>; comments on Munday's style and dialogue, and suggests allusion to <u>Zelauto</u> in <u>Much Ado about Nothing</u> (pp. 16-29).

2061   THOMAS, HENRY. "English Translations of Portuguese Books before 1640." <u>Library</u>, 4th Ser., 7 (June 1926), 1-30.
        Notes that <u>Palmerin of England</u> is translated from Jacque Vincent's French version and that <u>Palladine of England</u> is an abridged version of Claude Colet's <u>L'Histoire Palladienne</u>. Also discusses Munday's translations of <u>Amadis of Gaul</u>.

2062   THOMAS, HENRY. "English Translations of Portuguese Books before 1640," in <u>Miscelânea de estudos em honra de D. Carolina Michaëlis de Vasconcellos</u>. Revista da Universidade de Coimbra, 1. Coimbra, Portugal: Universidad de Coimbra, 1933, pp. 690-711.
        Discusses dating and sources of Munday's translations of <u>Palmerin of England</u> and <u>Palladine of England</u>. Argues that Pyott and Munday are not the same.

2063   THOMAS, HENRY. <u>Spanish and Portuguese Romances of Chivalry: The Revival of the Romance of Chivalry in the Spanish Peninsula, and Its Extension and Influence Abroad</u>. Cambridge: Cambridge University Press, 1920, 343pp.
        Provides overview of Munday's translations of Spanish romances and the commercial impetus behind his work. Notes allusions to his translations in plays (passim). In Appendix II ("Anthony Munday and Lazarus Pyott," pp. 310-15) argues that Pyott was not Munday's pseudonym.

*2064   TURNER, JULIA CELESTE. "Anthony Mundy: A Study in the Elizabethan Profession of Letters." Ph.D. dissertation, University of California, Berkeley, 1928.
        <u>See</u> 2065.

2065   TURNER, [JULIA] CELESTE. <u>Anthony Mundy, an Elizabethan Man of</u>
        <u>Letters</u>. University of California Publications in English,
        2, no. 1. Berkeley: University of California Press, 1928,
        234pp.
            Examines Munday's prose fiction in context of his life
        and works: discusses his style, his sources, and his
        handling of the original text in his translations. In-
        cludes Appendix II, "The Chronology of Mundy's Romances"
        (pp. 180 83) and "A List of the Works of Anthony Mundy,"
        pp. 201-15 (with title page transcriptions and locations of
        copies). <u>See</u> 2070.

2066   UNDERHILL, JOHN GARRETT. <u>Spanish Literature in the England of</u>
        <u>the Tudors</u>. Columbia University Studies in Literature.
        New York: Macmillan Co. for Columbia University Press,
        1899, 448pp.
            Includes general overview of Munday's translations of
        Spanish prose fiction works (passim).

2067   WHITE, MARGARET IMOGINE ZECHIEL. "The Influence of John Lyly's
        <u>Euphues</u> upon Selected Pieces of Elizabethan Prose Fiction."
        Ph.D. dissertation, University of Illinois at Urbana-Cham-
        paign, 1971, 332pp.
            Examines influence of Lyly's style, themes, didacticism,
        and narrative techniques and devices on <u>Zelauto</u>.

2068   WRIGHT, [JULIA] CELESTE TURNER. "'Lazarus Pyott' and Other
        Inventions of Anthony Munday." <u>PQ</u>, 42 (October 1963),
        532-41.
            Discusses reasons for Munday's use of Lazarus Pyott as
        pseudonym, especially in his translation of <u>Amadis of Gaul</u>.

2069   WRIGHT, [JULIA] CELESTE TURNER. "Mundy and Chettle in Grub
        Street." <u>Boston University Studies in English</u>, 5 (Autumn
        1961), 129-38.
            Discusses circumstances surrounding publication of
        <u>Gerileon</u> and <u>Primaleon</u>, Part II.

2070   WRIGHT, [JULIA] CELESTE TURNER. "Young Anthony Mundy Again."
        <u>SP</u>, 56 (April 1959), 150-68.
            Includes discussion of publication of Munday's works in
        the context of his life. Supplements 2065.

<u>NASHE, THOMAS</u> (1567-1601?)

<u>The Unfortunate Traveller: Or, the Life of Jacke Wilton</u>. <u>STC</u> 18380-
    18381.

Nashe

Bibliographies

2071   FEHRENBACH, ROBERT J.   "Thomas Nashe," in The Predecessors of
        Shakespeare: A Survey and Bibliography of Recent Studies
        in English Renaissance Drama.   Edited by Terence P. Logan
        and Denzell S. Smith.   Lincoln: University of Nebraska
        Press, 1973, pp. 107-24.
            Includes overview of recent scholarship on Unfortunate
        Traveller and a selective bibliography.

2072   JOHNSON, ROBERT C.   "Thomas Nashe, 1941-1965," in Elizabethan
        Bibliographies Supplements, V: Robert Greene, 1945-1965;
        Thomas Lodge, 1939-1965; John Lyly, 1939-1965; Thomas Nashe,
        1941-1965; George Peele, 1939-1965.   Compiled by Robert C.
        Johnson.   London: Nether Press, 1968, 45-55.
            Provides chronological list of editions and criticism,
        1941-1965; supplements 2073.

2073   TANNENBAUM, SAMUEL A.   Thomas Nashe (A Concise Bibliography).
        Elizabethan Bibliographies, 21.   New York: Samuel A. Tan-
        nenbaum, 1941, 39pp.
            Provides classified list of editions and criticism.   Con-
        tinued by 2072.

Editions

2074   NASHE, THOMAS.   The Complete Works of Thomas Nashe.   Edited by
        Alexander B. Grosart.   Huth Library.   6 vols.   London:
        Privately Printed, 1883-1885, 335, 290, 282, 264, 308,
        304pp.
            Provides reprint of 1594 edition of Unfortunate Traveller
        (V, 1-186).   In "Memorial-Introduction--Critical," VI,
        vii-xxxix, discusses Nashe's style.

2075   NASHE, THOMAS.   The Unfortunate Traveller; or, The Life of
        Jack Wilton.   Edited by Edmund [W.] Gosse.   London: C.
        Whittingham & Co., 1892, 259pp.
            Provides reprint of unidentified edition.   In "An Essay
        on the Life and Writings of Thomas Nash," pp. vii-xlii,
        discusses work in context of Nashe's life and writings.

2076   NASHE, THOMAS.   The Works of Thomas Nashe.   Edited by Ronald
        B[runlees] McKerrow.   5 vols.   London: A. H. Bullen, 1904-
        1910 [Vol. V published by Sidgwick & Jackson], 402, 397,
        416, 484, 394pp.
            Provides critical edition based on second edition (1594)
        of Unfortunate Traveller (II, 187-328; notes, IV, 252-94).
        Provides analytical descriptions of early editions and

analysis of printing of second edition. In "Introduction,"
V, 1-159, argues that Unfortunate Traveller is not a picaresque novel influenced by Lazarillo de Tormes and doubts
that Nashe was influenced by Rabelais. Discusses Unfortunate Traveller in context of Nashe's life and works. Provides "Notes on Some Peculiarities of Nashe's Grammar,
Spelling, Style, etc." (Appendix F, V, 199-203) and "Notes
on Copies of the Early Editions of Nashe's Works" (Appendix
G, V, 204-208). See revised edition 2084.

2077   NASHE, THOMAS. The Vnfortvnate Traveller; Or, The Life of
        Jacke Wilton. Edited by H[erbert] F[rancis] B[rett] Brett-
        Smith. Percy Reprints, 1. Boston: Houghton Mifflin Co.,
        1920, 152pp.
            Provides annotated reprint of second 1594 edition with
        emendations from first 1594 edition. In "Introduction,"
        pp. v-xx, discusses Nashe's realism, his style, the influ-
        ence of the Italian novella and Lazarillo de Tormes on the
        work, and the variety of forms and subject matter which
        make up the work. Calls it the first English historical
        novel. Discusses printing and publication of 1594 editions.

2078   NASHE, THOMAS. The Unfortunate Traveler, or the Life of Jack
        Wilton. Introduction by Samuel C. Chew. Rogues' Bookshelf.
        New York: Greenberg, 1926, 222pp.
            Provides modernized text based on 1594 editions. In
        "Introduction," pp. vii-xxiii, discusses influence of pi-
        caresque and other earlier kinds of popular literature; ex-
        amines how Nashe's use of historical background and "local
        color" foreshadow later developments in prose fiction;
        comments on realism, satire, and style.

2079   NASHE, THOMAS. The Unfortunate Traveller, in Shorter Novels:
        Elizabethan and Jacobean. Introduction by George Saints-
        bury. Notes by Philip Henderson. Everyman's Library, 824.
        London: J. M. Dent & Sons; New York: E. P. Dutton & Co.,
        1929, pp. 261-356.
            Provides partly modernized reprint of 1594 edition. In
        "Notes," pp. xx-xxii, comments on Nashe's style and dis-
        cusses work as a picaresque novel. Reprinted in 65.

2080   NASHE, THOMAS. The Unfortunate Traveller. Edited by Philip
        Henderson. London: Verona Society, 1930, 193pp.
            Provides reprint of 1594 edition. In "An Account of the
        Life and Writings of Thomas Nashe," pp. ix-xxvi, discusses
        influence of picaresque romance on work and discusses it in
        context of Nashe's life and other writings.

337

Nashe

2081 NASHE, THOMAS. The Unfortunate Traveller or the Life of Jacke
Wilton. Introduced by Michael Ayrton. London: John
Lehmann, 1948, 121pp.
Reprints text from 2077. In "Introduction," pp. 5-10,
comments on work as "social journalism" and on Nashe's
originality. See 2182.

2082 NASHE, THOMAS. The Unfortunate Traveller, in Elizabethan Fiction. Edited by Robert Ashley and Edwin M. Moseley. San
Francisco: Rinehart Press, 1953, pp. 197-308.
Provide a partly modernized text based on 2076. In "Introduction" (pp. xiv-xvii) assert that Nashe's importance
to the development of prose fiction lies in his consistency
of tone and points of view and in his use of "realistic
diction."

*2083 NASHE, THOMAS. Le Voyageur malchanceux; ou, la vie de Jack
Wilton. Translated by Charles Chassé. Collection Bilingue
des Classiques Etrangers. Paris: Aubier, 1954, 315pp.
Not seen. Provides facing page translation with introduction and notes. Listed in NUC Pre-1956 Imprints, vol.
405, 431.

2084 NASHE, THOMAS. The Works of Thomas Nashe. Edited by Ronald
B[runlees] McKerrow. Corrected and Supplemented by F[rank]
P[ercy] Wilson. 5 vols. Oxford: Blackwell, 1958, 402,
397, 416, 484, 466pp.
Provides corrected reprint of 2076 with "A Supplement to
McKerrow's Edition of Nashe," an 84 page appendix to volume
V.

2085 NASHE, THOMAS. The Unfortunate Traveller; or The Life of Jack
Wilton. Edited by John Berryman. New York: Capricorn
Books, 1960, 159pp.
Provides normalized text based on 2076. In "Introduction," pp. 7-28, discusses faults of work, style, and tri-
adic structure. Argues that work had no influence on
development of novel and attempts to explain its continuing
appeal.

2086 NASHE, THOMAS. The Unfortunate Traveller, in Thomas Nashe:
Selected Writings. Edited by Stanley [W.] Wells. Stratford-upon-Avon Library, 1. Cambridge: Harvard University
Press, 1965, pp. 187-278.
Provides modernized text based on the first 1594 edition;
includes textual apparatus. In "Introduction," pp. 1-20,
describes the variety of styles and subject matter in the
work, declaring that The Unfortunate Traveller "has no or-
ganizing principle; it is not a unified work of art."

2087 NASHE, THOMAS. The Unfortunate Traveler: Or, the Life of
Jack Wilton, in Elizabethan Prose Fiction. Edited by
Merritt [E.] Lawlis. Indianapolis: Odyssey Press, Bobbs-
Merrill Co., 1967, pp. 435-547.
Provides partly modernized text based on 1593 edition.
(See textual notes, pp. 634-37, for discussion of changes
made in second edition and list of substantive emendations.)
In introductory note discusses the mixture of forms, calling
work "one of the most eclectic" in Renaissance prose fic-
tion. Suggests that this mixture leads to a "blurred con-
ception of the narrator-protagonist," the major flaw of the
work. Also discusses style.

2088 NASHE, THOMAS. The Unfortunate Traveller, 1594. Menston,
England: Scolar Press, 1971, not paginated.
Provides facsimile reprint of second edition (1594) with
selected pages from first edition.

2089 NASHE, THOMAS. The Unfortunate Traveller, in The Unfortunate
Traveller and Other Works. By Thomas Nashe. Edited by
J. B. Steane. Harmondsworth and Baltimore: Penguin Books,
1972, pp. 251-370.
Provides modernized, annotated text, apparently based on
2084. In "Introduction," pp. 13-44, discusses the cruelty
and "bad taste" of the Unfortunate Traveller and suggests
that the work is an "intuitive (rather than intellectual)
exploration of national character."

Studies

2090 ADOLPH, ROBERT. The Rise of Modern Prose Style. Cambridge:
M. I. T. Press, 1968, 372pp.
Compares Nashe's style to that of Bunyan and Defoe to
illustrate influence of utilitarianism on change in style
of prose fiction. Focuses on descriptive quality of Nashe's
language, finding him "more interested in generalized, highly personal sensory impressions than in abstract logical
distinctions" (pp. 268-88).

2091 ANDERSON, GEORGE MINOR. "The Use of Language and Rhetoric in
Thomas Nashe's The Unfortunate Traveller." Ph.D. dissertation, Yale University, 1961, 222pp.
Analyzes Nashe's neologisms and syntax, and his use of
loan words, rhetoric, puns, and colloquialisms; examines
"the extent to which Nashe employs formal rhetorical figures,
and how they serve to heighten the parodied situations of
his novel."

Nashe

2092   ARNOLD, AEROL. "Thomas Nashe's Criticism of the State of
       Learning in England." Ph.D. dissertation, University of
       Chicago, 1937.
           Includes discussion of Unfortunate Traveller in estab-
       lishing that "Nashe belonged to the humanistic tradition of
       Cheke which emphasized the importance of the classics both
       as sources of knowledge and as standards of excellence."

2093   ATKINS, J[OHN] W[ILLIAM] H[EY]. "Elizabethan Prose Fiction,"
       in The Cambridge History of English Literature, III:
       Renascence and Reformation. Edited by A[dolphus] W[illiam]
       Ward and A[lfred] R[ayney] Waller. Cambridge: Cambridge
       University Press, 1909, 339-73.
           Includes discussion of Nashe's style and Unfortunate
       Traveller as a picaresque novel and as "a novel of manners."
       Calls work "the first historical novel" in England (pp. 362-
       67).

2094   AYRTON, MICHAEL. "The Deadly Stockado." The London Magazine,
       4, no. 7 (July 1957), 40-45.
           Provides an appreciation of Nashe as man and author;
       comments briefly, but enthusiastically, on the vitality,
       influence, and style of Unfortunate Traveller.

2095   BAKER, ERNEST A[LBERT]. The History of the English Novel,
       Vol. II. London: H. F. & G. Witherby, 1929, 303pp.
           Devotes Chapter X ("Thomas Nashe," pp. 153-69) to an ex-
       amination of Nashe's place in the development of realistic
       fiction. Examines his style and illustrates how The Unfor-
       tunate Traveller parodies the types of fiction then popular.

2096   BAWCUTT, N. W. "Nashe and Bodin." N&Q, NS, 14 (March 1967),
       91.
           Suggests Jean Bodin's The Republic as a possible source
       for the Cutwolf episode.

2097   BAWCUTT, N. W. "Possible Sources for The Unfortunate Travel-
       ler." N&Q, NS, 7 (February 1960), 49-50.
           Suggests possible sources for the Cutwolf episode.

2098   BEER, E. S. DE. "Thomas Nashe: The Notices of Rome in The
       Unfortunate Traveller." N&Q, 185 (31 July 1943), 67-70.
           Provides historical and topographical notes to section
       on Rome.

*2099 BENTON, V. J. "The Prose Style of Thomas Nashe." Ph.D. dis-
       sertation, University of Leeds, 1970.
           Abstract not available.

2100   BHATTACHERJEE, M. M.   "Italy in Elizabethan Pamphlets."   CalR,
       83 (May 1942), 129-35.
          Focuses on anti-Italian comments in Unfortunate Travel-
       ler, suggesting reasons for adverse statements about Italian
       society and manners.

2101   BLOOR, R[OBERT] H[ENRY] U[NDERWOOD].   The English Novel from
       Chaucer to Galsworthy.   University Extension Library.   Lon-
       don: I. Nicholson and Watson, 1935, 248pp.
          Includes discussion of amorality, "elasticity," and style
       of Unfortunate Traveller; suggests that it is the closest
       to a realistic novel produced in the Elizabethan period
       (pp. 89-99).

2102   BOWERS, FREDSON T[HAYER].   "Thomas Nashe and the Picaresque
       Novel," in Humanistic Studies in Honor of John Calvin Met-
       calf.   University of Virginia Studies, 1.   Charlottesville:
       University of Virginia, 1941, pp. 12-27.
          Compares Unfortunate Traveller with Spanish picaresque
       novels and examines form of work, characterization of Wil-
       ton, and satire to argue that "even in a partly imperfect
       shape, Nashe produced the first English picaresque novel."

2103   BRADISH, GAYNOR FRANCIS.   "The Hard Pennyworth: A Study in
       Sixteenth Century Prose Fiction."   Ph.D. dissertation,
       Harvard University, 1958, 194pp.
          Analyzes Nashe's use of theme of "learning through ex-
       perience" in Unfortunate Traveller; analyzes relationships
       of style and structure to theme and examines influences upon
       Nashe's treatment of theme.

2104   BROWN, LEWIS.   "The Unfortunate Traveller by Thomas Nashe
       (XVI Century)."   Journal of Jewish Lore and Philosophy, 1
       (1919), 241-53.
          Discusses Zadoch episode, pointing out how it reflects
       contemporary English, not Roman, life and arguing that the
       episode "was suggested to Nashe by the rumorous overture to
       the Lopez trial" in the spring and summer of 1593. See
       2175.

2105   BROWNE, THOMAS ARTHUR.   "Thomas Nashe and the Traditions of
       Plain-Speaking."   Ph.D. dissertation, University of Minne-
       sota, 1961, 226pp.
          Argues that Nashe "is a serious and consistent social
       critic, and that the role he takes in his writings is that
       of the 'plain-speaker.'"   Examines Wilton as a plain-speaker
       and suggests that through him "Nashe seems to be defending
       his own ideas of right conduct."

341

Nashe

2106   CHANDLER, FRANK WADLEIGH. The Literature of Roguery. 2 vols.
        Boston: Houghton, Mifflin and Co., 1907, 602pp.
            Includes discussion of Unfortunate Traveller as the
        earliest English example of picaresque romance. Examines
        Nashe's realism, satire, and style (I, 192-98).

2107   CLUETT, ROBERT. "Arcadia Wired: Preliminaries to an Elec-
        tronic Investigation of the Prose Style of Philip Sidney."
        Lang&S, 7 (Spring 1974), 119-37.
            Presents "a partial quantitative account of Sidney's
        style in prose fiction measured against those of Lodge,
        Lyly, and Nashe." Concentrates analysis on syntax and word
        classes.

2108   COFFMAN, GEORGE R. "A Note on Shakespeare and Nash." MLN, 42
        (May 1927), 317-19.
            Suggests that Nashe's description of Surrey's horse at
        the tournament held to defend Geraldine's beauty is the
        source of two similes in Vernon's description of Hal and
        the King's forces (1 Henry IV, 4.1.97-110). See 2134.

2109   COOLIDGE, JOHN S. "Martin Marprelate, Marvell, and Decorum
        Personae as a Satirical Theme." PMLA, 74 (December 1959),
        526-32.
            Discusses Martin's use of decorum personae as "basis for
        a defense of satire," arguing that in developing the "device
        of using a theatrical, comic mask in non-dramatic writing"
        the anonymous author influenced the development of Eliza-
        bethan prose fiction "in an important way," particularly
        through possible influence on Nashe's creation of Jack
        Wilton.

2110   CROSTON, A. K. "The Use of Imagery in Nashe's The Unfortunate
        Traveller." RES, 24 (April 1948), 90-101.
            Examines Nashe's imagery, finding that his "prose is far
        more concerned with the interplay between 'tenor' and 've-
        hicle,' placing the stress, where over-balancing takes
        place, on the 'vehicle.'" Also investigates sources of
        imagery, finding that "Learning" and "Daily Life" predomin-
        ate.

2111   DAVIS, GWENN. "The Satiric Technique of Thomas Nashe." Ph.D.
        dissertation, University of Michigan, 1966, 206pp.
            Examines subjects, characteristics, form, and techniques
        of Nashe's satire. Discusses Unfortunate Traveller "in the
        context of Nashe's other satire as a narrative with strong
        resemblances to the anatomy form which is ordered by a
        speaker who is a parody of the kind of repentant sinner

Greene presented and an adaptation of the kind of narrative
voice used by Nashe in his other works."

2112   DAVIS, ROBERT GORHAM. "The Sense of the Real in English Fic-
       tion." CL, 3 (Summer 1951), 200-17.
            Discusses briefly The Unfortunate Traveller in the de-
       velopment of realism, noting that Nashe's "documentation
       from histories and travelers' reports is presented as in-
       teresting in its own rights" and "anticipates Defoe's
       mingling of history, journalism, and fiction."

2113   DAVIS, WALTER R[ICHARDSON]. Idea and Act in Elizabethan Fic-
       tion. Princeton: Princeton University Press, 1961, 311pp.
            Analyzes Nashe's use of "destructive juxtaposition," the
       structure of The Unfortunate Traveller and its relationship
       to changes in narrative technique, the function of role-
       playing, the function of the narrator and Wilton's relation-
       ship to the audience, and the style (pp. 210-37).

2114   DEMADRE, A. "Le Récit dans The Unfortunate Traveller de Thomas
       Nashe," in Récit et roman: Formes du roman anglais du XVIe
       au XXe siècle. Études Anglais, 42. Paris: M. Didier,
       1972, pp. 9-15.
            Examines relationships between the plot and Nashe's nar-
       rative methods. Analyzes the narrative voice and Nashe's
       integration of the comic and the realistic.

2115   DENT, R[OBERT] W. John Webster's Borrowing. Berkeley: Uni-
       versity of California Press, 1960, 323pp.
            Provides detailed analysis of Webster's use of Unfor-
       tunate Traveller as a source (passim).

*2116 DOUB, DONALD VALENTINE, JR. "Unfortunate Travellers: Origins
       of the Picaresque Novel in England." Ph.D. dissertation,
       Harvard University, 1967.
            Abstract not available.

2117   DREW, PHILIP. "Edward Daunce and The Unfortunate Traveller."
       RES, NS, 11 (November 1960), 410-12.
            Suggests Daunce's A Brief Discourse of the Spanish State
       (1590) as source for some incidents, especially Esdras's
       revenge on Cutwolf.

2118   DUNCAN-JONES, KATHERINE. "Nashe and Sidney: The Tournament
       in The Unfortunate Traveller." MLR, 63 (January 1968), 3-6.
            Examines tournament at Florence as "a mosaic of refer-
       ences to tournaments and single combats in the Arcadia" and
       argues Nashe is providing a burlesque of chivalric conven-
       tions.

Nashe

2119   DURHAM, CHARLES W. III. "Character and Characterization in
           Elizabethan Prose Fiction." Ph.D. dissertation, Ohio Uni-
           versity, 1969, 147pp.
               Examines Nashe's methods of characterization.

2120   EBBS, JOHN DALE. "A Note on Nashe and Shakespeare." MLN, 66
           (November 1951), 480-81.
               Notes similarity between passage in description of rape
           of Heraclide on top of her husband's corpse and lines in
           Titus Andronicus (2.3.129-30); suggests Nashe had either
           seen the play or Shakespeare had read Nashe's manuscript.
           See 2192.

2121   EIN, RONALD BORIS. "The Serpent's Voice: Commentary and
           Readers' Beliefs in Elizabethan Fiction." Ph.D. disserta-
           tion, Indiana University, 1974, 273pp.
               Analyzes implied narrator commentary in "the narrator
           summary" at the beginning of Unfortunate Traveller.

2122   FEASEY, LYNETTE. "The Unfortunate Traveller." TLS, 20 October
           1948, p. 555.
               Discusses bibliographical history of the work and refer-
           ences to current affairs.

2123   FEASEY, LYNETTE, and EVELINE [I.] FEASEY. "Nashe's The Unfor-
           tunate Traveller: Some Marlovian Echoes." English, 7,
           no. 39 (1948), 125-29.
               Points out references to Marlowe and echoes of his works:
           argues "that in the figure of the Earl of Surrey Nashe is
           paying deliberate tribute to Christopher Marlowe" and "that
           the supposed defence of Aretine is...a defence" of Marlowe.

*2124   FIEBACH, RENATA-MARIA. "Der stilistische Wert der Funktion-
           verschiebung bei Thomas Nashe." Ph.D. dissertation, Univer-
           sity of Berlin, 1957.
               Abstract not available.

2125   FRIEDERICH, REINHARD H. "Myself Am Centre of My Circling
           Thought: Studies in Baroque Personae (Burton and Donne)."
           Ph.D. dissertation, University of Washington, 1971, 194pp.
               Argues that because of "character credibility and flexi-
           bility rather than plot manipulation" The Unfortunate Tra-
           veller and Gascoigne's Master F. J. "succeed, whereas Greene
           and Deloney fail since their static characters cannot gener-
           ate more than didactic or simply cumulative structures."

2126   FRIEDERICH, REINHARD H. "Verbal Tensions in Thomas Nashe's The
           Unfortunate Traveller." Lang&S, 8 (Summer 1975), 211-19.

344

Argues that <u>Unfortunate Traveller</u> must be analyzed through Nashe's use of language rather than through generic or structural approach. Analyzes several episodes to illustrate how "the verbal construct...develops the ultimate effect" of a passage.

2127   GIBBONS, SISTER MARINA, O.P. "Polemic, the Rhetorical Tradition, and <u>The Unfortunate Traveller</u>." <u>JEGP</u>, 63, no. 3 (1964), 408-21.
Examines influences on and ranges, subjects, and techniques of Nashe's use of polemic. Discusses relationship between Nashe's contentiousness and the satire in the work.

2128   GISELA, JUNKE. "Formen des Dialogs im frühen englischen Roman." Ph.D. dissertation, University of Köln, 1975, 150pp.
Examines form and use of dialogue in <u>Unfortunate Traveller</u>. <u>See</u> 208.

2129   GOHLKE, MADELON SPRENGNETHER. "Narrative Structure in the New <u>Arcadia</u>, <u>The Faerie Queene</u> I, and <u>The Unfortunate Traveller</u>." Ph.D. dissertation, Yale University, 1972, 356pp.
Defends <u>Unfortunate Traveller</u> against charge of formlessness by arguing that structure of the work "cannot be understood 'spatially,' since the reader is not placed outside the action, but rather within it, approximating the experience of the figures within the fiction." Suggests that "structure emerges in conjunction with the progressive revelation of the thematic organization of the work."

2130   GOHLKE, MADELON S[PRENGNETHER]. "Wits Wantonness: <u>The Unfortunate Traveller</u> as Picaresque." <u>SP</u>, 73 (October 1976), 397-413.
Argues that Nashe's resolution of "the central problem of...the apparent split between rhetorical cleverness and moral action" "involves a sophisticated handling of...picaresque." Identifies Nashe's subject as "the relationship between wit and wisdom" and argues that work is highly structured through a developing pattern of misfortune.

2131   GREBANIER, BERNARD. <u>The Truth about Shylock</u>. New York: Random House, 1962, 381pp.
Argues that although Nashe's treatment of Zadoch and Zachary reflects "a bigotry that was certainly fashionable in some quarters," his primary intention was to make the two comic characters (pp. 55-63).

2132   HABEL, URSULA. <u>Die Nachwirkung des picaresken Romans in England (von Nash bis Fielding und Smollett)</u>. Sprache und

Nashe

> Kultur der Germanischen und Romanischen Völker, A. Anglis-
> tische Reihe, 4. Breslau: Priebatsch, 1930, 75pp.
>   Examines place of Unfortunate Traveller in the develop-
> ment of the picaresque novel in England (pp. 16-24).

2133 HARLOW, C. G. "Nashe's Visit to the Isle of Wight and His
      Publications of 1592-4." RES, NS, 14 (August 1963), 225-42.
        Suggests delay between entry in Stationers' Register and
      publication of Unfortunate Traveller "may be the direct re-
      sult of Nashe's persecution [by the Lord Mayor of London]
      followed by his stay" in the Isle of Wight.

2134 HARLOW, C. G. "Shakespeare, Nashe, and the Ostrich Crux in
      1 Henry IV." SQ, 17 (Spring 1966), 171-74.
        Provides further evidence (see 2108) showing that Unfor-
      tunate Traveller was Shakespeare's source for I Henry IV
      (4.1.97-110) and identifies Samuel Daniel's The Worthy
      Tract of Paulus Jovius as Nashe's source for his allusion
      to the ostrich.

2135 HARMAN, EDWARD GEORGE. Gabriel Harvey and Thomas Nashe. Lon-
      don: J. M. Ouseley & Son, 1923, 287pp.
        Includes discussion of Unfortunate Traveller in context
      of Harvey-Nashe controversy. Argues that descriptions in
      work indicate that Nashe was a "traveller" (passim).

2136 HIBBARD, G[EORGE] R. Thomas Nashe: A Critical Introduction.
      London: Routledge and Kegan Paul, 1962, 274pp.
        In chapter on The Unfortunate Traveller (pp. 145-79) ar-
      gues that the work is neither a picaresque romance nor a
      novel. Discusses structure in detail, concluding that Nashe
      was an "improviser" whose basic element was the scene. Ana-
      lyzes influence of literary forms and social conventions on
      work, Nashe's intention in various scenes, and connections
      with Nashe's other works; in the process, takes issue with
      several of Latham's conclusions (2157).

2137 HILL, ROWLAND MERLIN. "Realistic Descriptive Setting in Eng-
      lish Fiction from 1550 through Fielding." Ph.D. disserta-
      tion, Boston University, 1941, 344pp.
        Examines how "Nashe bolsters reader-faith in the proba-
      bility of his picaro's occasionally ultra-sensational esca-
      pades by skillfully utilizing" realistic historical setting.

2138 HOWARTH, R[OBERT] G[UY]. Two Elizabethan Writers of Fiction:
      Thomas Nashe and Thomas Deloney. Cape Town: University of
      Cape Town Editorial Board, 1956, 60pp.

Examines <u>Unfortunate Traveller</u> as an historical novel;
discusses Nashe's characterization of Wilton, his style,
and the structure of work (which he calls "formless"). Provides running commentary on work. Discusses Nashe's "power
to chill the soul with horror which is not just sensation"
(pp. 1-31).

2139 HUNTER, G. K. "Notes on Webster's Tragedies." <u>N&Q</u>, NS, 4
(February 1957), 53-55.
In note 10 identifies passage in <u>Unfortunate Traveller</u>
as source for the <u>Duchess of Malfi</u>.

2140 HUNTER, J. B. "The Unfortunate Traveller of Thomas Nashe as
a Sidelight on Elizabethan Security." <u>N&Q</u>, 196 (17 February
1951), 75-76.
Suggests that Edward de Vere is the cider merchant and
that the "'syder' which this lord purveys to the troops is
'desire' in anagram; in other words patriotic propaganda."

2141 IMBERT-TERRY, H. M. "Thomas Nashe, Satirist." <u>Transactions
of the Royal Society of Literature</u>, 18, Part 3 (1897),
177-214.
Comments on <u>Unfortunate Traveller</u> in providing overview
of Nashe's work as satirist: discusses style and suggests
that importance of Nashe's works "must lie in the varied
pictures they present of contemporary life and manners."

2142 JOHNSON, WILLIAM JACKSON. "Stylistic Development in the Prose
of Thomas Nashe." Ph.D. dissertation, University of Texas
at Austin, 1967, 238pp.
Examines <u>Unfortunate Traveller</u> in the context of an analysis of characteristics of Nashe's style and the changes in
it.

2143 JONES, DOROTHY. "An Example of Anti-Petrarchan Satire in
Nashe's <u>The Unfortunate Traveller</u>." <u>YES</u>, 1 (1971), 48-54.
Discusses satire on Petrarchan attitudes in Surrey's
sonnet "If I must die" and its relationship to the work as
a whole.

2144 JUSSERAND, J[EAN] J[ULES]. <u>The English Novel in the Time of
Shakespeare</u>. Translated by Elizabeth Lee. Revised edition.
London: T. Fisher Unwin, 1890, 433pp.
Discusses characteristics of Nashe's style and influence
of Rabelais upon it. Examines <u>Unfortunate Traveller</u> as
picaresque tale (pp. 295-327).

Nashe

2145 JUSSERAND, J[EAN] J[ULES]. "Le Roman au temps de Shakespeare."
      RDM, 187 (1 February 1887), 573-612.
      Discusses Unfortunate Traveller as picaresque novel; dis-
      cusses Nashe's style and the weakness of the structure of
      the work (pp. 602-10).

2146 KAULA, DAVID. "The Low Style in Nashe's The Unfortunate Tra-
      veler." SEL, 6 (Winter 1966), 43-57.
      Suggests that Nashe uses a structure corresponding to
      "the usual tripartite arrangement of the Christian cosmos"
      (the paradisiac, the human, and the infernal) to parody the
      process of "fall, purgation, and repentance." Analyzes the
      characteristics of Nashe's low style ("Wilton's true speak-
      ing voice") and the contrast with various styles parodied
      by Nashe. Suggests that the low style mirrors Nashe's per-
      ception of human action "as violent, fragmentary, and acci-
      dental."

2147 KINSMAN, ROBERT S. "Priscilla's 'Grote': An Emendation in
      Nashe's Unfortunate Traveller." N&Q, NS, 7 (February 1960),
      50-51.
      Suggests that Priscilla's "grate" in Wilton's description
      of Rome is a misprint for Priscilla's "grote" or "grotto,"
      an area near Rome.

2148 KLEIN, KARL LUDWIG. Vorformen des Romans in der englischen
      erzählenden Prosa des 16. Jahrhunderts. FAGAAS, 13.
      Heidelberg: C. Winter, 1969, 260pp.
      Provides detailed analysis--by episode--of Unfortunate
      Traveller. Provides overview of scholarship, analyzes nar-
      rative forms and techniques used by Nashe, discusses point
      of view, and examines concern for decorum (pp. 127-250).

2149 KOLLMAN, W. "Nash's Unfortunate Traveller und Head's English
      Rogue: Die beiden Hauptvertreter des englischen Schelmen-
      romans." Anglia, 22 (1899), 81-140.
      Examines Nashe's realism in discussing Unfortunate Tra-
      veller as picaresque novel.

2150 KOPPENFELS, WERNER VON. "Thomas Nashe und Rabelais." Archiv,
      207, no. 4 (1970), 277-91.
      Includes examination of parallels between Unfortunate
      Traveller and Gargantua and Pantagruel in arguing that Nashe
      was influenced directly by Rabelais.

2151 KOPPENFELS, WERNER VON. "Two Notes on Imprese in Elizabethan
      Literature: Daniel's Additions to The Worthy Tract of
      Paulus Iovius; Sidney's Arcadia and the Tournament Scene in
      The Unfortunate Traveller." RenQ, 24 (Spring 1971), 13-25.

348

Discusses Nashe's "creative imitation" of passages from
Sidney's Arcadia, particularly in the description of the
imprese in the tournament episode.

2152   KOPPENFELS, WERNER VON. "Zur zeitgenössischen Aufnahme des
        elisabethanischen 'Romans': Nashes Unfortunate Traveller
        in der Literatur der Shakespeare-Epoche." Anglia, 94,
        nos. 3-4 (1976), 361-87.
            Examines influence of Unfortunate Traveller on later
        prose fiction and on plays of Shakespeare and Webster.

2153   KRAPP, GEORGE PHILIP. The Rise of English Literary Prose.
        New York: Oxford University Press, 1915, 565pp.
            Includes examination of Nashe's style and discussion of
        The Unfortunate Traveller as a mixture of original and tra-
        ditional "motives." Also discusses element of realism in
        the work (pp. 482-92, passim).

2154   LANHAM, RICHARD [ALAN]. "Opaque Style in Elizabethan Prose
        Fiction." PCP, 1 (1966), 25-31.
            Discusses the irony which is the result of the contrast
        between style and plot in Unfortunate Traveller.

2155   LANHAM, RICHARD A[LAN]. "Tom Nashe and Jack Wilton: Personal-
        ity as Structure in The Unfortunate Traveller." SSF, 4
        (Spring 1967), 201-16.
            Approaching The Unfortunate Traveller through an analysis
        of Wilton and his relationship to society--elements provid-
        ing both subject and structure--discerns a pattern of "so-
        cial disenfranchisement and violence." However, argues that
        the work culminates in no definable meaning, only the
        "imitation of a truly neurotic personality."

2156   LARSON, CHARLES [HOWARD]. "The Comedy of Violence in Nashe's
        The Unfortunate Traveller." CahiersE, No. 8 (October 1975),
        pp. 15-29.
            Analyzes "the nature of...the violent comedy of the
        events in Italy" to argue that Nashe, through the use of
        imagery, stereotypes, and technical virtuosity, invites his
        reader to feel "that it is not only permissible but also de-
        sirable...to achieve psychic release in the process of
        laughing at a series of fictional events which he hopes
        will never befall him in life."

2157   LATHAM, AGNES M[ARY] C[HRISTABEL]. "Satire on Literary Themes
        and Modes in Nashe's Unfortunate Traveller." E&S, NS, 1
        (1948), 85-100.
            Analyzes work as "a spirited parody of popular literary
        themes and styles of the day." See 2136.

Nashe

2158   LEA, KATHLEEN, and ETHEL SEATON.   "'I saw young Harry.'"   RES,
        21 (October 1945), 319-22.
            Cites parallel between Nashe's description of Surrey's
        horse and Vernon's description of Hal and his companions
        (I Henry IV), noting briefly that Nashe has adapted "Pliny
        and Gesner to the sights and the prowess of the tiltyard."

2159   LEGGATT, ALEXANDER.   "Artistic Coherence in The Unfortunate
        Traveller."   SEL, 14 (Winter 1974), 31-46.
            Suggests that although the work lacks tight structural
        unity, Nashe does use structural techniques which later
        writers used more effectively in achieving unity. Finds a
        consistent pattern of imagery ("the frailty of the flesh"),
        "interrelated strands of action," and rudimentary attempts
        at creating a character who develops. Suggests that Wilton
        does not reform; instead, he is the vehicle for "a narrative
        voice which changes its tone to fit the changed nature of
        the events described."

2160   LIEDSTRAND, FRITHJOF.   Metapher und Vergleich in The Unfortun-
        ate Traveller von Thomas Nashe und bei seinen Vorbildern
        François Rabelais und Pietro Aretino.   Weimar: G. Uschmann,
        1929, 149pp.
            Provides detailed, classified comparative listing of
        metaphors and images in the works of the three writers to
        illustrate influence of Rabelais and Aretino on Nashe's
        style in Unfortunate Traveller.

2161   LOISEAU, JEAN.   "Deux attitudes élisabéthaines devant le voy-
        age: Lyly (Euphues) et Nashe (Jack Wilton)," in Le Voyage
        dans la littérature anglo-saxonne. Actes du Congrès de
        Nice (1971).   Société des Anglicistes de l'Enseignement
        Supérieur. Paris: M. Didier, 1972, pp. 13-19.
            Examines treatment of and attitude toward travel and
        foreign countries in Unfortunate Traveller.

2162   LYONS, NATHAN.   "Thomas Nashe, the Antic Stylist."   MQR, 10
        (Spring 1971), 113-18.
            Analyzes characteristics of Nashe's prose style, empha-
        sizing how he manipulates the schemata of medieval rhetoric
        and how he utilizes qualities of oral tradition.

2163   McGINN, DONALD J.   "Nashe's Share in the Marprelate Contro-
        versy."   PMLA, 59 (December 1944), 952-84.
            Provides detailed analysis of Nashe's prose style, par-
        ticularly of his vocabulary and sentence construction.

2164   MACKERNESS, E. D. "A Note on Thomas Nashe and 'Style.'" *Eng-lish*, 6, no. 34 (1947), 198-200.
       Discusses general characteristics of Nashe's prose style.

2165   MALHOTRA, K. K. "'The Picaresque's Progress': A Study of *Jack Wilton* and *Jonathan Wild*." *PURBA*, 2, no. 2 (1971), 39-47.
       Analyzes the *Unfortunate Traveller* as a picaresque romance, emphasizing Nashe's "traditional" approach to the form. Compares Nashe's work with Fielding's *Jonathan Wild*.

2166   MARCUS, HANS. "Thomas Nash über Deutschland." *Archiv*, 192 (1955), 113-33.
       Discusses Nashe's depiction of Germany in *Unfortunate Traveller* and examines reasons for his distortions.

2167   MILLER, STUART. "A Genre Definition of the Picaresque Novel." Ph.D. dissertation, Yale University, 1963, 325pp.
       Utilizes *Unfortunate Traveller* as one example in attempt to define "the picaresque novel as a genre." Examines plot, character, point of view, and rhythm.

2168   MILLER, STUART. *The Picaresque Novel*. Cleveland: Press of Case Western Reserve University, 1967, 172pp.
       Refers throughout to *Unfortunate Traveller* in attempting to construct "a model of the typical picaresque novel." Discusses the "rhythm of events," the pattern of "love and loneliness," and the relationship between narrator and picaro in the work (passim).

2169   MONTESER, FREDERICK. "An Examination of Thomas Nashe's Literary Development." Ph.D. dissertation, Arizona State University, 1968, 185pp.
       Includes discussion of *Unfortunate Traveller* in "an analysis of Nashe's literary progress": discusses "characterization, subject matter, vocabulary and style."

2170   MONTESER, FREDERICK. *The Picaresque Element in Western Literature*. Studies in the Humanities, 5. University, Alabama: University of Alabama Press, 1975, 160pp.
       Includes discussion of *Unfortunate Traveller* as a picaresque novel and argues that Nashe was "inspired" by *Lazarillo de Tormes* (passim).

2171   MORROW, PATRICK. "The Brazen World of Thomas Nashe and *The Unfortunate Traveller*." *JPC*, 9 (Winter 1975), 638-44.
       Analyzes movement of work from comic through serio-comic to serious episodes; suggests that *Unfortunate Traveller* is

Nashe

close to modern black humor. Concludes that because Nashe
was "unable to write within the conventions of any established genre, he turned to satirizing them through the pro-
jection of his literary personality as persona."

2172 MURRAY, P. J. M. "Countries of the Mind: The Travellers of
Nashe and Swift." Words, 3 (1970), 46-61.
Compares Nashe's use of Wilton as a fictional traveller
with Swift's use of Gulliver to argue that Nashe is too intent on artifice to present a developed satiric vision
"capable of informing a coherent literary work."

2173 MUSTARD, W. P. "'Agrippa's Shadows.'" MLN, 43 (May 1928),
325.
Suggests reference to description of Agrippa's necromancy
in Unfortunate Traveller as the best commentary on Lyly's
allusion to "Agrippa his shadows" in the second prologue to
Campaspe.

2174 MUSTARD, W. P. "Notes on Thomas Nashe's Works." MLN, 40
(December 1925), 469-76.
Includes notes on sources and analogues of passages in
Unfortunate Traveller.

2175 NEWMAN, LOUIS I. "Richard Cumberland on Thomas Nashe's Unfortunate Traveller." Journal of Jewish Lore and Philosophy,
1 (1919), 414-17.
Notes Cumberland's quotation of passage (Zadoch-Zachary
dialogue) in The Observer (1785); supports Brown's suggestion (2104) that Lopez was the original of Zadoch.

2176 ORMOND, JEANNE DOWD. "The Knave with a Hundred Faces: The
Guises of Hermes in Nashe, Fielding, Melville, and Mann."
Ph.D. dissertation, University of California, Irvine, 1974,
187pp.
Argues that "the structure of Nashe's Unfortunate Traveller becomes clear...[if one realizes that it] is not that
Nashe fails in an attempt to make his picaresque into a
bildungsroman...[but that] at the crucial moment, he suc-
ceeds in allowing his hero to discover his fictive freedom"
by transforming the work "into a novel of the Hermetic
mode."

2177 OTTEN, KURT. Der englische Roman vom 16. zum 19. Jahrhundert.
Grundlagen der Anglistik und Amerikanistik, 4. Berlin:
E. Schmidt, 1971, 184pp.
Includes general critical discussion of Unfortunate Tra-
veller in context of examination of development of the Eng-
lish novel (pp. 30-35).

2178   PARRILL, WILLIAM BRUCE. "The Elizabethan Background of Hell,
        the Devil, the Magician, and the Witch, and Their Use in
        Elizabethan Fiction." Ph.D. dissertation, University of
        Tennessee, 1964, 321pp.
            "[S]tudies the uses which Nashe, Greene, Dekker, Lodge
        and the other fiction writers made of the wide variety of
        material available" on the topics. Finds that use was
        largely satirical.

2179   PEÑUELAS, MARCELINO C. "Algo mas sobre la picaresca: Lázaro
        y Jack Wilton." Hispania, 37 (1954), 443-45.
            Compares Lazarillo de Tormes with Unfortunate Traveller
        to demonstrate that the differences between the two works
        arise from attitude toward life. Compares nature of major
        characters, their relationship with women, and the source
        of their humor. Concludes that Wilton does not dare to
        look at life face to face.

2180   PISK, GEORGE MICHAEL. "Rogues and Vagabonds in Tudor England:
        A Study in Fact and Fiction." Ph.D. dissertation, Univer-
        sity of Texas at Austin, 1968, 405pp.
            Includes discussion of Unfortunate Traveller.

*2181   POELL, MARGRIT. "Wortformen und Syntax in Thomas Nash Unfor-
        tunate Traveller. Ein Vergleich mit der Sprache Shake-
        speares." Ph.D. dissertation, University of Graz, 1950,
        172pp.
            Abstract not available.

2182   PRITCHETT, V. S. "Books in General." New Statesman and Na-
        tion, 35 (10 April 1948), 297.
            Discusses Nashe's style and the violence in Unfortunate
        Traveller. Takes issue with Ayrton's suggestion of parallel
        between violence in Nashe's work and in post World War II
        society (2081).

2183   RALEIGH, WALTER [ALEXANDER]. The English Novel: Being a Short
        Sketch of Its History from the Earliest Times to the Appear-
        ance of Waverley. London: J. Murray, 1894, 310pp.
            Examines Nashe's style and his place in the development
        of the novel (pp. 71-86).

2184   RANDOLPH, GERALD RICHARD. "An Analysis of Form and Style in
        the Prose Works of Thomas Nashe." Ph.D. dissertation,
        Florida State University, 1962, 193pp.
            Discusses Unfortunate Traveller in context of detailed
        examination of aspects of Nashe's style and his adaptation
        of style to genre.

Nashe

2185 RE, ARUNDELL DEL. "Realism in Elizabethan Fiction--II:
Thomas Nashe." Studies in English Literature (Imperial
University of Tokyo), 9 (1920), 172-92.
Discusses the unity of Unfortunate Traveller and provides
a detailed plot summary to support his contention that
Nashe was "a creator of the realistic novel based upon the
observation and portrayal of life." Claims that the work
is "the first complete and realistic prose tale in which
the true and the fanciful are happily blended."

2186 RE, ARUNDELL DEL. "Two Elizabethan Realists: Robert Greene
and Thomas Nashe," in The Secret of the Renaissance and
Other Essays and Studies. By Arundell del Re. Tokyo:
Kaitakusha, 1930, pp. 72-112.
Discusses Unfortunate Traveller as a "realistic novel
based upon the observation and portrayal of life." Examines
Nashe's style, his "realistic description," and structural
unity.

2187 RICHARDS, ALFRED E. "The English Wagner Book of 1594." PMLA,
24 (March 1909), 32-39.
Suggests possibility that Nashe is author of The Second
Report of Doctor John Faustus, noting "similarity of style
and expression" to Nashe's works.

2188 RIDDELL, JAMES A. "Some Late 16th- and Early 17th-Century
Antedatings of the OED." AN&Q, 10 (May 1972), 131-32.
Includes two words ("collachrimation" and "deuolution")
from Unfortunate Traveller.

2189 ROSENBERG, EDGAR. "The Jew in Western Drama." BNYPL, 72
(September 1968), 442-91.
Examines Nashe's treatment of Jews in The Unfortunate
Traveller. Analyzes the "element of the Italianated Jew,"
i.e., "the identification of Jew with political depravity,
specifically 'Italian' depravity," which is more pronounced
in Nashe's work than in any other of the Elizabethan period.

2190 RÜHFEL, JOSEPH. Die Belesenheit von Thomas Nash. München:
Manz, 1911, 48pp.
Provides list of allusions to classical and modern authors in Nashe's works as means of indicating the breadth
of his reading.

2191 SCHLAUCH, MARGARET. Antecedents of the English Novel, 1400-
1600 (from Chaucer to Deloney). Warsaw: PWN--Polish Scientific Publishers; London: Oxford University Press, 1963,
264pp.
Discusses Nashe's use of rhetorical figures (pp. 212-16).

2192   SCHRICKX, W.   "Titus Andronicus and Thomas Nashe."   ES, 50
        (February 1969), 82-84.
            Provides evidence that suggests Shakespeare's indebted-
        ness in Titus Andronicus (2.3.129-30) to Nashe's description
        of Heraclide's rape atop her husband's dead body.   See 2120.

2193   SEAMAN, GERDA REE SEGALL.   "The Equivocal Satire of Thomas
        Nashe."   Ph.D. dissertation, University of California,
        Davis, 1974, 174pp.
            Includes discussion of Unfortunate Traveller in analyzing
        "the disparity between logical assertion and rhetorical im-
        plication" in Nashe's works.   Finds that "[d]espite his
        overt championing of the received values of the Elizabethan
        hierarchy, Nashe, in most of his works, seems to be lauding
        the individual at the expense of the system."

2194   SIERACKI, CHARLES ALFRED.   "The Narrator in Elizabethan Prose
        Fiction: Gascoigne and Nashe."   Ph.D. dissertation, Uni-
        versity of Illinois at Urbana-Champaign, 1971, 185pp.
            Analyzes "how...[Nashe in Unfortunate Traveller] shapes
        the identity of the narrator and manipulates this persona
        to expose the comic nature of the other characters and,
        thereby, to shape the satiric theme" of the work.   Argues
        that Unfortunate Traveller "has a unified structure as a
        Menippean satire; that it is not simply a burlesque of
        literary themes and modes but a satire that remains effec-
        tive...in its exposure and ridicule of human perversity."

2195   SMITH, GEORGE WELLINGTON.   "The Prose Satire of Thomas Nashe."
        Ph.D. dissertation, University of Virginia, 1932.
            Examines subjects of Nashe's satire and his methods in
        Unfortunate Traveller.   Concludes that "many elements in...
        The Unfortunate Traveller admit of interpretation as bur-
        lesques and, in some cases, as parodies."

2196   SMITH, JOHN DALE.   "Narrative Technique in the Realistic Prose
        Fiction of Greene, Nashe, and Deloney."   Ph.D. dissertation,
        University of Wisconsin, 1968, 323pp.
            Discusses influences on narrative of Unfortunate Travel-
        ler.   Concludes that "[b]ecause of its use of history, its
        linguistic brilliance, and its first-person point of view,
        The Unfortunate Traveller is the most important of the
        Elizabethan proto-novels."   Examines Nashe's place in the
        development of the novel.

2197   SPLAINE, CYPRIAN.   "Nashe."   Athenaeum, No. 2957 (28 June
        1884), p. 834.
            Lists some "curious" words in Unfortunate Traveller.

355

Nashe

*2198   STALKER, ARCHIBALD. Shakespeare and Thomas Nashe. Stirling,
         1935.
              Not located. Listed in Samuel A. Tannenbaum, "Shake-
         speare and His Contemporaries," Shakespeare Association
         Bulletin, 11 (1936), 18.

*2199   STALKER, ARCHIBALD. Shakespeare, Marlowe, and Nashe. Stir-
         ling: Learmonth, 1937.
              Not located. Listed in MHRA Annual Bibliography, 18
         (1937), #2320.

2200   STAMM, FANNY. Der Unfortunate Traveller des Thomas Nashe:
         Eine Studie über das Verhältnis der englischen zur italien-
         ischen Renaissance. Basel: Schwabe, 1930, 60pp.
              Examines Nashe's treatment of Italy and Italians; traces
         sources of and influences on his treatment.

2201   STANZEL, FRANZ K. "Nashe: The Unfortunate Traveller," in Der
         englische Roman: Vom Mittelalter zur Moderne, Vol. I.
         Edited by Franz K. Stanzel. Düsseldorf: Bagel, 1969, 54-
         84.
              Examines Unfortunate Traveller in context of Elizabethan
         prose fiction and in context of Nashe's other works. Dis-
         cusses structure, picaresque elements, narrative voice (par-
         ticularly the role of Wilton), and depiction of Italy.
         Argues that work is both a "Trivialroman und Anti-Trivial-
         roman."

2202   STATON, WALTER F., JR. "The Characters of Style in Elizabethan
         Prose." JEGP, 57, no. 2 (1958), 197-207.
              Discusses Nashe as "the Elizabethan writer who most fully
         exploited the low style," but argues he used it not out of
         preference but because of demand of subject matter.

2203   STATON, WALTER F., JR. "The Significance of the Literary
         Career of Thomas Nashe." Ph.D. dissertation, University of
         Pennsylvania, 1955, 198pp.
              Discusses Unfortunate Traveller in examination of "the
         meaning that Nashe's various works had for his contempor-
         aries as well as the purpose he had in writing and publish-
         ing them." Concludes "that Nashe regarded himself and was
         regarded by his fellows as a sort of virtuoso rhetorician...
         [and] that his writings are hortatory rather than intellec-
         tual."

2204   STEBBINS, HENRY MARTIN. "The Soldier in the English Novel."
         Ph.D. dissertation, University of Pittsburgh, 1934.

Includes discussion of Nashe's treatment of the soldier in Unfortunate Traveller. Finds that Nashe "devoted some effort to picturing the professional life of the army man" and "sympathized with the hard life of the common private."

2205   STEVENS, F. G. "Parolles and Jack Wilton's Captain." Shakespeare Review, 1 (1 July 1928), 190-96.
Suggests that Shakespeare based Parolles on Nashe's depiction of the braggart Captain in Unfortunate Traveller.

2206   STEVENSON, RUTH MacDONALD. "The Duality of Thomas Nashe." Ph.D. dissertation, Duke University, 1972, 410pp.
Uses history of ideas approach "to discover basic concepts which reveal his [Nashe's] attitudes about his world and which thereby reflect the influential ideas of his time." Discusses Unfortunate Traveller in context of examination of Nashe's "growing concern...with destructive forces which threaten, dominate, and destroy the principles of life and order and induce his ultimate retreat to the idea of art--a personal, aesthetic alternative to chaos."

2207   SUMMERSGILL, TRAVIS L. "The Influence of the Marprelate Controversy upon the Style of Thomas Nashe." SP, 48 (April 1951), 145-60.
Argues that "as a result of borrowing certain stylistic devices, attitudes toward the reader, and concepts of the function of literature from the Puritan writer [of the Marprelate tracts], he [Nashe] achieved a conversational ease and offhand brilliance hitherto unknown in English prose." (See: Donald J. McGinn, "Thomas Nashe and the Marprelate Controversy: A Correction," SP, 48 [October 1951], 798; and reply by Summersgill, pp. 798-99.)

*2208   SUMMERSGILL, TRAVIS L. "Studies in the Craftsmanship of Thomas Nashe." Ph.D. dissertation, Harvard University, 1948.
Abstract not available.

2209   SUTHERLAND, JAMES. On English Prose. The Alexander Lectures, 1956-1957. Toronto: University of Toronto Press, 1957, 133pp.
Suggests that in his prose, Nashe "is a good deal less interested in making things easy for the reader than in enjoying his own superiority over him.... He takes more delight in self-expression than in communication." Analyzes basic characteristics of Nashe's prose style (pp. 48-52, passim).

Nashe

2210   UTTER, ROBERT PALFREY. "The Beginnings of the Picaresque
            Novel in England." Harvard Monthly, April 1906, pp. 96-114.
            Argues against assumption that Unfortunate Traveller was
            influenced directly by Lazarillo de Tormes; suggests that
            work was descended from "vagabond books and conny-catching
            pamphlets." Examines lack of unity, "apparent uncertainty
            of purpose," and characterization.

2211   WEIMANN, ROBERT. "Jest-Book und Ich-Erzählung in The Unfor-
            tunate Traveller: Zum Problem des point of view in der
            Renaissance-Prosa." ZAA, 18, no. 1 (1970), 11-29.
            Analyzes Nashe's experimentation with point of view in
            Unfortunate Traveller.

2212   WOODWARD, PARKER. Euphues the Peripatician. London: Gay and
            Bird, 1907, 208pp.
            In Chapter VII ("The Peripatician," pp. 111-32) argues
            that Bacon was author of Unfortunate Traveller.

2213   YORK, ERNEST C. "Nashe and Mandeville." N&Q, NS, 4 (April
            1957), 159-60.
            Suggests that the description of the "banqueting house"
            in Unfortunate Traveller is based on "the description of
            the castle and garden of Catolonabes" in Mandeville's
            Travels.

2214   YORK, ERNEST C. "Shakespeare and Nashe." N&Q, 198 (September
            1953), 370-71.
            Suggests that Shakespeare used the rape of Heraclide as
            a source for Titus Andronicus.

2215   ZELLER, HILDEGARD. Die Ich-Erzählung im englischen Roman.
            Sprach und Kultur der Germanischen und Romanischen Völker,
            A. Anglistische Reihe, 14. Breslau: Priebatsch, 1933,
            107pp.
            Includes examination of Unfortunate Traveller in context
            of discussion of development of first person narrator in
            pre-eighteenth-century prose fiction (pp. 12-26).

THE NOBLE HYSTORY OF KYNGE PONTHUS OF GALYCE AND LYTELL BRYTAYNE

    STC 20107-20108.

Editions

2216   BRIE, FRIEDRICH. "Zwei frühneuenglische Prosaromane." Archiv,
            118 (1907), 318-28.

Provides transcript of fragment of 1510? edition of
Ponthus (STC 20107.5). See also: Friedrich Brie, "Zu
Surdyt," Archiv, 121 (1908), 129-30.

2217 "King Ponthus and the Fair Sidone: A Critical Edition." Edited by Edith Smith Krappe. Ph.D. dissertation, University
of Pennsylvania, 1953, 891pp.
      Provides reprint of 1511 edition and examines source of
text.

Studies

2218 MATHER, FRANK JEWETT, JR. "King Ponthus and the Fair Sidone."
PMLA, 12, no. 1 (1897), i-lxx, 1-150.
      In introduction to edition of English version preserved
in Bodleian MS. Digby 185, discusses relationship between
manuscript and 1511 edition, which was apparently a close
translation of a printed French version.

NORTH, THOMAS

Bidpai, The Morall Philosophie of Doni. STC 3053-3054.

Editions

2219 BIDPAI. The Earliest English Version of the Fables of Bidpai:
The Morall Philosophie of Doni. Translated by Thomas North.
Edited by Joseph Jacobs. Bibliothèque de Carabas. London:
David Nutt, 1888, 337pp.
      Provides old-spelling text based on 1570 edition. In
"Introduction" (pp. xi-lviii) traces spread of fables
throughout Eastern and Western literatures and discusses
North's style and the unity of the work.

Studies

2220 BELLORINI, MARIA GRAZIA. "Thomas North traduttore di Anton
Francesco Doni." Aevum, 38 (1964), 84-103.
      Examines North's handling of text (particularly his am-
plifications) and his style.

2221 CHITANAND, T. P. "North's The Morall Philosophie of Doni."
Indian Journal of English Studies, 3, no. 1 (1962), 112-15.
      Comments briefly on contents, style, and structure
(noting the "Oriental framework").

North

2222   COLVILE, KENNETH NEWTON. "Thomas North," in Fame's Twilight:
        Studies of Nine Men of Letters. By Kenneth Newton Colvile.
        London: P. Allan & Co., 1923, pp. 30-64.
            Includes discussion of North's style in The Moral
        Philosophy of Doni.

2223   GREENLAW, EDWIN A. "The Sources of Spenser's Mother Hubberd's
        Tale." MP, 2 (January 1905), 411-32.
            Argues that Spenser did not use North's Moral Philosophy
        of Doni as a source.

PAINTER, WILLIAM (1540?-1594)

The Palace of Pleasure. STC 19121-19125.

Editions

2224   PAINTER, WILLIAM. The Palace of Pleasure. Edited by Joseph
        Haslewood. 3 vols. London: R. Triphook, 1813, 544, 801pp.
            Provides partly modernized reprint of 1575 edition of
        Part I and of 1580? edition of Part II. In "Preliminary
        Matter," I, 3-34, provides bibliographical descriptions of
        sixteenth-century editions, notes on sources, and discussion
        of influence on later works.

2225   PAINTER, WILLIAM. "The Novel of Rhomeo and Julietta" and "The
        Story of Giletta of Narbona," in Shakespeare's Library: A
        Collection of the Romances, Novels, Poems, and Histories
        Used by Shakespeare as the Foundation of His Dramas, Vol.
        II. Edited by J[ohn] Payne Collier. London: T. Rodd,
        1843, separately paginated.
            Provides reprint based on 1567 edition for "Romeo and
        Julietta" and on 1566 edition for "Giletta." In "Introduc-
        tion [to "Romeo and Julietta"]," pp. i-viii, discusses
        Painter's style and his handling of the story. Reprinted
        in 2228.

2226   PAINTER, WILLIAM. "Giletta of Narbona," in The Works of Wil-
        liam Shakespeare, Vol. VII. By William Shakespeare. Edited
        by James O[rchard] Halliwell[-Phillipps]. London: C. & J.
        Adlard for the Editor, 1857, 4-9.
            Provides reprint of tale from 1566 edition of Palace of
        Pleasure.

2227   PAINTER, WILLIAM. "The Goodly History of the True and Constant
        Love between Rhomeo and Julietta," in The Works of William
        Shakespeare, Vol. XIII. Edited by James O[rchard]

Halliwell[-Phillipps]. London: C. & J. Adlard for the
Editor, 1864, 94-120.
Provides reprint from unidentified edition of Palace of
Pleasure.

2228　PAINTER, WILLIAM. "The Novel of Rhomeo and Julietta" and "The
Story of Giletta of Narbona," in Shakespeare's Library: A
Collection of the Plays, Romances, Novels, Poems, and His-
tories Employed by Shakespeare in the Composition of His
Works. 6 vols. Edited by John Payne Collier. 2d edition
revised. Edited by W[illiam] Carew Hazlitt. London:
Reeves and Turner, 1875, I, 205-260; III, 138-51.
Reprints 2225.

2229　PAINTER, WILLIAM. "Rhomeo and Iulietta," in Originals and
Analogues, Part I: Romeus and Iuliet, Arthur Brooke;
"Rhomeo and Iulietta," William Painter. Edited by P. A.
Daniel. New Shakspere Society, Publications, Ser. 3, no. 1.
London: N. Trübner for the New Shakspere Society, 1875,
pp. 93-144.
Provides a reprint based on 1580? edition collated with
modern editions. In "Introduction," pp. iii-xxxix, compares
the two versions of the story.

2230　PAINTER, WILLIAM. The Palace of Pleasure: Elizabethan Versions of Italian and French Novels from Boccaccio, Bandello,
Cinthio, Straparola, Queen Margaret of Navarre, and Others.
Edited by Joseph Jacobs. 3 vols. London: D. Nutt, 1890,
1319pp.
Provides old-spelling text based on a collation of 1575
edition with 2224. In "Introduction," pp. xi-xxxvi, discusses development of novella, popularity and influence
(especially on drama) of The Palace of Pleasure, and Painter's style. In "Analytical Table of Contents," pp. lxiii-
xci, provides notes on sources, parallels, and derivative
works for each of the tales. Reprints preliminary matter
from Haslewood's edition (2224). See 2244 and 2255.

*2231　PAINTER, WILLIAM. The Goodly History of the True & Constant
Love between Rhomeo & Julietta. Nelson, New Hampshire:
Monadnock Press, 1903, 84pp.
Not seen. Provides modernized reprint based on 2229.
Listed in NUC Pre-1956 Imprints, vol. 33, 500.

2232　An Elizabethan Story-Book: Famous Tales from The Palace of
Pleasure. Edited by Peter Haworth. New York: Longmans,
Green, 1928, 272pp.

Painter

> Provides modernized texts of "Giletta of Narbona,"
> "Romeo and Julietta," "Coriolanus," "Appius and Virginia,"
> "The Duchess of Malfi," "A Lady of Bohemia," "Ansaldo and
> Dianora," "Alexander de Medici and the Miller's Daughter,"
> "Sophonisba," and "A Doctor of the Laws." In "Introduc-
> tion," pp. ix-xvi, stresses use of work as a source by
> dramatists and the sensationalism of the stories.

2233 PAINTER, WILLIAM. The Palace of Pleasure. Edited by Hamish
Miles. 4 vols. London: Cresset Press, 1929, 226, 254,
264, 234pp.
Provides reprint of unidentified editions. In "Introduction," I, vii-xxv, discusses Painter's style and influence
of Palace of Pleasure; provides tabular listing of sources.

2234 PAINTER, WILLIAM. "The Duchesse of Malfi," in The Duchess of
Malfi. By John Webster. Edited by John Russell Brown.
Revels Plays. Cambridge: Harvard University Press, 1964,
pp. 175-209.
Provides reprint from 1567 edition with notes on substantive changes in 1575 edition. In "Introduction," pp. xvii-
lxxii, discusses Webster's use of tale as source.

2235 PAINTER, WILLIAM. "The Story of Giletta of Narbona" and "The
Story of Romeo and Julietta," in Elizabethan Love Stories.
Edited by T[erence] J. B. Spencer. Penguin Shakespeare
Library. Harmondsworth: Penguin Books, 1968, pp. 41-95.
Provides modernized texts based on 1566 and 1567 editions
respectively. In "Introduction," pp. 7-31, discusses rela-
tionship of stories to Shakespeare's All's Well that Ends
Well and Romeo and Juliet.

Studies

2236 ADDY, S. O. "The Decameron in English." N&Q, 73 (2 January
1886), 3-4.
Points out that only ten of Painter's tales are translations from Boccaccio.

2237 BAWCUTT, N. W. "The Revenger's Tragedy and the Medici Family."
N&Q, NS, 4 (May 1957), 192-93.
Suggests that version of life of Alessandro de' Medici in
Palace of Pleasure might have served as Tourneur's source.

2238 BISWAS, DINESH CHANDRA. Shakespeare's Treatment of His Sources
in the Comedies. Calcutta: Jadavpur University, 1971,
299pp.
Examines Shakespeare's use of Novel 38 as a source for
All's Well that Ends Well (pp. 99-108).

2239 BLUESTONE, MAX. From Story to Stage: The Dramatic Adaptation of Prose Fiction in the Period of Shakespeare and His Contemporaries. SEngL, 70. The Hague: Mouton, 1974, 341pp.
Includes examination of the adaptation and transformation of several of Painter's tales by Shakespeare in All's Well that Ends Well, by Marston and Barkstead in The Insatiate Countess, and by Heywood in The Royal King and Loyal Subject and A Woman Killed with Kindness (passim).

2240 BOKLUND, GUNNAR. The Duchess of Malfi: Sources, Themes, Characters. Cambridge: Harvard University Press, 1962, 199pp.
Includes examination of Webster's use of Palace of Pleasure as source (passim).

2241 BOOTHE, BERT E. "The Contribution of the Italian Novella to the Formation and Development of Elizabethan Prose Fiction, 1566-1582." Ph.D. dissertation, University of Michigan, 1936.
Provides detailed analysis of Painter's translations of Italian tales: examines factors affecting his selection of tales, his handling of the originals (especially his variations), his moral tone, and his narrative types.

2242 BUCHERT, JEAN R[UTH]. "Cinthio in the Palace of Pleasure: William Painter's Translations from Gli Hecatommithi." RenP 1969, pp. 1-8.
Examines Painter's tales of "Two Maidens of Corinth" and "Euphimia of Corinth," discussing their thematic and structural relationships to the work as a whole and Painter's handling of Cinthio's text (particularly his additions).

*2243 BUCHERT, JEAN RUTH. "A Critical Study of Painter's Palace of Pleasure." Ph.D. dissertation, Yale University, 1957.
Abstract not available.

2244 BUSH, DOUGLAS. "The Classical Tales in Painter's Palace of Pleasure." JEGP, 23, no. 3 (1924), 331-41.
Identifies sources of classical tales, correcting list in Jacob's edition (2230).

2245 BUSH, DOUGLAS. "William Painter and Thomas Heywood." MLN, 54 (April 1939), 279-80.
Notes editions and studies which continue to give a list of incorrect sources of Palace of Pleasure.

2246 CHICKERA, ERNST DE. "Palaces of Pleasure: The Theme of Revenge in Elizabethan Translations of Novelle." RES, NS, 11 (February 1960), 1-7.

Painter

Examines attitudes toward revenge in translations, distinguishing two types of revenge stories. Tale of President of Grenoble represents that in which "the wrong or injury comes back to the wrong-doer in almost equal measure." The tale of the revenge of a Captain on the Lords of Nocera represents that "in which the wrongdoer is punished with a severity out of all proportion to the offence."

2247   CLEMONS, W. H. "The Sources of Timon of Athens." Princeton University Bulletin, 15 (1904), 208-23.
Discusses Painter's tale of Timon in context of other Elizabethan treatments and examines Shakespeare's use of the tale as a source for the play.

2248   CRANFILL, T[HOMAS] M[ABRY]. "Barnaby Rich's 'Sappho' and The Weakest Goeth to the Wall." University of Texas Studies in English, 1945-1946, pp. 142-71.
Examines Rich's extensive borrowings from Painter's Palace of Pleasure.

2249   CUNLIFFE, JOHN W. "Gismond of Salerne." PMLA, 21 (June 1906), 435-61.
Discusses relationship between Painter's version of story and Boccaccio's to show that authors of Tancred and Gismunda used latter as source. Notes several inaccuracies in Painter's translation.

2250   DELIUS, N[IKOLAUS]. "Shakespeare's All's Well that Ends Well und Paynter's 'Giletta of Narbonne.'" Shakespeare-Jahrbuch, 22 (1887), 27-44.
Analyzes Shakespeare's use of Painter's tale as a source.

2251   DENT, R[OBERT] W. John Webster's Borrowing. Berkeley: University of California Press, 1960, 323pp.
Provides a detailed analysis of Webster's use of Palace of Pleasure as a source (passim).

2252   DICKENS, LOUIS GEORGE. "The Story of Appius and Virginia in English Literature." Ph.D. dissertation, University of Rochester, 1963, 328pp.
Includes examination of Painter's use of story.

2253   FELLHEIMER, JEANETTE. "The Source of Richard Lynche's 'Amorous Poeme of Dom Diego and Gineura.'" PMLA, 58 (June 1943), 579-80.
Argues on basis of similarity of wording of passage that Lynche's source was Painter's translation.

2254   FOSSEN, R. W. VAN. "Introduction," in <u>A Woman Killed with</u>
        <u>Kindness</u>. By Thomas Heywood. Edited by R. W. van Fossen.
        Revels Plays. Cambridge: Harvard University Press, 1961,
        196pp.
              Discusses Heywood's use of various tales from <u>Palace of</u>
        <u>Pleasure</u> as sources (pp. xvii-xxvi).

2255   FOWLER, MARY. "The Story of Sophonisba." <u>MLN</u>, 32 (June 1917),
        374-75.
              Corrects Jacobs (2230) and Scott (37), noting that Paint-
        er's source of the story is Petrarch's <u>Africa</u>, not his
        <u>Triumphs</u>.

2256   GALIGANI, GIUSEPPE. "Il Boccaccio nel Cinquecento inglese,"
        in <u>Il Boccaccio nella cultura inglese e anglo-americana</u>.
        Edited by Giuseppe Galigani. Florence: L. S. Olschki,
        1974, pp. 27-57.
              Discusses Painter's use of Boccaccio as source; examines
        Painter's handling of text, especially the effect of his
        moral emphasis.

2257   GUBAR, SUSAN DAVID. "Tudor Romance and Eighteenth-Century
        Fiction." Ph.D. dissertation, University of Iowa, 1972,
        243pp.
              Includes examination of structure and style of <u>Palace of</u>
        <u>Pleasure</u>: discusses reader response and how the tales "call
        attention to their own literariness." Also discusses how
        'Mrs. Manley's adaptations of Painter's stories reveal the
        nature of eighteenth-century objections to romance."

2258   GUSKAR, H. <u>Fletchers Monsieur Thomas und seine Quellen, Teil</u>
        <u>III</u>. Halle: Karras, 1905, 54pp.
              Includes examination of Fletcher's use of <u>Palace of</u>
        <u>Pleasure</u> as source (passim).

2259   GUSKAR, H. "Fletchers <u>Monsieur Thomas</u> und seine Quellen."
        <u>Anglia</u>, 28 (1905), 397-420; 29 (1906), 1-54.
              Examines Fletcher's use of Painter as a source. (<u>See</u>
        <u>also</u>: Arthur Ludwig Stiefel, "Zur Quellenfrage von John
        Fletcher's <u>Monsieur Thomas</u>," <u>Englische Studien</u>, 36 [1906],
        238-43; and O. L. Hatcher, "On the Sources of Fletcher's
        <u>Monsieur Thomas</u>," <u>Anglia</u>, 30 [1907], 89-102.)

2260   HOOK, FRANK S. "Introduction," in <u>The French Bandello: A</u>
        <u>Selection. The Original Text of Four of Belleforest's His-</u>
        <u>toires tragiques Translated by Geoffrey Fenton and William</u>
        <u>Painter, Anno 1567</u>. Edited by Frank S. Hook. University
        of Missouri Studies, Vol. 22, no. 1. Columbia: University
        of Missouri, 1948, pp. 9-51.

Painter

Discusses Painter's treatment of Belleforest's text and his style. Reprints four tales translated by both Painter and Fenton.

2261 HOOPER, GIFFORD. "Heywood's A Woman Killed with Kindness, Scene XIV: Sir Charles's Plan." ELN, 11 (March 1974), 181-88.
Uses Painter's tale of Salimbene and Angelica, the source of Heywood's subplot, as support for argument that Sir Charles plans to marry his sister to Sir Francis, not to prostitute her.

2262 HORNÁT, JAROSLAV. Anglická renesanční próza: eufuistická beletrie od Pettieho Paláce Potěchy do Greenova Pandosta [Renaissance Prose in England: Euphuistic Fiction from Pettie's Palace of Pleasure to Greene's Pandosto]. Acta Universitatis Carolinae, Philologica, Monographia 33. Prague: Universita Karlova, 1970, 173pp.
Discusses blend of entertainment and didacticism in Palace of Pleasure, Painter's literalness in translation, and the euphuistic characteristics of his style (pp. 19-27).

2263 KÄMPFER, OSCAR. Das Verhältnis von Thomas Heywoods The Royal King and the Loyal Subject zu Painters Palace of Pleasure. Halle: Druck von Wischan & Wettengel, 1903, 52pp.
Provides detailed examination of Heywood's use of Palace of Pleasure as source.

2264 KIESOW, KARL. "Die verschiedenen Bearbeitungen der Novelle von der Herzogin von Amalfi des Bandello in den Literaturen des XVI. und XVII. Jahrhunderts." Anglia, 17 (1895), 199-258.
Includes discussion of Painter's adaptation of Belleforest's version and Webster's use of Painter as a source for Duchess of Malfi.

2265 KIMMELMAN, ELAINE. "The Palace of Pleasure." Boston Public Library Quarterly, 2 (1950), 231-44.
Describes copy of first edition acquired by Boston Public Library, outlines contents, and characterizes use by playwrights as source-book.

2266 KOEPPEL, EMIL. Quellen-Studien zu den Dramen Ben Jonson's, John Marston's, und Beaumont's und Fletcher's. Münchener Beiträge zur Romanischen und Englischen Philologie, 11. Erlangen and Leipzig: Deichert, 1895, 158pp.
Includes discussion of use of Palace of Pleasure as source by Marston, Beaumont and Fletcher, Thomas Heywood, and Massinger (passim).

2267   KOEPPEL, EMIL. <u>Studien zur Geschichte der italienischen
Novelle in der englischen Litteratur des sechzehnten Jahr-
hunderts</u>. Quellen und Forschungen, 70. Strassburg: K. J.
Trübner, 1892, 106pp.
  Identifies Painter's Italian sources and discusses his
style (pp. 1-12).

2268   LAGARDE, FERNAND. <u>John Webster</u>. 2 vols. Publications de la
Faculté des Lettres et Sciences Humaines de Toulouse, Série
A, 7. Toulouse: Association des Publications de la
Faculté des Lettres et Sciences Humaines de Toulouse, 1968,
1418pp.
  Includes discussion of Webster's use of <u>Palace of Plea-
sure</u> as a source for <u>Duchess of Malfi</u> (pp. 436-40, 443-49,
passim).

2269   LAWRENCE, WILLIAM WITHERLE. "The Meaning of <u>All's Well that
Ends Well</u>." <u>PMLA</u>, 37 (September 1922), 418-69.
  Discusses analogues of story of Giletta of Narbona.

2270   LUNDEBERG, OLAV K. "The True Sources of Robert Dodsley's <u>The
King and the Miller of Mansfield</u>." <u>MLN</u>, 39 (November 1924),
394-97.
  Suggests that "King Mansor of Morocco" and "Alexander de
Medici and the Miller's Daughter" were used as sources for
the play.

2271   MARTIN, ROBERT G. "A New Source for <u>A Woman Killed with Kind-
ness</u>." <u>Englische Studien</u>, 43, no. 2 (1911), 229-33.
  Examines Heywood's use of Painter's tale of "A Fair Lady
of Turin" as a source for the main plot.

2272   MAXWELL, J[AMES] C[LOUTTS]. "William Painter's Use of Mexía."
<u>N&Q</u>, NS, 1 (January 1954), 16.
  Points out that Novel I, 26 is from Claude Gruget's
French translation of Mexía's <u>Silva de varia lección</u>. Notes
that Painter also used Mambrino da Fabriano's Italian translation.

2273   MERLE, ALFRED. <u>Massingers The Picture und Painter II, 28</u>.
Halle: Hofbuchdruckerei von C. A. Kaemmerer, 1905, 55pp.
  Analyzes Massinger's use of Painter's tale of "Lady of
Bohemia" as source.

2274   MIGLIOR, GIORGIO. "Bandello e Painter." <u>Studi e Ricerche di
Letteratura Inglese e Americana</u>, 1 (1967), 21-45.
  Examines Painter's use of tales by Bandello: discusses
his choice of tales, his style, his didacticism, and his

Painter

> handling of text. (Focuses on tale of Countess of Celant.)
> Also considers influence on Elizabethan drama.

*2275 ÖFTERING, MICHAEL. Die Geschichte der "Schönen Irene" in den
       modernen Litteraturen. Würzburg: Stürtz, 1897, 56pp.
         Not seen. Listed in NUC Pre-1956 Imprints, vol. 426,
       695.

2276 PATTERSON, McEVOY. "Origin of the Main Plot of A Woman Killed
      with Kindness." University of Texas Studies in English, 17
      (July 1937), 75-87.
         Argues that Heywood used "A Punishment More Rigorous than
      Death" and "A Gentleman of Perche" as sources.

2277 PRESSON, ROBERT K. "Marston's Dutch Courtezan: The Study of
      an Attitude in Adaptation." JEGP, 55, no. 3 (1956), 406-13.
         Focuses on differences between play and Painter's story
      of Countess of Celant, Marston's probable source.

2278 PRICE, JOHN EDWARD. "William Painter's 'Giletta of Narbona'
      and 'Rhomeo and Julietta': An Analytical Study with Com-
      parison of Sources and Analogues." Ph.D. dissertation,
      Loyola University of Chicago, 1970.
         Analyzes the two works "to define their literary quali-
      ties...and...to place them in the historical development of
      the legends to which they belong."

2279 PRUVOST, RENÉ. Matteo Bandello and Elizabethan Fiction.
      Bibliothèque de la Revue de Littérature Comparée, 113.
      Paris: H. Champion, 1937, 349pp.
         Analyzes Painter's style, treatment of the text, and ad-
      ditions in his translations of Bandello. Examines in par-
      ticular his moral emphasis. Compares his translation of
      several tales with later translations/adaptations and dis-
      cusses influence of Painter on development of Elizabethan
      prose fiction (passim).

2280 ROBERTS, ARTHUR J. "The Sources of Romeo and Juliet." MLN,
      17 (February 1902), 41-44.
         Compares Painter's version with Brooke's poem, finding
      that the latter is a much superior treatment of the story
      and that Shakespeare owed nothing to Painter.

2281 RODAX, YVONNE R. "The Real and the Ideal in Novelle of Italy,
      France, and England." Ph.D. dissertation, New York Univer-
      sity, 1968, 221pp.
         See 2282.

2282   RODAX, YVONNE [R.]. <u>The Real and the Ideal in the Novella of</u>
        <u>Italy, France, and England: Four Centuries of Change in</u>
        <u>the Boccaccian Tale</u>. UNCSCL, 44. Chapel Hill: University
        of North Carolina Press, 1968, 144pp.
            Examines Painter's naturalization of the tales, his
        style, and his tendency to moralize without regard for a
        relationship to plot (pp. 94-99).

2282a   ROSSI, SERGIO. "Goodly histories, tragicall matters, and other
        morall argument: La novella italiana nel Cinquecento
        inglese," in <u>Contributi dell'Istituto di filologia moderna</u>.
        Edited by Sergio Rossi. Pubblicazioni della Università
        Cattolica del Sacro Cuore, Serie Inglese, 1. Milan: Vita
        e Pensiero, 1974, pp. 39-112.
            Surveys publications of 1566-1567 to place <u>Palace of</u>
        <u>Pleasure</u> and Fenton's <u>Certain Tragical Discourses</u> in context
        of continuing development of literature with a moral empha-
        sis. Discusses significance of "Palace" in title, Painter's
        structure and purpose, his treatment of the original texts,
        and the dramatic qualities of the tales.

2283   SHERBO, ARTHUR. "<u>The Knight of Malta</u> and Boccaccio's <u>Filo-</u>
        <u>colo</u>." <u>ES</u>, 33 (1952), 254-57.
            Argues that the <u>Palace of Pleasure</u> is not the source of
        the play; rather it is Boccaccio's <u>Filocolo</u>, probably in
        Grantham's translation. Compares Painter's story of Don
        John of Mendoza with Grantham's version.

2284   SHERWOOD, CLARENCE. <u>Die Neu-Englischen Bearbeitungen der</u>
        <u>Erzählung Boccaccios von Ghismonda und Guiscardo</u>. Berlin:
        Sittenfeld, 1892, 56pp.
            Includes discussion of Painter's handling of text (es-
        pecially his expansions and alterations); compares Painter's
        treatment of story with Boccaccio's (pp. 11-21).

2285   SMALLWOOD, R. L. "The Design of <u>All's Well that Ends Well</u>."
        <u>ShS</u>, 25 (1972), 45-61.
            Examines how Shakespeare uses and transforms Painter's
        tale of Giletta of Narbona, a source of the play.

2286   STARNES, D. T. "Barnabe Riche's 'Sappho Duke of Mantona': A
        Study in Elizabethan Story-Telling." <u>SP</u>, 30 (July 1933),
        455-72.
            Analyzes Rich's use of Painter's collection (especially
        "The Duchess of Malfi") as source for his story.

2287   TURNER, ROBERT Y. "Dramatic Conventions in <u>All's Well that</u>
        <u>Ends Well</u>." <u>PMLA</u>, 75 (December 1960), 497-502.

Painter

> Discusses changes made by Shakespeare in his use of
> "Giletta of Narbona." Notes that in tale "there is no pur-
> gation or alteration of character whatsoever"; the emphasis
> is on Giletta's fitness as wife to the Count.

2288 WAITH, EUGENE M. "A Tragicomedy of Humors: Fletcher's The
>   Loyal Subject." MLQ, 6 (September 1945), 299-311.
>   Compares Painter's story of Ariobarzanes with Fletcher's
>   treatment.

2289 WILKES, G. A. "The Sources of Fulke Greville's Mustapha."
>   N&Q, NS, 5 (August 1958), 329-30.
>   Points out that Mustapha story was available through
>   Painter's tale of "Sultan Soliman," a translation of Nicho-
>   las Moffan's Soltani Solymanni.

2290 WILSON, HAROLD S. "Dramatic Emphasis in All's Well that Ends
>   Well." HLQ, 13 (May 1950), 217-40.
>   Discusses Shakespeare's use of Painter's tale of Giletta
>   of Narbona as source.

2291 WRIGHT, HERBERT G[LADSTONE]. Boccaccio in England from Chaucer
>   to Tennyson. London: Athlone Press, University of London,
>   1957, 509pp.
>   Includes discussion of Painter's handling of text in his
>   translations from the Decameron: examines Painter's altera-
>   tions and his didacticism. Finds that second volume of
>   Palace of Pleasure has more coherence than first.

2292 WRIGHT, HERBERT G[LADSTONE]. "The Indebtedness of Painter's
>   Translations from Boccaccio in The Palace of Pleasure to
>   the French Version of le Maçon." MLR, 46 (July & October
>   1951), 431-35.
>   Discusses Painter's reliance on Le Maçon's translation.

PARKER, HENRY (1476-1556)

[Masuccio Salernitano, Novella 49 from Novellino. British Library MS.
  Royal 18.A.62.]

Editions

2293 BRIE, FRIEDRICH. "Die erste Übersetzung einer italienischen
>   Novelle ins Englische durch Henry Parker, Lord Morley (ca.
>   A.D. 1545)." Archiv, 124 (1910), 46-57.
>   Provides transcription of Parker's translation (British
>   Library MS. Royal 18.A.62) of the forty-ninth novella of

Masuccio's <u>Novellino</u>. Discusses work in context of English translation of Italian novelle.

PARRY, ROBERT (fl. 1588-1597)

Moderatus: <u>The Most Delectable & Famous Historie of the Blacke Knight</u>. STC 19337.

Diego Ortuñez de Calahorra et al, <u>Myrrour of Knighthood</u>, Parts II-VI, IX. <u>STC</u> 18862-18868, 18871.

Studies

2294 ATKINSON, DOROTHY F. "The Authorship of <u>The Mirror of Knight-hood</u>, Part Nine." <u>MLQ</u>, 6 (June 1945), 175-86.
      On basis of style, sentence structure, and vocabulary, argues that R. P. (not L. A.) translated ninth part. Supplements earlier evidence identifying R. P. as Robert Parke (2296).

2295 ATKINSON, DOROTHY F. "Busirane's Castle and Artidon's Cave." <u>MLQ</u>, 1 (1940), 185-92.
      Discusses "the nature and extent of Spenser's debt [in <u>Faerie Queene</u> (III, xi-xii)]...to the first (1578) and second (1585) parts of the <u>Mirrour</u>."

2296 ATKINSON, DOROTHY F. "One R. P." <u>MLQ</u>, 6 (March 1945), 3-12.
      Identifies R. P. as Robert Parke on basis of similarity of vocabulary and style between R. P.'s translation of the <u>Mirror</u> and Parke's translation of <u>The History of China</u>.

2297 ATKINSON, DOROTHY F. "The Pastorella Episode in <u>The Faerie Queene</u>." <u>PMLA</u>, 59 (June 1944), 361-72.
      Argues that Claridiano pastoral of fourth and fifth parts, and portions of second, of <u>Mirror</u> is source for Pastorella section. Observes that although the <u>Mirror</u> is a collection of familiar stories, "its redaction of these stories presents new details which make the <u>Mirrour</u> an independent vehicle for the transmission of the old tales."

2298 BROWN, ELAINE V. BEILIN. "The Uses of Mythology in Elizabethan Romance." Ph.D. dissertation, Princeton University, 1973, 336pp.
      Analyzes Parry's use of the Venus myth in <u>Moderatus</u>.

2299 EVANS, DOROTHY A[TKINSON]. "Some Notes on Shakspere and <u>The Mirror of Knighthood</u>." <u>Shakespeare Association Bulletin</u>, 21 (October 1946), 161-67; 22 (April 1947), 62-68.

Parry

  Examines Shakespeare's possible use of the <u>Mirror</u>, Parts III and V, in <u>Much Ado about Nothing</u>, <u>The Tempest</u>, <u>Cymbeline</u>, and <u>Hamlet</u>.

2300 GOLDER, HAROLD. "Bunyan's Valley of the Shadow." <u>MP</u>, 27 (August 1929), 55-72.
  Uses examples from <u>Mirror</u> to illustrate influence of earlier romances on narrative framework of <u>Pilgrim's Progress</u>. Discusses, in particular, the conventional elements of the descent into a cave or dark valley.

2301 O'CONNOR, JOHN J. "Three Additional <u>Much Ado</u> Sources," in <u>Essays in Literary History Presented to J. Milton French</u>. Edited by Rudolf Kirk and C. F. Main. New Brunswick: Rutgers University Press, 1960, pp. 81-91.
  Suggests three different episodes in Parry's translation of <u>Mirror</u> that Shakespeare might have used as sources for the Hero-Claudio plot.

2302 PEROTT, JOSEPH DE. "<u>The Mirrour of Knighthood</u>." <u>RR</u>, 4 (October-December 1913), 397-402.
  Suggests that first three Books were published by 1579. Explains allusion to <u>Mirror</u> in Lyly's <u>Euphues</u>.

2303 PEROTT, JOSEPH DE. "Über eine Anno 1587 Erschienene Heute aber Gänzlich Vergessene Novelle als Quelle von Massinger's <u>A Very Woman</u>." <u>Anglia</u>, 39 (1916), 201-208.
  Examines Massinger's use of <u>Mirror</u>, Part III, as source.

2304 THOMAS, HENRY. <u>Spanish and Portuguese Romances of Chivalry: The Revival of the Romance of Chivalry in the Spanish Peninsula, and Its Extension and Influence Abroad</u>. Cambridge: Cambridge University Press, 1920, 343pp.
  Includes discussion of the translation of the various parts of the <u>Mirror</u>, allusions to the work in drama, and its use as a source in various plays (passim).

2305 WELD, JOHN SALTAR. "Studies in the Euphuistic Novel, 1576-1640." Ph.D. dissertation, Harvard University, 1940, 304pp.
  Characterizes <u>Moderatus</u> as "an amazing compound of chivalry, euphuistic courtship, and pastoral verse." Traces sources of work.

<u>THE PARSON OF KALENBOROWE</u>
 By P. Frankfurter.

 <u>STC</u> 14894.5.

Pasquils Jests Mixed with Mother Bunches Merriments

Editions

2306   SCHRÖDER, EDWARD. "Der Parson of Kalenborow und seine niederdeutsche Quelle." Jahrbuch des Vereins für Niederdeutsche
Sprachforschung, 13 (1887), 129-52.
       Provides reprint of major part of extant fragment and
examines relationship with source.

Studies

2307   FERRARA, FERNANDO. Jests e Merry Tales: Aspetti della narrativa popolaresca inglese del sedicesimo secolo. Nuovi
Saggi, 27. Rome: Editrice dell'Ateneo, 1960, 257pp.
       Examines place of Parson of Kalenberg in development of
sixteenth-century jest book; discusses style and structure
of work (pp. 100-105).

2308   HERFORD, CHARLES H. Studies in the Literary Relations of
England and Germany in the Sixteenth Century. Cambridge:
Cambridge University Press, 1886, 456pp.
       Includes comparison of the Parson of Kalenberg with the
German Volksbuch to illustrate that the English version is
not a mere translation "but a free and independent handling
of the story" (pp. 275-81).

PASQUILS JESTS MIXED WITH MOTHER BUNCHES MERRIMENTS

   STC 19451-19453.3. Wing P655.

Editions

2309   Pasquils Jests Mixed with Mother Bunch's Merriments, in
Shakespeare Jest-Books, Vol. III. Edited by W[illiam]
Carew Hazlitt. London: Willis & Sotheran, 1864, 84pp.
(separately paginated). [Also published separately.]
       Provides an annotated reprint of a transcript of the
1603 edition. In "Introduction," III, 2-6, discusses the
bibliographical history of the work and suggests that Breton was the author.

Studies

2310   FRIEDMAN, ARTHUR. "Goldsmith and the Jest-Books." MP, 53
(August 1955), 47-49.
       In discussion of sources·for "four unexplained stories
in his [Goldsmith's] writings" suggests jest of "A Notable
Young Rogue" as analogue to "A Flemish Tradition," Bee,
No. IV.

Paynell

PAYNELL, THOMAS (fl. 1528–1567)

The Moste Excellent Booke Entituled: The Treasurie of Amadis of
Fraunce. STC 545.

Studies

*2311 HIRTEN, WILLIAM J. "The Life and Works of Thomas Paynell."
       Ph.D. dissertation, Yale University, 1943.
          Abstract not available.

2312   THOMAS, HENRY. "English Translations of Portuguese Books
       before 1640." Library, 4th Ser., 7 (June 1926), 1–30.
          Notes that Paynell's Amadis of France is translated from
       one of the editions of Le Thresor des douze livres d'Amadis
       de Gaule.

2313   THOMAS, HENRY. "English Translations of Portuguese Books
       before 1640," in Miscelânea de estudos em honra de D. Caro-
       lina Michaëlis de Vasconcellos. Revista da Universidade de
       Coimbra, 1. Coimbra, Portugal: Universidad de Coimbra,
       1933, pp. 690–711.
          Discusses dating of Paynell's translation of Amadis.

PEELE, GEORGE (1556–1596)

Merrie Conceited Jests of George Peele. STC 19541–19544.5. Wing
P1053–1054.

Bibliographies

2314   JOHNSON, ROBERT C. "George Peele, 1939–1965," in Elizabethan
       Bibliographies Supplements, V: Robert Greene, 1945–1965;
       Thomas Lodge, 1939–1965; John Lyly, 1939–1965; Thomas Nashe,
       1941–1965; George Peele, 1939–1965. Compiled by Robert C.
       Johnson. London: Nether Press, 1968, 57–63.
          Provides chronological list of editions and criticism,
       1939–1965; supplements 2315.

2315   TANNENBAUM, SAMUEL A. George Peele (A Concise Bibliography).
       Elizabethan Bibliographies, 15. New York: Samuel A.
       Tannenbaum, 1940, 46pp.
          Provides classified list of editions and criticism. Con-
       tinued by 2314.

Editions

2316 PEELE, GEORGE. Merrie Conceited Iests, of George Peele.
      London: Singer and Triphook, 1809, 33pp.
          Provides reprint of 1627 edition.

2317 PEELE, GEORGE. Peele's Merry Conceited Jests, in The Works of
      George Peele, Vol. II. By George Peele. Edited by Alexan-
      der Dyce. 2d edition. London: William Pickering, 1829,
      263-302.
          Provides modernized text based on 1627 edition. In
      "Some Account of George Peele and His Writings," I, i-xxxix,
      discusses biographical value of work.

2318 PEELE, GEORGE. Peele's Merry Conceited Jests, in The Dramatic
      and Poetical Works of Robert Greene & George Peele. By
      Robert Greene and George Peele. Edited by Alexander Dyce.
      London and New York: Routledge, Warne, and Routledge, 1861,
      pp. 607-20.
          Provides modernized text of 1627 edition. In "Some Ac-
      count of George Peele and His Writings" (pp. 323-46) notes
      that the Jests is "a work of fiction."

2319 PEELE, GEORGE. Merrie Conceited Jests of George Peele, in
      Shakespeare Jest-Books, Vol. II. Edited by W[illiam] Carew
      Hazlitt. London: Willis & Sotheran, 1864, 261-310.
          Provides a slightly modernized, annotated reprint of
      1607 edition. In brief introductory note discusses the
      bibliographical history of the work.

2320 PEELE, GEORGE. Merry Conceited Jests of George Peele, in The
      Old Book Collector's Miscellany: Or a Collection of Read-
      able Reprints of Literary Rarities, Illustrative of the
      History, Literature, Manners, and Biography of the English
      Nation During the Sixteenth and Seventeenth Centuries, Vol.
      I. Edited by Charles Hindley. London: Reeves and Turner,
      1871, 48pp. (separately paginated).
          Provides modernized reprint of 1630? edition.

2321 PEELE, GEORGE. Merry Conceited Jests of George Peele, in The
      Works of George Peele, Vol. II. By George Peele. Edited
      by A[rthur] H[enry] Bullen. London: J. C. Nimmo, 1888,
      373-404.
          Provides annotated, modernized reprint of 1627 edition.
      In "Introduction" (I, xiii-xliii) suggests that work has
      some biographical value.

Peele

Studies

2322   CHRISTIAN, MILDRED GAYLER. "Middleton's Acquaintance with
         the Merrie Conceited Jests of George Peele." PMLA, 50
         (September 1935), 753-60.
             Discusses Middleton's use of Merry Conceited Jests as
         source for A Mad World, My Masters, Your Five Gallants, and
         The Puritan.

*2323   CHRISTIAN, MILDRED GAYLER. "Non-Dramatic Sources for the
         Rogues in Middleton's Plays." Ph.D. dissertation, Univer-
         sity of Chicago, 1932.
             Abstract not available; see 2322.

2324   HORNE, DAVID H. "The Life," in The Life and Minor Works of
         George Peele. Edited by David H. Horne. The Life and Works
         of George Peele, Vol. I. By George Peele. Edited by
         Charles Tyler Prouty. New Haven: Yale University Press,
         1952, pp. 1-131.
             Examines sources and analogues of Merry Conceited Jests
         in an attempt to ascertain what elements are biographical.
         Suggests that some jests include biographical material and
         that author of work had negative attitude toward Peele.

2325   LEE, A. COLLINGWOOD. ["The Puritan."] N&Q, 129 (21 February
         1914), 156-57.
             Points out that play is partly based on jest of Peele
         and the barber.

2326   WILLIAMSON, MARILYN L. "Middleton's Workmanship and the Au-
         thorship of The Puritan." N&Q, NS, 4 (February 1957),
         50-51.
             Suggests that use of Merry Conceited Jests as a source
         for The Puritan is supporting evidence of Middleton's au-
         thorship.

PETTIE, GEORGE (1548-1589?)

A Petite Pallace of Pettie His Pleasure: Conteyning Many Pretie Histories. STC 19819-19823.

Editions

*2327   PETTIE, GEORGE. "The Tale of Tereus and Progne," Referred to
         Several Times by Shakespeare. Edited by J[ames] O[rchard]
         Halliwell[-Phillipps]. London: n.p., 1866, 36pp.
             Not seen. Issued in 11 copies. Listed in NUC Pre-1956
         Imprints, vol. 453, 650.

2328   PETTIE, GEORGE. <u>A Petite Pallace of Pettie His Pleasure</u>.
        Edited by I[srael] Gollancz. King's Classics. 2 vols.
        London: Chatto and Windus, 1908, 230, 200pp.
            Reprints slightly modernized text of 1576 edition and
        provides collations with editions of 1586?, 1590?, and 1608.
        In "Preface" (I, ix-xxvi) discusses Pettie's euphuistic
        style, the sources of the tales, and the bibliographical
        history of the work.

2329   PETTIE, GEORGE. "Tereus and Progne," in <u>Elizabethan Tales</u>.
        Edited by Edward J[oseph] O'Brien. London: G. Allen &
        Unwin, 1937, pp. 95-109.
            Provides modernized text based on unidentified edition.

2330   PETTIE, GEORGE. <u>A Petite Pallace of Pettie His Pleasure</u>.
        Edited by Herbert Hartman. Oxford: Oxford University
        Press, 1938, 361pp.
            Reprints text of 1576 edition with collations from the
        other sixteenth- and seventeenth-century editions. In the
        notes, traces sources of plots and proverbs. In "Introduc-
        tion," pp. ix-xxxiv, discusses the bibliographical history
        of the work; Pettie's use of <u>questioni d'amore</u>, <u>exempla</u>, and
        <u>sententiae</u>; and his euphuistic style.

Studies

2331   BOND, R[ICHARD] WARWICK. "<u>Euphues</u> and Euphuism," in <u>The Com-
        plete Works of John Lyly</u>, Vol. I. By John Lyly. Edited by
        R[ichard] Warwick Bond. Oxford: Clarendon Press, 1902,
        119-75.
            Includes discussion of characteristics of Pettie's style
        and finds in <u>Petite Palace</u> "an exact model of the style of
        <u>Euphues</u>."

2332   BORINSKI, LUDWIG. "Diego de San Pedro und die euphuistische
        Erzählung." <u>Anglia</u>, 89, no. 2 (1971), 224-39.
            Analyzes influence of San Pedro's <u>Arnalte y Lucenda</u> and
        <u>Cárcel de amor</u> upon form, style, subject matter, and themes
        of tales in <u>Petite Palace</u>.

2333   BORINSKI, LUDWIG. "The Origin of the Euphuistic Novel and Its
        Significance for Shakespeare," in <u>Studies in Honor of T. W.
        Baldwin</u>. Edited by Don Cameron Allen. Urbana: University
        of Illinois Press, 1958, pp. 38-52.
            Credits Pettie with the development of the euphuistic
        novel and examines the influence of Belleforest and <u>The
        Goodly History of the Lady Lucrece</u> on Pettie's tales. Ana-
        lyzes characteristics of the euphuistic novel.

Pettie

2334 BUSH, DOUGLAS. "The Petite Pallace of Pettie His Pleasure."
      JEGP, 27, no. 2 (1928), 162-69.
          Identifies sources and isolates general characteristics
      (subject matter, plot, style, moralizing, etc.) of tales.
      Also considers influence of Belleforest.

2335 BUSH, J. N. DOUGLAS. "Martin Parker's Philomela." MLN, 40
      (December 1925), 486-88.
          Discusses Parker's close dependence on tale of Tereus
      and Progne as source.

2336 BUSH, J. N. DOUGLAS. "Pettie's Petty Pilfering from Poets."
      PQ, 5 (October 1926), 325-29.
          Points out "that certain aspects of...[Pettie's] euphuism
      owe something to his study of the verse of his age."

2337 DICKENS, LOUIS GEORGE. "The Story of Appius and Virginia in
      English Literature." Ph.D. dissertation, University of
      Rochester, 1963, 328pp.
          Includes examination of Pettie's use of story.

2338 GUBAR, SUSAN DAVID. "Tudor Romance and Eighteenth-Century
      Fiction." Ph.D. dissertation, University of Iowa, 1972,
      243pp.
          Includes examination of structure and style of Petite
      Palace: discusses reader response and how the tales "call
      attention to their own literariness."

2339 HORNÁT, JAROSLAV. Anglická renesanční próza: eufuistická
      beletrie od Pettieho Paláce Potěchy do Greenova Pandosto
      [Renaissance Prose in England: Euphuistic Fiction from
      Pettie's Palace of Pleasure to Greene's Pandosto]. Acta
      Universitatis Carolinae, Philologica, Monographia 33.
      Prague: Universita Karlova, 1970, 173pp.
          Analyzes euphuistic characteristics of Pettie's style.
      Provides detailed examination of tale of Sinorix and Camma
      to illustrate "construction of plots and elements of compo-
      sition typical of the euphuistic 'love pamphlets' popular
      in Elizabethan England after Pettie and Lyly" (pp. 28-36).

2340 HORNÁT, JAROSLAV. "George Pettie, eufuista před Eufuem"
      [George Pettie, an Euphuist before Euphues]. ČMF, 42
      (1960), 143-57.
          Analyzes Pettie's style, plot construction, and "elements
      of composition" to illustrate that Petite Palace includes
      the basic characteristics of euphuism. Shows how Pettie's
      stories "reveal a vigorous tendency to suppress the dynamic
      components of plot and to stress the rhetorical devices of
      ornamental and well-balanced speeches...which represent the

quintessence of an euphuistic narrative." Includes English summary.

2341 KOEPPEL, EMIL. Studien zur Geschichte der italienischen Novelle in der englischen Litteratur des sechzehnten Jahrhunderts. Quellen und Forschungen, 70. Strassburg: K. J. Trübner, 1892, 106pp.
Identifies Italian sources of Petite Palace and discusses Pettie's style (pp. 21-29).

2342 PRUVOST, RENÉ. Matteo Bandello and Elizabethan Fiction. Bibliothèque de la Revue de Littérature Comparée, 113. Paris: H. Champion, 1937, 349pp.
Examines the influence of Bandello on Pettie, his "use of sentimental and moralizing rhetoric," and his detachment toward moral issues (passim).

2343 RINGLER, WILLIAM [A.]. "The Immediate Source of Euphuism." PMLA, 53 (September 1938), 678-86.
Argues that euphuism was developed and perfected by John Rainolds in his Latin lectures, which provided the model for the euphuistic style of Lyly, Pettie, Gosson, and Lodge.

2344 STARNES, D. T. "Literary Features of Renaissance Dictionaries." SP, 37 (January 1940), 26-50.
Includes detailed examination of Pettie's use of Cooper's Thesaurus as a source for at least six of his stories.

2345 SWART, J. "Lyly and Pettie." ES, 23 (1941), 9-18.
Provides a statistical analysis of sentence structure, alliteration, and sound patterns in comparing the styles of the two writers. Finds "in Pettie's use of rhetorical devices a lack of restraint."

2346 TILLEY, MORRIS PALMER. Elizabethan Proverb Lore in Lyly's Euphues and in Pettie's Petite Pallace with Parallels from Shakespeare. University of Michigan Publications, Language and Literature, 2. New York: Macmillan Co., 1926, 471pp.
Provides lists of proverbs in Petite Palace. Discusses Lyly's borrowing of proverbs from Pettie and in Appendix A (pp. 357-82) traces passages from Petite Palace in the Maxwell Younger Manuscript (1586). Proverbs from Petite Palace later subsumed in: Morris Palmer Tilley, A Dictionary of the Proverbs in England in the Sixteenth and Seventeenth Centuries: A Collection of Proverbs Found in English Literature and Dictionaries of the Period (Ann Arbor: University of Michigan Press, 1950), 866pp.

Pettie

2347   TOOR, DAVID SYDNEY. "Euphuism in England before John Lyly."
       Ph.D. dissertation, University of Oregon, 1965, 197pp.
          Includes discussion of Petite Palace, which "shows full-
       flowered euphuism," in examination of development of the
       style in English prose.

2348   VINCENT, C[HARLES] J[ACKSON]. "Pettie and Greene." MLN, 54
       (February 1939), 105-11.
          Provides evidence of Greene's borrowings from Pettie,
       arguing that Petite Palace, rather than Lyly's Euphues, is
       the main source of Greene's prose style.

PHILLIPS, EDWARD

Juan Perez de Montalván, The Illustrious Shepherdess; The Imperious
   Brother. Wing P1469.

Studies

2349   HONE, RALPH E. "Edward and John Phillips: Nephews and Pupils
       of John Milton." Ph.D. dissertation, New York University,
       1955, 920pp.
          "[D]iscuss[es] the works of the brothers biographically,
       historically, critically, and bibliographically."

THE PINDER OF WAKEFIELD: BEING THE MERRY HISTORY OF GEORGE A GREENE

   STC 12213.

Editions

2350   The Pinder of Wakefield. Edited by E. A. Horsman. English Re-
       prints Series, 12. Liverpool: Liverpool University Press,
       1956, 107pp.
          Provides annotated reprint of 1632 edition. In "Intro-
       duction," pp. vii-xii, discusses relationship between Pinder
       of Wakefield, the play, and the manuscript romance ("The
       Famous History of George a Greene"). Also discusses folk-
       lore sources of the work.

Studies

2351   GARKE, ESTHER. The Use of Songs in Elizabethan Prose Fiction.
       Bern: Francke Verlag, 1972, 132pp.
          Draws frequently on Pinder of Wakefield for examples in
       analysis of types of songs, their relationships to plot and

structure, and their functions (to complement or contrast
setting, to present character relationships, to characterize
singer and audience).

2352 NELSON, MALCOLM ANTHONY. "The Robin Hood Tradition in English
Literature in the Sixteenth and Seventeenth Centuries."
Ph.D. dissertation, Northwestern University, 1961, 274pp.
See 2353.

2353 NELSON, MALCOLM A[NTHONY]. The Robin Hood Tradition in the
English Renaissance. ElizS, 14. Salzburg: Institut für
Englische Sprache und Literatur, Universität Salzburg,
1973, 269pp.
Discusses Pinder of Wakefield in context of the Robin
Hood tradition; examines eclecticism of anonymous author,
who drew upon folklore, folk games, jest book tradition,
and earlier Robin Hood works (pp. 191-205).

2354 O., T. P. "The Pinder of Wakefield." N&Q, 41 (15 January
1870), 57-58.
Provides transcription of title page and first chapter
of 1632 edition.

2355 PÄTZOLD, KURT-MICHAEL. "Thomas Deloneys Thomas of Reading und
das Jest-Book The Pinder of Wakefield: Eine vergleichende
Interpretation." NM, 72 (1971), 113-26.
Examines Deloney's use of Pinder of Wakefield as source.

THE PLEASANT HISTORY OF CAWWOOD THE ROOKE

STC 4889. Wing P2548-2549.

Editions

2356 The Pleasant History of Cawwod the Rooke, in Short Fiction of
the Seventeenth Century. Edited by Charles C[arroll] Mish.
Stuart Editions. New York: New York University Press,
1963, pp. 339-63.
Provides modernized reprint of 1640 edition. In a brief
introductory note, discusses the relationship with Reynard
the Fox. See 60.

A PLEASANT HISTORY OF THE LIFE AND DEATH OF WILL SUMMERS

STC 22917.5. Wing P2551.

A Pleasant History of...Will Summers

Studies

2357   MISH, CHARLES C[ARROLL]. "Will Summers: An Unrecorded Jest-
       book." PQ, 31 (April 1952), 215-18.
           Describes structure and contents of unique copy of 1637
       edition.

RATSEIS GHOST: OR THE SECOND PART OF HIS MADDE PRANKES AND ROBBERIES

   STC 20753a.

Editions

2358   Ratseis Ghost, or the Second Part of His Madde Prankes and
       Robberies (1605). Introduction by H. B. Charlton. John
       Rylands Facsimiles, 5. Manchester: Manchester University
       Press and John Rylands Library, 1932, not paginated.
           Provides facsimile reprint of 1605 edition. In "Intro-
       duction," pp. vii-xiii, discusses work as rogue literature.

2359   Ratseis Ghost, in The Life and Death of Gamaliel Ratsey, 1605.
       Introduction by S. H. Atkins. Shakespeare Association Fac-
       similes, 10. London: Oxford University Press for the
       Shakespeare Association, 1935, not paginated.
           Provides facsimile reprint of 1605 edition. In "Intro-
       duction," pp. v-xii, discusses the notoriety of Ratsey and
       the popularity of works about him.

Studies

2360   LIEVSAY, JOHN LEON. "Newgate Penitents: Further Aspects of
       Elizabethan Pamphlet Sensationalism." HLQ, 7 (November
       1943), 47-69.
           Traces use of Greene's works as sources for Ratsey's
       Ghost. Argues that Samuel Rowlands was the author. See
       2361.

2361   O'CONNOR, JOHN J. "On the Authorship of the Ratsey Pamphlets."
       PQ, 30 (October 1951), 381-86.
           Argues against Lievsay's identification of Samuel Row-
       lands as author (2360). Traces sources of Ratsey's Ghost.

REYNOLDS, JOHN (fl. 1620-1640)

The Triumphs of Gods Revenege against the Crying and Execrable Sinne
   of Murther. STC 20942-20946. Wing R1308-1313, R1303.

The Flower of Fidelitie: The Various Adventures of Three Foraign
  Princes. Wing R1304-1307.

"Love's Laurell Garland" (British Library Add. MS. 34,782).

Editions

2362 REYNOLDS, JOHN. "Don Juan and Marsillia" [from Triumphs of
       God's Revenge], in Short Fiction of the Seventeenth Century.
       Edited by Charles C[arroll] Mish. Stuart Editions. New
       York: New York University Press, 1963, pp. 193-234.
         Provides modernized text from 1670 edition. In brief
       introductory note, discusses the moralistic nature of the
       tale and suggests possible influence of the drama on Rey-
       nold's works. See 60.

Studies

2363 BABCOCK, C. MERTON. "An Analogue for the Name Othello." N&Q,
       196 (24 November 1951), 515.
         Argues against Triumphs of God's Revenge as Shakespeare's
       source for the name.

2364 BRYANT, JERRY H. "John Reynolds of Exeter and His Canon."
       Library, 5th Ser., 15 (June 1960), 105-17.
         In establishing Reynolds's canon, discusses the dating,
       publishing history, and popularity of Triumphs of God's
       Revenge and Flower of Fidelity. Also establishes that the
       unpublished romance "Love's Laurell Garland" is by Reynolds.
       See 2365.

2365 BRYANT, JERRY H. "John Reynolds of Exeter and His Canon: A
       Footnote." Library, 5th Ser., 18 (December 1963), 299-303.
         Includes plate made from Reynolds's unpublished romance
       "Love's Laurell Garland." Briefly notes similarity of hand-
       writing to that in other manuscripts he argues were written
       by Reynolds. See 2364.

2366 BRYANT, JERRY H. "John Reynolds of Exeter's 'Love's Laurell
       Garland': An Unpublished Romance." Manuscripta, 8 (Novem-
       ber 1964), 131-45.
         Describes manuscript; discusses Reynolds's use of con-
       ventions from Arcadian, Greek, and chivalric romances; sug-
       gests possible sources and analogues; and analyzes style and
       structure.

2367 CHRIST, KARL. Quellenstudien zu den Dramen Thomas Middletons.
       Leipzig: R. Noske, 1905, 141pp.

383

Reynolds

Includes discussion of Middleton's use of <u>Triumphs of God's Revenge</u> as source for <u>The Changeling</u> (pp. 92-99). In Appendix, reprints tale of Don Pedro from 1629 edition (pp. 112-30).

2368   FARR, DOROTHY M. "<u>The Changeling</u>." <u>MLR</u>, 62 (October 1967), 586-97.
Discusses Middleton's modifications of story of Beatrice Joanna (<u>Triumphs of God's Revenge</u>), a source of the play.

2369   FORSYTHE, ROBERT STANLEY. <u>The Relation of Shirley's Plays to the Elizabethan Drama</u>. Columbia University Studies in English and Comparative Literature. New York: Columbia University Press, 1914, 497pp.
Includes detailed analysis of Shirley's use of tale of Antonio and Berinthia (<u>Triumphs of God's Revenge</u>) as source for <u>The Maid's Revenge</u> (pp. 136-49).

2370   [MISH, CHARLES CARROLL.] "John Reynold's [sic] <u>The Triumphs of Gods Revenge</u>." <u>SCN</u>, 10 (1952), 37.
Provides brief overview of contents and discusses popularity of work. Suggests two topics for further investigation: sources of tales and relationship between tales and drama of time.

2371   NAKANO, NANCY YOSHIKO. "The Authority of Narrative: Technique and Argument in Milton, Bunyan, Dryden, and John Reynolds." Ph.D. dissertation, University of California-Los Angeles, 1973, 203pp.
Analyzes narrative in <u>Triumphs of God's Revenge</u>. Discusses work as "a sustained effort to demonstrate the unfailing vengeance of God against murderers." Examines how "the portrayal of character is designed to arouse the maximum of indignation against the guilty, while the narrator's viewpoint remains appropriately moralistic and admonitory."

2372   SCHOENBAUM, SAMUEL. <u>Middleton's Tragedies: A Critical Study</u>. New York: Columbia University Press, 1955, 285pp.
Summarizes tale of Alsemero, Beatrice-Joanna, and De Flores, the source of <u>The Changeling</u>; concludes that the story is "[t]old without insight or irony, [and] its complete disregard for human motivation is matched only by its utter lack of artistry."

2373   WALLIS, ALFRED. "A Famous Exeter Author." <u>Notes and Gleanings</u>, 1 (16 January 1888), 1-3.
Discusses publishing history of <u>Triumphs of God's Revenge</u> and its influence.

RICH, BARNABY (1542-1617)

The Adventures of Brusanus Prince of Hungaria. STC 20977-20977.5.

Riche His Farewell to Militarie Profession. STC 20996-20997.

A Right Exelent and Pleasaunt Dialogue betwene Mercury and an English Souldier. STC 20998.

The Straunge and Wonderfull Adventures of Don Simonides. STC 21002-21002a.

Editions

2374   RICH, BARNABY. "Phylotus and Emelia," in Philotus: A Comedy. Edited by John Whitefoord Mackenzie. Bannatyne Club Publications, 50. Edinburgh: Ballantyne, 1835, pp. 7-32.
        Provides reprint based on 1583 edition of Farewell with some readings from 1606 edition.

2375   RICH, BARNABY. "The Historie of Apolonius and Silla," in Shakespeare's Library: A Collection of the Romances, Novels, Poems, and Histories Used by Shakespeare as the Foundation of His Dramas, Vol. II. Edited by J[ohn] Payne Collier. London: T. Rodd, 1843, 25-49.
        Provides reprint from 1606 edition of Farewell.

2376   RICH, BARNABY. Eight Novels [i.e., Rich His Farewell to Military Profession] Employed by English Dramatic Poets of the Reign of Queen Elizabeth. Edited by J[ohn] Payne Collier. Shakespeare Society Publications, 33. London: Shakespeare Society, 1846, 240pp.
        Provides modernized reprint of 1581 edition. In "Preface," pp. x-xvi, discusses use of work as source for Elizabethan dramas.

2377   RICH, BARNABY. "Of Apolonius and Silla," in The Works of William Shakespeare, Vol. VII. By William Shakespeare. Edited by James O[rchard] Halliwell[-Phillipps]. London: C. & J. Adlard for the Editor, 1857, 230-42.
        Provides reprint based on 1581 edition of Farewell with some readings from 1606 edition.

2378   RICH, BARNABY. "Apolonius and Silla," in Shakespeare's Library: A Collection of the Plays, Romances, Novels, Poems, and Histories Employed by Shakespeare in the Composition of His Works, Vol. I. Edited by John Payne Collier. 2d edition

Rich

revised. Edited by W[illiam] Carew Hazlitt. London:
Reeves and Turner, 1875, 387-412.
Provides reprint from 1581 edition of Farewell.

2379 RICH, BARNABY. "Of Apolonius and Silla," in Twelfe Night. By
William Shakespeare. Edited by Horace Howard Furness.
New Variorum. Philadelphia: J. B. Lippincott Co., 1901,
pp. 328-39.
Provides reprint from 2376. Includes overview of scholarship on Shakespeare's use of the tale as a source (pp.
326-27). See 2416.

2380 RICH, BARNABY. Rich's "Apolonius & Silla," an Original of
Shakespeare's Twelfth Night. Edited by Morton Luce.
Shakespeare Classics, 13. London: Chatto & Windus, 1912,
108pp.
Provides modernized reprint based on 1581 and 1606 edi-
tions. In "Introduction," pp. 1-51, briefly discusses
Shakespeare's use of work as source.

2381 RICH, BARNABY. "Of Gonsales and His Vertuous Wife Agatha,"
in How a Man May Chuse a Good Wife from a Bad. Edited by
A. E. H. Swaen. Materialien zur Kunde des Älteren Dramas,
35. Louvain: A. Uystpruyst, 1912, pp. XXV-XLII.
Reprints text of tale from 2376. In "Introduction,"
pp. VI-XLIII, discusses use of Rich's tale as source of the
play.

2382 RICH, BARNABY. "Apolonius and Silla," in Great Short Novels
of the World: A Collection of Complete Tales Chosen from
the Literatures of All Periods and Countries. New York:
McBridge, 1927, pp. 202-17.
Provides modernized reprint from 1581 edition of Farewell.

2383 RICH, BARNABY. "Apolonius and Silla," in Elizabethan Tales.
Edited by Edward J[oseph] O'Brien. London: G. Allen &
Unwin, 1937, pp. 125-53.
Provides modernized text based on unidentified edition.

2384 RICH, BARNABY. Rich's Farewell to Military Profession, 1581.
Edited by Thomas Mabry Cranfill. Austin: University of
Texas Press, 1959, 441pp.
Provides facsimile reprint of 1581 edition with extensive
notes. In "Introduction," pp. xv-lxxxii, analyzes Rich's
adaptation and modification of three tales from Cinthio's
Gli Hecatommithi (provides detailed investigation of sources
and analogues in appendix, pp. 339-50). Discusses

dramatists' use of <u>Farewell</u> as source and the popularity of
the work in the sixteenth and seventeenth centuries. Provides detailed bibliographical analysis of early editions,
including notes on revisions.

2385   RICH, BARNABY. "Apolonius and Silla," in <u>Shakespeare and His</u>
        <u>Sources</u>. Edited by Joseph Satin. Boston: Houghton
        Mifflin, 1966, pp. 317-35.
            Provides modernized reprint based on 1581 edition of
        <u>Farewell</u>.

2386   RICH, BARNABY. "Of Apolonius and Silla," in <u>The Sources of</u>
        <u>Ten Shakespearean Plays</u>. Edited by Alice Griffin. New
        York: Crowell, 1966, pp. 209-26.
            Provides modernized reprint of tale from unidentified
        edition of <u>Farewell</u>.

2387   RICH, BARNABY. "Of Apolonius and Silla," in <u>Elizabethan Prose</u>
        <u>Fiction</u>. Edited by Merritt [E.] Lawlis. Indianapolis:
        Odyssey Press, Bobbs-Merrill Co., 1967, pp. 189-225.
            Reprints partly modernized text from 1581 edition of
        <u>Farewell</u>. (<u>See</u> p. 630 for list of substantive emendations.)
        In introductory note examines work in the tradition of the
        novella and romance.

2388   RICH, BARNABY. "The Story of Apolonius and Silla," in <u>Eliza-</u>
        <u>bethan Love Stories</u>. Edited by T[erence] J. B. Spencer.
        Penguin Shakespeare Library. Harmondsworth: Penguin Books,
        1968, pp. 97-117.
            Provides modernized text based on 1581 edition of <u>Fare-</u>
        <u>well</u>. In "Introduction," pp. 7-31, discusses relationship
        with Shakespeare's <u>Twelfth Night</u>.

Studies

2389   BASKERVILL, C. R. "Source and Analogues of <u>How a Man May</u>
        <u>Choose a Good Wife from a Bad</u>." <u>PMLA</u>, 24 (December 1909),
        711-30.
            Argues that Rich's "Gonsales and Agatha" is source for
        play. Notes that Rich follows Cinthio closely, sometimes
        expanding a phrase for the purpose of illustration or ex-
        planation. Examines possible influence of Rich's story on
        several other plays.

2390   BASKERVILL, C. R. "The Source of the Main Plot of Shirley's
        <u>Love Tricks</u>." <u>MLN</u>, 24 (April 1909), 100-101.
            Argues that <u>Farewell</u> is the primary source of the main
        plot of Shirley's play.

Rich

2391   BECKER, GUSTAV. "The Adventures of Don Simonides: Ein Roman
       von Barnabe Rich und seine Quelle." Archiv, 131 (1913),
       64–80.
           Provides detailed summary of work and traces Rich's
       sources.

2392   BISWAS, DINESH CHANDRA. Shakespeare's Treatment of His Sources
       in the Comedies. Calcutta: Jadavpur University, 1971,
       299pp.
           Examines Shakespeare's use of "Apolonius and Silla" as a
       source for Twelfth Night (pp. 90–98).

2393   BLUESTONE, MAX. From Story to Stage: The Dramatic Adaptation
       of Prose Fiction in the Period of Shakespeare and His Con-
       temporaries. SEngL, 70. The Hague: Mouton, 1974, 341pp.
           Includes examination of the adaptation and transformation
       of "Apolonius and Silla" in Shakespeare's Twelfth Night and
       of "Sappho Duke of Mantona" in The Weakest Goeth to the
       Wall (passim).

2394   BROWN, ELAINE V. BEILIN. "The Uses of Mythology in Elizabethan
       Romance." Ph.D. dissertation, Princeton University, 1973,
       336pp.
           Analyzes Rich's use of the Venus-Diana myth in Don
       Simonides.

2395   BRUCE, DOROTHY HART. "The Merry Wives and 'Two Brethren.'"
       SP, 39 (April 1942), 265–78.
           Provides detailed analysis of parallels between "Of Two
       Brethren" in Farewell and Falstaff's adventures in Merry
       Wives to argue that Shakespeare used Rich's story as a
       source.

2396   CALKINS, ROGER W. "The Renaissance Idea of 'Imitation' and
       Shakespeare's Twelfth Night," in Twenty-Seven to One: A
       Potpourri of Humanistic Material Presented to Dr. Donald
       Gale Stillman on the Occasion of His Retirement from Clark-
       son College of Technology. Edited by Bradford B. Broughton.
       [New York: Ryan Press,] 1970, pp. 52–65.
           Discusses the "Puritanical nature of Riche's attack on
       the immorality of the love conventions" in "Apolonius and
       Silla." Notes "dissimilarity of tone and attitude" between
       Rich's story and Twelfth Night.

2397   CONRAD, HERMANN. "Zu den Quellen von Shakespeares Twelfth
       Night." Englische Studien, 46, no. 1 (1912), 73–85.
           Examines Shakespeare's knowledge of "Apolonius and Silla"
       and argues that it is not the main source of the play.

2398   CRAIGIE, JAMES. "Rich's Farewell to Military Profession."
        TLS, 1 November 1934, p. 755.
            On basis of letter of 18 June 1595 from George Nicolson
        to Robert Bowes, speculates that there was a 1594 edition
        which is not extant.

2399   CRANFILL, T[HOMAS] M[ABRY]. "Barnaby Rich: An Elizabethan
        Reviser at Work." SP, 46 (July 1949), 411-18.
            Examines types of changes made in 1594 edition of Fare-
        well. Argues that the corrections, which are characterized
        by "aimlessness, inconsistency, capriciousness, poor judg-
        ment, perverseness, and pedantry" were not done by Rich but
        possibly by an "over-zealous corrector at the press."

2400   CRANFILL, T[HOMAS] M[ABRY]. "Barnaby Rich and King James."
        ELH, 16 (March 1949), 65-75.
            Discusses James's reasons for displeasure with references
        to Scotland and its king in the story of Balthasar (Fare-
        well, 1581, 1583, 1594) and Rich's changes in the story in
        the 1606 edition.

2401   CRANFILL, THOMAS MABRY. "Barnaby Rich's Farewell and the
        Drama." Ph.D. dissertation, Harvard University, 1944,
        148pp.
            Traces sources used by Rich for each of the stories and
        examines use of Farewell as source in seventeenth-century
        drama.

2402   CRANFILL, T[HOMAS] M[ABRY]. "Barnaby Rich's 'Sappho' and The
        Weakest Goeth to the Wall." University of Texas Studies in
        English, 1945-1946, pp. 142-71.
            Examines Rich's sources for "Sappho Duke of Mantona"
        (including Painter, Pettie, and his own "Lady of Chabry");
        analyzes the flaws in Rich's story; and discusses use of
        the work as a source for the anonymous play The Weakest
        Goeth to the Wall.

2403   CRANFILL, THOMAS M[ABRY], and DOROTHY HART BRUCE. Barnaby
        Rich: A Short Biography. Austin: University of Texas
        Press, 1953, 145pp.
            Examines autobiographical significance of Rich's prose
        fiction; discusses his prose fiction in the context of his
        life and works. See 2414.

2404   DAVIS, WALTER R[ICHARDSON]. Idea and Act in Elizabethan Fic-
        tion. Princeton: Princeton University Press, 1969, 311pp.
            Analyzes the "testing of ideas...by experience" in Rich's
        fiction. Discusses influence of Lyly on Rich (pp. 126-31).

Rich

2405   FORSYTHE, ROBERT STANLEY. <u>The Relations of Shirley's Plays to</u>
       <u>the Elizabethan Drama</u>. Columbia University Studies in Eng-
       lish and Comparative Literature. New York: Columbia Uni-
       versity Press, 1914, 497pp.
           Includes detailed analysis of Shirley's use of tale of
       Phylotus and Emilia (<u>Farewell</u>) as source for <u>Love Tricks</u>
       (pp. 117-36, passim).

2406   GHALL, SEAN. "Barnaby Rich and Ireland." <u>DM</u>, NS, 1, no. 3
       (1926), 3-10; no. 4 (1926), 4-12; 2, no. 2 (1927), 44-58.
           Provides an overview of Rich's works and discusses refer-
       ences to Ireland in <u>Mercury and an English Soldier</u>.

2407   GUBAR, SUSAN DAVID. "Tudor Romance and Eighteenth-Century
       Fiction." Ph.D. dissertation, University of Iowa, 1972,
       243pp.
           Includes examination of structure and style of Rich's
       prose fiction; discusses reader response and how the works
       "call attention to their own literariness."

2408   HARRISON, T. P., JR. "Shakespeare and Montemayor's <u>Diana</u>."
       <u>University of Texas Studies in English</u>, No. 6 (December
       1926), pp. 72-120.
           Points out instances of Shakespeare's use of "Apolonius
       and Silla" in <u>Twelfth Night</u>.

2409   HELGERSON, RICHARD. "Lyly, Greene, Sidney, and Barnaby Rich's
       <u>Brusanus</u>." <u>HLQ</u>, 36 (February 1973), 105-18.
           Discusses Rich's borrowings from a manuscript of the
       <u>Old Arcadia</u> and from Greene's <u>Gwydonius</u>, concluding that
       although Rich was influenced by both the Arcadian and eu-
       phuistic movements, <u>Brusanus</u> is a piece of hack-work, not
       an attempt to assimilate the two traditions. Suggests that
       Rich carries on the process begun by Greene of diluting
       "euphuistic rhetoric with action." Argues for 1592 as date
       of composition.

2410   JORGENSEN, PAUL A. "Barnaby Rich: Soldierly Suitor and
       Honest Critic of Women." <u>SQ</u>, 7 (Spring 1956), 183-88.
           Discusses how Rich blends literary roles of "blunt
       soldier" and honest man in appealing to both male and fe-
       male audience in <u>Farewell</u>.

2411   JORGENSEN, PAUL A. "The Courtship Scene in <u>Henry V</u>." <u>MLQ</u>, 11
       (June 1950), 180-88.
           Discusses Rich's attitude toward the soldier (especially
       his "advocacy of the soldier's worthiness in love") in <u>Fare-</u>
       <u>well</u> and suggests that the work influenced Shakespeare's

treatment of the courtship scene. Argues that Rich did
much to free the soldier from popular contempt.

2412   KITTLE, WILLIAM. Edward de Vere, Seventeenth Earl of Oxford,
       1550-1604. Washington, D. C.: Buchanan Co., 1935, 252pp.
       Argues that Rich is satirizing Gascoigne (i.e., Oxford)
       in Farewell (pp. 167-70).

2413   LEWIS, ROBERT JOHN. "The Narrative Art of Barnaby Riche."
       Ph.D. dissertation, University of Notre Dame, 1971, 223pp.
       Provides a critical estimate of each of Rich's prose
       fiction works; discusses influences on his works, style,
       and the development of his narrative art.

2414   LIEVSAY, JOHN LEON. "A Word about Barnaby Rich." JEGP, 55,
       no. 3 (1956), 381-92.
       Argues against attempt of Cranfill and Bruce (2403) to
       elevate Rich to status of "major minor" Elizabethan; ques-
       tions whether he is "a serious and independent artist" and
       whether his work "possesses integrity of thought and dis-
       tinctive charm of praise."

2415   MUIR, KENNETH. "The Sources of Twelfth Night." N&Q, NS, 2
       (March 1955), 94.
       Suggests that Dedicatory Epistle to Farewell is a source
       for the characterization of Aguecheek.

2416   NEILSON, WILLIAM ALLAN. "The Variorum Twelfth Night." Atlan-
       tic Monthly, 89 (May 1902), 715-18.
       Devotes major portion of review to arguing against Fur-
       ness's conclusion that Shakespeare had not used Rich's
       Farewell as source (2379). Discusses Shakespeare's use of
       "Apolonius and Silla" and "Of Two Brethren."

2417   PRUVOST, RENÉ. "The Beginning of Barnabe Rich's Military
       Career: A Correction to the D.N.B." RES, 9 (April 1933),
       190-91.
       Points out that Rich's comment "It is now thirty yeares
       sith I became a souldier" in Adventures of Brusanus means
       thirty years before date of publication (1592) rather than
       composition (1585) of work.

2418   PRUVOST, RENÉ. Matteo Bandello and Elizabethan Fiction.
       Bibliothèque de la Revue de Littérature Comparée, 113.
       Paris: H. Champion, 1937, 349pp.
       Examines Rich's debt to Bandello in several of his tales,
       his style, and his mingling of didactic and narrative ele-
       ments in Don Simonides. Also examines his place in the de-
       velopment of Elizabethan prose fiction (passim).

Rich

2419   PRUVOST, RENÉ. "The Two Gentlemen of Verona, Twelfth Night,
        et Gl'Ingannati." EA, 13, no. 1 (1960), 1-9.
            Discusses Shakespeare's use of "Apolonius and Silla" as
        source for Twelfth Night.

2420   SALINGAR, L. G. "The Design of Twelfth Night." SQ, 9 (Spring
        1958), 117-39.
            Discusses relationship of "Apolonius and Silla" to
        Shakespeare's treatment of Viola.

2421   SAMSON, DONALD C. "Rich's Farewell to Military Profession."
        Expl., 34 (September 1975), item 1.
            Explicates Rich's use of word "romer" in "Apolonius and
        Silla."

2422   SMITH, G. C. MOORE. "Riche's Story 'Of Phylotus and Emilia.'"
        MLR, 5 (July 1910), 342-44.
            Notes similarities between Rich's story and Gli Ingan-
        nati; suggests several plays for which Farewell was source.

2423   STARNES, D. T. "Barnabe Riche's 'Sappho Duke of Mantona': A
        Study in Elizabethan Story-Making." SP, 30 (July 1933),
        455-72.
            Analyzes Rich's use of a form of the Eustace legend,
        stories from Painter's Palace of Pleasure, and Underdowne's
        Aethiopian History as sources. Suggests that Rich's pro-
        cedure in composing stories was to draw from commonplace
        book in which he had copied plot summaries, "felicitous
        passages," and notes from his wide reading in fiction of
        his time.

2424   THOMPSON, D. W. "Belphegor in Grim the Collier and Riche's
        Farewell." MLN, 50 (February 1935), 99-102.
            Argues Rich followed version of Straparola in Tredici
        piacevoli notti (1550), not that of Machiavelli. Also ar-
        gues that Rich's version is not the source of Grim the
        Collier.

2425   WEBB, HENRY J. "Barnabe Riche--Sixteenth Century Military
        Critic." JEGP, 42, no. 2 (1943), 240-52.
            Notes that in Dialogue between Mercury and an English
        Soldier Rich imitates "the pattern of the Old-French love-
        vision" and that he borrowed from Peter Whitehorne's trans-
        lation of Machiavelli's The Art of War.

2426   WELD, JOHN SALTAR. "Studies in the Euphuistic Novel, 1576-
        1640." Ph.D. dissertation, Harvard University, 1940, 304pp.

Points out Rich's debt to Pettie in Farewell and traces
sources of Brusanus. Characterizes the latter work as "the
first of a series of novels in which the familiar euphuistic
motifs of Greene and Lyly are diluted with large amounts of
chivalric romance."

2427 WOLF, MELVIN H. "Introduction," in Faultes Faults and Nothing
Else but Faultes (1606). By Barnaby Rich. Edited by Melvin
H. Wolf. Gainesville, Florida: Scholars' Facsimiles &
Reprints, 1965, pp. 9-76.
Places Rich's prose fiction in the context of his life
and other writings; provides detailed chronology and gives
bibliographical description of "one copy of the earliest
edition" of each of Rich's works.

ROBERTS, HENRY (fl. 1585-1606)

A Defiance to Fortune: Proclaimed by Andrugio, Noble Duke of Saxony.
STC 21078.

Haigh for Devonshire: A Pleasant Discourse of Sixe Gallant Marchants.
STC 21081-21081a.

Honours Conquest: Wherein Is Conteined the Famous Hystorie of Edward
of Lancaster. STC 21082.

Pheander, The Mayden Knight: Describing His Honourable Travailes.
STC 21086-21087. Wing R1597A, M600.

Editions

2428 ROBERTS, HENRY. "Eine kritische Edition von Henry Roberts'
A Defiance to Fortune (1590)." Edited by Giselher Tiegel.
Ph.D. dissertation, University of Köln, 1973, 304pp.
Provides critical old-spelling edition based on 1590 edi-
tion. Analyzes work in context of prose fiction of the
time: examines plot, motifs, style, and characterization.
(Abstract in: English and American Studies in German:
Summaries of Theses and Monographs, 1973. Edited by Werner
Habicht. Tübingen: M. Niemeyer Verlag, 1974, pp. 63-64.)

2429 ROBERTS, HENRY. "Henry Robarts Pheander, the Mayden Knight:
Kritische Edition und Interpretation." Edited by Klaus
Dieter Matussek. Ph.D. dissertation, University of Köln,
1975, 367pp.
Provides critical edition based on 1595 text. Analyzes
relationship to romance tradition, narrative technique, and

Roberts

theme. Concludes that "Pheander shows the characteristics
of a quasi-autonomous work of art as well as of a literary
product conditioned by the historical, social, and ideologi-
cal situation of late 16th century bourgeois society in
England." (Abstract in: English and American Studies in
German: Summaries of Theses and Monographs, 1975. Edited
by Werner Habicht. Tübingen: M. Niemeyer Verlag, 1976,
pp. 73-74.)

Studies

2430   HAZLITT, W[ILLIAM] CAREW. "Pheander, the Mayden Knight." N&Q,
       32 (19 August 1865), 149.
            Lists editions (1595, 1617, 1661) he knows and asks if
       there are others.

2431   MISH, CHARLES C[ARROLL]. "A Seventeenth-Century Fiction Re-
       print." N&Q, NS, 4 (March 1957), 104.
            Identifies Marianus, or Love's Heroic Champion (1641) as
       merely an unacknowledged reprint, with alterations in para-
       graphing and names of characters and places, of Pheander
       (1617).

2432   RYE, W. B. "Devonshire Bibliography: Henry Robert's Haigh
       for Deuonshire, 1600." The Western Antiquary; or, Devon
       and Cornwall Notebook, 4 (February 1885), 181-83.
            Describes copy of 1600 edition and lists contents.

2433   WELD, JOHN SALTAR. "Studies in the Euphuistic Novel, 1576-
       1640." Ph.D. dissertation, Harvard University, 1940, 304pp.
            Suggests that it is unlikely that Roberts was author of
       Defiance to Fortune; identifies sources of work and discus-
       ses its influence.

2434   WRIGHT, LOUIS B. "Henry Robarts: Patriotic Propagandist and
       Novelist." SP, 29 (April 1932), 176-99.
            Surveys Roberts's four prose fiction works, particularly
       as they reveal his bent for patriotic propaganda. Argues
       that Roberts did not plagiarize Haigh for Devonshire from
       Deloney's Thomas of Reading.

ROBIN GOODFELLOW, HIS MAD PRANKES AND MERRY JESTES

    STC 12016-12017.

Editions

2435   The Mad Pranks and Merry Jests of Robin Goodfellow: Reprinted
        from the Edition of 1628. Edited by J[ohn] Payne Collier.
        Percy Society, 2. London: C. Richards for the Percy So-
        ciety, 1841, 65pp.
            Reprints text of 1628 edition. In "Introduction," pp.
        v-xx, discusses date of work.

2436   Life of Robin Goodfellow, in Illustrations of the Fairy Mythol-
        ogy of A Midsummer Night's Dream. Edited by James Orchard
        Halliwell[-Phillipps]. Shakespeare Society Publications,
        26. London: Shakespeare Society, 1845, pp. 120-54.
            Reprints text from 2435.

2437   Life of Robin Goodfellow, in Fairy Tales, Legends, and Romances
        Illustrating Shakespeare and Other Early English Writers.
        Edited by W[illiam] C[arew] Hazlitt. London: F. & W.
        Kerslake, 1875, pp. 173-207.
            Provides reprint of text from 2435.

2438   Robin Good-Fellow; His Mad Pranks and Merry Jests, in The
        Sources and Analogues of A Midsummer Night's Dream. Edited
        by Frank Sidgwick. Shakespeare Classics, 9. New York:
        Duffield; London: Chatto & Windus, 1908, pp. 81-121.
            Provides modernized, annotated reprint of 2435.

Studies

2439   M., J. "Robin Goodfellow." N&Q, 30 (29 October 1864), 343.
            Locates known copies and describes woodcut which is
        present in only his copy.

ROBINSON, RICHARD (fl. 1576-1603)

A Record of Auncient Histories, Intituled in Latin: Gesta Romanorum.
    STC 21288-21290a. Wing R631-640.

Editions

2440   Gesta Romanorum: A Record of Auncient Histories Newly Perused
        by Richard Robinson. Translated by Richard Robinson. In-
        troduction by John [Saltar] Weld. Delmar, New York:
        Scholars' Facsimiles & Reprints, 1973, not paginated.
            Provides facsimile reprint of 1595 edition (with addi-
        tions from later editions). In "Introduction," pp. v-xi,
        discusses popularity of translation and Robinson's alteration
        of allegory to make "it conform with Protestant teaching."

Rowland

ROWLAND, DAVID

The Pleasaunt Historie of Lazarillo de Tormes. STC 15336-15339.

Editions

2441   The Pleasaunt Historie of Lazarillo de Tormes. Translated by
        David Rowland. Edited by J[ohn] E[rnest] V[ictor] Crofts.
        Percy Reprints, 7. Oxford: Blackwell, 1924, 78pp.
            Provides emended reprint of 1586 edition. In "Introduc-
        tion," pp. v-xii, discusses publishing history of work and
        examines Rowland's treatment of the text and his use of
        Saugrain's French translation.

2442   Lazarillo de Tormes. Translated by David Rowland. In Spanish
        Short Stories of the Sixteenth Century in Contemporary
        Translations. Edited by J[ohn] B[rand] Trend. World's
        Classics, 326. Oxford: Oxford University Press, 1928,
        pp. 1-71.
            Provides modernized text based on unidentified edition.

S., J.

Clidamas, or the Sicilian Tale. STC 21501.

Giovanni Francesco Loredano, The Life of Adam. Wing L3067.

Editions

2443   LOREDANO, GIOVANNI FRANCESCO. The Life of Adam. Translated
        by J. S. Introduction by Roy C. Flannagan and John Arthos.
        Gainesville, Florida: Scholars' Facsimiles & Reprints,
        1967, not paginated.
            Provides facsimile reprint of 1659 edition. In "Intro-
        duction," pp. v-xxi, discuss analogues with Paradise Lost.

Studies

2444   O'CONNOR, JOHN J. "A Note on the Meaning of 'Novel' in the
        Seventeenth Century." N&Q, 198 (November 1953), 477-78.
            Discusses use of "novel" in sense of fiction of some
        length in Clidamas; notes that use antedates first recorded
        appearance in OED.

THE SACK—FULL OF NEWES

Wing S223.

Editions

*2445   The Sack Full of Newes: An Old Jest—Book Originally Printed
in the Sixteenth Century: Now First Reprinted since 1673
from a Copy Supposed to Be Unique. Edited by J[ames]
O[rchard] Halliwell[-Phillipps]. London: Printed for the
Editor by Whittington and Wilkins, Chiswick Press, 1861,
40pp.
Not seen. Listed in NUC Pre—1956 Imprints, vol. 513,
389.

2446   The Sack—Full of Newes, in Shakespeare Jest—Books, Vol. II.
Edited by W[illiam] Carew Hazlitt. London: Willis &
Sotheran, 1864, 163—87.
Provides annotated reprint of 1673 edition. In brief
introductory note discusses bibliographical history of the
work.

2447   The Sackful of News, in Elizabethan Prose Fiction. Edited by
Merritt [E.] Lawlis. Indianapolis: Odyssey Press, Bobbs—
Merrill Co., 1967, pp. 13—30.
Provides partly modernized reprint of 1673 edition. In
introductory note, discusses the work as an example of the
collection of detached jests, suggesting that Sackful "is
unusual in its moral neutrality." Considers the kinds of
humor and the range of subjects.

SALES, SIR WILLIAM

Theophania: Or Severall Modern Histories. Wing S371.

Studies

2448   C[ROSSLEY, JAMES]. "Theophania." N&Q, 5 (24 January 1852),
88—89.
Responds to earlier query (Henry Kersley, "Theophania,"
N&Q, 1 [12 January 1850], 174), identifying Sales as author
and noting presence of a manuscript key in his copy.

2449   SHEARER, AUGUSTUS HUNT. "Theophania: An English Political
Romance of the Seventeenth Century." MLN, 31 (February
1916), 65—74.

Sanford

Examines the work as "a mildly partizan account of the
early years of the Civil War," identifying characters and
places. Argues that the work was composed during the latter part of 1645 and suggests Clarendon as possible author.

SANFORD, JOHN

Ludovico Guicciardini, The Garden of Pleasure. STC 12464-12465.

Studies

2450   TILLEY, M[ORRIS] P[ALMER]. "Borrowings in Grange's Golden
       Aphroditis." MLN, 53 (June 1938), 407-12.
           Points out Grange's borrowings from The Garden of
       Pleasure.

SCOGGIN, JOHN (fl. 1480)

The Jestes of Skogyn. STC 21850.3-21850.7.

Scoggins Jestes. STC 21851. Wing B3750.

Editions

2451   SCOGGIN, JOHN. Scoggin's Jests, in Shakespeare Jest-Books,
       Vol. II. Edited by W[illiam] Carew Hazlitt. London:
       Willis & Sotheran, 1864, 37-161.
           Provides annotated reprint of 1626 edition. In "Intro-
       duction," II, 38-55, discusses the bibliographical history
       of the work and allusions to it.

Studies

2452   BRIE, FRIEDRICH. Eulenspiegel in England. Palaestra, 27.
       Berlin: Mayer & Müller, 1903, 160pp.
           Includes discussion of influence of Howleglas on Scog-
       gin's Jests (pp. 80-94). See 2461.

2453   BRITTEN, JAMES. "'Scoggins' [sic] Heirs.'" N&Q, 39 (22 May
       1869), 484.
           Explains allusion to Scoggin's Jests in Gerard's Herbal.

2454   BROOKS, NEIL C. "Scogan's Quem Quaeritis and Till Eulenspieg-
       el." MLN, 38 (January 1923), 57.
           Replies to Farnham's article (2459), noting that the
       source of the jest is William Copland's Howleglas but with

an anti-Catholic bias added. Points out that the jest is not of English, but probably of Continental clerical, origin.

2455 CLOUSTON, W[ILLIAM] A[LEXANDER]. "Eastern Origin of a Jest of Scogin." N&Q, 59 (19 April 1879), 302-303.
      Traces origin of "What Shifts Scoggin and His Fellows Made when They Lacked Money" to a tale in the Pantcha Tantra and Vishnusarman's Hitopadesa. Suggests the version in Scoggin was adapted from the one in the Middle English translation of the Gesta Romanorum. See 2456, 2457, and 2463.

2456 CLOUSTON, W[ILLIAM] A[LEXANDER]. "Eastern Origin of a Jest of Scogin." N&Q, 59 (17 May 1879), 382-83.
      Revises earlier note (2455); now suggests origin was William Copland's Howleglas.

2457 CLOUSTON, W[ILLIAM] A[LEXANDER]. "Eastern Origin of a Jest of Scogin." N&Q, 59 (31 May 1879), 426.
      Cites analogue of "What Shifts Scoggin and His Fellows Made when They Lacked Money" from Ser Giovanni. See 2455 and 2456.

2458 FARNHAM, WILLARD EDWARD. "John (Henry) Scogan." MLR, 16 (April 1921), 120-28.
      Attempts to identify historical Scoggin, considers internal evidence for dating jests, and provides annotated list of editions of Jests of Scoggin.

2459 FARNHAM, WILLARD [EDWARD]. "Scogan's Quem Quaeritis." MLN, 37 (May 1922), 289-92.
      Discusses importance of an English version of the Easter Quem Quaeritis preserved in "How Scoggin Set a Whole Town Together by the Ears" (1613 edition only). See 2454.

2460 FERRARA, FERNANDO. Jests e Merry Tales: Aspetti della narrativa popolaresca inglese del sedicesimo secolo. Nuovi Saggi, 27. Rome: Editrice dell'Ateneo, 1960, 257pp.
      Examines place of Scoggin's Jests in development of sixteenth-century jest book: discusses its assimilation of preceding jest book traditions, its use of fool figure to give coherence to work, its structure, and its importance to the development of jest-biography (pp. 126-39).

2461 HASSELL, J[AMES] WOODROW, JR. "On the Influence in England of Henri Estienne and Bonaventure des Périers: The Sources of Scoggins Jestes (1613)," in Mediaeval Studies in Honor of

Scoggin

Urban Tigner Holmes, Jr. Edited by John Mahoney and John
Esten. UNCSRLL, 56. Chapel Hill: University of North
Carolina Press, 1965, pp. 79-88.
Identifies T. D.'s Mirror of Mirth and Henri Estienne's
The Stage of Popish Toys as sources. Provides additions and
corrections to discussion of sources in 2452.

2462 MAGOON, MARIAN WAITE. "Some Analogues to Elizabethan Jest
Books in Medieval Ecclesiastical Literature." Ph.D. dissertation, University of Michigan, 1931.
Traces analogues in Medieval collections of exempla to
several tales in Scoggin's Jests.

2463 R., R. "Eastern Origin of a Jest of Scogin." N&Q, 60 (25 Oc-
tober 1879), 331-32.
Cites version of "What Shifts Scoggin and His Fellows
Made when They Lacked Money" in Dialogues of Creatures
Moralized and oral version heard c. 1845. See 2455-57.

2464 SCHULZ, ERNST. Die englischen Schwankbücher bis herab zu
Dobson's Drie Bobs (1607). Palaestra, 117. Berlin:
Mayer & Müller, 1912, 238pp.
Includes discussion of sources and organization of Jests
of Scoggin (pp. 59-66).

2465 [THOMS, WILLIAM J.] "'Where Scoggin Looked for His Knife,'
&." N&Q, 11 (3 March 1855), 167.
In reply to query, notes that quotation in one of the
volumes of State Trials refers to Scoggin's Jests.

2466 WARDROPER, JOHN. "Borde and Scoggin," in Jest upon Jest: A
Selection from the Jestbooks and Collections of Merry Tales
Published from the Reign of Richard III to George III.
Edited by John Wardroper. London: Routledge & Kegan Paul,.
1970, pp. 198-99.
Examines evidence in favor of Borde as compiler of
Scoggin's Jests.

THE SECOND REPORT OF DOCTOR JOHN FAUSTUS

STC 10715.

Bibliographies

2467 HENNING, HANS. Faust Bibliographie, I: Allgemeines, Grundlagen, Gesamtdarstellungen. Das Faust-Thema vom 16. Jahrhundert bis 1790. Berlin: Aufbau-Verlag, 1966, 530pp.

The Second Report of Doctor John Faustus

Includes list of editions of (p. 167) and works about
(pp. 163-64) the Second Report.

Editions

2468 The Second Report of Dr. John Faustus, in A Collection of
      Early Prose Romances, Vol. III. Edited by William J. Thoms.
      London: William Pickering, 1828, 114pp. (separately pagi-
      nated). [Also published separately.]
         Provides reprint of 1680 edition. In introductory note
      (pp. iii-vii) comments on publishing history of work. Re-
      printed in 2470.

2469 The Second Report of Doctor John Faustus, in Studies in English
      Faust Literature, I: The English Wagner Book. By Alfred E.
      Richards. Literarhistorische Forschungen, 35. Berlin: E.
      Felber, 1907, pp. 31-176.
         Provides annotated reprint of 1594 Jeffes's edition. In
      introductory comments, establishes that there are two sepa-
      rate 1594 editions; provides bibliographical description
      of both and traces publishing history of work (pp. 3-30).

2470 The Second Report of Doctor John Faustus, in Early English
      Prose Romances. Edited by William J. Thoms. Revised and
      enlarged edition. London: G. Routledge and Sons; New York:
      E. P. Dutton and Co., [1907], pp. 885-958.
         Reprints 2468.

2471 The Second Report of Faustus, Containing His Appearances and
      the Deeds of Wagner, in The History of the Damnable Life
      and Deserved Death of Doctor John Faustus, 1592. Together
      with The Second Report of Faustus: Containing His Appear-
      ances and the Deeds of Wagner, 1594. Edited by William
      Rose. Broadway Translations. London: G. Routledge; New
      York: E. P. Dutton, 1925, pp. 213-319.
         Provides modernized text based on 2469.

Studies

2472 DÉDÉYAN, CHARLES. Le Thème de Faust dans la littérature euro-
      péene, Vol. I. Les Cahiers des Lettres Modernes. Paris:
      Lettres Modernes, 1954, 290pp.
         Provides a lengthy synopsis of The Second Report to
      illustrate the anonymous author's originality in handling
      the story (pp. 124-34).

2473 GREENLAW, EDWIN [A.]. "Britomart at the House of Busirane."
      SP, 26 (April 1929), 117-30.

The Second Report of Doctor John Faustus

>   Suggests portions of Chapters I and VIII of Second Re-
> port are derived from Faerie Queene, III, xi-xii.

2474   JANTZ, HAROLD. "An Elizabethan Statement on the Origin of
the German Faust Book." JEGP, 51, no. 2 (1952), 137-53.
    Argues that the Second Report is more important to the
development of the Faust tradition than the German Wagner
Book (1593) and that the English work "offers us the earliest printed evidence on the origin and corruption of the
Faust book." Suggests that "the first book" in introduction
of Second Report refers to the 1587 German edition, which
was a "garbled and corrupted" translation of an Italian
original. Also suggests that section on pact between Faust
and Mephistophiles "correctly follows the Latin original."
Considers author's probable acquaintance with Wittenberg
customs and relationship of work to Marlowe's play.

2475   RICHARDS, ALFRED E. "The English Wagner Book of 1594." PMLA,
24 (March 1909), 32-39.
    Observes that although History of Doctor John Faustus
has "no special literary importance" The Second Report of
Doctor John Faustus "possesses a certain literary character." Notes the dramatic quality of latter and examines
various literary influences on work. Suggests possibility
that Nashe is author.

2476   RICHARDS, ALFRED E. "A Literary Link between Thomas Shadwell
and Christian Felix Weisse." PMLA, 21 (December 1906),
808-830.
    Notes importance of description of the stage hell-mouth
in the Second Report and use of work as source for Will
Mountfort's farce The Life and Death of Doctor Faustus,
1696.

2477   RICHARDS, ALFRED E. "Some Faustus Notes." MLN, 22 (February
1907), 39-41.
    Includes some comparisons of Second Report to other six-
teenth-century treatments of the Faust legend.

2478   STEADMAN, JOHN M. "Sources of the 'Fountain-of-Oblivion' Episode in the English Wagner Book." Archiv, 196 (1959),
145-46.
    Traces sources to Ariosto's Orlando Furioso and to "tra-
ditional representations of Father Time and Kairos."

2479   STEADMAN, JOHN M. "Stanzaic Patterns in the English Wagner
Book." N&Q, NS, 4 (September 1957), 376-77.
    Suggests Second Report was composed between 1592 and
1594.

2480   TILLEY, M[ORRIS] P[ALMER]. "On the Name 'Seignior Prospero.'"
       MLN, 26 (June 1911), 196-97.
          Suggests that the "Seignior Prospero" of Second Report
       is the name of a "foreign horseman" who is mentioned in
       other Renaissance works.

2481   WALZ, JOHN A. "An English Faustsplitter." MLN, 42 (June
       1927), 353-65.
          Suggests that the mention of Faust's tree by Fynes Mory-
       son (Itinerary) confirms the claim of the author of the
       Second Report "that he had direct personal information
       about Wittenberg."

SHELTON, THOMAS

Miguel de Cervantes Saavedra, The History of Don Quixote. STC 4915-
   4917. Wing C1776-1777.

Editions

2482   CERVANTES SAAVEDRA, MIGUEL DE. The History of the Valorous
       and Witty Knight-Errant Don Quixote of the Mancha. Trans-
       lated by Thomas Shelton. Introduction by Justin Huntly
       McCarthy. 4 vols. Philadelphia: J. B. Lippincott Co.,
       1895, 340, 356, 371, 305pp.
          Provides modernized reprint based on 1612 and 1620 edi-
       tions. In "Preface," I, vii-x, praises Shelton's as the
       best of the English translations.

2483   CERVANTES SAAVEDRA, MIGUEL DE. The History of Don Quixote of
       the Mancha. Translated by Thomas Shelton. Introductions
       by James Fitzmaurice-Kelly. 4 vols. Tudor Translations,
       1st Ser., 13-16. Edited by W. E. Henley. London: David
       Nutt, 1896, 328, 294, 323, 290pp.
          Provides reprint of Part I from 1612 edition and of
       Part II from 1620 edition. In "Introduction to the First
       Part," I, ix-li, provides critical estimate of Shelton's
       translation; discusses his style, identifies his source as
       the 1607 Brussels edition, and comments on the influence of
       the translation. In "Introduction to the Second Part," III,
       xi-l, provides critical estimate of Shelton's translation
       and identifies his source as the 1616 Brussels edition.

2484   CERVANTES SAAVEDRA, MIGUEL DE. The History of the Valorous &
       Witty Knight-Errant Don Quixote of the Mancha. Translated
       by Thomas Shelton. Introduction by Alfred W[illiam] Pol-
       lard. 3 vols. Library of English Classics. London:

Shelton

> Macmillan and Co.; New York: Macmillan Co., 1900, 381,
> 373, 359pp.
> Provides modernized text based on 1620 edition. In
> "Bibliographical Note," I, v-viii, comments briefly on edi-
> tions of Shelton's translation.

2485 CERVANTES SAAVEDRA, MIGUEL DE. The History of the Valorous
and Witty Knight-Errant Don Quixote of the Mancha. Translated by Thomas Shelton. Introduction by Royal Cortissoz.
4 vols. New York: Scribner's, 1906-1907, 453, 432, 409,
437pp.
Provides modernized reprint of unidentified edition.

2486 CERVANTES SAAVEDRA, MIGÜEL DE. The First Part of the Delight-
ful History of the Most Ingenious Knight Don Quixote of the
Mancha. Translated by Thomas Shelton. Edited by Charles W.
Eliot. Harvard Classics, 14. New York: Collier & Son,
1909, 545pp.
Provides modernized text based on unidentified edition.

2487 CERVANTES SAAVEDRA, MIGUEL DE. The History of Don Quixote of
the Mancha. Translated by Thomas Shelton. Introduction by
F[rederick] J[oseph] Harvey Darton. 2 vols. London:
Navarre Society, 1923, 568, 538pp.
Provides modernized reprint based on 1612 and 1620 edi-
tions.

2488 CERVANTES SAAVEDRA, MIGUEL DE. The History of the Valorous
and Wittie Knight-Errant Don Quixote of the Mancha. Translated by Thomas Shelton. 2 vols. Chelsea: Ashendene
Press, 1927-1928, 282, 266pp.
Provides reprint of 1612 edition of Part I and 1620 edition of Part II.

Studies

2489 ADOLPH, ROBERT. The Rise of Modern Prose Style. Cambridge:
M. I. T. Press, 1968, 372pp.
Compares Shelton's translation with those by Phillips
and Motteux in terms of style and point of view. Discusses
lack of "distance between characters and narrator" and of
concreteness in Shelton's translation (pp. 262-67).

2490 ALLEN, JOHN J. "Cide Hamete's English Translators." HR, 35
(October 1967), 366-67.
Notes mistranslation of passage in Cave of Montesinos's
episode in English translations of Don Quixote, including
that by Shelton.

2491   ANON. "Shelton's Don Quixote." TLS, 17 August 1922, p. 536.
       Provides bibliographical particulars on and locates
       copies of 1612 edition of Part I. (See also: "Early Edi-
       tions of Cervantes," TLS, 22 June 1922, p. 416.)

2492   B., R. O. "Notes on Acquisitions: The Ashendene Press Don
       Quixote, 1927-28." HLQ, 8 (May 1945), 321-22.
       Briefly discusses typography of work in report on gift
       of a vellum copy of 2488.

2493   BAWCUTT, N. W. "Don Quixote, Part I, and The Duchess of Mal-
       fi." MLR, 66 (July 1971), 488-91.
       Argues for Webster's use of Shelton's translation as a
       source for the play.

2494   COLES, J. "Translations of Don Quixote." N&Q, 90 (25 August
       1894), 145.
       Describes Frome Literary and Scientific Institution copy
       of 1612 edition of Shelton's translation.

2495   CUNNINGHAM, GRANVILLE C. "Don Quixote." Baconiana, 15
       (January-April 1917), 110-27.
       Seems to argue that Bacon was Shelton and composed Don
       Quixote in English, which Cervantes then translated into
       Spanish.

2496   DUFF, E[DWARD] GORDON. Notes on the Hitherto Undescribed
       First Edition of Shelton's Translation of Don Quixote, 1612-
       1620. [London: E & S, 19--], 19pp.
       Provides detailed "bibliographical history of the English
       editions." Analyzes publication history of editions of
       Shelton's translation and provides analytical bibliographi-
       cal descriptions of the editions.

2497   FREEHAFER, JOHN. "Cardenio, by Shakespeare and Fletcher."
       PMLA, 84 (May 1969), 501-13.
       Discusses indebtedness of original Cardenio to 1612 edi-
       tion of Shelton's translation.

2498   KNOWLES, EDWIN B., JR. "Allusions to Don Quixote before 1660."
       PQ, 20 (October 1941), 573-86.
       Provides chronological list of 49 allusions (through
       Shelton's translation) in English literature (1611-1660)
       and argues against assumption of "'instantaneous popularity'"
       of work in England. Reprinted in 2503.

2499   KNOWLES, EDWIN B. "Cervantes and English Literature," in
       Cervantes across the Centuries: A Quadricentennial Volume.

Shelton

Edited by Angel Flores and M. J. Benardete. New York: Dryden Press, 1947, pp. 267-93.
Includes discussion of critical reception of Don Quixote (through Shelton's translation) in seventeenth-century England.

2500 KNOWLES, EDWIN B. "Cervantes y la literatura inglesa." Realidad, 2 (1947), 268-97.
Includes discussion of Shelton's translation, noting that it is disfigured by abundant errors.

2501 KNOWLES, EDWIN B. "Don Quixote Abridged." PBSA, 49 (First Quarter 1955), 19-36.
Includes description of two late seventeenth-century abridgments based on Shelton's translation.

2502 KNOWLES, EDWIN B., JR. "The First and Second Editions of Shelton's Don Quixote Part I: A Collation and Dating." HR, 9 (April 1941), 252-65.
Lists and describes nature of variants in wording between the two editions and provides evidence for dating the publication of the second edition 1620. Reprinted in 2503.

2503 KNOWLES, EDWIN B., JR. Four Articles on Don Quixote in England. New York: New York University, 1941, 115pp.
In "Don Quixote in England before 1660," pp. 3-12, argues against commonly accepted notion that Shelton's translation was immediately popular. Includes reprints of 2498 and 2502.

2504 KNOWLES, EDWIN B., JR. "Some Textual Peculiarities of the First English Don Quixote." PBSA, 37, no. 3 (1943), 203-14.
Provides bibliographical description of 1612 edition of Part I and lists variants discovered as the result of collation of seventeen copies.

2505 KNOWLES, EDWIN B. "Thomas Shelton, Translator." Studies in the Renaissance, 5 (1958), 160-75.
Suggests that the "deere friend" for whom Shelton translated Don Quixote was Richard Nugent.

*2506 KNOWLES, EDWIN B., JR. "The Vogue of Don Quixote in England from 1605 to 1660." Ph.D. dissertation, New York University, 1939.
Abstract not available.

2507 PEERS, E. ALLISON. "Cervantes in England." BHS, 24 (October 1947), 226-38. [Translated as: "Cervantes en Inglaterra," in Homenaje a Cervantes, Vol. II. Valencia, 1950, 279-86.]

Includes discussion of circumstances surrounding Shelton's translation and the looseness with which he handles the text.

2508 R., R. "Don Quixote." N&Q, 61 (6 March 1880), 206.
      Notes prices of two editions of Shelton's translation illustrated with engravings.

2509 R., R. "Don Quixote: Shelton's Translation." N&Q, 63 (7 May 1881), 378.
      Notes that the Laing copy of Shelton's translation of Don Quixote was offered by Pickering, the bookseller, in catalogue of 1881.

2510 SALAZAR CHAPELA, ESTEBAN. "Clasicos espanoles en Inglaterra." CA, 11, no. 1 (1952), 256-61.
      Includes discussion of influence of Shelton's Don Quixote on English literature.

2511 SALAZAR SANTACOLOMA, EDGARDO. "En torno al Quijote." BCB, 10 (1967), 843-50.
      Presents imaginary dialogue between Verstegan and Shelton, in which Verstegan points out errors in Shelton's Don Quixote.

2512 SOLLY, EDWARD. "Cervantes' Farewell." N&Q, 56 (25 August 1877), 146.
      Corrects Shelton's mistranslation of final sentence of the preface to Don Quixote.

2513 THORNBURY, WALTER. "Did Shakespeare Ever Read Don Quixote?" N&Q, 44 (9 September 1871), 201.
      Speculates that Shakespeare probably read Shelton's translation of Part I. (See: 2517; J. Henry Shorthouse, "Did Shakespeare Ever Read Don Quixote?," N&Q, 44 [7 October 1871], 295; Walter Thornbury, "Did Shakespeare Ever Read Don Quixote?," N&Q, 44 [25 November 1871], 444.)

2514 TODD, F. M. "Webster and Cervantes." MLR, 51 (July 1956), 321-23.
      Argues for Webster's use of Don Quixote as source for The Duchess of Malfi; suggests possibility that Webster might have seen Shelton's translation in manuscript.

2515 TOLE, F. A. "Don Quixote." N&Q, 61 (10 January 1880), 43.
      Calls attention to a copy of Shelton's translation "illustrated with a set of French plates" which sold at Laing's sale for £55.

Shelton

2516　WATTS, H. E.　"Cervantes and His Translators."　N&Q, 44 (11
　　　　November 1871), 392.
　　　　　　Praises Shelton's translation for coming "nearer the
　　　　genius of the author [i.e., Cervantes] than any of the Eng-
　　　　lish translations."　(See J. Henry Shorthouse, "Cervantes
　　　　and His Translators," N&Q, 44 [2 December 1871], 456-57.)

2517　WATTS, H. E.　"Did Shakespeare Ever Read Don Quixote?"　N&Q,
　　　　44 (7 October 1871), 295.
　　　　　　Supports Thornbury's speculation (2513) that Shakespeare
　　　　read Part I of Shelton's translation.

2518　WILSON, EDWARD M.　"Cervantes and English Literature of the
　　　　Seventeenth Century."　BH, 50 (1948), 27-52.
　　　　　　Discusses use of Shelton's translation of Don Quixote by
　　　　Edmund Gayton in his Pleasant Notes upon Don Quixote.

*2519　WRIGHT, ALEXANDER TREMAINE.　Thomas Shelton, Translator.
　　　　London:　Privately Printed, 1898, 6pp.
　　　　　　Not located.　Cited in 2505.

SHEPPARD, SAMUEL (fl. 1646)

The Loves of Amandus and Sophronia.　Wing S3167.

Studies

2520　ROLLINS, HYDER E.　"Samuel Sheppard and His Praise of Poets."
　　　　SP, 24 (1927), 509-55.
　　　　　　Discusses briefly Amandus and Sophronia in context of
　　　　Sheppard's life and other works.　Characterizes it as "an
　　　　undistinguished work told in undistinguished prose inter-
　　　　rupted by mediocre poems."

SIDNEY, SIR PHILIP (1554-1586)

The Countesse of Pembrokes Arcadia.　STC 22539-22550.　Wing S3768-
　　　　3770.

Bibliographies

2521　GODSCHALK [i.e., GODSHALK], WILLIAM L[EIGH].　"Bibliography of
　　　　Sidney Studies since 1935," in Sir Philip Sidney as a
　　　　Literary Craftsman.　By Kenneth [Orne] Myrick.　2d edition.
　　　　Lincoln:　University of Nebraska Press, 1965, pp. 352-58.
　　　　　　Provides annotated author list of books and articles.

2522 GODSHALK, WILLIAM L[EIGH]. "Recent Studies in Sidney." ELR,
2 (Winter 1972), 148-64.
Reviews important scholarship on Arcadia and lists
studies published between 1945 and 1969.

2523 GUFFEY, GEORGE ROBERT. "Sir Philip Sidney, 1941-1965," in
Elizabethan Bibliographies Supplements, VII: Samuel Daniel,
1942-1965; Michael Drayton, 1941-1965; Sir Philip Sidney,
1941-1965. Compiled by George Robert Guffey. London:
Nether Press, 1967, 30-48.
Provides chronological list of criticism, 1941-1965;
supplements 2525.

2524 JUEL-JENSEN, BENT. "Some Uncollected Authors, XXXIV: Sir
Philip Sidney, 1554-1586." BC, 11 (1962), 468-79; 12
(1963), 196-201.
Discusses lack of availability of bibliographical data
on Sidney's works and provides an annotated "Check-List of
Editions of Arcadia to 1739" (23 items).

2525 TANNENBAUM, SAMUEL A. Sir Philip Sidney (A Concise Bibliography). Elizabethan Bibliographies, 23. New York: Samuel
A. Tannenbaum, 1941, 77pp.
Provides classified list of editions and criticism. Con-
tinued by 2523.

2526 WASHINGTON, MARY ALDRIDGE. "A Bibliography of Criticism of
Sir Philip Sidney, 1940-1965." Ph.D. dissertation, Univer-
sity of Missouri, Columbia, 1969, 346pp.
See 2527.

2527 WASHINGTON, MARY A[LDRIDGE]. Sir Philip Sidney: An Annotated
Bibliography of Modern Criticism, 1941-1970. University of
Missouri Studies, 56. Columbia: University of Missouri
Press, 1972, 200pp.
Lists 215 items alphabetically by author in section
headed "Arcadia" (pp. 58-103). Other works on Arcadia scat-
tered throughout; see especially "Editions" (pp. 51-52) and
"Foreign Studies" (pp. 169-71).

Editions

2528 SIDNEY, PHILIP. The Countess of Pembroke's Arcadia. London:
S. Low, Marston, & Co., 1867, 512pp.
Provides modernized, abridged version based on unidentified edition. In "Introductory and Biographical Essay,"
pp. vii-xxxii, anonymous writer discusses Sidney's style
and lack of clear structure of work.

Sidney

2529   SIDNEY, PHILIP. The Countess of Pembroke's Arcadia. Edited
           by H[einrich] Oskar Sommer. London: Kegan Paul, Trench,
           Trübner, and Co., 1891, 786pp.
              Provides facsimile reprint of 1590 edition. In "Intro-
           duction," pp. 1-45, traces bibliographical history of work
           from 1590 to 1867.

2530   SIDNEY, PHILIP. The Countess of Pembroke's Arcadia. Edited
           by Ernest A[lbert] Baker. London: G. Routledge and Sons;
           New York: E. P. Dutton & Co., 1907, 718pp.
              Provides modernized reprint of 1739 London edition;
           includes continuations by Alexander and Beling. In "Intro-
           duction," pp. vii-xxvi, discusses affinity of work "in its
           style and in the purely imaginative nature of the story, the
           characters, and the life depicted" with poetry. Examines
           influence of romance on work, its publishing history, its
           popularity and influence, and its place in development of
           English prose fiction.

2531   SIDNEY, PHILIP. The Complete Works of Sir Philip Sidney.
           Edited by Albert Feuillerat. 4 vols. Cambridge English
           Classics. Cambridge: Cambridge University Press, 1912-
           1926, 584, 405, 453, 414pp.
              Provides editions of New Arcadia (based on 1590 edition;
           vol. I), the conclusion to the 1593 edition (vol. II, 1-
           207), and the Old Arcadia from the Clifford MS.(vol. IV).
           See 2549.

2532   SIDNEY, PHILIP. The Countess of Pembrokes Arcadia. Introduc-
           tion by Carl Dennis. Kent: Kent State University Press,
           1970, not paginated.
              Provides facsimile of text of 2529. In "Introduction,"
           pp. v-lxxiii, discusses genre, the function of the settings,
           characterization, themes (especially love), structure, and
           style.

2533   SIDNEY, PHILIP. The Countess of Pembroke's Arcadia (The Old
           Arcadia). Edited by Jean Robertson. Oxford: Clarendon
           Press, 1973, 588pp.
              Provides critical edition with a modernized text based
           on St. John's College, Cambridge, MS. I.7. In "General In-
           troduction" (pp. xv-xli) discusses date of composition,
           sources, style and diction, genre, and influence on later
           works. In "Textual Introduction" (pp. xlii-lxxi) provides
           description of manuscripts and printed editions, and dis-
           cusses relationships among the texts.

Studies

2534 ADAMS, W[ILLIAM] DAVENPORT. "Sidney's Arcadia," in Famous
Books: Sketches in the Highways and Byeways of English
Literature. By W[illiam] Davenport Adams. London: W.
Glaisher, 1875, pp. 114-44.
Examines extremes in critical attitude toward Arcadia
and provides a general overview of the main aspects of the
work along with a lengthy synopsis.

2535 ADDLESHAW, PERCY. Sir Philip Sidney. London: Methuen & Co.,
1909, 395pp.
Discusses Arcadia in context of Sidney's life and times.
Stresses faults of work. Takes at face value Sidney's ex-
planation of manner of composition and asserts that because
of this piece-meal approach the work fails as an artistic
whole (passim).

2536 ALPERS, PAUL J. The Poetry of The Faerie Queene. Princeton:
Princeton University Press, 1967, 424pp.
Provides comparison between pastoral episode of Book VI
of Faerie Queene and Book I of Arcadia, arguing that Sidney's emphasis on the analytic mode and "moral consciousness
restricts...the interest and value of pastoral experience"
in his work (pp. 289-96, passim).

2537 AMOS, ARTHUR KIRKHAM, JR. "The Narrative Technique of Sir
Philip Sidney's New Arcadia." Ph.D. dissertation, University of Oregon, 1970, 238pp.
Examines the "structural metaphor" of each book and analyzes the relationship of overall structure to content and
meaning.

2538 AMOS, ARTHUR K[IRKHAM], JR. Time, Space, and Value: The Nar-
rative Structure of the New Arcadia. Lewisburg: Bucknell
University Press, 1976, 203pp.
Analyzes narrative structure and relationship to themes.
Analyzes the "ordering principle" of each book: I, "the
dyadic relationships of space"; II, "time"; III, "value."

2539 ANDERSON, D. M. "The Dido Incident in Sidney's Arcadia." N&Q,
NS, 3 (October 1956), 417-19.
Finds implications of rape and emasculation in incident
and suggests that the extant version might have been toned
down for publication. Examines place of incident in Arcadia, suggesting that the scene "show[s] us Pyrocles unre-
mittingly noble in a setting of passion and treachery."
Traces source of passage to Amadis de Gaule.

Sidney

2540   ANDERSON, D. M. "The Trial of the Princes in the Arcadia,
        Book V." RES, NS, 8 (November 1957), 409-12.
            Investigates "issues...fundamental to the political the-
        ory of the sixteenth century" behind the trial and cautions
        against interpreting trial in light of revision of earlier
        books.

2541   ANDREWS, MICHAEL C[AMERON]. "Jack Drum's Entertainment as
        Burlesque." RenQ, 24 (Summer 1971), 226-31.
            Discusses Marston's use of the Argalus-Parthenia tale as
        source for Jack Drum's Entertainment and suggests that the
        play was meant to burlesque both the Arcadia and The Trial
        of Chivalry, a play which was also based on Sidney's romance.

2542   ANDREWS, M[ICHAEL] C[AMERON]. "Sidney's Arcadia and Soliman
        and Perseda." AN&Q, 11 (January 1973), 68-69.
            Suggests Parthenia's death as Kyd's source for Perseda's
        death.

2543   ANDREWS, MICHAEL C[AMERON]. "Sidney's Arcadia and The Winter's
        Tale." SQ, 23 (Spring 1972), 200-202.
            Discusses story of Plangus as a source for a passage in
        The Winter's Tale (4.2.25 ff.).

2544   ANDREWS, MICHAEL CAMERON. "Sidney's Arcadia on the English
        Stage: A Study of the Dramatic Adaptations of The Countess
        of Pembroke's Arcadia." Ph.D. dissertation, Duke Univer-
        sity, 1966, 206pp.
            Analyzes use of Arcadia as source for nine plays.

2545   ANDREWS, MICHAEL C[AMERON]. "The Sources of Andromana." RES,
        NS, 19 (August 1968), 295-300.
            Compares story of Plangus in Arcadia to its use in Beau-
        mont and Fletcher's Cupid's Revenge and in the anonymous
        Andromana. Argues that Arcadia is less important as source
        than Cupid's Revenge.

*2546   ANON. "A Passage in Arcadia." N&Q, 38 (18 January 1869), 56.
            Not located. Listed in 2525.

2547   ANON. "Sidney, Spenser, and Elizabethan Romance." Tait's
        Edinburgh Magazine, 22 (October 1855), 577-82. [Reprinted
        as: "Sir Philip Sidney and the Arcadia." Eclectic Maga-
        zine, 36 (December 1855), 1051-57.]
            Provides general overview of Arcadia. Discusses Sidney's
        style and asserts that eclogues "are trivial, tedious, and
        mean" and "have no connexion with the story."

2548 ANON. "Sir Philip Sidney's Arcadia." Bookworm, 1 (1888),
      145-49.
      Gives popular account of moral value of work and of its
      composition and publication.

2549 APPLEGATE, JAMES. "Sidney's Classical Meters." MLN, 70
      (April 1955), 254-55.
      Calls attention to variety in Sidney's experiments with
      classical meters and notes that in Feuillerat's edition of
      Old Arcadia (2531) "the pattern notations for the elegiacs
      and the hexameters give no indication of variations which
      were allowable in classical practice and which Sidney in
      fact did admit into his."

2550 ARMSTRONG, WILLIAM A. "King Lear and Sidney's Arcadia." TLS,
      14 October 1949, p. 665.
      Argues that Pamela-Crecopia debate influenced Shake-
      speare's treatment of theme of nature in Lear and provided
      the direct source for 4.2.1-2. See 2860.

2551 ATKINS, J[OHN] W[ILLIAM] H[EY]. "Elizabethan Prose Fiction,"
      in The Cambridge History of English Literature, III:
      Renascence and Reformation. Edited by A[dolphus] W[illiam]
      Ward and A[lfred] R[ayney] Waller. Cambridge: Cambridge
      University Press, 1909, 339-73.
      Includes discussion of Sidney's treatment of love in
      Arcadia and influences on work; comments on form, style,
      popularity, and influence of work (pp. 351-55).

2552 BAKER, ERNEST A[LBERT]. The History of the English Novel,
      Vol. II. London: H. F. & G. Witherby, 1929, 303pp.
      In Chapter V ("Sidney's Arcadia," pp. 67-89), discusses
      Sidney's style and its affinity with poetry, influences on
      the two Arcadias, characterization, and the influence of
      Sidney's work on later Elizabethan fiction and the develop-
      ment of the novel.

2553 BARKER, WILLIAM. "Three Essays on the Rhetorical Tradition."
      Ph.D. dissertation, Brandeis University, 1968, 151pp.
      Examines conclusion of Arcadia in context of Renaissance
      attitude toward "artifice in speech." Analyzes how charac-
      ters "experience themselves in rhetoric, but...do not ex-
      perience the knowledge of the narrator and reader:...a
      Logos beyond words is ordering the structure of their
      world."

2554 BASKERVILL, C. R. "Sidney's Arcadia and The Tryall of Cheval-
      ry." MP, 10 (October 1912), 197-201.

Sidney

>   Discusses anonymous playwright's use of Arcadia (Argalus
>   and Parthenia episode) as a source.

2555   BAUGHAN, DENVER EWING. "Sidney's Defence of the Earl of
>   Leicester and the Revised Arcadia." JEGP, 51, no. 1 (1952),
>   35–41.
>   Discusses increased emphasis on genealogy in revised
>   Arcadia and argues that the Defence of the Earl of Leicester
>   (written 1584) "provided the occasion for, at least, the
>   genealogical emphasis in the revision, if not the whole
>   work."

*2556   BAUGHAN, DENVER E[WING]. "Sir Philip Sidney and the Two Ver-
>   sions of the Arcadia." Ph.D. dissertation, Yale University,
>   1934.
>   Abstract not available.

2557   BEATY, FREDERICK L. "Lodge's Forbonius and Prisceria and Sid-
>   ney's Arcadia." ES, 49 (February 1968), 38–45.
>   Argues that Lodge had access to a manuscript of the Old
>   Arcadia and was deliberately imitating it in Forbonius and
>   Prisceria. Points out similarities in plot, style, and
>   poetry between the two works.

2558   BECKETT, ROBERT DUDLEY. "The Narrative Structure of the Old
>   Arcadia and the New Arcadia of Sir Philip Sidney: An
>   Analytical Comparison." Ph.D. dissertation, University of
>   Colorado, 1967, 200pp.
>   "[A]nalyze[s] four aspects of narrative structure in each
>   work: ...the story-teller relationship...; the plot pattern
>   ...; archetypal plot...; characters."

2559   BEESE, MARGARET. "Manuscripts of Sidney's Arcadia." TLS, 4
>   May 1940, p. 224.
>   Describes briefly two manuscripts (British Library MS.
>   Add. 41,498 and MS. Jesus 150) of Old Arcadia.

2560   BENNETT, JOSEPHINE WATERS. The Evolution of The Faerie Queene.
>   Chicago: University of Chicago Press, 1942, 309pp.
>   Discusses influence of Arcadia on Spenser's poem (passim).

2561   BERGBUSCH, MARTIN LUTHER THEODORE. "Political Thought and Con-
>   duct in Sidney's Arcadia." Ph.D. dissertation, Cornell
>   University, 1971, 277pp.
>   Examines "extent [to which] Sidney's Arcadia embodies a
>   coherent political theory." Analyzes political topics to
>   determine Sidney's adherence to or departure from "English
>   orthodoxy."

2562　BERGBUSCH, MARTIN [LUTHER THEODORE]. "Rebellion in the New
　　　　Arcadia." PQ, 53 (January 1974), 29-41.
　　　　　　Examines Sidney's treatment of the uprisings in New Ar-
　　　　cadia and possible influences on his attitude toward rebel-
　　　　lion to argue that "[t]he specific influence of Huguenot
　　　　thought about civil insurrection upon Sidney is clear and
　　　　unmistakable."

2563　BILL, ALFRED H.　Astrophel; or, the Life and Death of the Re-
　　　　nowned Sir Philip Sidney. New York:　Farrar & Rinehart,
　　　　1937, 382pp.
　　　　　　Discusses briefly the composition and revision of Arcadia
　　　　in the context of Sidney's life (passim).

2564　BLOOR, R[OBERT] H[ENRY] U[NDERWOOD]. The English Novel from
　　　　Chaucer to Galsworthy. University Extension Library. Lon-
　　　　don:　I. Nicholson and Watson, 1935, 248pp.
　　　　　　Includes discussion of Sidney's style and didacticism in
　　　　Arcadia (pp. 73-82).

2565　BLUESTONE, MAX.　From Story to Stage:　The Dramatic Adaptation
　　　　of Prose Fiction in the Period of Shakespeare and His Con-
　　　　temporaries. SEngL, 70. The Hague:　Mouton, 1974, 341pp.
　　　　　　Includes an examination of the adaptation and transforma-
　　　　tion of portions of the Arcadia by Fletcher in Cupid's Re-
　　　　venge (passim).

2566　BOAS, FREDERICK S.　Sir Philip Sidney, Representative Elizabe-
　　　　than:　His Life and Writings. London:　Staples Press, 1955,
　　　　204pp.
　　　　　　Describes the extant manuscripts and printed editions
　　　　(up to 1926) of the Arcadia.　Provides a detailed synopsis
　　　　of both the Old and the New Arcadia, and gives a general
　　　　comparison of the two versions (pp. 56-130).

2567　BOKLUND, GUNNAR.　The Duchess of Malfi:　Sources, Themes,
　　　　Characters. Cambridge:　Harvard University Press, 1962,
　　　　199pp.
　　　　　　Includes discussion of Webster's use of Arcadia as source
　　　　(passim).

2568　BOND, WILLIAM HENRY.　"The Reputation and Influence of Sir
　　　　Philip Sidney." Ph.D. dissertation, Harvard University,
　　　　1941, 360pp.
　　　　　　Traces fluctuations in reputation and influence of
　　　　Arcadia.

415

Sidney

2569   BOURNE, H[ENRY] R[ICHARD] FOX. <u>A Memoir of Sir Philip Sidney</u>.
        London: Chapman and Hall, 1862, 573pp.
             Suggests that reading <u>Euphues</u> caused Sidney to think that
        he could produce a better work and thus wrote <u>Arcadia</u>. In-
        cludes general discussion of style, subject matter, and de-
        fects (pp. 322-48). Revised as 2570.

2570   BOURNE, H[ENRY] R[ICHARD] FOX. <u>Sir Philip Sidney: Type of</u>
        <u>English Chivalry in the Elizabethan Age</u>. Heroes of the
        Nations, 5. New York: G. P. Putnam's Sons, 1891, 402pp.
             Discusses <u>Arcadia</u> in the context of Sidney's life and
        times: treats work as a "'trifle.'" Examines, in general
        terms, Sidney's style, his characterization, and influences
        on the work (passim). Revision of 2569.

2571   BOWEN, MARY. "Some New Notes on Sidney's Poems." <u>MLN</u>, 10
        (April 1895), 236-46.
             Notes presence of eight <u>Arcadia</u> poems in Rawlinson MS.
        Poetic 85, suggesting these will have to be considered by
        a future editor of <u>Arcadia</u>.

2572   BRIE, FRIEDRICH. <u>Sidneys Arcadia: Eine Studie zur englischen</u>
        <u>Renaissance</u>. Quellen und Forschungen, 124. Strasbourg:
        K. J. Trübner, 1918, 346pp.
             Examines influences--particularly classical--on themes
        and form of <u>Arcadia</u>. Identifies autobiographical elements
        (including characters).

2573   BRIE, FRIEDRICH. "Das Volksbuch <u>Gehörnten Siegfried</u> und Sid-
        neys <u>Arcadia</u>." <u>Archiv</u>, 121 (1908), 287-90.
             Discusses anonymous author's use of Dametas-Clinias epi-
        sode in <u>Arcadia</u> (Opitz's translation) as source. (See:
        Gustav Brockstedt, "Zu der Abhandlung Friedrich Bries:
        'Das Volksbuch vom <u>Gehörnten Siegfried</u> und Sidneys <u>Arcadia</u>,'"
        <u>Archiv</u>, 123 [1909], 155-59.)

2574   BRIGGS, WILLIAM DINSMORE. "Political Ideas in Sidney's <u>Ar-
        cadia</u>." <u>SP</u>, 28 (April 1931), 137-61.
             Attempts to ascertain Sidney's "political ideas," par-
        ticularly his perception of the ideal relationship between
        ruler and subjects. Notes areas of agreement with <u>Vindiciae</u>
        <u>contra Tyrannos</u>. (See also: William Dinsmore Briggs,
        "Sidney's Political Ideas," <u>SP</u>, 29 [October 1932], 534-42.)

2575   BROWN, ELAINE V. BEILIN. "The Uses of Mythology in Elizabethan
        Romance." Ph.D. dissertation, Princeton University, 1973,
        336pp.
             Provides "interpretation of the mythology" in <u>Arcadia</u>.

2576 BROWN, JAMES NEIL. "Elizabethan Pastoralism and Renaissance
Platonism." AUMLA, No. 44 (November 1975), pp. 247-67.
Includes discussion of Arcadia in examination of influ-
ence of Neoplatonism on Elizabethan pastoral.

2577 BROWN, T. E. "Sir Philip Sidney: A Causerie." New Review,
12 (April 1895), 415-24.
Discusses the "pure Euphuism" of Arcadia.

2578 BRUCKL, O. "Sir Philip Sidney's Arcadia as a Source for John
Webster's The Duchess of Malfi." ESA, 8 (1965), 31-55.
Discusses Arcadia as source of "mood and atmosphere" and
"images and epithets" for Webster's play.

2579 BRUNHUBER, K[ASPAR]. Sir Philip Sidneys Arcadia und ihre Nach-
läufer: Literarhistorische Studie. Nürnberg: M. Edelmann,
1903, 63pp.
Provides notes on sources of Arcadia and traces its use
as a source in seventeenth- and eighteenth-century drama
and fiction.

2580 BUCHIN, ERNA. "Sidney's Arcadia als Quelle für Cymbeline."
Archiv, 143 (1922), 250-52.
Identifies two passages in Arcadia used by Shakespeare
as sources.

2581 BULLOUGH, GEOFFREY. "Introduction [to Hamlet]," in Narrative
and Dramatic Sources of Shakespeare, Vol. VII. Edited by
Geoffrey Bullough. London: Routledge and Kegan Paul; New
York: Columbia University Press, 1973, 3-59.
Suggests that episode treating Plexirtus's plot to have
Pyrocles and Musidorus murdered by ship captain was source
for Hamlet's "adventure with the pirates in Q2 and his good
relations with them."

2582 BULLOUGH, GEOFFREY. "Introduction [to King Lear]," in Narrative and Dramatic Sources of Shakespeare, Vol. VII. Edited
by Geoffrey Bullough. London: Routledge and Kegan Paul;
New York: Columbia University Press, 1973, 269-308.
Discusses Shakespeare's use of Arcadia (tale of blind
king of Paphlagonia, Plangus story, and Pamela-Crecopia
debate) as source for King Lear.

2583 BULLOUGH, GEOFFREY. "Introduction [to Pericles]," in Narrative
and Dramatic Sources of Shakespeare, Vol. VI. Edited by
Geoffrey Bullough. London: Routledge and Kegan Paul; New
York: Columbia University Press, 1966, 349-74.

417

Sidney

Suggests that Sidney had story of Apollonius of Tyre in mind when composing Arcadia; notes that Pyrocles's adventures "afford parallels to those of Apollonius."

2584   BUSH, DOUGLAS. "Marvell and Sidney." RES, NS, 3 (October 1952), 375.
In letter, notes that he had anticipated Martin (2816) in discussing parallels between Arcadia and Marvell's "The Definition of Love" in 141.

2585   BUTTERWORTH, WALTER. "Sir Philip Sidney and His Arcadia." Papers of the Manchester Literary Club, 23 (1897), 266-88.
Examines the influence of pastoral and heroic romances on Arcadia and discusses the "faults" and "excellences" of the work. Concludes that "the chiefest value of the work is that it is the truest biography of a period in the life of" Sidney.

2586   BUXTON, JOHN. "'A Draught of Sir Phillip Sidney's Arcadia,'" in Historical Essays, 1600-1750: Presented to David Ogg. Edited by H[enry] E[smond] Bell and R. L. Ollard. London: A. & C. Black, 1963, pp. 60-77.
Reprints text of anonymous seventeenth-century poem in which "the author adapts Sidney's...[Arcadia] to the circumstances which led to the outbreak of the civil war." Points out that the anonymous author regarded Sidney's work as a political allegory.

2587   BUXTON, JOHN. Elizabethan Taste. London: Macmillan; New York: St. Martin's Press, 1963, 384pp.
In section on Sidney's Arcadia (pp. 246-68) analyzes reasons for popularity from sixteenth to eighteenth century. Examines sixteenth-century attitudes toward the work--especially its rhetorical qualities.

2588   BUXTON, JOHN. "Sidney and Theophrastus." ELR, 2 (Winter 1972), 79-82.
Discusses briefly the influence of the Theophrastan character on the "comic or satiric descriptions of character" in Arcadia and describes "an elaborate [seventeenth-century manuscript] index to the Arcadia, made by someone familiar with the English imitators of Theophrastus."

2589   C[ARTWRIGHT, ROBERT]. "The Arcadia Unveiled." N&Q, 27 (6 June 1863), 441-43; (20 June 1863), 481-83; (27 June 1863), 501-503.
Treats work as an allegory, identifying various characters (e.g., Strephon as Spenser, Basilius as Lord Burghley, Crecopia as Mary Queen of Scots) and personal allusions.

2590   C[ARTWRIGHT, ROBERT]. "The Faerie Queene Unveiled." N&Q, 28
        (11 July 1863), 21-22; (25 July 1863), 65-66; (8 August
        1863), 101-103.
            Discusses influence of Arcadia on Faerie Queene, espe-
        cially Spenser's imitation of scenes and characters. As-
        serts that Pyrochles and Cymochles are "satire[s]" of
        Pyrocles and Musidorus, respectively.

2591   CARTWRIGHT, ROBERT. "Shakspere, Sidney, and Spenser," in
        Papers on Shakspere. By Robert Cartwright. London: J. R.
        Smith, 1877, pp. 17-27.
            Argues that "Philoclea is a lover's portrait of Miss
        [Frances] Walsingham" and that Parthenia is a portrait of
        Penelope Devereux.

2592   CASPARI, FRITZ. Humanism and the Social Order in Tudor Eng-
        land. Chicago: University of Chicago Press, 1954, 303pp.
            In Chapter VII ("Sir Philip Sidney," pp. 157-75), ana-
        lyzes Arcadia as heroic poem; examines ideals embodied in
        characters, which are designed as models for the reader to
        imitate. Examines influence of humanism on Sidney's con-
        ception of man and the state, and discusses political theory
        in work.

2593   CHALLIS, LORNA. "The Use of Oratory in Sidney's Arcadia." SP,
        62 (July 1965), 561-76.
            Analyzes several speeches to illustrate Sidney's exploi-
        tation of "the dramatic possibilities of classical oratory,"
        particularly in his "use of formal speech as an integral
        part of an imitation of human action." Concludes that "in
        treating argument and debate as an integral part of person-
        ality...he anticipates...the psychological realism which
        was to become an essential feature of drama and later of
        fiction."

2594   CHANG, H[SIN] C[HANG]. Allegory and Courtesy in Spenser: A
        Chinese View. Edinburgh University Publications, Language
        and Literature, 8. Edinburgh: Edinburgh University Press,
        1955, 237pp.
            In Chapter V, compares Spenser's treatment of certain
        elements of romance in Faerie Queene, Book VI, with Sidney's
        treatment in Arcadia. Examines, in particular, their re-
        spective attitudes toward, and use of, chivalry (pp. 114-
        51).

2595   CHARNEY, MAURICE. "Hawthorne and Sidney's Arcadia." N&Q, NS,
        7 (July 1960), 264-65.
            Corrects misinformation about Hawthorne's ownership of
        a copy of Arcadia.

Sidney

2596 CLEMEN, WOLFGANG. Shakespeares Bilder: Ihre Entwicklung und
ihre Funktionem im dramatischen Werk. Bonner Studien zur
Englischen Philologie, 27. Bonn: P. Hanstein, 1936, 347pp.
Includes discussion of Sidney's imagery in Arcadia (pp.
317-22).

2597 CLUETT, ROBERT. "Arcadia Wired: Preliminaries to an Elec-
tronic Investigation of the Prose Style of Philip Sidney."
Lang&S, 7 (Spring 1974), 119-37.
Presents "a partial quantitative account of Sidney's
style in prose fiction measured against those of Lodge,
Lyly, and Nashe." Concentrates analysis on syntax and word
classes.

2598 COFFEE, JESSIE A. "Arcadia to America: Sir Philip Sidney and
John Saffin." AL, 45 (March 1973), 100-104.
Discusses the seventeenth-century New England judge's
use of Arcadia as a source for aphorisms copied into his
commonplace book.

2599 COHEN, EILEEN ZELDA. "Gentle Knight and Pious Servant: A
Study of Sidney's Protestantism." Ph.D. dissertation, University of Maryland, 1965, 208pp.
Examines how "Sidney's humanism and moderate Anglicanism
are...apparent in...the Old Arcadia." Argues that "[c]er-
tain passages of the Old Arcadia can be meaningfully inter-
preted as specific denials of attitudes and ideas associated
with Puritans in the Elizabethan mind."

2600 COHEN, EILEEN Z[ELDA]. "The Old Arcadia: A Treatise on Mod-
eration." RBPH, 46, no. 3 (1968), 749-70.
Examines emphasis on order, law, tradition, and reason
to argue that in "the Old Arcadia, Sidney showed himself
the exemplar of the humanist, conservative tradition of his
faith--the Anglican Church." Also argues that Sidney was
not sympathetic toward the ideas in Mornay's A Defense of
Liberty against Tyrants.

2601 COLLIER, J[OHN] PAYNE. "Sir Philip Sidney and His Works."
Gentleman's Magazine, 188 (April 1850), 370-77.
Provides "bibliographical particulars" of 1590 edition
of Arcadia and compares contents with 1598 edition.

2602 COMITO, TERRY [ALLEN]. "The Lady in a Landscape and the Po-
etics of Elizabethan Pastoral." UTQ, 41 (Spring 1972),
200-18.
Examines Arcadia in arguing that the Urania myth which
animates the work "gives us a parable for understanding the

poet's aspirations—and also their necessary limits." Suggests that "[t]he incantation of memory and desire with which Sidney's romance begins is an attempt to find in the usual properties of the pastoral world not dead matter but a voice speaking of qualities otherwise 'unspeakeable.'"

2603 COMITO, TERRY ALLEN. "Renaissance Gardens and Elizabethan Romance." Ph.D. dissertation, Harvard University, 1968.
Includes examination of Arcadia, especially Sidney's treatment of "man's relation to the external world." Discusses work in context of examination of relationship between Renaissance gardens and the "ways in which the pastoral poet...imagines space and its possibilities."

*2604 COOKE, PAUL J. "The Spanish Romances in Sir Philip Sidney's Arcadia." Ph.D. dissertation, University of Illinois at Urbana-Champaign, 1939.
Abstract not available.

2605 COOPER, SHEROD M., JR. The Sonnets of Astrophel and Stella: A Stylistic Study. SEngL, 41. The Hague: Mouton, 1968, 183pp.
Analyzes comments in Arcadia on style (pp. 11-21).

2606 COULMAN, D. "'Spotted to Be Known.'" JWCI, 20 (1957), 179-80.
Provides "further proof of the identification of Sidney with Philisides" by noting that a manuscript copy of Abraham Fraunce's Insignium, Armorum, Emblematum, Hieroglyphicorum, et Symbolorum among Sidney's papers at Penshurst includes copy of Philisides's device identified as belonging to Sidney.

2607 COURTHOPE, W[ILLIAM] J[OHN]. A History of English Poetry, II: The Renaissance and the Reformation. London: Macmillan and Co., 1897, 457pp.
Includes general critical estimate of Arcadia: discusses the idealism of the work, its defects, and its contribution to the development of English drama. Also discusses Sidney's style (pp. 203-33).

2608 CRAIK, T. W. "Introduction," in Sir Philip Sidney: Selections from Arcadia and Other Poetry and Prose. By Philip Sidney. Edited by T. W. Craik. New York: Capricorn Books, 1966, pp. 1-18. [Published in Great Britain as: Sir Philip Sidney: Selected Poetry and Prose. London: Methuen, 1965.]
Discusses briefly style, "epic character," and revision, commenting on shift of emphasis from "romantic complications" to "opportunities of displaying heroic action and

heroic character." Provides annotated selections from New Arcadia (pp. 78-194).

2609   CRANZ, CORNELIA. "Sir Philip Sidney and His Arcadia." College Folio, 13 (December 1904), 79-89.
       Provides synopsis and discusses Sidney's style, the "rambling plot" of the work, and the "lack of characterization."

2610   CRAWFORD, CHARLES. "John Webster and Sir Philip Sidney." N&Q, 110 (17 September 1904), 221-23; (1 October 1904), 261-63; (15 October 1904), 303-304; (29 October 1904), 342-43; (12 November 1904), 381-82. [Reprinted in: Charles Crawford. Collectanea, First Series. Stratford-on-Avon: Shakespeare Head Press, 1906, pp. 20-46.]
       Examines Webster's use of Arcadia as source in his works.

2611   CROLL, MORRIS W[ILLIAM]. "Arcadia." MLN, 16 (February 1901), 62-63.
       Suggests Penshurst as original of description of Kalander's house.

2612   CROMPTON, N. J. R. "Sidney and Symbolic Heraldry." CoA, 8 (1965), 244-48.
       Explains symbolism behind Sidney's description of armor and emblems in Arcadia. (Continuation apparently not published.)

2613   [CROSSLEY, JAMES?] "The Countess of Pembroke's Arcadia... 1633...." Retrospective Review, 2, Part 2 (1820), Article 1, 1-44. [Reprinted as: Sir Philip Sidney and the Arcadia. London: Chapman and Hall, 1853, 85pp.]
       Provides lengthy synopsis of plot, examines characteristics of Sidney as writer, and discusses "faults" of the work.

2614   CUTTS, JOHN P. "Dametas' Song in Sidney's Arcadia." Renaissance News, 11 (Autumn 1958), 183-88.
       Transcribes musical setting of song from Thomas Ravenscroft's Pammelia and speculates that such a setting raises possibility that "behind the first book [of Old Arcadia] there is the shadow of an earlier masque-like entertainment" or "that the manuscript of the first book...inspired a semi-dramatic performance."

2615   CUTTS, JOHN P. "Introduction," in Loves Changelinges Change: An Anonymous Play Based on Sidney's Arcadia. North American Mentor Texts and Studies Series, 2. Fennimore, Wisconsin: James Westburg & Associates, 1974, pp. vii-xix.

Discusses appearance in text of play versions (not elsewhere extant) of three poems from Arcadia. Examines anonymous author's use of New Arcadia as a source, particularly
his tendency to copy passages verbatim or merely to trans-
pose word order.

2616 CUTTS, JOHN P. "More Manuscript Versions of Poems by Sidney."
      ELN, 9 (September 1971), 3-12.
      Discusses variants in versions of three Arcadia poems
      preserved in manuscript play "Loves Changelinges Change."
      Examines anonymous author's close reliance on New Arcadia
      as source.

2617 CUTTS, JOHN P. "Pericles in Rusty Armour, and the Matachine
      Dance of the Competitive Knights at the Court of Simonides."
      YES, 4 (1974), 49-51.
      Suggests possibility that "Sidney's treatment of chival-
      ric conventions in the Phalantus affair [New Arcadia] may...
      have influenced in some odd practical details Shakespeare's
      presentation of the tournament of knights in Pericles."

2618 DANA, MARGARET E[LIZABETH]. "Heroic and Pastoral: Sidney's
      Arcadia as Masquerade." CL, 25 (Fall 1973), 308-20.
      Analyzes the various effects of Sidney's use of disguise,
      arguing that it is "an essential and complex element of the
      fictional world of the Arcadia." Suggests that use of dis-
      guise allows Sidney to avoid the limitations of heroic nar-
      rative: "[h]e has been able to explore reaches of wit and
      playfulness which would not have been in keeping with the
      dignity of his heroes under normal circumstances."

2618a DANA, MARGARET E[LIZABETH]. "The Providential Plot of the Old
      Arcadia." SEL, 17 (Winter 1977), 39-57.
      Argues that the plot of Old Arcadia "is based upon the
      workings of providence, as mediated through the ambiguous
      voice of the oracle." Examines role of narrator, describing
      him "as ironic, sympathetic, and just." Analyzes conclusion
      to argue that it is meant "to give...a sense of life's para-
      doxes."

2619 DANA, MARGARET ELIZABETH. "Sidney's Two Arcadias: From Ro-
      mance Towards Epic." Ph.D. dissertation, University of
      California, Riverside, 1971, 257pp.
      Analyzes Sidney's attempt to synthesize epic and romance
      in both versions. Examines relationship of works to Italian
      and English criticism and to Orlando Furioso and the Aeneid.
      Argues that in his revision, Sidney moved away "from some
      of the romance elements towards the epic as the sixteenth
      century conceived it."

Sidney

2620   DANBY, JOHN F[RANCIS]. "The Poets on Fortune's Hill: Litera-
        ture and Society, 1580-1610." Cambridge Journal, 2 (1949),
        195-211.
            Discusses Sidney as the example of "the poet above the
        need for patronage,...with no desire to cater for any au-
        dience but himself." Incorporated into 2621.

2621   DANBY, JOHN F[RANCIS]. Poets on Fortune's Hill: Studies in
        Sidney, Shakespeare, Beaumont & Fletcher. London: Faber
        and Faber, 1952, 212pp. [Also published as: Elizabethan
        and Jacobean Poets: Studies in Sidney, Shakespeare, Beau-
        mont & Fletcher. London: Faber and Faber, 1954, 212pp.]
            Analyzes Arcadia as an elite work, a "Great House Ro-
        mance," and as a compendium in which the "material is de-
        liberately moralized." Provides a running analysis in which
        he examines Sidney's concern for "the inner environment of
        man," illustrates how the structure is "organized on a basis
        of contrasts and complements," analyzes characterization and
        style, and discusses Arcadia as a political, moral, and
        Christian treatise.

2622   DANCHIN, F. C. "Les Deux Arcadies de Sir Philip Sidney."
        Revue Anglo-Américaine, 5 (October 1927), 39-52.
            Examines, in a general manner, the relationships between
        the Old Arcadia and the revision. Discusses narrative
        technique.

2623   D[AVENPORT], A[RNOLD]. "Possible Echoes from Sidney's Arcadia
        in Shakespeare, Milton, and Others." N&Q, 194 (24 December
        1949), 554-55.
            Suggests echoes in works of Shakespeare, Milton, Drummond
        of Hawthornden, and Fuller.

2624   DAVIDSON, CLIFFORD. "Nature and Judgment in the Old Arcadia."
        PLL, 6 (Fall 1970), 348-65.
            Analyzes Sidney's treatment of Nature in the Old Arcadia,
        arguing that the work "dramatizes...the renaissance argument
        over Nature, especially in the area of ethics" and that
        "[i]t is Sidney's paradoxical and ambivalent treatment of
        this argument which underlies his analysis of the heroic
        life as against the retreat to a pastoral world."

2625   [DAVIS, SARAH MATILDA.] The Life and Times of Sir Philip Sid-
        ney. Boston: Ticknor and Fields, 1859, 282pp.
            Provides lengthy synopsis of Arcadia and offers general
        comments on style (pp. 152-94).

2626   DAVIS, WALTER R[ICHARDSON]. "Actaeon in Arcadia." <u>SEL</u>, 2
(Winter 1962), 95-110.
  Provides detailed analysis of allusion to Actaeon in
cave episode of Book III, showing that "Sidney not only
plays variations on the elements of plot in the myth, but
also draws on all the various interpretations of self-
knowledge, curiosity, and lust in order to make his meaning
clear."

2627   DAVIS, WALTER R[ICHARDSON]. <u>Idea and Act in Elizabethan Fic-
tion</u>. Princeton: Princeton University Press, 1969, 311pp.
  Analyzes juxtaposition of actual and ideal in <u>Arcadia</u>,
the functions of role-playing and disguises, and the influence on the development of pastoral romance. Argues that
"<u>Arcadia</u> is an explicit exploration of the possibilities of
love" and that Sidney places his emphasis on "the intellectual [as opposed to actional] content of his pastoral"
(passim).

2628   DAVIS, WALTER R[ICHARDSON]. <u>A Map of Arcadia: Sidney's Romance in Its Tradition</u>, in <u>Sidney's Arcadia</u>. By Walter
R[ichardson] Davis and Richard A[lan] Lanham. YSE, 158.
New Haven: Yale University Press, 1965, pp. 1-179.
  Analyzes in detail the plot of <u>Arcadia</u>. Discusses work
as a pastoral romance: places <u>Arcadia</u> in history of genre,
examines influence of previous pastoral romances on Sidney,
and defines his contribution as "the moralization of plot."
Argues that focus of work is "the perfection of the hero
through love." Analyzes relationship of pastoral and
chivalric episodes and political element to main plot.
<u>See</u> 2710.

2629   DAVIS, WALTER R[ICHARDSON]. "Thematic Unity in the <u>New Ar-
cadia</u>." <u>SP</u>, 57 (April 1960), 123-43.
  Analyzes in detail episodes added in <u>New Arcadia</u> to illustrate how the new material clarifies and/or amplifies
plot and/or theme. Suggests that these new episodes provide
"amplification whereby the matter of the original plot is
diffused, reflected, moralized, and generally clarified."

2630   DAVISON, MARY CAROL. "The Metamorphoses of Odysseus: A Study
of Romance Iconography from the <u>Odyssey</u> to <u>The Tempest</u>."
Ph.D. dissertation, Stanford University, 1971, 474pp.
  Analyzes <u>Arcadia</u> as it exemplifies "Renaissance aesthetic
theories in both literature and the visual arts"; examines
"Sidney's use of iconographic scenes."

Sidney

2631   DELASANTA, RODNEY KENNETH. "The Epic Voice." Ph.D. disserta-
        tion, Brown University, 1962, 242pp.
        See 2632.

2632   DELASANTA, RODNEY [KENNETH]. The Epic Voice. DPL, Series
        Maior, 2. The Hague: Mouton, 1967, 140pp.
        In Chapter III ("The Arcadia," pp. 60–81) examines the
        "narrative artistry" and structural design of the New Ar-
        cadia; analyzes the effect of Sidney's use of restricted
        narration on characterization, plot design, and "psycho-
        logical verisimilitude."

2633   DENKINGER, EMMA MARSHALL. "The Arcadia and 'The Fish Torpedo
        Faire.'" SP, 28 (April 1931), 162–83.
        By investigating possible sources of references to tor-
        pedo, attempts to determine depth and extent of Sidney's
        scholarship. Explicates use of fish as Amphialus's device
        and identifies Sidney's "immediate source" as "the impresa
        of Bernardo Tasso."

2634   DENKINGER, EMMA MARSHALL. Immortal Sidney. New York: Bren-
        tano's, 1931, 329pp.
        Briefly discusses Arcadia as work written for the enter-
        tainment of the Countess of Pembroke (passim).

2635   DENKINGER, EMMA MARSHALL. "Some Renaissance References to Sic
        Vos non Vobis." PQ, 10 (April 1931), 151–62.
        Discusses use of phrase as Musidorus's impresa in Old
        Arcadia and suggests diplomatic negotiations surrounding
        Elizabeth's French marriage as reason for change of impresa
        in revised Arcadia.

2636   DENT, R[OBERT] W. John Webster's Borrowing. Berkeley: Uni-
        versity of California Press, 1960, 323pp.
        Provides detailed analysis of Webster's use of the Ar-
        cadia as a source (passim).

2637   DIPPLE, ELIZABETH [DOROTHEA]. "The Captivity Episode and the
        New Arcadia." JEGP, 70, no. 3 (1971), 418–31.
        Discusses differences in structure, style, tone, and plot
        between captivity episode and earlier part of work, suggest-
        ing that Sidney stopped of his own accord because of prob-
        lems of integrating these changes into a conclusion. Points
        out how Sidney transfers "sexual fall" from Pyrocles and
        Musidorus to Amphialus and suggests changed conception of
        latter is responsible for change in style of episode.

2638   DIPPLE, ELIZABETH [DOROTHEA]. "The 'Fore-Conceit' of Sidney's
        Eclogues," in Literary Monographs, I. Edited by Eric
        Rothstein and Thomas K. Dunseath. Madison: University of
        Wisconsin Press, 1967, 1–47.
            Examines relationship of eclogues to Old Arcadia, par-
        ticularly the ways in which "they serve to clarify what
        Sidney considered the pertinence of his prose tale." Ex-
        amines various parallels and contrasts between eclogues and
        prose.

2639   DIPPLE, ELIZABETH [DOROTHEA]. "Harmony and Pastoral in the
        Old Arcadia." ELH, 35 (September 1968), 309–28.
            Discusses the contrast between the harmony of the static
        pastoral setting and the disharmonic symbolism of the "po-
        litical narrative romance or dramatic sequence" in examining
        Sidney's transformation of the pastoral conventions.

2640   DIPPLE, ELIZABETH [DOROTHEA]. "Metamorphosis in Sidney's
        Arcadias." PQ, 50 (January 1971), 47–62.
            Examines Sidney's "structuring of action on the idea of
        metamorphosis," particularly "radical physical change," in
        discussing the "disparity" of the two versions. Concludes
        that "[i]n the New Arcadia...metamorphosis is an infinitely
        elastic theme which serves the ideas of love, faithfulness,
        and unity of being, whereas in the Old Arcadia it had served
        the idea of fragmentation and failure."

*2641   DIPPLE, ELIZABETH DOROTHEA. "Sidney's Changing Concept of
        Arcadia: The Redemption of a Landscape." Ph.D. disserta-
        tion, Johns Hopkins University, 1963.
            Abstract not available.

2642   DIPPLE, ELIZABETH [DOROTHEA]. "'Unjust Justice' in the Old
        Arcadia." SEL, 10 (Winter 1970), 83–101.
            Examines the changes in the narrative voice and the
        events of Books IV and V to illustrate the "ironies of in-
        justice" in the Old Arcadia. Argues that Sidney explores
        "the imperfection of justice" and that the princes are both
        guilty and not guilty.

2643   DISHER, M. WILLSON. "The Trend of Shakespeare's Thought."
        TLS, 20 October 1950, p. 668; 27 October 1950, p. 684;
        3 November 1950, p. 700.
            Discusses influence of Arcadia on Shakespeare's thought
        and plays.

2644   DOBELL, BERTRAM. "New Light upon Sir Philip Sidney's Arcadia."
        Quarterly Review, 211 (1909), 74–100.

Sidney

Reports on three manuscripts of Old Arcadia (heretofore unknown). Discusses differences between original version and revision, the superior structure of the Old Arcadia, and the Countess of Pembroke's editing of the 1593 edition. Discusses the autobiographical significance of the Philisides episode and transcribes portions of the manuscripts (particularly the sections including unpublished poems).

2645   DOBELL, BERTRAM. "Sidney's Arcadia." Athenaeum, No. 4167 (7 September 1907), p. 272.
Announces discovery of Ashburnham manuscript of Old Arcadia and comments briefly on contents.

2646   DOBELL, BERTRAM. "Sidney's Arcadia." Athenaeum, No. 4169 (21 September 1907), p. 336.
Answers Greg (2704) by pointing out that Old Arcadia "is a quite finished and coherent work." Comments on dramatic structure and intended appeal to female audience.

2647   DOBSON, AUSTIN. "Pamĕla: Pamēla." N&Q, 110 (30 July 1904), 89–90.
Points out pronunciation was Pamēla in Arcadia.

2648   DORAN, MADELEINE. "Elements in the Composition of King Lear." SP, 30 (January 1933), 34–58.
Examines Shakespeare's use of Arcadia as source in both original version and revision of play. Discusses, in particular, influence of the moral and political philosophy of Sidney's romance on Shakespeare's revision.

2649   DORSTEN, JAN A[DRIANUS] VAN. "Gruterus and Sidney's Arcadia." RES, NS, 16 (May 1965), 174–77.
Discusses reference to Arcadia in epigram by Janus Gruterus, suggesting he had seen Sidney's work in manuscript.

2650   DORSTEN, J[AN] A[DRIANUS] VAN. Terug naar de toekomst. Leiden: Universitaire Pers, 1971, 25pp.
Examines autobiographical significance of Philisides's song and discusses relationship of song to Old Arcadia.

2651   DOWLIN, CORNELL MARCH. "Sidney and Other Men's Thoughts." RES, 20 (October 1944), 257–71.
Discusses background of Sidney's conception of prose romances as heroic poems.

2652   DUHAMEL, P[IERRE] ALBERT. "Sidney's Arcadia and Elizabethan Rhetoric." SP, 45 (April 1948), 134–50.

Applies method suggested by John Brinsley (<u>Ludus Liter-arius</u>) for analysis of rhetoric to passage from <u>Arcadia</u>. Analyzes Sidney's use of <u>inventio</u> and <u>dispositio</u> to show that Sidney, unlike most of his contemporaries, emphasized the ornamental rather than the probative value of rhetoric. Analyzes passage from <u>Euphues</u> as contrast.

2653 DUHAMEL, PIERRE ALBERT. "Sir Philip Sidney and the Traditions of Rhetoric." Ph.D. dissertation, University of Wisconsin, 1945, 166pp.

Examines style in <u>Arcadia</u> to show that "a correlation is revealed between...[Sidney's] stylistic practice and the several conceptions of rhetoric that stemmed from his familiarity with various traditions of thought" (particularly Ramistic and Aristotelian theory).

2654 DUNCAN-JONES, E. E. "Henry Oxinden and Sidney's <u>Arcadia</u>." <u>N&Q</u>, 198 (August 1953), 322-23.

Identifies Letter 143 of <u>The Oxinden Letters, 1604-1642</u> as "a mosaic of unacknowledged quotations from Sidney's <u>Arcadia</u>." Notes that Oxinden's use provides "a striking indication of the vogue of Sidney's romance in 1640."

2655 DUNCAN-JONES, KATHERINE. "Nashe and Sidney: The Tournament in <u>The Unfortunate Traveller</u>." <u>MLR</u>, 63 (January 1968), 3-6.

Examines tournament at Florence in <u>Unfortunate Traveller</u> as "a mosaic of references to tournaments and single combats in the <u>Arcadia</u>" and argues Nashe is burlesquing chivalric conventions.

2656 DUNCAN-JONES, KATHERINE. "Sidney in Samothea: A Forgotten National Myth." <u>RES</u>, NS, 25 (May 1974), 174-77.

Explains Sidney's use of Samothea (birth-place of Philisides in <u>Old Arcadia</u>) as representation of "a legendary British civilization believed to be older than Greece itself, and the source of Greek letters."

2657 DUNCAN-JONES, KATHERINE. "Sidney's Urania." <u>RES</u>, NS, 17 (May 1966), 123-32.

Suggests that Urania is essentially allegorical and represents Heavenly Beauty and that the love she embodies contrasts with that engaged in by Pyrocles and Musidorus. Examines "changing conception of her role" concluding: "[o]nly in Urania do the discrepancies between different levels of presentation appear to be imperfectly reconciled."

Sidney

2658 DUNLOP, JOHN [COLIN]. The History of Fiction: Being a Critical Account of the Most Celebrated Prose Works of Fiction,
from the Earliest Greek Romances to the Novels of the
Present Age, Vol. III. Edinburgh: Longman, Hurst, Rees,
Orme, and Browne, 1814, 436pp.
        Includes discussion of mixing of forms in Arcadia, the
influence of the work, and Sidney's style, sources, and
characterization (pp. 164-78). See 182 and 183.

2659 DUNN, UNDINE. "The Arcadian Ethic." Ph.D. dissertation,
Indiana University, 1968, 423pp.
        Analyzes the ethic of Old Arcadia and examines relation-
ship between it and Sidney's own beliefs and "the received
code of his class." Suggests that Sidney began composition
in August or early September, 1579, and that Philoclea "may
have been Mary Agarde." Discusses influence of Plautus and
Terence on structure of Old Arcadia.

2660 DURHAM, CHARLES W. III. "Character and Characterization in
Elizabethan Prose Fiction." Ph.D. dissertation, Ohio University, 1969, 147pp.
        Examines Sidney's methods of characterization.

2661 EAGLE, R[ODERICK] L. "The Arcadia (1593)--Spenser (1611)
Title Page." Baconiana, 29 (1945), 97-100.
        Interprets title-page compartment: identifies figures
as Musidorus (as Dorus) and Pyrocles (as Zelmane) and argues that the pig-marjoram emblem is meant to signify that
the work is not for the vulgar. See 2936.

2662 EAGLE, RODERICK L. "The Arcadia (1593) Title-Page Border."
Library, 5th Ser., 4 (June 1949), 68-71.
        Analyzes the figures of the title-page border. Suggests
that the pig-marjoram emblem is intended to point out that
the work is not for the vulgar and identifies the two
figures as representations of Pyrocles and Musidorus.

2663 ELTON, WILLIAM R. King Lear and the Gods. San Marino:
Huntington Library, 1966, 381pp.
        In Chapter III ("Sidney's Arcadia: Four Attitudes to
Providence," pp. 34-62) examines four major attitudes expressed in Arcadia toward providence: "(1) the prisca
theologia, or virtuous-heathen view...; (2) the atheistic
view; (3) the superstitious view; and (4) the view which
falls into none of the previous categories but is the result of human reactions to the effects of the hidden
providence."

430

2664   ELTON, WILLIAM [R.]. "<u>King Lear</u> and the Gods: Shakespeare's
        Tragedy and Renaissance Religious Thought." Ph.D. disser-
        tation, Ohio State University, 1957, 302pp.
            Examines attitudes toward providence in <u>Arcadia</u> and
        their influence on Shakespeare: finds that <u>Arcadia</u> contains
        "expressions of the new questioning of Providence" and "an-
        ticipates the major attitudes toward Providence of Shake-
        speare's characters, whose beliefs coincide with those which
        the Renaissance conventionally assigned to heathens."

2665   ESTRIN, BARBARA. "The Lost Child in Spenser's <u>The Faerie
        Queene</u>, Sidney's <u>Old Arcadia</u>, and Shakespeare's <u>The Winter's
        Tale</u>." Ph.D. dissertation, Brown University, 1972, 271pp.
            Examines Sidney's use of the motif in <u>Old Arcadia</u> and
        argues that the work "equivocates between romance and
        comedy." Also analyzes the "role of the poet's persona...
        as it emerges" in the work.

2666   EWING, S. B., JR. "Burton, Ford, and <u>Andromana</u>." <u>PMLA</u>, 54
        (December 1939), 1007-17.
            Discusses anonymous author's use of Plangus episode as
        source for <u>Andromana</u>. Observes that in Arcadia, the episode
        is "told simply as divertisement," with emphasis on plot,
        not character.

2667   FADER, DANIEL NELSON. "Apthonius and Elizabethan Prose Ro-
        mance." Ph.D. dissertation, Stanford University, 1963,
        265pp.
            Analyzes influence of "the formal prescriptions for one
        or another of the exercises in Apthonius's <u>Progymnasmata</u>"
        on <u>Euphues</u>, <u>Arcadia</u>, and <u>Rosalynde</u>. Finds that the "rela-
        tionship between the exercises and the romances is one im-
        portant source of the lack of vital movement which
        characterizes all three of the narratives; the more eclectic
        the author's use of the rhetorical schemes, the more lively
        his story."

2668   FLÜGEL, EWALD. <u>Sir Philip Sidney</u>. Halle: M. Niemeyer, 1888,
        91pp.
            Discusses <u>Arcadia</u> in context of Sidney's life. Includes
        description of 1598 edition of <u>Arcadia</u> (pp. LXXVIII-LXXX).

2669   FOGEL, EPHIM G[REGORY]. "Milton and Sir Philip Sidney's <u>Ar-
        cadia</u>." <u>N&Q</u>, 196 (17 March 1951), 115-17.
            Examines Milton's use of <u>Arcadia</u> as a source for the
        opening lines of <u>Samson Agonistes</u>; argues that "[i]n actual-
        ity, Milton seems to have admired the <u>Arcadia</u>."

Sidney

2670   FOGEL, EPHIM GREGORY. "The Personal References in the Fiction
       and Poetry of Sir Philip Sidney." Ph.D. dissertation, Ohio
       State University, 1958, 495pp.
            Attempts "to separate the probable personal references
       in...Arcadia...from those that have been alleged but seem
       improbable; to put the references in the context of...
       literary traditions; and in general to elucidate their bi-
       ographical and artistic significance." Concludes that "Sid-
       ney's personal references...enable him to achieve a fusion
       of the actual and the ideal in his art."

2671   FORD, PHILIP JEFFREY. "Paradise Lost and the Five-Act Epic."
       Ph.D. dissertation, Columbia University, 1967, 289pp.
            Includes examination of the influence of the theories of
       fifteenth-century Italian critics on Sidney's use of five-
       act structure in Old Arcadia. Also discusses characteris-
       tics of work.

2672   FORD, P[HILIP] JEFFREY. "Philosophy, History, and Sidney's
       Old Arcadia." CL, 26 (Winter 1974), 32-50.
            Examines Old Arcadia in light of Defense of Poetry to
       argue that Sidney was experimenting with epic in the orig-
       inal version. Analyzes relationship between narrative and
       analytic structure of Old Arcadia.

2673   FORSYTHE, ROBERT STANLEY. The Relation of Shirley's Plays to
       the Elizabethan Drama. Columbia University Studies in Eng-
       lish and Comparative Literature. New York: Columbia Uni-
       versity Press, 1914, 497pp.
            Includes detailed analysis of Shirley's use of Arcadia
       as a source for his The Arcadia (pp. 268-79).

2674   FRASER, RUSSELL A. "Sidney the Humanist." SAQ, 66 (January
       1967), 87-91.
            Discusses Sidney's utilitarian, didactic purpose in the
       Arcadia and the relationship of these qualities to his view
       of Sidney as "the humanist par excellence."

2675   F[ULLER], H. DE W. "Sidney's Arcadia." Nation, 96 (20 Febru-
       ary 1913), 174-77.
            Criticizes Arcadia because of Sidney's lack of close-knit
       structure and "critical purpose," praises the comic elements,
       examines characterization, and discusses Sidney's style.

2676   G., A. B. "Sir Philip Sidney's Arcadia." N&Q, 49 (16 May
       1874), 396.
            Criticizes J. Hain Frisworth's edition (apparently 2528)
       because of omission of poems.

2677   GAAF, W. VAN DER. "Gill's Mopsae." ES, 16 (1934), 59.
       Suggests that Gill's use of "mopsae" to mean "women whose
       speech is characterized by what he considers mannerisms and
       affectations" (Logonomia Anglica) is based on Sidney's
       Mopsa. Notes that Gill provides a "'phonetic' transcrip-
       tion" of two passages from Arcadia.

*2678 GALM, JOHN ARNOLD. "Sidney's Arcadian Poems." Ph.D. disserta-
       tion, Yale University, 1963.
       See 2679.

2679   GALM, JOHN A[RNOLD]. Sidney's Arcadian Poems. Salzburg
       Studies in English Literature, ElizS, 1. Salzburg: Insti-
       tut für Englische Sprache und Literatur, Universität Salz-
       burg, 1973, 229pp.
       Slightly revised version of 2678. Examines Sidney's in-
       tegration of the poems into the narrative of Arcadia, the
       thematic and other relationships between the poetry and the
       prose, and the value of the poems for interpreting action.

2680   GARKE, ESTHER. The Use of Songs in Elizabethan Prose Fiction.
       Bern: Francke Verlag, 1972, 132pp.
       Draws frequently on Arcadia for examples in analysis of
       types of songs, their relationships to plot and structure,
       and their functions (to complement or contrast setting, to
       present character relationships, to characterize singer and
       audience) in pastoral romances and courtly fiction.

2681   GARNETT, JAMES M. "Notes on Elizabethan Prose." PMLA, 4,
       no. 1 (1889), 41-61.
       Finds lengthy sentences and "lack of correct syntax"
       major faults in Sidney's style in New Arcadia.

2682   GENOUY, HECTOR. L'Arcadia de Sidney dans ses rapports avec
       l'Arcadia de Sannazaro et la Diana de Montemayor. Paris:
       H. Didier, 1928, 211pp.
       Examines influences of Arcadia and Diana on Sidney's
       work: compares structure, subject matter, style, themes,
       characters, and form of three works to isolate Sidney's
       indebtedness and his originality.

2683   GEORGAS, MARILYN DAVIS. "Sir Philip Sidney and the Victorians."
       Ph.D. dissertation, University of Texas at Austin, 1969,
       434pp.
       "[T]races...Sidney's Victorian reputation...as a writer
       of prose fiction"; examines the generally negative critical
       attitude toward Arcadia.

Sidney

2684   GEULEN, HANS. "'Arcadische' Simpliciana: Zu einer Quelle
        Grimmelshausens und ihrer strukturellen Bedeutung für
        seinen Roman." Euphorion, 63, no. 4 (1969), 426-37.
            Discusses Grimmelshausen's use of Opitz's translation of
        Arcadia as source.

2685   GEULEN, HANS. Erzählkunst der frühen Neuzeit: Zur Geschichte
        epischer Darbietungsweisen und Formen im Roman der Renais-
        sance und des Barock. Tübingen: Rotsch, 1975, 322pp.
            Includes discussion of Arcadia as example of courtly
        literature; discusses influence of Greek romance on work
        and Sidney's irony (pp. 140-47).

2686   GIRARDIN, SAINT-MARC. Cours de littérature dramatique ou de
        l'usage des passions dans le drame, Vol. III. Paris:
        Charpentier, 1862, 415pp.
            In Chapter XLVI includes discussion of Arcadia; examines
        Sidney's use of pastoral elements, his treatment of love,
        and his mixture of comic and idyllic (pp. 273-85). (Earlier
        editions not available.)

2687   GISELA, JUNKE. "Formen des Dialogs im frühen englischen Ro-
        man." Ph.D. dissertation, University of Köln, 1975, 150pp.
            Examines form and use of dialogue in Arcadia. See 208.

2688   GODSHALK, W[ILLIAM] L[EIGH]. "Gabriel Harvey and Sidney's
        Arcadia." MLR, 59 (October 1964), 497-99.
            Argues that the marginalia in so-called Harvey copy of
        1613 Arcadia are not in Harvey's hand. Discusses briefly
        the nature of the manuscript notes.

2689   GODSHALK, WILLIAM LEIGH. "Sidney and Shakespeare: Some
        Central Concepts." Ph.D. dissertation, Harvard University,
        1964.
            Compares treatment of kingship, heroism, and pastoralism
        in Arcadia with Shakespeare's treatment of concepts in his
        plays. Concludes that the two are similar in attitude to-
        ward heroism and pastoralism but that Shakespeare is more
        conservative in examination of politics. Examines elements
        of the story of Paphlagonian king not used by Shakespeare
        in Lear.

2690   GODSHALK, WILLIAM LEIGH. "Sidney's Revision of the Arcadia,
        Books III-V." PQ, 43 (April 1964), 171-84.
            In arguing for Sidney's responsibility for revisions,
        examines circumstances and "literary quarrel" surrounding
        publication of editions of 1590 and 1593, Hugh Sanford's
        "editing" of 1593 edition, and nature of revisions.

2691   GOHLKE, MADELON SPRENGNETHER. "Narrative Structure in the New
       Arcadia, The Faerie Queene I, and The Unfortunate Traveller."
       Ph.D. dissertation, Yale University, 1972, 356pp.
           Defends New Arcadia against charge of formlessness by
       arguing that structure of work "cannot be understood 'spa-
       tially,' since the reader is not placed outside the action,
       but rather within it, approximating the experience of the
       figures within the fiction." Suggests that "structure
       emerges in conjunction with the progressive revelation of
       the thematic organization of the work."

2692   GOHN, ERNEST S. "Primitivistic Motifs in Sidney's Arcadia."
       Papers of the Michigan Academy of Science, Arts, and Let-
       ters, 45 (1960), 363–71.
           Examines Sidney's use of cultural and chronological
       primitivism in setting and in emphasis on chivalric ideal.
       Suggests that the unreconciled opposition between Sidney's
       attempt "to lead men on the paths of virtuous action" and
       his "wistful hankering for a past when life was easier and
       issues were simpler" "is a cause of the singularly inco-
       herent impression one has of" Arcadia.

2693   GOLDMAN, MARCUS SELDEN. "Sidney and Harington as Opponents of
       Superstition." JEGP, 54, no. 4 (1955), 526–48.
           Examines Sidney's skepticism toward occult arts in Ar-
       cadia. Argues that "the condemnation of the credulity of
       various personages" in the work—an outgrowth of Sidney's
       emphasis on the need for self-discipline—is a "vigorous
       protest against the superstitions of sixteenth-century
       England."

2694   GOLDMAN, MARCUS SELDEN. Sir Philip Sidney and the Arcadia.
       ISLL, Vol. 17, nos. 1-2. Urbana: University of Illinois,
       1934, 236pp.
           Interprets Arcadia in context of Sidney's life and times.
       Surveys criticism of Arcadia from seventeenth through nine-
       teenth centuries, discusses work as an heroic romance, ex-
       amines Sidney's use of materials from "contemporary life,"
       and analyzes his use of Malory's Morte d'Arthur as source.

*2695 GOLDMAN, MARCUS S[ELDEN]. "Sir Philip Sidney and the Arcadia:
       A Study in Elizabethan Action and Thought." Ph.D. disser-
       tation, University of Illinois at Urbana-Champaign, 1931.
       See 2694.

*2696 GRAVES, ISABEL. "Sir Philip Sidney's Use of Arcadianism and
       Its Source." Ph.D. dissertation, University of Pennsyl-
       vania, 1899.
       Abstract not available.

Sidney

2697   GREAVES, MARGARET. The Blazon of Honour: A Study in Renais-
        sance Magnanimity. London: Methuen & Co., 1964, 142pp.
            In Chapter IV ("That Most Heroicke Spirit," pp. 62-74)
        analyzes Arcadia as a study of the magnanimous character,
        particularly as realized in Pyrocles and Musidorus. Finds
        that in Arcadia Sidney makes use of the traditional quali-
        ties of magnanimity and adds "a further quality only rarely
        glimpsed in earlier studies of the magnanimous character--
        the love of learning and art." Concludes that in the work
        "magnanimity acquires the greatest depth and extension of
        meaning that has yet occurred in its history."

2698   GREEN, GLADYS. "Trollope on Sidney's Arcadia and Lytton's The
        Wanderer." Trollopian, No. 3 (September 1946), pp. 45-54.
            Transcribes Trollope's note on Arcadia from the flyleaf
        of the third volume of his copy (Dublin, 1739). Trollope's
        note includes comments on the style, on the importance of
        the work, and on the difficulty he had in finishing it.

2699   GREENBLATT, STEPHEN J. "Sidney's Arcadia and the Mixed Mode."
        SP, 70 (July 1973), 269-78.
            Examines the relationship between the mixture of genres
        and the complexity of the world Sidney presents; argues that
        through "shifting generic perspectives, Sidney exposes the
        limitations of modes of conduct and versions of reality."

2700   GREENLAW, EDWIN [A.]. "The Captivity Episode in Sidney's
        Arcadia," in The Manly Anniversary Studies in Language and
        Literature. Chicago: University of Chicago Press, 1923,
        pp. 54-63.
            Argues that "[t]he episode as a whole refers...to Sid-
        ney's sense of the peril in the French marriage that seemed
        imminent at the time when he wrote Arcadia, while the debate
        between Crecopia and Pamela introduces an attack upon the
        Lucretian philosophy." See 2790.

2701   GREENLAW, EDWIN [A.]. "Shakespeare's Pastorals." SP, 13
        (April 1916), 122-54. [Reprinted in: Pastoral and Romance:
        Modern Essays in Criticism. Edited by Eleanor T(erry) Lin-
        coln. Englewood Cliffs, New Jersey: Prentice-Hall, 1969,
        pp. 83-107.]
            Discusses influence of Arcadia on Faerie Queene, espe-
        cially the Calidore-Pastorella story, and argues that Phi-
        lisides of the Old Arcadia was Shakespeare's model for
        Jaques.

2702   GREENLAW, EDWIN A. "Sidney's Arcadia as an Example of Eliza-
        bethan Allegory," in Anniversary Papers by Colleagues and

Pupils of George Lyman Kittredge. Edited by F. N. Robinson. Boston: Ginn and Co., 1913, pp. 327-37.
Argues that revised Arcadia was written as a serious heroic poem, as Sidney and his contemporaries understood the term. Discusses influence of Xenophon's Cyropaedia on the work and examines Sidney's conception of the virtues of the public and the private man.

2703   GREG, WALTER W[ILSON]. Pastoral Poetry & Pastoral Drama: A Literary Inquiry, with Special Reference to the Pre-Restoration Stage in England. London: A. H. Bullen, 1906, 476pp.
Includes discussion of the pastoral elements in and style of Arcadia. Examines use of Arcadia as a source in later pastoral drama (pp. 147-54, 319-34, passim).

2704   GREG, W[ALTER] W[ILSON]. "Sidney's Arcadia." Athenaeum, No. 4168 (14 September 1907), p. 303; No. 4170 (28 September 1907), p. 368.
Discusses briefly early publishing history and suggests that manuscripts of Old Arcadia represent an "uncorrected draft." See 2645 and 2646.

2705   GUBAR, SUSAN DAVID. "Tudor Romance and Eighteenth-Century Fiction." Ph.D. dissertation, University of Iowa, 1972, 243pp.
Includes examination of structure and style of Arcadia: discusses reader response and how the work "call[s] attention to [its]...own literariness." Also examines how Stanley's modernized Arcadia "reveal[s] the nature of eighteenth century objections to romance."

2706   HAGAN, ENID MARGARET. "Pastoral and Romance in Sidney's Two Arcadias." Ph.D. dissertation, University of Washington, 1971, 171pp.
Examines the mingling of pastoral and romance in both versions. Analyzes the "parallel political and love plots" in Old Arcadia and the additional "romantic material appropriate for an heroic poem" in New Arcadia. Finds that in New Arcadia Sidney "appears to be moving toward a more favorable attitude toward love."

2707   HAINSWORTH, G[EORGE]. "L'Arcadia de Sidney en France: Trois nouveaux témoignanges de son succès." RLC, 10 (1930), 470-71.
Notes three seventeenth-century French allusions to Arcadia.

Sidney

2708 HALLAM, GEORGE WALTER, JR. "Functional Paradox in Sidney's
Revised Arcadia." Ph.D. dissertation, University of
Florida, 1959, 266pp.
Analyzes structure, arguing that if work is examined
"in light of paradoxes of situation functioning conceptually
in accordance with certain principles of Ramistic logic,...
the revised Arcadia is seen to have a unity that derives
from an interrelationship of theme, structure, plot and
style."

2709 HALLIWELL[-PHILLIPPS], JAMES O[RCHARD]. A Brief Account of an
Unique Edition of Sir Philip Sydney's Arcadia. Brixton
Hill: For Private Circulation, 1854, 7pp.
Describes copy of 1605 edition.

2710 HAMILTON, A. C. "Et in Arcadia Ego." MLQ, 27 (September
1966), 332-50.
Review article on works by Davis (2628), Lanham (2778),
and Kalstone (2756). Objects to Davis's use of 1598 edition and "the strong Christian reading forced upon the
text." Criticizes Lanham for ignoring "the larger dramatic
context."

2711 HAMILTON, A. C. "Sidney's Arcadia as Prose Fiction: Its Relation to Its Sources." ELR, 2 (Winter 1972), 29-60.
In arguing that Arcadia is "a work of comparative literature, the first in English prose," analyzes assimilation
of the sources which "provide the 'imitative patterns' upon
which Sidney structures the" Old and New Arcadia.

2712 HAMM, DIETER. "Sir Philip Sidneys Old Arcadia: Die Selbstthe-
matisierung der Literatur." Ph.D. dissertation, University
of Konstanz, 1972, 184pp.
Argues that Old Arcadia is "an Apologie for Poetrie sui
generis." Examines influence of Sidney's concern for literary theory on plot, structure, and characterization. (Abstract in: English and American Studies in German:
Summaries of Theses and Monographs, 1972. Edited by Werner
Habicht. Tübingen: M. Niemeyer Verlag, 1973, pp. 49-50.)

2713 HAMPSTEN, ELIZABETH MORRIS. "A Study of Romance." Ph.D.
dissertation, University of Washington, 1965, 296pp.
Includes examination of Arcadia in an attempt "to define
...[the] literary mode of romance." Argues that "[t]he
lesson set forth in...Arcadia is the obligation of the man
of power toward society;...[it is an] anti-war book...,
reflecting the tragic consequences for a society of its
leaders' no longer being able, or willing, to wield their
power effectively."

2714 HANFORD, JAMES HOLLY, and SARA RUTH WATSON. "Personal Allegory in the Arcadia: Philisides and Lelius." MP, 32 (August 1934), 1-10.
Discusses Queen of Iberia's tournament, arguing that Lelius is Sir Henry Lee and that both Helen and Queen of Iberia represent Elizabeth. Argues that the episode reveals "Sidney's mixed attitude of loyalty and hostility toward his queen." Suggests the tournament is based on Queen's Day tournament of 1581.

*2715 HANSSEN, SELBY. "An Analysis of Sir Philip Sidney's Metrical Experiments in the Arcadia." Ph.D. dissertation, Yale University, 1942, 372pp.
Abstract not available.

2716 HARKNESS, STANLEY. "The Prose Style of Sir Philip Sidney," in Studies by Members of the Department of English. University of Wisconsin Studies in Language and Literature, 2. Madison: [University of Wisconsin], 1918, pp. 57-76.
Analyzes the "length,...types, and...syntactical irregularity" of sentences in Arcadia, using Sidney's Apology as contrast. Finds little concern "with the rigors of sentence-form." Discusses Sidney's adaptation of style to subject matter.

2717 HARMAN, EDWARD GEORGE. The Countesse of Pembrokes Arcadia (with a Chapter on Thomas Lodge). London: Cecil Palmer, 1924, 243pp.
Provides episode by episode analysis to support contention that Francis Bacon is author.

2718 HARRISON, T. P., JR. "The Relations of Spenser and Sidney." PMLA, 45 (September 1930), 712-31.
Examines similarity of character between New Arcadia and Spenser's works (especially Faerie Queene), concluding that: the two authors "agree upon the function of epic poetry... [and] voice a similar ethical ideal"; the Braggadoccio episode parallels the Crecopia-Pamela episode in the historical, but not moral, allegory; the political ideas of the two works "belong invariably to the traditional thought of the time." Concentrates analysis on the disputation between Crecopia and Pamela. Suggests ultimately that it is impossible to determine which author influenced the other. (See: J. M. Purcell, "The Relations of Spenser and Sidney," PMLA, 46 [September 1931], 940; Mally Behler, "Die Beziehungen zwischen Sidney und Spenser," Archiv, 146 [1923], 53-59.)

Sidney

2719   HARRISON, T. P., JR. "A Source of Sidney's _Arcadia_." _University of Texas Studies in English_, No. 6 (December 1926), pp. 53–71.
Examines indebtedness of both versions of _Arcadia_ to Montemayor's _Diana_ for pastoral elements and "for some details of general structure, technical device, and plots, many of which have hitherto been attributed to his [Sidney's] reading of the Greek romances."

2720   HAZARD, MARY ELIZABETH. "'Pregnant Images of Life': Sidney's Use of Visual Imagery in _The New Arcadia_." Ph.D. dissertation, Bryn Mawr College, 1970, 310pp.
Analyzes Sidney's use of "the iconographic portrait, the pageant and procession, tilts, masques,... dreams," and emblems as vehicles for his visual imagery.

2721   HAZLITT, WILLIAM. _Lectures Chiefly on the Dramatic Literature of the Age of Elizabeth_. London: Stodart and Steuart, 1820, 364pp.
Includes discussion of defects--particularly in style and in thought--of _Arcadia_. Characterizes the work as "not romantic, but scholastic; not poetry, but casuistry; not nature, but art, and the worst sort of art, which thinks it can do better than nature" (pp. 265–78).

2722   HELGERSON, RICHARD. _The Elizabethan Prodigals_. Berkeley: University of California Press, 1976, 188pp.
Includes examination of autobiographical elements of _Old_ and _New Arcadia_; discusses changes in _New Arcadia_ which take the author out of the work and suggests that Sidney left the revision unfinished "[o]ut of moral compunction." Suggests that Sidney also follows the Prodigal paradigm in his writings (pp. 125–55).

2723   HELGERSON, RICHARD. "Lyly, Greene, Sidney, and Barnaby Rich's _Brusanus_." _HLQ_, 36 (February 1973), 105–18.
Discusses Rich's borrowings from a manuscript of _Old Arcadia_. Argues that Rich composed _Brusanus_ in 1592; hence, his use of a manuscript is not evidence of the early influence of Sidney's work on prose fiction.

2724   HELGERSON, RICHARD. "The Prodigal Son in Elizabethan Fiction." Ph.D. dissertation, Johns Hopkins University, 1970, 197pp.
Examines Sidney's use of Prodigal Son motif.

2725   HELTZEL, VIRGIL B. "The Arcadian Hero." _PQ_, 41 (January 1962), 173–80.

Analyzes the qualities of Sidney's conception of the ideal Arcadian hero; finds that Sidney "gives pre-eminence to beauty and greatness of mind" and emphasizes valor and courtesy.

2726   HERBST, CARL. Cupid's Revenge by Beaumont und Fletcher und Andromana, or the Merchant's Wife in ihrer Beziehung zu einander und zu ihrer Quelle. Königsberg: Hartungsche Buchdruckerei, 1906, 74pp.
Includes analysis of use of Arcadia as source for the plays.

2727   HERPICH, CHA[RLE]S A. "Shakespeare's 'Virtue of necessity.'" N&Q, 109 (6 February 1904), 110-11.
Traces source of this and other passages to Arcadia.

2728   HERPICH, CHA[RLE]S A. "Sonnet III and Sidney's Arcadia." N&Q, 116 (31 August 1907), 164.
Suggests passages in Arcadia as source for Shakespeare's sonnet.

2729   HILL, HERBERT WYNFORD. Sidney's Arcadia and the Elizabethan Drama. University of Nevada Studies, Vol. 1, no. 1. Reno: University of Nevada, 1908, 59pp.
Discusses sources, structure, and popularity of Arcadia. Examines influences on Sidney's style and its characteristics. In Part II, analyzes influence on drama to 1642.

2730   HOGAN, PATRICK G[ALVIN], JR. "Sidney and Titian: Painting in the Arcadia and the Defence." SCB, 27, no. 4 (1967), 9-15.
Argues that while writing Arcadia, Sidney often recalled paintings by Titian or other examples of graphic arts. Examines "iconographic parallels" between selected references to paintings in the New Arcadia and the paintings of Titian and other Renaissance artists.

2731   HOGAN, PATRICK G[ALVIN], JR. "Sidney/Spenser: A Courtesy-Friendship-Love Formulation." ForumH, 9, no. 1 (1971), 64-69.
Discusses similarity of concepts of love, friendship, and courtesy in Arcadia and Faerie Queene.

2732   HOGAN, PATRICK GALVIN, JR. "Sir Philip Sidney's Arcadia and Edmund Spenser's Faerie Queene: An Analysis of the Personal, Philosophic, and Iconographic Relationships." Ph.D. dissertation, Vanderbilt University, 1965, 534pp.
Examines the writers' "assimilation...of the concepts of Renaissance Christian Neo-Platonism" and use of common iconographic sources.

Sidney

2733   HOLLIDAY, CARL. English Fiction from the Fifth to the Twenti-
        eth Century. New York: Century Co., 1912, 461pp.
            Includes discussion of "beauty" in Arcadia, Sidney's
        style, the looseness of structure of work, and its influence
        on later prose fiction (pp. 164-73).

2734   HOLZINGER, WALTER. "Der Abentheurliche Simplicissimus and Sir
        Philip Sidney's Arcadia." CollG, No. 2 (1969), pp. 184-98.
            Examines Grimmelshausen's use of Arcadia (through Martin
        Opitz's translation) as a source for Simplicissimus.

2735   HOWELL, ROGER. Sir Philip Sidney: The Shepherd Knight.
        London: Hutchinson, 1968, 318pp.
            Discusses Arcadia in context of Sidney's life and times.
        Argues that Sidney intended Old Arcadia to delight more than
        to teach and set about "transforming it into a more serious
        work." Discusses briefly the publishing history of the work
        and Pembroke's editorship (pp. 162-71, passim).

2736   HOY, CYRUS. "Shakespeare, Sidney, and Marlowe: The Metamor-
        phoses of Love." VQR, 51 (Summer 1975), 448-58.
            Examines the transformations (both ennobling and degrad-
        ing) caused by the power of love in characters in Arcadia.
        Points out similar transformations in Shakespeare's plays.

2737   HUDSON, HOYT H[OPEWELL]. "Introduction," in Directions for
        Speech and Style. By John Hoskins. Edited by Hoyt H[ope-
        well] Hudson. Princeton Studies in English, 12. Princeton:
        Princeton University Press, 1935, 166pp.
            Examines Hoskins's quotations from Arcadia (see also
        "Notes," pp. 53-101). Concludes that Hoskins's work "re-
        mains chiefly as a document witnessing to the charm exerted
        by the person and writings of Sir Philip Sidney."

2738   HUDSON, HOYT H[OPEWELL]. "An Oxford Epigram Book of 1589."
        HLQ, 2 (January 1939), 213-17.
            Quotes epigram addressed to Greville in De Caede et In-
        teritiv Gallorum Regis, Henrici Tertii (1589) which "fur-
        nished direct evidence" that Greville saw the 1590 Arcadia
        through the press. Also notes that epigram refers to work
        as a poem.

2739   HUGHES, MERRITT Y. "New Evidence on the Charge that Milton
        Forged the Pamela Prayer in the Eikon Basilike." RES, NS,
        3 (April 1952), 130-40.
            Uses bibliographical evidence to argue that Milton did
        not forge prayer.

2740   HÜSGEN, HILDEGARDIS. <u>Das Intellektualfeld der deutschen Ar-</u>
       <u>cadia und in ihrem Englischen Vorbild</u>. Münster: F. Mas-
       sing, 1935, 95pp.
          Provides classified listing of concepts and topics and
       examines handling of these in German translation by Opitz.

2741   ISLER, ALAN D[AVID]. "The Allegory of the Hero and Sidney's
       Two <u>Arcadias</u>." <u>SP</u>, 65 (April 1968), 171-91.
          Argues that "<u>Arcadia</u>, in the best tradition of classical
       and Renaissance heroic poems, is built upon the courage
       wisdom, passion reason, Achilles-Ulysses, and related po-
       larities." Analyzes how Pyrocles and Musidorus, and Pamela
       and Philoclea manifest these polarities (especially that of
       passion-reason).

2742   ISLER, ALAN D[AVID]. "Heroic Poetry and Sidney's Two <u>Arcadias</u>.
       <u>PMLA</u>, 83 (May 1968), 368-79.
          Examines problems of genre of the two <u>Arcadias</u>, arguing
       against viewing <u>Old Arcadia</u> as romance and <u>New Arcadia</u> as
       epic. Concludes that both are heoric poems if judged by
       Elizabethan notion of type.

2743   ISLER, ALAN D[AVID]. "Moral Philosophy and the Family in
       Sidney's <u>Arcadia</u>." <u>HLQ</u>, 31 (August 1968), 359-71.
          Examines theme of harmony/disharmony in family unit (par-
       ticularly Basilius's household) and its reflection of order/
       lack of order in state and individual.

2744   ISLER, ALAN DAVID. "The Moral Philosophy of Sidney's Two
       <u>Arcadias</u>: A Study of Some Principal Themes." Ph.D. disser-
       tation, Columbia University, 1966, 205pp.
          Argues that from viewpoint of moral, didactic purposes
       both <u>Old</u> and <u>New Arcadia</u> are heroic poems. Analyzes ele-
       ments of the moral philosophy in both works.

2745   ISLER, ALAN D[AVID]. "Sidney, Shakespeare, and the 'Slain-
       Notslain.'" <u>UTQ</u>, 37 (January 1968), 175-85.
          Argues that in depiction of mob in Book II, Sidney was
       bound by decorum to treat episode comically, and that those
       who accuse him of cruelty in the description are guilty of
       misunderstanding Sidney's intention. Argues that the vic-
       tims are similar to the "slain-notslain" of cartoons.

2746   JEHENSON, YVONNE MYRIAM. "Sir Philip Sidney's <u>Arcadia</u> and
       Honore d'Urfe's <u>L'Astrée</u>: Studies in the Renaissance and
       Mannerist Pastoral." Ph.D. dissertation, Columbia Univer-
       sity, 1974, 164pp.

Sidney

> Analyzes the different "manner in which...[the] two au-
> thors present the same themes and valus which are tradi-
> tionally associated with the pastoral genre." Examines
> Sidney's treatment of the Nature/Civilization, Otium/Nego-
> tium, and Innocence/Passion conflicts, and shows that the
> "balance" and "harmony" of the New Arcadia are the result
> of "Sidney's concern for literary tradition."

2747   JONES, FREDERIC L. "Another Source for The Trial of Chivalry."
        PMLA, 47 (September 1932), 668-70.
           Notes that portion of Pyrocles-Musidorus adventures from
        Book I of New Arcadia was source for actions of Ferdinand
        and Pembroke.

*2748   JONES, WILLIAM BUFORD. "Nathaniel Hawthorne and English
        Renaissance Allegory." Ph.D. dissertation, Harvard Univer-
        sity, 1962.
           Abstract not available.

2749   JUDGE, CYRIL BATHURST. Elizabethan Book-Pirates. Harvard
        Studies in English, 8. Cambridge: Harvard University
        Press, 1934, 212pp.
           Discusses the circumstances surrounding 1599 Edinburgh
        piracy of Arcadia and Ponsonby's legal action. Includes
        transcription of legal documents in case (pp. 100-11, 156-
        59).

2750   JUEL-JENSEN, BENT. "Sidney's Arcadia, 'London, 1599': A Dis-
        tinguished 'Ghost.'" BC, 16 (1967), 80.
           Points out that 1599 edition listed in David Ramage's
        A Finding-List of English Books to 1640 in Libraries in the
        British Isles (Durham, 1958) is actually a copy of 1613 edi-
        tion to which Alexander Pope affixed a calligraphic title
        with 1599 date.

2751   JUEL-JENSEN, BENT. "Sir Philip Sidney's Arcadia, 1638: An
        Unrecorded Issue." Library, 5th Ser., 22 (March 1967),
        67-69.
           Describes "hitherto apparently unrecorded form of the
        preliminaries" of 1638 edition. (In letter to the editor
        ["Sidney's Arcadia, 1638," Library, 5th Ser., 22 (December
        1967), 355] notes provenance of volume.)

2752   JUSSERAND, J[EAN] J[ULES]. The English Novel in the Time of
        Shakespeare. Translated by Elizabeth Lee. Revised edition.
        London: T. Fisher Unwin, 1890, 433pp.
          Examines characteristics of Sidney's style (including
        his excesses), his depiction of love, his characterization,

and his lack of tight structure. Examines popularity and influence of Arcadia, particularly in France (pp. 217-83).

2753 JUSSERAND, J[EAN JULES]. "Le Roman au temps de Shakespeare." RDM, 187 (1 February 1887), 573-612.
Includes discussion of style, genre, and subject matter of Arcadia (pp. 595-602).

2754 KALSTONE, DAVID [MICHAEL]. "Introduction," in Sir Philip Sidney: Selected Poetry and Prose. By Philip Sidney. Edited by David [Michael] Kalstone. Signet Classic Poetry Series. New York and Toronto: New American Library; London: New English Library, 1970, pp. vii-xxx.
Discusses Pyrocles and Musidorus as "participants in and interpreters of their experience" and the "choric function" of the poems. Reprints selected poems from the 1598 edition of Arcadia (pp. 53-103).

*2755 KALSTONE, DAVID MICHAEL. "The Poetry of Sir Philip Sidney." Ph.D. dissertation, Harvard University, 1961.
See 2756.

2756 KALSTONE, DAVID [MICHAEL]. Sidney's Poetry: Contexts and Interpretations. Cambridge: Harvard University Press, 1965, 203pp.
In Part One ("The Poetry of Arcadia," pp. 7-101) discusses Sannazaro's Arcadia as background to Sidney's Arcadia and analyzes the tension between the demands of "pastoral love" and those of "heroic achievement." Discusses the relationship of the poems to the work as a whole.

2757 KALSTONE, DAVID [MICHAEL]. "The Transformation of Arcadia: Sannazaro and Sir Philip Sidney." CL, 15 (Summer 1963), 234-49.
Examines influence of Sannazaro's Arcadia on Sidney's conception of the pastoral lover (and particularly on "You Goat-herd Gods").

2758 KENNEDY, JUDITH M. "Introduction," in A Critical Edition of Yong's Translation of George of Montemayor's Diana and Gil Polo's Enamoured Diana. Edited by Judith M. Kennedy. Oxford: Clarendon Press, 1968, pp. xv-lxxx.
Discusses the influence of Diana on the structure, narrative technique, and themes of Sidney's Old and New Arcadia (pp. xxxiii-xxxix).

2759 KERLIN, ROBERT T. "Scott's Ivanhoe and Sydney's Arcadia." MLN, 22 (May 1907), 144-46.
Points out several correspondences between the two works.

445

Sidney

2760   KIMBROUGH, ROBERT. "Introduction," in <u>Sir Philip Sidney:</u>
       <u>Selected Prose and Poetry</u>. By Philip Sidney. Edited by
       Robert Kimbrough. New York: Holt, Rinehart, and Winston,
       1969, pp. ix–xxiii.
           Discusses composition and revision of <u>Arcadia</u> in context
       of Sidney's life and times. Argues that he stopped the re-
       vision because he found that the work "was taking on a kind
       of independent realism and significance which was no longer
       contained within his esthetic of Art, Imitation, and Exer-
       cise." Reprints selections from 1590 edition (pp. 247–539).

2761   KIMBROUGH, ROBERT. <u>Sir Philip Sidney</u>. TEAS, 114. New York:
       Twayne, 1971, 162pp.
           In Chapter III ("<u>The Lady of May</u> and <u>Old Arcadia</u>," pp.
       63–88) provides a running synopsis of <u>Old Arcadia</u>: dis-
       cusses structure, Sidney's use of "style to reveal person-
       ality," his "comic handling of material," and the "gradual
       impersonalization of the narrator." In Chapter VI ("<u>New</u>
       <u>Arcadia</u>," pp. 125–43) provides running synopsis of work,
       discussing changes made in revision. Examines change from
       comic to heroic mode, characterization, and nature of imi-
       tation in New <u>Arcadia</u>.

2762   KIRK, DAVID MORRISON. "The Digression: Its Use in Prose Fic-
       tion from the Greek Romance through the Eighteenth Century."
       Ph.D. dissertation, Stanford University, 1960, 268pp.
           Includes discussion of Sidney's use of digression in
       New Arcadia.

*2763 KIYOHARA, YOSHIMASA. "Sir Philip Sidney no <u>Arcadia</u> ni tsuite
       [On Sir Philip Sidney's <u>Arcadia</u>]." <u>Albion</u> (Kyoto-daigaku),
       NS, No. 8 (November 1961), pp. 11–27.
           Not seen. Listed in Kazuyoshi Enozawa and Sister Miyo
       Takano, "English Renaissance Studies in Japan, 1961–1963,"
       <u>RenB</u>, 1 (1974), 31.

2764   KNOLL, ROBERT E. "Spenser and the Voyage of the Imagination."
       <u>WHR</u>, 13 (Summer 1959), 249–55.
           Suggests, in passing, that painting of "Diana when Actae-
       on saw her bathing" in <u>Arcadia</u> is description of Titian's
       "Actaeon and Diana."

2765   KOEPPEL, E[MIL]. "Sidneiana." <u>Anglia</u>, 10 (1887), 522–23.
           Notes differences between some passages from <u>Arcadia</u> in
       Fraunce's <u>Arcadian Rhetoric</u> and the published version (1598
       edition).

2766 KOK, A. S. "Sir Philip Sidney." Onze Eeuw, 10 (May 1910),
223-60.
Includes general discussion of Arcadia with comments on
form and style.

2767 KOPPENFELS, WERNER VON. "Two Notes on Imprese in Elizabethan
Literature: Daniel's Additions to The Worthy Tract of
Paulus Iovius: Sidney's Arcadia and the Tournament Scene
in The Unfortunate Traveller." RenQ, 24 (Spring 1971),
13-25.
Examines Nashe's use of various tournaments in the Ar-
cadia as sources for the tournament scene in Unfortunate
Traveller.

2768 KRAPP, GEORGE PHILIP. The Rise of English Literary Prose.
New York: Oxford University Press, 1915, 565pp.
Includes discussion of the antecedents of Arcadia, the
characteristics of Sidney's style and its relationship to
the subject matter, and the nature of the didacticism in
the work. Compares Sidney's style to that of Lyly (pp. 366-
84, passim).

2769 KRAUSS, FRITZ. "Die schwarze Schöne der Shakespeare-Sonette."
Shakespeare-Jahrbuch, 16 (1881), 144-212.
Argues that Shakespeare used Arcadia as a source for the
Dark Lady sonnets.

2770 KRIEGER, GOTTFRIED. Gedichteinlagen im englischen Roman.
Ph.D. dissertation, University of Köln. Köln: n.p., 1969,
274pp.
Includes discussion of function and relation to theme
and structure of verse insets in Arcadia (passim).

2771 KUDCHEDKAR, S. L. "Castiglione's Courtier and Elizabethan
Literature." Indian Journal of English Studies, 3, no. 1
(1962), 12-24.
Discusses briefly Pyrocles and Musidorus as representations of Castiglione's ideal. Sees Argalus as "the most
complete, balanced courtier in Arcadia."

2772 KUIN, R. J. P. "Scholars, Critics, and Sir Philip Sidney,
1945-1970." British Studies Monitor, 2, no. 3 (1972), 3-22.
Includes survey of "trends and developments" in studies
on Arcadia. Observes in the criticism "a sense of a closed,
inbred world: of critics speaking solely to each other and
to a small number of dutiful students."

Sidney

2773 LaGUARDIA, ERIC. <u>Nature Redeemed: The Imitation of Order in</u>
<u>Three Renaissance Poems</u>. SEngL, 31. The Hague: Mouton,
1966, 180pp.
Includes discussion of treatment of conflict between
passion and purity (or nature and spirit) in <u>Arcadia</u> (pp.
40-45).

2774 LANCASTER, H. CARRINGTON. "Sidney, Galaut, La Calprenède: An
Early Instance of the Influence of English Literature upon
French." <u>MLN</u>, 42 (February 1927), 71-77. [Reprinted in:
<u>Adventures of a Literary Historian: A Collection of His</u>
<u>Writings Presented to H. Carrington Lancaster</u>. Baltimore:
Johns Hopkins University Press, 1942, pp. 177-86.]
Discusses the Philoxenus-Amphialus episode as the source
of Jean Galaut's play <u>Phalante</u>, which in turn was the source
of La Calprenède's <u>Phalante</u>.

2775 LANDMANN, FRIEDRICH. "Introduction," in Evphves: The Anatomy
of Wit. <u>To Which Is Added the First Chapter of Sir Philip</u>
<u>Sidney's</u> Arcadia. By John Lyly. Edited by Friedrich Land-
mann. Englische Sprach- und Literaturdenkmale, 4. Heilbronn: Verlag von Gebr. Henninger, 1887, pp. III-XXXII.
Contrasts style in <u>Arcadia</u> with euphuism and discusses
the influence of Montemayor's <u>Diana</u> on Sidney.

2776 LANGENFELT, GÖSTA. "The Attitude to Villeins and Labourers in
English Literature until c. 1600." <u>ZAA</u>, 8 (1961), 337-80.
Includes discussion of Sidney's "social prejudices" in
his contemptuous treatment of lower-class characters in <u>Old</u>
and <u>New Arcadia</u>.

2777 LANGFORD, GERALD. "John Barclay and His <u>Argenis</u>." Ph.D. dissertation, University of Virginia, 1940, 199pp.
Includes examination of influence of <u>Arcadia</u> on Barclay's
work.

2778 LANHAM, RICHARD A[LAN]. The Old Arcadia, in <u>Sidney's</u> Arcadia.
By Walter R[ichardson] Davis and Richard A[lan] Lanham.
YSE, 158. New Haven: Yale University Press, 1965, pp. 181-
410.
Examines questions of genre and degree of Sidney's seri-
ousness about the work. Analyzes structure and themes, the
painstaking integration of rhetorical speeches "into the
narrative and thematic progression of the romance," the
comic elements, the complexity of Sidney as narrator, the
style, the sources, and the relationship between <u>Old</u> and
<u>New Arcadia</u>. Labels work "a prose-fictional tragi-comical-
heroic-politico-pastoral drama" and argues that Sidney was

moving toward comic novel form. Argues throughout against
simplistic interpretation of work. See 2710.

2779   LANHAM, RICHARD [ALAN]. "Opaque Style in Elizabethan Prose
       Fiction." PCP, 1 (1966), 25-31.
          Discusses relationship between structure and rhetoric in
       Arcadia, especially the juxtaposition of event and speech.
       Argues that rhetoric is a theme of the work, but points out
       that it lacks "an unadorned normative style by which to
       judge the exaggerations in which...[Sidney's] characters...
       indulge."

*2780 LANHAM, RICHARD ALAN. "Sidney's Original Arcadia." Ph.D. dis-
       sertation, Yale University, 1963.
          See 2778.

2781   LAWRY, JON S. Sidney's Two Arcadias: Pattern and Proceeding.
       Ithaca: Cornell University Press, 1972, 320pp.
          In a book by book examination of the Old Arcadia and the
       New Arcadia as heroic poems, analyzes narrative techniques
       and structures, themes, patterns of conduct and action, and
       character. Emphasizes Ramist influence on structure of Old
       Arcadia and the icastic pattern of New Arcadia. Analyzes
       changes made in New Arcadia and the importance of the De-
       fense of Poetry to an understanding of the original and
       revised versions.

2782   LAWTON, HAROLD W. "Notes sur Jean Baudoin et sur ses traduc-
       tions de l'Anglais (1619; 1624-1625; 1626; 1648)." RLC, 6
       (1926), 673-81.
          Discusses the circumstances surrounding Baudoin's trans-
       lation of the Arcadia and the characteristics of his trans-
       lation. Briefly compares his work with the translation by
       Geneviève Chappelain.

2783   LEE, SIDNEY. "Sir Philip Sidney," in Great Englishmen of the
       Sixteenth Century. By Sidney Lee. New York: Charles
       Scribners' Sons, 1904, pp. 63-115.
          Discusses literary influences on Arcadia; the combination
       of pastoral, chivalry, and intrigue; and Sidney's style.

2784   LEED, JACOB. "Richardson's Pamela and Sidney's." AUMLA, 40
       (1973), 240-45.
          Provides detailed comparison between the two characters
       to show Richardson chose the name of the Arcadian princess
       "to call attention to certain features of his heroine's
       personality."

Sidney

2785   LEGOUIS, ÉMILE. "Le Premier traducteur Français de l'anglais
       littéraire." <u>Revue Anglo-Américaine</u>, 10 (June 1933), 418-
       21.
              Discusses briefly the treatment of the text of <u>Arcadia</u>
       by Jean Loiseau de Tourval, the first to translate Sidney's
       work into French.

2786   LEMMI, C. W. "Italian Borrowings in Sidney." <u>MLN</u>, 42 (Febru-
       ary 1927), 77-79.
              Points out that the sonnet describing Mopsa is an imita-
       tion of a poem by Francesco Berni and that the source of
       Dorus's comment that love "like a point in midst of a
       circle, is still of a nearness" is the eleventh chapter of
       Dante's <u>Vita Nuova</u>.

2787   LEVIN, HARRY. <u>The Myth of the Golden Age in the Renaissance</u>.
       Bloomington: Indiana University Press, 1969, 255pp.
              Includes discussion of Sidney's depiction of Arcadia
       (pp. 93-99).

2788   LEVINE, NORMAN. "Aspects of Moral and Political Thought in
       Sidney's <u>Arcadia</u>." Ph.D. dissertation, Columbia University,
       1972, 216pp.
              "[A]nalyzes many aspects of the moral and political
       teaching of the <u>Arcadia</u> and suggests how Arcadian doctrine
       for any one of these aspects accords with that of the
       others."

2789   LEVINE, ROBERT ERIL. <u>A Comparison of Sidney's Old and New</u>
       Arcadia. Salzburg Studies in English Literature, ElizS,
       13. Salzburg: Institut für Englische Sprache und Litera-
       tur, Universität Salzburg, 1974, 126pp.
              Examines genre of <u>Arcadia</u> and traces textual history of
       the versions. Compares setting, style, and narrative tech-
       nique of Book I of <u>Old</u> and <u>New Arcadia</u>; compares narrative
       structure of Book II; and compares treatment of insurrec-
       tion.

2790   LEVINSON, RONALD B. "The 'Godlesse Minde' in Sidney's <u>Ar-
       cadia</u>." <u>MP</u>, 29 (August 1931), 21-26.
              Argues against Greenlaw's contention (2700) for influ-
       ence of Lucretius on Pamela-Crecopia debate. Suggests that
       Sidney is drawing upon Cicero's <u>De Natura Deorum</u> and that
       Pamela's "godlesse minde" is a reference to Velleius, one
       of speakers in the dialogue.

2791   LEWIS, C[LIVE] S[TAPLES]. <u>English Literature in the Sixteenth
       Century Excluding Drama</u>. Oxford History of English Litera-
       ture, 3. Oxford: Clarendon Press, 1954, 704pp.

Discusses relationship among versions of Arcadia, influences, didacticism, form ("Arcadian epic"), style, and
characterization. Argues that "[t]he heart of the Arcadia
...is its nobility of sentiment" (pp. 331-42, passim).

*2792   LEWIS, PIERS INGERSOLL. "Literary and Political Attitudes in
        Sidney's Arcadia." Ph.D. dissertation, Harvard University,
        1964.
        Abstract not available.

2793   LILJEGREN, S. B. "Milton and the King's Prayer." Beiblatt
        zur Anglia, 37 (March 1926), 91-94.
        Takes issue with several of Smart's arguments (2907).

2794   LINDENBAUM, PETER ALAN. "The Anti-Pastoral Pastoral: The
        Education of Fallen Man in the Renaissance." Ph.D. disser-
        tation, University of California, Berkeley, 1970, 354pp.
        Analyzes "anti-pastoral sentiment" in both versions of
        Arcadia. Argues "that the two versions have more in common
        than is usually assumed, that there is reason to believe
        that the New Arcadia would end in a manner similar to the
        Old Arcadia, and that Sidney in both versions uses Pyrocles'
        and Musidorus' Arcadian sojourn so as to put them through an
        education in which they are brought to recognize their own
        limitations as fallen human beings."

2795   LINDENBAUM, PETER [ALAN]. "Sidney's Arcadia: The Endings of
        the Three Versions." HLQ, 34 (May 1971), 205-18.
        Argues that the conclusion of the Old Arcadia is "suc-
        cessful" and prepared for--not hasty, artificial, and con-
        ventional--by Sidney's "insistence on human limitations
        within the last sixty pages...[which] prepares us for some
        intervention by a higher power." Suggests that Sidney's
        revision of the episode in Philoclea's bedroom and elimina-
        tion of Musidorus's attempted rape of Pamela indicate that
        he "intended a considerable improvement in the princes'
        heroic and moral character and conduct" in the projected
        revision.

2796   LINDHEIM, NANCY ROTHWAX. "Sidney's Arcadia, Book II: Retro-
        spective Narrative." SP, 64 (April 1967), 159-86.
        Analyzes the structure of the retrospective narrative
        section in Book II and discusses the relationship of this
        section to the revised Arcadia as a whole. Analyzes how
        stories told by Pyrocles emphasize public virtues while
        those told by Musidorus emphasize private ones. Analyzes
        how the "two accounts [which] seem to present alternative
        views concerning the nature and exercise of moral virtue"
        illustrate the education of the prince.

451

Sidney

2797   LINDHEIM, NANCY ROTHWAX. "The Structures of Sidney's Arcadia."
        Ph.D. dissertation, University of California, Berkeley,
        1966, 332pp.
            Examines rhetorical, tonal, and narrative structures and
        their influence on "units of composition ranging from single
        clauses to whole books" and on themes.

2798   LINDHEIM, NANCY R[OTHWAX]. "Vision, Revision, and the 1593
        Text of the Arcadia." ELR, 2 (Winter 1972), 136–47.
            Argues "that any critical reading of the Arcadia must
        recognize the distinctions between main plot and episodes
        in the interest of working out some relation between them
        that will account for the text" of the 1593 edition; other-
        wise, one will be "blind to developments in Sidney's under-
        standing of the complexity of heroic and moral experience."
        Analyzes the Pyrocles-Philoclea debate on suicide and
        Musidorus and Pyrocles's acceptance of death as illustra-
        tion.

2799   LLOYD, JULIUS. The Life of Sir Philip Sidney. London: Long-
        man, Green, Longman, Roberts, and Green, 1862, 260pp.
            In Chapter IV ("Arcadia," pp. 89–116) discusses influ-
        ences on the work, Sidney's mixture of forms, and the "dig-
        nity of mind" exhibited in Arcadia.

2800   MACAULAY, ROSE. "Lyly and Sidney," in The English Novelists:
        A Survey of the Novel by Twenty Contemporary Novelists.
        Edited by Derek Verschoyle. London: Chatto & Windus,
        1936, pp. 29–47.
            Finds Sidney "a dull, even disastrous novelist" and dis-
        cusses briefly the "damage [caused by Arcadia] to literature
        and to literary taste and fashion."

2801   McCOY, DOROTHY SCHUCHMAN. Tradition and Convention: A Study
        of Periphrasis in English Pastoral Poetry from 1557-1715.
        SEngL, 5. The Hague: Mouton, 1965, 289pp.
            Examines Sidney's use of the high, middle, and low
        styles and his use of periphrasis in each (pp. 51–61,
        passim).

2802   MacCRACKEN, H. N. "The Sources of Ivanhoe." Nation, 92 (19
        January 1911), 60.
            Comments on Scott's use of Arcadia as source. See 2959.

2803   McKEITHAN, D. M. "King Lear and Sidney's Arcadia." University
        of Texas Studies in English, 14 (1934), 45–49.
            Suggests that "Shakespeare possibly took suggestions
        from the story of Plangus" for the means by which Edmund
        discredits Edgar to Gloucester.

2804   McNEIR, WALDO F. "The Behaviour of Brigadore: The Faerie
        Queene, V, 3, 33–34." N&Q, NS, 1 (March 1954), 103–104.
        Suggests possibility that description of Musidorus's
        manège is source for the passage.

2805   McNEIR, WALDO F. "Trial by Combat in Elizabethan Literature."
        NS, 15 (1966), 101–12.
        In examining how Elizabethan literature was "a mirror...
        of chivalric legal ceremony," discusses the various trials
        by combat in Arcadia, noting that "Sidney...regarded the
        legal manifestation of chivalry in trial by combat as unre-
        alistic."

2806   McPHERSON, DAVID C. "A Possible Origin for Mopsa in Sidney's
        Arcadia." RenQ, 21 (Winter 1968), 420–28.
        Suggests that in name "Sidney is making a kind of pun,
        humorously combining the name's Virgilian associations with
        those surrounding the Dutch word mops," which "means 'pug
        dog' and, formerly, by extension, meant 'country lout'
        also." Examines possible sources of Sidney's knowledge of
        meaning of Dutch word.

2807   MAGENDIE, MAURICE. Le Roman français au XVIIe siècle: De
        l'Astrée au Grand Cyrus. Paris: E. Droz, 1932, 457pp.
        Includes examination of influence of Arcadia on French
        prose fiction, 1620–1650 (pp. 71–77).

2808   MAHL, MARY R[OBERTA]. "Sir Philip Sidney's Scribe: The New
        Arcadia and the Apology for Poetry." ELN, 10 (December
        1972), 90–91.
        Reports that same scribe was responsible for the Norwich
        manuscript of the Apology and the Cambridge University
        Library manuscript of the New Arcadia.

2809   MARENCO, FRANCO. Arcadia puritana: L'uso della tradizione
        nella prima Arcadia di Sir Philip Sidney. Biblioteca di
        Studi Inglesi, 9. Bari: Adriatica, 1968, 238pp.
        Examines Old Arcadia against background of contemporary
        religious thought to argue that work is a moral treatise
        and an allegory of post-lapsarian man. Analyzes Sidney's
        use and rejection of conventions of pastoral and epic, his
        themes, and the structure (both moral and dramatic) of the
        work.

2810   MARENCO, FRANCO. "Double Plot in Sidney's Old Arcadia." MLR,
        64 (April 1969), 248–63.
        Provides "an analysis of the interaction of main plot
        and sub-plot...and an attempt to approach the spirit of the
        work through its dramatic structure."

Sidney

2811   MARENCO, FRANCO. "Per una nuova interpretazione dell'<u>Arcadia</u>
        di Sidney." <u>EM</u>, 17 (1966), 9-48.
            Discerns influence of Protestant Neoplatonism and Cal-
        vinistic thought in <u>Arcadia</u>. Argues that in work Sidney
        presents an allegory of the degradation of man. Compares
        <u>Arcadia</u> with John Davies's <u>Nosce Teipsum</u> and Fulke Gre-
        ville's <u>Treaty of Humane Learning</u>.

2812   MARENCO, FRANCO. "Sidney e l'<u>Arcadia</u> nella critica letteraria."
        <u>Filologia e Letteratura</u>, 12 (1966), 337-76.
            Provides topical overview of <u>Arcadia</u> criticism from the
        sixteenth century through 1966.

2813   MARENCO, FRANCO. "Sir Philip Sidney: Studi 1965-66."
        <u>Filologia e Letteratura</u>, 13, no. 2 (1967), 216-24.
            Includes survey of essays and books published during
        1965-1966 on <u>Arcadia</u>.

2814   MARINO, JAMES ARTHUR. "The Cult of Ideal Friendship in Three
        Elizabethan Novels." Ph.D. dissertation, Louisiana State
        University and Agricultural and Mechanical College, 1972,
        226pp.
            Examines Sidney's use of friendship "for narrative con-
        tent, thematic unity, and character development."

2815   MARSH, T. N. "Elizabethan Wit in Metaphor and Conceit: Sid-
        ney, Shakespeare, Donne." <u>EM</u>, 13 (1962), 25-29.
            Notes similarity of conceits in poem describing Mopsa
        and Donne's "The Anagram"; also notes use of conceit of
        "blood filling the wrinkles of a face" (<u>Arcadia</u>, Book I,
        Chapter 1) in Donne's <u>Divine Poems</u> and in Shakespeare's
        <u>Titus Andronicus</u>. Suggests that in latter instance, Sid-
        ney's "image is developed statically."

2816   MARTIN, L. C. "Marvell, Massinger, and Sidney." <u>RES</u>, NS, 2
        (October 1951), 374-75.
            Suggests possible influence of Philoclea's soliloquy on
        love for Zelmane on Marvell's "The Definition of Love."
        <u>See</u> 2584.

2817   MASSON, DAVID. <u>British Novelists and Their Styles: Being a
        Critical Sketch of the History of British Prose Fiction</u>.
        Boston: Gould and Lincoln; New York: Sheldon and Co.,
        1859, 312pp.
            Includes general appreciation of <u>Arcadia</u>: comments on
        Sidney's style and finds that the emphasis on the ideal is
        "the most memorable characteristic" of the work (pp. 69-77).

2818   MATHEWS, ERNST GARLAND. "Studies in Anglo-Spanish Cultural
        and Literary Relations, 1598-1700." Ph.D. dissertation,
        Harvard University, 1938.
            Includes examination of influence of Spanish romance
        (particularly Montemayor's Diana) on Arcadia. Suggests that
        "something of the fondness for pastoral scenes and lush
        descriptions, some of the centralizing devices and general
        structure, something of the tone even of a few knightly
        episodes...were at least influenced by the popular [Spanish]
        pastoral romances."

2819   MERMEL, ANN RAUCH. "Mythological Allegory in Sidney's Ar-
        cadia." Ph.D. dissertation, University of Houston, 1974,
        249pp.
            Argues "that in writing the Arcadia Sidney imitated
        mythological actions which, in turn, imitated divine Ideas."
        Examines how "Basilius, Pyrocles, Musidorus, Plangus, and
        Erona all have mythological counterparts, and [how] the
        major actions in which they participate have mythological
        parallels."

*2820   MILLER, PETER MacNAUGHTON, JR. "The Rhetoric of Sidney's
        Arcadia." Ph.D. dissertation, Princeton University, 1939,
        262pp.
            Abstract not available.

2821   MILLS, LAURENS J. One Soul in Bodies Twain: Friendship in
        Tudor Literature and Stuart Drama. Bloomington, Indiana:
        Principia Press, 1937, 480pp.
            Examines Sidney's use of friendship theme in Arcadia
        (pp. 214-20).

2822   MORISON, SAMUEL ELIOT. "The Reverend Seaborn Cotton's Common-
        place Book." Publications of the Colonial Society of Mas-
        sachusetts, 32 (1937), 320-52.
            Provides transcript of portion of the seventeenth-century
        Puritan's commonplace book, which includes several extracts
        from Arcadia.

2823   MORLEY, EDITH J[ULIA]. The Works of Sir Philip Sidney. Quain
        Essay. London: H. Rees, 1901, 60pp.
            Discusses style, characterization, and combination of
        pastoral and romance in Arcadia, as well as the place of
        the work in the development of the English novel.

2824   MORLEY, HENRY. English Writers, IX: Spenser and His Time.
        London: Cassell & Co., 1892, 472pp.

Sidney

> Discusses influences on Sidney's style in <u>Arcadia</u> and the influence of the work on later writers (pp. 124-31).

2825 MOUNT, C. B. "Sir Philip Sidney and Shakespeare." <u>N&Q</u>, 87 (22 April 1893), 305.
> Suggests <u>Arcadia</u> as source of a passage in <u>The Winter's Tale</u>.

2826 MUIR, KENNETH. "Introduction," in <u>King Lear</u>. By William Shakespeare. Edited by Kenneth Muir. Arden Shakespeare. Cambridge: Harvard University Press, 1952, pp. xv-lxiv.
> Discusses Shakespeare's use of <u>Arcadia</u> as source for the play.

2827 MUIR, KENNETH. <u>Shakespeare's Sources, I: Comedies and Tragedies</u>. London: Methuen & Co., 1957, 279pp.
> Includes discussion of Shakespeare's use of <u>Arcadia</u> as source for <u>King Lear</u> (pp. 141-66).

2828 MUIR, KENNETH. <u>Sir Philip Sidney</u>. Writers and Their Work, 120. London: Longmans, Green, & Co. for the British Council and the National Book League, 1960, 40pp.
> Analyzes characteristics of style in both <u>Old</u> and <u>New Arcadia</u> and compares style in the two versions. Finds that Sidney's "Arcadian style depends...on the intensive use of a wide variety of figures." Examines Sidney's "descriptive power" and the rhythm of his prose. Comments on didacticism.

2829 MUIR, KENNETH, and JOHN F[RANCIS] DANBY. "<u>Arcadia</u> and <u>King Lear</u>." <u>N&Q</u>, 195 (4 February 1950), 49-51.
> Suggests several passages from <u>Arcadia</u> which influenced Shakespeare in <u>Lear</u>.

2830 MYRICK, KENNETH [ORNE]. <u>Sir Philip Sidney as a Literary Craftsman</u>. Harvard Studies in English, 14. Cambridge: Harvard University Press, 1935, 330pp.
> Analyzes <u>New Arcadia</u> as an heroic poem both in form and in purpose: finds that both <u>Old</u> and <u>New Arcadia</u> "show a strong instinct for form" and analyzes in detail how "in subject and structure the <u>New Arcadia</u> follows Minturno's rules for the heroic poem." Includes discussion of relationship of work to Sidney's theory of poetry, of his ornamentation in style, and of his themes.

2831 MYRICK, KENNETH [ORNE]. <u>Sir Philip Sidney as a Literary Craftsman</u>. 2d edition. Lincoln: University of Nebraska Press, 1965, 363pp.
> Makes only minor revisions to 2830 and adds 2521.

2832 MYRICK, KENNETH ORNE. "Sir Philip Sidney: The Elizabethan
Courtier as Critic and Literary Artist." Ph.D. dissertation, Harvard University, 1934.
Analyzes New Arcadia as an heroic poem (particularly as
it follows "Minturno's requirements for the epic"). Examines "the imaginative quality of the New Arcadia, and relate[s] the work to...[Sidney's] theory of 'delightful
teaching.'" Finds that "[t]he allegory is far less important than Herr Brie and even Mr. Greenlaw have asserted;
but the teaching is more systematic than has been realized
by Mr. Zandvoort and by most other scholars."

2833 NEELY, CAROL THOMAS. "Speaking True: Shakespeare's Use of
the Elements of Pastoral Romance." Ph.D. dissertation,
Yale University, 1969, 226pp.
Examines structure, the "two communities," landscape,
and lovers in Old and New Arcadia to argue that both works
are "structurally and thematically unresolved."

2834 NELSON, T. G. A. "Sir John Harington as a Critic of Sir
Philip Sidney." SP, 67 (January 1970), 41-56.
Examines Harington's attitude toward and use of Arcadia.
Finds his preference was "for the satirical passages...
rather than the more elevated ones."

2835 NEWKIRK, GLEN ALTON. "The Public and Private Ideal of the
Sixteenth Century Gentleman: A Representative Analysis."
Ph.D. dissertation, University of Denver, 1966, 345pp.
Includes discussion of Arcadia in analysis of sixteenth-
century concept of the "gentlemanly ideal."

2836 NICHOLSON, BRINSLEY. "On Shakespeare's Pastoral Name." N&Q,
49 (7 February 1874), 109-10.
Brings forth evidence that Philisides is Sidney. (See
also: B[rinsley] Nicholson, "Philisides," N&Q, 56 [13 October 1877], 286.)

*2837 O'BRIEN, PAULINE W. "The 'Speaking Picture' in the Works of
Sidney." Ph.D. dissertation, Duke University, 1954, 185pp.
Abstract not available.

2838 O'CONNOR, JOHN J. Amadis de Gaule and Its Influence on Elizabethan Literature. New Brunswick: Rutgers University
Press, 1970, 318pp.
In Chapter X ("Amadis and Sidney's Arcadia," pp. 183-
201) argues that "the influence of Amadis upon the Arcadia
appears to be greater than hitherto realized." Argues that
Sidney based "his central narrative upon Amadis" but that

Sidney

he combined and transformed most of the episodes. Also examines influence on Sidney's "treatment of sexual love, his
sense of humor, and his prose style."

2839   O'CONNOR, JOHN J. "Studies in the Theory and Practice of Prose
       Fiction, 1600-1640." Ph.D. dissertation, Harvard University,
       1951, 184pp.
          Includes examination of "the vogue of Sidney's Arcadia
       in the early 17th century, and the several attempts to con-
       tinue that work and mine that vein."

2840   OGILVY, J. D. A. "Arcadianism in I Henry IV." ELN, 10 (March
       1973), 185-88.
          Suggests Hal's answer to Falstaff in tavern scene is
       parody of Arcadian style. Notes parallels between Hal's
       speech and opening paragraphs of Arcadia.

2841   O'HARA, JAMES EUGENE, JR. "The Rhetoric of Love in Lyly's
       Euphues and His England and Sidney's Arcadia." Ph.D. dis-
       sertation, University of Michigan, 1974, 210pp.
          Analyzes characteristics of Sidney's style and attempts
       to differentiate between arcadianism and euphuism.

2842   OSBORN, ALBERT W. Sir Philip Sidney en France. Bibliothèque
       de la Revue de Littérature Comparée, 84. Paris: H.
       Champion, 1932, 219pp.
          Examines influence of Amadis de Gaule on Arcadia, dis-
       cusses the French translations of the work, and traces its
       reputation in France and influence upon French literature.
       Reprints (from MS. Rawlinson D. 920) the fragment of Jean
       Loiseau de Tourval's translation.

2843   OTTEN, KURT. Der englische Roman vom 16. zum 19. Jahrhundert.
       Grundlagen der Anglistik und Amerikanistik, 4. Berlin: E.
       Schmidt, 1971, 184pp.
          Includes general critical estimate of Arcadia in context
       of discussion of development of the English novel (pp. 26-
       30).

2844   PARKER, ROBERT WESLEY. "Narrative Structure and Thematic De-
       velopment in Sidney's Original Arcadia." Ph.D. disserta-
       tion, Columbia University, 1965, 291pp.
          Examines narrative and thematic structure in an attempt
       to resolve the problem of the conclusion of the Old Arcadia.
       Discusses resemblances of plot to "structure of Roman and
       Renaissance comedy" and identifies the "crux of the problem
       (which would have been no problem for the Renaissance reader
       of comedy)...[as] the unreconciled conflict between the

expectations raised by the comic plot, and the moral themes
that plot is asked to develop."

2845   PARKER, ROBERT W[ESLEY]. "Terentian Structure and Sidney's
       Original Arcadia." ELR, 2 (Winter 1972), 61–78.
       Analyzes Sidney's use of the Terentian five-act structure
       to achieve a unified, causally linked plot. Argues that Old
       Arcadia is heroic, according to the Renaissance understand-
       ing of the term.

2846   PARRY, GRAHAM. "Lady Mary Wroth's Urania." PLPLS-LHS, 16,
       part 4 (1975), 51–60.
       Examines relationship of Urania to Sidney's Arcadia and
       examines significance of character of Urania to Wroth's
       title. Calls her style "almost indistinguishable from
       Sidney's."

2847   PATCHELL, MARY [F.]. The Palmerin Romances in Elizabethan
       Prose Fiction. Columbia University Studies in English and
       Comparative Literature, 166. New York: Columbia University
       Press, 1947, 171pp.
       Examines possible influences of Palmerin romances on New
       and Old Arcadia to argue against the assumption that, of
       Spanish fiction, Sidney was influenced by only Amadis
       (pp. 115–27).

2848   PATTISON, BRUCE. "Sir Philip Sidney and Music." M&L, 15
       (January 1934), 75–81.
       Discusses effect of music on Sidney's works and music
       allusions in Arcadia.

2849   PERKINSON, RICHARD H. "The Epic in Five Acts." SP, 43 (July
       1946), 465–81.
       Includes discussion of Sidney's use of five-act dramatic
       structure for his heroic poem. Suggests that Sidney's
       "classical conscience" was the cause of "his dissatisfaction
       with the structure of the Old Arcadia."

2850   PETTET, E. C. Shakespeare and the Romance Tradition. London:
       Staples Press, 1949, 208pp.
       Sees Arcadia as epitome of Elizabethan prose romance and
       anlyzes its characteristics. Traces influence on Shake-
       speare's plays (pp. 23–32, passim).

*2851 PHILLIPS, HELEN MARIE. "Human Nature and Art in Sidney's Ar-
       cadia." Ph.D. dissertation, Cornell University, 1933.
       Abstract not available.

Sidney

2852   PLOMER, HENRY R. "The Edinburgh Edition of Sidney's Arcadia."
        Library, 2d Ser., 1 (March 1900), 195–205.
            Discusses William Ponsonby's lawsuit over the piracy of
        Arcadia; examines the circumstances surrounding the print-
        ing, publication, and distribution of the 1599 Edinburgh
        edition.

2853   POIRIER, MICHEL. "Quelques sources des poèmes de Sidney." EA,
        11, no. 2 (1958), 150–54.
            Suggests sources for several passages in poems from
        Arcadia.

2854   POIRIER, MICHEL. "Sidney's Influence upon A Midsummer Night's
        Dream." SP, 44 (July 1947), 483–89.
            Suggests that Sidney's description of hunt in Book I of
        revised Arcadia is Shakespeare's source for Theseus and
        Hippolyta's comments on baying of the hounds at beginning
        of Act IV. See 2870.

2855   POIRIER, MICHEL. Sir Philip Sidney: Le Chevalier poète éliza-
        béthain. Travaux et Mémoires de l'Université de Lille, NS,
        26. Lille: Bibliothèque Universitaire de Lille, 1948,
        321pp.
            Analyzes Arcadia as a reflection of Sidney's moral, po-
        litical, and religious ideas. Discusses sources of and in-
        fluences on Arcadia, the structure and form of both Old and
        New Arcadia, the revisions in New Arcadia, themes, and
        style.

2856   PRAZ, MARIO. "The Duchess of Malfi." TLS, 18 June 1954,
        p. 393.
            Points out that the mock decapitation of Philoclea is
        not Webster's source for the scene "'with the dead hand and
        the mock corpse.'"

2857   PRAZ, MARIO. "Sidney's Original Arcadia." London Mercury, 15
        (March 1927), 507–14.
            Argues that Old Arcadia is superior to New Arcadia. Com-
        pares treatment of plot and style in two versions and dis-
        cusses Sidney's "euphuistic technique" in the New Arcadia.

2858   PRINCE, RONALD FRANK. "'The Knowledge of a Mans Selfe': A
        Reading of Sidney's Old Arcadia." Ph.D. dissertation, Uni-
        versity of Pittsburgh, 1972, 221pp.
            Argues that in Old Arcadia Sidney "employs the pastoral
        form to present the conflict between sexual passions and
        moral authority" and that he utilizes "a dialectic between

passion and reason which shapes the structural components
of the Old Arcadia." Analyzes structure and narrative
voice.

2859 PSILOS, PAUL DENNIS. "Sidney's Arcadia: A Critical Study."
      Ph.D. dissertation, Northwestern University, 1970, 222pp.
          Uses "Sidney's conception of the nature and function of
      poetry as expressed in the Defense of Poesie" as basis for
      interpreting the "narrative and logical consistency" of
      New Arcadia.

2860 PYLE, FITZROY. "King Lear and Sidney's Arcadia." TLS, 11
      November 1949, p. 733.
          Argues against direct influence of Pamela-Crecopia epi-
      sode on theme of nature in the play and on Lear, 4.2.1-2.
      See 2550.

2861 PYLE, FITZROY. "Twelfth Night, King Lear, and Arcadia." MLR,
      43 (October 1948), 449-55.
          Discusses influence of Sidney's work on plot, character,
      and tone of the two plays.

2862 RALEIGH, WALTER [ALEXANDER]. The English Novel: Being a
      Short Sketch of Its History from the Earliest Times to the
      Appearance of Waverley. London: J. Murray, 1894, 310pp.
          Discusses Sidney's style and his influence on later
      writers. Finds that introduction of comic characters is
      a fault in Arcadia (pp. 51-64).

2863 RAMAGE, CRAUFURD TAIT. "Sir Philip Sidney's Arcadia." N&Q,
      37 (30 May 1868), 516.
          In answer to query ("Sundrie Queries," N&Q, 37 [11 April
      1868], 342) suggests phrase "Making a perpetual mansion of
      this poor baiting-place of man's life" is adaptation from
      Cicero or Seneca. See 2901.

2864 READ, PATRICIA ELINOR. "The Disfigured Mind: A Study of Art
      and Moral Vision in Sir Philip Sidney's Old and New Ar-
      cadias." Ph.D. dissertation, Rice University, 1971, 257pp.
          Analyzes how Sidney's "treatment of moral vision and of
      the visual arts...reflects tension between Renaissance op-
      timism about the capacity of man to see clearly and to cre-
      ate reasonable order and Puritan pessimism about it."

2865 REES, JOAN. "Fulke Greville and the Revisions of Arcadia."
      RES, NS, 17 (February 1966), 54-57.
          Interprets Greville's letter to Walsingham as indicating
      possibility of two stages in revision of Arcadia: "one in

Sidney

which he [Sidney] changed some episodes in the later part
of the Old Arcadia on moral and artistic grounds; and a
second in which he decided to rewrite the whole thing."

2866   REES, JOAN. Fulke Greville, Lord Brooke, 1554-1628: A Critical Biography. Berkeley: University of California Press,
1971, 252pp.
Includes discussion of Greville's editorship of New Arcadia and his preference for the revised version. Examines
how "Greville's attitude towards...[Arcadia] reflects
strongly his own political interests and his assessment of
the moral value of literature" (pp. 45-57).

2867   REEVES, ROBERT NICHOLAS III. The Ridiculous to the Delightful:
Comic Characters in Sidney's New Arcadia. LeBaron Russell
Briggs Prize Honors Essays in English, 1973. Cambridge:
Harvard University Press, 1974, 61pp.
Analyzes Sidney's use of "humor and irony to achieve his
primary goal of 'delightful teaching.'" Examines the relationship of the comic subplot to the main plot, the central
themes of the work, and Sidney's didactic intent, finding
that "the low characters provide Sidney with a device to
expose the flaws as well as exalt the virtues of his heroes
and heroines." Concludes that "Sidney's primary comic
achievement" in the New Arcadia is his attempt to merge the
"delightful and the ridiculous." In Appendix speculates
about possibility that Shakespeare's depiction of Falstaff
owes something to Dametas.

2868   RIBNER, IRVING. "Machiavelli and Sidney: The Arcadia of
1590." SP, 47 (April 1950), 152-72.
Analyzes political doctrine expressed in several episodes in New Arcadia "to demonstrate that Sidney's doctrine
is essentially in agreement with that contained in the writings of...Machiavelli." Does not suggest that Sidney borrowed directly from Machiavelli but that Machiavelli's
ideas "were a part of the Elizabethan intellectual milieu."

*2869   RIBNER, IRVING. "Machiavelli and Sir Philip Sidney." Ph.D.
dissertation, University of North Carolina at Chapel Hill,
1950, 199pp.
Abstract not available.

2870   RIBNER, IRVING. "A Note on Sidney's Arcadia and A Midsummer
Night's Dream." Shakespeare Association Bulletin, 23 (October 1948), 207-208.
Supplements Poirier's argument (2854) for Shakespeare's
use of Arcadia as a source for the play by suggesting that

the "Philoclea-Zelmane-Basilius-Gynecia tangle" furnished a model for the "Lysander-Hermia-Demetrius-Helena love tangle."

2871   RIBNER, IRVING. "Sidney's Arcadia and the Machiavelli Legend." Italica, 27 (1950), 225-35.
        Examines villains in New Arcadia "to demonstrate (1) that the characteristics with which Sidney endows these villains have little relation to Machiavelli's actual writings, but are instead reflections of the prevalent popular misinterpretation, (2) that these villains all fail in their purposes not because they follow Machiavelli, but precisely because they fail to follow certain of Machiavelli's basic precepts, rules of conduct of which Sidney also evidently approved, and (3) that the 'Machiavels' of the Arcadia, rather than offer evidence that Sidney was opposed to Machiavelli's ideas, serve instead to reinforce the conclusion...that Sidney and Machiavelli were in essential agreement."

2872   RIBNER, IRVING. "Sidney's Arcadia and the Structure of King Lear." SN, 24 (1952), 63-68.
        Examines how Sidney's tale of the blind king of Paphlagonia, with its illustration of the "evils which will befall a kingdom when the ruler abandons his God-given responsibility," complements the main plot of the Arcadia. Notes that the Gloucester subplot in Lear complements the main plot in the same manner and argues that "Shakespeare used the Arcadia not only as a source of plot material, but also as a model for plot construction."

2873   RIBNER, IRVING. "Sir Philip Sidney on Civil Insurrection." JHI, 13 (April 1952), 257-65.
        Examines attitude in Arcadia toward obedience due the monarch. Argues that "in spite of Sidney's manifest endorsement of" the concept of limited monarchy, there is "strong evidence of Sidney's distaste for...armed insurrection against a king who...[did] not fulfill his obligations to his people." Concludes that Sidney's "attitude towards the problems of tyranny and civil insurrection" is that of the "traditional stand of the Elizabethan gentleman."

2874   RINGLER, WILLIAM A., JR. "Introduction," in The Poems of Sir Philip Sidney. By Philip Sidney. Edited by William A. Ringler, Jr. Oxford: Clarendon Press, 1962, pp. xv-lxvi.
        Discusses Arcadia as a mixture of genres, the dramatic form of Old Arcadia, and the relationship of the poems to the prose narrative. Also analyzes the characteristics of the Arcadia poems. Provides critical edition of all poems

463

Sidney

in <u>Arcadia</u>. In the "Commentary" discusses the dates of
composition of the <u>Old</u> and <u>New Arcadia</u>, the textual history
of the works, and the relationship between the surviving
texts of the <u>Old Arcadia</u> and the revision (pp. 364-83). In
the "Bibliography" provides detailed description of the
manuscripts and the early editions of the <u>Old</u> and the <u>New</u>
<u>Arcadia</u> (pp. 525-38).

2875   RINGLER, WILLIAM [A.]. "Master Drant's Rules." <u>PQ</u>, 29 (Janu-
       ary 1950), 70-74.
          Provides literal transcript of unpublished passage in
       Jesus College MS. 150 of <u>Old Arcadia</u>, in which Dicus and
       Lalus, at conclusion of first set of eclogues, "discuss the
       relative merits of quantitative and riming verse." Also
       provides literal transcript of unpublished "Nota" from St.
       John's College MS. 308 of <u>Old Arcadia</u>; concludes that the
       "Nota" is "Sidney's version of" Drant's rules for quantita-
       tive verse.

2876   RINGLER, WILLIAM [A.]. "Poems Attributed to Sir Philip Sid-
       ney." <u>SP</u>, 47 (April 1950), 126-51.
          Includes discussion of authorship of poems which were
       attributed to Sidney in seventeenth-century editions of
       <u>Arcadia</u> or which were identified in manuscripts as omitted
       from the <u>Arcadia</u>.

2877   ROBERTSON, JEAN. "Sidney and Bandello." <u>Library</u>, 5th Ser.,
       21 (December 1966), 326-28.
          Suggests that if Sidney was influenced by Bandello's
       tales in <u>Arcadia</u>, his source was one of the French versions.
       Describes Sidney's copy of the Boaistuau-Belleforest <u>His-
       toires tragiques</u> (Lyons, 1561).

2878   ROGERS, EVELYN GIBBS. "Sidney the Perfectionist Poet: Changes
       in Text and Context of the New <u>Arcadia</u> Poems." Ph.D. dis-
       sertation, University of Maryland, 1970, 264pp.
          Compares "the poems of the New <u>Arcadia</u> and their con-
       texts...with those poems and their settings in the Old
       <u>Arcadia</u>"; concludes that "Sidney [<u>i</u>s] constantly improving
       his art."

2879   ROSE, MARK [ALLEN]. <u>Heroic Love: Studies in Sidney and Spen-
       ser</u>. Cambridge: Harvard University Press, 1968, 168pp.
          Argues that Sidney, rather than pitting war against love
       as is common in the epic tradition, "cast[s] over love it-
       self the atmosphere of the heroic, transforming the torments
       of the soul aspiring to marriage into a struggle worthy of
       the epic hero." Analyzes balance between passion and reason

in <u>New Arcadia</u> to argue that for Pyrocles and Musidorus
"[l]ove is not in fact a diversion from their true goal, but
the final stage in their education, an experience arranged
by providence to prepare them for their lives as rulers of
states."

*2880 ROSE, MARK ALLEN. "Heroic Love: Studies in the Morality of
Love in Two Elizabethan Epics." Ph.D. dissertation, Harvard
University, 1967.
<u>See</u> 2879.

2881 ROSE, MARK [ALLEN]. "Sidney's Womanish Man." <u>RES</u>, NS, 15
(November 1964), 353-63.
Argues that "Sidney...intended his readers to find Pyrocles's disguise offensive" and "that the Amazonian dress is
not intended as a compliment but as a criticism of Pyrocles's
failings" and is symbolic of the ascendancy of passion over
reason.

2882 ROTA, FELICINA. <u>L'Arcadia di Sidney e il teatro: Con un
testo inedito</u>. Bibliotheca di Studi Inglesi, 6. Bari:
Adriatica Editrice, 1966, 390pp.
Examines use of <u>Arcadia</u> as source by several seventeenth-
century playwrights. Provides transcription of text of
"Loves Changelings Change," a manuscript play based on <u>Ar-
cadia</u>.

2883 ROWE, KENNETH THORPE. "The Countess of Pembroke's Editorship
of the <u>Arcadia</u>." <u>PMLA</u>, 54 (March 1939), 122-38.
Interprets prefatory address by H. S. in 1593 edition as
an "explicit statement" that Lady Mary did not add to or revise her brother's work; rather, her concern was for printing only what was Sidney's. Argues that she did not
bowdlerize work but probably "had special knowledge [likely
a manuscript revised by her brother] of Sidney's intentions
for revision of the last three books" of <u>Old Arcadia</u>.

2884 ROWE, KENNETH THORPE. "Elizabethan Morality and the Folio Revisions of Sidney's <u>Arcadia</u>." <u>MP</u>, 37 (November 1939),
151-72.
Discusses revisions in episodes treating consummation of
love by Pyrocles and Philoclea, and Musidorus's contemplated
attempt on Pamela's virginity. Argues against revision by
Countess of Pembroke on grounds that such a consummation
"was entirely conventional in Elizabethan literature" and
would not have offended Sidney's sister. Argues that Sidney
made revisions on ethical and artistic grounds in attempt to
present "supreme models of virtue."

Sidney

2885   ROWE, KENNETH THORPE. "The Love of Sir Philip Sidney for the
        Countess of Pembroke." <u>Papers of the Michigan Academy of
        Science, Arts, and Letters</u>, 25 (1939), 579-95.
            Rejects idea that Philisides episode is a representation
        of an incestuous relationship between Sidney and his sister;
        examines autobiographical associations in the episode.

2886   ROWE, KENNETH THORPE. <u>Romantic Love and Parental Authority in
        Sydney's</u> Arcadia. UMCMP, 4. Ann Arbor: University of
        Michigan Press, 1947, 58pp.
            Examines Sidney's treatment of the theme of "conflict
        between love and parental authority over marriage." Finds
        that <u>Arcadia</u> "is distinguished by an equal and balanced pre-
        sentation of the claims of romantic love and parental au-
        thority" but that Sidney "did not resolve this conflict, but
        left it a dilemma, with equal ethical support for both
        sides." Also discusses Evarchus as an example of the
        Renaissance conception of the governor.

2887   RUDENSTINE, NEIL L[EON]. <u>Sidney's Poetic Development</u>. Cam-
        bridge: Harvard University Press, 1967, 325pp.
            Examines relationship between themes of <u>Old Arcadia</u> and
        Sidney's correspondence with Languet, discusses treatment
        of love in <u>Old Arcadia</u>, analyzes the stylistic relationships
        between poetry and prose in <u>Arcadia</u>, and discusses the re-
        lationship of Sidney's concept of energia to his prose
        style.

*2888   RUDENSTINE, NEIL LEON. "Sir Philip Sidney: The Styles of
        Love." Ph.D. dissertation, Harvard University, 1964.
            Abstract not available. Published in revised form as
        2887.

2889   SAINTSBURY, GEORGE. <u>A History of English Prose Rhythm</u>. Lon-
        don: Macmillan and Co., 1912, 505pp.
            Notes that although "there are some good things in...the
        <u>Arcadia</u>...the sentences are, as a rule, heavy and clumsy,
        ill-constructed in themselves and ill-compacted into para-
        graphs" (pp. 138-40).

2890   SAVAGE, JAMES E. "Beaumont and Fletcher's <u>Philaster</u> and Sid-
        ney's <u>Arcadia</u>." <u>ELH</u>, 14 (September 1947), 194-206.
            Discusses <u>Old</u> and <u>New Arcadia</u> as source of "plot ma-
        terial and characterization" in Beaumont and Fletcher's
        <u>Cupid's Revenge</u> and as source of <u>Philaster</u> (through <u>Cupid's
        Revenge</u>).

2891   SAVAGE, JAMES E. "Notes on A Midsummer Night's Dream." UMSE,
        2 (1961), 65-78.
            Discusses Shakespeare's use of Arcadia as a source for
        the description of the hounds. Suggests that in the play
        "the designation 'Spartan' is chosen as an indirect tribute
        to the Arcadia and its author."

2892   SCHANZER, ALICE. "Influssi italiana nella letteratura inglese:
        Sir Philip Sidney." Rivista d'Italia, 8 (July 1901), 459-
        81.
            Discusses in general terms the influence of Sannazaro,
        Boccaccio, and Ariosto on Arcadia.

*2893   SCHINDL, ERIKA. "Studien zum Wortschatz Sir Philip Sidneys:
        Neubildungen und Entlehnungen." Ph.D. dissertation, Uni-
        versity of Wien, 1955.
            Abstract not available.

2894   SCHLAUCH, MARGARET. Antecedents of the English Novel, 1400-
        1600 (from Chaucer to Deloney). Warsaw: PWN--Polish Scien-
        tific Publishers; London: Oxford University Press, 1963,
        264pp.
            Discusses New Arcadia as Neo-Hellenic Arcadian romance,
        examining briefly structure, comic elements, style, and
        theme. Concludes that the work "has less kinship with the
        modern novel" than some of Caxton's translations of French
        romances (pp. 176-85).

2895   SCHLEINER, WINFRIED. "Differences of Theme and Structure of
        the Erona Episode in the Old and New Arcadia." SP, 70
        (October 1973), 377-91.
            Argues that in revising episode, Sidney was concerned
        not only with technical matters but also with making the
        story fit "a new expressive purpose...which grew out of
        some of his assumptions about social rank, politics, and
        society." Shows that purpose of earlier version was "to
        show the vindictiveness of Cupid"; the purpose of the later
        was to illustrate how "the discrepancy of rank...[was] a
        primary source of the couple's misfortune." Concludes that
        "the increased verisimilitude...of the new version results
        from closer attention to political and social dimensions of
        the action."

*2896   SCHLOSSER, J. F. H. "Über Opitz und Philip Sidney," in Aus
        der Nachlass von J. F. H. Schlosser, Vol. IV. Edited by S.
        Schlosser. Mainz, 1859, 94-128.
            Not located. Cited in 2525.

Sidney

2897   SCHNEIDER, PAUL STEPHEN. "The Labyrinth of Love: A Reading
of Sir Philip Sidney's New Arcadia." Ph.D. dissertation,
University of Wisconsin, Madison, 1973, 292pp.
      Provides "an extensive critical analysis of the New Ar-
cadia, attempting to explain the thematic significance of
the psychological realism in the revision and the thematic
relationship between the story of King Basilius' family and
the complicated narratives Sidney interspersed in that
story."

2898   SCRIBNER, SIMON. Figures of Word-Repetition in the First Book
of Sir Philip Sidney's Arcadia. Ph.D. dissertation, Catholic University of America, 1948. Washington: Catholic
University of America Press, 1948, 142pp.
      Attempts "a systematic and complete survey of the figures
of word-repetition" from viewpoint of sixteenth-century
rhetorical theory. Examines "the nature and extent of the
forms of composition" (narration, exposition, description)
and analyzes the relationship between "the theory of the
Defence and its application in the Arcadia."

2899   SEATON, ETHEL. "Introduction," in The Arcadian Rhetoric. By
Abraham Fraunce. Edited by Ethel Seaton. Luttrell Society
Reprints, 9. Oxford: Blackwell for the Luttrell Society,
1950, pp. vii-lv.
      Includes discussion of range of quotations from Arcadia
and the nature of the manuscript used by Fraunce (pp. xxxv-
xxxix).

*2900   SHAPAZIAN, ROBERT MICHAEL. "Sidney's Arcadia: The Metaphorics
of Artificiality." Ph.D. dissertation, Harvard University,
1970.
      Abstract not available.

2901   SHAW, J. B. "Passage in the Arcadia." N&Q, 38 (5 December
1868), 541.
      Notes that Cicero in De Senectute and Consolatio "has the
same simile, though scarcely the same sentiment" as phrase
from Arcadia. See 2863.

2902   SHEPHARD, OSCAR H. "Sir Philip Sidney." Papers of the Manchester Literary Club, 57 (1932), 1-25.
      Discusses Sidney's style (calling it "euphuistic") and
powers of description in Arcadia; admits, however, to not
having read entire work.

*2903   SHIMAMURA, KAORU. "Sir Philip Sidney: An Introduction."
ESELL, 51-52 (1967), 145-72.

Not located. Listed in <u>1971 MLA International Bibliog-</u>
<u>raphy</u>, I: #2703.

2904 SIDNEY, PHILIP. <u>A Cabinet of Gems, Cut and Polished by Sir</u>
<u>Philip Sidney; Now, for the More Radiance, Presented without</u>
<u>Their Setting</u>. Compiled by George MacDonald. Elizabethan
Library. Chicago: A. C. McClurg, n.d., 204pp.
Provides extracts, arranged by subject, from <u>Arcadia</u>.

2905 SIEBECK, BERTA. <u>Das Bild Sir Philip Sidneys in der englischen</u>
<u>Renaissance</u>. Schriften der Deutschen Shakespeare-Gesell-
schaft, NS, 33. Weimar: H. Böhlaus, 1939, 214pp.
Provides overview of themes in <u>Arcadia</u>, Sidney's treat-
ment of friendship and love, his depiction of the heroic
type and the ruler, and his style (pp. 25-33).

2906 SINNING, HEINRICH. Cupid's Revenge von Beaumont und Fletcher
und Sidney's Arcadia. Halle: n.p., 1905, 68pp.
Analyzes use of <u>Arcadia</u> as source.

2907 SMART, JOHN S. "Milton and the King's Prayer." <u>RES</u>, 1 (Octo-
ber 1925), 385-91.
Discusses presence of Pamela's prayer in <u>Eikon Basilike</u>,
noting variations from text in <u>Arcadia</u> which "give it a
definitely Christian character." In answer to Milton's
characterization of Pamela as a "heathen woman," asserts
that she is "Christian rather than Pagan." <u>See</u> 2793.

2908 STADLER, ULRICH. <u>Der einsame Ort: Studien zur Weltabkehr im</u>
<u>heroischen Roman</u>. BSDSL, 43. Bern: Francke, 1971, 119pp.
In Appendix "Grimmelshausen und die <u>Arcadia</u> Philipp Sid-
ney's," pp. 89-105, discusses Grimmelshausen's use of 1643
edition of Opitz's translation of <u>Arcadia</u> as source.

2909 STERNBERG, JOACHIM. <u>Untersuchungen zur Verwendung des antiken</u>
<u>Mythus in der Dichtung Sir Philip Sidneys als ein Beitrag</u>
<u>zur Interpretation</u>. Bonn: Friedrich-Wilhelms-Universität,
1969, 382pp.
Analyzes functions--idealistic, ironic-satiric, and
dramatic-elegaic--of Sidney's use of classical mythology
in <u>Arcadia</u>.

2910 STIGANT, WILLIAM. "Sir Philip Sidney," in <u>Cambridge Essays,</u>
<u>1858</u>. London: J. W. Parker and Son, n.d., pp. 81-126.
Suggests biographical identification of various charac-
ters (e.g., Musidorus as Fulke'Greville) in <u>Arcadia</u>, and
examines influences on the work, its genre, and Sidney's
style.

Sidney

2911 SYFORD, CONSTANCE MIRIAM. "The Direct Source of the Pamela-Crecopia Episode in the Arcadia." PMLA, 49 (June 1934), 472-89.
    Argues that Plutarch's Moralia served as inspiration for ideas and phrases in episode. Notes how Sidney alters Plutarch's "natural, scientific" emphasis to a "religiously aesthetic" one.

2912 SYFRET, ROSEMARY. "Introduction," in Selections from Sidney's Arcadia. By Philip Sidney. Edited by Rosemary Syfret. Hutchinson English Texts. London: Hutchinson Educational, 1966, pp. 14-56.
    Provides overview of publishing history of work; comments on style, structure, and characterization in Old Arcadia; discusses New Arcadia as a prose epic and comments on style and structure. Provides modernized, abridged text of New Arcadia.

2913 SYKES, H. DUGDALE. Sidelights on Elizabethan Drama. London: Oxford University Press, 1924, 237pp.
    Points out use of Arcadia as a source in plays by Webster, Heywood, and Field (passim).

2914 SYMONDS, J[OHN] A[DDINGTON]. Sir Philip Sidney. English Men of Letters. New York: Harper & Brothers, 1887, 194pp.
    In Chapter IV ("The French Match and The Arcadia," pp. 59-86) provides a synopsis of a portion of the plot and comments on style. Examines poems as embodiment of "the theories of the Areopagus."

2915 TALBERT, ERNEST WILLIAM. The Problem of Order: Elizabethan Political Commonplaces and an Example of Shakespeare's Art. Chapel Hill: University of North Carolina Press, 1962, 256pp.
    Includes examination of Sidney's political thought in Arcadia. Discusses it in context of relationships with contemporary political theories. Examines various aspects of political thought as represented through characters (pp. 89-117).

2916 TAYLOR, A. B. "A Note on Ovid in Arcadia." N&Q, NS, 16 (December 1969), 455.
    Points out that Sidney is indebted to Ovid's description of Daphne for his depiction of Philoclea fleeing from the lion.

2917 TAYLOR, ARVILLA KERNS. "The Manège of Love and Authority: Studies in Sidney and Shakespeare." Ph.D. dissertation, University of Texas, Austin, 1969, 467pp.

"[E]xplores the nature and the significance of manège imagery in the works of Sidney."

2918 TENNENT, J. EMERSON. "Sir Philip Sidney's Arcadia." N&Q, 37 (25 April 1868), 397.
Points out some "modern imitators" of a passage in Arcadia.

2919 [THOMPSON, FRANCIS.] "The Prose of Poets: Sir Philip Sidney." Academy, 61 (21 December 1901), 615-16.
Provides appreciative estimate of Sidney's prose style in Arcadia.

2920 TILLYARD, E[USTACE] M[ANDEVILLE] W[ETENHALL]. The English Epic and Its Background. London: Chatto and Windus, 1954, 558pp.
In Chapter X ("Sidney," pp. 294-319) observes that "the chief substance of the Old Arcadia concerns friendship and love, ethics not politics." Discusses New Arcadia as heroic poem: examines influence of medieval romance, of Greek romance on form and "heightened didactic tone," and of Italian theories of epic on revision. Defines main theme of New Arcadia as "the education of the four princely young people"; discusses political element of work and character.

2921 TILLYARD, E[USTACE] M[ANDEVILLE] W[ETENHALL]. "The English Epic Tradition." PBA, 22 (1936), 35-55.
Argues that Arcadia is a Renaissance epic; compares it to the Faerie Queene.

2922 TILLYARD, E[USTACE] M[ANDEVILLE] W[ETENHALL]. "Milton and Sidney's Arcadia." TLS, 6 March 1953, p. 153.
Points out in Paradise Lost "a reminiscence, doubtless unconscious, of a passage in the revised Arcadia." (See: J. B. Broadbent, "Milton and Sidney's Arcadia," TLS, 20 March 1953, p. 187.)

2923 TING, NAI TUNG. "Studies in English Prose and Poetic Romances in the First Half of the Seventeenth Century." Ph.D. dissertation, Harvard University, 1941, 360pp.
Includes examination of influence of Arcadia on style, structure, and content of seventeenth-century romances.

2924 TOLIVER, HAROLD E. Pastoral Forms and Attitudes. Berkeley: University of California Press, 1971, 401pp.
In Chapter III ("Sidney's Knights and Shepherds," pp. 45-62) examines structure and results of Sidney's combination of pastoral and romance elements.

Sidney

2925   TOWNSEND, FREDA L. "Sidney and Ariosto." PMLA, 61 (March
       1946), 97-108.
          Discusses the influence of Ariosto on Sidney's revision,
       noting that "the Furioso provided a structural pattern by
       which Sidney could write and rewrite his Arcadia."

2926   TUCKERMAN, BAYARD. A History of English Prose Fiction from
       Sir Thomas Malory to George Eliot. New York: G. P. Put-
       nam's Sons, 1882, 339pp.
          Includes discussion of Sidney's style, the comic elements
       in the Arcadia, and the work as a reflection of its time
       (pp. 90-101).

2927   TURNER, MYRON [MARTIN]. "The Disfigured Face of Nature: Image
       and Metaphor in the Revised Arcadia." ELR, 2 (Winter 1972),
       116-35.
          "[A]ttempts to explore some aspects of Sidney's imagery."
       "[E]mphazies his treatment of nature and, in particular,
       one of his central metaphors, the disfigured face of nature."

2928   TURNER, MYRON [MARTIN]. "The Heroic Ideal in Sidney's Revised
       Arcadia." SEL, 10 (Winter 1970), 63-82.
          Examines background of Sidney's conception of the heroic
       prince and his attempt "to reconcile the pride and self-
       sufficiency of the hero with Christian humility and de-
       pendence upon God." Finds that "Pamela is Sidney's most
       complete study in this reconciliation." Concludes that
       Pyrocles and Musidorus, although "godlike heroes," lack in-
       ternal balance and must learn, through love, to accept their
       human limitations.

2929   TURNER, MYRON MARTIN. "Majesty in Adversity: The Moral Struc-
       ture of Sidney's Arcadia." Ph.D. dissertation, University
       of Washington, 1965, 292pp.
          Examines Sidney's concept of the heroic and argues that
       in Arcadia "Sidney reveals the primacy of the heroic mind
       over heroic deeds." Finds that "[t]he center of Sidney's
       heroic conception is the reconciliation of the proud con-
       tempt and virtuous sulf-sufficiency of magnanimity with
       that humility and patience grounded in the Christian's de-
       pendence upon his God."

2930   VICKERS, BRIAN. "'In Search of Arcadia.'" Cambridge Review,
       89 (29 October 1966), 62-64.
          In review of Sidney's Arcadia (2628 and 2778) discusses
       style and "the confusion surrounding the two versions" as
       "barriers" to modern readers.

2931   WAGNER, BERNARD MATHIAS. "New Poems by Sir Philip Sidney."
       PMLA, 53 (March 1938), 118-24.
            Notes presence in MS. Harley 7392 of poems from both ver-
       sions of Arcadia. Provides text of "Singe neighbours singe,"
       suggesting that it might have been written for the revision
       of Arcadia, and of "Philisides, the Shepherd good & true,"
       calling it a "piece of 'Arcadiana,' which makes use...of
       the characters familiar from the old Arcadia."

2932   WALKER, D. P. "Ways of Dealing with Atheists: A Background
       to Pamela's Refutation of Crecopia." BHR, 17 (1955), 252-
       77.
            Examines Sidney's "liberal" attitude toward atheism in
       the context of analysis of techniques of dealing with athe-
       ists in contemporary anti-atheist works. Argues that Pamela
       is a prisca theologus--a good pagan--and examines how she
       uses natural reason in an attempt not to convert but to
       silence Crecopia.

2933   WALLACE, MALCOLM WILLIAM. The Life of Sir Philip Sidney.
       Cambridge: Cambridge University Press, 1915, 438pp.
            In Chapter XII ("Sidney a Man of Letters--The Arcadia
       and the Apologie for Poetrie," pp. 220-40) discusses bi-
       ographical significance of Arcadia and identifies Henry
       Sandford as the H. S. who wrote the prefatory address to
       the 1593 edition.

2934   WALLACE, MALCOLM W[ILLIAM]. "The Reputation of Sir Philip
       Sidney." The Johns Hopkins Alumni Magazine, 17 (November
       1928), 1-21.
            In tracing Sidney's early reputation, observes "it was
       the Arcadia which seemed...to bear most authentic witness
       to its author's virtues of many kinds." Discusses various
       reactions to Arcadia from Milton to the twentieth century.

2935   WALLER, G. F. "'This matching of contraries': Bruno, Calvin,
       and the Sidney Circle." Neophil, 56 (July 1972), 331-43.
            Argues that "in Sidney's work...we see clearly the
       philosophical tension" which results from the "confronta-
       tion of the Magical [epitomized by Bruno] and Calvinist
       traditions." Finds that in Arcadia Sidney favors the Cal-
       vinist tradition "but the work's atmosphere has been cre-
       ated by a unique tension between the ethos of Calvin and
       that of the Magical-courtly tradition."

2936   WALTERS, PERCY. "The Hidden Meaning of the Title Pages of
       Arcadia, etc." Baconiana, 29 (1945), 159-60.

Sidney

Argues against Eagle's conclusions (2661), and identifies title-page figures as "Queen Elizabeth and her husband, the Earl of Leicester, with their legitimate son Francis [Bacon] between them, identified by the head of the boar." Suggests Bacon was author of part of Arcadia.

2937 WARNLOF, JESSICA JEAN. "The Influence of Giordano Bruno on the Writings of Sir Philip Sidney." Ph.D. dissertation, Texas A & M University, 1973, 212pp.
Examines influence of Bruno on Arcadia: compares Sidney's work with Bruno's Lo spaccio and Eroici furori and finds "many verbal parallels."

2938 WARREN, C[LARENCE] HENRY. Sir Philip Sidney: A Study in Conflict. London: T. Nelson & Sons, 1936, 250pp.
Provides general discussion of Arcadia in context of Sidney's life (passim).

2939 WATERHOUSE, GILBERT. The Literary Relations of England and Germany in the Seventeenth Century. Cambridge: Cambridge University Press, 1914, 210pp.
In Chapter III ("Sidney's Arcadia in Germany," pp. 18-39) examines popularity and influence of Arcadia in Germany. Discusses translations by Valentinus Theocritus and Martin Opitz; compares two versions and argues that Theocritus was not pseudonym used by Opitz.

2940 WATSON, SARA RUTH. "Chivalry in Elizabethan Literature." Ph.D. dissertation, Case Western Reserve University, 1942.
Examines Sidney's use of chivalric trappings in Arcadia: analyzes how these chivalric elements "were used to present, allegorically, religious and political events and opinions."

2941 WATSON, SARA RUTH. "Shakespeare's Use of the Arcadia: An Example in Henry V." N&Q, 175 (19 November 1938), 364-65.
Traces source of description of Dauphin's horse to description of Argalus's horse in Arcadia. (For contradiction see: Joseph E. Morris, "Shakespeare's Use of the Arcadia," N&Q, 175 [3 December 1938], 409.)

2942 WATSON, SARA RUTH. "Sidney at Bartholomew Fair." PMLA, 53 (March 1938), 125-28.
Argues that although Crecopia's beheading trick is close to Reginald Scot's description of "'the decollation of Iohn Baptist'" (Discovery of Witchcraft), Sidney's probable source is an actual beheading stunt "'donne by one Kingsfield of London, at a Barholomewtide, An. 1582.'"

2943   WEINER, ANDREW DAVID. "'Erected Wit' and 'Infected Will': A
       Study of Sir Philip Sidney's <u>Old Arcadia</u>." Ph.D. disserta-
       tion, Princeton University, 1969, 249pp.
           Argues that <u>Old Arcadia</u> is not an heroic poem but "a
       pastoral which used romance materials in the comic mode."
       Sees main characters as "negative moral <u>exempla</u>" and dis-
       cusses "choral function" of eclogues.

2944   WEISS, ADRIAN. "The Rhetorical Concept of <u>Narratio</u> and Narra-
       tive Structure in Elizabethan Prose Fiction." Ph.D. disser-
       tation, Ohio University, 1969, 222pp.
           In investigation of "the influence of the rhetorical
       concept of <u>narratio</u> upon narrative structure" finds that
       Sidney's two <u>Arcadias</u> "are indebted to <u>narratio</u>, and that,
       indeed, <u>narratio</u> determined the very nature of" the works.

2945   WHITE, R. S. "'Comedy' in Elizabethan Prose Romances." <u>YES</u>,
       5 (1975), 46-51.
           Includes examination of meaning in Sidney's use of term
       in <u>Arcadia</u>.

2946   WHITEFORD, ROBERT NAYLOR. <u>Motives in English Fiction</u>. New
       York: G. P. Putnam's Sons, 1918, 390pp.
           Discusses Sidney's style, the episodic structure of <u>Ar-
       cadia</u>, and the influence of the work on later prose fiction
       (pp. 35-41).

2947   WHITMAN, ROBERT F. "Webster's <u>Duchess of Malfi</u>." <u>N&Q</u>, NS, 6
       (May 1959), 174-75.
           Discusses Webster's use of passage in <u>Arcadia</u> as source
       for the play.

2948   WHITNEY, LOIS. "Concerning Nature in <u>The Countesse of Pem-
       brokes Arcadia</u>." <u>SP</u>, 24 (April 1924), 207-22.
           Analyzes "Sidney's various answers to the two questions:
       first, 'what is nature?' and second, 'what is ethically
       right "according to nature?.'"'"

2949   WHITTEMORE, NENA [LOUISE] THAMES. "The Palm Tree Impresa in
       the New <u>Arcadia</u>." <u>AN&Q</u>, 14 (1975), 3-5.
           Suggests that the <u>impresa</u> on Argalus's shield "expresses
       the interdependent love of Argalus and Parthenia" and that
       "it foreshadows the coming events of the plot, and it sym-
       bolizes the nature of love."

2950   WHITTEMORE, NENA LOUISE THAMES. "Unity and Variety in Sir
       Philip Sidney's <u>New Arcadia</u> (1590)." Ph.D. dissertation,
       City University of New York, 1968, 261pp.

Sidney

>   Examines techniques through which Sidney, in his revi-
> sion, "achieves a synthesis of unity and variety." Analyzes
> structure of work.

2951   WILES, AMERICUS GEORGE DAVID. "The Continuations of Sir
>   Philip Sidney's Arcadia." Ph.D. dissertation, Princeton
>   University, 1934.
>   Examines the merits of the five continuations of Ar-
>   cadia; includes parallel analyses of the Old and New Ar-
>   cadia and an analysis of the style. Finds that "[t]he
>   continuations themselves have little literary merit and not
>   much merit as continuations."

2952   WILES, A[MERICUS] G[EORGE] D[AVID]. "James Johnstoun and the
>   Arcadian Style." RenP 1957, pp. 72-81.
>   Analyzes characteristics of Johnstoun's style in his
>   continuation of Sidney's Arcadia and evaluates his success
>   in imitating the characteristics of Sidney's style.

2953   WILES, A[MERICUS] G[EORGE] D[AVID]. "Parallel Analyses of
>   the Two Versions of Sidney's Arcadia, Including the Major
>   Variations of the Folio of 1593." SP, 39 (April 1942),
>   167-206.
>   Analyzes several parallel passages to illustrate differ-
>   ences in structure; discusses, in particular, the change
>   from chronological organization to "epic structure" and
>   Sidney's skillfulness in achieving artistic unity among the
>   various episodes and subplots.

2954   WILKINS, ERNEST HATCH. "Arcadia in America." PAPS, 101
>   (February 1957), 4-30.
>   Includes discussion of influence of Sidney's Arcadia on
>   Arcadia as place-name on Eastern Shore of Virginia.

2955   WILLIAMS, GEORGE WALTON. "The Printer of the First Folio of
>   Sidney's Arcadia." Library, 5th Ser., 12 (December 1957),
>   274-75.
>   Argues that John Windet, not Thomas Creede, was the
>   printer of 1593 folio edition.

2956   WILSON, MONA. Sir Philip Sidney. London: Duckworth, 1931,
>   328pp.
>   In Chapter VIII ("The Arcadia," pp. 135-55) provides a
>   general discussion of sources, composition and publication,
>   popularity, and style.

2957   WOLFF, SAMUEL LEE. The Greek Romances in Elizabethan Prose
>   Fiction. Columbia University Studies in Comparative

Literature. New York: Columbia University Press, 1912, 539pp.
  Provides detailed synopsis of Arcadia and examines in detail the influences (particularly on structure) of Greek romances on Old and New Arcadia. Also discusses changes made in revision of Old Arcadia and techniques Sidney used to revise the work (pp. 262-366). In Appendix B provides "Notes and Transcripts: 'Clifford' MS. of Sidney's Arcadia," pp. 470-76.

2958   WOLFF, SAMUEL LEE. "Scott's Ivanhoe and Sidney's Arcadia." PMLA, 26, Appendix, (1911), ix.
  Abstract of paper presented MLA Convention, 1910: points out that Scott used the "outline and several details of Sidney's episode of the captivity of Pamela, Philoclea, and Pyrocles" for "his own episode of the captivity of Rebecca, Rowena, and Ivanhoe."

2959   WOLFF, SAMUEL LEE. "The Sources of Ivanhoe." Nation, 92 (2 February 1911), 11.
  Discusses Scott's use of Arcadia as source. See 2802.

2960   WOOLF, VIRGINIA. "The Countess of Pembroke's Arcadia," in The Second Common Reader. By Virginia Woolf. New York: Harcourt, Brace, and Co., 1932, pp. 38-49.
  Discusses Sidney's language, his treatment of character, and his lack of tight control over structure. Observes that "[i]n the Arcadia, as in some luminous globe, all the seeds of English fiction lie latent."

2961   WRIGHT, THOMAS EDWARD. "The English Renaissance Prose Anatomy." Ph.D. dissertation, Washington University, 1963, 238pp.
  Examines Sidney's revision of Arcadia "through the use of anatomy forms."

2962   YATES, FRANCES A. "Elizabethan Chivalry: The Romance of the Accession Day Tilts." JWCI, 20 (1957), 4-25.
  Examines how "the richly woven word-picture of the Iberian annual jousts in...Arcadia is a reflection of Accession Day Tilt pageantry."

2963   YATES, FRANCES A. John Florio: The Life of an Italian in Shakespeare's England. Cambridge: Cambridge University Press, 1934, 370pp.
  Explicates Florio's attack on Sanford's editing of 1593 Arcadia; suggests possibility that Florio had been employed to edit 1590 edition (pp. 199-209).

Sidney

2964   ZANDVOORT, R[EINARD] W. "Fair Portia's Counterfeit." RLMC,
        NS, 2 (1951), 351-56. [Reprinted in: R(einard) W. Zand-
        voort. Collected Papers: A Selection of Notes and Articles
        Originally Published in English Studies and Other Journals.
        Groningen Studies in English, 5. Groningen: Wolters, 1954,
        pp. 58-62.]
            Examines Sidney's description of paintings in Arcadia;
        points out that he is working with a recognized rhetorical
        descriptive technique rather than describing actual paint-
        ings.

2965   ZANDVOORT, R[EINARD] W. Sidney's Arcadia: A Comparison be-
        tween the Two Versions. Amsterdam: Swets & Zeitlinger,
        1929, 227pp.
            Provides detailed comparison of two versions in studying
        "Sidney's methods and results" in revising the Old Arcadia.
        Examines "salient features of Sidney's thought as manifested
        in the two versions" and argues that Arcadia is not an al-
        legory. Traces sources and analyzes style of Old and New
        Arcadia. Provides annotated bibliography of studies of
        Arcadia.

2966   ZANDVOORT, R[EINARD] W. "The Two Versions of Sidney's Ar-
        cadia." Archiv, 157 (1930), 261.
            Summarizes main points of 2965.

2967   ZANDVOORT, R[EINARD] W. "What Is Euphuism?," in Mélanges de
        linguistique et philologie: Fernand Mossé in memoriam.
        Paris: Didier, 1959, pp. 508-17. [Reprinted in: R(einard)
        W. Zandvoort. Collected Papers II: Articles in English
        Published between 1955 and 1970. Groningen Studies in Eng-
        lish, 10. Groningen: Wolters-Noordhoff, 1970, pp. 12-21.]
            Examines differences between arcadianism and euphuism:
        finds that while Sidney occasionally uses euphuistic "pat-
        terns" for ornamentation, Lyly uses such as the "groundwork"
        of his style.

2968   ZEEVELD, W. GORDON. "The Uprising of the Commons in Sidney's
        Arcadia." MLN, 48 (April 1933), 209-17.
            Argues that the nature of the revisions of this passage
        (particularly in concealing the cause of the uprising) sug-
        gests that the original version was a protest against
        Elizabeth's proposed French marriage.

2969   ZOUCH, THOMAS. Memoirs of the Life and Writings of Sir Philip
        Sidney. York: Payne, Mawman, and Wilson, 1808, 389pp.
            Includes appreciative discussion of Arcadia: comments
        on moral purity of work as well as Sidney's style, charac-
        terization, and descriptive powers (passim).

SMYTHE, ROBERT

Matteo Bandello, <u>Straunge, Lamentable, and Tragicall Hystories</u>. STC
13524 (to be 1356.5 in new <u>STC</u>).

Studies

2970 PRUVOST, RENÉ. <u>Matteo Bandello and Elizabethan Fiction</u>.
Bibliothèque de la Revue de Littérature Comparée, 113.
Paris: H. Champion, 1937, 349pp.
  Examines Smythe's translation of Belleforest's text in
<u>Strange, Lamentable, and Tragical Histories</u> (pp. 78-83,
passim).

STANLEY, THOMAS (1625-1678)

Juan Perez de Montalván. <u>Aurora and the Prince</u>. Wing P1467-1468.

Bibliographies

2971 FLOWER, MARGARET. "Thomas Stanley (1625-1678): A Bibliog-
raphy of His Writings in Prose and Verse (1647-1743)."
<u>TCBS</u>, 1, part 2 (1950), 139-72.
  Includes analytical descriptions of the editions of
Stanley's <u>Aurora</u> and <u>The Prince</u>.

Studies

2972 CRUMP, GALBRAITH MILLER. "Introduction," in <u>The Poems and
Translations of Thomas Stanley</u>. By Thomas Stanley. Edited
by Galbraith Miller Crump. Oxford: Clarendon Press, 1962,
pp. i-lxiv.
  Provides detailed bibliographical analysis of the printed
editions of Stanley's works (pp. xlii-lv). Prints only the
poems from <u>Aurora</u> and <u>The Prince</u>.

*2973 CRUMP, GALBRAITH MILLER. "The Poems and Translations of
Thomas Stanley." Ph.D. dissertation, Oxford University-
St. John's College, 1960.
  Abstract not available. <u>See</u> 2972.

*2974 CUMMING, L. M. "Thomas Stanley: A Biographical and Critical
Study." Ph.D. dissertation, University of Edinburgh, 1924.
  Abstract not available.

2975 WRIGHT, LYLY H[ENRY]. "A Bibliographical Note." <u>HLQ</u>, 2
(January 1939), 231-32.

Style

        Points out that sheets from 1647 edition of <u>Aurora</u> were
    used in making up the 1647 edition of Stanley's <u>Poems and</u>
    <u>Translations</u>.

STYLE, WILLIAM

Lucas Gracian Dantisco, ["Axa and the Prince,"] in <u>Galateo Espagnol</u>
    <u>or the Spanish Gallant</u>. <u>STC</u> 12145.

Studies

2976   RANDALL, DALE B. J. "<u>Axa and the Prince</u>: A Rediscovered
            <u>Novela</u> and Its English Translator." <u>JEGP</u>, 60, no. 1 (1961),
            48–55.
            Discusses previously unnoticed novella "The Tale of the
        Great Soldan, and of the Loves of the Beautifull Axa and
        the Prince of Naples," included in William Style's <u>Galateo</u>
        <u>Espagnol</u>.

TALES AND QUICKE ANSWERES, VERY MERY AND PLEASANT TO REDE
    (enlarged as <u>Mery Tales, Wittie Questions, and Quicke Answeres</u>)

    <u>STC</u> 23665–23665.5.

Editions

2977   Shakespeare's Jest Book [i.e., Tales and Quick Answers]. Edit-
            ed by S. W. Singer. Chiswick: Whittingham, 1814, 192pp.
            Provides reprint of 1532? edition. In "To the Reader,"
        pp. vii–xvi, discusses didacticism and indecency in work.
        Identifies this as work alluded to in <u>Much Ado about Noth-</u>
        <u>ing</u>. In <u>Supplement to the</u> Tales and Quicke Answeres (Chis-
        wick: Whittingham, 1815, 39pp.) provides text of additional
        twenty-five tales from 1567 edition. <u>See</u> 639.

2978   The Hundred Merry Tales: or, Shakespeare's Jest Book. Lon-
            don: J. Chidley, 1831, 126pp.
            Provides reprint of 1532? edition of <u>Tales and Quick</u>
        <u>Answers</u>.

2979   <u>Tales and Quick Answers</u>, in <u>Shakespeare's Merry Tales</u>. London:
            Routledge, 1845, pp. 105–231.
            Provides modernized text based on 2977. In "Preface,"
        pp. iii–xiv, anonymous writer discusses popularity of work
        and paraphrases "To the Reader" in 2977.

Tales and Quicke Answeres

2980   Mery Tales and Quicke Answeres, in Shakespeare Jest-Books,
       Vol. I.   Edited by W[illiam] Carew Hazlitt. London:
       Willis & Sotheran, 1864, 162pp. (separately paginated).
          Provides annotated reprint of 1567 edition. In "Intro-
       duction," pp. i-x, discusses the bibliographical history of
       the work and allusions to it.

2981   Tales and Quick Answers, in A Hundred Merry Tales and Other
       English Jestbooks of the Fifteenth and Sixteenth Centuries.
       Edited by P. M. Zall. Lincoln: University of Nebraska
       Press, 1963, pp. 239-322.
          Provides modernized reprint of 1532? edition.

Studies

2982   BUSH, DOUGLAS. "Some Sources for the Mery Tales, Wittie Ques-
       tions, and Quicke Answers." MP, 20 (February 1923), 275-80.
          Traces "correct" sources of six tales.

2983   CHAPMAN, K. P. "Lazarillo de Tormes, a Jest-Book, and Bene-
       dik." MLR, 55 (October 1960), 565-67.
          Traces source of "Of the Blind Man and His Boy" (Merry
       Tales) to Lazarillo de Tormes and suggests that jest is
       source of Benedict's allusion to "blindman" (Much Ado about
       Nothing, 2.1.206-207).

2984   HAZLITT, W[ILLIAM] CAREW. Studies in Jocular Literature: A
       Popular Subject More Closely Considered. London: E.
       Stock, 1890, 238pp.
          Discusses the lack of original matter in Tales and Quick
       Answers and defends coarseness of work (pp. 117-20, 162-67,
       passim).

2985   KAHRL, STANLEY J[ADWIN]. "The Medieval Origins of the Six-
       teenth-Century English Jest-Books." Studies in the Renais-
       sance, 13 (1966), 166-83.
          Draws on Merry Tales and Quick Answers to illustrate
       "the similarities in both style and content between the
       jests and their forbears the exempla."

2986   LIPKING, JOANNA BRIZDLE. "Traditions of the Facetiae and
       Their Influence in Tudor England." Ph.D. dissertation,
       Columbia University, 1970, 477pp.
          Examines influence of facetiae on jest book. Suggests
       that A Hundred Merry Tales and Tales and Quick Answers "are
       best understood as imitations of the books of facetiae,
       showing the same organization, conception of the joke, and
       comic resources."

Tales and Quicke Answeres

2987   MAGOON, MARIAN WAITE. "Some Analogues to Elizabethan Jest
        Books in Medieval Ecclesiastical Literature." Ph.D. dis-
        sertation, University of Michigan, 1931.
            Traces analogues in Medieval collections of exempla to
        several tales in Tales and Quick Answers.

2988   MARCHAM, F. "Lyly's Euphues and His England." N&Q, 111 (13
        May 1905), 366.
            Traces source of a passage to Tales and Quick Answers.

2989   STIEFEL, A[RTHUR] L[UDWIG]. "Die Quellen der englischen
        Schwankbücher des 16. Jahrhunderts." Anglia, 31 (1908),
        453-520.
            Identifies source(s) of each tale in both editions of
        Tales and Quick Answers. Discusses dating of first edition.
        (See also: E. Koeppel, "Zu Anglia, XXXI, 456f," Anglia,
        32 [1909], 253-56; Arthur Ludwig Stiefel, "Zur Schwank- und
        Motivkunde," Anglia, 32 [1909], 491-502; and 2992.)

2990   STIEFEL, A[RTHUR] L[UDWIG]. "Zum Einfluss des Erasmus auf die
        englische Literatur." Archiv, 124 (1910), 58-64.
            Examines use of Erasmus's Ecclesiastes as source for
        several jests in Merry Tales.

2991   VOCHT, HENRY DE. De invloed van Erasmus op de engelsche
        tooneelliteratuur der XVIe en XVIIe eeuwen, eerste deel:
        Shakespeare Jest-Books, Lyly. Gent: A. Siffer, 1908,
        303pp.
            Examines use of works of Erasmus as source for tales in
        Merry Tales, Witty Questions, and Quick Answers (pp. 30-79).

2992   VOCHT, H[ENRY] DE. "Mery Tales, Wittie Questions and Quicke
        Answeres and Their Sources." Anglia, 33 (1910), 120-32.
            Provides additions and corrections to 2989. Argues
        against Stiefel's conclusion that Gast's Convivales Sermones
        was a principal source (2989). Suggests 1535 or earlier as
        date of first edition.

TARLTON, RICHARD (d. 1588)

Tarltons Jests. STC 23683.3-23684.

Editions

2993   TARLTON, RICHARD. Tarlton's Jests, in Tarlton's Jests and
        News Out of Purgatory: With Notes and Some Account of the

Life of Tarlton. Edited by James Orchard Halliwell[-Phil-
lipps]. Shakespeare Society Publications, 20. London:
Shakespeare Society, 1844, pp. 1-45.
  Provides expurgated reprint of 1611 edition. In "Introduction," pp. vii-xlvii, discusses biographical basis of
jests.

2994 TARLTON, RICHARD. Tarlton's Jests, in Shakespeare Jest-Books,
      Vol. II. Edited by W[illiam] Carew Hazlitt. London:
      Willis & Sotheran, 1864, 189-260.
        Provides annotated reprint of 1611 edition. Includes a
      list of "Notices of Richard Tarlton from Various Sources,"
      II, 254-60. In a brief introductory note discusses the
      bibliographical history of the work.

2995 TARLTON, RICHARD. Tarlton's Jests Drawn into These Three
      Parts, in Kemp's Nine Days Wonder by William Kemp; Tarlton's
      Jests; with A Pretty New Ballad, Entitled the Crow Sits upon
      the Wall. Introduction by J[ohn] P. Feather. New York:
      Johnson Reprint, 1972, not paginated.
        Provides facsimile reprint of 1613 edition (with D4^v-E4^v
      from 1638 edition). In brief "Introduction" discusses the
      bibliographical history of the work and the relationship of
      the jests to Tarlton.

Studies

2996 BOYCE, BENJAMIN. "News from Hell: Satiritic Communications
      with the Nether World in English Writing of the Seventeenth
      and Eighteenth Centuries." PMLA, 58 (June 1943), 402-37.
        Surveys treatment of theme in Elizabethan fiction, find-
      ing few works on classical model of Lucian. Notes that
      Elizabethan descriptions lack emphasis on character of neth-
      er world, e.g., in Tarlton's Jests the lower world is used
      only as framework for collection of tales.

TARLTONS NEWES OUT OF PURGATORIE

  STC 23685-23686.

Editions

2997 Tarlton's News Out of Purgatory, in Tarlton's Jests and News
      Out of Purgatory: With Notes and Some Account of the Life
      of Tarlton. Edited by James Orchard Halliwell[-Phillipps].
      Shakespeare Society Publications, 20. London: Shakespeare
      Society, 1844, pp. 47-105.
        Provides reprint of c. 1590 edition (?).

Tarltons Newes Out of Purgatorie

2998   Tarltons Newes Out of Purgatorie, in The Collected Works of
       Robert Armin. By Robert Armin. Introductions by J[ohn] P.
       Feather. 2 vols. New York: Johnson Reprint, 1972, not
       paginated.
            Provides facsimile reprint of 1590 edition of Tarlton's
       News. In "Introduction" to Tarlton's News presents evidence
       for Armin's authorship and discusses form of work.

2999   "Tarletons Newes Out of Purgatorie: A Critical Edition with
       Introduction and Commentary." Edited by David Nicholas
       Ranson. Ph.D. dissertation, Case Western Reserve Univer-
       sity, 1974, 233pp.
            Provides critical edition based on 1590 edition. Ex-
       amines printing history and style; argues that Robert Greene
       was the author.

Studies

3000   DAVIES, H. NEVILLE. "Introduction," in The Cobbler of Canter-
       bury: Frederic Ouvry's Edition of 1862 with a New Intro-
       duction by H. Neville Davies. Cambridge, England: D. S.
       Brewer; Totowa, New Jersey: Rowman and Littlefield, 1976,
       pp. 1-55.
            Provides detailed analysis of structure, which he sees
       as similar to five-act dramatic structure; reviews question
       of authorship; and examines The Cobbler of Canterbury as an
       "invective against" Tarlton's News.

3001   EVERITT, E. B. The Young Shakespeare: Studied in Documentary
       Evidence. Anglistica, 2. Copenhagen: Rosenkilde and
       Bagger, 1954, 188pp.
            Explores relationship between Tarlton's News and Cobbler
       of Canterbury. Seems to argue that Shakespeare was the au-
       thor of Tarlton's News (passim).

3002   FEATHER, JOHN [P.]. "A Check-List of the Works of Robert
       Armin." Library, 5th Ser., 26 (June 1971), 165-72.
            Ascribes authorship of Tarlton's News to Robert Armin.
       See 3006.

3003   FORSYTHE, ROBERT S. "The Merry Wives of Windsor: Two New
       Analogues." PQ, 7 (October 1928), 390-98.
            Discusses two analogues of story of "The Two Lovers of
       Pisa" in Tarlton's News.

3004   GALIGANI, GIUSEPPE. "Il Boccaccio nel Cinquecento inglese,"
       in Il Boccaccio nella cultura inglese e anglo-americana.

This Mater Treateth...Frederyke of Jennen

Edited by Giuseppe Galigani. Florence: L. S. Olschki, 1974, pp. 27-57.
Discusses use of Decameron as source for Tarlton's News.

3005 LAKE, D. J. "The Canon of Robert Armin's Works: Some Difficulties." N&Q, NS, 24 (March-April 1977), 117-20.
Argues that Armin's authorship of Tarlton's News is doubtful.

3006 LIPPINCOTT, H[ENRY] F[REDERICK]. "Bibliographical Problems in the Works of Robert Armin." Library, 5th Ser., 30 (December 1975), 330-31.
Supports Feather's (3002) attribution of Tarlton's News to Armin.

3007 McMILLAN, MARY EVELYN. "An Edition of Greenes Vision and A Maidens Dreame by Robert Greene." Ph.D. dissertation, University of Alabama, 1960, 188pp.
Examines relationship between Greene's Vision and Cobbler of Canterbury and Tarlton's News.

3008 MAGOON, MARIAN WAITE. "Some Analogues to Elizabethan Jest Books in Medieval Ecclesiastical Literature." Ph.D. dissertation, University of Michigan, 1931.
Traces analogues in Medieval collections of exempla to several tales in Tarlton's News.

3009 MARCO, SERGIO DE. "Il Boccaccio nel Settecento inglese," in Il Boccaccio nella cultura inglese e anglo-americana. Edited by Giuseppe Galigani. Florence: L. S. Olschki, 1974, pp. 93-111.
Discusses influence of Boccaccio on Tarlton's News, particularly in the use of the jester as a means for anti-Catholic polemic and for purposes of edification. Examines relationship of Tarlton's News to Cobbler of Canterbury.

THIS MATER TREATETH OF A MERCHAUNTES WYFE, AND WAS CALLED FREDERYKE OF JENNEN
(translation has been ascribed to Lawrence Andrewe)

STC 11361-11362.

Editions

3010 Frederyke of Jennen, in Die Historie von den vier Kaufleuten (Frederyke of Jennen). Die Geschichte von der vertauschten Wiege (The Mylner of Abyngton). By Josef Raith. Aus

This Mater Treateth...Frederyke of Jennen

Schrifttum und Sprache der Angelsachsen, 4. Leipzig: R.
Noske, 1936, pp. 107–23.
Provides reprint of 1560 edition. In commentary, dis-
cusses source of English translation, compares work with
Dutch and German versions, discusses its use by Shakespeare
as a source for Cymbeline, and suggests that translator was
Lawrence Andrewe.

3011 Frederyke of Jennen, in Cymbeline. By William Shakespeare.
Edited by J. M. Nosworthy. Arden Shakespeare. Cambridge:
Harvard University Press, 1955, pp. 198–211.
Provides reprint of 1560 edition based on 3010. In "In-
troduction," pp. xi–lxxxiv, discusses Shakespeare's use of
Frederyke of Jennen as source.

3012 Frederyke of Jennen, in Narrative and Dramatic Sources of
Shakespeare, Vol. VIII. Edited by Geoffrey Bullough.
London: Routledge & Kegan Paul; New York: Columbia Uni-
versity Press, 1975, 63–78.
Reprints text of 1560 edition. In "Introduction [to
Cymbeline]," pp. 3–37, discusses Shakespeare's use of work
as source for the play.

Studies

3013 ALMANSI, GUIDO. "Il Decameron, Cymbeline e il 'Cycle de la
gageure,'" in Il Boccaccio nella cultura inglese e anglo-
americana. Edited by Giuseppe Galigani. Florence: L. S.
Olschki, 1974, pp. 193–202.
Discusses treatment of the wager plot in Frederyke of
Jennen and the relationship of the work to Shakespeare's
Cymbeline.

3014 BERGEL, LIENHARD. "Shakespeare's Cymbeline and Boccaccio,"
in Il Boccaccio nella cultura inglese e anglo-americana.
Edited by Giuseppe Galigani. Florence: L. S. Olschki,
1974, pp. 203–18.
Discusses how Frederyke of Jennen is a modification--
especially in its anticatholicism--of its source in Boccaccio; examines Shakespeare's use of Frederyke as a source
for Cymbeline.

3015 BISWAS, DINESH CHANDRA. Shakespeare's Treatment of the Sources
in the Comedies. Calcutta: Jadavpur University, 1971,
299pp.
Examines Shakespeare's use of Frederyke of Jennen as a
source for Cymbeline (pp. 143–54).

3016   LEE, A. COLLINGWOOD. "Cymbeline: The Source of the 'Wager
        Incident.'" N&Q, 133 (29 April 1916), 342-43.
            Points out that Frederyke of Jennen includes a version
        of the wager story; suggests that Frederyke is a rendering
        of Von vier Kaufmännern.

3017   NOSWORTHY, J. M. "The Sources of the Wager Plot in Cymbeline."
        N&Q, 197 (1 March 1952), 93-96.
            Argues that Shakespeare used Frederyke of Jennen as a
        source.

3018   PROCTER, ROBERT. Jan van Doesborgh, Printer at Antwerp: An
        Essay in Bibliography. Illustrated Monographs, 2. London:
        Chiswick Press for The Bibliographical Society, 1894, 132pp.
            Provides bibliographical description of 1518 edition.
        Suggests that work was "probably a translation from the
        Dutch" and suggests that translator was Lawrence Andrewe.
        Provides notes on illustrations (passim).

3019   SCHLAUCH, MARGARET. "A Sixteenth-Century English Satirical
        Tale about Gdańsk." KN, 4 (1957), 95-120.
            Provides detailed analysis of linguistic features of
        Frederyke of Jennen. Compares it with The Deceit of Women
        and suggests both works were translated by the same person.

3020   STEIN, HAROLD. "Six Tracts about Women: A Volume in the
        British Museum." Library, 4th Ser., 15 (June 1934), 38-48.
            Provides bibliographical analysis of Vele's edition
        (1560) of Frederyke of Jennen.

3021   THRALL, WILLIAM FLINT. "Cymbeline, Boccaccio, and the Wager
        Story in England." SP, 28 (October 1931), 639-51.
            Compares Frederyke of Jennen with other versions of the
        wager story. Suggests that "the tale must be added to the
        list of significant analogues of Cymbeline."

THORNLEY, GEORGE

Longus, Daphnis and Chloe: A Most Sweet and Pleasant Pastorall Ro-
    mance for Young Ladies. Wing L3003.

Editions

3022   LONGUS. Daphnis & Chloe. Translated by George Thornley.
        Edited by J[ohn] M[axwell] Edmonds. In Daphnis & Chloe by
        Longus with the English Translation of George Thornley Re-
        vised and Augmented by J. M. Edmonds. The Love Romances of

Thornley

Parthenius and Other Fragments with an English Translation
by S. Gaselee. Loeb Classical Library. New York: G. P.
Putnam's Sons; London: W. Heinemann, 1916, pp. 1–247.
Reprints a corrected text of Thornley's translation. In
"Introduction," pp. vii–xxi, comments briefly on Thornley's
style and identifies text from which he translated.

3023   LONGUS. Daphnis & Chloe: A Most Sweet and Pleasant Pastorall
Romance for Young Ladies. Translated by George Thornley.
Waltham Saint Lawrence, Berkshire: Golden Cockerel Press,
1923, 108pp.
Provides reprint of 1657 edition.

3024   LONGUS. Daphnis & Chloe. Translated by George Thornley. Introduction by George Saintsbury. Abbey Classics, 13. London: Chapman & Dodd, 1923, 211pp.
Provides partly modernized reprint of 1657 edition.
Reprinted in 472.

3025   LONGUS. Daphnis & Chloe. Translated by George Thornley. New
York: Frank-Maurice; London: Geoffrey Bles, 1925, 200pp.
Provides reprint of 1657 edition.

*3026   LONGUS. Daphnis and Chloe. Translated by George Thornley.
London: A. Zwemmer, 1937, 213pp.
Not seen. Provides "revised and augmented" text based
on 1657 edition. Listed in NUC Pre-1956 Imprints, vol. 340,
415.

3027   LONGUS. Daphnis and Chloe. Translated by George Thornley.
New York: Pantheon, 1949, 175pp.
Provides modernized reprint based on 1657 edition.

TILNEY, EDMUND

A Brief and Pleasant Discourse of Duties in Mariage Called the Flower
of Friendshippe. STC 24076–24077a.5.

Editions

3028   TILNEY, EDMUND. "A Critical 3rd Edition of Edmund Tilney's
The Flower of Friendshippe, Published in 1577; Edited with
Introduction, Notes, and Glossary." Edited by Ralph Glass-
gow Johnson. Ph.D. dissertation, University of Pittsburgh,
1961, 279pp.
Provides critical edition based on text of 1577 edition.
Examines style, sources, and influence on later writers.

Studies

3029 BOAS, FREDERICK S. <u>Queen Elizabeth, the Revels Office, and
      Edmund Tilney</u>. Elizabeth Holland Lecture, 1937. London:
      Oxford University Press, 1938, 27pp. [Reprinted in:
      Frederick S. Boas. <u>Queen Elizabeth in Drama and Related
      Studies</u>. London: George Allen & Unwin, 1950, pp. 36–55.]
      Provides a synopsis of <u>Flower of Friendship</u> and discusses
      the work in the context of Tilney's life.

3030 CRANE, THOMAS FREDERICK. <u>Italian Social Customs of the Six-
      teenth Century and Their Influence on the Literatures of
      Europe</u>. Cornell Studies in English. New Haven: Yale
      University Press, 1920, 705pp.
      Includes a lengthy synopsis of <u>Flower of Friendship</u>
      to illustrate how characteristic it is of the "social di-
      versions of Italy" and to show the influence of Castiglione
      and Boccaccio on Tilney (pp. 506–11).

3031 HENDERSON, ARCHIBALD, JR. "Family of Mercutio." Ph.D. dis-
      sertation, Columbia University, 1954, 270pp.
      Examines ways in which M. Gualter "display[s] the traits
      of the mocker at love and at women."

3032 MIGLIOR, GIORGIO. "Edmund Tilney, prosatore elisabettiano."
      <u>ACF</u>, 8, no. 1 (1969), 68–90.
      Analyzes characteristics of Tilney's style and his treat-
      ment of marriage in <u>Flower of Friendship</u>. Examines influ-
      ence of humanism and of works of Castiglione, Erasmus, Pedro
      de Luján, and Marguerite de Navarre on form, style, and
      subject matter of work.

3033 MONCADA, ERNEST J[OSEPH]. "The Spanish Source of Edmund
      Tilney's <u>Flower of Friendshippe</u>." <u>MLR</u>, 65 (April 1970),
      241–47.
      Identifies source as Pedro de Luján's <u>Coloquios matri-
      moniales</u> and discusses the "dramatic interplay of the char-
      acters" in Tilney's work.

3034 TILNEY-BASSETT, J. G. "Edmund Tilney's <u>The Flower of Friend-
      shippe</u>." <u>Library</u>, 4th Ser., 26, nos. 2–3 (1945), 175–81.
      Establishes that there were at least two states of the
      1568 edition; compares 1568 with 1571 edition.

Tofte

TOFTE, ROBERT (1562-1620)

Nicolas de Montreux, Honours Academie: Or the Famous Pastorall of
   Julietta with Divers Histories. STC 18053.

Studies

3035   DENT, R[OBERT] W. "John Webster and Nicolas de Montreux."
          PQ, 35 (October 1956), 418-21.
             Examines Webster's use of Honor's Academy as a source
          for The White Devil.

3036   DENT, R[OBERT] W. John Webster's Borrowing. Berkeley: Uni-
          versity of California Press, 1960, 323pp.
             Provides detailed analysis of Webster's use of Honor's
          Academy as a source (passim).

*3037 FOX, CHARLES A. O. Notes on William Shakespeare and Robert
          Tofte. Swansea: Printed for the Author, 1956, 15pp.
             Not seen. Listed in Britism Museum Catalogue of Printed
          Books, 1956-1965, vol. 16, col. 79. See 3038.

3038   FOX, C[HARLES] A. O. Notes on William Shakespeare and Robert
          Tofte. 2d edition. Swansea: Printed for the Author,
          1957, 60pp.
             Provides list of allusions in Honor's Academy to Shake-
          speare's plays and poems and discusses Shakespeare's use of
          Honor's Academy as a source for The Tempest. Provides
          "Notes on Some Words and Phrases in Honours Academie,"
          pp. 38-40. Revision of 3037.

3039   WILLIAMS, FRANKLIN B., JR. "Robert Tofte." RES, 13 (July
          1937), 282-92; (October 1937), 405-24.
             In a survey of Tofte's life and works, briefly discusses
          Honor's Academy, noting that it is a hurriedly done, though
          faithful, translation, and was composed 1598-1599.

3040   WILSON, F[RANK] P[ERCY]. "Introduction," in The Batchelars
          Banquet: An Elizabethan Translation of Les Quinze joyes de
          mariage. Edited by F[rank] P[ercy] Wilson. Oxford:
          Clarendon Press, 1929, pp. vii-xlviii.
             Suggests that Tofte was translator.

THE TRUE HISTORY OF THE TRAGICKE LOVES ,OF HIPOLITO AND ISABELLA,
NEAPOLITANS
   (translation of Les Amours tragiques d'Hypolite et Isabelle.)

   STC 13516-13517

Studies

3041   MULRYNE, J. R.   "The French Source for the Sub-Plot of Middle-
       ton's <u>Women Beware Women</u>."   <u>RES</u>, NS, 25 (November 1974),
       439-45.
              Considers Middleton's possible use of <u>Hipolito and Isa-</u>
       <u>bella</u> in manuscript and examines relationship between two
       French versions and the English, concluding that translation
       is from the 1597 Rouen edition.

TURNER, RICHARD

Constant Lusina: The Amorous Passions of Paurinio.   STC 24344.

The Garland of a Greene Witte, Discovering the Constancie of Calipolis.
   STC 24345.

Studies

3042   WELD, JOHN SALTAR.   "Studies in the Euphuistic Novel, 1576-
       1640."   Ph.D. dissertation, Harvard University, 1940, 304pp.
              Traces sources of <u>Garland</u> and <u>Constant Lusina</u>.

TWINE (or TWYNE), LAURENCE (fl. 1576)

The Patterne of Painefull Adventures.   STC 709-710.

Editions

3043   TWINE, LAURENCE.   <u>The Patterne of Painefull Adventures</u>, in
       <u>Shakespeare's Library: A Collection of the Romances,</u>
       <u>Novels, Poems, and Histories Used by Shakespeare as the</u>
       <u>Foundation of His Dramas</u>, Vol. I.   Edited by J[ohn] Payne
       Collier.   London: T. Rodd, 1843, i-vi, 183-257.
              Provides reprint of 1594? edition.

3044   TWINE, LAURENCE.   <u>The Patterne of Painefull Adventures</u>, in
       <u>Shakespeare's Library: A Collection of the Plays, Romances,</u>
       <u>Novels, Poems, and Histories Employed by Shakespeare in the</u>
       <u>Composition of His Works</u>, Vol. IV.   Edited by John Payne
       Collier.   2d edition revised.   Edited by W[illiam] Carew
       Hazlitt.   London: Reeves and Turner, 1875, 229-334.
              Reprints 3043.

Twine

3045 TWINE, LAURENCE. <u>The Patterne of Painefull Adventures Gath-
ered into English by Laurence Twine</u>. New Rochelle, New
York: Elston Press, 1903, 79pp.
Reprints text of 1594? edition.

3046 TWINE, LAURENCE. <u>The Patterne of Painefull Adventures</u>, in
<u>Narrative and Dramatic Sources of Shakespeare</u>, Vol. VI.
Edited by Geoffrey Bullough. London: Routledge and Kegan
Paul; New York: Columbia University Press, 1966, 423–82.
Reprints text of 1594? edition. In "Introduction [to
<u>Pericles</u>]," pp. 349–74, identifies Twine's source as Tale
153 of the <u>Gesta Romanorum</u> and examines Shakespeare's use
of <u>Pattern of Painful Adventures</u> in <u>Pericles</u>.

Studies

3047 GRAY, HENRY DAVID. "Heywood's <u>Pericles</u>, Revised by Shakespeare." <u>PMLA</u>, 40 (September 1925), 507–29.
Discusses briefly Twine's work as source for brothel
scenes, concluding that here Twine's "story is finer than
the drama." Observes that his "Marina has a genuinely
pathetic and moving appeal."

3048 LEONARD, NANCY SCOTT. "Romance as Recovery: A Study of
Shakespeare's <u>Pericles</u>." Ph.D. dissertation, Indiana Uni-
versity, 1972, 262pp.
Includes examination of Shakespeare's use of <u>Pattern of
Painful Adventures</u> as source.

3049 MUIR, KENNETH. "The Problem of <u>Pericles</u>." <u>ES</u>, 30 (1949),
65–83.
Enumerates borrowings from Twine's <u>Pattern of Painful
Adventures</u> in Wilkins's <u>Painful Adventures of Pericles</u>.
Revised in 3192.

3050 PEASE, RALPH WILLIAMS. "The Genesis and Authorship of
<u>Pericles</u>." Ph.D. dissertation, Texas A & M University,
1972, 210pp.
Discusses Shakespeare's use of <u>Pattern of Painful Adven-
tures</u> as source.

3051 SEILER, GRACE ELIZABETH. "Shakespeare's Part in <u>Pericles</u>."
Ph.D. dissertation, University of Missouri, 1951, 329pp.
Discusses Shakespeare's use of <u>Pattern of Painful Adven-
tures</u> as a source and uses Twine's work to help establish
some idea of the earlier <u>Pericles</u> play.

3052   SINGER, S[AMUEL]. Apollonius von Tyrus: Untersuchungen über das Fortleben des antiken Romans in spätern Zeiten. Halle: Niemeyer, 1895, 234pp.
       Includes examination of Twine's sources as well as Shakespeare's use of Twine as a source (passim).

3053   SMYTH, ALBERT H. "Shakespeare's Pericles and Apollonius of Tyre." PAPS, 37 (January 1898), 206-312.
       Includes discussion of Twine's treatment of story (particularly his amplifications of the Latin Historia Apollonii Regis Tyri) in the context of a "complete historical sketch of [the treatments of] the romance."

3054   SPIKER, SINA. "George Wilkins and the Authorship of Pericles." SP, 30 (October 1933), 551-70.
       Analyzes pattern of Wilkins's borrowings from Twine: finds that they correspond to the Gower portions of Shakespeare's Pericles and to "changes of scene where the precise details of action or speech [from the play] might have been confused in Wilkin's [sic] memory."

3055   TOMPKINS, J. M. S. "Why Pericles?" RES, NS, 3 (October 1952), 315-24.
       Contrasts vehemence of Twine's Apollonius to patience of Shakespeare's Pericles and observes that "instability of fortune" is stressed in Twine's version.

TYLER, MARGARET

Diego Ortuñez de Calahorra, The Mirrour of Princely Deedes and Knighthood. STC 18859-18861.

Studies

3056   ATKINSON, DOROTHY F. "Busirane's Castle and Artidon's Cave." MLQ, 1 (June 1940), 185-92.
       Discusses "the nature and extent of Spenser's debt [in Faerie Queene (III, xi-xii)]...to the first (1578) and second (1585) parts of the Mirrour."

3057   GOLDER, HAROLD. "Bunyan's Valley of the Shadow." MP, 27 (August 1929), 55-72.
       Uses examples from Mirror to illustrate influence of earlier romances on narrative framework of Pilgrim's Progress. Discusses, in particular, the conventional elements of the descent into a cave or dark valley.

Tyler

3058   MACKERNESS, E. D. "Margaret Tyler: An Elizabethan Feminist."
        N&Q, 190 (23 March 1946), 112-13.
            Discusses Tyler's "bold assertion of woman's equality
        in reading and writing" in the Preface to her translation
        of the Mirror as "a document of some importance in the his-
        tory of women's rights." Suggests that her translation was
        done in response to demands of a lower- and middle-class
        female readership.

3059   PEROTT, JOSEPH DE. "Die Magelonen und die Sturmfabel."
        Shakespeare-Jahrbuch, 47 (1911), 128-31.
            Identifies Mirror, Part I, as a source of The Tempest.

3060   PEROTT, JOSEPH DE. "The Mirrour of Knighthood." RR, 4 (Octo-
        ber-December 1913), 397-402.
            Suggests first three Books were published by 1579. Ex-
        plains allusion to Mirror in Lyly's Euphues.

3061   PEROTT, JOSEPH DE. "The Probable Source of the Plot of Shake-
        speare's Tempest." Publications of the Clark University
        Library, 1, no. 8 (1905), 209-16.
            Argues that Mirror, Part I, was source.

3062   PEROTT, JOSEPH DE. "Professor Fitzmaurice-Kelly and the
        Source of Shakespeare's Tempest." RR, 5 (October-December
        1914), 364-67.
            Reiterates earlier identification (3059) of Mirror,
        Book I, as source of act I of The Tempest; provides "list
        of verbal borrowings."

3063   THOMAS, HENRY. Spanish and Portuguese Romances of Chivalry:
        The Revival of the Romance of Chivalry in the Spanish Penin-
        sula, and Its Extension and Influence Abroad. Cambridge:
        Cambridge University Press, 1920, 343pp.
            Includes discussion of the translation of the various
        parts of the Mirror, allusions to the work in drama, and
        its use as a source in various plays (passim).

UNDERDOWNE, THOMAS (fl. 1566-1578)

Heliodorus, An Aethiopian Historie. STC 13041-13046.

Editions

3064   HELIODORUS. An Aethiopian History. Translated by Thomas
        Underdowne. Introduction by Charles Whibley. Tudor Trans-
        lations, 5. Edited by W. E. Henley. London: David Nutt,
        1895, 322pp.

Provides reprint of 1587 edition. In "Introduction,"
pp. vii-xxix, discusses Underdowne's handling of text, his
style (including diction and rhythm), and popularity of the
work. Examines how Underdowne transformed, not translated,
the work. ("Introduction" reprinted as: "Heliodorus," in
Studies in Frankness, by Charles Whibley [New York: E. P.
Dutton & Co., 1912], pp. 49-97.)

3065   HELIODORUS. An Aethiopian History. Translated by Thomas
        Underdowne. Introduction by George Saintsbury. Abbey
        Classics, 23. London: Chapman & Dodd, 1924, 301pp.
            Provides reprint of 1587 edition. In "Introduction,"
        pp. vii-xvii, comments on Underdowne's handling of text and
        the "raciness" of his sidenotes.

3066   HELIODORUS. "An Aethiopian Historie, Written in Greeke by
        Heliodorus and Englished by Thomas Vnderdowne." Translated
        by Thomas Underdowne. Edited by Robert Riner Hellenga.
        Ph.D. dissertation, Princeton University, 1969, 691pp.
            Provides critical old-spelling text based on collation
        of 1569 and 1577 editions. Provides bibliographical analy-
        sis of early editions; discusses Underdowne's treatment of
        text and style; and examines influence of work on Renais-
        sance fiction and drama.

3067   HELIODORUS. "Thomas Underdowne's Translation of Heliodorus'
        An Aethiopian History: A Critical Edition." Translated by
        Thomas Underdowne. Edited by Edward Albert Herscher. Ph.D.
        dissertation, St. Louis University, 1973, 957pp.
            Provides critical edition based on 1577 edition. Pro-
        vides bibliographical analysis of early editions and dis-
        cusses Underdowne's treatment of the text.

Studies

3068   CORNEY, BOLTON. "Mr. Hazlitt's Hand-Book: Heliodorus, etc."
        N&Q, 37 (15 February 1868), 142-44.
            To illustrate inaccuracies of Hazlitt's Handbook (17),
        discusses errors and omissions in listing of editions of
        Underdowne's translation. See 3069 and 3072.

3069   CORNEY, BOLTON. "To Mr. W. Carew Hazlitt: A Paragraphic Re-
        joinder." N&Q, 37 (14 March 1868), 241-42.
            Replies to Hazlitt's rejoinder (3072), reasserting criti-
        cism in original note (3068).

3070   GESNER, CAROL. "Cymbeline and the Greek Romance: A Study in
        Genre," in Studies in English Renaissance Literature.

Underdowne

Edited by Waldo F. McNeir. LSUSHS, 12. Baton Rouge:
Louisiana State University Press, 1962, pp. 105-31.
Argues that in writing Cymbeline, Shakespeare "was pro-
foundly influenced by the Aethiopica" in Underdowne's translation.

3071 GESNER, CAROL. Shakespeare & the Greek Romance. Lexington:
University Press of Kentucky, 1970, 228pp.
Includes discussion of Shakespeare's use of Underdowne's
Aethiopian History as a source for Cymbeline; also considers
influence of work on other plays (pp. 98-115, passim).

3072 HAZLITT, W[ILLIAM] CAREW. "Mr. Hazlitt's Handbook." N&Q, 37
(29 February 1868), 201.
Answers Corney's criticisms (3068) by defending his original listing in Handbook (17) of editions of Underdowne's
translation. See 3069.

3073 HUGHES, MERRITT Y. "Spenser's Debt to the Greek Romances."
MP, 23 (August 1925), 67-76.
Discusses Underdowne's stress on Heliodorus's moral purpose and suggests that "[l]ike Spenser and Sidney, Underdowne was moved by the desire to give England an epic that
would contribute to the education of gentlemen."

3074 HUNTER, G. K. "A Source for The Revenger's Tragedy." RES,
NS, 10 (May 1959), 181-82.
Suggests incident in Cnemon's story (Aethiopian History,
Book I) was Webster's source for Lusurioso breaking into
bedchamber.

3074a OEFTERING, MICHAEL. Heliodor und seine Bedeutung für die
Literatur. Litterarhistorische Forschungen, 18. Berlin:
E. Felber, 1901, 176pp.
Includes discussion of influence of Underdowne's translation of Aethiopica on Renaissance drama and on the prose
fiction of Sidney, Warner, and Roger Boyle (pp. 92-100,
149-54).

3075 STARNES, D. T. "Barnabe Riche's 'Sappho Duke of Mantona': A
Study in Elizabethan Story-Telling." SP, 30 (July 1933),
455-72.
Analyzes Rich's use of Underdowne's Aethiopian History
as source.

3076 WHITE, R. S. "'Comedy' in Elizabethan Prose Romances." YES,
5 (1975), 46-51.
Includes examination of meaning of term in Underdowne's
Aethiopian History.

URQUHART, SIR THOMAS (1611-1660)

François Rabelais, The First [Second] Book of the Works of Mr. Francis
Rabelais (Urquhart's translation of Book III was published post-
humously in 1693). Wing R103-105, R108-110.

Editions

3077   RABELAIS, FRANÇOIS. The Complete Works of Doctor François
       Rabelais, Abstractor of the Quintessence; Being an Account
       of the Inestimable Life of the Great Gargantua, and of the
       Heroic Deeds, Sayings, and Marvelous Voyages of His Son the
       Good Pantagruel. Translated by Thomas Urquhart and Peter
       Motteux. Introduction by J. Lewis May. Abbey Library.
       London: Murray, n.d., 768pp.
            Provides modernized, annotated reprint of unidentified
       edition.

3078   RABELAIS, FRANÇOIS. The Works of Rabelais. Translated by
       Thomas Urquhart and Peter Motteux. London: Chatto and
       Windus, n.d., 668pp.
            Provides modernized reprint based on unidentified edi-
       tion.

3079   RABELAIS, FRANÇOIS. The Works of Rabelais. Translated by
       Thomas Urquhart and Peter Motteux. London: Published for
       the Trade, n.d., 956pp.
            Provides modernized reprint of Books I and II from 1653
       edition and Book III from 1693 edition.

*3080 RABELAIS, FRANÇOIS. The Romance of Gargantua and Pantagruel.
       Translated by Thomas Urquhart and Peter Motteux. Edited
       by Theodore Martin. Edinburgh: T. G. Stevenson, 1838,
       531pp.
            Not seen. Listed in NUC Pre-1956 Imprints, vol. 478,
       203.

*3081 RABELAIS, FRANÇOIS. The Life of Gargantua and the Heroic
       Deeds of Pantagruel. Translated by Thomas Urquhart and
       Peter Motteux. Introduction by Henry Morley. Morley's
       Universal Library. London: George Routledge and Sons,
       1883, 320pp.
            Not seen. Listed in NUC Pre-1956 Imprints, vol. 478,
       198.

3082   RABELAIS, FRANÇOIS. Five Books of the Lives, Heroic Deeds,
       and Sayings of Gargantua and His Son Pantagruel. Translated
       by Thomas Urquhart and Peter Motteux. Introduction by

Urquhart

        Anatole de Montaiglon. 2 vols. Bibliophilist's Library,
9-10. Philadelphia: Barrie, 189-, 378, 458pp.
        Provides modernized text based on 1653 edition of Books
I-II and 1693 edition of Book III. In "Introduction," I,
xxiii-liii, comments briefly on Urquhart's style.

3083   RABELAIS, FRANÇOIS. <u>Five Books of the Lives, Heroic Deeds,
and Sayings of Gargantua and His Son Pantagruel</u>. Translated
by Thomas Urquhart and Peter Motteux. Introduction by Ana-
tole de Montaiglon. 2 vols. London: Lawrence and Bullen,
1892, 389, 469pp.
        Provides reprint of unidentified edition. In "Introduc-
tion," I, xv-xlvi. comments briefly on Urquhart's translation.

3084   RABELAIS, FRANÇOIS. <u>The Works of François Rabelais</u>. Translated by Thomas Urquhart and Peter Motteux. Edited by
Alfred Wallis. 3 vols. London: Gibbings and Co., 1897,
353, 244, 308pp.
        Provides modernized reprint based on unidentified edi-
tion. In "Introduction," I, v-xv, comments appreciatively
on quality of Urquhart's translation.

3085   RABELAIS, FRANÇOIS. <u>Gargantua and Pantagruel</u>. Translated by
Thomas Urquhart and Peter Motteux. Introduction by Charles
Whibley. 3 vols. Tudor Translations, 1st Ser., 24-26.
Edited by W. E. Henley. London: David Nutt, 1900, 433,
265, 464pp.
        Provides reprint of Books I and II from 1653 edition and
Book III from 1693 edition. In "Introduction," I, vii-xcv,
provides a critical estimate of Urquhart's translation,
discusses his style, and examines his use of Cotgrave's
<u>Dictionary</u>.

*3086   RABELAIS, FRANÇOIS. <u>The Works of Francis Rabelais</u>. Translated
by Thomas Urquhart and Peter Motteux. Introduction by
George Saintsbury. London: Chatto & Windus for the Bibli-
ophilist Library, 1902, 695pp.
        Not seen. Listed in <u>NUC Pre-1956 Imprints</u>, vol. 478,
189.

*3087   RABELAIS, FRANÇOIS. <u>Master Francis Rabelais</u>. Translated by
Thomas Urquhart and Peter Motteux. 2 vols. London: Aldus
Society, 1903.
        Not seen. Provides reprint of Books I and II from 1653
edition and Book III from 1693 edition. Listed in <u>NUC Pre-
1956 Imprints</u>, vol. 478, 198.

3088   RABELAIS, FRANÇOIS. <u>Five Books of the Lives, Heroic Deeds,</u>
        <u>and Sayings of Gargantua and His Son Pantagruel</u>. Translated
        by Thomas Urquhart and Peter Motteux. 3 vols. London:
        A. H. Bullen, 1904, 286, 275, 319pp.
            Provides modernized reprint of Books I and II from 1653
        edition and Book III from 1693 edition. In "Introduction,"
        anonymous writer comments briefly on Urquhart's style and
        treatment of the text.

3089   RABELAIS, FRANÇOIS. <u>The Works of Mr. Francis Rabelais, Doctor</u>
        <u>in Physick, Containing Five Books of the Lives, Heroick</u>
        <u>Deeds, & Sayings of Gargantua and His Sonne Pantagruel</u>.
        Translated by Thomas Urquhart and Peter Motteux. 2 vols.
        London: Richards, 1904, 421, 394pp.
            Provides reprint of Books I and II from 1653 edition and
        of Book III from 1693 edition.

3090   RABELAIS, FRANÇOIS. <u>The Works of Mr. Francis Rabelais</u>. Trans-
        lated by Thomas Urquhart and Peter Motteux. 2 vols. Lon-
        don: Moring; Philadelphia: J. B. Lippincott, [1912], 490,
        478pp.
            Provides modernized reprint based on 1653 edition of
        Books I and II and 1693 edition of Book III.

3091   RABELAIS, FRANÇOIS. <u>The Lives, Heroic Deeds, & Sayings of</u>
        <u>Gargantua & His Son Pantagruel</u>. Translated by Thomas
        Urquhart and Peter Motteux. 3 vols. London: Chatto &
        Windus, 1921, 366, 300, 405pp.
            Provides reprint of Books I and II from 1653 edition and
        Book III from 1693 edition.

3092   RABELAIS, FRANÇOIS. <u>The Works of Mr. Francis Rabelais</u>. Trans-
        lated by Thomas Urquhart and Peter Motteux. 2 vols. Lon-
        don: Navarre Society, 1921, 490, 478pp.
            Provides modernized text based on unidentified edition.

3093   RABELAIS, FRANÇOIS. <u>The Lives, Heroic Deeds, & Sayings of</u>
        <u>Gargantua & His Son Pantagruel</u>. Translated by Thomas
        Urquhart and Peter Motteux. 3 vols. New York: Boni,
        1925, 366, 298, 408pp.
            Provides reprint of Books I and II from 1653 edition
        and Book III from 1693 edition.

3094   RABELAIS, FRANÇOIS. <u>Gargantua & Pantagruel</u>. Translated by
        Thomas Urquhart and Peter Motteux. Preface by Henri
        Clouzot. New York: Dodd, Mead, [1928], 836pp.
            Provides modernized reprint of unidentified edition.

Urquhart

3095   RABELAIS, FRANÇOIS. <u>The Lives, Heroic Deeds, & Sayings of</u>
        <u>Gargantua and His Son Pantagruel</u>. Translated by Thomas
        Urquhart and Peter Motteux. New York: Simon & Schuster,
        1928, 1057pp.
            Provides modernized text based on unidentified edition.

3096   RABELAIS, FRANÇOIS. <u>Gargantua and Pantagruel</u>. Translated by
        Thomas Urquhart and Peter Motteux. Introduction by D. B.
        Wyndham Lewis. 2 vols. Everyman's Library, 826–27. Lon-
        don: J. M. Dent; New York: E. P. Dutton, 1929, 758pp.
            Reprints modernized, unannotated text of Urquhart's
        translation of Books I and II (apparently from 1653 edition)
        and Book III (apparently from 1693 edition). In "Introduc-
        tion," I, vii–xvii, praises Urquhart's "transmutation" of
        the original, discusses briefly the kinds of alterations
        made by him, and calls Motteux's translation of Books IV
        and V "mediocre" in comparison to Urquhart's translation
        of Books I–III.

3097   RABELAIS, FRANÇOIS. <u>The Urquhart-Le Motteux Translation of</u>
        <u>the Works of Francis Rabelais</u>. Translated by Thomas Ur-
        quhart and Peter Motteux. Edited by Albert Jay Nock and
        Catherine Rose Wilson. 2 vols. New York: Harcourt, Brace,
        1931, 1144pp.
            Provides annotated text based largely on 1727 edition.
        In "Preface," I, 1–14, discuss Urquhart's handling of the
        text.

3098   RABELAIS, FRANÇOIS. <u>Gargantua and Pantagruel</u>. Translated by
        Thomas Urquhart and Peter Motteux. 3 vols. World's Clas-
        sics, 411–413. London: Oxford University Press, 1934,
        422, 402, 342pp.
            Provides partly modernized, annotated reprint of uniden-
        tified edition.

3099   RABELAIS, FRANÇOIS. <u>Gargantua and Pantagruel</u>. Translated by
        Thomas Urquhart and Peter Motteux. Great Books of the
        Western World, 24. Chicago: Encyclopaedia Britannica,
        1952, 330pp.
            Provides modernized text based on unidentified edition.

Studies

3100   BOSTON, RICHARD. "Introduction to The Admirable Urquhart," in
        <u>The Admirable Urquhart: Selected Writings</u>. By Thomas Ur-
        quhart. Edited by Richard Boston. London: Fraser, 1975,
        pp. 9–63.
            Includes discussion of Urquhart's style and handling of
        text in his translation of Rabelais.

*3101   BROUGHAM, ELEANOR M. Comments and Queries. London: Lane,
       1927, 124pp.
           Not seen. Includes essay on Urquhart. Listed in Hardin
       Craig, "Recent Literature of the English Renaissance," SP,
       26 (1929), 267.

3102   BROUGHAM, ELEANOR M. "Sir Thomas Urquhart." New Statesman,
       19 January 1927, pp. 569-70.
           Places Urquhart's translation of Rabelais's work in con-
       text of his life and writings, and praises quality of his
       translation.

3103   BROWN, HUNTINGTON. Rabelais in English Literature. Cambridge:
       Harvard University Press, 1933, 270pp.
           Examines Urquhart's use of Cotgrave's Dictionary, his
       style, and his handling of the original (pp. 111-26, passim).

3104   BROWN, HUNTINGTON. "Rabelais in English Literature through
       Sterne." Ph.D. dissertation, Harvard University, 1930.
       See 3103.

3105   C[ORDIÉ], C. "Urquhart e Rabelais." RLMC, 11 (June 1958),
       172-73.
           Notes briefly some critical discussions of Urquhart's
       translation.

3106   CUNNINGHAM, ROBERT NEWTON. Peter Anthony Motteux, 1663-1718:
       A Biographical and Critical Study. Oxford: B. Blackwell,
       1933, 227pp.
           Discusses Motteux's use of Urquhart's translation of
       Rabelais and compares the styles of the two translators
       (pp. 73-86).

3107   EDDY, WILLIAM A. "Rabelais,--A Source for Gulliver's Travels."
       MLN, 37 (November 1922), 416-18.
           Points out Swift's allusions to Rabelais; suggests
       Swift knew Urquhart's translation.

3108   KIDDE, C. A. "Rabelais in English: Urquhart and Kimes."
       N&Q, NS, 15 (March 1968), 104-105.
           Examines Kimes's revision of Urquhart's translation of
       Books I and II in an attempt to ascertain the nature of
       Urquhart's original translation of Book III, which is known
       only in Kimes's revised form.

3109   OAKLEY, J. H. I. "'Urchard,' the Translator of Rabelais."
       N&Q, 53 (8 January 1876), 32-33.
           Comments on various spellings of "Urquhart" and briefly
       traces the use of his translation by Motteux and Ouzell.

Urquhart

3111   OLIVER, RAYMOND. "Urquhart's Rabelais." SHR, 8 (1974), 317-
       28.
              Describes "Urquhart's approach to translation" by ana-
       lyzing influences of Rabelais's text, Randle Cotgrave's
       Dictionary, the euphuistic tradition, the "literary tradi-
       tion of Scottish flytings and related extravagance," and
       the English language per se on the translator's style.
       Analyzes how he translates "style, not language" by trans-
       forming "French stylistic effects into English ones."

3112   PAGE, CURTIS HIDDEN. "Introduction," in Rabelais. By François
       Rabelais. Translated by Thomas Urquhart and Peter Motteux.
       Edited by Curtis Hidden Page. French Classics for English
       Readers. New York: G. P. Putnam's Sons, 1905, pp. xiii-
       xli.
              Praises quality of Urquhart's translation, calling it
       "probably the closest reproduction ever made in English of
       the exact style and spirit of a foreign author." Provides
       abridgment of Urquhart's translation.

3113   POWYS, LLEWELYN. "Sir Thomas Urquhart," in Thirteen Worthies.
       By Llewelyn Powys. New York: American Library Service,
       1923, pp. 91-106.
              Includes discussion of Urquhart's style in his transla-
       tion of Rabelais.

3114   ROE, F[REDERICK] C. "A Double Centenary: Sir Thomas Urquhart
       and His Translation of Rabelais." Aberdeen University Re-
       view, 35 (1953), 121-29.
              Discusses Urquhart and Rabelais as "kindred spirits."
       Examines Urquhart's treatment of the original text and dis-
       cusses aspects of his style.

3115   ROE, F[REDERICK] C. Sir Thomas Urquhart and Rabelais. Tay-
       lorian Lecture, 1957. Oxford: Clarendon Press, 1957,
       23pp.
              Discusses Urquhart's translation in the context of his
       life and times. Examines his style, influences on his vo-
       cabulary, and his handling of the text.

3116   ROE, FREDERICK C. "Urquhart traducteur de Rabelais," in
       Association Guillaume Budé, Congrès de Tours et Poitiers,
       1954. Paris: Belles Lettres, 1954, pp. 143-45.
              Summary of paper in which Roe discusses Urquhart's
       qualifications--his life, tastes, intellectual sympathy,
       and style--as translator of Rabelais. Apparently a summary
       of a version of 3117.

3117   ROE, F[REDERICK] C. "Urquhart, traducteur de Rabelais." <u>ER</u>,
       1 (1956), 112-19.
            Discusses high quality and popularity of Urquhart's
       translation; examines, in general terms, his style. <u>See</u>
       3116.

3118   SAINÉAN, L[AZARE]. <u>L'Influence et la réputation de Rabelais</u>.
       Paris: J. Gamber, 1930, 330pp.
            Includes discussion of Urquhart's handling of text, es-
       pecially his vocabulary (pp. 68-74).

3119   SAINÉAN, LAZARE. "Les Interprètes de Rabelais en Angleterre
       et en Allemagne." <u>Revue des Études Rabelaisiennes</u>, 7
       (1909), 137-258.
            Includes analysis of Urquhart's translation of Rabelais's
       text; discusses Urquhart's retention of French terms, his
       handling of proverbial and idiomatic phrases, his mistrans-
       lations, and his additions and amplifications. Illustrates
       Urquhart's reliance on Cotgrave's <u>Dictionary</u>.

3120   SMITH, SYDNEY GOODSIR. "The Perfect Translator of Rabelais
       (Sir Thomas Urquhart of Cromartie)." <u>The Listener</u>, 50
       (10 December 1953), 1007, 1009.
            Provides general appreciation of Urquhart, with comments
       on prose style.

3121   TERRY, F. C. BIRKBECK. "Asses' Bridge." <u>N&Q</u>, 83 (11 April
       1891), 286.
            Notes <u>OED</u> antedating from phrase in Urquhart's transla-
       tion of Rabelais.

3122   WELLS, WHITNEY HASTINGS. "<u>Moby Dick</u> and Rabelais." <u>MLN</u>, 38
       (February 1923), 123.
            Provides parallel passages between <u>Moby Dick</u> (Chapter
       41) and Urquhart's translation (Book I, Chapter 10). Sug-
       gests Melville borrowed from Urquhart's translation.

3123   WHIBLEY, CHARLES. "Sir Thomas Urquhart." <u>New Review</u>, 17
       (July 1897), 21-38. [Reprinted in: Charles Whibley.
       <u>Studies in Frankness</u>. New York: E. P. Dutton & Co., 1912,
       pp. 227-62.]
            Discusses Urquhart's translation of Rabelais in context
       of his life and writings. Examines his style, discussing
       his peculiar affinity with Rabelais. Asserts that, along
       with the Authorized Version of the Bible, Urquhart's
       Rabelais is "the finest translation ever made from one
       language into another."

Urquhart

3124   WILLCOCK, JOHN. <u>Sir Thomas Urquhart of Cromartie, Knight</u>.
       Edinburgh and London: Oliphant, Anderson, & Ferrier, 1899,
       267pp.
             In Chapter VII ("Translation of Rabelais," pp. 184-207)
       discusses Urquhart's translation as "his great literary
       achievement." Examines style, handling of text (particu-
       larly amplifications), and publishing history.

<u>VIRGILIUS. THIS BOKE TREATH OF THE LYFE OF VIRGILIUS AND OF HIS DETH
AND MANY MARVAYLES THAT HE DYD BY WHYCHCRAFT</u>
(translated from Dutch?)

       STC 24828-24829.

Editions

3125   <u>Virgilius. This Boke Treateth of the Lyfe of Virgilius</u>.
       Edited by E[dward] V[ernon] Utterson. London: M'Creery,
       1812, 30pp.
             Provides reprint of 1518? edition.

3126   <u>The Lyfe of Virgilius</u>, in <u>A Collection of Early Prose Romances</u>,
       Vol. II. Edited by William J. Thoms. London: William
       Pickering, 1828, 56pp. (separately paginated). [Also pub-
       lished separately.]
             Provides reprint of 1518? edition. In introductory re-
       marks (pp. iii-xii) comments on origins of story and pub-
       lishing history.

3127   <u>Virgilius</u>, in <u>Early Prose Romances</u>. Edited by Henry Morley.
       Carisbrooke Library, 4. London: G. Routledge, 1889,
       pp. 207-36.
             Provides reprint of 1518? edition from 3126. In "Intro-
       duction" traces the development of the legend (pp. 18-20).

3128   <u>Virgilius</u>, in <u>Early English Prose Romances</u>. Edited by William
       J. Thoms. Revised and enlarged edition. London: G.
       Routledge and Sons; New York: E. P. Dutton and Co.,
       [1907], pp. 207-36.
             Reprints 3127.

Studies

3129   McNEIR, WALDO F. "Traditional Elements in the Character of
       Greene's Friar Bacon." <u>SP</u>, 45 (April 1948), 172-79.
             Draws on <u>Virgilius</u> in discussion of conventional ele-
       ments of the treatment of benevolent magicians in early
       romances.

3130   PROCTER, ROBERT. Jan van Doesborgh, Printer at Antwerp: An
       Essay in Bibliography. Illustrated Monographs, 2. London:
       Chiswick Press for The Bibliographical Society, 1894,
       132pp.
              Provides bibliographical description of Doesborgh's edi-
       tion of Virgilius; suggests that it was "probably a trans-
       lation of the Dutch version" and was printed in 1518.
       Suggests that Lawrence Andrewe was translator. Provides
       notes on illustrations (passim).

3131   SPARGO, JOHN WEBSTER. Virgil the Necromancer: Studies in
       Virgilian Legends. HSCL, 10. Cambridge: Harvard Univer-
       sity Press, 1934, 514pp.
              Includes examination of the relationship of the English
       Virgilius to the French and Dutch versions: argues that
       the English is a translation of the Dutch version but that
       the translator also used the French (pp. 237-51).

3132   STEADMAN, JOHN M. "Spenser and the Virgilius Legend: Another
       Talus Parallel." MLN, 73 (June 1958), 412-13.
              Cites parallel for Talus's iron flail in chapter "How
       the Emperor Asked Counsel of Virgilius."

["THE WANDERING JEW"]

   British Library MS. Add. 38,599.

Editions

3133   ANDERSON, GEORGE K. "The Wandering Jew Returns to England."
       JEGP, 45, no. 3 (1946), 237-50.
              Prints version of story from British Library MS. Add.
       38,599, suggesting that it may be based on the prose ver-
       sion entered in the Stationers' Register in 1612 but not
       extant, or on a French version.

3134   ANDERSON, GEORGE K. The Legend of the Wandering Jew. Provi-
       dence: Brown University Press, 1965, 503pp.
              In section on "The English Version of the Ahasuerus-
       Book" (pp. 60-66), provides literal transcript of version
       of story from British Library MS. Add. 38,599. Shows that
       the English text is based on a French version and discusses
       its relationship to the prose account entered in the Sta-
       tioners' Register in 1612.

Warner

WARNER, WILLIAM (1558–1609?)

Pan His Syrinx. STC 25086–25087.

Editions

3135   WARNER, WILLIAM. William Warner's Syrinx or a Sevenfold His-
          tory. Edited by Wallace A. Bacon. Northwestern University
          Studies, Humanities Series, 26. Evanston: Northwestern
          University Press, 1950, 311pp.
              Provides modernized critical text based on 1597 edition.
          In "Introduction" (pp. xi–lxxxv) examines work in context
          of Elizabethan prose fiction, influence of Lyly on Warner's
          style, influence of Heliodorus's Aethiopica on structure,
          nature of the revisions in 1597 edition, and influence of
          Syrinx on later prose fiction (especially that by Greene
          and Roberts) and drama.

Studies

3136   BACON, WALLACE A. "The Source of Robert Daborne's The Poor-
          Mans Comfort." MLN, 57 (May 1942), 345–48.
              Discusses Daborne's use of tale of Opheltes as source
          for main plot of play.

3137   WHITE, MARGARET IMOGINE ZECHIEL. "The Influence of John
          Lyly's Euphues upon Selected Pieces of Elizabethan Prose
          Fiction." Ph.D. dissertation, University of Illinois at
          Urbana–Champaign, 1971, 332pp.
              Examines influence of Lyly's style, themes, didacticism,
          and narrative techniques and devices on Pan His Syrinx.

3138   ZEITLER, WILLIAM IRVING. "The Life, Works, and Literary In-
          fluence of William Warner." Ph.D. dissertation, Harvard
          University, 1928.
              Includes discussion of Pan His Syrinx in context of
          Warner's life and other works.

WATSON, HENRY (fl. 1503–1509)

Hystorye of Olyver of Castylle and of the Fayre Helayne. STC 18808.

The Hystory of the Two Valyaunte Brethren Valentyne and Orson. STC
    24571.3–24573. Wing V28–33.

Editions

*3139   The History of Oliver of Castile: Reprinted from the Unique
        Copy of Wynkyn de Worde's Edition of 1518. Translated by
        Henry Watson. Edited by Robert Edmund Graves. London:
        Roxburghe Club, 1898, 177pp.
            Not seen. Listed in NUC Pre-1956 Imprints, vol. 429,
        667.

3140   Valentine and Orson, Translated from the French by Henry Wat-
        son. Translated by Henry Watson. Edited by Arthur Dickson.
        EETS, Original Series, 204. London: Oxford University
        Press for the Early English Text Society, 1937, 439pp.
            Provides reprint of 1555 edition; includes reprint of
        fragment of c. 1510 edition. In "Introduction," pp. ix-
        lxiii, traces publishing history of work, compares Watson's
        text with the French, analyzes language (sounds and spell-
        ings, inflections, vocabulary), and examines influence on
        Spenser, Shakespeare, and Bunyan.

Studies

*3141   DICKSON, ARTHUR. "Valentine and Orson: A Study in Late
        Medieval Romance." Ph.D. dissertation, Columbia University,
        1929, 309pp.
            See 3142.

3142   DICKSON, ARTHUR. Valentine and Orson: A Study in Late
        Medieval Romance. New York: Columbia University Press,
        1929, 317pp.
            In Appendix II ("Valentine and Orson in English," pp.
        284-98) provides annotated chronological list of English
        translations. Discusses briefly Watson's translation.

3143   McNEIR, WALDO F. "Traditional Elements in the Character of
        Greene's Friar Bacon." SP, 45 (April 1948), 172-79.
            Draws on Valentine and Orson in discussion of conven-
        tional elements in the treatment of benevolent magicians
        in early romances.

WEAMYS, ANNA

A Continuation of Sir Philip Sydney's Arcadia. Wing W1189.

Weamys

Studies

3144   MacCARTHY, B[RIDGET] G. <u>Women Writers: Their Contribution
to the English Novel, 1621-1744</u>. Cork: Cork University
Press, 1944, 288pp.
    Discusses style and plot of <u>Continuation</u>; contrasts
Weamys's style with that of Sidney (pp. 64-69).

3145   WILES, AMERICUS G[EORGE] D[AVID]. "The Continuations of Sir
Philip Sidney's <u>Arcadia</u>." Ph.D. dissertation, Princeton
University, 1934.
    Includes examination of Weamys's <u>Continuation</u>; finds
that it is inferior to Beling's and that it has little
literary merit.

WESTWARD FOR SMELTS: OR, THE WATER-MANS FARE OF MAD-MERRY WESTERN
WENCHES

    <u>STC</u> 25292.

Editions

3146   Westward for Smelts: <u>An Early Collection of Stories</u>. Edited
by James Orchard Halliwell[-Phillipps]. Percy Society, 22.
London: Richards for the Percy Society, 1848, 71pp.
    Provides an annotated reprint of the 1620 edition.

Studies

3147   DAVIES, H. NEVILLE. "Introduction," in The Cobbler of Canterbury: <u>Frederic Ouvry's Edition of 1862 with a New Introduction by H. Neville Davies</u>. Cambridge, England: D. S.
Brewer; Totowa, New Jersey: Rowman and Littlefield, 1976,
pp. 1-55.
    Examines influence of <u>The Cobbler of Canterbury</u> on the
structure of <u>Westward for Smelts</u>.

3148   KOEPPEL, EMIL. <u>Studien zur Geschichte der italienischen
Novelle in der englischen Litteratur des sechzehnten Jahr-
hunderts</u>. Quellen und Forschungen, 70. Strassburg: K. J.
Trübner, 1892, 106pp.
    Identifies Italian sources of <u>Westward for Smelts</u>.

3149   THRALL, WILLIAM FLINT. "<u>Cymbeline</u>, Boccaccio, and the Wager
Story in England." <u>SP</u>, 28 (October 1931), 639-51.
    Compares <u>Frederyke of Jennen</u> to other versions of the
wager story, including that in <u>Westward for Smelts</u>.

WHETSTONE, GEORGE (c. 1551–1587)

An Heptameron of Civill Discourses. STC 25337–25338.

The Rocke of Regard. STC 25348.

Editions

3150   WHETSTONE, GEORGE. "The History of Promos and Cassandra," in
        Shakespeare's Library: A Collection of the Romances,
        Novels, Poems, and Histories Used by Shakespeare as the
        Foundation of His Dramas, Vol. II. Edited by J[ohn] Payne
        Collier. London: T. Rodd, 1843, 51–62.
            Provides reprint from 1582 edition of Heptameron. Re-
        printed in 3152.

3151   WHETSTONE, GEORGE. The Rocke of Regard. [Edited by John
        Payne Collier.] N.p.: n.p., 1870, 331pp.
            Provides reprint of 1576 edition.

3152   WHETSTONE, GEORGE. "The History of Promos and Cassandra," in
        Shakespeare's Library: A Collection of the Plays, Romances,
        Novels, Poems, and Histories Employed by Shakespeare in the
        Composition of His Works, Vol. III. Edited by John Payne
        Collier. 2d edition revised. Edited by W[illiam] Carew
        Hazlitt. London: Reeves and Turner, 1875, 155–66.
            Reprints 3150.

3153   WHETSTONE, GEORGE. "Promos and Cassandra," in Elizabethan
        Tales. Edited by Edward J[oseph] O'Brien. London: G.
        Allen & Unwin, 1937, pp. 154–65.
            Provides modernized text based on unidentified edition
        of Heptameron.

3154   WHETSTONE, GEORGE. "A Critical Edition of George Whetstone's
        An Heptameron of Ciuill Discourses (1582)." Edited by
        David Napoleon Beauregard. Ph.D. dissertation, Ohio State
        University, 1967, 338pp.
            Provides "a critical old-spelling edition" based on
        1582 edition; omits second and sixth days' discourses.
        Discusses work as "an attempt to make the contents of mar-
        riage manuals...more entertaining and more palatable" and
        examines style and influences on work.

3155   WHETSTONE, GEORGE. "The Story of Promos and Cassandra," in
        Elizabethan Love Stories. Edited by T[erence] J. B. Spen-
        cer. Penguin Shakespeare Library. Harmondsworth: Penguin
        Books, 1968, pp. 119–27.

Whetstone

Provides modernized text based on 1582 edition of <u>Hepta-meron</u>. In "Introduction," pp. 7-31, discusses relationship with Shakespeare's <u>Measure for Measure</u>.

Studies

3156 BUDD, FREDERICK E. "Material for a Study of the Sources of Shakespeare's <u>Measure for Measure</u>." <u>RLC</u>, 11 (1931), 711-36.
Includes discussion of Whetstone's <u>Heptameron</u> as a possible source.

3157 CECIONI, CESARE G. "Un adattamento di due novelle del Boccaccio nello <u>Heptameron of Civil Discourses</u> di George Whetstone (1582)," in <u>Il Boccaccio nella cultura inglese e anglo-americana</u>. Edited by Giuseppe Galigani. Florence: L. S. Olschki, 1974, pp. 185-91.
Examines the tale of Monsieur Bergetto as an adaptation of two novelle from the <u>Decameron</u>; discusses the anticatholicism in Whetstone's adaptation and the structure of the <u>Heptameron</u>.

3158 CRANE, THOMAS FREDERICK. <u>Italian Social Customs of the Sixteenth Century and Their Influence on the Literatures of Europe</u>. Cornell Studies in English. New Haven: Yale University Press, 1920, 705pp.
Provides a lengthy synopsis of <u>Heptameron</u> to illustrate the influence of Italian culture and literature on Whetstone's work (pp. 511-20).

3159 DENT, R[OBERT] W. <u>John Webster's Borrowing</u>. Berkeley: University of California Press, 1960, 323pp.
Provides a detailed analysis of Webster's use of <u>Heptameron</u> as a source (passim).

3160 DENT, ROBERT W. "Webster's Borrowings from Whetstone." <u>MLN</u>, 70 (December 1955), 568-70.
Points out Webster's indebtedness to <u>Heptameron</u> as source for sententiae and images in <u>Duchess of Malfi</u>.

3161 DORAN, MADELEINE. <u>Endeavors of Art: A Study of Form in Elizabethan Drama</u>. Madison: University of Wisconsin Press, 1954, 496pp.
In Appendix III ("The Sources of <u>Measure for Measure</u>," pp. 385-89) discusses Shakespeare's use of <u>Heptameron</u> as a source.

3162 GALIGANI, GIUSEPPE. "Il Boccaccio nel Cinquecento inglese," in <u>Il Boccaccio nella cultura inglese e anglo-americana</u>.

Edited by Giuseppe Galigani. Florence: L. S. Olschki,
1974, pp. 27-57.
Discusses influence of Boccaccio on Heptameron; examines
structure of work.

3163   GARKE, ESTHER. The Use of Songs in Elizabethan Prose Fiction.
Bern: Francke Verlag, 1972, 132pp.
Draws frequently on Whetstone's works of prose fiction
for examples in analysis of types of songs, their relationships to plot and structure, and their functions.

3164   HENDERSON, ARCHIBALD, JR. "Family of Mercutio." Ph.D. dissertation, Columbia University, 1954, 270pp.
Examines ways in which Dr. Mossenigo (Heptameron) "display[s] the traits of the mocker at love and at women."

*3165   IZARD, THOMAS C. "George Whetstone, Mid-Elizabethan Gentleman
of Letters." Ph.D. dissertation, Columbia University,
1942, 297pp.
See 3166.

3166   IZARD, THOMAS C. George Whetstone: Mid-Elizabethan Man of
Letters. Columbia University Studies in English and Comparative Literature, 158. New York: Columbia University
Press, 1942, 307pp.
Includes discussion of Whetstone's prose fiction in context of his life and works. Discusses briefly relationship
of "Rinaldo and Giletta" and Gascoigne's Master F. J. Provides detailed examination of sources of Heptameron: analyzes work as a courtesy book and as an "examination of the
institution of marriage." Includes "Bibliography of Whetstone's Works," pp. 279-87, with transcription of title
pages and notes on modern editions.

3167   KOEPPEL, EMIL. Studien zur Geschichte der italienischen
Novelle in der englischen Litteratur des sechzehnten Jahr-
hunderts. Quellen und Forschungen, 70. Strassburg: K. J.
Trübner, 1892, 106pp.
Identifies Italian sources of Heptameron and discusses
Whetstone's style (pp. 30-40).

3168   PROUTY, CHARLES T[YLER]. "Elizabethan Fiction: Whetstone's
'The Discourse of Rinaldo and Giletta' and Grange's The
Golden Aphroditis," in Studies in Honor of A. H. R. Fair-
child. Edited by Charles T[yler] Prouty. University of
Missouri Studies, 21, no. 1. Columbia: University of
Missouri, 1946, pp. 133-50.

Whetstone

> Examines Whetstone's use of Gascoigne's Master F. J. and
> Ariosto as sources. Notes division of story into two dis-
> tinct parts. Argues that Whetstone's "interest was not in
> telling a story or in displaying character but in present-
> ing as much as possible of...stereotypes of love behavior
> and love language as he could."

3169   PROUTY, CHARLES T[YLER]. "George Whetstone and the Sources
        of Measure for Measure." SQ, 15 (Spring 1964), 131-45.
            Discusses Whetstone's depiction of "the low-life of Lon-
        don" in The Rock of Regard and its influence on his charac-
        terization in Promos and Cassandra.

3170   PROUTY, CHARLES T[YLER]. The Sources of Much Ado about Noth-
        ing: A Critical Study Together with the Text of Peter
        Beverley's Ariodanto and Ieneura. New Haven: Yale Univer-
        sity Press, 1950, 150pp.
            Discusses Whetstone's handling of the tale of Generva
        (in "Rinaldo and Giletta"), particularly his treatment of
        the deception (pp. 22-26).

3171   SCANLON, PAUL A. "Whetstone's 'Rinaldo and Giletta': The
        First Elizabethan Prose Romance." WP, 2 (1973), 195-206.
            Argues that with Whetstone's tale "Elizabethan prose
        fiction enters the realm of romance." Examines structure
        of work, Whetstone's combination of pastoral and chivalric
        elements, and his use of Gascoigne's Master F. J. and Ari-
        osto's Orlando Furioso.

WILKINS, GEORGE (fl. 1604-1608)

Jests to Make You Merie (with Thomas Dekker). STC 6541.

The Painfull Adventures of Pericles Prince of Tyre. STC 25638.5.

Editions

3172   WILKINS, GEORGE. Pericles Prince of Tyre: A Novel by George
        Wilkins, Printed in 1608, and Founded upon Shakespeare's
        Play. Edited by Tycho Mommsen. Introduction by J[ohn]
        Payne Collier. Oldenburg: Stalling, 1857, 118pp.
            Provides reprint of copy of 1608 edition held by Stadt-
        bibliothek, Zurich. In "Preface of the Editor," pp. I-XXV,
        discusses correspondences between play and novel, and Wil-
        kins's use of Twine and the play as a source.

3173   WILKINS, GEORGE, and THOMAS DEKKER. <u>Jests to Make You Merie</u>,
in <u>The Non-Dramatic Works of Thomas Dekker</u>, Vol. II. By
Thomas Dekker. Edited by Alexander B. Grosart. Huth
Library. London: Printed for Private Circulation, 1885,
267-359.
Provides reprint of 1607 edition.

3174   WILKINS, GEORGE. <u>The Painfull Adventures of Pericles Prince
of Tyre</u>. Edited by Kenneth Muir. Liverpool Reprints, 8.
Liverpool: University Press of Liverpool, 1953, 125pp.
Provides reprint of 1608 edition. In "Introduction,"
pp. iii-xv, reviews scholarship on relationship between
Wilkins's work and <u>Pericles</u>. Suggests that "Shakespeare
and Wilkins may have been borrowing from the source-play;
but it seems more probable that the reporters of the play
or the compositors of Q[uarto, 1609] made use of the novel
to correct the copy."

3175   WILKINS, GEORGE. <u>The Painfull Adventures of Pericles Prince
of Tyre</u>, in <u>Narrative and Dramatic Sources of Shakespeare</u>,
Vol. VI. Edited by Geoffrey Bullough. London: Routledge
and Kegan Paul; New York: Columbia University Press, 1966,
492-546.
Reprints text of 1608 edition, with some modification
of punctuation. In "Introduction [to <u>Pericles</u>]," pp. 349-
74, discusses Wilkins's use of Twine's <u>Pattern of Painful
Adventures</u> and stage version of <u>Pericles</u> as sources. Notes
that Wilkins's "method was to interweave passages from
Twine and from the play." In "Appendix: <u>Pericles</u> and the
Verse in Wilkins's <u>Painfull Adventures</u>," pp. 549-64, attempts to reconstruct verse passages which Wilkins seems to
be quoting or paraphrasing from a version of <u>Pericles</u> an-
terior to that published in 1609.

Studies

3176   BAKER, HARRY T. "The Relation of Shakspere's <u>Pericles</u> to
George Wilkins's Novel, <u>The Painfull Aduentures of Pericles,
Prince of Tyre</u>." <u>PMLA</u>, 23 (March 1908), 100-18.
Notes that Wilkins copied several passages, generally
descriptive, from Twine's <u>Pattern of Painful Adventures</u>,
and criticizes Wilkins's lack of "dramatic technic." Discusses relationship between Wilkins's novel and Shakespeare's <u>Pericles</u>, arguing that in latter part of novel
Wilkins was following his own dramatic version of the
Pericles story and not Shakespeare's. Notes that most
echoes of <u>Pericles</u> in latter part of Wilkins's novel are
commonplace expressions. Lists in Appendix resemblances
between <u>The Painful Adventures</u> and Shakespeare's play.

Wilkins

3177 BARKER, GERARD A. "Themes and Variations in Shakespeare's
     Pericles." ES, 44 (December 1963), 401–14.
     Analyzes theme of kingship in Wilkins's work; suggests
     that emphasis on the theme is the result of Wilkins's use
     of an Ur-Pericles play as a source. Discusses points of
     contrast with earlier versions of the Pericles story.

3178 BULLOUGH, GEOFFREY. "Pericles and the Verse in Wilkins's
     Painfull Adventures." Bulletin de la Faculté des Lettres
     de Strasbourg, 47 (1969), 799–812.
     By using the verse-relics in Wilkins's novel, attempts
     to reconstruct passages of the source play Wilkins used.

3179 COLLIER, J[OHN] PAYNE. Farther Particulars Regarding Shake-
     speare and His Works: In a Letter to the Rev. Joseph
     Hunter. London: T. Rodd, 1839, 68pp.
     Examines Wilkins's use of Pericles as source for Painful
     Adventures; discusses value of Wilkins's work in emending
     text of play (pp. 33–54). See 3180.

3180 COLLIER, J[OHN] PAYNE. "Shakespeare's Pericles, and Wilkins's
     Novel Founded upon It." N&Q, 16 (4 July 1857), 3–4.
     Expands earlier argument (3179) that Wilkins's novel was
     "probably derived from short-hand notes taken at the Globe
     Theatre during the representation" of Pericles.

3181 CRAIG, HARDIN. "Pericles and The Painfull Adventures." SP,
     45 (October 1948), 600–605.
     Compares treatment of brothel scene in play with that in
     Painful Adventures to argue that Pericles was revised after
     Wilkins composed his work.

3182 CRAIG, HARDIN. "Pericles Prince of Tyre," in If by Your Art:
     Testament to Percival Hunt. Edited by Agnes Lynch Starrett.
     Pittsburgh: University of Pittsburgh Press, 1948, pp. 1–14.
     Accepts theory that Wilkins based his novel on an Ur-
     Pericles.

3183 DELIUS, N[IKOLAUS]. "Ueber Shakespeare's Pericles, Prince of
     Tyre." Shakespeare-Jahrbuch, 3 (1868), 175–204.
     Examines relationship of Wilkins's novel to the play.
     Argues that Wilkins wrote original play, which was altered
     by Shakespeare; rather than lose credit for his work, he
     composed the prose version.

3184 EDWARDS, PHILIP. "An Approach to the Problem of Pericles."
     ShS, 5 (1952), 25–49.

Argues that <u>Painful Adventures</u> is based on the "play given by the King's Men that is also reported in the Quarto of <u>Pericles</u>." Suggests that Wilkins frequently relied on his own imagination, rather than a lost play, to amplify episodes imperfectly remembered. Discusses value of <u>Painful Adventures</u> in emending 1609 edition of play.

3185 FLEAY, F. C. "On the Play of <u>Pericles</u>." <u>New Shakspere Society's Transactions</u>, 1 (1874), 195-209.
       Lists verse-fossils in <u>Painful Adventures</u> and argues that Wilkins used the play as a source.

*3186 GREENE, GUY SHEPARD. "George Wilkins." Ph.D. dissertation, Cornell University, 1926, 37pp.
       Abstract not available.

3187 HASTINGS, WILLIAM T. "Exit George Wilkins?" <u>Shakespeare Association Bulletin</u>, 11 (April 1936), 67-83.
       Argues that "The <u>Painful Adventures</u> is...a reissue of Twine's <u>Pattern of Painful Adventures</u>, extensively revised and modified to make it pass as a paraphrase of" Shakespeare's <u>Pericles</u>. Suggests that publication of Wilkins's book was the result of a frustrated attempt to publish a pirated edition of the play.

3188 HOENIGER, F. D. "Introduction," in <u>Pericles</u>. By William Shakespeare. Edited by F. D. Hoeniger. Arden Shakespeare. London: Methuen, 1963, pp. xiii-xci.
       Discusses relationship between <u>Pericles</u> and <u>Painful Adventures</u>, arguing that Wilkins used a play behind the 1609 quarto as source but was more dependent on Twine's <u>Pattern of Painful Adventures</u>. Discusses episodes in which Wilkins's account "may be more accurate than that of" the 1609 quarto.

3189 HONIGMAN, E. A. J. <u>The Stability of Shakespeare's Text</u>. Lincoln: University of Nebraska Press, 1965, 224pp.
       In Appendix B ("George Wilkins and <u>Pericles</u>," pp. 193-99) discusses Wilkins's prose style.

3190 MAXWELL, J[AMES] C[LOUTTS]. "Introduction," in <u>Pericles, Prince of Tyre</u>. By William Shakespeare. Edited by J[ames] C[loutts] Maxwell. Cambridge: Cambridge University Press, 1969, i-xxxix.
       Argues that Wilkins's novel is based not on an Ur-<u>Pericles</u> but on a reported text of the 1609 quarto of Shakespeare's play.

Wilkins

3191   MUIR, KENNETH. "The Problem of Pericles." ES, 30 (1949), 65–
          83.
               Enumerates Wilkins's borrowings from Twine's Pattern of
          Painful Adventures. Discusses the relationship between
          Wilkins's Painful Adventures and Shakespeare's Pericles,
          arguing that Wilkins based his prose fiction work on an Ur-
          Pericles, a play which he himself had written.

3192   MUIR, KENNETH. Shakespeare as Collaborator. New York:
          Barnes & Noble, 1960, 178pp.
               In Chapter IV ("Shakespeare's Hand in Pericles," pp. 56–
          76—a revision of 3191) points out that Wilkins made use of
          Twine's Pattern of Painful Adventures for material not in
          the play and argues that The Painful Adventures was based
          largely on an early version of the play.

3193   MUIR, KENNETH. Shakespeare's Sources, I: Comedies and
          Tragedies. London: Methuen & Co., 1957, 279pp.
               Includes discussion of relationship of Painful Adventures
          to Shakespeare's play. Argues that Wilkins based his work
          on an earlier version of the play and that by comparing
          Painful Adventures with the printed text of Pericles it is
          possible to "roughly estimate the nature of Shakespeare's
          alterations" (pp. 225–31).

3194   MUNRO, JOHN. "Some Matters Shakespearian—III." TLS, 11 Oc-
          tober 1947, p. 528.
               Examines relationship between Painful Adventures and
          Shakespeare's play: points out that because Wilkins's prose
          lapses into verse in other works the verse-fossils in Pain-
          ful Adventures cannot be positive proof that the prose ver-
          sion was based on a play.

3195   OSBORN, JAMES M. "Edmund Malone and the Dryden Almanac Story."
          PQ, 16 (October 1937), 412–14.
               Transcribes note by Malone in his copy of The Critical
          and Miscellaneous Prose Works of John Dryden in which he
          discusses version of the anecdote found in Jests to Make
          You Merry. See 3196.

3196   OSBORN, JAMES M. "Edmund Malone and the Dryden Almanac Story."
          PQ, 17 (January 1938), 84–86.
               Reprints text of earlier note (3195), omitting transcrip-
          tion of one jest.

3197   PARROTT, THOMAS MARC. "Pericles: The Play and the Novel."
          Shakespeare Association Bulletin, 23 (July 1948), 105–13.

Argues that Wilkins's Painful Adventures was based on
Shakespeare's play and that the novel was published in an
attempt to capitalize on the popularity of the play.

3198   PEASE, RALPH WILLIAMS. "The Genesis and Authorship of
        Pericles." Ph.D. dissertation, Texas A & M University,
        1972, 210pp.
            Argues that Wilkins "used a report of the play" and ex-
        amines his use of Twine as a source.

3199   SEILER, GRACE ELIZABETH. "Shakespeare's Part in Pericles."
        Ph.D. dissertation, University of Missouri, 1951, 329pp.
            Argues that Painful Adventures was "based on notes which
        Wilkins made at a theatrical production of the original
        play." Uses Painful Adventures to help establish some idea
        of the earlier play.

3200   SPIKER, SINA. "George Wilkins and the Authorship of Pericles."
        SP, 30 (October 1933), 551-70.
            Examines relationship of Wilkins's Painful Adventures to
        Shakespeare's Pericles and Twine's Pattern of Painful Adven-
        tures. Concludes that Wilkins was recalling from memory a
        performance of the play. Analyzes plagiarism from Twine to
        show that his borrowings follow a pattern: they correspond
        to the Gower portions of the play and to "changes of scene
        where the precise details of action or speech [from the
        play] might have been confused in Wilkin's [sic] memory."

3201   SYKES, H. DUGDALE. "Wilkins and Shakespeare's Pericles, Prince
        of Tyre," in Sidelights on Shakespeare: Being Studies of
        The Two Noble Kinsmen, Henry VIII, Arden of Feversham, A
        Yorkshire Tragedy, The Troublesome Reign of King John, King
        Leir, Pericles Prince of Tyre. Stratford-upon-Avon:
        Shakespeare Head Press, 1919, pp. 143-203.
            Provides detailed examination of correspondences between
        play and Painful Adventures to argue that "the play is a
        dramatization of the novel." Interprets Wilkins's title to
        mean "the true and original version of the story of Pericles
        used in the play." Points out Wilkins's borrowings from
        Sidney's Arcadia.

3202   THOMAS, DANIEL LINDSEY. "On the Play Pericles." Englische
        Studien, 39 (1908), 210-39.
            Argues that Wilkins wrote Painful Adventures to capital-
        ize on the popularity of the play.

3203   TOMPKINS, J. M. S. "Why Pericles?" RES, NS, 3 (October 1952),
        315-24.

Wilkins

> Observes that like Shakespeare, Wilkins "emphasizes the
> gentleness and courtesy of Pericles," which suggests that
> Wilkins "consciously evoked...the bearing of Burbage in the
> part."

3204   WOOD, JAMES O. "Pericles, I.ii." N&Q, NS, 14 (April 1967),
        141-42.
           Uses Painful Adventures to support interpretation of a
        passage in Quarto 1.

[WILLIAM OF PALERMO, A PROSE ROMANCE]

  STC 25707.5.

Editions

3205   BRIE, FRIEDRICH. "Zwei frühneuenglische Prosaromane." Archiv,
        118 (1907), 318-28.
           Provides diplomatic transcript of Bodleian collotype of
        fragment of William of Palermo. Discusses relationship to
        English poem.

WILSON, SIR THOMAS (1560?-1629)

Jorge de Montemayor, "Diana de Monte Mayor: Done out of Spanish by
    Thomas Wilson" (British Library Add. MS. 18,638).

Editions

3206   THOMAS, H[ENRY]. "Diana de Monte Mayor: Done out of Spanish
        by Thomas Wilson." Revue Hispanique, 50 (December 1920),
        367-418.
           Transcribes Wilson's translation of Book I from British
        Library Add. MS. 18,638. In brief introductory notes, com-
        ments on Wilson's vocabulary. See 3207.

Studies

3207   ANDERSON, D. M. "Sir Thomas Wilson's Translation of Monte-
        mayor's Diana." RES, NS, 7 (April 1956), 176-81.
           Describes manuscript, comments on low quality of trans-
        lation, and provides supplementary notes to Thomas's edition
        (3206).

3208   THOMAS, HENRY. "English Translations of Portuguese Books be-
        fore 1640," in Miscelânea de estudos em honra de D. Carolina

<u>Michaëlis de Vasconcellos</u>. Revista da Universidade de
Coimbra, 1. Coimbra, Portugal: Universidad de Coimbra,
1933, pp. 690–711.
　　Includes discussion of Wilson's <u>Diana</u> and speculates on
possibility of Shakespeare's use of it as a source for <u>Two
Gentlemen of Verona</u>.

<u>WOTTON, HENRY</u> (fl. 1578)

Jacques Yver, <u>A Courtlie Controversie of Cupids Cautels</u>. <u>STC</u> 5647.

Studies

3209　ATKINSON, DOROTHY F. "The Source of <u>Two Gentlemen of Verona</u>."
　　　　<u>SP</u>, 41 (April 1944), 223–34.
　　　　　Proposes story of Claribel and Floradine as one of
　　　　sources of play; provides scene by scene comparison of play
　　　　with story to show the resemblance "in general structure"
　　　　between the works. <u>See</u> 3215.

3210　BOAS, FREDERICK S. "Introduction," in <u>The Works of Thomas Kyd</u>.
　　　　By Thomas Kyd. Edited by Frederick S. Boas. Oxford:
　　　　Clarendon Press, 1901, pp. xiii–cvii.
　　　　　Discusses Kyd's use of Wotton's <u>Courtly Controversy</u> as
　　　　a source for <u>Soliman and Perseda</u> (pp. lvi–lxi, passim).

3211　CAMPBELL, KILLIS. "The Sources of Davenant's <u>The Siege of
　　　　Rhodes</u>." <u>MLN</u>, 13 (June 1898), 177–82.
　　　　　Examines <u>Courtly Controversy</u> as possible source.

3212　CORSER, THOMAS. "Wotton's <u>Courtlie Controversie of Cupid's
　　　　Cautels</u>." <u>N&Q</u>, 14 (29 November 1856), 428–29.
　　　　　Briefly describes work in query for biographical informa-
　　　　tion on Wotton.

3213　HENDERSON, ARCHIBALD, JR. "Family of Mercutio." Ph.D. dis-
　　　　sertation, Columbia University, 1954, 270pp.
　　　　　Examines ways in which Sir Fleur d'Amour "display[s] the
　　　　traits of the mocker at love and at women."

3214　MYERS, KAREN W. "The False Steward in the 'Second Historie'
　　　　of Wotton's <u>Cupids Cautels</u>: A Neglected <u>Hamlet</u> Source."
　　　　<u>ESRS</u>, 15 (1966), 18–26.
　　　　　Examines parallels between Wotton's work and the Ophelia
　　　　plot of the play to argue for Shakespeare's use of <u>Courtly
　　　　Controversy</u> as a source.

Wotton

3215 POGUE, JIM C. "The Two Gentlemen of Verona and Henry Wotton's
A Courtlie Controuersie of Cupids Cautels." ESRS, 10,
no. 4 (1962), 17-21.
Supplements Atkinson's article (3209) by adding further
instances of Shakespeare's use of Courtly Controversy as a
source.

3216 SARRAZIN, GREGOR. Thomas Kyd und sein Kreis. Berlin: Felber,
1892, 126pp.
Discusses use of story of Perseda as source for Soliman
and Perseda. Reprints lengthy extract of tale from 1578
edition of Courtly Controversy (pp. 8-48).

3217 SIEPER, ERNST. "Die Geschichte von Soliman und Perseda in der
neueren Litteratur." Zeitschrift für Vergleichende Lit-
teraturgeschichte, NS, 9 (1895), 33-60; 10 (1896), 151-74.
Discusses Wotton's style and his translation of the tale
of Soliman and Perseda from French version; discusses Kyd's
use of Courtly Controversy as source for Spanish Tragedy
and Soliman and Perseda.

3218 WELD, JOHN S[ALTAR]. "Some Problems of Euphuistic Narrative:
Robert Greene and Henry Wotton." SP, 45 (April 1948),
165-71.
Discusses Greene's borrowings from Courtly Controversy
in Mamillia.

3219 WELD, JOHN SALTAR. "Studies in the Euphuistic Novel, 1576-
1640." Ph.D. dissertation, Harvard University, 1940, 304pp.
Suggests that "by joining to [the "natural history
similes" found in Le Printemps D'Yver]...a schematic sentence structure, Wotton bridged the gap between Pettie's
purely structural euphuism and Lyly's mixture of schemata
and bestiary." Suggests that Wotton "may have influenced
Lyly's style."

WROTH, LADY MARY (c. 1586-1640)

The Countess of Mountgomeries Urania. STC 26051.

Studies

3219a GARTENBERG, PATRICIA, and NENA [LOUISE] THAMES WHITTEMORE.
"A Checklist of English Women in Print, 1475-1640." BB, 34
(January-March 1977), 1-13.
Include listing for Urania. Note that Urania is "[t]he
one published original work of prose fiction by a woman"

Authors/Translators/Titles

Young

during the period. Point out that the "female viewpoint is
entirely original and fresh."

3220 KOHLER, CHARLOTTE. "The Elizabethan Woman of Letters: The
Extent of Her Literary Activities." Ph.D. dissertation,
University of Virginia, 1936.
    Includes discussion of Wroth's Urania in Chapter IV.
Suggests that Elizabethan "women writers [including Wroth]
were not able to create new thoughts and images in their
minds, [but that] they did uphold and illumine the models
which they set themselves."

3221 MacCARTHY, B[RIDGET] G. Women Writers: Their Contribution to
the English Novel, 1621-1744. Cork: Cork University Press,
1944, 288pp.
    Examines how Wroth consciously patterned Urania on Sid-
ney's Arcadia, analyzes her introduction of realistic
novella-like digressions, and discusses her satire of her
contemporaries (pp. 47-64).

3222 O'CONNOR, JOHN J. "James Hay and The Countess of Montgomerie's
Urania." N&Q, NS, 2 (April 1955), 150-52.
    Discusses importance to Lord Hay's biography of Wroth's
depiction of his private life under the guise of the
father-in-law of Sirelius.

3223 PARRY, GRAHAM. "Lady Mary Wroth's Urania." PLPLS-LHS, 16,
part 4 (1975), 51-60.
    Examines relationship of work to Sidney's Arcadia, ana-
lyzes significance of title, and discusses her style, which
is "almost indistinguishable from Sidney's." Also discusses
work as "a product of the courtly-chivalric ethos."

3224 TING, NAI TUNG. "Studies in English Prose and Poetic Romances
in the First Half of the Seventeenth Century." Ph.D. dissertation, Harvard University, 1941, 360pp.
    Finds that Urania "was not a mere reproduction of the
Arcadia, but rather an awkward jumble of sentimental pastoralism and chivalric extravagances of the Spanish type."
Concludes that "[d]esultoriness, dullness, and the tinsel
of an exaggerated Arcadian style justly doomed the work to
oblivion."

YOUNG, BARTHOLOMEW (fl. 1577-1600)

Jorge de Montemayor and Gaspar Gil Polo, Diana. STC 18044.

Giovanni Boccaccio, Amorous Fiammetta. STC 3179.

521

Young

Editions

3225   BOCCACCIO, GIOVANNI. <u>Amorous Fiammetta</u>. Translated by
       Bartholomew Young. Edited by Edward Hutton. London:
       Navarre Society, 1926, 416pp.
           Provides modernized text based on 1587 edition. In "In-
       troduction," pp. vii–lix, discusses briefly Young's style
       and places translation in context of his life and other
       works.

3226   BOCCACCIO, GIOVANNI. <u>Amorous Fiametta</u>. Translated by Bar-
       tholomew Young. Edited by K. H. Josling. London: Mandrake
       Press, 1929, 212pp.
           Provides "a faithful reprint of the 1587 edition."

3227   GIL POLO, GASPAR. Diana Enamorada <u>(1564) Together with the</u>
       <u>English Translation (1598) by Bartholomew Yong</u>. Translated
       by Bartholomew Young. Edited by Raymond L. and Mildred B.
       Grismer. Minneapolis: Burgess Publishing Co., 1959, 325pp.
           Provides annotated reprint of 1598 edition.

3228   MONTEMAYOR, JORGE DE. <u>A Critical Edition of Yong's Translation</u>
       <u>of George of Montemayor's</u> Diana <u>and Gil Polo's</u> Enamoured
       Diana. Translated by Bartholomew Young. Edited by Judith
       M. Kennedy. Oxford: Clarendon Press, 1968, 548pp.
           Provides critical edition based on 1598 edition. In
       "Introduction," pp. xv–lxxx, discusses vogue of <u>Diana</u> in
       England and its influence on Elizabethan fiction, drama,
       and poetry. Analyzes Young's treatment of the original
       text, discussing in particular his expansions.

Studies

3229   HARRISON, T. P. "Bartholomew Yong, Translator." <u>MLR</u>, 21
       (April 1926), 129–39.
           Discusses translations in context of his life and works.
       Suggests that motive in translating <u>Diana</u> was to offer
       tribute to memory of Sidney.

3230   HARRISON, T. P., JR. "Concerning <u>Two Gentlemen of Verona</u> and
       Montemayor's <u>Diana</u>." <u>MLN</u>, 41 (April 1926), 251–52.
           Argues, in general terms, for Shakespeare's indebtedness
       to the <u>Diana</u>, although not specifically to Young's transla-
       tion.

3231   MATHEWS, ERNST GARLAND. "Studies in Anglo-Spanish Cultural
       and Literary Relations, 1598–1700." Ph.D. dissertation,
       Harvard University, 1938.

Includes discussion of Young's translations; calls his
"prose...excellent, sensitive to variations in his originals, and uncursed by euphuism or Arcadianism.

3232   SALAZAR CHAPELA, ESTEBAN. "Clasicos espanoles en Inglaterra."
       CA, 11, no. 1 (1952), 256-61.
       Includes discussion of influence of Young's Diana on
       English literature.

3233   THOMAS, HENRY. "English Translations of Portuguese Books be-
       fore 1640." Library, 4th Ser., 7 (June 1926), 1-30.
       Discusses various other English translations of Diana
       that Young might have known.

3234   UNGERER, GUSTAV. "Bartholomew Yong, Mannerist Translator of
       Spanish Pastoral Romances." ES, 54 (October 1973), 439-46.
       Suggests that Young's close connections with prominent
       recusants caused him to translate Diana. Discusses reasons
       for dedicating Diana to Penelope Devereux, its popularity
       among female readers, and Mannerist traits of Young's style.

3235   WALES, JULIA GRACE. "Shakespeare's Use of English and Foreign
       Elements in the Setting of The Two Gentlemen of Verona."
       TWA, 27 (1932), 85-125.
       Discusses, in passing, several parallels between Young's
       Diana and the play.

3236   WRIGHT, HERBERT G[LADSTONE]. "The Italian Edition of Boccac-
       cio's Fiammetta Used by Bartholomew Young." MLR, 38 (Oc-
       tober 1943), 339-40.
       Suggests that Young used the 1558 or 1565 edition;
       discusses nature of Young's marginal notes.

Index

App, August Joseph, 1589, 2021
Applegate, James, 2549
Applegate, James E., 1252-53
Apthonius, 1692, 1837, 2667
Apuleius (see William Adlington)
Arber, Edward, 1214, 1613, 1770,
  1784
Ardolino, Frank, 1058
Aretino, Pietro, 2123, 2160
Ariosto, Lodovico, 351, 1088,
  2478, 2619, 2892, 2925,
  3168, 3171
Aristotle, 2653
Armes, William D., 1785
Armin, Robert, 502-17
Armstrong, Archibald, 518-20
Armstrong, William A., 2550
Arnold, Aerol, 2092
Arthos, John, 2443
Ascham, Roger, 1004, 1855-56,
  1886, 1897
Ashbee, Edmund William, 712,
  1611
Ashley, Robert, 53, 85, 642,
  825, 1051, 1775, 2082
Ashmore, Basil, 940
Ashton, John, 54
Ashworth, Robert A., 86
Assarsson-Rizzi, Kerstin, 988
Atkins, John William Hey, 87,
  829, 1786, 2093, 2551
Atkins, S. H., 1631, 2359
Atkinson, Dorothy F. (see also
  Dorothy Atkinson Evans),
  441, 1170, 2294-97, 3056,
  3209
Aurelio and Isabel (see The
  Historie of Aurelio and of
  Isabell)
Aurner, Robert Ray, 1787
Austin, Warren B., 672-75,
  1254-58
Ayres, Harry Morgan, 1513
Ayres, Philip J., 88
Ayrton, Michael, 2081, 2094

B

B., A., 521
B., C. C., 1788-89
B., G., 1604

B., R., 1257
B., R. O., 2492
B., W., 522-524
B., W. C., 1529, 1790
Babcock, C. Merton, 2363
Bache, William B., 830-31
Bacon, Francis, 1493, 1698,
  1763, 1796, 1974, 2212,
  2495, 2717, 2936
Bacon, Roger, 986, 993
Bacon, Wallace A., 1259, 1791,
  3135-36
Bahlsen, Leo, 89
Bailey, James Osler, 1129
Bailey, Philip James, 965
Baily, Johnson, 1792
Baird, Donald, 4
Baird, Ruth Cates, 1667
Bakeless, John Edwin, 943
Baker, Ernest Albert, 90-92,
  488, 549, 572, 779, 832,
  1260, 1668, 1793, 2095,
  2530, 2552
Baker, Harry T., 3176
Baker, Sheridan, 93-95
Bald, R. C., 1620
Baldwin, Charles Sears, 96
Baldwin, Edward Chauncey, 1657
Baldwin, Spurgeon Whitfield, Jr.,
  97
Baldwin, Thomas W., 1261
Baldwin, William, 525-33
Bandello, Matteo (see Sir Geof-
  frey Fenton; William Painter;
  Robert Smythe), 330, 1076,
  1429, 1915, 2342, 2418, 2877
Bang, W., 772, 1794
Banquet of Jests, or Change of
  Cheare, A, 73, 534-35
Barclay, John (see Sir Robert Le
  Grys; Kingsmill Long), 196-97,
  264, 596, 606-607, 694,
  1551, 2777
Barish, Jonas A., 1795
Barker, Gerard A., 3177
Barker, Richard Hindry, 2029
Barker, William, 2553
Barkstead, William, 2239
Barley, Alfred H., 1796
Barley, William, 536
Barnard, Dean Stanton, Jr.,
  1165-66

Cortissoz, Royal, 2485
Cotgrave, Randle, 3085, 3103, 3111, 3119
Cotterell, Sir Charles, 727
Cotton, Seaborn, 2822
Cottrell, G. W., 574
Coulman, D., 2606
Courthope, William John, 1820, 2607
Cowper, William, 1788
Craig, Hardin, 3101, 3181-82
Craigie, James, 2398
Craik, T. W., 2608
Crane, Ronald Salmon, 10-11, 164-66
Crane, Thomas Frederick, 1297, 1682, 1821, 3030, 3158
Crane, William G., 167-69, 570, 575-77, 1822
Cranfill, Thomas Mabry, 2248, 2384, 2399-2403
Cranz, Cornelia, 2609
Crawford, Bartholow V., 170
Crawford, Charles, 2610
Crawford, D. A. E. L., 1823
Crede, 1824
Creede, Thomas, 2955
Creigh, Geoffrey, 2038, 2044
Crockett, Harold Kelly, 171
Croft, Henry Herbert Stephen, 925
Crofts, John Ernest Victor, 2441
Croll, Morris William, 1774, 1825-26, 2611
Crompton, N. J. R., 2612
Cross, Wilbur L., 172
Crosse, G., 841
Crossley, James, 656, 2448, 2613
Croston, A. K., 2110
Crouch, Laura Ernestine, 1133
Crouch, Nathaniel, 1120, 1148
Crow, Joan, 544
Crump, Galbraith Miller, 2972-73
Crupi, Charles, 615
Cudworth, Ralph, the elder, 657
Cumberland, Richard, 2175
Cumming, L. M., 2974
Cunliffe, John W., 1047-48, 1063, 2249

Cunningham, Granville C., 2495
Cunningham, Robert Newton, 3106
Curtis, G. B., 1298
Cutts, John P., 616, 2614-17
Cuvelier, Eliane, 1683

D

D., C., 1299-1300
D., T., 72, 728-31
Daborne, Robert, 3136
Da Crema, Joseph J., 1827
Daghistani, Y., 172a
Dahl, Torsten, 842-43
Dallington, Sir Robert, 732-36
Dalziel, Margaret, 173
Damon, Phillip, 1072
Dana, Margaret Elizabeth, 2618-19
Danby, John Francis, 2620-21, 2829
Danchin, F. C., 2622
Daniel, George Bernard, Jr., 729
Daniel, P. A., 2229
Daniel, Samuel, 2134
Dannenberg, Friedrich, 1828
Dante Alighieri, 1308, 1466, 2786
Danter, John, 690, 1463
Darton, Frederick Joseph Harvey, 36, 464, 1119, 1584, 2487
Daunce, Edward, 2117
D'Avenant, Sir William, 3211
Davenport, A., 1504
Davenport, Arnold, 1684, 2623
Davenport, Robert, 1306, 1353, 1412
Davidson, Clifford, 2624
Davies, Charles, 591
Davies, H. Neville, 508, 697-98, 1134-35, 3000, 3147
Davies, Sir John, 2811
Davies, John, of Kidwelly, 737-38
Davis, C. A. C., 1301
Davis, Gwenn, 2111
Davis, Herbert, 589
Davis, Robert Gorham, 2112
Davis, Sarah Matilda, 2625
Davis, Walter Richardson, 174, 677, 844, 908, 1064,

H

Howard, Henry, Earl of Surrey, 2123
Howard, Sir Robert, 633
Howard, Thomas, 1524
Howarth, Robert Guy, 65, 349, 824, 857, 2138
[Howe Howleglas Served a Taylor], 1546-48
Howell, James, 1549-54
Howell, Roger, 2735
Howleglas (see William Copland; Howe Howleglas Served a Taylor)
Howlett, Timothy Reed, 614
Hoy, Cyrus, 2736
Hudson, Hoyt Hopewell, 235, 2737-38
Hughes, Helen Sard, 279
Hughes, Merritt Y., 236, 2739, 3073
Hughes, R. J., 450
Hughes, Walter, 959
Hume, Martin Andrew Sharp, 237-38
Hundred Merry Tales (see A C. Mery Talys)
Hunt, Mary Leland, 789-90
Hunt, T. W., 1859
Hunter, G. K., 239, 1348, 1709, 1860-1862, 2139, 3074
Hunter, J. B., 2140
Huntley, Frank Livingstone, 1766
Huppé, Bernard F., 1863
Hurrell, John Dennis, 240, 702, 1622
Hurwood, Bernhardt J., 645
Hüsgen, Hildegardis, 2740
Hutton, Edward, 746, 748, 1189, 3225
Hyde, Edward, Earl of Clarendon, 2449
Hystorie of Hamblet, The, 1555-69

I

IJsewijn, Jozef, 197
Image of Idleness (see A Lyttle Treatyse Called the Image of Idlenesse)

Imbert-Terry, H. M., 2141
Ingleby, Clement Mansfield, 667, 1212, 1349
Iota Rho, 2051
Irwin, Larry Wayne, 2027
Isler, Alan David, 2741-45
Isocrates, 1801, 1908, 1965
Izard, Thomas C., 1028, 3165-66

J

Jacke of Dover His Quest of Inquirie, 1570-71
Jackson, William A., 19, 1443
Jacobs, Joseph, 739, 2219, 2230
Jaggard, Isaac, 861
James I, 2400
James, Henry, 1052
Jamieson, T. H., 518
Jantz, Harold, 2474
Jeaffreson, John Cordy, 1350
Jeffery, Violet May, 1864
Jeffes, Abel, 2469
Jehenson, Yvonne Myriam, 2746
Jenkins, Harold, 681, 1351
Jenkinson, J. A., 1710
Jennings, John, 1572
Jest Books (see also appropriate author and title listings), 4, 22, 32, 52, 54, 56-57, 70, 72-73, 84, 90, 97, 133, 147-49, 156, 176, 192, 220, 224, 235, 250, 278, 286, 298, 332, 339, 345, 356, 358, 360, 381-82, 391, 401, 422, 438-40, 816, 819, 826, 868, 879, 2030, 2353
Jewkes, W. T., 241
Johnson, H. H., 1751
Johnson, Ralph Glassgow, 3028
Johnson, Reginald Brimley, 242
Johnson, Richard, 1573-1608
Johnson, Robert C., 1040, 1199, 1640, 1768, 2035, 2072, 2314
Johnson, Ronald Conant, 1077
Johnson, Thomas, 887
Johnson, William Jackson, 2142
Johnston, Arthur, 243-44
Johnstoun, James, 1609
Jones, Claude E., 20

Index